10,000

GARDEN QUESTIONS

ANSWERED BY 15 EXPERTS

10,000
GARDEN QUESTIONS
ANSWERED BY 15 EXPERTS

WITH 400 ILLUSTRATIONS AND
TEMPERATURE AND
PLANTING MAPS

F. F. Rockwell
EDITOR

ASSOCIATE EDITORS

Montague Free, T. H. Everett, Esther C. Grayson

VOLUME 2

Published by
THE AMERICAN GARDEN GUILD, INC.
and
DOUBLEDAY & COMPANY, INC.
Garden City   *New York*

PRINTED IN THE UNITED STATES OF AMERICA

Who They Are

THE horticultural authorities who have planned and guided the preparation of *10,000 Garden Questions Answered* are well known to the American gardening public. Their combined experience covers pretty much the entire range of gardening activities. In the preparation of this book they have had, in addition to their own broad background of knowledge upon which to draw, the services of a score of specialists in certain lines.

F. F. ROCKWELL, editor in chief of the American Garden Guild and of *The Home Garden,* has long been familiar to this country's amateur gardeners through a score or more of books and his lectures, articles, and natural-color photographs. At GrayRock, the country place of the Rockwells, extensive experiments and tests are carried on. Mr. Rockwell is also a past president of the Men's Garden Clubs of America.

R. S. LEMMON, long an editor of *The Home Garden,* formerly published *Real Gardening,* and is one of the country's most widely and favorably known garden editors and lecturers. He has specialized in the field of native plants and wildflowers, and was one of the organizers of the American Rock Garden Society.

P. J. McKENNA was for many years assistant horticulturist of the world-famous New York Botanical Garden, and is now chairman of horticulture for the Federated Garden Clubs of New York State, Inc. He is in wide demand as a lecturer and teacher on many horticultural subjects, and is ex-president of the Men's Garden Club of New York.

W. E. THWING, is well known for his work with wildflowers, and his natural-color motion pictures of wildflowers have won him wide recognition in the field of photography.

MONTAGUE FREE for more than twenty-five years was horticulturist of the great Brooklyn Botanic Garden; is now staff horticulturist of *The Home Garden.* He is a nationally known authority on all phases of gardening, a popular lecturer, and a leading figure among garden writers.

T. H. EVERETT has long been horticulturist at the famous New York Botanical Garden, a post which has brought him exceptionally broad contacts with the problems of amateur gardeners. His organization and direction of the Garden's courses in practical horticulture have been one of the highlights of his career.

R. C. ALLEN, secretary of the American Rose Society and formerly on the staff of the Department of Floriculture and Ornamental Horticulture at Cornell University, is a well-known specialist in flowering plants, particularly roses and delphiniums.

ALEX LAURIE'S official post is professor of floriculture at Ohio State University. But further than that, he is internationally famous as an authority on soil and its fertility, plant feeding, and related subjects which have to do with the practical phases of plant growth.

C. H. CONNORS heads the Department of Horticulture at Rutgers University, besides being ornamental horticulturist of the New Jersey Agricultural Experiment Station; an all-around plant-growing authority of long and varied experience.

DONALD WYMAN is horticulturist of the world-renowned Arnold Arboretum at Harvard University, where he has earned a national reputation in the field of trees, shrubs, and other woody plants.

T. A. WESTON, deceased, was the author of the famous *One Man's Garden,* and one of America's leading authorities on growing all types of bulbs and on the principles and practices of most other phases of flower gardening.

CYNTHIA WESTCOTT, best known to many gardening readers as "The Plant Doctor," is a foremost authority on the prevention and control of plant insect pests and diseases. She is always in close personal contact with the actual practice of what she preaches.

ESTHER C. GRAYSON is known to gardeners all over the country as an expert on flower arrangement, home cookery, canning, and the growing and use of herbs. Of equal importance is her wide knowledge and experience in growing vegetables and flowers.

HELEN VAN PELT WILSON, author of *A Garden in the House* and a favorite writer on many phases of home gardening, is especially conversant with plants for the house and hardy flowers.

HELEN S. HULL, ex-president of the National Council of State Garden Clubs, operates large gardens of her own and knows every detail in them.

Other well-known authorities who have assisted in answering questions are:

MILTON CARLETON, of Vaughan's Seed Store in Chicago, is a famous, capable gardener in his own right, with unusually broad experience. FRANCIS C. COULTER is an executive of one of the country's largest seed concerns, but has also found time to become a gardening author whose books and articles are both popular and accurate. ALEX CUMMING, who was widely known as a specialist in the production of fine chrysanthemums and author of a successful book on these popular plants, long headed a New England nursery which has served the gardening public for many years. HENRY E. DOWNER has practiced and taught horticulture in this country for a quarter century. He is horticulturist and superintendent of grounds at Vassar College.

DR. DAVID C. FAIRBURN is horticulturist of the Missouri Botanical Garden, one of the leading institutions of its kind in the world. KATHLEEN N. MARRIAGE is widely known as an authority on rock gardening and the native flora of the Western highlands. JOHN MELADY is a noted specialist in lawns and all that goes into their establishment and maintenance. H. DEWEY MOHR is a specialist in dahlias and has developed many outstanding new varieties.

H. STUART ORTLOFF, landscape architect and coauthor with H. B. Raymore of several excellent books and numerous articles on garden and grounds design, planting, and maintenance, combines the artistic and the practical angles of his profession with unusual success. To him, "Will it work?" is really the acid test.

DAVID PLATT was manager of a highly successful seed store, knew professional horticulture, and was equally familiar with the amateur's ambitions and many problems.

HILDEGARD SCHNEIDER, head gardener at The Cloisters in New York, is an all-around plantswoman of long experience.

DR. GEORGE L. SLATE, associate in research in the Division of Pomology, New York State Agricultural Experiment Station, is a noted authority on lilies as well as fruits. His best-known book, *Lilies for American Gardens,* is recognized as the leading work in its field. PROFESSOR LEE A. SOMERS, associate in the Vegetable Gardening Extension work at Illinois College of Agriculture, knows food gardens and gardening in the most practical way— from personal experience and many contacts with beginners as well as experts. VICTOR A. TIEDJENS is associate professor of vegetable gardening at Rutgers University. P. J. VAN MELLE has a particular flair for native plants, rock gardening, and accurate knowledge of plant histories and types. THOMAS A. WILLIAMS, was known to hundreds of thousands of radio fans as "The Old Dirt Dobber," for his C.B.S. program, heard nationally. PROFESSOR PAUL WORK, of the Department of Vegetable Crops, New York State Agricultural Experiment Station, "knows his onions" literally as well as figuratively. Dr. J. H. Clark, associate pomologist of the New Jersey State Agricultural Experiment Station, has a prominent part in the extensive fruit-testing and experiment program at that institution.

Other specialists and gardeners who have contributed valuable experience and knowledge to the preparation of this volume are: John H. Beale, George A. Buchanan, George E. Burkhardt, L. C. Chadwick, Dr. A. S. Colby, Lillian Meyferth Cronk, Charles F. Doney, Professor E. V. Hardenburg, D. C. Kiplinger, Stuart Longmuir, Harriet K. Morse, George D. Oberle, E. L. Reber, Roy P. Rogers, Kenneth D. Smith, Nancy Ruzicka Smith, John V. Watkins, Robert E. Weidner, Natalie Gomez, and John Wingert.

Artists who have prepared illustrations are: George L. Hollrock, Pauline W. Kreutzfeldt, Helen Reddy, Carl Sigman, William Ward, Eva Melady, Tabea Hofmann, H. B. Raymore, Natalie Harlan Davis, Frederic F. Rockwell, Laurence Blair, and Russell J. Walrath, who did the temperature and frost maps, adapted from data by the U. S. Department of Agriculture.

Foreword

OFTEN there is an interesting story back of the making of a book, and that is true of the present volume. Twenty-five thousand home gardeners not only made its publication imperative but actually helped to create it. This is the way it all came about:

When the charter subscription list of *The Home Garden* was being made up, the publishers invited subscribers to send in, for answering in the magazine's question-box department, the gardening questions that most often puzzled them. Rather to the astonishment of all concerned, the result was an avalanche of more than 25,000 questions from every state in the Union. Four full pages in the magazine every month are devoted to answers, but at that rate it would take nearly six years to complete the job, and it seemed likely that people who needed information might not care to wait that long for it. Here was a genuine need and an authentic cry for help that could not be denied. It was fair to assume that these thousands of questions did not represent the problems only of the gardeners who asked them, but were a typical cross section of the information needs of average amateur gardeners throughout the country.

So it seemed that a real service could be rendered to American gardeners by making available to them all the authoritative answers to these universal questions. And one method appeared feasible—to put questions and answers in a book.

The Editorial Board of *The Home Garden* had expected, rather optimistically as it turned out, to answer all questions received. But to answer accurately so large a number, in so short a time, was obviously beyond their capacity. Therefore, help was sought from other prominent horticultural authorities in all parts of the country—a happy necessity, because it brought into the volume a far broader combined experience. Instead of the fifteen experts originally engaged in this effort and indicated in our title, a

ix

group of more than fifty earnest workers labored on this really gigantic task and poured into the book a sum total of knowledge and experience seldom, if ever, equaled.

It seems appropriate to mention here one other point that may be of interest to readers of this book. *10,000 Garden Questions Answered* is the first of a series of garden books planned and prepared by the American Garden Guild, Inc. The Guild was organized to bring together a group of leaders in American horticulture for the purpose of instructing and aiding the amateur gardeners of America. Through the books already published and in preparation, the American Garden Guild hopes to maintain a standard and create a service long needed in American amateur gardening.

W. E. T.

Contents

xi

Introduction

THE PREPARATION OF *10,000 Garden Questions Answered* has
been a somewhat herculean task. It was undertaken, in response
to numerous requests, because it seemed worth while to present,
in some organized and permanent form, the wealth of information which the answers to these questions convey.

The original plan was to list the questions, with their answers,
in alphabetical order—A to Z. It soon became evident, however,
that this would not accomplish our purpose, which was to make
the information available to the reader in a way that would
enable him not only to refer to it quickly, but to find readily all
the information on any particular subject. The most practical
method of attaining this objective, it seemed to us—after carefully studying several plans which suggested themselves—was to
arrange this widely diversified mass of material in ten general
categories that would cover the whole field. These sections or
divisions are:

    I   Soils and Fertilizers

   II   Ornamental Plants and Their Culture

  III   Ten Leading Garden Flowers

   IV   Lawns and Turf Areas

    V   The Home Vegetable Garden

   VI   Home-Grown Fruits

  VII   House Plants

 VIII   Plant Troubles and Their Control

   IX   Regional Garden Problems

    X   Landscaping and Miscellaneous

The "Introductions"

For each of these sections an introduction which gives general information on the subject covered has been prepared. The introductions are *based upon the questions most generally asked* concerning the subject discussed. In other words, these questions, instead of being answered individually, have been answered in a composite reply that presents the general principles involved and provides a background for the more specific questions which follow.

This treatment has two distinct advantages. In the first place, it enables the reader to get much more from the answers to the individual questions; in the second, it has saved a great amount of space. Even by handling the material in this way, it was found necessary to increase the size of the volume from the 1,280 pages originally planned to 1,488. Actually, the *answers* to more than 12,000 questions are contained in the present volume.

The advantages of having questions answered by experts widely experienced in many lines are obvious. Too often such answers are compiled from outdated reference books. The answers in this volume are by persons who are actually *doing* the things they write about. Many of them are recognized internationally as authorities in their respective fields. At the same time, with few exceptions, their work brings them into direct contact with the problems of amateur gardeners the country over.

An Advance Word to Critics

With some fifty different persons contributing information of one sort or another, it is inevitable that many differences of opinion have arisen. In so far as possible, the recommendations and suggestions made on any specific subject have been brought into harmony by correspondence or discussion. There are cases where this has not been possible. The result is honest differences of opinion such as would be forthcoming on almost any garden question that might be asked of any group of experts—differences similar to those that would be found in every field of human endeavor, in any science or art, and horticulture partakes of both.

Unfortunately, too, we have in this country no generally recognized single authority in the realm of plant nomenclature. An attempt in this direction has been made in the publication of *Standardized Plant Names*. Botanists in general have been unwilling to follow the recommendations of the hard-working committee which has for many years unselfishly struggled with this perplexing problem. Excellent as has been the intention of this committee, many of its recommendations—particularly in abolishing, changing, and creating new common or English names—have not seemed acceptable even to the non-botanist. Nevertheless, those authorities who will not recognize *Standardized Plant Names* as the last word cannot agree among themselves on any other single authority. Thus this entire subject still remains in a very chaotic state.

Even the least-informed beginner can imagine, with this condition existing, and with half a hundred contributors, each with his or her own ideas on the subject, what a problem we have faced in regard to nomenclature. In general, *Standardized Plant Names* has been followed; but in many instances—where it seemed that following its recommendations could only make "confusion worse confounded"—it has not.

The result, we realize, will leave the door wide open to the critics. However, our primary concern has been for the amateur reader; and where he can get the *meaning* of a question or an answer, we are content to let the scientists and botanists wrangle with us—and with each other—as to names, spelling, precedents, and authorities.

The botanically minded critic, too, will find some gall for his ink when it comes to botanical terms. For the most part the questions have been left in the dirt gardener's terminology in which they were written, and often the answers are in kind. Where the questioner has asked about how to plant a dahlia "tuber," for instance, it has not been deemed necessary to instruct him that he should have said "root" (or, more accurately, "bulbous root"). A too-strict adherence to botanical terminology often tends to confuse the beginner rather than to enlighten him, and this volume is primarily for beginners.

I wish to take this opportunity, also, to express my appreciation of the co-operation we have had from the group of contributors who have made possible this volume, and especially to the assistant editors, Montague Free, T. H. Everett, and Esther C. Grayson, and also to my personal assistant, Lillian Meyferth Cronk, for the untiring effort they have put into the work of handling the thousands of details involved in its preparation.

Our aim has been to present the amateur gardener with *practical* information in readily available form, on his own personal problems. To the extent that this has been accomplished, we will have succeeded in making the kind of book we set out to create.

F. F. R.

10,000

GARDEN QUESTIONS

ANSWERED BY 15 EXPERTS

Home-Grown Fruits

INTRODUCTION

BY C. H. CONNORS

WILD FRUITS formed an important part of the diet of primitive peoples. Some fruits—as dates, bananas, and plantains—still supply a considerable part of the food supply of certain races. Even today tremendous quantities of wild fruits, such as cranberries, blueberries, grapes, plums, crabapples, elderberries, blackberries, and others, are gathered in the wild, not only to increase the food supply but to make viands more palatable and to add pleasure to eating. What would turkey be without cranberries? Or roast pork without applesauce? We have come to think of these as concomitant. Originally they were used as condiments, to help subdue wild flavors.

As families migrated from one part of the world to another, an accompaniment deemed as essential as tools for work, or seeds of vegetables, were plants or cuttings or seeds of fruiting plants. Sometimes these would thrive in the new environment, and sometimes not. Then new varieties had to be sought as substitutes for those that could not be grown.

The nutritionists value highly the inclusion of fruits in the diet. Some of them, such as citrus fruits and strawberries, yellow peaches and apricots, are especially valued for their vitamin content. All supply sugars of several types in easily digestible form. Most are esteemed for the acids that add tone to the system. Minerals are found abundantly in many. Above all, the flavors and aromas that abound, while they may not add anything essential to the diet, certainly contribute something that makes of eating a little less of a chore that must be performed three times a day.

Why Grow Your Own?

Home-grown fruits, if properly cultivated and handled, are,

as a rule, much superior to market fruits. Fruits for shipment must be picked in a slightly immature condition, so that they may be able to stand packing and handling. They must often be harvested before the sugars and flavors are developed up to the point where the ripening process will continue after the fruit is removed from the tree. This is especially true of the more perishable fruits, such as the berries. One has not really had peach ice cream until he has picked from the tree a suitable variety, so fully ripe that it would squash in the hand, and used this for the making of a most delectable dish, quite different from the drugstore product. Or, with blackberries, there is absolutely no comparison between the fruit as purchased in the market and those ripened on the canes to the point where a touch will make them fall off.

A fruit that is allowed to develop on the plant, under the proper environmental conditions, until it is fully ripe, has quality, flavor, and nutritional value that cannot be attained in fruits that must be picked for shipment.

Of course location with respect to production has a bearing. If the homeowner is situated in a region where fruits are harvested and delivered to a local market, the quality will more nearly approach that of home-grown fruits; but even for such local handling many sorts must be picked before fully mature.

Limiting Factors

The successful culture of fruits depends upon space, the time available for care, climate, soil, and site.

Space Limits. One having only a limited space which may be used for fruit will be wise not to attempt to grow any of the fruit trees, as these require much more space than the small garden affords. A standard apple tree, fully developed, occupies a space 35 to 40 ft. square; a pear, 24 to 30 ft. square; a peach, 20 to 25 ft. square, and so on. Not only is the space occupied to be considered, but also the effect of the tree upon the surroundings. The roots always extend beyond the spread of the branches. The shade cast by the tree may seriously affect plants grown near it.

In addition to the space required there is another factor, known as self-incompatibility. Most of the varieties of apples, pears, sweet cherries, and some of the plums will not set a satisfactory crop of fruit to their own pollen. Consequently, if there is not in the immediate neighborhood a compatible variety, in addition to the variety wanted, one must have 2 trees of the same fruit, of different but compatible varieties; otherwise the results will be very disappointing.

Dwarfing stocks have been in use for years. In general, these are suited for special situations. They require some space for cultivation. Dwarf apple trees require special attention; otherwise they are likely to become standard trees. Many situations may be suitable for cordon or espalier trees. These, too, are grown on dwarfing roots, and they require much more care in training than do standard trees. The yields, from the quantity standpoint, are apt to be disappointing.

It would be well, then, for the person with a small area to limit the fruit plantings to the small fruits, as they are called.

Strawberries are best for a small area. They can even be worked into a perennial border as an edging, or in other ways. A yield of about 40 quarts may be expected from a row 50 ft. long. The so-called everbearing varieties at present available are not so high in quality as the spring-fruiting sorts, nor do they produce so heavily.

The cane or bramble fruits are less satisfactory for very limited space. While they may be used in rows as separations between areas, they will spread by shoots arising from the roots, or by rooting at the tips. For this reason they should not be planted too near a property line, as they may become a nuisance in a neighbor's garden. Raspberries become very ragged in appearance after the fruit is harvested, as the fruit-bearing canes die. Blackberries are very rampant in growth. Dewberries do best in a light, sandy soil. Boysenberry is a variety of dewberry that is a little more tender to cold.

Currants and gooseberries are very prolific bearers and for the average family only a few plants of each would be required. These can very well be used in the shrub border, or as specimen plants, or at the edge of the garden.

Grapes can be worked into the landscape scheme about as well as any plant. They can be used to cover a pergola or to form a shaded arcade. On trellis or fence the vines form a good screen, or a separation between areas.

Blueberries are very exacting in their requirements of soil and moisture, so they do not fit into the general garden picture. However, if they can be given the proper environment, they are satisfactory. If space and proper provision for culture are given to rhododendrons and azaleas, blueberries may well be companions, for they have the same cultural requirements. And the blueberries, while they are deciduous, are handsome plants, both when in flower and when the foliage turns color in the autumn.

Time Limitation. No one should plant fruit on faith alone. Time must be available, at the proper seasons, for cultivation, for pruning, and, above all (especially in the case of tree fruits), for the spraying required in the control of insects and diseases. Such control also involves proper equipment, for ordinary garden equipment will not suffice for trees. Wherever dwarf fruits are grown, whether to develop normally or trained as cordons or espaliers, much more attention must be paid to both top and root. The top must be skillfully pruned and trained to secure maximum production. The roots must be given at least annual attention to make sure that the scion or top is not forming roots above where it joins the dwarfing understock.

Climatic Limitation. Climate has a very great bearing upon the kinds and varieties of fruits that may be grown; such factors as rainfall and temperature must be taken into consideration.

Rainfall, of course, is important. Where it is more than 20 ins. a year, fruits may be successfully grown. This embraces the region from the eastern margin of the Great Plains to the Atlantic Ocean and southward to the Gulf of Mexico. In the Great Plains region the rainfall decreases from more than 30 ins. to the east to 15 ins. on the western border. Where the rainfall is below 20 ins., irrigation must be practiced. In the plateau province (from the Great Plains to the coastal range) the rainfall is usually less than 20 ins., so no fruits, generally speaking, will be possible unless they are irrigated. On the Pacific coastal belt the rainfall may vary from 100 ins. in Washington to about 10 ins. in the San Joaquin Valley. The variation may be as great as this in California alone. In Washington the rainfall will be 100 ins. on the coast and 10 to 15 ins. east of the coastal range.

Temperature limits the distribution of fruit plants. Citrus fruits, pomegranates, and figs will not grow in Vermont; nor will the apples at home in Vermont do well in the deep South.

Low temperature affects fruit production by bud injury, by injury to woody parts above ground, and by root injury.

Buds of peaches will usually be killed at 10° to 15° below zero, depending upon the growth conditions of the buds. Flower buds of sweet cherry will probably all be killed at 15° below. Flower buds of apples may be killed at low temperatures, but there is a considerable variation among varieties. Susceptibility, according to the development of the bud, will have a bearing. Some varieties of grapes lose their flowers at low temperatures. Currants and gooseberries are very hardy. Apricot is very tender.

Wood injury at low temperatures will vary with the age of the trees, culture and latitude, soil moisture, wind velocity; apples are most resistant, peaches most susceptible, among the tree fruits. Of course the tropical and subtropical fruits cannot stand much frost.

Temperature affects fruit setting also. The varieties of peaches grown in the East and in the middle section of California will not develop flower buds unless they are subjected to chilling to complete the process known as after-ripening, so they do not do well in some parts of Florida, for instance.

Absolute and accumulated temperatures have an effect on initiation of growth and upon maturity. Baldwin may be a good variety of apple for Vermont, while Delicious will not do well in the colder parts of that state.

Soil and Site

In general, fruits require a loamy soil with good drainage, but retentive of moisture. Even though the cranberry must be flooded at certain times, the soil should be well drained. The dewberry does not grow well except in sandy soil. Apple varieties will vary somewhat; summer varieties in general do better on a sandier soil than do winter varieties.

A soil reaction that is slightly acid is best for most fruits. The blueberry, which does best in very acid soil, is an exception.

Site is important, as it affects drainage both of water and of air. A pocket or depression may be too moist. Peaches and other early-blooming fruits, such as the apricot, will be injured by late frosts in such a situation.

Where there are large bodies of water, the movement of air results in a warmer condition on the leeward side. This is notable in the Michigan fruit belt and along the shores of Lake Erie and Lake Ontario. In the latter area, the fruit belt is 6 to 10 miles wide. South of it, fruit cannot be grown for some distance.

Elevation is also important. Sometimes a difference in elevation of even less than 50 ft. may mean success or failure with peaches. Apples may be grown on high elevations in states which normally would not be considered suitable, as New Mexico.

Sunlight is an exceedingly important factor. Fruits must have plenty of sunlight, and do best when exposed to direct sunlight for the full daily period. Some varieties are affected in maturing by the total hours of sunlight. For instance, apple varieties adapted to growing in England will seldom prove satisfactory over most of this country, and vice-versa.

Planting

The season when planting may best be done varies with the climate. In regions of fairly early and severe winters, spring planting will usually be best for most fruits. In milder climates, fall planting seems to be best. There may be variations with kinds and within states. Sweet cherries in a fairly mild climate will do better if planted in the fall, while sour cherries may do better if planted in the spring. In other states, the reverse may be true.

With tree fruits, it is best to plant trees 1 or 2 years old. If they are older than that, there is a tremendous setback, unless great pains, at considerable expense, are taken in moving them. So-called bearing-size trees, if moved with bare roots, will probably have a high mortality and will not yield as quickly as young trees properly planted and handled.

Buy from a reliable nursery and as near home as possible. Most fruit plants lose a great deal in drying out during shipment, even though they may be carefully packed. Furthermore, especially with the brambles, there are mosaic diseases that will cause trouble. The reliable nursery will have rogued the planting to eliminate as thoroughly as possible the danger from this source.

Insects and Diseases

It is not possible to produce good fruits without careful attention to control of insects and diseases, but the seriousness of injury from these sources varies with climate and soil. Fire blight of pear, apple, and quince is usually less severe on heavy soils of good drainage and with a relatively low nitrogen content. Codling moth, which attacks apples, is so serious in a few sections of the country that a continuous coating of insecticide must be maintained on the fruits.

The pests may be seasonal or permanent. Many of the Agricultural Colleges and Experiment Stations issue up-to-the-minute information on the development of insects and diseases. All issue spray schedules, with time of application based on stage of development of the plants and of the pests concerned.

There are systemic diseases, such as mosaic and wilt diseases, which affect the whole plant. Here eradication is the only means of control.

Some diseases affect the leaves (cherry leaf spots, peach leaf curl, scab of apples), causing destruction of leaf tissue, the malformation of leaves, or premature leaf drop, thus reducing the power of the tree to manufacture carbohydrates. Other diseases affect the fruit, sometimes causing injury that may mar only the appearance (as sooty mold of apple, apple scab); or (as with brown rot of peach, plum, cherry) invading the deep tissue and resulting in the eventual destruction of the fruits.

Insects are of many different types. Some bore into the stem. Some, as the cane borers of the brambles, are controlled by the removal of the affected parts. Others, as apple-tree borers, are sometimes sought out and killed in place. Still others are destroyed by fumigants, as nicotine paste injected into the holes (for leopard-moth larva), and paradichlorbenzene for peach-tree borers. Sucking insects—such as aphids, leafhoppers, and psyllas—may kill or cripple leaves and malform fruits. Various scales injure or even kill young wood. Leaf-eating insects—as currant worm, Japanese beetle, tent caterpillar, webworms—reduce the ability of the plants to manufacture sugars. Some destroy the fruits from within or without, as codling moth of pome fruits and curculio of stone fruits. These often cause premature ripening and dropping of tree fruits, which results in considerable nuisance on the home grounds, where an adequate spray schedule is not followed.

Generally speaking, the nearer home fruit plantings are to commercial plantings, or to where there are, or have been, abandoned commercial plantings, the more likelihood there is of damage by pests.

The Question of Varieties

The gardener desiring to grow fruits on his home place, in deciding which kinds to attempt, will be limited first of all by the controlling factors of climate and site. In the selection of varieties, the same natural factors will have a bearing. For instance, the Cuthbert raspberry, while subject to mosaic disease, might be hardy in one state and not in another. Delicious apple will do well in the climate of Philadelphia and under irrigation in the apple section of Washington, but will not do at all well in the colder parts of New Hampshire. Most of the Agricultural Colleges and Experiment Stations have available lists of varieties of fruits that are adapted to areas within their limits.

The next consideration should be quality and yield. One of the objects of growing fruits on the home grounds is to produce specimens of really superior eating quality. So only the varieties producing fruits of the highest quality and capable of good yields should be selected.

Then should come resistance to disease. If a strawberry variety is of highest quality and yield, but susceptible to the red stele disease, it would be folly to plant that variety in a situation where the disease is present. The Cuthbert raspberry is susceptible to mosaic disease. It should not be planted unless assurance is given that the plants have been carefully selected for freedom from that disease, and then only where the disease is not prevalent.

Herewith are given some lists of varieties for home planting.

They are merely suggestions, as all of them will not do equally well in all conditions under which the particular class of fruit will survive the climate. For this reason, in selecting a list of fruits for the home garden, the planter will do well to check with his state Experiment Station (see list in Section X) before sending in his order.

APPLE: Yellow Transparent, Gravenstein, Wealthy, Melba, McIntosh, Delicious, Stayman, Jonathan, Baldwin, Winesap.

PEAR: Seckel, Elizabeth, Bartlett, Clapp Favorite, Winter Nelis, Kieffer.

PEACH: Cumberland, Golden Jubilee, Halehaven, Belle, Elberta, Lizzie.

APRICOT: Moorpark, Blenheim.

CHERRY, SOUR: Montmorency.

CHERRY, SWEET: Governor Wood, Coe, Napoleon, Schmidt, Windsor, Black Tartarian.

PLUM: Abundance, Red June, Reine Claude, Italian Prune, Lombard, Stanley, Shropshire Damson.

QUINCE: Orange.

GRAPES: Fredonia, Delaware, Brighton, Niagara, Portland, Concord, Catawba, Seneca, Sheridan.

RASPBERRY, RED: Sunrise, Latham, Indian Summer. BLACK: Bristol, Cumberland. RASPBERRY PURPLE-CANE: Columbian, Sodus, Potomac.

BLACKBERRY: Alfred, Blowers, Brewer.

DEWBERRY: Lucretia, Boysen.

CURRANT: Red Lake, Wilder, Fay.

GOOSEBERRY: Chautauqua, Poorman.

STRAWBERRY: Pathfinder, Fairfax, Catskill. Everbearers: Wayzata, Gem, Mastodon.

BLUEBERRY: June, Rancocas, Stanley, Concord, Rubel, Jersey.

ORCHARD

SOIL

How can soil for orchard fruits be built up? Grow corn or other cultivated crops on the ground for a year or two. Each fall plant a cover crop of rye to be turned under in the spring. This will increase the humus content of the soil.

Does sandy soil retard growth of apples and peach trees? Mine are 4 years old and only about 5 ft. tall. Will other soil put around the trees help any? Apple and peach trees will grow well in sandy soil if it is properly fertilized, provided it contains ample moisture. Adding heavy soil might help, but it would require a great deal. It would be more feasible to improve the soil by adding lime (if it needs it), then a 5–10–5 commercial fertilizer at the rate of about 800 lbs. per acre. If the soil is dry, either irrigate with a sprinkler system or mulch with some strawy material to conserve moisture. Build up the humus content of the soil by turning under a yearly cover crop.

Will fruit trees grow in a scrub-oak section on Long Island? The soil in question is probably low in fertility, but with good care might produce enough fruit for home use. Liberal applications of stable manure, annual fertilizing, and mulching to conserve moisture should make it possible to produce fruit on this soil.

Our soil is mostly sand. Would it be suitable for the raising of strawberries, red raspberries, and fruit trees? A sandy loam soil, or even a loamy sand, is suitable for these fruits if it has a reasonable supply of moisture. If it is very dry, sandy soil you will probably have poor results unless you irrigate. Peaches will thrive in sandier soil than is needed for apples.

Will fruit trees grow in muck ground? Yes, provided the muck is well drained, not too acid, and contains the necessary nutrient elements in sufficient quantities. Muck land is usually low; hence cold air may "drain" into such an area and result in frost damage. Fruit trees should have good "air drainage," so are usually set on relatively high land.

Is there any reason why fruit trees will not grow on soil adjacent to black-walnut trees? There is some sketchy evidence that black-walnut trees may have an adverse effect on plants set near by, but the general belief is that no fruit plants should be set near any shade trees. The roots reach out and compete for plant-food materials and water, and the shade cast seriously affects the fruitfulness of plants as well as their growth.

FERTILIZER AND MANURE

Must fruit trees (such as apple and peach) be heavily manured?   Fruit trees should have sufficient manure (or commercial fertilizer) to supply any nutrient elements which may be deficient in the soil in which they are growing. However, it is easy to overfertilize these fruits. They do not require as heavy fertilization, for instance, as is needed by most vegetable crops.

Should manure be placed on a new garden plot on which fruit trees and berries are to be planted?   A good coat of manure would be about the best treatment you could give.

How is nitrate of soda applied when used for fruit trees? Nitrate of soda is usually used for fruit trees at the rate of ¼ lb. for 1- to 2-year-old trees, to 5 to 10 lbs. for trees 20 to 30 years old.

Can you give some data on fertilizer to help fruit trees produce well, and at younger age? (Illinois.)   Good production will be secured only if the trees have the proper supply of nutrients, and that in turn will depend a great deal on the natural fertility of the soil. Check with your county agricultural agent for specific recommendations for your particular soil. No particular type of fertilizer will cause the trees to bear at a younger age. The age of bearing can be delayed, however, by applying too much nitrogen, or by heavy pruning.

What type of fertilizer should be used for fruit trees in acid soil?   Most fruit trees in the East are grown in acid soil; that is, soil which is below the neutral point of pH 7.0. If soil is very acid (below pH 5.5), lime should be added to bring the reaction to around pH 6.0, then use ordinary commercial fertilizer as required.

I have heard that fruit trees do not require lime. Is that correct?   Fruit trees require lime as much as any other plants. Whether it should be used or not depends on the acidity and calcium content of the soil. The pH should be between 5.5 and 6.0.

Is it true that a little salt given to fruit trees helps to better the fruit? If so, how much should be given?   Ordinary table salt (sodium chloride) would be likely to cause injury if used in any considerable quantity. Small amounts would not cause injury but would not be of any value to the tree.

PLANTING

What is the best age at which to buy apple, peach, cherry,

plum, and pear trees for setting in the home garden? Apple, 1 or 2 years; peach, 1 year; cherry, 1 or 2 years; plum, 2 years; pear, 2 years. Larger trees are not recommended, and nothing is gained by planting so-called "bearing-age" trees.

How many fruit trees will be necessary to supply a family of 4 with an adequate amount for the year? This will vary greatly according to personal preferences. Six apple, 2 pear, 6 peach, 1 sour cherry, and 2 plum trees would provide about as much as the ordinary family would want, if varieties with a succession of ripening dates are chosen, and if the trees are on suitable soil and well cared for.

How early in spring should fruit trees and berries be planted? Plant just as early as the soil can be worked. There is no danger of planting too early, provided the soil has dried out enough to be worked into good tilth.

How far apart should fruit trees be planted? I plan to plant about 10 acres. Planting distances of fruit trees depend on the kinds of fruits, and, to some extent, on soil and climate. The following are average: Apple, 35 to 40 ft.; pear, 24 to 30 ft.; peach, 20 to 25 ft.; plum, 22 to 24 ft.; cherry (sour), 22 to 24 ft.; cherry (sweet), 24 to 30 ft.; apricot, 22 to 24 ft.; quince, 18 to 20 ft.

Just how should I go about planting a fruit tree? How big a hole should I dig for an apple tree? A hole 12 to 15 ins. deep and 15 ins. across should be large enough for the average nursery tree. If the roots are too long to fit in a hole this size, cut them back. As the soil is filled in, jiggle the tree up and down a little so that all the roots will make contact with the soil. When the hole is half full, and again when it is full, step on the soil around the trunk of the tree in order to compact it. Finish filling the hole. If the soil is at all dry, pour in a pail of water before the hole is quite full.

How should fruit trees and berry bushes be planted in new ground just cleared of timber? (North Dakota.) The ideal way would be to start with the ground cleared and all stumps removed. Then a 4- to 6-in. covering of farm manure, plus a dressing of superphosphate, 20 lbs. per 1,000 sq. ft. or 1,000 lbs. an acre, could be plowed under. A rough harrowing, then a dressing of ground limestone, 40 lbs. per 1,000 sq. ft. or 2,000 lbs. per acre, thoroughly worked into the surface, and the land is ready to plant. If the stumps are not yet removed and you wish to plant standard fruit trees, measure off and stake the spots where the trees will be planted (see question on distance to plant) and remove the stumps from this area. Dig in some manure, plus superphosphate, as previously suggested; plant the trees and put a mulch of straw or the like in a 2-ft. radius around each tree. The remainder of the stumps can then be removed at leisure, and the area plowed. In the absence of manure, plant cover crops for humus. Also have the soil tested for lime needs before liming. The area for the berry bushes will first have to be entirely cleared before planting.

How should nursery-grown trees be treated upon receipt? Remove from packing at once and plant immediately or heel in. Examine carefully. If the plants are dried out, soak in water, completely immersed, if possible, for 24 hours. If they do not plump up, return them.

Received nursery-stock fruit trees in fall. What is best way to hold until spring? If they cannot be planted at once, heel them in. Dig a trench wide enough and deep enough so that the root systems will almost go in them. Place plants in the trench, packed close together, at an angle of about 45°. Place loose soil about roots, work down and pack tight, then mound. No grass or weeds against roots. Object is to keep roots moist during winter.

How large does a body of water have to be to cause conditions to be favorable for fruit growing? The moderating effect of the body of water is caused by the changes in temperature oc-curing in air masses as they move across the water toward the fruit-growing section. If prevailing winds do not blow across un-frozen water long enough to have their temperature raised, then there will be no effect on temperatures in the orchard. This means a body of water will have to be several miles wide and remain unfrozen in order to have very much effect.

Can fruit trees be used as decorative specimens on the home grounds? Quite often crabapples are used to good advantage. Some people use peach, cherry, and apple trees as part of the decorating scheme.

Is locality taken into consideration with regard to the types of trees which should be planted? Yes indeed. Fruits which thrive in Louisiana would not survive the winters in New Eng-land, and New England varieties would not do well in Louisiana. Cultural methods also vary greatly in different localities.

SPRAYING

We have a new orchard of fruit trees. What should they be sprayed with, and when? The damage likely to be caused by certain pests varies a great deal in different localities, hence spraying recommendations vary from one producing section to another. Each Agricultural Experiment Station has developed spraying directions to fit conditions within the state. These directions may change from year to year as new methods are developed. Get on your station's mailing list to receive spray schedules.

How and how often should orchard trees be sprayed? They should have a minimum of 4 sprayings, with a good pressure sprayer. One dormant spray should be given, and at least 3 before and while fruit is forming. Commercial growers use as many as 11 sprays in one season.

Does the Japanese beetle do much harm to fruit trees? What spray can be used against it? It seems almost impossible to protect the fruits that ripen during the beetle season, if the infestation is heavy. It is possible to protect trees. Young trees, especially, should be protected with oleate-coated arsenate of lead during the beetle season. Otherwise they may be defoliated, and the trees suffer accordingly.

MULCHES AND COVER CROPS

How does a mulch of straw or peatmoss provide more water to young trees? No more water is provided, but what is already there is conserved. The mulch prevents wind and sun from striking the ground and evaporating moisture from the surface. It also prevents the growth of weeds and grass which would compete for water with the trees. During a very hard rain the mulch prevents or lessens surface runoff.

How should fruit trees be mulched? They were 3-year-old trees when planted, and have been growing in a yard for 3 years. By mulching is meant the placing of enough strawy material around the tree to keep down weeds and grass and thus conserve moisture. The mulch is usually applied from the trunk to a point under the tips of the branches, hence the area mulched increases as the tree increases in size. Straw, spoiled hay, lawn clippings, or leaves may be used. If leaves are used, place some hay or brush over them to prevent their blowing away. Mice often injure mulched trees, so it is best to rake the mulch away from the trunk in the fall (a distance of 3 or 4 ft.) and spread it again in the spring.

Should the ground under orchard fruit trees be kept cultivated? Apples and pears are often grown in sod ground, but most other fruits do better where the ground is cultivated. Cultivation is kept up during the early part of the year. It ceases about July, or when cover crop is sown.

Is the growing of fruit trees in grass sod satisfactory in a small

orchard?   Peach trees should be on cultivated land, but apples and pears may be grown in sod if the soil is normally fairly moist. If the soil is inclined to be dry, then frequent cultivation or the mulch system (keeping the ground around the trees covered with hay or straw) should be used.

What is the best ground cover for a young orchard of 2-year-old trees?   If the soil is sandy or rather level, cultivate during the summer, and seed a cover crop (such as rye) in the fall. If the soil is rather heavy or moist, start a permanent grass or alfalfa sod; cultivate just around the trees, or mulch them to conserve moisture.

I have 6 acres; expect to plant about 1 acre orchard. What is a good cover crop for the rest that could be plowed under? Ground is clay mixed. (Michigan.)   There are several from which you might choose, depending on local soil and climatic conditions. One combination would be soybeans in summer followed by rye in the fall. Or use buckwheat in summer.

PRUNING AND TRAINING

How and how often should fruit trees be pruned?   Pruning is done yearly, usually while the trees are dormant, but some pinching off is done throughout the growing season. Pruning is done to train the tree for shape, or to produce growth for fruit— as in the case of the peach. In pruning, cross branches and all dead or diseased wood are cut out, as well as water sprouts or "suckers." It takes a knowledge of trees to do a good pruning job.

When and how much should I trim or cut back grafted fruit trees—4-ft. pear and 5-ft. apple planted this fall?   If these are the so-called bearing-size trees, they should be pruned rather severely at time of transplanting to compensate for the roots which are unavoidably lost when the trees are dug. The tops should be reduced by at least ½ of the twig growth. This is taking for granted that the trees were dug with a large ball of soil, held on by being wrapped with burlap, thus reducing root losses to a minimum. The trees will probably need very little additional pruning during the first 2 or 3 years after transplanting.

Is it advisable to cut the heart or center limb out of a fruit tree to prevent its growing too tall?   Peach trees are usually trained to an open center, so the central leader is cut out. Apple trees are well adapted to the modified leader system, in which the leader is allowed to grow to a height of 8 to 10 ft. before it is cut out.

How should fruit trees be pruned so that branches will not bend down or break off when fruit gets large? We would like to make the branches stronger and not lose more fruit than necessary. The branches are bound to bend down if a crop is being produced. However, heading back the long, leggy branches will reduce their length in relation to their diameter. Such branches will not bend or break so badly because the leverage exerted by the load of fruit is not so great. Breakage may also be prevented by propping with poles and by thinning off excess fruit.

Is root pruning the proper way to reduce wood and leaf growth on a fruit tree? Root pruning is seldom justified unless the tree is growing in a greenhouse, or is used as an ornamental where its size must be strictly limited. If a tree is making too much wood growth, it can usually be checked satisfactorily by withholding nitrogen from the fertilizer application.

How is root pruning of a fruit tree done? In a young tree the roots may be cut by inserting a sharp spade to full depth all around the tree, at a distance from the trunk equal to about ⅔ of the spread of the branches. If the tree is older, or if the soil is hard and stony, it will be necessary to dig a trench some 18 ins. deep around the tree. Cut all the roots to a depth of 2 ft., then fill in the trench with good soil.

Set out fruit trees last May 15, the largest I could buy. Should I have trimmed or cut them back? Was May 15 early enough to set out in western Maine? Always set trees as early as you can get the ground in condition, which might be a little earlier than May 15. Fruit trees should always be pruned back at planting time to compensate for loss of roots, which always occurs when trees are dug.

What is meant by "ringing" of fruit trees? Taking out a ring of bark around the trunk or one or more main limbs of a tree —usually an apple tree. This causes carbohydrates synthesized in the leaves to stay in the top of the tree, above the ring. The result usually is a heavy set of fruit buds followed by a large crop, but the roots are starved for carbohydrates, so the tree is weakened. It will die if the ring is too wide to heal over in one season, therefore scoring by cutting through the bark in one or more places, all around the trunk, but without actually removing any bark, is a safer method. Ringing or scoring is usually used only on filler trees which are to be removed in 2 or 3 years anyway.

PROTECTION

Does it harm a young fruit tree to have its branches tied together in a compact column when covering them with burlap to protect them from winter sunscald?   If the branches are flexible and not frozen, they may be tied up. When frozen, they are brittle and will snap off.

Is whitewash beneficial to fruit trees? How should it be applied?   It might be in some localities, where sunscald occurs. Sunscald may be caused by absorption of heat on sunny side, followed by rapid drop in temperature as the sun goes down on bright but cold winter days. A whitewashed trunk will absorb less heat, so there will be less drop in temperature. A rapid drop in temperature will sometimes injure plant tissues. Whitewash probably has no other beneficial effect. It may be applied with a brush, or by means of a sprayer.

What is a good formula for whitewash for the trunks of trees? An old standard formula is as follows: Slake fresh quicklime in water; thin to a paste with skim milk; add 2 or 3 handfuls of salt to a pail.

Would it be advisable to use a good white-lead and oil paint on fruit trees?   No paint should be used on fruit trees except possibly on pruning wounds over 2 ins. in diameter. Most commercial growers do not paint wounds unless they are much larger than that. The paint does not cause the wound to heal faster but may help to keep the exposed wood from decaying before the new bark grows over the wound and seals out decay organisms.

Young apple trees protected against injury from rabbits by tar-paper cylinders tied around them.

How are young fruit trees best protected from mice in the winter?   Remove mulch and loosen plant material from around the trunk for a foot or more. Use strychnine-poisoned oats in the runways under matted grass. Sometimes snap mousetraps placed in the runs and baited with rolled oats will catch them.

What is the best protection against rabbits, for young fruit trees, other than using wire netting? The Fish and Wild Life Service of the United States Department of the Interior, Chicago, Illinois, has developed a satisfactory repellent paint which can be secured from that service.

POLLINATION AND FRUITING

What is cross-pollination? Cross-pollination is the transfer of the pollen of one variety to the pistil in the blossom of another variety.

What is meant when you say that a plant is self-sterile or self-unfruitful? The two terms are commonly used synonymously, but there is a difference. Self-sterile means that a variety will not form seeds with its own pollen. Self-unfruitful means that it will not form fruits with its own pollen.

Is there any explanation why a variety may be self-unfruitful? It is based on genetic factors. Sometimes the pollen may be sterile, i.e., not capable of germinating. In other cases it will be able to germinate but will fail to function.

Which fruit trees are not self-fertile? Fruits that are not self-fertile are many apples; all varieties of the European pear and its hybrids; a few varieties of peaches; all sweet cherries and Duke cherries; many of the European plums, most of the Japanese plums, and many of the hybrids arising from American plum species.

Will any variety of apple cross-pollinate another? No. There are certain varieties that definitely will not pollinate themselves, nor will they act as pollinators, because of a weakness in the pollen. Varieties that bear a close relationship, as Delicious, Starking, and Richared (the last two being bud sports of Delicious), will not cross-pollinate each other.

Are there some varieties of apples and cherries that will act as pollinators for one variety and not for another? Delicious forms good pollen but will not cross-pollinate its bud sports, Starking and Richared. Among sweet cherries there are a number of varieties that are selectively cross-fruitful.

Why do seedlings of fruit trees differ so much from the parents in fruit quality? Nearly all of our fruits are of complicated parentage, so that when seeds are sown all sorts of varieties may be expected to occur. Often the weakest qualities of the genus show up, or susceptibility to disease. Some do come relatively alike; Elberta peach seedlings, for instance, may all resemble Elberta in shape and color, but many will be clingstones and many will be of poor quality.

What is the latest on chemical fertilization of fruit blossoms? How expensive, if O.K.? Chemical sprays do not actually fertilize fruit-tree blossoms, but they may cause the fruit to hang on and develop without seeds. This is still in the experimental stage.

For how many years can the following fruit trees be expected to bear heavily: apple, pear, peach, sour cherry, sweet cherry, plum, quince? Will depend somewhat upon variety, and definitely upon climate, site, soil, culture. Apple, 50 to 75 years; pear, 35 to 50 years; quince, 25 to 30 years; peach, 15 years; plum, 30 years; sour cherry, 30 to 40 years; sweet cherry, 50 to 60 years. Profitable commercial production may be less.

Can I have young transplanted fruit trees bearing in a year or two? Fruit production of young trees depends on age. Four to 6 years for common tree fruits.

I have many fruit trees, some 3, 4, and 5 years old, and they do not produce yet. How can I make them produce? Many varieties of fruit trees do not normally produce fruit until the trees are 5 or 6 years old. Keep them growing well, but not too vigorously.

My fruit trees were set out 2 years ago but seem to show small progress. What should I do to get more rapid growth? (Tennessee.) Give them good growing conditions by cultivating and applying fertilizer, and lime if the soil needs it. It may be necessary to spray to control pests. Dry weather may have been a factor; if so, mulching will help.

How can I develop fruit trees quickly? I set out 15 trees 2 years ago and have had poor results. Fruit trees normally develop rather slowly; apple trees, for instance, taking 4 to 12 years, depending on the variety, to come into bearing. Give them good growing conditions, full sun, sufficient moisture, and the fertilizer needed by your particular soil.

I have a few fruit trees: peach, pear, and plum; none bear any fruit. Why? There might be several reasons: too young; weak, because of faulty nutrition; over-vegetative, because of too heavy pruning or too much nitrogen in the fertilizer; injury to buds or blossoms by low temperatures; injury by pests.

I have a home fruit orchard: apples, peaches, pears, plums,

and cherries. **The fruit seems small. How can the size be increased?** Size will depend on the variety, planting distance, natural fertility of soil, fertilizer treatment, moisture supply, and amount of pruning and thinning. Try to determine which factors were responsible, then improve conditions with respect to those factors. The system under which they are grown is a factor, whether on sod, cultivated, or mulch. Build up the humus content of the soil by the use of cover crops if the trees are on cultivated soil. If the soil is light and tends to dry out, use the mulch system and apply fertilizer early in spring. Trees in their first years should be well grown to eventually make vigorous trees.

Can I get quick returns from berries and grapes? Second season for berries, third for grapes. Fertilizers high in phosphorus and potash are important on sandy soils.

Does covering berry bushes with cheesecloth to keep birds away retard growth and ripening of fruit? Cheesecloth to keep birds away from berry bushes should be put on just as the fruit starts to ripen, and at this stage it will not appreciably retard growth or date of ripening.

How may heavily laden branches of fruit trees be prevented from breaking? Proper thinning of the fruits should be done after the so-called "June drop"; if still heavy, prop with stout crotched stakes.

HARVESTING AND STORING

What is the right time to pick apples, cherries, pears? For home use, most apple varieties may be left on the tree until ripe enough to use, or until they start to drop; pick cherries as soon as they are ripe enough to eat; most varieties of pears should be picked when fully grown but still relatively hard—when the first few specimens begin to acquire a yellowish tinge and start to drop.

How should fruit be harvested which is to be stored for winter? Each apple or pear should be picked from the tree, by hand or with a picker, before it is dead ripe. Avoid bruises, scratches, and cuts. Store only perfect fruit.

Where apples are stored in fruit cellar and temperature is controlled only by opening windows to outside air, but where humidity can be controlled, what degree of humidity should be maintained? Give as much ventilation as possible, and a relative humidity of 85 per cent.

Should the door of a fruit house (built into a bank, with stone

sides, wooden roof, ventilating opening in roof, concrete floor) be kept closed in early fall for apple storage; or open?   Close on warm days and open at night on cold days, to bring the temperature down close to 32° F.

Should apples in storage be kept dry or moist?   The air should circulate, and the room should be ventilated. The air should, if possible, have a relative humidity of around 85 per cent.

Should apples in storage be sprayed with water?   Apples in storage are sometimes sprayed with water, if the air becomes dry and there is danger of shriveling.

Will apples keep longer if waxed?   Commercial-wax emulsions will reduce shriveling in storage but may increase "scald" if not properly used. Moisture-proof cellophane wraps will also reduce shriveling. The best assurance of good keeping is to store a long-keeping variety where the air is moist and as near 32° F. as possible.

Should apples be wrapped when stored?   Wrapping will help to prevent shriveling and will keep decay from spreading if a few bad apples are mixed with the good ones. Special oil-treated wraps will prevent scald. Most apples stored commercially for any length of time are wrapped in oiled paper or have oil-impregnated paper strips scattered through the package.

Apples placed in a cold storage room looked fine when they came out, but 2 days later they looked as if they had been dipped in hot water. Why?   This is a storage trouble known as apple scald. It is worse if the fruit is picked before it is fully matured and colored. Some varieties are much more susceptible than others. Good ventilation in the storage will help to some extent. Wrapping the apples in thin paper impregnated with oil will prevent scald almost entirely. The immediate cause seems to be certain gases given off by the apples themselves, and the oil in the wraps will absorb these gases.

I have had some very fine apples, but no place to store them; cellar too warm, attic and garage too cold. How can they be stored inexpensively somewhere outdoors?   You could build an insulated storage room in the cellar, about a window. Or they can be stored in a barrel pit. (See Storage.)

EXHIBITING

How are tree fruits selected for shows?   Usually shown as plates of 5. Select fruits that are typical in form, size, coloring for the variety and vicinity; that are uniform in form, size, and color, and free from insect and disease injury. Do not wash or polish: dirt may be wiped off, but even this may mar the natural appearance.

PROPAGATION

What are Malling rootstocks?   At the East Malling Research Station in England have been collected all of the apple rootstocks that may be vegetatively propagated. Many of these are dwarfing stocks. They are given Roman numerals. VIII is a French Paradise, very dwarfing. V is Improved Doucin, a semi-dwarfing, etc. These are being tried in this country to test the adaptability of American varieties on the various types of stock.

Where can Paradise apple rootstock be obtained?   The Paradise apple rootstocks produce dwarfed trees, but the stock is much mixed. Any Agricultural Experiment Station in an apple-growing state that is testing the Malling stocks might be willing to distribute some.

Can grapes, peaches, cherries, and apples be grown from seeds obtained when you get them from the fruit you buy? All fruits are originally grown from seeds. They seldom resemble their parents, and more often than not are decidedly inferior.

How and when should seeds of cherry, peach, plum, apple, and pear be planted?   Mix with sand in the fall and place outdoors, where they will be kept moist. Freezing is beneficial but not essential; however, the temperature should not rise above 51° F.

How can I sprout apple seeds?   Seeds of apple may be mixed with moist sand, placed in a box, and set out of doors in winter. In the spring, plant the seeds in a nursery row and they should germinate that same season.

What is the difference between "budding" an apple tree and "grafting" one?   Both budding and grafting are used by nurserymen in growing young fruit trees. In the former case a bud (with a sliver of bark attached) is used; in grafting, a small section of a branch or shoot, with several eyes (called a scion). Both budding and grafting are also used when it is desired to add one or more varieties to an older tree.

Would it be practical for me, as an amateur, to attempt budding or grafting named varieties of apples on some young wild apple trees growing on my place?   Yes indeed; neither process is very difficult, though in this, as in most things, "practice makes

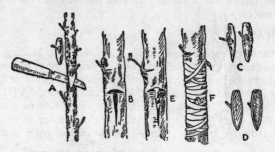

BUDDING

Budding is the simplest method of propagating a desired variety upon another of the same (or a closely related) species. (A) Bud stick; (C and D) different views of bud, after being cut from bud stick; (B) T-shaped cut in bark, on stock (stem or branch that is to be budded); (E) bud inserted; (F) bud bound in tight with raffia or rubber band.

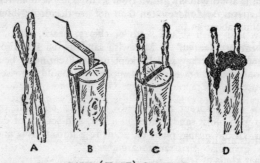

BARK (CLEFT) GRAFTING

A simple method of grafting for the amateur. (A) Scions, or sections of small branches of the variety it is desired to obtain. (B) Heel of grafting tool holding open the split or cleft in the end of branch on which graft is to be grown. (C) Scions cut to wedge shape and inserted so that bark layers of branch and scions come into direct contact. (D) Grafting wax applied to protect wound and prevent drying out.

perfect." For details of the operations, see illustrations on page 780, and below.

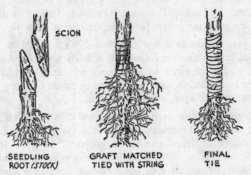

SCION

SEEDLING   GRAFT MATCHED   FINAL
ROOT *(STOCK)*   TIED WITH STRING   TIE

Steps in grafting a young fruit tree.

WHAT TO GROW

Can I grow orchard fruits on a small place?   Yes. There are numerous nurseries advertising trees with 3 or 4 varieties of apples grafted on one trunk. Pears, peaches, and plums require small space. Apple trees are set about 40 ft. apart; pear, peach, and plum about 20 ft. apart.

Which are the best kinds of tree fruits for home gardens in northern New Jersey?   This will depend somewhat on the personal preferences of the gardener. If there is room for only 1 or 2 trees, the apple would probably be most generally satisfactory: it makes a fair shade tree and can stand neglect better than the peach. Most pear varieties blight badly, except Seckel and Kieffer. The sour cherry Montmorency is fairly easy to grow, but birds are likely to get a good share of the fruit.

What kinds of fruit trees shall I plant in a space 75 × 150 ft. to give our family of 5 the best selection of fruit and assure fertilization of the blossoms? (New York.)   The varieties, and to some extent the kinds of fruit to plant, will depend on how cold it gets during the winter. If you are in a part of the state where peaches can be grown, try the following plan: Row 1 (4 ft. from fence), strawberries. Row 2 (8 ft. from first row), raspberries, currants, or other bush fruits. Row 3 (10 ft. from second row), grapes. Row 4 (20 ft.), 4 peach, 2 sour cherry, 2 pear. Row 5 (23 ft.), 6 apple trees. This will make the apple row 10 ft. from the edge of the plot, which may be too close or not, depending on who owns the adjoining land and the purpose for which it is used. There will be no pollination problem with the small fruits or sour cherries. With peaches and pears, planting of more than one variety will practically insure a satisfactory supply of pollen. McIntosh, Delicious, Cortland, Grimes, and many others are good pollinizers for other varieties of apples.

We plan to put in a few fruit trees. What would be a good selection for an amateur? Our soil is fairly good but somewhat shady. Do not plant fruits in the shade. Suggested kinds are listed in Introduction, and in questions on Kinds of Fruits. These, however, require open, sunny situations.

In planting a new orchard (of as few as 6 trees) on a place having no fruit at present, what would you advise? (Illinois.) Your choice of fruits should be governed by your soil and climatic conditions. Plant what is already growing well in your community, or consult your county agent.

What fruits can be grown in cold and short-growing season? Elevation 5,700 ft. (Montana.) Only the hardiest varieties such as some of the new fruits produced by breeding at the Minnesota and South Dakota Experiment stations. Write to your own Experiment Station for a list of recommended varieties.

APPLE

PLANTING

When is the proper time to plant apple trees? Some say fall, others spring. Either spring or fall. If you can get the plants and you live in a region where the autumn is long, fall will perhaps be better, as the soil can be handled and the trees planted when there is not much pressing work.

Can an apple tree be transplanted without injury to it if it had apples for the first time this year? Transplanting any tree is a shock, and if a tree has been bearing, transplanting (unless the entire root system is taken with it) may result in rapid vegetative growth that will retard fruiting.

Can apple trees (Anoke) safely be moved after they are 5 years old? Any tree can be moved with proper precautions. A tree as old as that should be trenched and moved with balled roots, either ball and burlap or frozen ball.

What is meant by "trenching" a tree for moving? Trenching is a process of preparing a tree for moving 1 year before the moving is done. Dig a trench completely around the tree 2 ft. wide and a little deeper than the roots extend (2 to 3 ft.). Cut off all roots clean. Fill the trench with good topsoil and tamp it down. New fibrous roots to replace those cut off will grow in this new soil.

In trenching a tree for moving, how far from the trunk should the trench be made? This will depend somewhat upon the size of the tree, the distance of the moving, and the equipment available. Balls of soil are heavy. Not any closer than ½ the distance from the trunk to the margin of the branches; better ⅔.

What is meant by a frozen ball? After trenching, when one growing season has elapsed, the tree may be moved in the late autumn or early winter. Dig a trench at the edge of the previous trench wide enough to work in, at the same time digging an inclined place so the ball can be pulled out of the hole. Now cut the soil off the ball, uniformly, until roots can be seen. Undercut at the bottom so that the ball is resting on ⅓ or less of its diameter. This cannot be done unless there is enough moisture in the soil to hold it together. Put some straw or other material in the bottom so the connecting section of soil will not freeze too hard. Wait until the ball is frozen solid, and will remain frozen, before attempting to move it. The new hole will have been dug, the soil placed under cover or protected so it will not freeze, and some straw placed in the bottom of the new hole to prevent deep freezing. If the distance is only a few feet, a trench can be made between the old hole and the new and the ball drawn through this. Otherwise, put it on a sledge or platform to move.

How should a 13-year-old apple tree be fertilized? Apple trees require a complete fertilizer treatment containing the important nutrient elements. The amount of each element needed is determined by the natural fertility of the soil and its past treatment. Therefore the requirements of a 13-year-old tree might vary from nothing in a very fertile soil to 20 lbs. of a 5–10–5 formula on a light sand. (See Fertilizer.)

When hog manure is spread in an apple orchard which comes into bearing age, is it necessary to apply lime or chemical fertilizer to prevent acidity of the soil? If so, how much should be applied? Make sure that enough lime is present so soil is not very acid. Use 20 per cent superphosphate, 400 to 600 lbs. to the acre, to balance the hog manure. (See Lime.)

What is the best time to plant apple and pear trees in state of Connecticut? Also best time of year to prune such trees? Prune and plant in very early spring before the buds begin to swell.

PRUNING APPLES

When is the best time to prune apple trees?   Any time during the dormant season is satisfactory. Actually the best pruning weather is likely to be in late fall, just after the leaves have dropped, and before the weather becomes too cold.

When is the proper time to prune apple trees in the Berkshires?   Late winter or early spring.

What are the main points to keep in mind when pruning a bearing apple tree?   Do not remove a branch unless there is a good reason why it should come off. Some varieties will require very little pruning. Take out limbs that are dead, broken, or badly diseased, too low, or too high; remove water sprouts from trunk and main limbs, thin out a little in the top, if necessary, to admit light to the lower limbs; remove slender, obviously weak twigs.

How can I prune so there will not be a lot of water sprouts? If large branches are to be removed, take them out gradually, over 2 or 3 years. This will result in fewer water sprouts, and these can be detected and rubbed off before they become large.

Is it true that fall pruning of fruit trees cuts down sucker growth?   Fruit trees react the same to dormant pruning regardless of whether it is done soon after the leaves fall in the autumn or just before growth starts in the spring.

What happens when apple spurs are pruned off?   Most of the fruit in certain varieties is borne on short, crooked growths known as spurs. These spurs start to form on 2-year-old wood and grow very slowly. If spurs are pruned off a particular section of a limb, they will not be replaced, and that part of the tree cannot produce any fruit.

Is summer pruning of trees advisable to make them bear fruit earlier?   Most experiments have indicated that dormant pruning is preferable. Certainly summer pruning is not of any practical value as a means of hastening fruit production by young trees.

How often should apple trees, just planted, be pruned? Prune at planting time, and early each spring thereafter.

Should bearing-age apple trees, which were pruned when shipped from nursery, be further pruned when planted?   It may be necessary if the trees are shipped bare root. If there appears to be any drying out, more pruning may be necessary—back

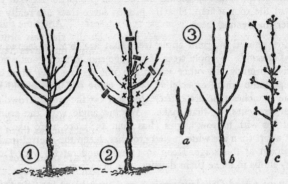

APPLE TREE PRUNING

(1) A 2-year-old nursery-grown tree, as received and planted. (2) The same tree after being pruned. The "X" signs indicate branches removed entirely. (3) Effects of cutting back compared with thinning. (a) Twig severely cut back. (b) Growth from cut-back twig is all vegetative (no flowers). (c) Growth from tree with thinning pruning only; nice balance of twig growth and flowering spurs is clearly evidenced.

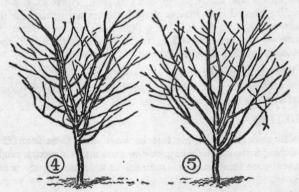

(4) Neglect of early training results in poor framework. A Stayman apple about 6 years old with three "leaders" (very undesirable), pole-like growths, and bad crotch. To correct these faults now means a high head. (5) Early training results in good form. Stayman apple about 6 years old; good spacing of scaffold branches. Central leader still present. Note development of secondary branches.

to live wood. The top should be reduced proportionately to the size of the root system. Heavily pruned large trees are really no better than young trees.

How should I prune apple trees that are in their second or third season?   Apple trees of this age should receive only corrective pruning. In other words, do not remove any branches except those which especially need to come off. This would include branches that are broken, too low on the trunk, crowding other branches, or that make a narrow angle with the trunk. Crotches with narrow angles (less than 45°) are more likely to split apart than are wide-angled crotches. Keep the central leader dominant at this stage. Head in (prune moderately) very long, leggy limbs to make them develop side branches.

I have a Red Delicious apple 3 or 4 yrs. old, about 8 ft. high. What is proper method to prune? Would like to keep it as low as possible.   You could take out some of the top shoots in order to keep the top low, but do as little pruning as possible. Very much pruning at this age will keep the tree vegetative and delay the time at which it will come into bearing.

After planting a Dolgo crab tree 3 ft. high, does one prune it the first year, and how much? What care does it need in winter?   Crabapples are hardy. They don't require winter care. Only pruning needed is to remove those branches not needed for the framework. Select the 3, 4, or 5 branches that are to form the frame so they are spaced 8 to 12 ins. apart on the trunk, thus avoiding crotches. Remove the rest.

When is the proper time to prune old apple trees?   Renovation pruning can be done any time during the dormant period; that is, while the leaves are off the trees.

CULTURE

Can mulching an apple tree be overdone?   Seldom. If a mulching material that will pack down too much is used, it might prevent root aeration. Loose material to a depth of 4 to 12 ins. is good.

What special care do apple trees need in the spring?   Proper pruning and spraying, and then attention to the fertilization of the soil. (See Fertilizer.)

How should the fruit of an apple tree be thinned? What is the best method and time?   Thin when the young apples are about the size of hulled walnuts. Leave at least 6 or 7 ins. between fruits. The small apples may be removed by snapping the stem with thumb and finger, being careful not to injure the spur. Special thinning shears are available, and very useful.

Can bearing-size fruit trees, such as apple, cherry, or peach, be purchased at a nursery? Some nurseries advertise bearing-size trees. They are seldom satisfactory unless handled with ball and burlap. (See Introduction.)

How soon after the autumn planting of "bearing-age" apple and pear trees should they be permitted to bear fruit? Usually the trees will determine this themselves. They must reach a balance of growth and food storage before they will produce.

I have just purchased a 6-ft. McIntosh apple tree. How many years, approximately, until it bears fruit? With good care it should bear in the 6th year, in the orchard.

How much should a Red Delicious apple tree grow a year if planted at 2 years of age? The first year it should increase its height about 2½ ft.; the next year 2 ft. Ordinarily, 3 to 6 shoots, 30 to 48 ins. long may be produced in the first year.

An apple tree bears fruit by halves—that is, first one side bears apples and the next year the other side. How do you explain this? (New York.) Some varieties bear a full crop in alternate years. In the case of your tree, something happened to upset the periodicity on one side. This is a desirable condition.

We have an Astrachan apple tree that bore no fruit last year. It is about 12 years old and bore abundantly the previous year. We have lived here for 1½ years. Would you have any explanation? Red Astrachan is generally an alternate-year bearer.

Have two early apple trees bearing only every other year, but together. Can I change the bearing years of one of them? The only certain way is to remove practically all the flowers, or small fruits from one of them. There are promises of deflorating sprays, but none is yet completely effective.

What can be done to an apple tree (about 5 years old) to get it to blossom and bear fruit? It is now about 10 to 11 ft. high. Any variety of apple must reach a particular state of internal development before it will set fruits. Do only corrective or formative pruning, and do not fertilize too heavily with nitrogen. When the proper balance is reached, the tree will fruit; to use means to hasten this might prove dangerous.

What causes a young medium-size apple tree to have only one large flawless apple? Probably it is a self-unfruitful variety and needs to be pollinated by a compatible variety.

We have a Wealthy apple tree about 8 years old that seems to produce a lot of foliage but few apples. What is the reason? Wealthy is one of the earliest varieties to bear. Probably too much nitrogen, or too heavy pruning. Inexperienced persons have been known to prune off the fruiting spurs also.

Have a Grimes Golden apple tree in yard 8 years old. Has been pruned by experienced nursery 1940 and 1941, yet will not bloom; hence, no fruit. Why?   Grimes Golden should bear at about 5 or 6 years in the orchard. Probably the pruning was too heavy and encouraged vegetative growth.

I have a Golden Delicious apple tree 10 years old which has had only 5 apples on it. Tree looks fine; 12 ft. high. Why no apples?   Delicious apples will not set a crop of fruit to their own pollen. Some compatible variety must be grown nearby.

I have 10 apple trees, 16 years old, which do not bear any fruit. This is a small orchard by itself. Can anything be done to make it bear? (Wisconsin.)   This may be due to winter injury; if so, there is little chance of correcting the condition. If a tree is making a very vigorous growth and does not form fruit buds, it may be caused by pruning too heavily, or by using too much nitrogenous fertilizer, in which case the remedy is evident.

How can immature apples be prevented from dropping? Nearly all species of fruiting trees lose some fruits by dropping when the fruits are small; this is called the June drop. The reason is that more fruits are formed than the tree can support. Sometimes the drop is because of imperfect fertilization by pollen. Sometimes it is caused by codling moth or curculio, which can be prevented by spraying. (See Section VIII.)

What new spray is used to prevent dropping of premature fruits, such as apples?   Various commercial brands of hormone sprays or pre-harvest sprays may be obtained. The active agent in most of these is napthalene acetic acid. These are for premature dropping of nearly mature fruits.

My 2 apple trees have full bloom, but when the apples form they fall off. Spraying helps very little. Can you offer a solution?   If the fruits attain a size of ½ to ¾ ins., the spraying may be with the wrong material, or applied at the wrong time, or otherwise inadequate. If they drop at smaller size, it may be a question of incompatible pollination or too rapid growth.

How old must a Northern Spy apple tree be to produce fruit? What is the matter if an apparently healthy tree does not yield? Northern Spy apple requires the longest period of any variety to reach the stage of fruitfulness. This may be as much as 15 or 20 years in some instances.

What is best method to make apple and pear trees 50 to 60 years old profitable? Pruning, spraying, soil enrichment, etc. If they have been long neglected, might be better to start anew. They may be too tall for profitable handling, and then many new and better varieties have come along since these were planted. If in fair condition, a renovation pruning with lime and fertilizer and spraying may bring them back.

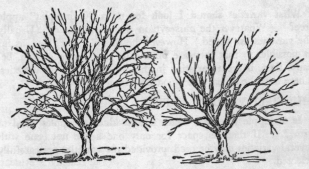

Old neglected fruit trees can be cut back severely to form new, lower heads, thus making them easier to care for.

How about apple trees that have been neglected for several years and no longer bear fruit fit to eat? Can these trees be brought back to a normal condition? If so, how? Renovation pruning, lime (probably), fertilization, and proper spraying are indicated. These measures will gradually restore the trees to vigor, provided, of course, they are not too old.

How can I preserve an old apple tree that is beginning to decay? Cut and scrape off all decayed material down to sound wood, and paint large cuts with a good tree paint. If there are bad crotches, it will pay to secure the limbs with a chain or a bolt brace. It seldom pays to fill large cavities.

How can I tell flower buds from leaf buds on apple trees in the summer? Apples form most of their flower buds at the ends of short spurs. Some varieties may form them laterally, on longer twigs of the current season's growth. Flower buds are plump and more rounded than the narrow-pointed leaf buds.

Is there any way to keep apple trees from blooming too early? Frost always gets our blossoms. There is no practical way to delay the blooming date. Certain varieties, such as Rome Beauty and Ralls, bloom later than most. Consult your State Experiment Station as to hardy varieties for your locality. You may be in a place where the climate does not permit apples to be grown successfully.

Is it possible to determine the variety of apples by the appearance of the leaf on a "Quintuplet" apple tree?   Probably only a few men in the country are qualified to determine, negatively or positively, some varieties of apples by their foliage. It would require an unusual knowledge in this field.

What varieties should I look for on a "Quintuplet" apple tree?   Whatever the nurseryman chooses to put on. (Usually the varieties are stated.) However, he should select these, as far as possible, so that they are practically uniform in growth, because there is great variation in the growth of various varieties. There must be at least one good pollinator in the lot.

MULTIPLE-VARIETY TREES

Is an apple tree that bears several kinds of apples good to grow?   If there is space for only one apple tree, one with several varieties may be used, provided the varieties are carefully selected.

About how much room is needed for a "5-in-1" apple tree?   Since these are grafted on standard roots, they will require a space about 35 × 45 ft.

How soon can I expect fruit from a 5-in-1 apple tree?   Depends upon the varieties used. Some varieties will produce fruits in 3 to 5 years after planting; others require 5 to 8 years, and sometimes more. Growth conditions, as governed by site, soil, and fertilization will also have an effect.

Will a "5-in-1" apple tree continue to bear heavily over a long period of years?   If properly cared for, it should bear as long as if the same varieties were planted individually.

What precautions should be taken in pruning a non-bearing "Quintuplet" apple tree?   Try to secure as uniform a development of each variety as possible. If one is weaker than the others, prune it more lightly than the more vigorous kinds. Only prune in winter, but pinch back rapid growths in summer to act as a stopper.

My "Quintuplet" apple tree is lopsided. Why?   The varieties are such as do not grow at a uniform rate, or the union on one may not be as good as with the others. The exposure as related to shading may affect one more than another. (See above.)

INSECTS AND DISEASES

See Section VIII.

My apple tree is turning green around the trunk. What is the cause? What is the remedy? The green color is probably caused by moss or lichens growing on the dead outer bark. It will do no harm, but may indicate poor circulation of air, or too much shade. Possibly pruning has been neglected. This condition usually does not occur on sprayed trees.

What causes hard brown spots in apples? The trees appear healthy, but the apples are not fit to use. Probably "bitter pit," usually associated with excessive tree growth late in the season. Some varieties especially susceptible, such as Baldwin or Northern Spy. In some localities lack of boron in the soil may cause brown spots in the flesh of the apple.

Is it the same kind of aphis that we have on other plants that curl up apple leaves? These are "green" and "rosy" apple aphids. If they are present, the eggs may be killed by a dormant spray of dinitro cresol or dinitro phenol compound, which is miscible in oil or water. This spray also kills scales and mites. A summer infestation may be controlled with a nicotine spray.

Are there borers that attack apple trees? There are 3 that may: Round-headed apple-tree borer, flat-headed apple-tree borer, and leopard-moth borer. The round-headed usually attacks young trees, and the laying of eggs may be prevented by means of repellent paint, or covering the trunks with fine-meshed wire or with paper. The flat-headed usually works in old, neglected trees. The leopard moth attacks young trees or branches. Examine the trees frequently, and if sawdust is seen near the trunk, look for the hole. Sometimes the larvae may be killed in the hole with a fairly stiff wire; but carbon disulphide or a nicotine paste made especially for the purpose will usually be effective.

My apples all have worms in them. What shall I do? These are probably codling moth, and are controlled by spraying with arsenate of lead at the proper stage of flower and fruit development. When there is only one brood, the critical stages are petal fall and 10 days after; incidence of this insect varies, and there may be more than one brood, requiring several sprays. Consult your county agricultural agent or Agricultural College or Experiment Station.

What causes young apples to fall off? They have crescent-

shaped marks on them.   This is the egg-laying mark of curculio. Arsenate of lead is the control, used with other materials
for additional insects and diseases. Pink-bud and petal-fall spray
are important, but others may be necessary in different localities.
Consult your county agent, Agricultural College, or Experiment
Station for spray schedule.

In July, when I approach my apple trees, myriads of little flies
come out. What are they?   They may be leaf hoppers. Keep
watch just after bloom. The nymphs cannot then fly, but are
very shy and sidle away. This is the time to kill them with a
nicotine spray. They are not easy to kill as adults.

What is San Jose scale?   A sucking insect which forms a
hard circular covering that attacks orchard fruits and related
plants, especially apple, peach, pear. It may kill young trees of 2
or 3 years. It is indicated by scurfy appearance when the scales
are thickly clustered on young twigs. There may be a reddish
discoloration along veins of leaves, or small circular red spots on
fruits. Control is lime-sulphur or miscible oil as dormant spray.
Which to use depends upon whether other insects or diseases
need to be controlled with the same application.

How can I get rid of tent caterpillars?   Apple-tree tent
caterpillars east of the Rockies, and a similar species west, infest
wild cherries, apples, etc. In regularly sprayed orchards they are
usually no problem, but in home fruit gardens they may be. Do
not burn them, as this will injure the tree. Spray with arsenate
of lead when the nests are about the size of a silver dollar. Better
still, follow the regular spray schedule for your state.

What are the brown and somewhat star-shaped spots on my
apples?   This is apple blotch, prevalent in the South and
Southeast. Spray with Bordeaux mixture, if the variety will
tolerate it, during petal fall. A regular spray schedule with
wettable sulphur and lime sulphur usually gives control.

Why do they order cedar trees cut down near apple orchards?
The Red Cedar and the apple are alternate hosts for the so-
called cedar rust which is indicated by light-yellow spots changing to orange on apple leaves and fruits in spring and summer;
cedar "galls" on cedar in winter, developing to release spores in
early spring. Spraying is not effective. If you prefer Red Cedars,
keep them and destroy the apple trees; or vice versa.

What makes the leaves on some of the twigs of my apple trees
turn black and dry up, just as if they had been burned?   This
is fire blight, a bacterial disease. Cut these off well back from the
dead part. Use a solution of zinc chloride to sterilize tools after

each cut. Look for cankers on the trunk or limbs and clean these out. Regulate the growth of the trees so that it is not too vigorous. Spraying with Bordeaux mixture while the trees are in full bloom will often prevent infection through this means.

What is apple scab? It appears as dark-gray, irregular spots on the fruits, but it is carried over winter on fallen leaves. It may completely defoliate trees. A severe infestation makes fruit unsalable and sometimes inedible. Wettable sulphur for pink bud and for petal fall sprays is the most important control. Many Experiment Stations release dates of spraying based on the development of the disease.

VARIETIES

What is best and quickest-growing apple tree? If you have only a small garden space, it might be inadvisable to plant an apple tree. (See Introduction to this section.) A variety that would suit your purpose might be even more important than earliness of fruit bearing. Golden Delicious usually bears fruit at 4 years, Wealthy at 5 years after planting.

Which varieties of apples have proved suitable in New York? The McIntosh family of apples are all good in the Northeastern states. Melba ripens in August, Milton in September, McIntosh, Cortland, and Macoun in early winter. Rhode Island Greening and Northern Spy are good winter varieties.

For a family which likes crisp, hard, slightly tart, and very juicy, old-fashioned apples, and which has room for only 2 or 3 trees, which varieties would you recommend for central New Jersey? You might try Wealthy for medium early, Jonathan for early winter, and Stayman for a late variety.

What is the best all-round or all-purpose apple tree to plant in New England? Baldwin.

APRICOT

Can apricots be grown in central Massachusetts? Yes. They have been growing for many years at the Arnold Arboretum in Boston. However, late spring freezes frequently kill the flowers. The new "Scout" variety is said to be one of the hardiest, but another variety should be planted with it for cross-pollination purposes.

We have 2 apricot trees 8 to 10 years old. What can I do to prevent fruit rotting just before it becomes ripe? (California.) Spray with wettable sulphur when calyx or shuck splits, again in 10 days, and twice more at 2- to 3-week intervals.

CHERRY

SOILS AND PLANTING

Under what conditions of soil and climate can sweet cherries be grown successfully?   They need a sandy loam, deep and well drained. Climate is even more important. The shores of the Great Lakes, the Hudson Valley of New York, and the Pacific coast are the areas where sweet cherries are grown commercially. They are susceptible to winter injury and late frosts and do not like extremely hot summers.

Are sour cherries fussy as to soil and climate?   These can be grown over most of the Atlantic coast and in the Mississippi Valley. Commercially, they are grown in New York, Wisconsin, and Michigan. They can be grown on sandy or heavy soils, if well drained, and can stand drought better than sweet cherries.

When should young cherry trees be fertilized to bring them most quickly into bearing?   If young cherry trees need fertilizing, do it in early spring. As a general rule they would start bearing at an earlier age if they were grown a bit slowly. It is desirable to grow good-sized trees as quickly as possible, in order to get a large crop; hence the trees are usually forced while young, thus sacrificing very early bearing for the larger size of tree.

What is a good fertilizer for cherries and how should it be applied?   On sandy soil of average fertility a complete fertilizer such as a 5–10–5 might be used at the rate of 300 to 500 lbs. per acre. Then use nitrate of soda or some other readily available nitrogenous material in quantity sufficient to maintain good, vigorous growth. Broadcast complete fertilizer in early spring, the nitrate of soda later as needed.

What is the best age to buy cherry trees and when should trees be planted?   One- or 2-year-old trees. Plant in early spring in the North. Farther South, in late autumn.

PRUNING; GENERAL CULTURE

Should cherry trees be pruned and at what age?   Cherry trees should be pruned each year, but removal of a few undesirable twigs may be all the pruning needed. They require less pruning than the apple or peach.

When is the best time to prune cherry trees?   At any time during the dormant season. The best time is in early spring— during the latter part of March.

How should cherry trees be pruned? With sweet cherries little need be done except to remove dead or injured branches and twigs that are growing in an undesirable position as too high or tending to make a weak crotch. Sour cherries should be started as delayed open-center trees with a short trunk about 6 ft. high and several well-spaced scaffold limbs. Besides the "corrective" pruning as recommended for sweet cherries some thinning of tops will be needed to keep trees from becoming too dense and so shading out fruit-bearing wood in lower part. If trees are pruned every year, not a great deal of cutting will be needed at any one time.

I have been told a Bing sweet cherry will not produce fruit when planted by itself. What variety will? I don't want more than 1 tree. No sweet cherry will produce fruit to its own pollen. Nearly all sweet varieties will pollinate others. You might top-work (graft) Windsor or Black Tartarian on a branch of the Bing. This will provide enough pollination for 1 tree.

I have a Black Tartarian cherry tree surrounded with plums, peaches, Oka cherry, Rocky Mountain cherry, and apples. Does it need any other cherry for fertilization? None of these is an effective pollinator. You could use Bing, Windsor, Napoleon, and Wood.

Will the Oka cherry act as a cross-pollinator for the Elephant Heart plum? Possibly. The Oka is said to be ¾ sand cherry and ¼ Japanese plum. Another Japanese plum variety would probably be better than the Oka, however.

What do you recommend doing for white cherry tree when very small green cherries fall off before maturing? Plant another variety to act as a pollinator.

What causes the small green cherries (sour cherry) to drop off the tree? May be lack of pollination or attacks by curculio. (See Cherry—Chapter VIII.)

I planted 3 cherry trees and 2 days later we had frost. How should I protect these trees from frost? If the trees were dormant, as they should have been for transplanting, frost a few days after planting would not hurt them.

I have a 15-year-old sweet cherry tree. Why does it bear only a few large fruits? This tree is located in a strip 4 ft. wide separating two cement driveways. This is a very poor location for a tree. Probably there is no other sweet cherry tree in the near neighborhood to act as a pollinator.

Will fruit trees be injured by sulphur from coal smoke? We

live in a railroad town.   Too much gas in the atmosphere, from burning coal or other sources, might be unfavorable for tree growth. However, it has to be pretty concentrated and continuous to cause injury. Many so-called railroad towns have nice trees.

How long does it take for a cherry tree to blossom?   A sour cherry should produce its first blossoms 3 or 4 years after planting. A sweet cherry tree may take 1 to 3 years longer.

How can I retard the blooming of cherry, peach, plum, and apricot trees?   There is no practical method of retarding blooming dates of fruit trees in order to avoid frost injury. Some varieties naturally bloom a little later than others.

We raised a cherry tree from a pit; it is 3 years old. Will it bear fruit?   It will bear eventually but is not likely to resemble the parent.

A sour cherry tree bore fruit 1 year and none the next. Why? The blossoms or buds were probably injured by cold weather.

I have 4 cherry trees which bloom but have only a dozen or so cherries. Why?   Probably because of imperfect pollination. If your trees are all of one variety, plant some other. There are 7 distinct groups which will not pollinate each other, so the variety must be selected with care and also as to possibility of frost injury.

I accidentally broke a branch in the lower part of a cherry tree that left a groove in the bark; the sap keeps running out at foot of tree. What must I do to correct this?   Sap will run from any kind of an injury on a cherry tree. There is no practical method of repairing an injury such as the one described. If the tree is growing vigorously, the wound may heal over eventually.

What is the height of Carolina cherry tree?   There is a sweet cherry variety named Caroline. It is described as upright, spreading, and vigorous, so would probably attain a height of 25 to 30 ft.

PESTS AND DISEASES

How can I keep my cherries free of insects and diseases? Plum curculio and brown rot are worst. (See Section VIII for control.) Cherry leaf spot appears first as yellow spots—in the leaves. These turn brown and fall out. They look like shot holes. Leaves turn yellow and fall. Sometimes tree is completely defoliated. Lime sulphur or wettable sulphur sprays in the regular schedule should control this.

I have a cherry tree that blooms every year; the cherries start forming, then wither and fall off tree.   Sounds like injury by plum curculio, which attacks the small fruits. It may be controlled by spraying with arsenate of lead soon after the blossoms fall. Ask your Experiment Station for spraying recommendations.

How can I keep birds from eating my cherries and other fruits?   This is a hard question to answer. The only 100 per cent way is to build a cage around the tree or stay and guard it from sunup until sundown. Scarecrows of various kinds will help some, especially if put up before the birds get a taste of the fruit. Tethering a captive hawk in or near the tree is one method which works well—if you can find the hawk. Hanging up objects, such as inflated paper bags, which will blow about in the wind, is sometimes successful but not always.

What are the principal insects and diseases of cherries?   See Chapter VIII.

PEACHES

What kind of soil is needed for peach trees?   Any good soil that is well drained. They prefer sandy loam or light clay, however.

Should I mix fertilizer with the soil when I plant a peach tree?   Do not mix fertilizer with soil used to fill in around roots, as it might cause some injury. Dig it under before the tree is planted or work into soil around newly planted tree, but outside limits of the hole in which it was planted.

Would it be all right to allow leaves of a peach tree to remain on the ground to be used with fertilizer?   The leaves of any tree, if not infected with a serious disease, may be used for soil improvement.

Should I plant a peach orchard in spring or fall?   In general, except where winters are quite mild, spring planting is best. (See Introduction.)

Is it wise to plant new peach trees in the same places from which old ones have just been removed?   It is better not to. If there seems to be a special reason for putting a new tree where an old one was taken out, dig in some lime, superphosphate and well-rotted manure. This will counteract, to some extent, the partial exhaustion of soil fertility caused by the old tree.

I have a bearing peach tree. When can I move it?   Moving a bearing-age peach tree is hazardous. It must be pruned heavily and might be as long coming into bearing again as a new tree. It can be moved in fall, but very early spring would be better.

How should I care for a peach tree that produced its first crop last year?   Prune it moderately, cultivate, apply what fertilizer may be needed for your particular soil conditions. You will probably also need to apply a treatment for borers and do some spraying in order to get fruit of good quality.

How does one care for a peach tree in a suburban back yard? Ideal treatment would include cultivation of soil around tree; use of a complete fertilizer; lime if necessary; adequate pruning; some spraying and thinning of fruit whenever a heavy crop is set. Control of peach borer, which works in the trunk just above level of soil, is very important.

I have 3 5-year-old, thrifty peach trees: Early Crawford and Hale. Why do they bloom well but bear only 5 or 6 peaches? The variety might be self-sterile, as J. H. Hale. If other varieties are near to furnish pollen, then there must be some other reason for failure. Blossoms may have been killed by frost. Give them another chance.

My peach tree has 3 main trunks at ground level, forming a sort of cup which is filled with gum. How shall I treat it? Probably result of killing the leading shoot when tree was a year or two old. Best cut away 2 of them as close as possible and arrange drainage so water will not stand in "cup" if one is left. Paint the wounds.

I have a Halehaven peach tree which has had only ½ doz. peaches. Could you explain why and what to do to improve fruit? The tree may be too young to bear a full crop. It should have a full crop by the fourth year if it is making good growth and has not been injured by cold weather.

Why do some peach trees fail to bear? (California.) Might be due to any one or more of these factors: lack of enough winter cold to complete the rest period, frost injury to buds or flowers, lack of pollination (if a self-sterile variety), or faulty nutrition.

I have a 3-year-old peach tree about 8 ft. high with no blossoms on it yet. It grew from a Halehaven pit. When will it bear fruit, or must I graft it? Peaches usually bear at 3 or 4 years of age. Whether a seedling will bear good fruit is a matter of chance. Seedlings are budded in their first season's growth to standard varieties. (See Budding.)

Have 6 peach trees which grew from Elberta seeds. What could I do to them to assure successful blooms and fruit? The best method would be to bud them to some desirable variety.

Why do my young peach trees (2 years old) drop all leaves and then start up from roots? These trees have been sprayed 5 times with wettable sulphur from early spring. It is possible something in the spray has caused leaves to drop. A 2-year-old tree should not ordinarily need 5 sprays, as there would be no fruit to protect at this age.

What is the approximate life of a peach tree? With good care peaches can be made to produce for about 20 to 25 years.

I have a young peach tree about 12 ft. away from a large oak tree. Will it grow and produce fruit there as well as it would in the open, or should it be moved? You have two handicaps: competition of roots, and shade. Better move it. Peaches need full sun.

Will a peach tree which came up from seed ever bear good peaches? It may or may not. If it is a seedling of Elberta, it will resemble that variety.

My peach tree is simply loaded with fruit but it never gets large enough to amount to anything. The fruit should be thinned when a little larger than a robin's egg. Take off all small or stunted peaches, leaving at least 6 ins. between the fruits that remain on the tree. Thinning will result in larger size, better color, and less breakage of limbs.

What is the best method of "domesticating" wild grown or neglected 2- to 3-year-old peach trees? Probably better to start anew if badly neglected. If not too bad, plow, lime (if needed), fertilize soil, prune, and give good spraying. Take out very bad trees and replace.

How can a peach tree 4 years old be changed to another variety? Peaches can be top-worked (see Grafting), but cleft grafting used for apples or pears is not successful with peaches. The way to proceed is to cut off branches 2 or 3 ins. in diameter in late winter. During the summer, shoots will appear, and these can be budded in July, August, or early September, just as seedling peaches are budded. (See Division II—Propagation.)

Will peach-tree roots block up a drain or sewer? Peach roots will not seek out a drain or sewer; but roots of any tree planted above or very close to a loose-joint sewer will enter it

PRUNING PEACHES

When and how should I prune newly planted peach trees?
Prune just before the trees are planted or just after. Small nursery
trees, 3 to 4 ft. high, should be pruned to a "whip" (a single
stem) and cut back to a height of 24 to 30 ins. Larger trees, 5 to
6 ft., should be cut back to about 30 to 36 ins., but instead of
cutting off all side branches leave 3, suitably spaced to be used
as scaffold limbs, and cut them to stubs 4 to 6 ins. long.

What is the proper way to prune a young peach tree?   Develop an open center, bowl-shaped type of tree with lowest scaffold limb at least a foot from the ground. Remove limbs that are
too low, that head in and tend to fill up the center, or that crowd
other limbs and make any part of tree too dense. Tallest limbs
should be headed to side branches pointing outward in order to
get maximum spread and keep center open.

**What time and method should be used in pruning old peach
trees?**   Pruning may be done during late fall, winter or early
spring. Old peach trees have general type of tree already established, hence pruning at this stage is to maintain vigor, thin crop,
and remove weak twigs. Pruning should be more severe than for
younger trees. Cut out weak twigs and limbs, thin out year-old
shoots by taking out weaker ones. Cut back shoots that are longer
than 12 ins. As tree gets older, severe pruning needed to maintain vigor may cause it to be smaller than it was as a younger
tree.

When is the best time to remove a limb from a peach tree?
Any time it seems necessary, although it is usually done during
the dormant season.

**What is the best way to fix a peach-tree limb which was
broken because of the heavy crop?**   If the branch can be
spared, cut if off. If it is split in the middle, prop it up and put
in a few small bolts with washers.

Should one cut all dead limbs from peach trees?   All dead
limbs should be removed from all trees, as they present a disease
and insect hazard. You should have no dead limbs if you prune
peach trees properly.

How do you prune a nectarine tree?   A nectarine is essentially a peach without fuzz, and is pruned in the same way
as a peach.

SPECIAL PROBLEMS

Must peach trees be cross-pollinated?   Only varieties J. H. Hale and the Mikado must be cross-pollinated.

Do peach trees need a mulch for winter?   Mulching soil about peach trees will have no appreciable effect on their susceptibility to injury by cold weather.

What is the best method to protect young peach trees from freezing in winter and from rabbits?   There isn't much that can be done in a practical way to protect peach trees from freezing. If they are of a hardy variety and in good growth condition, they will be as resistant to cold as it is possible to make them. Rabbits usually are not so likely to bother peach trees as apple trees. Mechanical protection by use of wirecloth, building paper, or even newspapers wrapped around trunk is probably most satisfactory.

What is the best method of propagation for peaches? Peaches are usually budded on seedlings grown from wild peach seeds. (See Budding.)

When I cut open peaches that appear to be sound, why are there little pink worms in them?   These are the larvae of the Oriental peach moth. Gather up and destroy all fruits at end of season. Treatment of trees for borer will kill some. No satisfactory control by spraying or dusting yet developed.

What are the main insects and diseases that trouble peaches? See Section VIII.

VARIETIES

What are the best varieties of peach trees to plant?   See Introduction.

Which is best, Southhaven or J. H. Hale peach?   It all depends on what you want. Southhaven is earlier and hardier; J. H. Hale is larger and more attractive. J. H. Hale is male sterile. It requires a pollinator to produce fruits.

PEAR

When does one fertilize young pear trees to bring them into early bearing?   The trees will bear earlier if making a moderate growth than if growing too vigorously. Overfertilization is also conducive to fire blight. If soil is poor, make a light application of a complete fertilizer in early spring. Otherwise, if tree is making good growth, do not use fertilizers.

What soil is best for pear trees?   Heavy sandy loam or clay loam with plenty of humus which will hold moisture, yet assure good drainage.

When is the best time to plant Bartlett pears?   Plant trees early in the spring as the soil can be prepared. Planting should be completed by time fruit-tree buds begin to expand.

How can I plant, care for, and prune Bartlett pear trees? Am setting out 100 trees this spring.   A hundred trees of Bartlett pears will involve considerable care and expense. It would be advisable, therefore, to get rather complete information from your Experiment Station as to fertilizing, spraying, etc., under your particular local conditions. When making planting plans, some provision should be made for cross-pollination by planting at least 5 or 6 trees of another variety.

Why has a pear tree which bore fine pears when first planted 3 years ago had none since?   A pear tree would not be expected to bear until 3 to 5 years after it is planted. Give it good growing conditions and it will start producing at the proper time, barring damage by frost and pests.

Our 5-year-old Bartlett pear has twice borne fruit sparingly. It is of good size and leaves look healthy. Why are leaves very small and few?   This tree is doing well to have borne fruit twice the first 5 years. Bartlett leaves are normally rather small, so perhaps the tree has nothing wrong with it. If you stimulate its growth too much, you may have trouble with the disease known as fire blight.

Will one pear tree alone in a garden bear fruit?   Most varieties of pears will bear a much better crop if cross-pollinized, so in making a new planting it would be highly desirable to include at least 2 varieties unless there are other varieties growing in the immediate neighborhood. However, single trees sometimes prove to be fairly reliable croppers.

Is Bartlett pear self-fertile? If not, what variety should I plant near it?   Bartlett will set a much better crop if cross-fertilized. Any of the common varieties, such as Seckel, Bosc, or Anjou would be satisfactory pollinizers.

Does a Duchess pear need cross-pollination?   Experiments in New York and in California indicate that this variety may bear a fair crop if self-pollinized but a better crop if cross-pollinated.

PRUNING PEARS

How should mature pear trees be pruned?   Mature pear trees of most varieties require very little pruning and are likely to be injured by fire blight if pruned too heavily. Simply remove dead and broken branches. If trees become too high, leaders may be cut back a little to a side branch.

How do you prune pear trees at planting time?   One-year trees will be unbranched whips. Head a 5-ft. tree back to 3½ or 4 ft. Two-year nursery trees will have 2 to 6 side branches; remove all side branches below 30 ins., save 2 to 4 of the stronger ones well distributed around the trunk and spaced at least 4 ins. apart. Remove the rest, head the leader back by about ⅓.

Our pear and plum trees have not had very much fruit for several years. They have never been pruned. How and when should this be done?   The lack of fruit is probably due to other factors than lack of pruning, such as frost injury, insects, or disease pests. Pruning would probably result in larger fruit. Remove dead, very weak, or broken branches, limbs that are too low or that rub and crowd other branches. If trees are getting too high, tallest limbs should be cut back to side branches. Avoid overpruning. The pear may be injured by blight if cut too hard. If there is a great deal of cutting needed, spread it over 2 or 3 years. If soil is fairly fertile, withhold fertilizers during years when heavy pruning is done.

How should I prune a young Seckel pear tree?   The Seckel pear makes a rather dwarfish, compact tree which requires very little pruning. Remove only dead or broken twigs and those branches which are definitely out of place (too low, rubbing, too high, etc.).

When pruning pear trees, is it harmful to remove some of the branches which had borne fruit during the past summer? It is claimed that this helps the growth of trees.   Pruning will stimulate growth, but if tree grows too vigorously, it will be more susceptible to fire blight. Pear trees usually need very little pruning. Just remove dead and broken branches and those which are too low or interfering with other branches. Tips of main limbs may need to be cut back slightly from time to time to prevent tree from growing too tall. No effort should be made to remove those branches which have borne fruit, as they should continue to bear for many years.

The trunk of our 20-year-old pear tree has produced 3 offshoots this year. If I cut them off and set them in a container of

mud and water, will roots develop?   The pear will not readily root from cuttings.

INSECTS AND DISEASES

Is it necessary to spray pears to secure good fruits?   Pears are attacked by San Jose scale, codling moth, and fire blight. (See Apple for control.) Fire blight is serious. Pear psylla is sometimes called a jumping plant louse. A black fungous grows in the excreta on leaves. Apply a dormant spray of lime sulphur; and also summer sprays of Black Leaf 40 (1 to 1,000) with soap after showers.

VARIETIES

What pear varieties are suitable for home-garden planting? See list in Introduction.

Can you give information on the Du Comice pear?   The Doyenne Du Comice pear has excellent fruit but the tree is a poor grower, subject to blight, and not very hardy. It is a valuable commercial variety on the Pacific coast but likely to prove disappointing in the East.

What is the best pear for the Lake George region? (New York.)   Flemish Beauty and Clapp Favorite are suggested for the Lake George region. Two varieties are necessary to provide cross-pollination.

PLUM

Do plums require a special type of soil?   Heavy loam for European; lighter loam for American and Japanese varieties.

How should young plum trees be fertilized to bring them into early bearing?   Young fruit trees usually make a rather vigorous growth if soil is reasonably fertile. Addition of fertilizer, if not carefully regulated, may make growth too vigorous and delay bearing instead of hastening it. Fertilize only enough to maintain good growth and trees will bear early. On sandy soils, of course, fertilizer will be needed every year if good growth is to be secured. The fertilizer program must be adapted to local soil conditions.

What is proper way to plant plum trees?   Order 1- or 2-year-old trees and plant in early spring 20 ft. apart (or a little less for Damsons).

Can a single plum tree bear fruit?   A few varieties such as Yellow Egg and Reine Claude will set fruit if self-pollinated.

Most varieties of plums, however, will set a very poor crop, or none at all, unless blossoms are fertilized by pollen from another variety of the same species of plum. Bees will carry the pollen for some distance, but it is better to have trees close together to insure cross-pollination.

I have a young plum tree which bloomed last spring but no fruit followed. Can you tell me the reason?   There are various possible reasons for the failure to produce fruit. The variety may be self-sterile and require another variety to pollinize it. Frost may have injured blossoms and prevented them from setting fruit. A young tree may sometimes be overvegetative and fail to set on that account. Pruning would make the tree more vegetative and would not induce fruiting.

We have a plum tree that blooms but never sets fruit. What causes this and what can be done to set fruit on this tree?   It is probably a self-sterile variety requiring pollen from a tree of another variety. If this is a Japanese plum, plant another Japanese variety near and let the bees do the rest.

Does the purple-leaf plum bear fruit?   Yes, if pollinized by another plum.

Why does my Elephant Heart plum tree not bear fruit? It is healthy, almost 5 years old.   The answer may be self-sterility unless some of the other plums near are of the Japanese type. If they are, they should provide cross-pollination and some other explanation would have to be formed.

I have a plum tree and think it needs pruning. Should I cut the branches short or just thin them out?   Some cutting back may be needed to prevent the tree from getting too tall and "leggy." Most of the pruning should be a thinning out to remove undesirable branches and keep top from becoming too dense.

How should a Japanese plum tree be pruned?   This type of plum grows and bears much like the peach and should be pruned a good deal like it. Train young tree to an open center and practice fairly heavy annual pruning to keep top from becoming too dense. This will help maintain vigor of tree and size of fruit.

I have several year-old plum trees grown from pits. May I expect these to bear in time, or should I have planted only grafted trees?   As the seedlings may not bear fruits worth having, it is much better to plant trees of known variety.

When and how should sand (or cherry) plum seed be planted? If you want named varieties of plum, they must be budded onto seedlings, as seedlings do not "come true." To produce seedlings for budding purposes, plant seed in the fall in furrows about 2 ins. deep. If only a few seeds are to be handled, it will be better to stratify (that is, mix the seed with sand and bury in a well-drained place). It may be protected against rodents by wire-cloth. Take up seed in early spring and plant in shallow furrows.

What causes my plums to rot and fall off?   This is the brown rot of stone fruits. More difficult to control on plum than on peach (which see) because of smooth skin.

Why are my plums wormy?   See Control of Plum Curculio under Peach.

What caused my Italian plums all to drop off? The tree is 6 years old.   The chances are that some pest is responsible, probably plum curculio, if the plums drop when small; or possibly brown rot if they are practically mature when they fall. Follow the spray schedule recommended by your Experiment Station.

DWARF AND ESPALIER FRUIT TREES

What is an espalier fruit tree?   It is a tree trained in formal shape to a given number of branches, usually in a vertical plane. The tree is planted against a wall, building, or trellis where it takes up little space and provides decoration as well as fruit. It may be trained to a single shoot or to 2 shoots opposite each other, or in fan or other shapes. The training is begun when the tree is very young. Espalier fruit trees have always been popular in Europe, where the protection afforded by wall training makes it possible to grow orchard fruits in climates less favorable than those in this country.

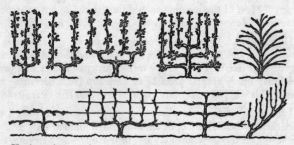

Various forms of espalier (or trained) fruit trees. These are usually grown against walls, or secured to wires or trellises.

Are espalier trees practical for the average home garden?

If you want fruit trees on a small place, they may do. But most of them are on dwarfing stocks and require a great deal more time and care in pruning and training. The yields are never plentiful.

What is the place of espalier fruit trees in the garden picture? Where there is limited space or if novelty design is wanted or in climates where severe weather changes prevail, this type of tree has its place.

What part of the season is fertilizer applied to dwarf fruit trees?   Two to 4 weeks before trees come into bloom.

How much fertilizer and how is it applied to dwarf trees on sod land?   One lb. chemical fertilizer per 1,000 sq. ft. for sod and ¼ lb. for each year's growth (age of tree). Broadcast under tree, beginning 2 ft. from trunk and extending to the outer spread of the branches. Chicken manure, 3 lbs. for the sod and 1 lb. for each year's growth of tree, may be used instead.

What fertilizer materials are used to feed dwarf fruit trees? Nitrogen has been found to be the main element in the growing of tree fruits. Apply a complete fertilizer high in nitrogen, such as 5–10–5. If unable to obtain this, apply dried chicken manure.

How is feeding applied to dwarf fruit trees on cultivated land? Same quantity as advised for age of tree for sod land, but omit the quantity for the sod.

How is feeding applied to dwarf fruit trees under the mulch system?   Broadcast the material on top of mulch as per the suggestions given for cultivated land. Water in if dry weather is encountered.

How should espalier trees be pruned?   The object is to maintain the skeleton form into which the tree has been trained. This means frequent pruning at an early stage to prevent undesired branches and suckers from getting a start.

Will dwarf fruit trees continue to bear as many years as regular-size fruit trees?   With proper attention to pruning (top and root), training, fertilization, and spraying, they might. However, the general expectation is that they will not.

If one wishes to train his own espalier trees, which are the most suitable varieties of apple, pear, peach, and apricot to use? Any varieties can be used, but only those of highest quality and best yield for your locality should be chosen. The fruits mentioned should be on dwarfing roots. The standard tree grows too vigorously to permit the intensive pruning an espalier is subject to.

Where may dwarf fruit trees be obtained?   Any first-class nursery in your neighborhood should be able to supply them.

SMALL FRUITS

STRAWBERRY

In what sort of soil should strawberries be planted? What advance fertilization is necessary?   A sandy loam soil is good, but any well-drained soil that is fairly retentive of moisture can be made to produce good strawberries. Turn under manure or commercial fertilizer before the plants are set.

Do strawberries require an acid soil? I have a patch that does not do very well, as my soil has a tendency to be alkaline. Would it be O.K. to use aluminum sulfate?   Try using ammonium sulfate as a source of nitrogen in your fertilizer program. If the soil is not too alkaline, the ammonium sulfate should do the trick.

Is lime needed for strawberries?   There is a popular belief that lime may be injurious to strawberries, but actually they will respond to lime about as well as other crops. If the soil is alkaline or only mildly acid (pH 5.6 or above), then lime won't be needed, and might even be harmful. But if the pH is down around 4.0 to 5.6, then by all means use lime.

Should you use fertilizer on strawberry plants? What is the best kind to use?   A complete fertilizer, such as 5–10–5, at the rate of 2 to 4 lbs. per 100 sq. ft., should be broadcast and worked into the soil before planting. A similar application should be made each spring.

Is animal manure too alkaline for dressing strawberries for winter?   A straw mulch after the ground is frozen is better for winter. Manure is best put on in early fall.

How can a strawberry planting be tied in with a vegetable garden?   A good plan is to have it adjacent to the vegetable garden, with strawberries next to vegetables. When an old row of strawberries is removed, vegetables may take their place, as it is not desirable to keep strawberries in one place too long.

How much space should be planted in strawberries for each person in the family?   Twenty-five ft. of row per person in fruit, and another 25 ft. of young plants coming along for the following year.

I have a slope in the back of my yard which I wish to have

covered with strawberries. If I plant them at the bottom, will
they climb? Do the leaves stay green in winter? Better to
plant in rows 2 ft. apart across the slope. As runners form, you
can place them where needed, to cover soil. The leaves remain
more or less green over winter, depending upon site; in cold regions, will need to be covered.

**I plan on starting a strawberry patch for a family of 2. I want
some for canning. How many plants do I need?** One hundred ft. of row would take 40 plants, set 30 ins. apart, and would
yield 30 to 40 quarts if all goes well. Decide how many quarts
you want and compute the number of plants needed. Don't forget
that you will want some for preserves, or to give to your friends.

When is the best time to plant strawberries? As early in
spring as the soil can be broken up and got into the proper condition. Strawberries should be set out with the very first garden
planting.

**If strawberry plants are planted early in the spring, will they
bear fruit the first year?** Spring-set plants will bear fruit the
first year if the blossoms are not cut off, but such plants will be so
exhausted by producing fruit before they are well established that
very few runners will be produced. Therefore removal of blossoms is common practice to prevent fruiting the first year.

**Is spring transplanting of strawberries as favorable as sum-
mer or fall planting?** Spring transplanting is much to be preferred. Late-summer or fall planting is likely to be unsuccessful
unless the runner plants have been rooted in pots. August would
be the second choice of season.

**Can a person put strawberry plants out until the ground freezes
up, or do they have to get a start before freezing weather?**
Spring planting is preferable. If you start to plant in the fall, do
so by early October, so roots will start growing before the ground
freezes. Mulch the plants as soon as the ground freezes. Even
then they may heave some during the winter; hence the preference for spring planting.

**If ground is not frozen, can strawberries be planted in Virginia
in December?** Yes, especially in sandy soil, although a somewhat later date, such as early March, would be better. If there
is a great deal of alternate freezing and thawing during the
winter and early spring, December-set plants are likely to heave
out of the ground.

How far apart are strawberry plants set? Varieties which
do not make runners freely (especially the Everbearers), about

SETTING OUT STRAWBERRY PLANTS

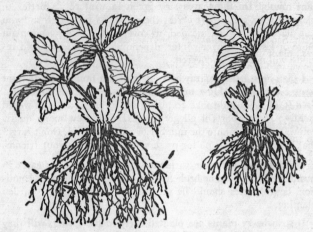

Old leaves removed and roots trimmed back.

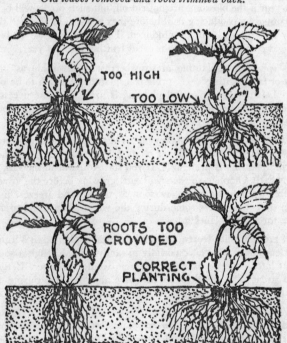

18 ins. apart; fair plant takes 24 ins.; good plant takes 30 ins. The rows 36 to 48 ins. apart.

How should strawberries be planted? Have soil in good tilth. Scoop out a hole with a garden trowel to a depth of 4 or 5 ins.; plant firmly, being sure that roots are well spread and extend down into the hole and are well covered. Plants should be set as deeply as possible without covering the crown. If set too deeply, plants will be smothered; if not deeply enough, part of roots will be exposed and dry out.

What is considered the best system of setting strawberry plants in small gardens—200 to 250 plants? The matted-row system is the easiest to develop and is favored by most commercial growers as well as home gardeners. Many home gardeners, however, like the hill system, as it produces a higher percentage of fine, large berries.

What is the matted-row method of strawberry growing? Plants are set 18 to 30 ins. apart in rows 30 to 48 ins. apart. The runners are allowed to develop and take root, forming a "matted row" 18 to 30 ins. wide, of plants which will produce fruit the following season.

Setting out a narrow border of strawberry plants to be grown by the hill system.

What is the hill method of strawberry growing? Set plants close together, 12 to 15 ins. apart, in rows 18 to 24 ins. apart. *Keep all runners cut off as they form.* The plants will each make several crowns and a large number of leaves. This system will give fancy fruit and high yields but requires a considerable amount of labor.

How long is a strawberry bed good for when using hill method of planting? If properly cared for, a bed may be kept productive for 3 or 4 years; the first crop will be the best, and later crops will be successively poorer. It is best to set new plants each spring, let them fruit the following spring, and then spade them under.

Is it necessary to plant more than one variety of strawberries? I plan to put in 200 of the Starbright variety. Practically all modern varieties, including Starbright, are perfect flowered and do not require another variety for pollination purposes.

How often should strawberries be renewed to maintain an abundant yield? At least every 2 years, and better every year.

CULTURE, STRAWBERRY

Should strawberry runners be removed to prevent them from sapping the strength of the plants? The production of runners by strawberry plants is a perfectly natural process and is not necessarily devitalizing. In the hill systems of growing, all runners should be removed in order to keep the plants properly spaced. In the common matted-row system the only runners removed are those in excess of the number required to produce a matted row with plants spaced at least 7 to 8 ins. apart. Each runner soon produces leaves and roots of its own, and becomes a "self-supporting," individual plant.

When is the best time to thin out strawberry plants? Begin to space and thin out as soon as the first runners take root. To get a properly spaced bed, go over it every 2 or 3 weeks for rest of growing season.

How many runners should be allowed to develop from each mother plant in the matted-row system? Allow at least 7 or 8 ins. (in all directions) between runner plants. If plants are 30 ins. apart in rows, allow 12 to 14 runner plants to develop from each mother plant. The excess runners should be cut off, preferably before they take root.

What shall I do when my June-bearing strawberries grow too thick? Keep the runners spaced and thinned so plants will stand at least 7 or 8 ins. apart in matted row. Usually beds are replanted every year or two, setting runner plants in a new location.

How often is it necessary to make a new strawberry bed? Is it better to make new beds, or clean and refill old ones? All things considered, it is better to plant a new bed each year and spade under the bed planted the year previously. If the plants are especially good, vigorous, and relatively free of weeds, it may be worth while to fertilize and cultivate them and keep them for a second fruiting year.

We have been advised to cut strawberry leaves off in the fall. Is this correct? The leaves definitely should not be cut off in the fall. They are the organs in which are manufactured those foods which feed the plant. Cutting off the leaves "starves" the rest of the plant.

How can I distinguish sex of strawberries? Most modern varieties are "perfect" flowered; that is, they have both stamens and pistils. When such varieties are in bloom, center of flower will consist of a rounded mass of light-green pistils surrounded by large yellow anthers (full of pollen) at ends of stamens. The "imperfect" or pistillate varieties at the same stage of development will have only the pistils; no anthers.

Can strawberries be weeded in the spring? If they were properly mulched, they will need little weeding, as the mulch will keep most of the weeds from growing. If they were not mulched, they may need weeding, but it should be done without disturbing soil about strawberry roots. In some cases a sharp hoe may be used to "shave" off weeds without stirring soil.

Why did my strawberry plants bloom so profusely but set no berries? Just a few tiny ones. Set new bed just last year. The variety may be pistillate and unable to set fruit without being pollinated by another variety. If it is a perfect flowered variety, then the blossoms may have been touched by frost, which, without injuring the petals, often kills the part which will develop into fruit.

My strawberry plants blossom and set berries, but they do not develop after being half grown. Why? The failure to size up might be due to dry weather. If berries are misshapen and knotty, they were probably touched by frost when in bloom, or possibly were poorly pollinated because of rainy weather during the blossoming season.

I seem to have no luck with strawberries. They do not bear very heavily. First be sure you have a productive variety and one *adapted to your soil and climate;* set a new bed frequently and keep the soil well, but not too heavily, fertilized. Do not let the plants crowd in the matted row. Plant only in spring.

How are strawberries propagated? Strawberry plants produce in summer long, stringlike growths called "runners," at the tips of which grow new plants. These send roots into the soil. They are allowed to develop until the following spring, when they are dug up and set out in new beds. Some varieties make many runners, others but few—the everbearing variety Rockhill (or Wayzata) practically none. It does, however, form several crowns. In propagating, these are separated, each with a piece of root attached, and planted in a new bed.

How should strawberry runners be cared for before they are set out in a new bed? If using runners from your own beds, dig only when ready to plant. Thin off old ragged or dead leaves, leaving the small leaves at the tip of the crown. If you purchase plants, try to plant them as soon as received. If this cannot be done, "heel in" in a shallow trench and keep them well watered until planting time.

Pot-grown strawberry plants for August setting.

Method of rooting strawberry runner in pot buried in soil.

How can runners be rooted in pots? Fill 2½- or 3-in. pots with a good composted soil and sink them in the ground about the mother plants. Place a runner tip over each pot and hold in place by putting a stone or clod on the runner near the tip, or bend or twist wires into hairpin shape and peg the runners down, or use clothespins. When new plant is well developed, the runner may be severed from the old plant.

Are potted strawberry plants any better than those runner

plants which have been allowed to become well established in the garden before transplanting? For starting a new bed in late summer or early fall only potted plants will stand transplanting satisfactorily. However, spring planting of ordinary runner plants is to be preferred.

Can strawberry seeds or plants be started in spring and produce worth-while results the same year? There are certain small-fruited European varieties which "come true" from seed and will fruit the same year the seed is planted. The common garden strawberry of North America, however, does not "come true" from seed. Plants do not produce full crops until the second year.

MULCHING STRAWBERRIES

Should strawberries be taken care of during the winter? Mulching is advisable to prevent winter injury, conserve moisture, and keep the berries clean the following spring. Plants are more likely to heave out during alternate freezing and thawing on heavy soils than on sandy soils, hence mulching is more essential on the heavier soils. Apply after a sharp freeze, when the soil is frozen to a depth of 2 to 3 ins.

Is it necessary to cover strawberry plants for the winter if they are grown in matted rows? Mulching is highly desirable, although unmulched beds may "get by" some years, especially if covered with snow during the coldest part of the winter. Plants will heave more in some soils than in others. Mulching has so much to recommend it, however, that it should be considered an essential part of strawberry culture.

Should strawberries that have been planted this fall be mulched to insure earlier fruiting? Strawberries planted in fall should be mulched to prevent them from heaving out of ground as soil freezes and thaws. They will not ripen any earlier than unmulched plants; in fact, not quite so early, but they will be more vigorous and better able to produce a crop.

What is the best material to use for a winter mulch on a strawberry bed? The ideal mulch is one that is easily handled, will remain in place, will not pack down so much that air cannot circulate, and that will be there in spring to keep soil moist, restrain weeds, and keep berries clean.

What are some suitable mulching materials? Salt hay, rye straw, wheat straw, oat straw, pine needles (used widely on the Eastern coastal plain), spoiled hay, leaves of trees. These may suggest materials that will be available to you.

How is mulching material applied to a strawberry bed?
Lay some twiggy branches over the rows to keep the material
from matting down on plants, and then sprinkle the material
lightly over the branches. Lay a few more branches on to hold the
covering in place. *Do not cover thickly,* or the plants will rot
underneath.

**What are the advantages of mulching strawberries with salt
hay, and when should it be applied?**   Salt hay makes a good
mulch because it is easy to spread, does not blow off readily, and
does not wear out quickly under the pickers' feet. Such a mulch
should be applied after first sharp freeze in order to give plants
some protection during winter. In spring it will conserve moisture and keep berries clean.

Is it all right to mulch the strawberry plants with tree leaves?
Leaves from hardwood trees (such as oak) make a suitable mulch
to apply between the rows of plants. Better to have them partly
decomposed. If only leaves are available for covering plants, use
layer of twigs before placing leaves, then twigs on top to hold.

**Are maple leaves suitable for covering strawberries for winter
protection?**   Maple leaves are about the poorest mulching
material because they mat down when wet. The plants are apt
to rot underneath.

How soon is the mulch removed from the strawberry bed?
As soon as danger of frost is over, remove from over the plants,
place it between the rows, and leave it there. It keeps soil cool,
retains moisture, and, above all, keeps down weeds. It will decay
and can be worked in the soil for the new planting.

**What is the proper winter care for strawberry plants in New
York climate? Should they be mulched?**   Yes, apply about 2
ins. of loose straw over the plants after the soil is frozen. The
mulch will have to be raked from the plants into the space between the rows before the leaf growth starts in the spring.

EVERBEARING STRAWBERRIES

What are "everbearing" strawberries?   These are varieties
that form a crop of fruit in the spring and another in late summer. The total yield is smaller than that of one-season berries,
and most of the varieties are not of so good quality.

Are everbearing strawberries successful?   They do not live
up to the descriptions in some of the catalogues, but if you like
strawberries well enough to put up with the faults of everbearing
varieties, then they may be termed "successful." One of the

faults is that crop is produced over such a long period that only a very small picking can be made on any one day.

Are everbearing strawberries as prolific as the ordinary kind? If the plants are grown in hills and the blossoms removed until the middle of July, most varieties will produce a fairly large crop per plant. The fruit will then ripen over a period of 2 to 3 months but the picking on any one day will be rather small. If the blossoms are not removed, plants will exhaust themselves by producing heavily during the hot midsummer months. Fruit produced in cooler fall weather will be of better quality than that produced in midsummer.

Should the runners be removed from everbearing strawberry plants? A maximum fall crop will be produced if plants are set close together, about 12 to 15 ins. apart, in rows 2 ft. apart, and all runners removed as they form. This is known as the hill system.

How, and when, are everbearing strawberries thinned? Most varieties will need no thinning unless grown in hills, in which case all the runners should be kept off. Set a new bed each spring rather than try to rejuvenate the old one.

Should the first blossoms be removed from everbearing strawberry plants? When should they be allowed to bear? Best results will be secured if all blossoms are removed up to the latter part of July. The first fruit would then ripen about the middle of August.

If I transplant everbearing strawberry plants in the spring, will they bear the same season? Yes, they should bear their maximum crop in the fall of the year in which they are planted.

My everbearing strawberries do not have the flavor of standard strawberries. Are there any that compare with usual spring berries? Most of the everbearing varieties are of rather poor quality. The Rockhill (Wayzata) has very good quality, but makes very few runners and in the East is not so productive as some of the poor-quality sorts, such as Mastodon.

What care should be given everbearing strawberries to keep them bearing from year to year? It can't be done. You could get some fruit for 2 or even 3 years, but many plants would die and the others would get progressively weaker. Don't count on one planting to produce more than one fall crop, followed by a spring crop.

What care should be given everbearing strawberries through winter? Do they thrive better in moist ground or dry? They should be winter mulched like any other strawberries. Ever-bearers are getting ready, during hot, dry weather of midsummer, to produce a fall crop, hence they must have ample moisture or the results will be disappointing.

Are the Mastodon and Gem, everbearing strawberry plants, perfect flowering? If not, which variety should be planted with them?   Yes, they are perfect flowering, so do not need another variety for a pollinizer.

What are several varieties of everbearing strawberries? Mastodon is one of the best known. Others are Rockhill (Wayzata), Gem, Berri-Supreme, and Gemzata.

What is the best everbearing strawberry for this climate to be used in a small garden? (New York.)   Rockhill (Wayzata) is the best-flavored everbearing strawberry for home use. Gem is another good variety, but is rather sour.

PLANTING IN BARRELS

Could I plant strawberries in top and side holes of small barrels, about 12 ins. wide and 24 ins. high, that can be easily turned to the sun at will? What soil, number, and kind of plants? Yes, if you want to grow the plants in a barrel as a novelty. Fill with good composted soil and distribute the holes so plants will be 8 to 9 ins. apart; keep soil moist throughout barrel. Choose a variety that is well adapted to your particular locality.

I have a 50-gal. oak barrel in which I want to grow strawberries. How would I prepare the soil and set the plants? How far apart for the holes?   Beginning 1 ft. from the bottom, bore holes, at irregular intervals, 9 ins. apart and large enough to hold a plant without cramping. Bore a number of smaller holes in the bottom for drainage, and set the barrel on flat bricks. Put in 6 ins. of drainage material—coarse gravel or cinders, topped with finer material. Mix good garden soil with ⅓ its bulk of old rotted manure or the like and ⅓ screened cinders. To every bushel add 1 lb. of a complete fertilizer. It is not necessary to fill whole interior with this soil. Maintain a 6-in. thickness around the inside, and fill center with any old gravelly material available. Planting and filling are done at the same time. Begin by covering the drainage with soil to level of first holes. Push plants through from inside, spread roots, and cover with soil. Repeat to within 12 ins. of the top; fill this with good soil and plant entire top. See that moisture conditions are uniform.

What variety should be used in a strawberry barrel? How should the plants be wintered over?   Select a variety of high quality adapted to your climatic conditions. If you like a sweet variety, try Fairfax. It is desirable to use potted plants if you can get them. Mulch with straw over the top; protect side plants if possible with straw or burlap after the first heavy freeze. Check moisture conditions occasionally to prevent drying out.

What is the proper way to handle strawberry plants in a strawberry jar after they are through bearing? Remove the old plants and replace a little later with newly formed runner plants rooted in small pots.

INSECTS AND DISEASES

Do strawberries need to be sprayed? Probably not—only if certain pests (such as leaf roller or weevil) are bad. Most strawberries in the home garden do quite well without being sprayed.

What causes the purplish spots on the leaves of my strawberry plants? One of two diseases—either leaf spot or leaf scorch. During most seasons the modern varieties will not be injured enough to make it worth while to spray.

What causes the buds to drop from my strawberry plants before they bloom? The strawberry weevil, a tiny insect, lays an egg in the bud and then cuts the stem just back of the bud. Control can be secured by dusting with 5 parts dusting sulphur to 1 part arsenate of lead, applied when the first buds are out.

Are any strawberry varieties resistant to the red stele root rot? Very few. Aberdeen, Pathfinder, and Sparkle are really resistant.

VARIETIES, STRAWBERRY

What are the best and hardiest types of strawberries? All of the so-called standard varieties will be hardy enough to withstand winter temperatures if properly mulched. There is no one best variety. Some are especially good for the commercial grower, others for the home garden; some people like tart berries, others sweet. Plant varieties that succeed in your immediate locality; or try several and then discard all but the best. For a small test plot the following varieties would be worth trying: Howard 17 (Premier), Dorsett, Fairfax, and Catskill.

What strawberries are best for a beginner's garden? Varieties vary in their adaptability. Try Pathfinder, Fairfax, Catskill. All good quality and productive.

What are best varieties of early strawberries for raising on bottom land? Strawberries are very sensitive to local conditions, so that a variety may be satisfactory on one farm and unsatisfactory on another farm a short distance away. Therefore, if you have not grown strawberries before it would be advisable to try several varieties, even if just a few plants of each. Early sorts worth trying would include Howard 17 (Premier), Blakemore, Pathfinder, and Maytime.

What strawberry varieties should we plant for table and home use?   Howard 17, Dorsett, Fairfax, and Catskill are good varieties. Consult your neighbors or your county agricultural agent to find out whether these varieties will do well in your particular locality.

What are good strawberry varieties for freezing in a home storage cabinet?   Sparkle and July Moon are good. Dorsett and Catskill are fairly good for this purpose.

What is the best variety of strawberry for the state of Maine? Howard 17, with Gem as the best fall-bearing variety.

What varieties of strawberries should I plant in a home garden in northern New Jersey? I want some for canning.   For early table use plant Pathfinder; for late and for canning and jam, plant Sparkle.

Are "bush" strawberries practical, and how much do they bear?   Strawberries do not grow on bushes. One plant sometimes sold as "bush strawberry" is one of the brambles. The fruit looks a little like a strawberry, but the edible quality is poor and the yield small.

Can wild strawberries be transplanted in a regular bed? If so, do they give a good crop?   Wild strawberries in cultivation, that is, fertilized and weeded, will give better yields than in the wild, but it requires a good many to fill a quart basket.

GRAPES

What soil is most suitable for cultivation of grapes?   A good loam or sandy loam is probably ideal, but grapes will grow satisfactorily on a wide range of soil types provided the moisture supply is adequate. Extremely dry or extremely wet soils are to be avoided.

Do grapes like alkaline or acid soil?   Grapes thrive on soils showing rather wide ranges of soil reaction. On the whole, acid soils seem preferable to alkaline soils.

Will grapes grow on muck soil?   Grapes are never grown commercially on muck soil. Grapevines are usually planted on slopes because they will not tolerate poor drainage, and most muck soils offer drainage problems at some seasons of the year. Also, grapes should have good air drainage, and the level surfaces of muck soils do not favor air drainage.

What fertilizer is best for feeding new grapes? Where it can be obtained, barnyard manure is as good a fertilizing material for young grapevines as any, and is safer to use than commercial fertilizer. It should be applied in the winter or early spring, and worked into the ground around the young vines. It is not wise to place manure in the holes when grapes are planted.

When should I fertilize young grapevines to bring them into bearing early? Applying 1 to 2 oz. of nitrate of soda or sulfate of ammonia to each vine about the time the growth starts in the spring will stimulate growth and hasten their reaching bearing size. If these materials are not available, a good covering of barnyard manure should be applied to the soil around each vine, in winter or early spring, and worked into the soil. Hoeing and cultivating to keep down weeds are necessary also.

What is a good fertilizer for grapes? This will depend on your soil and its natural fertility. A 5–10–5 commercial fertilizer is a good general-purpose formula which will be suitable for grapes. On a soil of average fertility use about 600 to 800 lbs. per acre or 1½ lbs. per vine, applied in early spring.

What is the best way to apply fertilizer to grapes? Broadcast the fertilizer, covering an area from a foot from the trunk out to 4 or 5 ft. away from the trunk. Spade fertilizer under or cultivate it in.

My Caco grapevine is 5 years old, has made wonderful growth, but it bears no grapes. What fertilizer should I use on it? The fact that your grapevine is making wonderful growth indicates that it does not need more fertilizer, but, on the contrary, needs to have all such materials withheld from it. It is possible that you have been pruning it too closely. Leave at least 40 buds on it the next time you prune it. Also reduce the amount of hoeing, to discourage excessive growth. This treatment may bring the vine out of its extreme vegetative condition and throw it into a fruiting condition.

What location is best suited for grapes? Do they grow well near trees? The ideal location for a vineyard is gently sloping land. Air and water drainage must be good to avoid danger of late spring frosts and "wet feet." Steep slopes should be avoided because they favor erosion unless rows are planted on the contour. Southern exposures favor earlier starting of growth in spring and earlier ripening of fruit, but are more susceptible to late-spring frost injury and to summer drought. Northern slopes are less susceptible to injury from late-spring frosts and summer droughts, but ripen their crops later than southern slopes. Deep, sandy soils that contain a good amount of organic matter will give best results for grapes. Soils too poor for other crops are not good grape soils. Planting grapes close to trees is usually not a good practice because the trees compete with the vines for water and soil nutrients as well as furnish cover for insects which may attack grapes. Shade from trees may favor diseases and delay ripening of the fruit.

Where should grapes be planted?   On fences, trellises that mark boundaries, or on arbors especially constructed for the purpose.

Do grapevines need much sun?   Grapes are sun-loving plants, as is shown by their tendency to climb over tops of tall trees. The outstanding grape regions of the world are in areas which have much clear, sunny weather and few fogs. Lack of sunlight favors the spread of mildew and black rot and retards ripening of fruit. However, grapevines will do fairly well if they receive direct sunlight at least half of the day. The vines will require more constant care under such conditions.

Will grapevines grow well in shade?   Though grapevines may grow fairly well in partial shade they will not thrive under such conditions. Shading favors the spread of diseases, delays ripening, and gives fruit of lower sugar content and quality.

How far apart should grapes be planted?   In the past many vineyards were planted at 8 × 8 ft. spacing, but now most plantings are made at 8 × 10 ft. spacing. More vigorous varieties (such as Fredonia, Golden Muscat, Buffalo, and Niagara) will show less crowding if planted at a 10 × 10 ft. spacing. In the home garden 6 ft. in the rows and 7 ft. between the rows would be all right.

How should grapevines be planted?   After the ground has been prepared and the rows have been marked, dig holes of sufficient size to accommodate the roots of the vines after they have been cut back to within 8 ins. of the trunk. The top should be cut back to a single strong cane of 2 buds' length. The vine is then placed in the hole and the roots spread out evenly. A few shovels of dirt are then thrown in on roots while the stem is shaken gently to sift fine dirt in around the fine roots. More topsoil is then thrown into hole and thoroughly tamped into place with the feet. Holes should then be well filled.

My Concord grapevines, now 5 years old, should be moved to a better location. When is best time? Will it destroy them if their root systems are cut? Any time in the fall after the vines are fully dormant. A good-sized ball of earth should be moved with the vine, so that as many roots be kept intact as possible. The tops should be cut back severely in order that the top growth be kept in balance with the greatly reduced root system. Vines should not be allowed to bear fruit the first year after moving, and only a light crop the following year.

At what time do you transplant Concord grapes which are several years old? How do you transplant and prune them? Large Concord grapevines should be moved after they are fully dormant in the fall. It is well to set them slightly deeper than they were in their original location. (See previous question on transplanting.)

Will an old grapevine live and bear if transplanted in the fall? Transplanting old grapevines can be done successfully if a large ball of earth is moved with them in order to keep as many of the roots intact as possible. (See preceding questions.)

How many grapevines will a family of 4 need? This will depend on how you use the fruit. For table use, etc., include 2 plants of very early varieties, 2 early, 6 to 10 mid-season for jelly and juice, and 2 to 4 late to very late.

Is it necessary to dig around grapevines? In a moist, fertile soil grapes may make a satisfactory growth with no cultivation. If they do not make satisfactory growth, however, soil should be cultivated out to a distance of 3 ft. from the trunk. In sandy soils, cultivation is imperative during early summer.

What treatment should I give my grapes? They are fruiting poorly on clay soil. The fact that grapes are not fruiting well on clay soil indicates that vines are probably not making enough growth to permit heavy fruiting. As a rule, grapes prefer lighter and sandier soils, but many good vineyards are found on clay soils. Fertilize vines with ⅓ lb. of nitrate of soda or sulfate of ammonia per vine. Apply when shoots are starting growth in spring. Apply barnyard manure about vines during winter or early spring, and work into soil. Frequent cultivation to keep down weeds and close pruning will encourage more vine growth and eventually result in heavier fruiting.

What can I do to make my grapevines bear heavily? An application of proper fertilizers, plus cover cropping and cultivation, should result in vigorous vines capable of bearing good crops of fruit. Pruning vines properly to not more than 40 buds per vine should enable them to set good crops. Spraying to control mildews, black rot, and leaf hoppers favors ripening of such heavy crops.

How soon, and how much, will grapes bear?   Grapevines should not be allowed to bear any fruit until their third season, and then only a small crop. The fourth season may be expected to give a good crop of fruit, and by the fifth season, if vines are well grown, they may be expected to have reached full production. This may be from 10 to 20 lbs. per vine. An average of 10 lbs. per vine would give about 3 tons per acre for vines spaced 8 to 10 ft. apart.

Why do grapes grow all to vines and bear no fruit? How often and at what season should they be trimmed?   Vines have probably been thrown into an overvegetative stage by being grown on too rich a soil, by overfertilization, or by being pruned too closely. Correct this condition by withholding all fertilization, by leaving at least 40 buds per vine when you prune, and by growing a summer cover crop to discourage excessive vine growth. Grapevines require pruning only once each year, when the vines are fully dormant. Dense shading encourages excessive vine growth and tends to discourage fruiting.

Concord grapevines, 15 years old, in recent years have ripened fruit very unevenly, with green and ripe berries of uneven sizes on each bunch. What is the cause and remedy?   Causes for the production of the small green berries on Concord grapevines and uneven ripening are not fully understood. It is thought that cool, rainy conditions at blossoming time, which interfere with fertilization of flowers, are usually responsible for the trouble. Vines having an insufficient supply of nitrogen often show more of this trouble than those more vigorous. Other than to keep vines in good, healthy condition there is little that one can do to correct this trouble inasmuch as one can do nothing to control the weather at blossoming time.

What is necessary to have grapes grow in nice bunches and have all the grapes ripen near the same time?   Uniform ripening of fruit is more likely to occur when vine does not bear too heavy a crop. This is controlled by pruning vines each year so that no more than 40 buds are left on such vigorous varieties as Concord or Fredonia, and about 30 buds, or fewer, on less vigorous varieties such as Delaware or Diamond. Spraying to prevent leaves from being attacked by mildew, black rot, or leaf hoppers will also favor uniform ripening.

How can I recognize flowers of grapes? My 3-year Caco vine has shown wonderful growth but no grapes. If you will look at the young shoots on grapevines when they are 6 to 10 ins. long, you will find tiny green structures which have much the appearance of a small bunch of grapes. These are rudimentary flowers and are borne opposite the lower 3 or 4 leaves on each of the shoots. As shoots grow, the flower clusters enlarge and expand. About 6 weeks after the shoots start to grow, individual blossoms appear. In opening, the petals, which remain greenish in color, are shed, leaving only pistil and anthers. The reason for non-fruiting may be overfertilization, which produces lush, soft growth at expense of fruit.

We have Tokay grapes that crack open before ripening and are sour; also some dry up. The bunches are very large and crowded. Cracking of the berries followed by souring is due to clusters being too compact. The only remedy is to reduce the cluster by pinching some of the berries from each cluster soon after they are set in the spring. A good plan is to remove ¼ to ⅓ of the branches of the cluster. This will reduce the size, and should loosen it enough to prevent cracking.

What pre-winter care should be given to grapevines? In regions where grapes are not injured by winter temperatures, no special fall treatment, except possibly sowing of a cover crop, is necessary. In the far North, if tender varieties are grown, they will need to be laid down and covered for winter protection. In such regions it will probably be more satisfactory to grow a hardy variety, even though such varieties may be of somewhat lower quality.

What causes my grapes to remain red instead of getting blue as they are supposed to do? Grapes color normally if they have sufficient leaf surface in proportion to fruit being produced. Therefore, failure to ripen may be due to pruning too lightly, which will result in an excessive crop or to loss of leaves caused by grape leaf hopper or Japanese beetle.

PRUNING GRAPES

When is the best time of year to prune grapevines? Grapevines should be pruned when vines are fully dormant, in late fall, winter, or early spring. Pruning in late winter, the canes which have suffered from winter injury can easily be detected and cut out, thus leaving only sound canes on the vine. Spring pruning is not recommended, because as buds begin to swell they become brittle and break off easily, thus reducing size of crop.

How should a mature grapevine be pruned?   Leave a main trunk to the top wire of the Kniffin trellis (see Index) and a 1-year-old cane in each direction on each wire—a total of 4 canes. Leave a 2-bud spur on the trunk near the base of each cane. Remove all other canes. Cut the 4 canes retained, to a length of 8 buds each for those on lower wire and 10 buds for those on top wire.

How do you prune Concord grapes? Should some new shoots be cut off after they start to grow?   Concord grapes should be pruned back to about 40 buds per vine. Usually 4 canes having 10 buds each are left on each vine.

Should 2-year-old grapevines be cut back? If so, in fall or spring?   The extent to which a 2-year-old vine should be cut back depends on amount of growth it has made. If good growth has been made, a cane long enough to reach to upper wire of trellis should be selected for trunk. If side shoots have developed on this stem, 2 should be selected near upper wire and 2 near lower wire. These should be cut back to 3 or 4 buds in length. If no side shoots have developed during second year of growth, such shoots should be selected shortly after growth starts the following spring. All other shoots should be broken off in order to favor growth of 4 shoots left. Pruning should be done in late fall or winter, long before buds start to swell in spring.

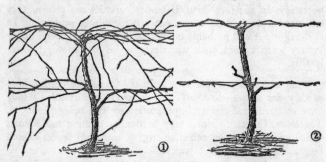

GRAPE PRUNING

(1) Concord grapevine (several years old) before pruning. (2) Same vine, pruned back during winter (Kniffen system).

Is it necessary to trim back grapes every year for 3 or 4 years, when started from cuttings?   Amount of cutting back to be done depends on amount of growth vine makes. Pruning is dwarfing in its effect on vine and should be done only as long as is necessary to aid in properly shaping it. The first year or two vine is cut back in order to prevent it from bearing fruit and to force all growth into 1 or 2 new shoots. Pruning for third year of growth should be less severe. By end of third season vine should have made enough growth to permit its being fully shaped and trained, and to permit bearing of a moderate crop.

How should a grapevine in its third season be pruned? By end of season vines should have made enough growth to enable one to select a strong cane for the trunk. This is run to top wire of trellis and cut at that height. If any side branches have developed on this trunk, select 2 near top wire and 2 near lower wire. Cut back these to 3 or 4 buds each, and tie to wires of trellis. The following season 4 more canes will be selected as close to the trunk as possible and left (after cutting back to 8 or 10 buds each).

How far should grapevine 5 years old be cut back each year? Your grapevine should be pruned back each year by removing all wood except 4 canes of preceding year's growth. Each of these canes should be cut back to 8 or 10 buds. These canes should be located in positions which favor easy tying to the trellis.

Should some of the new shoots in a grapevine be cut back in spring to prevent overgrowth of vines? Prune only when dormant. (See above.)

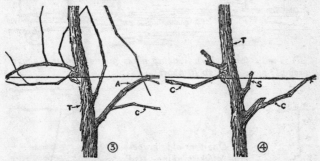

(*3*) *Detail, before pruning. T—main stem or trunk; A—arm, or lateral, 2-year-old wood; C—cane, 1-year-old wood. (4) Detail, after pruning. T—trunk; C—renewal cane, 1-year-old wood, tied to wire; S—spur, 1-year-old wood, cut back to 2 buds.*

Have read that in pruning grapes, the vines that bore last year should be cut off. Does this mean the entire cane near the ground, or merely the side-arm branches of the cane? Only side arms (side branches) should be cut back each year. Cutting back entire trunk would also destroy crop for the next year. Cut back

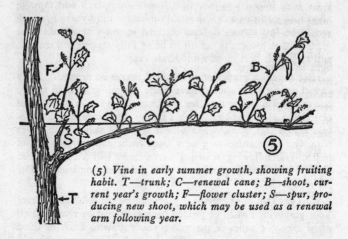

(5) *Vine in early summer growth, showing fruiting habit. T—trunk; C—renewal cane; B—shoot, current year's growth; F—flower cluster; S—spur, producing new shoot, which may be used as a renewal arm following year.*

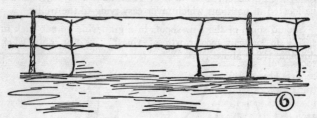

(6) *Trellis for Kniffen system; wires 30 and 60 ins. above ground; posts 15 to 20 ft. apart.*

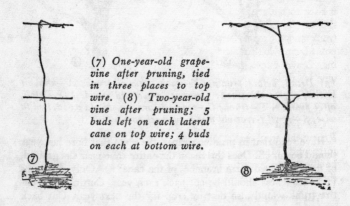

(7) *One-year-old grapevine after pruning, tied in three places to top wire.* (8) *Two-year-old vine after pruning; 5 buds left on each lateral cane on top wire; 4 buds on each at bottom wire.*

arms to a strong cane of the preceding year's growth. These canes become the new arms and should each be cut back to about 10 buds' length. These bear the next crop of fruit.

I have been told to prune my grapes in the summer to let the light in to the fruit. Is that necessary? It is not only unnecessary but undesirable. The fruit will color normally even if no light at all gets to it—quite different from the apple in this respect. Furthermore, removal of leaf surface at this time of year will delay or prevent normal ripening; hence defeat the very purpose for which it is done.

Would you recommend thinning foliage on grapevines in fall to hasten ripening of fruit before frost? Thinning the foliage would not hasten ripening of the fruit but would delay ripening, inasmuch as leaves are the food-manufacturing organs of the plant. Nothing can be done at this stage of the season to hasten ripening of fruit. Thinning crop shortly after blossoming might have speeded up ripening of remaining fruit if vine had set too heavy a crop.

How do you trim grapevines which have been neglected for years? Neglected grapevines should be renewed by cutting the old trunk back to the ground. New shoots will start from roots. Only 3 of these should be allowed to grow, and at the end of first season the strongest one should be selected for a new trunk and the others removed. The new trunk should be cut back to desired length and 4 side branches, of about 10 buds' length each, are then selected.

How can I best revitalize an old, neglected grapevine? Cut back the old vine severely. If the old trunk is in bad shape, cut it back to the ground and start a new trunk from one of the new shoots. If you do not care to cut it back that severely, and if the trunk and old arms are still in fair condition, cut vine back to point from which most vigorous shoots, closest to trunk, are arising. Leave a few, preferably 4, spurs of 2 buds each when the vine is cut back to provide new growth. It will be necessary to sacrifice a year's crop in order to get vine back to a desirable form and fruiting condition.

Can I cut an old grapevine stem that has grown too long? Renew the trunk of the old vine (see above) by cutting it back to ground. Many new shoots will start, but only about 3 should be allowed to grow the first season. The next winter remove 2 of these.

Will you please advise me as when to trim and how to trim

Scuppernong grapevines?   Scuppernong grapevines are usually trained on overhead trellises or arbors in home plantings. This system calls for a single trunk running to overhead trellis. At that height 8 arms, radiating from trunk like the spokes of a wheel from the hub, are selected and trained to grow out over trellis. After arms have been established they are pruned by cutting back all side branches on them to short spurs 2 or 3 buds long. As arms become older it may be desirable to renew some of them by cutting them back to a strong lateral cane near trunk. It is a good plan to renew one arm each year in this way. The best time to prune is in late winter, after danger of severe freezing. At that time one can easily tell which wood is alive. Avoid leaving injured wood. Pruning after the buds begin to swell is not desirable because the buds break off easily.

SPECIAL PROBLEMS

How can I prune and train new grapes to get the best quality? (New Jersey.)   The best training system for grapes in your section is what is known as the single-stem 4-cane Kniffin system. This employs a 2-wire, fence-type trellis with the wires stretched 3 and 5 ft. above the ground. A single stem is run to the top wire and cut at that point. Two side canes are selected at the upper wire and 2 at the lower wire, and cut back to 8 or 10 buds each. These are tied to wires in such a way as to give the idea of a capital T with two crossbars. The pruning should be done when vines are fully dormant.

How do you construct the standard grape trellis?   The standard grape trellis in the East is the Kniffen trellis. This is simply 2 wires, one 30 ins. from the ground and the other 30 ins. above the first, supported by posts every 18 to 20 ft. No. 9 wire is the best size for this purpose.

Do grapes cross-pollinate? If so, how close may different varieties be planted?   Yes, grapes frequently cross-pollinate when several vines are planted near each other. This is true in spite of the fact that most commercially important varieties are self-fruitful. Grape pollen is very light and fluffy and is easily scattered about by winds and is carried about by many small insects. However, you need have no fear that the pollen of one variety will in any way influence the fruit of another variety. It has been shown many times that there is no immediate effect produced by pollen of one variety being placed on pistils of another variety. Only the seedlings produced from such cross-pollination will show any effect.

How should grape cuttings be handled?   Make cuttings

during March of vigorous 1-year-old canes with 3 nodes or buds per cutting. Cut at base of cutting just below a bud, at tip about 1 in. beyond the bud. Tie in bundles like asparagus with butts all the same direction and bury upside down in a sandy soil, with about 2 ins. of soil over the cuttings. As soon as soil warms up take cuttings out, open up the bundles, and put the cuttings about 6 ins. apart in the nursery row, right side up, of course. Cuttings should be set deeply enough so that only tip bud is above surface of soil.

Should all grapevines be grafted? In some sections grapes should be grafted on rootstocks that are resistant to the grape phylloxera or root louse. Where this insect is not prevalent, vines may be grown from cuttings. Consult your Experiment Station concerning your own locality.

How can I get another vine started from the one I have? The easiest way is to lay a cane on the ground, peg it down if necessary, and cover a portion of it with soil. Roots will form at joints which are covered, and cane can be cut loose from old vine and used as a new plant. Most vines are propagated commercially by means of cuttings.

What is the best way to get grape cuttings started and set out so they will grow? Should grafting wax be used? Select straight, vigorous, well-matured, 1-year-old wood of pencil size. Cut into sections 3 buds long, making lower cut through node opposite lowest bud and upper cut about an inch above third bud. Tie cuttings in bundles of 50 and bury them in a trench, butt ends up, and cover with 6 ins. of soil during winter. After ground has warmed in spring, set cuttings in well-prepared soil so that they are about 3 ins. apart and with only upper bud above the soil. Hoe, cultivate, and water them during summer as needed. On good soil they should make enough growth in one season to permit transplanting them to the vineyard the next spring. No grafting wax or other materials need be used on cuttings handled in the manner described.

PESTS AND DISEASES

What causes grapes on vines to shrivel up and drop off until not one good grape is left? Shriveling of the grapes is caused by black rot, a disease which attacks the fruit, shoots, and foliage. (See Grapes—Section VIII.)

My grapes turn to mummies right on the vines. Why do they look like raisins but don't taste like them? Your grapes have been affected by the black rot disease which is caused by a fungus. It can be controlled by spraying with Bordeaux mixture. The most important times to spray are when new shoots are about 1 in. long, when they are 12 ins. long, right after blooming, and again 10 days later. (See Grapes—Section VIII.)

How can I keep bees from destroying ripe grapes without using poisonous sprays?   As a rule bees do not attack sound and uninjured berries. Only after some of the berries have cracked from overripeness or excess rainfall are bees apt to attack the fruit. When fruit reaches such a stage it must be harvested anyway to prevent spoiling. On a small scale injury by bees can be prevented by covering clusters with 1- or 2-lb. paper bags of type used in grocery stores.

Is there any method of protecting grapes from the ravages of wasps aside from bagging? I was told sulphur dust would protect them.   Wasps as a rule do not attack sound fruit. Only after berries have cracked from some other reason are these pests apt to attack fruit. Application of lime sulphur might have a repelling action, if applied heavily, but in such concentrations it would be objectionable on fruit and might injure the fruit and leaves.

If I plant some grapevines, will they have to be sprayed? You can't expect to have perfect fruit without spraying, but many home-garden grapevines produce a pretty fair crop in spite of the fact they are never sprayed. Why not start your vines and then spray if you find it necessary?

What causes my grape leaves to turn brown and drop a month before the first frost?   Grape leaf hoppers in all probability. These are sucking insects about the size of mosquitoes. They feed on under sides of leaves, causing them to appear first yellowish, then brown, after which they drop. The remedy is a contact spray such as nicotine directed at the under sides of the leaves. (See Grapes—Section VIII.)

VARIETIES OF GRAPES

Is there a seedless Concord grape on the market?   There is a variety of grape available to growers which is known as Concord Seedless. It is thought that it originated as a sport or mutation of Concord grape. The berries are much smaller than those of Concord and have only very rudimentary seeds, which are hardly noticeable.

How is the new Sheridan grape compared with our Concord grape?   Where it can be grown properly the Sheridan grape is an improvement over Concord. It has a larger berry and cluster, a more compact bunch, is more attractive, has a finer flavor, tougher skin, and will keep in fine condition in common storage until January. It requires a long season to mature, however, ripening about 2 weeks after Concord in central New York.

Are there any varieties of grapes which will keep better than Concord, either on the vine or after picking? Seneca, a very early white grape and Sheridan, a late, blue-black variety are especially good keepers.

What grape variety is usually made into grape juice? The most common sweet grape-juice variety throughout the East is the Concord.

What are some good modern grapes? There are many varieties of grapes which differ from each other in color, size, shape, flavor, ripening season, quality, and many other characters. Among the varieties considered to be of fine quality are Concord, Fredonia, Ontario, Delaware, Diamond, Buffalo, Worden, and Seneca.

Which are the best grapes for northern New York around the Thousand Islands? The relatively short growing season in this area will mature only very early varieties. Van Buren and Fredonia are early blue varieties. Portland, Ontario, and Seneca are green varieties. The two latter varieties may need winter protection.

I should like to grow some of the California varieties of grapes in New Jersey. Do they require special culture? Not so much special culture as special climate. Winters are too cold and summers too cloudy in New Jersey for most California varieties. American varieties or hybrids between American and European (California varieties are mostly of European origin) are most satisfactory in the East. Some varieties of this type are Fredonia, Niagara, Concord, and Delaware.

Will Scuppernong grapes grow in Pennsylvania? You are too far north for this type, which is widely grown in the South. The northern limit of the Scuppernong or Muscadine type is southern Virginia.

What kind of grape will pollinize with California Tokay grape? The vine is no more than 10 years old and covers Jasper Walnut tree. (Michigan.) The Tokay grape is self-fruitful and does not require cross-pollination. This California variety is not hardy enough to withstand the winters in Michigan. Therefore, I doubt whether you have a Tokay grapevine. My opinion is that you planted a vine of this variety which was grafted on a hardy American rootstock. Probably the Tokay graft has been killed and the vine has sprouted out from the hardy rootstock. Many of the hardy rootstocks used for grafting are male vines and never set fruit. This may account for the fact that your vine fails to bear a crop even though it may blossom profusely. If this is the case, there is nothing you can do except to replace the vine with another vine or to cut it off at the ground and graft a scion of the desired variety onto it. If another Tokay scion is grafted onto it, the Tokay top would need to be given winter protection to prevent it's being killed.

Can the California grapes like Tokay, Malaga, etc., be grown in eastern United States?   No, for two reasons. The root louse (phylloxera) will destroy vines on their own roots; and the season is not long enough to ripen the fruit. Certain new hybrids between the American varieties and the European vinifera vines, however (notably the new Golden Muscat), can be depended upon to ripen their fruits if a season 10 days longer than the normal season for ripening Concords can be expected in your locality.

Are there any grape varieties hardy enough to be grown in northern Minnesota?   Your own Experiment Station at Minneapolis is breeding for hardiness in grapes. Write to the Department of Horticulture there for recommendations.

CANE FRUITS

What is meant by the term "bramble or cane fruits"?   This group includes the fruits belonging to the genus Rubus; the red, black, and purple raspberries, the dewberry, and the bush and trailing blackberries. The loganberry, boysenberry, etc., may be classified as dewberries.

Have the "brambles" any preference as to soil?   Raspberries and bush blackberries do best in heavier soils; dewberries like sandy soils and will not thrive on heavy soils.

Can cane fruits be grown successfully in a sandy soil?   A sandy loam soil is satisfactory, but coarse sands are too subject to drought and are low in fertility.

What fertilizer is needed in planting cane fruits?   A complete fertilizer or barnyard manure.

Where should cane fruits be planted?   Cane fruits like cool growing conditions where the air drainage is good and the soil is rich, loamy texture. They can be planted near perennial vegetables such as rhubarb and asparagus, preferably on west or north side of these, so as not to shade low•growers.

Can you plant berry bushes during the winter when ground is soft? It could be done, but if soil has much clay in it it will be too sticky to do a good job. If there is much freezing and thawing afterward plants might heave out of ground unless mulched and surrounded with soil. Fall or early-spring planting would be preferable.

How much space should be planted with cane fruits for a family of 4? Personal tastes must be considered, of course, but here is one suggested assortment: plants 3 ft. apart in row, in rows 5 to 8 ft. apart. Red raspberries, 50 ft. of row; black raspberries, 24 ft. of row; blackberries, bush, 50 ft. of row.

Can raspberries be planted near pine trees? If there is distance enough between them so that there is no root competition or shade. The lime and fertilizer required for fruits might not favor the pine.

What berry bushes thrive in shade? No plants that bear fruit will thrive in much shade. The more sun they receive, the better the crops.

Should loganberry, raspberry, blackberry, boysenberry, bushes, etc., be planted north, south, east, or west? It makes very little difference. If the land slopes, plant across the slope or around it to prevent erosion or to facilitate irrigation.

When do you plant everbearing raspberries? Everbearing raspberries may be set either in the fall or spring and should have the same care that the ordinary one-crop varieties receive.

What bramble or cane fruits could be grown in a very small city garden? None of them are really adapted to such conditions as they will all spread, either by suckering or by tip rooting. Possibly black raspberries would be easiest to keep under control.

Do cane fruits need support? Cane fruits do not require support, but most growers use some means of training to keep them from growing too "ragged" and occupying too much space in the garden.

How would you construct a trellis for dewberry vines? A 5-ft. stake driven 1 ft. into the ground beside each plant will be quite satisfactory. Cut out old, dead canes and tie up new, vigorous canes in early spring, cutting them off at top of the stake.

How should I care for the new Indian Summer raspberries which I set out last spring? How should they be pruned and sprayed? (Vermont.)   Indian Summer raspberry is pruned in the same manner as the one-crop varieties. (See question on pruning raspberries.) Spraying is not necessary. The season in Vermont is too short to ripen the fall crop of Indian Summer.

What is correct yearly cultural care of established cane fruits? Constant shallow cultivation to control weeds is important. Mulching is a good plan, using well-rotted manure. Prune living canes only where necessary for training of plants. Prune out all dead canes after fruiting season. Apply nitrate of soda (or a similar high-nitrogen fertilizer) in spring, 1 to 2 lbs. per 100 ft. of row.

Will the application of whitewash or paint to a lattice fence harm Lucretia dewberries trained on the fence?   No harm will be done to the plants.

How often should berries be picked?   Pick red raspberries every day, blackcaps and blackberries every third day.

What pre-winter care should be given raspberries?   Raspberries should have cover crop sown between the rows.

How can I increase my stock of cane fruits?   Layering is often practiced by growers. Bend the cane down to the ground and put a shovel of earth over it, just back of the growing tip (the end of the plant). This will form roots. If plants are free from disease, the young sucker growths of raspberries can be transplanted.

How often should cane fruits be renewed in order to maintain an abundant yield?   As they run out; probably every 5 to 10 years.

VARIETIES OF CANE FRUITS

What kind of fruit bushes can I grow on a strip 3 × 40 ft.? (New York.)   If the area is exposed to full sunlight, you could grow any of the small fruits; such as grapes, strawberries, raspberries, currants, or gooseberries, or combinations of the ones you like best. For instance, 3 currant bushes would take up about 10 ft., leaving 30 ft. for strawberries if you particularly like these two fruits; or all may be planted to raspberries or blackberries.

Our garden is in Maine, rather far east on the coast. Can you give information on varieties of small fruits?   Howard 17 (Premier), Catskill, and Fairfax are good home-garden strawberries. Latham, Newburgh, Indian Summer and Taylor are good red raspberries. Bristol and Cumberland are the best black raspberries, while Sodus is the best purple variety.

What would be a profitable fruit planting, producing in about 3 or 4 years, which could be tended on week ends and will produce for at least 10 years without replanting? There are 2 acres and full sun, ½ mile from ocean. The acreage is too small for tree fruits. A combination of red raspberries and strawberries has been profitable for some growers, but strawberries have to be planted each year for best results. You might make a miscellaneous fruit planting for your own and sell the surplus. In that case, choose the fruits you like and take a part of your "profit" in personal satisfaction. If profit is the main objective, secure enough land to make an economic farm unit.

What different kinds of berries should be planted in order to have a continuous supply from late spring until frost? Start off with strawberries, then raspberries, currants, gooseberries, bush blackberries, trailing blackberries. These will cover the season until early August. Everbearing strawberries and raspberries will fill out the rest of the season but they are not too satisfactory. It might be better to depend on grapes or tree fruits during the fall.

Are boysenberries worth an amateur week-end gardener's efforts? Boysenberry is a form of dewberry that requires sandy soil. It is not reliably hardy in the North. It must be given adequate winter covering.

What kind of everbearing raspberries are suggested for south of Boston? The best variety at the Massachusetts State College at Amherst is Ranere or St. Regis. These are really fall bearing. The fall crop is produced at the tips of the new canes and next summer the same canes bear another crop.

Can we grow the Oregon Evergreen blackberry in this state? (Massachusetts.) It would kill to the ground during any but the mildest winter. The Brainerd is a variety of this type which is somewhat hardier.

What is the best variety of blackberry for Maine? Eldorado.

What is the best variety of raspberry for Maine? Latham raspberry.

What are the best varieties of cane fruits to grow? See Introduction.

BLACKBERRY

Will blackberries grow on any soil? They do best on good soil containing plenty of humus, but well drained. Heavy loam is preferable to sandy soils.

Can manure be used on blackberries?   Yes, manure or complete fertilizer can be used to improve poor soils on which blackberries are grown. A yearly cover crop, turned under in spring, or the turning under of summer mulch adds needed humus to the soil.

When is the best time to transplant blackberry or raspberry bushes?   Early spring, although fall planting may be successful if plants are set rather deeply and mounded somewhat to prevent heaving during winter. This applies to red raspberries; black raspberries should be set in the spring.

How far apart should raspberries and bush blackberries be planted?   Three ft. apart in the row and rows 7 to 8 ft. apart are standard distances.

How far apart should blackberries of the trailing type be planted?   Trailing blackberries such as Black Diamond (called Oregon Evergreen in the West) and Brainerd need plenty of room. Set plants at least 6 ft. apart in rows 6 to 8 ft. apart.

When and how should blackberries be pruned?   In June tips of new shoots are pinched off at a height of 3 ft. to make them branch. The following spring the branches are cut back to a length of about 15 ins. After crop is harvested, canes that have borne fruit are removed.

Why do some blackberries blossom and not have any berries? The cause of the trouble is not known. It is rather prevalent among blackberries in some seasons.

Are the trailing blackberries, that is, dewberry, boysenberry, Himalaya blackberry, etc., propagated the same way as the regular blackberries?   These are usually propagated by tip layering.

Can the suckers that come up from the roots of blackberries be used to make plants of the same variety?   Yes. Usually the nurserymen use root cuttings 3 to 4 ins. long and the thickness of a lead pencil. (See Division.)

Why do blackberry leaves get a bright orange color and then seem to die?   The orange color is made up of spores of a disease known as orange rust. Infected plants will die. The only control is to dig out diseased plants before spores have been discharged to infect other plants. Be sure to dig out the roots, as shoots coming up from these would be diseased.

Is it satisfactory to transplant wild blackberry bushes for home use?   This is all right if you can find really superior wild bushes, otherwise you will have much better results by planting named varieties. Wild blackberries sometimes do not do so well under cultivation as they do in the wild. Try such varieties as Blowers or Alfred.

Is the thornless Black Diamond blackberry as good as the thorny type?   Much better, as it is practically identical with the older type of Black Diamond, and thornlessness is a very valuable asset, as can be attested by anyone who has pruned the thorny type.

Would raspberry and blackberry plants make a good ground cover for a steep embankment?   Red raspberries would not do because of dying canes. Blackcap raspberry would fill the bill except that it is liable to be wiped out by mosaic disease. If soil is sandy and climate right, dewberry would be excellent. Black Diamond, or any trailing variety of blackberry would make a fine cover. Probably would need to be gone over every 3 or 4 years with a brush scythe.

BOYSENBERRIES

How can the boysenberry be a cross between the raspberry, dewberry, and blackberry?   It can't be. The story given out about its origin is rather misleading. It was admitted to be a chance seedling and is probably a straight dewberry seedling (at least that is what breeding experiments indicate).

What soil *p*H do thornless boysenberries require to yield best results?   Boysenberries are not particular as to the acidity of the soil, and this matter may be disregarded unless the soil is an extreme type.

How should boysenberries be fed?   Boysenberries may be fertilized with nitrate of soda or sulfate of ammonia at the rate of 1 lb. per 100 sq. ft. Failing these fertilizers, use 5 lbs. dried chicken manure.

Have some boysenberries, set out last spring, which I would like to move. When can this be done?   Boysenberries can be moved in late fall or early spring before growth starts. In mild climates, they may be moved any time during the winter.

Do boysenberry plants need protection during their first winter?   Boysenberries are not winter hardy in Northern states. The canes should be covered during winter months with straw or earth. They are covered after several hard freezes and before ground freezes. The covering is removed in early spring after the severe cold of winter is past and before growth starts.

How are boysenberries pruned out and trained? Boysenberries are a trailing vine. The canes grow one year, bear fruit
second, and then die, another crop taking their place. To facilitate harvesting of fruit and tillage operations fruiting canes are
tied up to a trellis at beginning of second season. A suitable
trellis consists of a wire 3 or 4 ft. above the ground. Canes are
gathered together and tied at top to this wire. The ends are cut
off or tied along wire. Canes may also be tied up to 5-ft. posts,
ends being cut off at top of post. After crop is off, fruiting canes
are removed and new canes, that will fruit following year, tied in.

**What is proper method for growing boysenberries? I saved
one plant out of 3 which I bought from nursery.** Boysenberries are best planted in early spring as soon as soil can be
worked. Culture consists of keeping down weeds, pruning, and
training. (See questions on Pruning and Training.)

**I am having trouble getting boysenberry to start growing. I
planted according to directions. Why?** Plants are easy to start
if they are in good condition when planted. No special care is
needed.

**Should the new thornless boysenberries be grown in shade,
semi-shade, or full sun, or should they be grown in acid soil?**
Boysenberries, thornless or thorny, should be grown in the sun.
The acidity of soil is not important.

**Do you believe it worth time and space for small garden to
plant boysenberries? Do they grow on tall briers or on ground
vine? (New York.)** Boysenberries are not hardy enough in
New York to deserve space in a small garden. Raspberries and
strawberries are better. Boysenberries grow in long runners that
are usually supported on a trellis.

Is boysenberry prolific enough to be profitable? The
boysenberry is productive where the plants are hardy. It is being
extensively planted commercially in California.

**Are boysenberries worth investing in, or do raspberries make
better profits?** Where boysenberries are hardy, they are
profitable. Raspberries are more reliable in the Northern states.

**Last spring we planted boysenberries. Sometime later I read
an article by someone who said they weren't fit to eat. Is this
true?** The man who did not like them had a perverted taste.
They are excellent.

**My boysenberries produce miles of runners and hardly any
berries. Why? (Michigan.)** Boysenberries are not winter
hardy in the Northern states and fruiting canes are killed each

winter. The roots which are uninjured produce vigorous new shoots the following year.

Why aren't boysenberries grown commercially in this part of the country? (New Jersey.) They aren't quite hardy enough to stand the winters without some protection, the yield isn't large enough to be profitable, and fruit is too soft to ship well. This variety may be grown in the home garden, by those who particularly like the flavor, by giving it a little extra care including some protection during winter.

Can boysenberries be grown in western Pennsylvania? Boysenberries can be grown in western Pennsylvania if canes are covered with earth or straw for winter protection.

Have 6-year-old boysenberry bushes, which were planted close to young shade trees and now are shaded too much. Can I transplant this coming spring? The plants are very large and strong. Can I divide them and make more plants? Old berry plants do not transplant and re-establish themselves readily. Either buy new plants or cover tips of new canes with soil in late summer. Roots will form at tips. New plants may be severed from parent plant following spring and moved to their permanent location. Dividing old plants is hardly practical.

How should nectarberries be cultivated? Nectarberries are very similar to boysenberries and should have the same care.

DEWBERRIES

What are dewberries? Are they a desirable cane fruit for the home garden? Trailing or procumbent blackberries. They are a week or two earlier than other blackberries, with large berries but of a poorer flavor than high-growing types.

Where should dewberries be planted? Dewberries are happiest on sandy soils south of central Pennsylvania. In the Northern states winter protection is advisable where reliable snow cover is lacking.

What is the planting distance for dewberries? The plants are set 5 ft. apart each way for training on stakes or 7 × 2 ft. if they are to be grown on a trellis.

Can dewberries be trimmed in some way so that the branches do not cling so close to the ground? The dewberry naturally trails on ground. The second or fruiting year canes may be tied to a 5-ft. stake and cut off at top. Sometimes they are tied to a wire 3 or 4 ft. from the ground.

How far should dewberry branches be allowed to spread? During the first season, when canes are trailing on ground, they are not restricted. (See next question.)

Last spring I planted some dewberry plants along the edges of my vegetable garden. How do you care for the straggly growth, to keep it within bounds? Dewberry canes are tied up to a trellis or a stake for the fruiting year. The first year canes trail on the ground.

RASPBERRY

Will young black raspberry bushes grow well if planted in fresh brown sandy loam fill? If the soil used in filling is subsoil, it is hardly suitable for berries of any kind. If it is topsoil, berries should do well in it.

When is the best time to plant red raspberry bushes? Red raspberries may be set in late fall if soil is mounded around plants to a height of several ins. to prevent heaving from frost action. In spring soil is worked down level. Raspberries may also be set in early spring.

When is the best time to transplant black raspberries? Tip plants are set in spring, but "transplants" may be set either in spring or in fall.

How far apart should raspberries be planted? Plant suckering varieties 3 ft. apart, in rows 5 or 6 ft. apart; blackcaps, 4 or 5 ft. apart, in rows 6 or 7 ft. apart.

Can raspberry bushes which were not planted in the fall be held over until spring without heeling them in? They must be heeled in, or packed in moist material such as sphagnum moss, and stored in a cellar where the temperature stays near 32° F. Roots must not be allowed to dry out, and temperature must be low enough to prevent canes from sprouting.

Is it possible to plant between the rows of raspberries? It seems as if there is space going to waste. There will be no waste space between rows of raspberries 6 or 7 ft. apart after the first season. The roots spread out farther than the canes.

Should raspberries and blackberries be pruned in the summer? Red raspberries should not be summer pruned. Blackcaps and bush blackberries should have their canes pinched back when they reach the height at which branching is desired. This would usually be at 24 to 30 ins. for black raspberries and 30 to 36 ins.

for bush blackberries. If pinching is done at proper time, it will consist of merely nipping out growing tip of cane with the fingers.

How should red raspberries be pruned and trained? Red raspberries are commonly tied to stakes or a wire trellis in the garden, but support is not necessary. Plants should be grown in hedgerows not over 1 ft. in width. In early spring canes which grew previous season are cut back about ¼ of their height. Weaker canes should be removed so that remaining canes are spaced about 6 ins. apart in rows 1 ft. in width. Canes which fruited previous summer should be removed if this was not done after the crop was harvested. Red raspberry plants send up a multitude of suckers between rows and unless these are subdued by vigorous use of hoe a veritable thicket will result.

How should black raspberries be pruned? Remove canes that are dead, broken, obviously diseased, or that grow at such an angle that they will bend to the ground when in fruit. Cut back good canes to about 24 to 30 ins. and then shorten the lateral branches to about 4 ins. in length.

Do red raspberries need a trellis? Not necessarily. If they are pruned rather short (cut back about ½ if 5 to 6 ft. tall), they will hold themselves up. However, a trellis of one wire on each side of row, supported by posts and crosspieces, will hold canes up during storms, prevent breakage, and keep berries from getting into mud.

Last summer I planted some Sodus purple raspberries. They have grown to a length of 9 to 12 ft. How far and when should they be cut back? In early spring canes should be cut back to a length of 4 or 5 ft. and tied up to a stake or wire trellis. To eliminate need for support, pinch off tips of new shoots when they reach a height of 30 ins. This makes canes branch and they are sturdier and self-supporting. The following spring cut branches back to a length of 10 or 12 ins. and no support will be needed.

What, if any, winter protection should be given 1-year-old black raspberry bushes? (New York.) Black raspberries are hardy without winter protection except in the coldest parts of the country like northern New York.

How can I protect raspberries over winter? (Massachusetts.) Hardy raspberry varieties should not need protection in Massachusetts. If protection is desired, bend canes down and cover tips with soil. In this position snow will provide protection. Where snow blows off, straw or earth may be used to cover the canes.

Are leaves or natural fertilizer better as a mulch dressing for raspberry bushes?   Straw, old hay, or leaves are good mulching materials for raspberries. Manure, if used in sufficient amounts to be of value as a mulch, will stimulate such a strong growth that winter injury may result. Manure is, of course, an excellent material for fertilizing raspberries.

At about what date in spring should mulch be removed from raspberries?   The best time to remove mulch is when unmulched plants begin to start growth.

Do everbearing raspberries bear more than once in a season? Two crops are borne, the first in July on canes which grew previous season, second or fall crop in September and October on tips of current season's canes.

My red raspberry patch has grown so profusely. Would it be wise to take out every other row and start a new patch?   It is rather difficult to subdue and restore order in a raspberry patch that has run wild. It will be easier and more satisfactory to take up healthy sucker plants and set a new patch, resolving to take care of it and keep suckers in bounds. Have rows in the new patch 6 or 7 ft. apart and keep rows of plants about 1 ft. in width.

Can shoots of red raspberry be cut away from parent plant and transplanted in the spring? If so, how and when?   New shoots of red raspberries may be taken up in June after they have reached a height of 6 or 8 ins. Care should be taken to get part of the old root. Cloudy, moist weather is essential and the plants should be watered in. This method of starting raspberries is not successful in hot, dry weather.

When is the best time to propagate wild red raspberries? Red raspberry sucker plants may be taken up and set either in late fall or early spring.

How can I get new plants to renew my raspberry planting? Red raspberries are propagated from suckers from the roots of old plants. These are dug up, the large root severed, and new plants set in place. Black and purple cane raspberries are propagated by tip layers. (See Division.)

Will red and black raspberries mix if planted close?   No, not at all.

PESTS AND DISEASES

How can I keep the birds from devouring my red raspberries? Cover plants with netting or cheesecloth.

How can I keep rabbits from gnawing raspberry bushes dur-

ing the winter? Fence them out with poultry netting 30 ins high.

What causes the so-called mosaic disease of raspberries? This is a virus disease spread from one plant to another by aphids. The only remedy is to keep digging out and destroying diseased plants. Be sure to take out roots, as all the shoots coming up from roots of a diseased plant will also be diseased.

What causes a hard, woody knot to grow at the ground level on my raspberry bushes? This is caused by the disease known as crown gall. There is no cure for a diseased plant, and the disease will live in the soil for some time. So set clean, inspected plants in soil that has not recently grown any of the bramble fruits.

What causes tips of my Latham raspberry plants to wilt over? The raspberry cane borer, a beetle, lays an egg near the tip of the cane, then cuts a girdle just above and just below the egg which usually causes the tip to wilt and die. The most practical control consists of breaking off wilted tips and burning them. Break or cut a couple of inches below the girdle in order to get the larva, which will start to bore down through the pith of the cane as soon as it hatches.

My blackcap raspberries have gray spots on the canes and on the fruit. What can I do? This is the disease known as anthracnose. A delayed dormant spray of lime sulphur, 1 to 20, when the buds are out about ½ in. in the spring, will usually give control. In severe cases put on a 3-6-50 Bordeaux mixture spray just before the first blossoms open. Remove old fruiting canes as soon as crop is picked.

Why aren't red and black raspberries supposed to be grown together? Because of certain diseases, mosaic in particular, which are carried by the reds and readily transmitted to the blacks. Mosaic infection may not injure a red variety very rapidly but will kill a blackcap in a much shorter time (that is, the reds act as carriers of the disease). The blacks would be much safer a couple of hundred yards away, far enough so aphids will not get from one to the other.

Why aren't the purple raspberries more widely grown? They are susceptible to the mosaic disease. They are not very attractive in the box and do not sell well. Those who know them frequently prefer them to the reds and blacks.

VARIETIES OF RASPBERRIES

Are everbearing raspberries more desirable than standard

sorts? For the home gardener, everbearing sorts are desirable to extend the season. They should be used to supplement the regular sorts rather than in place of them. Indian Summer is considered the best everbearing variety.

What black raspberries are the best producers for home use? Bristol and Cumberland are both productive, high-quality varieties.

What red raspberry do you consider best for home garden and market garden? (Wisconsin.) For Wisconsin, Latham is a standard variety. Newburgh should also be tried.

Is the Columbian the best purple raspberry? (Pennsylvania.) It used to be the standard variety of this type, but the newer varieties Sodus and Potomac are better.

What are good early and late red raspberries? Sunrise for early and Latham for late would make a good combination.

What is a good everbearing raspberry? There are only 2 commonly grown. Ranere (also known as St. Regis) is an old variety. The fall crop is rather uncertain, depending on the season. Indian Summer is a newer variety that seems to be pretty good in New York but in some regions farther South is inclined to be dark and crumbly. The fall crop of either variety is not very large or likely to be very profitable.

What is the culture of youngberry? Youngberries are similar to boysenberries and should have the same care.

Are thornless youngberries as satisfactory as the ones with thorns in respect to production and hardiness? The thornless are said to be less productive, but the evidence on this point is not conclusive.

BLUEBERRY

SOILS AND FERTILIZERS

What is an ideal blueberry soil? A well-aerated mixture of sand and peat with the water table 2 or 3 ft. below the surface. In such a soil there is excellent drainage near the surface, but water is always available within reach of roots. A plentiful supply of peatmoss means plenty of organic matter and usually the required acid reaction of pH 4.5 to 5.5. Such soil conditions are seldom available in the home garden, so they have to be approximated by spading in peat or leafmold, and by mulching or irrigation, or all three.

How can I make the soil sufficiently acid for successful blueberry culture?   Soil should be moist, full of peat or other organic material, and with a reaction of about pH 5.0. Soil may be made acid through the use of acid peatmoss, oak leafmold, and chemicals. Most chemicals are dangerous, as an excess is apt to be harmful. Sulphur and aluminum sulfate are among the best, but the quantities necessary have to be calculated in relation to the composition of the soil and its pH reaction.

How can hybrid blueberries be grown on neutral soil? Limestone soils vary. Sometimes, if the underlying rock is limestone, the topsoil may be acid. If the soil is deep and of limestone origin, the conditions are different. Investigate. Why try something that may be troublesome in later years? For instance, you might make the soil acid enough originally, but if it is necessary to irrigate, and the water is hard, trouble will develop. Excavate a bed 4 ft. wide and 2 ft. deep, put in a layer of 6 or 8 ins. of acid peatmoss or acid leafmold. Fill with soil that has been acidified chemically or by being composted with acid peat or leafmold. Use water that does not contain lime.

What is the pH requirement for Rubel Blueberry, Juneberry and Highbush Cranberry?   The ideal pH range for the highbush blueberry is usually from 4.5 to 5.5. The Juneberry and Highbush Cranberry do not require an especially acid soil, although (so far as we know) no experiments to determine optimum pH for these plants have been conducted, whereas several workers have studied the pH requirements of the blueberry.

Having limestone soil, how shall I prepare for growing blueberries successfully?   First get your soil tested, for it may not be as alkaline as you think. If it is not more alkaline than pH 5.5, no special treatment will be needed. If it is around pH 6.0, you can probably get satisfactory results by using ammonium sulfate as a fertilizer. If the pH is about 6.5 or 7.0, you will have to acidify by bringing in a plentiful supply of acid organic matter, or by chemical means. Acidity isn't the only soil requirement, however. Proper fertilization and a relatively constant and ample supply of moisture are necessary.

Just how is ordinary soil prepared for growing blueberries? Is there any way to test it?   Most State Agricultural Experiment Stations will test soil for residents of the state. Methods of acidifying the soil are elsewhere discussed. In many cases it will not be necessary to acidify artificially, and then the main requirement is assurance of a uniformly plentiful supply of moisture. If the soil is dry, it may be necessary to irrigate. If it is fairly moist, a permanent mulch of straw or hay will give best results by conserving what moisture there is.

Our soil is too rich for blueberries. What can we do about it? It probably isn't too "rich," as blueberries will grow in very fertile soil provided other conditions are right. Your soil may be alkaline, deficient in some one or more elements, or it may be too wet or too dry.

Would you recommend blueberries for an acid garden section? Blueberries will do excellently in an acid garden, and will usually be an asset to it. They require the same cultural conditions as azaleas and rhododendrons.

Is the soil in Cleveland all right to raise blueberries and boysenberries? Ground quite clayey. (Ohio.) Boysenberries can be grown in clay if humus is added, provided drainage is good. Lighter soils are better, of course. Allow plenty of room; the vines are enormous. Blueberries probably will not grow successfully in unmodified Ohio clays. They are lowland plants that like acid soils stuffed with humus and with a strong acid reaction. To grow them successfully will probably require the use of a good pH indicator. (Consult your county agent or a first-class seed store for details.) Dig a trench about 5 ft. wide and at least 2 ft. deep. Fill with a mixture of ⅓ soil, ⅓ rotted oak leaves or peat, and ⅓ sand. Maintain a pH of between 4.9 and 5.6, if possible, but always below 6.0.

We are much interested in trying to raise blueberries in an ashy soil in a dry climate; have plenty of water to irrigate, but the atmosphere is very dry. Can it be done? (Idaho.) Your main difficulty would be in getting your soil acid enough. It would be best to start in a small way first.

How should blueberries, already planted, be fed and cared for? We will take it for granted that your soil conditions are favorable; if not, you will probably be unsuccessful. Unless moisture conditions are ideal, put on a permanent straw mulch. Broadcast a good complete fertilizer, such as a 5–10–5 formula, at the rate of about 15 to 20 lbs. per 1,000 sq. ft. if your soil is of only average fertility, applying part in early spring and the remainder about a month later.

What is the best fertilizer for blueberries? I have a field of very fine native lowbush berries in Maine, which I wish to improve for marketing. Experiments at the Maine Agricultural Experiment Station have indicated the value of a complete fertilizer for lowbush blueberries provided weeds are kept under control. Since this is to be a commercial venture, write for the latest recommendations from the Maine Station.

What is proper fertilizer to use for cultivated blueberries? When should it be used? The amount and kind of fertilizer that would be sufficient for other berry bushes, such as raspberries, on your particular soil should also be good for blueberries on the same soil.

CULTURE

How and when should blueberry shrubs 3 years of age be pruned? Prune during late fall, winter, or early spring. Three-year-old bushes will need comparatively little pruning. Remove small, rather weak lateral twigs to prevent their fruiting. Long shoots, well covered with fruit buds, may need to be cut back to leave only 2 or 3 fruit buds. Remember that 1 fruit bud will produce a cluster of flowers and of fruit. If the fruit buds are not thinned by pruning, too many berries will be set, the fruit will be small and late in maturing, and the bush will be weakened.

When is the best time to make blueberry cuttings, and how are they cared for? Make hardwood cuttings in late winter or early spring and place them in peatmoss, or ½ sand and ½ peat, in ground beds under a lath house, or in a special raised propagating frame. Cuttings should be about 6 ins. long of good 1-year-old twigs, preferably without fruit buds. Place them at an angle in the moss, with at least ⅔ of the cutting covered. Great care must be taken in watering and ventilating, especially in raised frames which are covered with hotbed sash and kept closed in the early stages of rooting.

Is it necessary to plant at least 7 blueberry bushes in order to have them fruit? Two bushes, 1 each of 2 different varieties, would be enough to effect cross-fertilization. At least 7 bushes might be necessary to get a succession of fruit from early, medium, and late varieties, but the fruit on any 1 bush would not be any better than if there were only 2 bushes.

Are 2 blueberry bushes sufficient to assure fruit, or is it necessary to have more than that number? If so, how many? Two bushes are enough if they are different varieties which bloom at the same time. If only 1 variety is planted, a fair set might be obtained, but the berries would probably be a little smaller than if they had been cross-pollinated.

Is any progress being made in adapting blueberries to dry land? The only way this can be accomplished is by crossing those which require moist soil with one of the dry-land types. This work has been started. The cultivated blueberry has been crossed with the lowbush blueberry of Maine, a dry-land type, and also with 2 or 3 dry-land species of the South. Eventually there should be varieties adapted to ordinary agricultural soil and possibly even to the sandy coastal plains soils.

What are the requirements of hybrid blueberries?   The so-called hybrid blueberries are essentially like other plants with respect to most of their requirements, the two principal exceptions being that they require a rather acid soil and an ample and uniform moisture supply.

Where should blueberries be planted in the home garden?
Blueberries require acid soil, good drainage, and aeration. They need a space of 8 ft. between bushes.

Can blueberries be cultivated in a limited space under favorable conditions?   Yes. Favorable conditions, however, include full exposure to sunlight, which is not always possible in a very limited area.

How can I promote faster growth of blueberry bushes?   Be sure growing conditions are favorable with respect to soil fertility and moisture supply. Some varieties grow more rapidly than others, but all are rather slow growing compared, for instance, with a peach tree.

Will blueberries grow under tall, large oaks in semi-shade?
They will grow in this environment, but the yield of fruit will not be equal to that of plants grown in the open.

How are weeds controlled in the blueberry regions of Maine where cultivation isn't practical?   By burning over the blueberry fields every other year or every third year. Straw is spread thinly over the area and burned when conditions are right for a quick fire which will not injure the blueberry roots.

I have 2 acres of well-drained swampland; how and when should I plant highbush blueberries?   Be sure the swampland is well drained but not too dry; blueberries are very sensitive to moisture conditions. Plant as early in the spring as the soil can be got into condition. Set the plants carefully, slightly deeper than they were in the nursery row, about 5 ft. apart in rows 8 ft. apart.

We have very large blueberries in a pasture. Can they be moved to a garden with good results?   Very large bushes would be difficult to move, but you could move smaller ones. Some would need to be split up to make several plants. The size, color, and quality of the fruit are not likely to be as satisfactory as that from the named varieties, plants of which you can buy. Be sure your soil is properly prepared before digging the wild bushes.

Cultivated blueberry plants have been neglected for approximately 3 years. Will transplanting and proper care revive these plants? They could probably be brought back to normal by proper care without transplanting. Transplanting would result in some loss of plants and considerable delay in achieving really satisfactory growth.

How often should a planting of blueberries be renewed? Blueberries, with good care, should be as permanent as tree fruits, that is, 15 to 25 years or more.

Under ideal conditions are the leaves of blueberries light or dark green? Could yellowish-green color be due to any factor other than incorrect soil reaction? Varieties differ somewhat. Grover, for instance, always has light yellowish-green foliage. Once you are familiar with a variety, you can tell if the foliage is abnormally yellowish. The yellowish color might be due to too alkaline or a wet, poorly aerated soil, lack of sufficient nitrogen, or possibly a disease.

I have blueberries which are not doing well. What can be done? Check the following, which may be responsible: soil not acid enough; lacking in fertility, especially nitrogen; too dry; too wet; injury by low temperatures or by some pest.

How can I grow blueberries successfully in Ohio? For soil requirements, see previous questions. Plant 5 ft. apart in row, using balled and burlapped stock, either in fall or spring. Always plant 2 or more varieties to insure good pollination. Water once a week if rain does not fall for the first season. Cultivate shallowly, as roots grow close to surface. In spring apply about 1 lb. cottonseed meal to smaller shrubs, or 2 lbs. to mature specimens. Use ammonium sulfate (about ½ this rate) if cottonseed meal is not available. Supplement with ½ to 1 lb. any good mixed fertilizer. Use peatmoss or well-rotted oak leaves as a mulch. After plants are in full bearing, remove old, unfruitful branches during the winter.

Will the large blueberries grown in south Jersey do as well in northern New Jersey? Yes, if proper growing conditions are provided. However, there is not nearly so much good blueberry soil in the northern part of the state as in the southern part.

Does the blueberry make a good ornamental shrub? Yes,

it is attractive in bloom, when the fruit is ripe, and when the leaves turn red in the fall. The twigs in winter are also striking. Results will be disappointing, however, if growing conditions are not right. If they are favorable, it may be possible to raise a nice crop of fruit on a border of ornamental shrubs.

What are the advantages of mulching blueberries?   Maintenance of uniform moisture conditions is the most important. Weeds are kept from growing, and a supply of organic matter is built up. Blueberries are very shallow rooted, and cultivation, unless it is very shallow, will cause considerable damage to the roots; mulching eliminates entirely the need for cultivation. Some plant food will be furnished by the mulching material as it decays.

Would it be advisable to put burlap around blueberry bushes for winter in a location where the frost kills forsythia buds, so they do not bloom?   Blueberry buds are very hardy, while the flower buds of forsythia are susceptible to injury by low temperatures. No protection is necessary for blueberries.

VARIETIES OF BLUEBERRIES

What is meant by hybrid blueberries?   The term is commonly used to designate the named varieties of the type known as the highbush, swamp, or cultivated blueberry. Most of these varieties are simply selections from the wild or selections from crosses between wild bushes. Only a few, such as Rancocas, are actually hybrids between species.

What variety of large blueberries can be grown successfully in the home garden?   It is better to have more than 1 variety to secure cross-pollination and a long fruiting period. The following should be satisfactory: June for early, Rancocas for second early, Stanley and Concord for midseason, and Jersey for late.

I have seen blueberries growing in western Florida. What kind are they?   This is the so-called rabbit-eye blueberry, *Vaccinium virgatum,* a vigorous, dry-land type. It has been cultivated rather extensively, but its maximum development awaits the production by breeding of really superior varieties.

What is the difference between the cultivated blueberries and the ones that grow in Maine?   The species usually meant when the term "cultivated blueberries" is used is *Vaccinium corymbosum,* otherwise known as the highbush or swamp blueberry. The ones commonly seen in Maine belong to the species *Vaccinium angustifolium,* the lowbush type, which grows in dry upland.

Are cultivated blueberry bushes desirable as a hedge separating my land from my neighbor's? Not unless your neighbor is growing plants of similar soil requirements adjacent to them. The neighbor may object to their hanging over his property. This would necessitate shearing one side. The plants would be injured and fruiting retarded.

What are the important blueberry-producing states? New Jersey, North Carolina, and Michigan produce the most cultivated blueberries. There are some commercial plantings in Massachusetts, New York, and Maryland. Maine is in the lead in the production from wild lowbush blueberries. Nurseries in New Jersey, Michigan, Massachusetts, Maryland, North Carolina, and New York are propagating blueberry varieties.

CRANBERRY

Is the American cranberry worth planting for jelly? This requires special conditions—bog—so is not suitable for most gardens. Unless a fairly large suitable area is available, the yield would not be worth while.

Where is the cranberry native? There are 2 species used for jelly, etc.: *Vaccinium oxycoccus,* native to northern Europe, northern Asia, and North America, as far south as Pennsylvania, Michigan, and Wisconsin; and *Vaccinium macrocarpum* (the kind mostly sold), native to Newfoundland, south to North Carolina, Michigan, and Minnesota.

What are the soil requirements of the cranberry? Cranberries are grown in acid peat bogs which can be flooded. A level peat bog with a clay subbase is selected. Growth of weeds is killed by flooding for a year. Clear sand is added to a depth of 2 or 3 ins., and cuttings are thrust through this into the peaty soil beneath, 12 to 18 ins. apart. They fruit in about 3 years. Bogs are flooded from December to April or May, and at other times to control insects, to prevent frost, and to harvest loose berries. Bogs are fertilized every year or two and are sanded at intervals to prevent too-rapid, tangled growth.

Can cranberries be grown from seeds? Cranberries can be grown from seeds stratified in the fall.

What is the Highbush Cranberry, and what good is it? The Highbush Cranberry is *Viburnum trilobum* (*americanus*). The fruits are edible, having a distinctive taste liked by some people. Varieties are being selected and tested for culinary use.

How should Highbush Cranberries be pruned?   Highbush Cranberries require very little pruning. The method is to cut out, close to the ground, the oldest canes. This will permit the growth of renewal shoots from the base of the plant. Pruning is done in winter.

CURRANT AND GOOSEBERRY

Are currants and gooseberries particular as to soil?   Wherever good vegetables can be grown, currants and gooseberries do well.

Do gooseberries and currants require fertilizer?   Lime should be applied if the soil is very acid. A complete fertilizer (5–10–5) at the rate of 2 to 4 lbs. per 100 sq. ft., broadcast in the spring.

Should bush fruits be fertilized each year?   It is advisable to fertilize each year. Use a complete commercial fertilizer (3–8–7 or 5–10–5) at the rate of 4 lbs. per 100 sq. ft. broadcast and worked into the soil.

Where should bush fruits be planted?   Gooseberries and currants may be used in edging garden plots or in the shrub border, provided they have light enough and room to develop.

When should currant and gooseberry bushes be planted? These plants start growth very early in the spring, so they should either be set in the fall or by the latter part of March.

How far apart are currants and gooseberries planted?   Five ft. apart in the row; rows 6 ft. apart.

Can gooseberries and currants be planted near pine trees? In regions where white-pine blister rust is serious, the planting of gooseberries and currants may be forbidden. (See also same question under Raspberries, this section.)

How many currant and gooseberry bushes should be planted per person in the home garden?   Currants—2 plants. Gooseberries—2 plants.

What care is given in spring to currant bushes?   Prune, fertilize, and start cultivation. If the bushes are infested with scale, put on a spray of dormant-strength lime sulphur before growth starts.

Do red currants need to be cultivated?   Currant bushes sometimes struggle along in sod and produce some fruit, but they will do much better if weeds and grass are suppressed by cultivation.

Should I purchase bearing-size currant bushes? Good 1- or 2-year plants are much superior to bearing-age transplants. They are cheaper and more likely to survive.

How often should currants and gooseberries be picked? These berries ripen so they can all be picked at once, but they may remain on the bushes for several days without becoming overripe.

I planted 6 gooseberry bushes 3 years ago; gave each plant lots of space, but never a blossom or berry on them. What is wrong? Most gooseberry varieties should bear by the time the plants are 3 years old. Do not overfertilize, and if the plants don't bloom next spring send a branch to your Experiment Station. Some kind of pest might be causing the trouble. It is possible the nursery made a mistake and sent some ornamental shrubs instead of gooseberry bushes.

My gooseberry bushes are about 5 years old and produce hardly any fruit, despite good attention. What could be wrong? Most gooseberry varieties should be in full production at 5 years of age. Possibly you are "killing them with kindness." It would be possible by heavy pruning plus heavy fertilization to keep them in an excessively vegetative and unproductive condition. If you have been doing that, try no pruning and no fertilizers for 2 years.

Can gooseberries be successfully handled by a small gardener? Gooseberries are easy to grow and have few pests. The plants are very compact, so that the few needed by an average family will not require much room.

Why are gooseberry bushes not grown more in Massachusetts? Currants and gooseberries are alternate hosts for white-pine blister rust, a serious disease in New England as well as other parts of the country. Various state and federal laws provide for eradication of these plants in certain areas, and in Massachusetts state authorities have the right to remove them when deemed necessary, thus aiding in the control of this disease.

At what time of year should currant bushes be pruned? Late fall, winter, or very early spring. Since so many things have to be done in the spring, autumn is the most practical time.

What is the best method of pruning red currant bushes? Remove canes 4 years old or older; low-growing canes that droop to the ground when heavy with fruit; broken or diseased canes; the weaker 1-year shoots. After pruning, an ideal bush might consist of about 5 1-year shoots, 4 2-year canes, 3 3-year canes, and possibly 2 or 3 4-year canes, if they are vigorous.

Do red currant bushes that have borne heavily for 3 years have to be trimmed? They don't seem to have any dead wood. When the canes get to be about 4 years old they usually weaken and become unproductive. Such canes should be taken out, down to the ground, before they actually die.

Do gooseberry bushes need pruning?   They may continue to produce for a long time without pruning, but the bushes will be more vigorous and the fruit larger if they are pruned.

When should gooseberries be pruned?   At any time during the dormant season; that is, after the leaves fall and before growth starts in the spring.

How does one prune gooseberry bushes?   Remove dead or broken canes, then those branches that are borne around lower part of bush, low enough to touch ground when loaded with fruit. Canes more than 4 years old usually are too weak to be productive, so they should be cut out. This will usually be all the pruning needed, although it may be desirable to remove a few twigs here and there to shape up the bush, or open up a crowded part of it.

Are currants raised from cuttings?   That is the usual method—hardwood cuttings taken in late winter. Cuttings are made of 1-year canes, and are usually 6 to 8 ins. long. Currants can also be propagated by layers; that is, low-growing branches covered with soil except for the tips. After roots have formed, cut branch from plant and set where desired.

Will gooseberry bushes root from cuttings?   Hardwood cuttings are usually used, but they will also root from half-ripe cuttings in summer. (See Section II.)

What causes warts to grow on the top surface of currant leaves? These wartlike growths are the result of aphids feeding on the undersides of the leaves. As soon as brownish swellings first appear, spray with a contact insecticide such as nicotine sulfate. Direct the spray upward, as only those insects actually hit will be killed.

We have found our currant bushes stripped entirely bare of leaves. What causes this?   This is undoubtedly the work of the imported currant worm, which usually works in large numbers and can strip a bush in a very few days. Watch your bushes carefully in early summer, and when the greenish worms start work dust with rotenone, or spray with hellebore. Follow directions on the package.

Do early browning and dropping of leaves from currant bushes

mean the bushes have died? Or will they come out again next spring? The leaf-spot disease and injury by the currant aphis may make leaves turn brown and drop prematurely. If the twigs are still plump and the bark, when scraped, is bright green, you can expect the leaves to come out again next spring.

We have been told that currant and gooseberry bushes and pines do not mix. Must one or the other necessarily be host of attacking disease? Currants and gooseberries are the winter host for the white-pine blister rust, which attacks only those species of pines that have 5 needles in a bundle. The disease is limited in areas, and where not present, the fruits may be grown. Black currant is the worst, gooseberry next, and the red currant is permitted except in seriously infested areas. State laws should be consulted.

What varieties of currants are recommended for the home garden? Try Red Lake, one of the newer varieties.

What is a good gooseberry variety? (Pennsylvania.) Poorman is a good red-fruited variety. Chautauqua is very large fruited and yellowish green when ripe.

ELDERBERRY

Is the Adams Elderberry worth planting for fruit for pies and canning? Yes. Elderberries are ornamental, and many people like the blossoms for wine and the fruits for pies and jelly. They are of easy culture, growing almost anywhere. Can be used as a hedge.

Does the Adams Elderberry spread and become a nuisance? All elderberries spread by means of suckers from the roots. With watchful care these can be eliminated. Adams is not so aggressive as the wild types.

JUNEBERRY

Is the juneberry worth planting for fruit? Juneberry, also known as serviceberry or shadbush, will scarcely bear enough fruit to pay, but it is a good native ornamental shrub or small tree.

CHINESE JUJUBE (OR DATE)

What is the Chinese Date fruit like? How old are the trees before they fruit. (Kentucky.) Fruit of the Chinese Date, more commonly called the Chinese Jujube, is a drupe (stone fruit) oblong up to 2 ins. long with a sweet, whitish flesh of applelike flavor. The trees bear early, second or third year, where growing conditions are favorable. (See United States Department of Agriculture *Bulletin 1215*, "The Chinese Jujube.")

MISCELLANEOUS FRUITS

FIGS

What is the best fertilizer for a fig tree in acid soil?   One of the best fertilizers is well-rotted manure. A good garden fertilizer, such as 5–10–5, used at the rate of 1 lb. per 50 sq. ft., will probably supply sufficient nutrients.

What is the best time to prune a fig tree growing in a tub? If it's in a forcing house, at any season when it is not maturing fruits. If out of doors, prune in early spring.

How are fig trees pruned? (Maryland.)   Figs require very little pruning. Most of this is done in training the tree while it is young. It is especially desirable in regions where winter injury is probable and the trees must be protected. If trained to 3 or 4 branches, low, it is easy to lay these down and cover them with soil, mounding up over the center point, for protection from cold.

How can one keep a fig tree from freezing in the winter? (New York.)   Many methods are used, depending upon the protection afforded by buildings. One way is to tie up the branches and wrap them with several layers of burlap. Or heavy waterproof paper may be used. Surest way is to train the plant so it branches close to the ground. These branches may then be pressed to the ground, fastened, and covered with a foot or more of soil, with soil mounded over the central point.

Should fig tree on Long Island, on side of house, be covered for winter?   Fig trees will need good winter protection on Long Island. (See previous question.)

What is method of propagating fig tree by layering? (Pennsylvania.)   Bend a branch over in the early spring until a portion that is 2 years old may be fastened down and covered with soil. A notch in the underside of the covered portion, held open by a sliver of stone, may help. Keep this covering of soil moist. Roots should form by the middle of summer, when the new plant may be detached and planted.

In what parts of the country will figs bear successfully for the

home garden? In the southeastern Atlantic and Gulf states, in parts of California, much of Arizona, and New Mexico. In Northern states figs need winter protection, and usually bear little fruit.

What is treatment for fig trees under glass? The soil should be a good compost, and it is advisable to keep this mulched with well-rotted manure. Early temperature, 50° F. night, 65° F. day. Later increased to 65° F. night and 70° F. day. Figs must have plenty of air and moisture until the fruit is set.

Have a fig tree, which is covered every winter, but only few of the figs ripen before frost. Is there any way of forcing them to ripen earlier? (Ohio.) The variety factor enters here. Some varieties, such as Brown Turkey, mature fruits earlier than others.

How may I learn the variety of fig trees I have? (California.) Your State Agricultural College could probably identify the variety.

MULBERRIES

What are the chief uses of the mulberry? The berries are edible, though uninteresting in flavor. The trees make good screens or windbreaks, also provide food for birds. Weeping mulberries make fine decorative specimens.

Are mulberries easy trees to grow? Yes, they like almost any soil, and thrive under varying conditions.

How many kinds of mulberries are there in cultivation? Probably not more than 5 to 10 species although about 100 have been described. Two species, *Morus rubra* (Red Mulberry) and *M. celtidifolia* or *M. microphylea* (Texas Mulberry), are native to the United States. There are, of course, numerous varieties mostly belonging to *M. alba* (White Mulberry). This is the species used in feeding silkworms.

Did the so-called Russian mulberry actually come from Russia, or is it just a name? Yes, it really came from Russia. It was brought to the Western states by Russian Mennonites in 1875 to 1877.

Where did the Weeping Mulberry originate? On the grounds of John C. Teas, Carthage, Missouri, about 1883; it was called Teas' Weeping Mulberry. It is a chance seedling of the Russian mulberry.

Is the Weeping Mulberry of natural growth? No, this is the result of grafting variety described in previous answer high up on the trunk of a Russian mulberry.

Is it true that there are male and female mulberry trees? Must you have both to have berries? Also is there a difference in the foliage?   Yes, the sexes are separate, but there is little difference in the foliage. Both should be present to insure fruiting.

We have 2 mulberry trees planted about 30 ft. apart. They are over 15 years old. Why are they full of blossoms every spring but never set fruit?   Mulberries are often dioecious, that is, staminate (male) and pistillate (female) flowers on separate trees, though generallly both sexes are borne on the same tree. The failure to set fruit is undoubtedly due to lack of pollination. Both your trees may either have all flowers of one sex, or the male and female flowers do not mature at the same time. If you cannot judge, cut a small branch of each tree just before the flowers open and submit them to a botanist for examination.

How can a mulberry tree which has sprouted from the bottom (top dead) be cultivated to grow right? It is about 2 years old.   Cut off all but the strongest sprout. If the stub of the original stem remains, cut this (with a sloping cut) close to the shoot which was selected to carry on.

What are best varieties of mulberry for fruit production?   Trowbridge and New American for the North; Downing for the South.

PERSIMMONS

Are persimmons reliably hardy?   They are native from southern New England and Iowa to Florida and Texas. Oriental persimmons are grown chiefly in the South.

Is the persimmon tree worth growing for its fruit?   The native persimmon (*Diospyros virginiana*) bears very small fruit, which draws the mouth if eaten unripe, but which is very delicious after having been touched by frost. Fruit of Oriental type is much larger, but trees are less hardy.

Is the persimmon tree fussy about soil?   No; it will grow on good farm land with adequate drainage. It must have moisture, however.

How should a persimmon tree be transplanted?   With a burlapped ball of earth, even if the tree is of small size; in early spring.

How should persimmons be cared for in order to insure fruits?   Cover crop or other humus dug in around trees each year will keep soil in good condition. Complete fertilizer can be applied each spring.

Are persimmon trees staminate and pistillate varieties? Persimmons are usually dioecious; that is, staminate and pistillate flowers on different trees. Some pistillate trees produce parthenocarpic (seedless fruits) without having been pollinated.

I have some persimmon seeds. How should I start them? Plant the seeds about 1 in. deep as soon as they are ripe.

QUINCE

Does the quince make a good home-garden fruit? It is subject to all the pests of apples and pears, and is not generally satisfactory. Very limited in use.

What soil does the quince require? How are trees planted? Quince needs somewhat heavy, moist soil. Set 1- or 2-year specimens, in early spring, 8 to 10 ft. apart.

Are the quinces of an ornamental flowering quince bush edible? Or useful for jelly or quince honey? They can be used in any way the ordinary quince is used. In addition, they may be dried and used among linen for their aroma.

How and when are quince trees pruned? Quinces require very little pruning. Remove dead twigs and those which are growing "out of bounds"—too low, too high, etc. The bush form is probably preferable to the tree form. Prune in early spring.

I wish to cut back a tall quince tree. How many branches should I leave? It is difficult to spray as is. Remove a few of the tallest branches one year and a few more the next, so as to reduce the height gradually. Too-severe pruning all at once will probably result in an outbreak of fire blight.

How do you graft a quince bush? It is not necessary to graft quinces, as they can be propagated by cuttings—a much easier method of getting new plants.

NUT TREES

What is the best soil for nut trees? I have an open field. Any well-drained soil that will produce good farm crops is suitable for nut trees. The native walnut especially prefers fertile bottom-land soils, while the Persian (English Walnut) is thought to need limestone soils. Poor, eroded soils are not suitable for nut trees.

What is the general care for nut trees? The principal care required is to eliminate weed competition by cultivation or mulching. If the soil is not fertile, an annual application of nitrate of soda or sulfate of ammonia, at the rate of ¼ lb. for each inch of trunk diameter, should keep the trees growing.

Will the planting of nut trees in a fruit orchard react against either the fruit or nut trees in the presence of each other? Nut trees are too vigorous and grow too large to be grown in the same orchard with fruit trees.

Can nut trees be grown as far North as Brunswick, Maine? Those best suited are the native hazelnuts, the shagbark hickory, and butternuts.

How can nut trees be grafted? Several methods of grafting are used in nut-tree propagation. Splice grafting or whip grafting (see Grafting Section) is used when propagating young Persian Walnuts in nurseries in the West and for young pecans in the South. Scions are grafted onto a 1-year-old seedling understock. In the Persian Walnut the union is waxed but not tied; in the pecan, the union is tied with raffia. Soil that was removed from around the seedlings before grafting is pushed back, and the scions completely covered to a depth of 2 ins. When trees are being top-worked to another variety, the cleft graft method is used. This method, however, has been largely supplanted by that known as bark grafting (See Grafting).

Is there a miniature nut tree? No dwarfing stock for nut trees has as yet been introduced.

What kind of nut trees will grow in the East? (New Jersey.) Black walnuts and Chinese Chestnuts are probably the most satisfactory. Hickories are slow growing, and the hardy varieties of pecans and Persian Walnuts are thick shelled and not especially satisfactory.

What kinds of nuts can be successfully grown in south Pennsylvania climate? How to get such an orchard started? Is it necessary to purchase trees from nurseries, or can they be grown successfully from nuts? All of the common nut trees can be grown in south Pennsylvania, but getting commercially profitable crops is something else. Better consult your county agricultural agent or someone already in the business in your locality. With most of the nuts it would be essential to secure the best grafted varieties. The propagating and growing of young trees are highly specialized, and even though some are expensive to buy, you would be better off in the long run to purchase them than to try to propagate them yourself.

What are several quick-producing nut trees that can stand

cold and strong wind? (New York.) Filberts will bear nuts in 4 or 5 years, and are about as hardy as peaches. Grafted black walnuts also bear young, but will not produce many nuts until the trees develop sufficient bearing surface, which takes 8 or 10 years.

ALMOND

Can almond trees be grown in this country? Commercially, only in California. They are almost as hardy as the peach, but because they bloom earlier, they are especially susceptible to damage by late spring frost. Care and culture are the same as for peach.

Will almond come true from seeds? (Oregon.) No. Named varieties are increased by budding them on to seedling almonds or seedling peaches.

BUTTERNUT

Would you advise the home gardener to plant butternut trees? Butternut (*Juglans cinerea*) belongs to the walnut family but is hardier than our native black walnut, growing from New Brunswick to Arkansas. It is a good choice for the home garden in the north. The oblong nuts have a rich but delicate flavor, preferred by many to the stronger-flavored black walnut. Trees reach 50 to 75 ft. in height.

CHESTNUT

What kind of soil do chestnuts need? Well-drained, acid soil.

Are the blight-resistant Chinese Chestnuts hardy? Less so than our native chestnut. They may suffer injury in winter in northern United States. Oriental chestnuts have smaller nuts of inferior flavor, but since the native tree has been all but destroyed by blight, the blight-resistant Oriental sorts offer our only opportunity to grow healthy chestnuts today.

Have the Chinese Chestnuts which I see advertised been definitely proven to be blight resistant? Chinese Chestnuts are generally sufficiently resistant to blight to permit their culture in regions where the blight has destroyed the native American chestnut. Many of the Chinese Chestnuts in the trade are seedlings instead of grafted trees, and exhibit considerable variation in blight resistance.

Where can I get Chinese Chestnuts and the thin-shelled black walnut and pecan? A list of nurseries specializing in named varieties of nut trees may be had from the Northern Nut Growers' Association, Experiment Station, Geneva, New York.

Will any chestnut stand the climate of Montreal, Canada?
It is doubtful if any chestnut trees are hardy enough for Montreal.

I have in my garden a chestnut tree severely afflicted with blight. Is there any effective treatment which might be applied to save this tree?   If this is an American Chestnut, it is useless to attempt to save it.

We have an American Chestnut tree which bears many false (empty) burs. If a Chinese Chestnut were planted, would it fertilize the American? This tree has died down several times, but sent up a few shoots, which would live about 3 years and then die.
No treatments will save the American Chestnut. It will send up shoots for many years, but these will die as they become infected with blight. Planting another tree alongside this one would have no effect whatever on it.

FILBERT (HAZELNUT)

Will hazelnut (filbert) trees grow in this country? What varieties are best suited?   The American Hazelnut is hardy over a large part of the country and will produce nuts. Rush is considered about the best variety. Several varieties should be planted. The European hazelnut will grow vigorously, but it blooms so early in the spring that it produces nuts only in favored climates, usually not much north of Washington, D.C. Mostly grown in the Pacific Northwest. Barcelona, Du Chilly, and Italian Red are good varieties.

Where should filbert trees or bushes be planted?   They may be planted along a north or west boundary of the vegetable garden where they form an informal hedge or windbreak.

Should filbert (hazelnut) trees be trimmed to tree shape, or allowed to grow as bushes?   They may be grown either as trees or bushes; the former is thought to be more productive.

How should filberts be pruned?   The nuts are borne on wood of one year's growth. The pruning is done in late winter or early spring. Head back non-fruitful twigs and prune out old wood that has borne fruit.

Are filberts gathered before or after frost?   Filberts are gathered when they are ready to drop off the plant; it makes no difference when the frost occurs.

HICKORY

What hickories are worth growing for their nuts?   In the North the shagbark (*Carya ovata*), a handsome tree with bark which shreds from the trunk, giving it its name. Nuts are fair size with very hard shells. Shellbark (*C. laciniosa*) is also good eating. The pecan, the best varieties of which are grown only in the South, is also a hickory (*Carya*). (See Pecan.)

Where should one report good nut trees, when found, that they may be preserved? Such, for instance, as hickory or black walnut?   Northern Nut Growers' Association, Experiment Station, Geneva, New York.

MACADAMIA

What is the macadamia nut?   This is an edible nut of a species of Australian tree (*Macadamia ternifolia*). It is commonly called the Queensland Nut.

Is the macadamia nut tree grown in this country?   Yes, these nut trees are cultivated in California and in parts of Florida. They thrive in rich, loamy soil with plenty of moisture, although they have been reported as growing in dry sections as well. The tree is an evergreen, and is ornamental as well as useful.

PECAN

Are pecans successfully grown in the North?   There are hardy varieties which will stand fairly low temperatures, but the nuts are small and thick shelled. The thin-shelled varieties can be grown only in the South.

Of several small pecan trees planted, all have died but one. Is there some special way to dig holes or set them out to make them live and grow well? (Georgia.)   Vigorous pecan trees that have been carefully dug and not allowed to dry out should not be difficult to establish. Set the trees in the fall; firm the soil tightly against the roots; keep down weeds; and water and mulch the trees when drought threatens during the first year or two.

When is correct time to set out pecan trees? (North Carolina.) Pecan trees may be set in your section in the fall, or any time during the winter when the temperature is above freezing.

What should be done for pecan trees when the nuts do not fill properly? They hull themselves as they should, but do not fill out. (Virginia.)   Try fertilizing the trees with a complete fertilizer at the rate of ¼ lb. for each inch of trunk diameter. The 6–8–4 formula is suggested, and the rate of application is 40 lbs. to a 10- or 12-year-old tree, or 600 to 800 lbs. per acre.

Will inserting lye about 2 ft. deep and 20 ft. from the trunk of pecan trees help bearing?   Lye will certainly not benefit your pecan tree.

How old does a soft-shell pecan tree have to be before bearing nuts? Do you know of a nursery that has these trees for sale? A list of nurseries supplying pecan trees may be had from the Northern Nut Growers' Association, Geneva, New York. Age of bearing depends on the variety of tree, but not many nuts will be had until the trees are 6 or 8 years of age.

How should pecans be grafted? (Alabama.)   Varieties of pecan are propagated almost entirely upon seedling stocks of pecan species. Stocks of certain varieties are said to have some influence upon the growth of the grafted tree. Various pecan stocks are used in Texas. In Louisiana some use is made of the water hickory as a stock. Study local conditions as to stock used. (For grafting process see Section II.)

PISTACHE

In what part of the country can the pistachio nut tree be grown?   Only in California and Mexico. It needs a climate like that required by olive trees.

BLACK WALNUT

Is the black walnut a good tree for the home garden?   If you live where winter temperatures do not drop too low and want a handsome specimen tree which will produce nuts, the black walnut is a good choice. Though individual specimens live for years in New York State and similar sections, black walnuts are not considered reliably hardy where winter temperatures drop below 20° F. Butternut (which see) is hardier.

What special requirements has the black walnut?   Wild specimens are often found growing in dry, rocky upland pastures as well as in woodland. To produce nuts, this tree needs good soil, well drained, with regular supplies of moisture. A wild tree, in a dry, unfertile location, if subjected for a few years to fertilization and sufficient moisture, will increase its yield tremendously.

What are the dirty-white worms all through the outer shells of my black walnuts? What can I do to get rid of them? (New York.)   These are the maggots of the walnut-husk fly, distributed throughout the East to the Kansas-Nebraska line, on black walnuts and butternuts. A closely related species attacks the central and western black and English Walnuts. Flies, a little smaller than house flies, with transparent, black-banded wings, lay their eggs in the husks in August. The maggots tunnel through the husk for several weeks, drop to ground before or with nuts, and pupate several inches down in soil. They emerge as flies the next summer, or wait until second or third summer. They do little injury to kernels, but they stain surface of nut. Trees may be sprayed with cryolite in July. Drop infested nuts in water to drown the worms.

How can I grow native walnut seedlings from walnuts? So far have had no luck. (Missouri.) Plant seeds in the fall about 2 ins. deep. If squirrels are troublesome, store nuts in a box of moist sand outdoors and cover with wire netting to keep out rodents. Plant nuts in the spring.

How can I tell a young walnut tree from the Tree-of-Heaven? Crush the leaves or rub the bark of the walnut twig, and the odor will identify it immediately.

ENGLISH WALNUT

Is the English Walnut hardy? Commercially, it is not grown where temperatures drop below 40° F. In the home garden it may survive freezing temperatures if they are not too low —20° F. is considered the limit of cold which it will endure with‑ out injury.

Can I grow English Walnuts and Chinese Chestnuts in south‑ eastern Massachusetts? Temperatures below 20° F. are likely to prove injurious to both species.

What are the soil and cultural requirements of the English Walnut? Good, deep loam, well drained but with plenty of moisture to produce large crops of nuts. Winter temperatures which do not drop far below freezing. (See previous questions.)

Are English Walnut trees harmful near shrubs? The Per‑ sian (English) Walnut is not considered to be harmful to shrubs, but of course it will compete with them for plant food and mois‑ ture.

I have an English Walnut tree 14 years old. Never bore until last 2 years. All nuts fell off both years when they were quite small, but nuts inside were formed. Why does this happen? The nuts may not have been pollinated. If no English Walnut is near this tree, another should be planted to provide pollination.

What can I do to have more walnut nuts mature? The tree sets plenty of fruit, but nearly all drop off when they reach the size of large cherries. Lack of cross-pollination may be the cause of the trouble. Another variety of the same species should be set near by. The tree may need fertilizing to increase its vigor. Nitrate of soda or sulfate of ammonia at the rate of ¼ lb. for each inch of trunk diameter may be tried.

Is the English Walnut self-pollinating? Persian (English)

Walnuts usually require cross-pollination by another variety, since its own pollen often is not shed at the time when the pistils are receptive.

Must 2 (male and female) English Walnut trees be planted side by side? The male and female flowers of the Persian (English) Walnut are on the same tree, but the blooming periods of the male and female flowers on the same tree may not coincide. It is necessary, therefore, to set another tree to provide pollen when it is needed.

How are English Walnuts washed and dried to be stored for the winter? Remove the husks promptly and wash the nuts immediately. Lay the nuts out one layer deep in an airy room until they are thoroughly dried. Keep them in a cool, dry place.

We have an English Walnut tree. Is there some way to treat the nuts to prevent mold while drying and to keep nut meats white? The nuts should not mold if they are husked promptly, washed, and thoroughly dried in an airy place.

Do you know a good soft-shelled walnut—better than Manchurian—that will stand 10° or 20° below zero if need be? Usually 10° above. (Washington.) The Broadview variety of the English Walnut and the Carpathian strain of the same species are thought to be somewhat hardier than the usual varieties and may be worth trying.

What variety of English Walnut will thrive in the vicinity of New York? The Carpathian Walnut is the hardiest of these, and is the one to grow.

JAPANESE WALNUT

Can you give some information about a Japanese Walnut? The Japanese Walnut is a rapid-growing, very handsome tree. The nut is elongated, smooth, cracks poorly, and is inferior in quality to other walnuts. The Heartnut, a supposed sport of the Japanese Walnut, is much superior in cracking quality.

SECTION VII

House Plants

INTRODUCTION

BY HELEN VAN PELT WILSON
AND
ESTHER C. GRAYSON

THE ATTRACTIVENESS of plants indoors depends first of all on their health, and then upon how they are grouped or arranged. To be satisfactory, potted plants should be green and flourishing and, in the case of flowering types, in bloom for as long a period as possible.

To attain these ends, the selection of varieties tolerant of special unalterable conditions of light, heat, and humidity is most important. Only after this problem has been solved comes the artistic arrangement of plants at windows, so that as a group they may present an effective, arresting, even a changing and colorful picture as the autumn weeks give way to winter, and winter passes into the life-stirring months of early spring.

Although plants suitable for indoor culture have to a degree different requirements, there are certain basic needs shared by them all. There are conditions of light, heat and humidity, moisture, food, and rest, which are common to all. The window-garden enthusiast, therefore, keeps these basic factors in mind, while yet interpreting them for each plant as observation reveals its special and individual nature. Sometimes contradictions develop. Thus the general practice is to pot flowering plants "closely" (that is, in pots that keep their roots restricted), since a little root cramping tends to promote bloom. The African-violet, if crowded, however, fails entirely to keep in blossom. Another idiosyncrasy of this plant is a great need for water. Thus "do not let standing water remain in the plant saucer" is another general rule contradicted by the calla, violet, and cyclamen. All these appear at their best when there is a constant inch of water always at their disposal in a pebble-filled saucer under the pot.

So it happens that the gardener often learns but to unlearn; and the printed word becomes but a guide which only the actualities of experience can make valuable.

Light

All plants require a fully light location. Fresh-from-the-greenhouse specimens hung on a bracket in a dark hall or set at the mantel ends of a dim living room are destined, no matter what their original condition, for a short life—and not a very merry one. Light permits the plant organism to work effectively in transferring certain substances into usable foods. There are, of course, a number of excellent foliage plants which need no direct sun. The wax begonia and the patience plant will bloom to some extent in a fully light location, without direct sunshine, but for most flowering plants sunshine is required—not an occasional hour or so, but every bit a southern or eastern window can afford. Without a maximum of sunlight, the geranium will fail to bud, while the gardenia and cactus will tend to enduring green.

Temperature

The consistent coolness of our houses during these war days is a boon to house plants, which have long suffered from the high temperatures which many people felt were essential to their own comfort. Grown at 60° to 65° F., almost every house plant is better off than at 70° or 75° F., while a night drop to 55° F., similar to nature's outdoor falling of temperature after sunset, is a further cultural benefit. Many of the most decorative plants can be grown in a really cold house window where the average is 50° to 60° F. Indeed, if sunrooms in winter continue to be almost completely unheated, flourishing indoor gardens will still be possible there.

On record, for example, is one where night temperatures dropped to 35° and 40° F., and where only a small amount of electric radiation supplemented the effects of the sun during the day. Here begonias and geraniums bloomed incessantly. The cyclamen, with never a yellow leaf, opened bud after bud for a full 3 months. Primroses and Paperwhite Narcissi kept fresh for extra weeks, while ivies, Waxplants, *Asparagus sprengeri,* many ferns (even Maidenhairs), and Strawberry-begonias, maintained marvelous health. Of course these plants were all set back somewhat from the glass and, if outdoor temperatures threatened to go below 20° F., they were covered at night with newspapers.

When plants develop weak, soft, spindly growth, foliage color is light, and buds blast or fall prematurely, it is very often because they are suffering from too warm an atmosphere.

Humidity

The greatest foe to successful indoor gardening is, however, lack of humidity. Outdoors the air is moist. Inside, with modern heating devices what they are, it is usually much too dry. This results in parched foliage, especially on English ivy, even when the owner has never neglected moistening the soil.

Now how can humidity be increased? Various makeshifts are helpful when no real humidifying devices exist. If one has a hot-air central-heating system, a bucket or pan of water may be suspended under the register, and kept filled with a long-necked watering can. Supplying the window garden with a galvanized-iron or zinc tray fitted to the sill and filled with pebbles is probably the most effective means of increasing humidity. Where it is possible, the plants are set in the tray on top of a 1- or 2-in. layer of little stones. Excess water from the pots runs through to these, and more is added as needed. This serves as a source of evaporation for constantly moistening the air circulating about the plants.

An occasional cleansing of the foliage with a forceful stream from the hose is important in keeping house plants in good condition and free from insect pests.

Keeping deep bowls of water on the radiators is also a good plan; or extra-large, pebble-filled saucers or water-holding fiber mats may be set under each plant. Furthermore, humidity as well as cleanliness is increased if plants are frequently sprayed from a bulb syringe, or set under shower or faucet. Usually this can be managed only weekly, while a light syringing may be a daily matter. But again there must be interpretation according to individuals. The hairy-leaved African-violet, gloxinia, and rex begonia, and the tightly crowned cyclamen or pandanus, are more often harmed than benefited by showering or syringing.

Watering

The question most often asked by house-plant growers is, "How often should I water my house plants?" or, "Is there a rule, so much water for so much soil?"

Only in a very general way can a rule be offered. *When the topsoil feels dry to the touch, then is the time to water.* Then water so thoroughly that the entire root system is saturated and in a little while excess seeps out into the pot saucer. Except in a few cases, it is best immediately to empty this excess from the saucer.

The most important "Beware" in connection with watering applies to the little-and-often method. Pouring water on plants just for the fun of it does them no good. Often it results in a too-wet upper half of soil and a too-dry lower. Especially is this true of thick-rooted plants such as palms; or very large specimens of almost any plant, particularly those of the shrubby type— gardenias, azaleas, and the like. All such are wisely set, about once a week, in a pail filled with water to within an inch of the pot rim. Here they remain until enough moisture has been drawn up to make the surface *feel* moist. Then they are removed in a thoroughly refreshed condition.

Daily attention to every plant in the window garden, with a moderate amount of water applied where needed, is one of the secrets of success with house plants.

Most plants are safely moistened by applying water at the edge of the pot rim. Some with thick crowns, like the cyclamen or Staghornfern, are better moistened from below by pouring water into the saucer and letting the plant draw it up according to its need. Saved rainwater is better than faucet water, especially in places where the local supply has been treated with chemicals, the residue from which often collects on the soil and discolors the containers. Room-temperature water also is better than cold, which may have a retarding effect on growth. Most plants, however, are fairly tolerant, and, given *regular* care, will not be too fussy about the type of water supplied, only the amount. Actually, most amateurs tend to overwater rather than to neglect. Experience reveals which plants, like the gardenia or cyclamen, want a "just-moist" soil at all times; while others, notably the jade-plant, many of the cacti, the sansevieria, and geranium, thrive only when allowed to become quite dry between drinks.

In addition to the drinking habits of the plant itself, other factors influencing the amount of water required are: the size of pot (little ones dry out faster); the type of pot (glazed ones permit less evaporation); the stage of plant growth, whether active or resting; and the temperature of the room. The weather is also a factor: on sunny days more water is required than during dull ones. All these conditions are to be taken into consideration. Complicated as all this may sound, however, it soon becomes second nature to water the tiny poinsettia twice a day and the big jade-plant but once in 10 days, when the *feel* of the soil is made the actual guide.

Ventilation

A close atmosphere is very hard on house plants. Even when the weather is definitely cold, they require some fresh air. The best plan then is to admit fresh air indirectly through a window or door in an adjoining room, or through a canvas ventilator in the same room, but not directly beside the plants. It is most important to provide an abundance of fresh air for several weeks after plants are first brought in in autumn; and again in spring, as the midday hours become increasingly warm.

Where gas is used for heating and cooking, plenty of fresh air is especially necessary; but even this will not counteract the effects of escaping gas, the fumes of which spell ultimate death to most plants. Some of them are extremely allergic to gas. The Jerusalem-cherry, for instance, is one of these. First they drop all their fruit, then the leaves shrivel, and finally the plant dies. Such plants as the aspidistra, sansevieria, and Bostonfern will prove more tolerant, especially where there is good daily ventilation.

Air is essential to the roots as well as to the tops of plants. A constant loose condition of the surface soil, and hence aeration of the roots, is readily obtained by a weekly stirring with a discarded kitchen fork.

Pruning and Training

Plants are kept shapely by being turned frequently so that all sides receive an equal amount of light, and by the cutting back of overlong growth which tends to make ungainly specimens. Sometimes, too, a drastic pruning back is necessary to promote health. Thus in autumn the summer geraniums are cut back to stubs 3 to 6 ins. long, while the dormant poinsettia in spring is started all over again by hard pruning.

Fertilizing

Extra fertilizer is not nearly so important as good texture and structure of soil and proper potting. Sickly plants especially are more likely to be suffering from too much heat and water, or from some insect pest, than from starvation. Usually a plant from the florist requires no extra nutrients for a month or more. If a plant is at a standstill when, by all the rules of its own nature and the time of year, it should be growing, or when its buds are not maturing, or its foliage color is poor—although a proper system of culture is maintained—then extra feeding definitely is to be considered. Generally speaking, flowering plants require more nutrients than foliage ones, at least up to the time the buds show color. For slow-growing plants occasional light top dustings of complete fertilizer are good. Plant tablets, or one of the "complete" fertilizers especially prepared for house plants, are excellent, provided directions are carefully followed and it is not assumed that because a little is good for a plant a lot will be better. Nor should a resting plant be "pushed" with a quick-acting fertilizer when the need is for quiet and not for action. Thus the summer-weary geranium or wax plant in fall requires not fertilizer, but coolness and time to resuscitate itself.

Certain items are *not* suitable fertilizers—notably tea, coffee, oysters, cigar ashes, and castor oil.

Repotting

When a plant has actually outgrown its living quarters (when, after the pot is removed, a fine web of roots is seen on the outside of the earth ball), that plant needs another container, but probably one only a size larger. Usually established plants need shifting but once a year; some but once in 2 years. Often worn-out soil can be carefully washed from the roots, and the plant then repotted in the same size pot again.

Repotting is not a panacea. A too-large pot with unneeded amounts of soil and moisture more often kills an ailing plant than cures it. The best general policy is to keep plants in as small pots as possible. Overlarge antique specimens of plants, dear as they may be sentimentally, are rarely, when dispassionately viewed, very attractive in themselves or as part of the general window-garden arrangement. Institutional-size plants do not belong in people's houses, nor do sickly plants which, outside a greenhouse, will be unlikely to regain health under the trying conditions of our houses in winter.

The best time for repotting is in spring; then the resulting shock is offset by months of ideal outdoor life. In May, when the weather is settled, a practical plan is to take all the plants outdoors, discard some, divide others (repotting the divisions into *smaller* pots), and then shift the remainder into larger pots.

Arranged in a row, small to large, with a few pots on hand larger than any already in use, plants are easily repotted—the largest plants going into the new pots (which have first been soaked in a pail of water for 24 hours), and the others, successively, to the outgrown pots, which are thoroughly scrubbed out before receiving new occupants.

Plants are readily depotted for examination or repotting if they are first watered and then inverted on the gardener's left hand, with the main stem placed between the index and middle fingers. The pot rim is then knocked sharply against table or step. So loosened, the pot is lifted off by the right hand, and the root condition examined.

When needed, a larger pot is fitted with an arching piece of broken flower pot above the drainage hole and, if it is above a 3-in. size, a few more pieces of broken crock over this. In very large pots a handful of gravel or small cinders or pebbles is placed above the "crocking." (When pots have no drainage hole, a drainage layer of some of this coarse material is especially necessary in the bottom; also a bit of charcoal to insure sweetness.)

When the drainage layer is in place, a sifting of soil is added. Then the plant is centered in the pot, and extra soil firmly pressed around it with a potting stick—a piece of lath or an old ruler. The soil is kept ½ in. or so below the rim of the pot, this space being needed to receive water.

Potting Soil

Although there are almost as many soil formulas as there are types of house plants, it is a matter of experience that plants try to accustom themselves to any soil which is of proper texture or friability, and well drained. A generally good formula (which may be altered in its proportions according to type of plant to be grown) consists of 2 parts loam from vegetable or flower garden and 1 part well-rotted cow manure, leafmold, commercial humus, or peatmoss, with enough sand to make the mixture porous. Unless cow manure is used, add 2 qts. commercial cow manure to each bushel. For further enrichment, a 4-in. pot of complete fertilizer or bone meal to a wheelbarrowload of soil, or 1 teaspoonful to an 8-in. pot of soil.

The loam contains nutrients, sand facilitates drainage and

aeration of roots, while the other elements increase the water-holding capacity and thus prevent too-rapid evaporation of moisture and caking of soil. Humus also helps to produce a light, mellow mixture which roots can easily penetrate. To these essentials may be added, when convenient, a little charcoal to sweeten the soil (especially in pots lacking a drainage hole), and tobacco dust to discourage root aphis. Apartment gardeners can procure ready-made soil mixtures from florists or 10-cent stores.

If the plants have heavy roots—such as those of pandanus, sansevieria, or palm, also the geranium—less sand and more loam is used, because such roots have force enough to penetrate a firm mixture, and the plants prefer it. The fibrous-rooted ferns, begonias, and fuchsias thrive in a lighter medium—about ½ leafmold or peatmoss, ½ loam, and plenty of sand.

Acid-loving plants—the blue hydrangeas, camellias, heaths, and azaleas—require equal parts of soil and *acid* peat or hardwood leafmold, while bone meal is omitted.

Summer Quarters

Summer is the ideal time for all plants with real *future* possibilities to be resuscitated after the trying months indoors. Summer quarters may be established on porches, in window boxes, or in garden beds. (Even a cool, light window indoors will do, if plenty of fresh air is afforded.) Wherever placed, the plants are out of the way of strong winds, and are grouped to facilitate watering and syringing. Pots are not removed because house plants, freed of their containers, develop in an open garden bed such ranging root systems that autumn repotting becomes almost impossible.

Plunging in a garden bed which offers suitable gradations of light for the varying needs of the sun-loving geraniums and shade-requiring fern is, in general, the most healthful procedure. A location under some open-leaved tree, like an apple or an elm, with branches not too low, is ideal. Nearest to the trunk, where the shade is deepest, go the ferns; below the open branches in light shade are set resting geraniums and heliotrope, vines, foliage plants, and most of the flowering subjects: gardenias, azaleas, fuchsias, and shade-loving begonias; near the edge, but not under the drip, where sun daily penetrates, are placed the young geraniums, semperflorens begonias, and poinsettias.

A bed is dug deep enough to contain the largest pot to be plunged, plus a 3- to 6-in. layer of stones, cinders, or other worm-deterring drainage material. Here the plants are arranged according to their light requirements, and around them is packed light soil containing plenty of water-holding humus, preferably peat-moss. When plunging is completed, pot rims remain slightly above the soil surface. About once a week each plant is turned. This prevents anchoring roots from taking hold through the drainage hole, and also facilitates the development of shapely tops.

When the weather warms up, house plants—after repotting (where needed) and a thorough going over for insect pests —are best transferred to the open.

House plants cannot be forgotten in summer. Even when plunged, they require, because of their restricted root systems and location under tree branches, more frequent watering than average summer rainfall supplies. Some pruning may be required to promote shapely growth, and insect pests must always be watched for. Usually frequent hose syringing deters them but sometimes, as in winter, aphids or mealy bugs must be sprayed with an insecticide.

Lifting Plants in Autumn

Plants are prepared for winter well before frost. It is a good precaution to remove the pot from each specimen and, if necessary, to renew the drainage arrangements. At this season, however, roots are disturbed as little as possible.

Plants are brought inside before the first touch of frost. Many of the best ones, such as the poinsettia, are from the tropics, and hence are easily harmed by cool fall weather. During the first weeks indoors much attention is given to ventilation and syringing. Now more than at other times plants are particularly inclined to resent the dry, close air of the house. Falling leaves and blossoms are signs of unfavorable reaction. A thorough drenching under a faucet will often immediately check leaf dropping.

Rest Period

All plants have growth cycles which include periods of rest. As trees lose their leaves in fall and enter into a dormant period, so do house plants at some time rest in greater or lesser degree. In winter, ferns and palms are less active and produce fewer new leaves than in spring. In early fall many of the cacti remain utterly quiet. After flowering, poinsettias and cyclamens appear on the point of death, when really they are only going to sleep.

All plants which are resting require less water and warmth than when they are in a period of active growth. Many can be left entirely dark and dry. None are fed at this time. The resting condition of plants is not always an easy one to identify, but constant observation of each variety eventually reveals it, and the indoor gardener is accordingly guided in the treatment she gives them.

HOUSE PLANTS

SOIL

Are all house plants potted in the same soil mixture?   No, there are variations in soil mixtures for various types of plants. (See following questions.)

What is a good standard potting mixture for house plants? Two parts good garden loam, 1 part leafmold or peatmoss, 1 part sharp sand. For general use add 1 pt. complete fertilizer (or bone meal) and 2 qts. dried cow manure, or well-rotted cow manure, to each bushel of mixture. For plants requiring special soils see following questions.

What mixture of soil is best for azaleas and other acid-loving plants?   An *acid mixture*. Add to standard potting mixture (see previous question) 25 per cent in bulk acid (hardwood) leafmold and to each bushel add 2 qts. commercial or well-rotted cow manure and 1 pt. complete fertilizer.

What mixture of soil do I need for ferns grown indoors?   A *fibrous mixture*. Add to the standard potting mixture 25 per cent in bulk humus or peatmoss, 2 qts. well-rotted or commercial manure and 1 pt. complete fertilizer.

How shall I sweeten the potting mixture for house plants which need an alkaline soil? Herbs, for instance.   Make an *alkaline mixture*. To each bushel of standard mixture add 1 qt. raw ground limestone, 1 pt. bone meal, and 2 qts. well-rotted or commercial cow manure. Make up mixture 2 weeks or more before use to permit limestone to alkalize soil.

What potting soil shall I use for cacti and other succulents? A *sandy mixture*. Add 25 per cent in bulk sharp sand or crushed soft stone (or crushed flower pots) to standard potting mixture (see previous question). Add to each bushel 1 qt. raw ground limestone and 1 pt. complete fertilizer, or bone meal. Make up mixture 2 weeks or more before use. (See Cacti.)

Do tender bulbs, such as amaryllis, tuberous-rooted begonias, etc., need a special potting soil? Yes. Place 1 to 2 ins. of well-rotted cow manure in bottom of pot, and as potting soil use sifted, well-rotted compost. If compost and cow manure are not available, use 1 part garden loam, 1 part peatmoss or leafmold, and add to each bushel 3 qts. commercial cow manure and 1 pt. complete fertilizer.

Which house plants prefer peatmoss in the soil? Please add information concerning its use. All house plants like peatmoss in the soil except those which prefer an alkaline soil. (See previous questions, for information concerning its use.)

How shall soil on house plants be prevented from getting solid? Is there danger of cutting rootlets if soil is dug in, to loosen it? Stir the surface frequently. Use soil mixtures recommended in previous questions.

POTTING AND REPOTTING

What size pots are best for winter-blooming plants? Depends on the plant. Good primroses can be grown in 4½- to 5-in. pots. Wax-type begonias the same. Most flowering plants give more bloom if grown in pots just big enough to hold the roots.

Should the soil on a potted plant be changed? If so, how often? See Introduction to this section.

When should house plants be repotted? Varies with kind of plant. Good general rule is to repot at beginning of growing season. Fast-growing plants (as geraniums) may need a second or even third shift during season. Some (as agapanthus) need attention only every few years.

How can I tell when my plants need repotting? When plants are knocked gently from pots (see Introduction) root system shows whether repotting is necessary. If roots have formed a thick, dry web on outside of root ball, repot. If visible roots are few and appear succulent and healthy, repotting is not needed.

When repotting house plants, how much larger should the new pot be?   Usually one size larger. In the case of very fast-growing plants, two sizes larger can be used. Gently remove a little of the old soil in order to make room for more fresh potting mixture. (See Introduction.)

What size pots should I use when repotting in spring so my house plants will not have to be repotted again in autumn? Use pot two sizes larger in spring for plants which are to be sunk in garden beds in their pots. Cut back when they are brought into the house in the fall. Fast-growing plants may need fall repotting in spite of this precaution.

How should tender bulbs be potted for indoor bloom?   Most of these bulbs, such as amaryllis, callas, and tuberous-rooted begonias, are planted with the top of the bulb exposed.

With some bulbs (such as amaryllis) and other plants in large pots, the soil is renewed, without repotting, by removing as much as possible of the old soil, and then refilling with new soil.

How can I provide good drainage in the pots of my house plants?   Place a bit of broken flower pot, convex side up, on the bottom of small pots before potting plants. For medium-sized pots, use several pieces of this "crocking"; for large bulb pans and large pots, cover the entire bottom with broken bits of pot, always being sure the piece which covers the drainage hole is so placed as to allow free ingress and egress of water. In forcing bulbs and other plants which like manure, placing large pieces of well-rotted manure over the crocking before adding soil will help to assure good drainage.

I have a lot of house plants. Is there a suitable paint for covering flower pots to make them colorful? Ordinary paints peel off. Doubtless the Duco type ot enamel will last if it is applied when pots are dry. Ordinary house paint is not suitable.

FEEDING

When shall I feed my house plants?   See Introduction.

When shall I give fertilizer to flowering house plants?   See Introduction.

What fertilizers are best for house plants?   In the questions on Soil in this section and in the Introduction, recommendations are made for fertilizing the soil mixtures. In addition to this, complete fertilizers may be given in liquid or tablet form according to package directions, or liquid manure (which see) may be used. (See Culture of Specific Plants.)

Do you think liquid manure is a good fertilizer for house plants?   Yes. It gives excellent results. Use it sparingly once a week on plants which prefer a pot-bound condition (amaryllis, pandanus, palms, nerine, etc.) and on flowering plants until blooms show color.

How is liquid manure prepared for use on house plants? Place a bushel of cow manure in a burlap bag and steep it in a tub of water for 3 weeks. For use on plants, dilute to the color of weak tea.

Why does Vigoro kill my begonias?   Properly used, Vigoro or other complete fertilizers will not kill begonias or other house plants. Your begonias may have been unthrifty before you applied the fertilizer, or too much may have been given. Vigoro is a reliable complete fertilizer which, if properly used, gives consistently good results.

Several of my house plants look very sick indeed. Shall I give them fertilizer?   No. Cut them back; withhold water. Repot if pot-bound. Examine for pests. When new growth begins, a complete fertilizer can be given sparingly, according to directions on package.

What is the proper means of feeding plants that were slipped as house plants to carry over until spring?   Plants propagated for carrying over to spring, or old plants cut back and potted for the same purpose, don't need feeding during winter. Keep cool and don't encourage growth. Water no more than is necessary to prevent wilting; much depends upon the kind of plant.

What fertilizer is best for house plants (cacti, ferns, begonias)? Cacti: sandy potting mixture with fertilizer suggested. Ferns: fibrous potting mixture with fertilizer suggested. Begonias: standard potting mixture with fertilizer suggested.

Is black tea of any value to ferns?   No.

WATERING

What is a good general rule for watering house plants?

Water only when plant *needs* water, not whenever it seems that it may stand watering. Whenever water is supplied, give enough to saturate thoroughly the whole ball of soil. Never merely sprinkle the surface.

How often does one water house plants, namely, ferns, wax begonias, and geraniums?   Watering is governed by the temperature and humidity of a room. Keep geraniums on the dry side if not actively growing; begonias and ferns in a room of 60° to 70° F. will need water almost every day. Feeling the soil, judging the weight of the pot, or rapping the pot with the knuckles are other ways of telling when to water. A pot of soil that is wet sounds dead; if dry, it gives an empty ring.

Can you tell me why growing house plants rot or decay from the roots up?   This sounds like overwatering. Do not permit the plants to stand with their roots soaking in water. Surplus water should be poured from saucer after each watering, and water given only when surface of soil feels dry.

What can be done to counteract the effect of watering house plants with the hard water we have in this locality? There is so much lime in it.   If the hardness of the water is merely due to lime, use an acid fertilizer such as sulfate of ammonia.

Do flowers kept in cellar in winter need much water?   If the cellar is poorly lighted and not warm, plants should, as a rule, be kept fairly dry. If they are not actively growing, keep on the dry side.

How can I give enough water to azaleas, hydrangeas, and other house plants which seem to dry out completely?   Once a week place potted plant in bucket of water until soil is thoroughly soaked. (See Introduction.)

How can I keep my house plants from having "wet feet"?   Place a handful of large pebbles or gravel in the saucer under each pot, or in the tray or on the shelf on which pots are set. If there is surplus water, the pebbles will provide good drainage.

Must all flower pots have drainage?   Plants can be grown in pots without drainage and no outlet for surplus water, but they won't thrive for long because of lack of air. During the winter and spring narcissi and some other bulbs can be grown in pebbles in pots without a hole at the bottom.

How should house plants in glazed pots be watered?   More sparingly than those in unglazed pots. Though glazed pots hold water longer, they do not provide aeration of the soil.

TEMPERATURE

What temperature is best for most house plants? Most flowering house plants are happiest at 55° F. or lower. Cinerarias and calceolarias prefer 45° F. That's why so many people fail with house plants in hot rooms. It also explains why cyclamen, Jerusalem-cherry, decorative peppers, etc., last such a short time after coming from the florist. If your home is kept at 70° F. or above, day and night, grow semi-tropical foliage plants, cacti and succulents, African-violets, and poinsettias. If a low night temperature can be maintained, many plants preferring a cool temperature will do quite well.

Why do my house plants die within a short time? All except Chinese Evergreen and some ivy, both in water. I tried different soil, plant tablets. I put them in the sun and in the shade with no result. They grow nicely outside in summer but die in the house even in summertime. Probably too high temperature, poor drainage, or too much water. (See previous questions.)

What house plants thrive in a day temperature of 70° F. or more? Poinsettias, African-violets, and other tropicals such as most of the foliage plants; cacti and succulents. Begonias and geraniums if night temperature drops to 60° F.

What house plants, if any, will survive a night temperature of 26° F., day temperature of 50° to 60° F.? No house plant will continue to show green foliage if it must endure a night temperature below freezing. Only hardy perennials will stand this (lavender, thyme, dianthus, viola, etc.). You might have a few very dwarf or seedling evergreens, either coniferous or broad-leafed, and English Ivy for a bit of green through the winter.

What plants can be grown in unheated sun porch? I am trying geraniums, sweet marjoram, parsley, sage, winter savory, and ivies. Your suggestions will be appreciated. (New Jersey.) Such a porch in winter is hopeless, as in severe weather everything will freeze solid. Even the hardiest of plants will give up when in pots and exposed to fluctuating temperatures day and night.

Will house plants survive in a home with a modern heating system? They may survive or even do well if the temperature is kept below 70° F. in the daytime, below 60° F. at night. But if high temperatures are the rule, house plants are apt to develop many difficulties such as falling leaves and buds, pests and diseases, and general unthriftiness. Tropicals such as African-violets, poinsettias, semi-tropical foliage plants, etc., are exceptions to the rule.

Why do house plants do best in country farmhouses? Because the temperature is low, especially at night, and the humidity high, due to lack of central heating. The steaming kettle on the farm kitchen range is a first-class humidifier.

Is a very cool sun porch suitable for house plants in winter? If the night temperature is safely above freezing, house plants which prefer coolness (see individual plants) will be far happier there than indoors. (See previous questions.)

VENTILATION

Do my house plants need fresh air in winter? Yes, decidedly. See that fresh air is admitted daily to the room where they are kept, but avoid direct drafts. A window or door opened for half an hour each day in an adjoining room will provide the needed ventilation. (See Introduction.)

How can I give my house plants fresh air without chilling them by a direct draft? If air must be admitted from a near-by window in the room in which they are kept, use a window ventilator or a screen to prevent drafts.

SUMMER CARE

What shall I do with my house plants in summer? See Introduction.

How can I arrange my house plants outdoors in a garden bed so that they will receive the right amount of sunshine and shade? Choose a location near a water supply where part of the bed receives morning sun and part shade. Place geraniums, semperflorens begonias, and other flowering, sun-loving plants in sunniest location. Ferns, foliage plants, and other shade lovers go in the shade.

What house plants suffer from being sunk in a garden bed in summer? African-violets, Calla Begonias, and other "difficult" plants which cannot endure beating rains and winds. Place these on a sheltered porch or in an open window.

What house plants prefer a bed of cinders to garden soil when placed outdoors in their pots in summer? Cacti and succulents.

Will house plants take care of themselves if sunk in garden beds in summer? Yes, if there is adequate rainfall. In drought, they must be watered slowly and deeply by letting the hose run into the ground about them with the nozzle removed. Keep weeds down and cultivate soil occasionally.

AUTUMN CARE

When should house plants be brought indoors in autumn? At least 2 or 3 weeks before you plan to turn on the heat, and of course before frost. This permits the plant to acclimate itself gradually to the new environment.

How shall I prepare my house plants for the autumn move to the house? Two weeks before they come in, loosen the pots in the ground. Prune back long, unsightly branches. If plants tend to wither, prune more severely. At the end of a week, lift the pots and place plants on a sheltered porch or against a retaining wall where they will have outdoor light and air. At the end of 2-week period from first loosening pots in ground, remove to house.

Do house plants need special care when they first come indoors in autumn? Yes, the leaves of glossy-foliaged plants should be frequently syringed. Water moderately. Ventilation should be good. Pests are apt to appear now. Keep a close watch and have a spray gun handy.

Is it possible to leave coleus, geraniums, and begonias in the ground during the winter (covering them for protection), or should they be taken into the house? (New Jersey.) Positively will die however well you protect them. There is only one begonia that is hardy with protection, the tuberous *B. evansiana*.

What shall I do with fuchsias, lantanas, and other summer bloomers when they come indoors in fall? Place in a cool cellar window. Water very sparingly until new growth appears. Then cut them back and bring to light and give more water.

What shall I do for house plants that turn brown when brought in the house during winter? I am losing all of my plants. Keep them cool. Do not overwater. See that they get fresh air. Cut back withered portions.

EXPOSURE

What flowers and vines are suitable for a sunny window box? Geraniums, heliotropes, petunias, lantanas, abutilons, coleus, ageratum, morningglories, nasturtiums, Little Pickles, Kenilworth-ivy, *Campanula isophylla,* browallias.

Which house plants will grow in a window in winter? It has all of the morning sun. Flowering plants that will keep blooming if the temperature is not high (55° F. at night) are primulas in variety, callas, bouvardias, begonias, and all kinds of bulbs which potted in the fall will keep up a succession, including Paperwhite and other narcissi, amaryllis, veltheimia, etc.

What house plants will blossom with only 2 or 3 hours of sunshine during the winter months?   The small-flowered begonias are dependable; also various bulbs potted in the fall will help out. Saintpaulia will bloom without direct sunshine.

What house plants would you suggest for east windows partially shaded most of the time, and in a steam-heated room which is consistently overheated?   Why expect the impossible? Plants will not tolerate extreme heat unless they are tropical subjects which require high humidity, which almost never prevails in overheated rooms. About the only things we can suggest are sansevieria (Snake-plant) and the Kangaroo-vine (*Cissus antarctica*). Both can stand dryness and warmth to an unusual degree.

What house plants are suitable for rooms having little sunshine?   Much depends upon the temperature maintained. Dry, hot rooms will kill anything, but if temperature is moderate and you maintain fair humidity, you can grow small palms, ferns, ivies, and many of the so-called dish plants florists use.

What plants can be grown in a sun porch without southern exposure?   Almost anything you fancy if there is sufficient heat during winter to keep the night temperature around 45° F. Both blooming and foliage plants from the florists will get along in such a porch.

What flowers and vines are suitable for a shaded window box? Begonias, lobelia, English ivy, German-ivy, variegated panicum, Strawberry-geranium, trailing fuchsia, Creeping Fig, Grape-ivy, Ground-ivy (*Nepeta hederacea*), Kenilworth-ivy, ceropegia, chlorophytum, palms. Keep the night temperature down to 55° F. if possible.

What house plants may be grown successfully without a great amount of sunshine?   Other than wax begonias and saintpaulias you won't find many that will bloom in poor light. The room temperature counts for a lot, and if never above 65° F. in day and 50° to 55° F. at night, you can expect all kinds of ferns, palms and ivies to get along nicely.

Can I keep house plants in a west window?   Yes, plants which do not need full sunlight, such as African-violets, large-leaved begonias, foliage plants, ivies, etc.

What plants other than Chinese Evergreen and nephthytis

will grow in water in a northern exposure? Wanderingjew (tradescantia), English Ivy, Grape-ivy, redwood burls, and Umbrella-plant (*Cyperus alternifolius*).

What can I grow in a north window? All kinds of ferns, ivies, saintpaulias for blooming, maybe fuchsias also, as well as many of the green and variegated foliage plants carried by florists.

ENVIRONMENT

What are the conditions under which my house plants will flourish in winter? See Introduction.

I have a steam-heated house and have difficulty getting house plants to live. What is the trouble? Place humidifiers on your radiators, or stand open dishes of water near your house plants to increase humidity. See that they get fresh air daily, without direct drafts.

Does coal gas injure house plants? Yes, it is deadly, even in very small amounts.

Does cooking gas affect house plants? Artificial or manufactured gas has a bad effect on house plants. Natural gas does not affect them adversely, according to statistics.

I use gas for heating and cooking. The gasman says there are no leaks, but my house plants don't thrive. It is not too hot and dry nor too cold or dark where I have them. What is wrong? If the temperature and humidity as well as light are right, there may be a gas leak too small to be detected by human beings. Raise some tomato seedlings, or get some sizable, healthy tomato plants from your florist. If they hang their leaves and look sad after a short time, you can be sure gas is present.

What is the easiest flowering house plant to raise, having to use gas for cooking in the house? Geraniums, fuchsias, and semperflorens begonias are pretty easy, but a lot depends upon where you grow the plants, and the temperature. If you have a room that is 50° to 55° F. at night, 10° higher by day, with plenty of light and not too dry, your chances are good in spite of gas cooking, but don't expect plants to thrive in a kitchen that is 80° or more in the daytime and 20° or 30° lower at night.

What climbing plant, such as ivy, can one grow in the house with gas furnace? The Kangaroo-vine is about the toughest house vine we know. If that won't thrive with you, nothing will.

Our new home has gas hot-air heat. Will I be able to keep my gardenias, palms, and other house plants healthy during the

winter?   If there is no leak of unburned gas. If you maintain high humidity, you will find it good for the plants as well as yourself.

How can one grow house plants in a chimneyless house where the only available heat is from open natural gas stoves?   The atmosphere may be too hot and dry. Keep shallow pan filled with water near plants. If the temperature is 70° F. or more, humidity low, few plants will last long.

Is the cold from windows injurious to plants?   Definitely so if the plants are tender kinds; take out of the window at night or place thick paper in front of the glass. Cold drafts are very bad.

Do oil stoves in rooms injure house plants? The temperature varies from 40° to 80°. I do not have much luck with house plants.   The fumes of oil stoves are not good for house plants. If stove is kept in first-class working condition, plants will suffer less. Give them as much fresh air as possible without direct drafts. Eighty degrees is too high a temperature. (See questions on Temperature.)

What house plants can be easily kept in a hot, dry room with only a small amount of diffused sunlight?   No plant can thrive in a hot, dry room, but some of the cacti and succulents can put up with a lot if not kept too moist.

Do plants grow under electric light?   Yes, electric light can be used as a substitute for sunlight, though plants do better under natural conditions.

Why do my house plants have luxuriant foliage but the buds dry up and fall off before opening?   This may be due to high temperatures, irregular or too heavy watering, or gas fumes. (See Watering, Temperature, and Sanitation.)

What causes the lower leaves on a small palm plant to turn brown and then die? What is the remedy?   Unsuitable soil. Dryness at the root. Dry atmosphere. If possible have local greenhouseman or florist diagnose trouble, then correct offending condition.

How can I prevent plants, grown indoors from seeds or cuttings, from growing spindly?   This is caused by too much warmth and not enough light and humidity. Direct sunshine is needed by most plants.

INSECTS AND DISEASES

How can I prevent pests from getting a start on my house plants?   Examine all house plants before bringing them in.

If any specimens from the garden or purchased from a florist are infested with pests of any sort, segregate them and get them entirely clean before letting them join other healthy plants. Make it a habit to look all plants over weekly for possible pests.

How can disease and pests be well controlled in growing house plants? By providing the best possible cultural conditions. By applying early, simple methods of control. Sponging with soap and water at intervals checks such pests as scale, mealy bugs, and red spider. Keep all dead leaves picked off.

What shall I use to get rid of aphids on house plants? Black Leaf 40, used according to directions on bottle. (See Section VIII.)

Mealy bug, one of the most annoying of house-plant pests, is controlled by applying alcohol with a small swab.

What is the best method to clean mealy bugs off plants? Place plant in bathtub, and wash off bugs by directing a spray of water at them forcibly. With very hairy-leaved subjects brush off bugs with small, soft paintbrush dipped in 60 percent alcohol.

A small bulb syringe is very convenient for keeping the foliage of house plants clean and healthy.

How can I get rid of red spider on my house plants? Syringe with clear, cold water forcibly applied. If badly infested, dip the tops of the plants quickly, 2 or 3 times in succession, in water heated to 140°. Or spray or dust with rotenone.

What is the brown scalelike pest which adheres closely to the leaves and stems of ivy, and which seems to attract ants? What will kill this pest? Have used nicotine sulfate and pyrote but neither one was successful.   Brown scale is the name of the pest. It may be removed by sponging the leaves with soapy water to which Black Leaf 40 (nicotine sulfate) is added at the rate of a teaspoonful to a gallon).

What is the pin-point black insect that attacks nephthytis and causes the leaves to turn yellow and then dry up?   Sounds like a small scale insect. If adult insect is incapable of movement, this diagnosis is correct. Remove scales by sponging with Black Leaf 40 used according to manufacturer's directions.

What can be done about white jumping insects in soil of house plants?   These usually breed in the organic matter in the soil. Try standing the pots in a vessel of water kept at 110° F. for a few minutes. This temperature is fatal to many insects, and most plants are unaffected by it even when completely immersed.

How can one kill white flies? Do these flies hatch in the earth or on the leaves of plants?   They are difficult to control on house plants. Repeated sprayings with a nicotine insecticide is the best procedure. The eggs are small, translucent bodies laid on the under sides of the leaves. (See Section VIII.)

SANITATION

How often should house plants be syringed or washed under spigot?   Glossy-leaved plants profit from a weekly syringing or sponging. Fuzzy-leaved plants should be dusted with a camel's-hair brush.

In washing of leaves of house plants, should soap be added to water?   Many green-fingered gardeners do use soapy water in sponging off the foliage of glossy-leaved house plants. Plain water is just as good if all dust is removed, unless the plant is infested with red spider, scale, or other pests, when soapy water helps to remove them.

How can house plants be cleaned without injuring the plant, as certain plants are not to be touched with hands or most instruments?   Brush dust from fuzzy-leaved plants with a fine camel's-hair brush.

What causes the white and brownish moldlike substance on the outside of flower pots?   The white film is the lime or alkali in the clay. Wipe the pots occasionally; use wire brush if necessary.

Spraying with kerosene emulsion (¼ lb. soap dissolved in 1 pt. water. Add ½ gal. water and 1 gal. kerosene) keeps foliage clean, and controls many plant pests.

Why does the soil of house plants get moldy?   It is not mold, but algae, the spores of which are in the air and perhaps in the water. Keep the surface stirred, and once a month water with permanganate of potash, ½ teaspoonful to 1 gal. of water. Wipe off the pots occasionally.

Why does the soil in my house-plant pots smell sour and musty, and sometimes have a green, mosslike coating on the top? See Introduction to this section on Potting Soils. Bits of charcoal mixed through the soil will help keep it sweet. Do not overwater; try to admit fresh air daily, without direct drafts.

How can small seeds, such as orchid and begonia, be disinfected before growing them in cultural media of agar-agar? Calcium hypochlorite, 10 gm. to 160 c.c. of distilled water. Shake several minutes, and filter. Place seeds in tube and enough filtrate to wet all. After shaking and allowing to soak 15 minutes, transfer from solution with a platinum needle to the agar-agar.

Should the dirt be heated so as to kill bugs and worms before using for house plants?   No, this should not be necessary if you have good clean garden loam. This precaution is sometimes taken when preparing a soil mixture for starting difficult seeds or rooting cuttings.

PROPAGATION See also Section II.

How should I take slips from house plants and make them grow?   Take shoots or tops of plants 4 to 6 ins. long with firm, but not hard, stem growth. Fill a pot with sandy soil and insert cuttings around the edge. Make the holes with a stick and press soil around cutting firmly. Sink about 1 in. Shade from sun and keep only just moist. When growth starts, pot singly. (See also Section II: Propagation.)

Is there any way of dividing very large house plants so they will not take up so much room in the house?   It is usually better to root cuttings, discarding the unwieldy parent plant. Geraniums and many others can be pruned back very severely.

What can I feed house plants that will encourage blooms? I have a fairly cool room and southern exposure. My geraniums and fuchsias refuse to bloom during the dreary winter months. I have taken my rosemary indoors, but it will not grow in spite of all my efforts.   If your geraniums and fuchsias have been in bloom outdoors in summer, they are now resting. Start slips in summer for late winter bloom. Rosemary can also be readily rooted by slipping, and the young plants will grow more thriftily than the old, sometimes even coming into bloom.

Which blooming house plants can be started in March?   If you have ample light, a temperature not above 60° F., and understand the rudiments of plant raising, you can have fair success with begonias, gloxinias, and primulas. For lower temperatures, cinerarias and calceolarias can be tried.

What is the procedure for starting house plants from seeds, rather than from the usual slips?   Use light, sandy, not over-rich soil. Sow each kind thinly in a pot, making soil fairly firm and level beforehand. Water by standing in a vessel of water and then cover with glass. Give shade, and temperature of 60° to 70° F. Always water from the bottom. Transplant into other pots or boxes when true leaves show. Best time for sowing such seeds is between January and March; but some, like primroses, can be sown in June, and cinerarias and calceolarias in August or September.

Can seeds, taken from the garden in the fall be used indoors during the winter, or do they have to be dormant for a certain

period before they will grow? Seeds can be planted immediately, but most growers like to give them a short rest.

Can the soil in which seeds are planted indoors be permitted to dry off? Keep constantly moist, until the seed has germinated.

What is "damping off," and how can it be prevented? This is a fungous disease prevented by sterilizing the soil or treating the seed with a disinfectant such as Semesan or copper oxide. (See Section VIII.)

How can one start bougainvillea cuttings in the house? Take short side growths or tips 6 ins. long. Insert in sandy soil in a small pot, or several around the edge. After watering, stand in a box or big pot and cover with a sheet of glass, giving a warm position. Don't overwater but never allow to dry.

How can one take slips from a rubber tree? *Ficus elastica* can best be propagated by air-layering. Make a slanting cut halfway through the stem with a sharp knife; insert a toothpick to keep open, and bind around with a ball of damp sphagnum moss. Keep damp. While rooting, stake the branch to avoid breakage. When rooted, sever and pot in soil.

How can I propagate "Pick-a-back" plant? The small plants on the leaves will quickly root if the leaf is taken off the plant and pegged on the surface of soil in a pot. About the easiest of things to propagate.

PLANNING AND ARRANGING THE WINDOW GARDEN

How can I make a window garden? Have a wide shelf built to fit in a sunny bay or deep-silled window. Line the shelf with metal, or give several coats of bathtub enamel, after the cracks have been puttied up. It is well to have a rim built around the shelf to keep pots, pebbles, etc., from falling off. If entirely waterproof, the shelf may be lined with pebbles in which the pots are set. Pebbles are kept moist. If not completely waterproof, set pots on shelf, each in its own saucer. A "fountain" or a wide dish of water in the center will help keep a humid atmosphere if the shelf is not waterproof.

What sort of indoor window box do you recommend? A box with a metal lining. Fill the container with damp peatmoss or with standard potting soil (which see) in which bits of charcoal have been mixed. Sink potted plants to the rims in the soil or peatmoss.

Which flowers may be grown in the house throughout the year?
I have an inside flower bed about 8 × 4 ft.; the earth being
about 3 ft. deep with drainage.   A box of this size needs
to be in a glassed porch or greenhouse. In any ordinary window
the light would be insufficient to permit healthy growth of all
the plants the box would hold. Unless your room is especially
well provided with windows, don't expect all plants to be a success. In such a box, in a dwelling room, trouble is certain. At best,
a room is only a makeshift for plant growing. Window plants are
best grown in pots, which permits moving them around.

*Fancy-leaved caladiums, streptocarpuses, and gloxinias
are three of the less well-known plants which the experienced amateur will find interesting to grow.*

What are sure-to-bloom winter window garden flowers?
Semperflorens begonia, crown-of-thorns, and impatiens.

**What are ten good plants for providing a long succession of
blooms during the winter?**   Begonia Preussen, *Begonia froe-
beli*, zonal geraniums, Paperwhite and Soleil d'Or Narcissi, Christmas Cactus, *Crassula lactea* and C. *multicava*, marica, *Begonia
feasti*, amaryllis and primroses.

**What blooming flowers may I put in my fernery to keep in
the house during the winter?** I have it in front of south windows,
but have Venetian blinds which I keep tilted just a trifle—the
sun is not there all day because of the next house.   Better give
up the idea of flowering plants in a fernery that gets no sun, but
you might try the African-violet (saintpaulia) or some of the
winter-blooming begonias (which see). Forced bulbs are also a
possibility though they will not last so long as though they had
some sun.

**What flowers and other plants can be grown in a window box
in the heart of the city?**   Begonias, geraniums, lobelias, chlorophytum, English Ivy, Japanese Honeysuckle, sansevieria, German-
ivy, and Kenilworth-ivy.

**What house plants will survive in a city apartment with little
or no sunshine?**   Snake-plant, aspidistra, Chinese Evergreen,

English Ivy, pothos, Wanderingjew, palms, fatsia, dieffenbachia, Grape-ivy, dracaena, rubber plant (*Ficus elastica* and *Ficus pandurata*), pandanus, monstera, and peperomia.

What house plants require a great deal of moisture?   Callalily, Chinese Evergreen, ferns, spireas, hydrangeas, primulas, cinerarias, African-violets, cyclamen, Jerusalem-cherry.

Which house plants do well if kept on the dry side?   Aloe, agave, crassula, sedum, sansevieria, and other succulents including most cacti (excepting the orchid cactus).

How can I supply needed humidity in the room where I keep my house plants?   By fitting humidifiers to the radiators; by placing shallow trays or wide saucers filled with pebbles or sand (which must be kept moist) beneath the pots; by spraying the plants over each day with a fine atomizer.

Is there any way of safely leaving house plants during a vacation of a week to 10 days without care? Would it be harmful to leave them standing in saucers of water so that they do not dry out?   This would not be harmful in most cases. An alternative is to water the plants well and then stand the pots in a box packed around with wet paper or peatmoss. Place in a shaded place not subjected to drafts.

What are the names of some house plants that are easy to raise? (Washington.)   If your rooms have ordinary windows and in winter are heated to 70° F. or more, plant growing is not easy. All depends on light, temperature, and humidity, plus careful watering. For winter and early spring, various bulbs are relatively easy to flower, but their season is brief. If you want all-year-around plants, grow ferns, ivies, sansevierias, cacti, and succulents. Geraniums, fuchsias, and similar flowering plants are easy to raise from cuttings.

Which low-growing plants would be suitable for house use in small containers without drainage holes? (Michigan.)   Containers without drainage or vent at the bottom will soon sour the soil. If not carefully watered, air is driven from in the soil, and no plants can stand that. With care you may, for a time, keep ivies, saintpaulias, cacti, and succulent plants in variety in good shape. Succulents and cacti need very little water.

What plants would be good to plant in fancy china figures like rabbits, etc. What kinds would stand the shade?   For sunny positions, Babystears, cacti, and succulents in small sizes. For shady windows, various small ferns, peperomias, cryptanthus, pilea, small-leaved ivies, *Saxifraga sarmentosa*.

What dwarf plants are best suited for growing in small containers to keep on glass window shelves? (Maine.) Small-leaved ivies, Kenilworth-ivy, grevillea seedlings, various ferns, cacti, and succulents in variety; saintpaulia and many others according to fancy, room conditions, light, etc.

How shall I place the house plants in a window garden with a southern exposure? Put the flowering plants which need full sun close to the glass. On the edge of the shelf, facing the room, use small-leafed ivies or other vines which do not need sun. Against the walls on each side can go foliage plants with colored leaves to give variety of color. When the forced bulbs are ready for bloom, these can be placed just behind the ivy away from the full heat of the sun. Such flowers as callas, amaryllis, primulas, and fuchsias can also occupy this less sunny space when they are in bloom.

The only place I have for a window garden gets little sun. Is there any special way to arrange the plants? If plants are used which do not need sun, these can be placed to give the best effect. Large plants can go against the walls or be silhouetted against the glass. Vines are trained around the window frames and along the edge of the garden facing the room. Low plants are placed just behind this edge. Use foliage plants with variegated and colored leaves.

MINIATURE GARDENS

TERRARIUMS

What type of soil should I use in planting a terrarium? Half sandy loam, half peatmoss, or leafmold, with bits of charcoal added.

How can one make a terrarium? Use any large glass container and cover top with sheet of glass in the day; open at night. Place small rocks or coarse gravel on bottom of container, covered with soil, as above.

How should the interior of a terrarium be arranged? After the drainage layer and soil have been placed in the bowl, a grade may be established which will make it possible to have all the plants visible at one time to the eye of the observer. Perhaps stones, moss, or lichens can be used to give the effect of a miniature landscape. By arranging a slope instead of a flat surface, seedling trees or shrubs and other erect growers can go in on the low side, with creeping and low-growing plants on the higher level and between the taller ones.

What five plants do you consider most suitable and satisfactory for growing in a terrarium, since overheated living-room windows preclude all but desert-type varieties?   If the glass container is large enough, ferns come first; with small crotons, peperomias, dracaenas, and saintpaulias to provide color.

What cultivated plants are suitable for terrariums?   Various ferns, small palms, pellionias, selaginellas, *Begonia imperialis*, cryptanthus, small ivies, pileas, *Saxifraga sarmentosa*, *Festuca glauca* (grass), fittonias, marantas, and whatever plant appreciates humid conditions. Some of the plants soon outgrow their quarters, so remaking at intervals is necessary.

What wild plants can be used in a terrarium?   Wood wildings such as partridge-berry, wintergreen, pipsissewa, rattlesnake-plantain, hepatica, ground-pine, moss, lichens (on bits of bark or half-decayed wood), seedling evergreens, and tiny wild ferns do very well in a glass garden.

What seed can I sow in a woodsy terrarium?   It is not customary to sow seeds in a terrarium, but such a container is ideal for raising ferns from spores. The spores usually found on the back of fern fronds shaken in a terrarium will start as green flattened growth from which tiny ferns will duly emerge.

What is the proper way to care for a terrarium?   Keep in a not-too-sunny position and cover with a sheet of glass during the day; partly open at night. Water very sparingly, especially if the container is topped with glass. Don't wet the foliage when watering. Wipe glass top dry each day, also the sides if there is a great deal of condensation.

ORCHIDS IN TERRARIUMS

Can I grow orchids in the house? If so, how?   Providing you have a suitable terrarium and give the plants careful attention, a wide variety will thrive. Excellent results have been obtained with cattleyas, cypripediums, calanthes, *Odontoglossum grande,* and others.

How can orchids be raised in the house?   Satisfactory results are obtained by growing them in a terrarium built so that ventilation can be given both at top and sides. The orchids are grown in pots which stand on slat shelves over a tray holding water. Terrarium is placed near window. Temperature should average 55° to 65° F.

How often must I water a potted orchid growing in a terrarium?   On an average about once a week, but this will vary somewhat with prevailing weather conditions, amount of artificial heat in room, and the condition of the plant itself. Most orchids have a resting period during which they need little water.

DISH GARDENS

What plants are suitable for dish or tray gardens?   Cacti, succulents such as small specimens of crassulas, gasterias, echeverias, kalanchoes, and sedums. *Saxifraga sarmentosa,* cryptanthus, ferns, myrtle, seedling evergreens, pileas, small *Begonia semperflorens,* peperomias. Go to the florist and select any very small potted plants which will fit in your dish or tray. Or try small plants from your own garden or window garden.

How is a dish or tray garden arranged?   A shallow dish or tray is lined with coarse gravel or small pebbles, over which is placed a thin layer of light garden loam, sandy for cacti and succulents, mixed with peatmoss or leafmold for woodland plants. The plants are set in to simulate a miniature landscape and earth is packed firmly about their roots. Moss can be used to cover the bare soil of the surface.

How should the tray or dish garden be watered?   When the garden is made, enough water should be given to moisten thoroughly the roots of the newly set plants, but not enough to leave them soggy and waterlogged. After first watering, give water sparingly when soil feels dry to the touch. Pour water directly to the roots with a small pitcher or long-spouted watering can.

How can I keep the soil sweet in my dish garden?   Mix small pieces of charcoal through the soil mixture which you are using.

How long will the plants survive in a dish garden?   That depends on the plants used and the care given. Cacti or succulents often live for months if planted in sandy loam and watered sparingly. Foliage plants do not last quite so long, but if given proper care will remain fresh and green for some weeks.

LIVING PLANT ARRANGEMENTS

What is a living plant arrangement?   An arrangement of flowers and foliage, or of foliage plants, actually growing in a container instead of cut and placed in water, as with the usual flower arrangement.

How should a living plant arrangement be made?   Place gravel or pebbles in the bottom of the container which you select—preferably a bowl or dish deep enough to receive comfortably the roots of the plants. Arrange the flowers and foliage plants to make an interesting design, just as you would in arranging cut flowers. Fill in with soil around the roots, covering soil with a ground cover such as myrtle or moneywort.

What flowering plants are suitable for living plant arrangements? Fuchsias, African-violets, semperflorens begonias, browallias, torenias, minor bulbs (grapehyacinth, crocus, snowdrops, species tulips), sternbergias, colchicums.

What foliage plants are suitable for living plant arrangements? Small specimens of any of the foliage plants with decorative leaves (see Foliage Plants), myrtle, moneywort or Creeping Jenny, Babystears, partridge-berry, small-leaved ivies, tradescantia, pteris ferns.

What wild plants can I use in a living plant arrangement? Violets, hepaticas, springbeauties, arbutus, marshmarigolds, pipsissewa, partridgeberry, wintergreen, ferns; seedling blueberries, evergreens, and deciduous trees; also moss and lichens. Use a mossy rock or lichen-covered root or piece of stump to give a natural effect in placing the wild material.

THE KITCHEN-WINDOW HERB GARDEN

What herbs can I grow in my sunny kitchen window? Annuals: parsley, sweet marjoram, basil, anise, coriander. Perennials: mint, chives, thyme, sage, lemon balm, tarragon. Tender perennial shrubs: scented geraniums, lemonverbena, rosemary.

Should annual herbs in the kitchen-window herb garden be started from seed? Not unless seeds have been planted in summer so that the plants have a good start before going indoors. Before being brought to the kitchen they should be well established and happy in the pots or boxes in which they are to grow on through the winter. The double shock of transplanting and bringing indoors is apt to be too much for them.

What kitchen-window herbs can be grown from seed? If planted early enough to produce plants before cold weather, sweet marjoram, parsley, basil, anise, coriander.

What kitchen-window herbs must be purchased as plants? Rosemary, lemonverbena (tender shrubs), tarragon, mint, chives, thyme, sage, and lemon balm are perennials and must be purchased as plants or grown on in advance from seed so that you have plants ready to bring in for use during the winter.

Where can I purchase herb plants; seed for growing indoors in winter? Most leading seed houses now carry lists of herbs.

What kind of soil is necessary for herbs grown indoors? See alkaline potting mixture in Soil, this section.

Can herbs be grown in a window box or should they be kept in pots?   In general, pots are more successful. Basil or parsley may be grown in a box, especially if started from seed during summer. To be reasonably successful, the room must be cool— below 60°, preferably 50° to 55° F., for all but the tender perennial shrubs. (See previous question.)

Can chives be grown indoors in winter? If so, how?   Yes, chives do well in the kitchen herb garden. Bring in a clump of bulbs from the garden, setting it in a bulb pan of light, sweet soil. Cut back the foliage and let new growth start. Grow on in a sunny window, at a low temperature—preferably 55° F. Keep on the dry side.

Can I grow scented geraniums in the kitchen herb garden? Yes. See Geraniums.

Do you think one should bring in lemonverbena during winter? I did, potted it and kept in basement near a window, watered once a week. Am I doing the correct thing? (Michigan.) Being a native of Argentina and Chile, the lemonverbena would not winter over out of doors in Michigan. Most likely you are doing the right thing with it, if it stays alive all winter in the basement. It can be cut back when brought in from the garden and grown on through the cold weather in a sunny window. It can stand a higher temperature than that preferred by most herbs.

How can parsley plants be grown in the house during the cold months? Cut back, lift, and pot strong plants in the fall and give them a well-lighted window with a temperature never above 55° F. Don't overwater and don't feed with fertilizer.

Why does house-grown parsley become very pale, with long, weak stems? I give fertilizer every 2 or 3 weeks. It probably lacks sun and is grown too warm. Parsley grown indoors is almost always weaker and less thrifty than that grown in the garden. It wants plenty of sun, a temperature of not more than 55° F., enough but not too much water (keep it rather on the dry side), and *no* commercial fertilizer.

Should parsley and chives be kept very moist grown in a kitchen window? No. Be careful with watering; with a little practice you can tell by the weight of the container or the feel of the soil if it needs water or not.

Does it injure tarragon, rosemary, and pot marjoram to pot them every winter for use indoors? It does not injure them if they get the proper care and the plants are not too large. They should be set into the garden again in spring to recuperate. Eventually they will get too big to pot up, and cuttings should be propagated to produce young plants, leaving the parents in the herb garden out of doors. If the young plants are left in their pots, plunged in the garden through the summer, they will sustain less shock when brought indoors in autumn.

What is the truth about growing herbs indoors? The truth is that few herbs do well indoors unless they have the conditions which they prefer; namely, a night temperature of not over 55° F., plenty of light and sunshine, sufficient humidity, good air circulation, and regular care. These conditions are hard to provide in the average centrally heated home. A sun porch, cool window, or lean-to greenhouse offer more possibilities.

FLOWERING PLANTS

ABUTILON

Does abutilon or flowering-maple make a good house plant? Abutilon was one of Grandmother's favorite house plants. It also makes a good garden subject, growing tall and bushy and blooming freely in sunny, open beds. In autumn it may be so large that cuttings must be taken for rooting instead of bringing in the overgrown parent plant. Cuttings root readily. If the old plant comes in, cut it back very severely to prevent wilting and to encourage new growth. The variegated foliage and bell-shaped flowers are most attractive. It rapidly becomes pot-bound and therefore needs a lot of water. It is subject to white fly (which see). Repot in standard potting mixture. (See Soil, this section.)

I have a small plant with leaves almost exactly like a maple. Set it outdoors in July, it thrived, producing orange-colored flowers like "Japanese lanterns," on long, fine, drooping stems. What is it? What winter protection does it need? (Pennsylvania.) The plant is abutilon or flowering-maple. Not hardy, and must be grown as a pot plant in your section. Give average room conditions in winter, at 50° to 60° F. Flowers freely in winter. Root cuttings to make new plants. Grows quite large.

How can abutilon or flowering-maple be raised from seed as a house plant? Sow the seed in a pot in February or March, in sandy soil, barely covering. Place sheet of glass on pot and keep in a warm room. Give some light when germination starts, but use care in watering, as the seedlings are tiny. Transplant into another pot 1 in. apart when in rough leaf, and grow on like any other tender plant.

AFRICAN-VIOLET

CULTURE

Does the African-violet prefer a neutral, acid, or alkaline soil?
Saintpaulia specialists use medium-acid leafmold, loam, coarse
sand, and old cow manure, and a fertilizing formula of 2 5-in.
pots bone flour, 1 lb. muriate of potash and 1 lb. pulverized limestone (never hydrated lime) to 1 cu. yd. soil mixture, added at
potting time. Between pottings no other fertilizer is applied. This
soil mixture reacts above pH 6.0. The amateur with one or only
a few plants will discover that a light soil mixture full of humus
soil scraped from the top 2 in. under a privet hedge gives fine
results especially if a little bone flour (about 1 teaspoonful to a
5-in. pot of soil) is added at the 3-in. pot stage. Soil from the
woods is good too. To be avoided is a stiff, clayey soil which roots
cannot penetrate.

**What fertilizer is best for African-violets? Is aluminum sulfate
satisfactory?**   Except for a possible light addition of bone
meal or bone flour in the potting mixture, or on the soil surface
where growth is going well, extra plant food seems unnecessary,
especially when crown division gives an opportunity to provide
some fresh humusy soil about every 6 months. Aluminum sulfate
is too acid.

What is the best temperature for African-violets?   The
minimum night temperature in winter should be 60° to 65° F.
At 50° to 55° F. saintpaulias only struggle along. The day temperature is immaterial so long as it is not below night figures.

Will an African-violet thrive with no sunshine?   Frequently
these plants bloom even at north windows, but more prolific
results are obtained with plants grown at a sunny eastern exposure, with pots set back a little from the glass.

How should African-violets be watered?   Because of its
thick crown and velvety leaves, moisture is avoided around the
heart of the plant, and water supplied from the saucer or on the
edge of the pot. Either enough is given with each application to
keep the surface soil moist, or a little water is kept in the saucer
at all times—in which case a layer of sand or pebbles under the
pot assures good drainage.

**If African-violets require water in the saucer constantly, how
do you avoid damping off and loss of plant? Care is taken not
to allow moisture on the leaves.**   Regardless of what some

claim, saintpaulias do not want to be soaking wet all the time. Soil in such a condition lacks air and the roots will go bad.

Is cold water bad for African-violets?   Lukewarm water is better.

My African-violet has white rings and spots on the leaves. Is this a disease, or fertilizer deficiency?   Neither. It is caused by application of cold water on the leaf. If you must water the leaves, use lukewarm water. Otherwise, apply water only to the soil. It is not necessary to water African-violets from below, but it is important to avoid wetting the crown or heart of the plant.

Please tell me how to get African-violets to bloom. My plants remain green and healthy, but shortly after they leave the florist they cease flowering. Shall I repot them?   The difference in humidity between a greenhouse and ordinary living room is probably the reason for non-blooming. Best flowering is had on plants kept standing on moist pebbles which afford a constant "aura" of humidity. Faded flowers must also be promptly snipped to prevent seed formation, which is always a deterrent to further bud development. Plenty of fresh air indirectly admitted in cold weather is likewise important. Repotting may be necessary, but other factors in culture are first considered.

Should African-violets be kept "root-bound," and in small pots?   Unlike many flowering plants which tend to bloom more freely when the potting is close, African-violets flower better when somewhat overpotted. A plant entering its third year should flower well in a 6- or 7-in. pot. Young flowering plants do well in 3-, 4-, or 5-in. pots, depending on size of plant.

Does keeping an African-violet plant in a glazed flower pot prevent it from blooming?   In such a pot, even if it has a drainage hole, the plant will not dry out so readily; but it does not do so well in glazed pots as in porous clay pots, because air circulation in the soil is poorer.

What is the best location for African-violets in summer? They are either set in a light north window in a room where windows are kept open over long periods, or else on the sheltered porch; never are they "plunged" in the garden.

How are plants kept free of dust, if spraying is harmful to the hairy leaves?   Dust is removed with a soft brush. A flat camel's-hair paintbrush is ideal.

What causes a gnarly condition on African-violets? New leaves and blossoms have no stems, just grow out from the base of the plant.   Need of division might be the explanation, but more likely the cyclamen mite is at work. Spread a layer of napthalene flakes for a time in the saucer under the pot. These will act as a fumigant.

What makes the blossoms of an African-violet fall off while they are still fresh?   It is natural for them to do so. They fertilize or pollinate readily, and after that happens they slide off.

Why do African-violets drop their blooms before they open? Probably the temperature or humidity is too low. They want 60° F. or higher at night.

Will gas heat cause the buds to fall from African-violets? Leaking manufactured gas, however slight, will make any plant drop its leaves or buds.

How can one keep the leaves of African-violets from drooping onto the edge of the pot and thereby rotting away where contact is made?   It's natural for the leaves to droop over, and usually such fleshy leaves rot because of the dampness. Maybe you grow your plant too cool, which causes the leaves to sag. With 60° F. at night, the leaves will perk up more.

Why do the leaves of my African-violet rot and drop? No blooms either.   Too chilly a temperature; probably too much water.

What is wrong with an African-violet plant whose leaves curl? No sign of aphis.   Probably red-spider mites (see Index), which are almost invisible. It may be due to too cool a temperature, exposure to sun, or wetting the foliage.

My African-violet develops 10-in. stems which break in pieces. How can stronger stems be developed?   Such stem growth is most unusual. Very likely plants are in too cold or too shaded a location, with the center of the plant overcrowded with leaves. The overlarge foliage could be cut away and the plant divided.

INSECTS AND DISEASES

See Section VIII.

How can I clean up mildew on leaves and mold on stems of African-violets? What causes these?   These thick-leaved velvety plants are often a prey to mildew and mold without any apparent cause, although poor ventilation and insufficient sunlight seem to be contributing factors. Badly affected sections are sharply cut away and the plant, upper and under side, dusted with fine sulphur, or one of the dusts with sulphur as an active ingredient.

Why do mold spots form on the stems of my African-violets? Your mold spots are mealy bugs. (See Insects and Diseases, this section; also following question.)

How can mealy bug be cleaned up on African-violets? The end of a skewer or matchstick is wrapped with cotton and dipped in wood alcohol (or in a little toilet water). This is applied to all affected sections of the plant. Repeat as needed.

I have 7 African-violets which had blossoms steadily for 3 years, but now are infested with a webby substance on the under side of the leaf. Leaves are spotted yellow. What causes this? This sounds like red spider, a minute insect forming colonies of red dots on the under side of the foliage where webs are formed for protection. Increase humidity in room. Forceful syringing with clear, lukewarm water or with a rotenone preparation, to break the web and wash away the insects, is effective. Nicotine sprays are not helpful.

PROPAGATION

Can African-violets be successfully divided? Readily. Indeed, as soon as the crown gets overthick, flowering usually wanes. Carefully reset, each fair-sized repotted section usually begins to flower again immediately. It is also easy to maintain your stock by rooting leaf cuttings. (See following questions.)

Which is the better time to divide African-violets, in the spring or the fall? The spring is better. The divisions then grow on into good plants by the following winter.

What is the best method of propagating a large number of African-violets? Leaves may be sharply cut with their long stems from the base of the plant at any time (although florists prefer October and November). These are inserted in small separate pots, in a large bulb pan of light soil, or in a Wardian case. Half sand and half peatmoss seems to give the quickest results. Leaves are inserted the length of the stem. Soil is kept warm and moist while rooting takes place in a light place. Covering with a drinking glass or Mason jar helps to maintain ideally quick, humid rooting conditions; or pots may all be set in a box containing a layer of sand always kept moist. If warm weather makes outside growing safe, the plants are moved to a sheltered outdoor porch. When roots are formed, new leaves will begin to appear at the base of the old one. The glass is then removed and the plants shifted to 3-in. pots of leafmold. When these are root-filled, 4-in. pots are supplied, a good size for young plants of first flowering size. Generally speaking, it takes about 5 weeks for roots to develop and 5 weeks more for the first new leaves to appear. The first blossom by this method will show at 4 to 6 months.

PROPAGATION OF AFRICAN-
VIOLET

(Left to right) Leaf cutting inserted in pot of sandy compost. Method of keeping compost moist, by inserting small pot (with bottom hole loosely plugged) and applying water through this. (Below) Potted young plant, with saucer for watering from beneath. Plant, repotted, has reached flowering size.

How can African-violets be rooted in water?   Mature leaves cut with plenty of petiole or leaf stem will root if placed in a glass with just enough water to cover the end of the stem but not up to the leaf. As soon as roots develop, the "plant" is moved to a small pot of sandy soil. This method is slower than inserting leaves in soil at the outset.

VARIETIES

How many African-violets are there, and what are their names?   Varieties we know of are: Amethyst, Blue Boy, Blue Girl, Neptune, Orchid Beauty, Pink Beauty, and White Lady, as well as the original species *Saintpaulia ionantha*.

Where did the African-violet originate?   *Saintpaulia ionantha* was first discovered in East Africa in 1893 by Baron Walter von Saint Paul. Forms of it introduced at that time were *purpurea,* dark purple; *grandiflora violacea,* large flowered; and *albescens,* white tinted pink. These forms seemingly were all lost, as up to the time Blue Boy was originated in California the only form known was *S. ionantha,* the species, usually grown from seed in a small way and *S. kewensis,* a hybrid.

ANTHURIUM

What are the requirements of an anthurium plant to make it bloom?   In an ordinary room you have as much chance to flower this plant as you have with cattleya orchids. Anthuriums are tropical and demand high humidity and heat while in active growth with cooler conditions while in flower. The pot must be well drained and compost of sphagnum, peat, fibrous loam, and sand should be used. Crown must be above soil, and as stem base rises it should be wrapped with moss. If you succeed in flowering it, you are good.

BEGONIAS

SOIL AND FERTILIZER

What is the best soil mixture for begonias?   A loose, humusy mixture suits most begonias best. One part good loam, 2 parts leafmold, 1 part sand, ¼ part small lump charcoal, ¼ part dried cow manure, plus bone meal at the rate of 1 pt. to the bushel is satisfactory.

What type of soil do rex begonias need?   Mellow, porous, and rich in humus. One part good loam, 1½ parts leafmold, 1 part sand, ½ part old, rotted cow manure, and a generous helping of broken charcoal mixed in.

Fibrous-rooted begonias: type of soil and amount of moisture? Room temperature and humidity? Should they be kept in a sunny window or shaded?   Light, humusy, well-drained soil. Never permit soil to become really dry, but avoid saturated condition, 55° to 70° F. Sun in winter; shade in summer.

How should I feed begonias growing in pots?   They respond best to organic fertilizers, one of the best of which is diluted liquid cow manure; but any complete standard fertilizer that will dissolve in water may be used. Never feed plants that have not filled their pots with healthy roots.

How often should begonias grown as house plants be fertilized? Providing the plants are healthy and their roots are matting around the insides of their pots, about once a week during the active growing season and once every 2 or 3 weeks during the winter.

POTTING, CARE, AND CULTURE

What are the rules for repotting a healthy, fibrous-rooted begonia that has filled pot with roots?   (1) Water thoroughly few hours before repotting; (2) new pot should be only an inch or two wider than old; (3) put crocks (drainage material) in new pot; (4) avoid damaging roots; (5) moderately firm soil about root ball; (6) water thoroughly; keep warmer. Shade and spray with water for few days.

What is the proper care for begonias? They grow well but hardly ever blossom. About once a year they bud and then drop off.   Bud dropping suggests lack of light, or too low temperature. Most begonias need a minimum of 55° F., and a good light position. In summer, shade from strong sunshine is needed.

Can begonias in the house be pinched back severely to prevent them from growing leggy, or does this condition indicate some cultural defect?   Pruning back can be done. Some varieties (the coccineas, for example) send up long, canelike growths. Lack of light and too high temperatures may also be responsible for legginess.

Where in the house do begonias do best?   A sunroom where the night temperature is not below 50° F. and the day temperature not above 65° F. is ideal. Otherwise a light window (with the plants not too close to a radiator) is best.

How should fibrous-rooted begonias be watered?   Soil should be kept moist but not waterlogged. When water is given, thoroughly saturate whole ball of soil (preferably by immersing pot in pail), then give no more water until soil begins to show signs of dryness. Use water at room temperature.

How do you take care of begonias? My plants are withering up.   Begonias that have tuberous roots die down and rest for a period each year. Most others thrive in 55° to 70° F., providing atmosphere is not too dry and light is reasonably good. Soil should be light and humusy and moderately moist.

Should begonias have a rest; if so, when and what care should follow?   Impossible to generalize. The tuberous kinds need a complete rest through the winter. *Socotrana* and some South African kinds rest during summer. Many benefit from a partial rest (but are not dried off), while others continue growth the year round.

What is your method for growing a Callalily Begonia? One person's directions contradict the others. (New Jersey.) Place the plant in the window of a New England home and have the housewife care for it! This prima donna seems to do best under these conditions. Professional gardeners often fail, especially south of New Haven, Connecticut. A west window in a room with a night temperature not below 60° F., reasonable humidity and fresh air, with moderate watering from below (or without wetting heart of plant), may keep it alive.

Why is it so difficult to grow the Calla Begonia south of New England? This seems to be due to the extremes of summer weather. Like sweetpeas, delphiniums, and some other garden plants, this house plant abhors spells of weather when both days and nights are hot and humid.

How can I keep a Christmas Begonia over summer so it will bloom next winter? Rest for few weeks after blooming; cut back and repot in light soil in spring; grow on in humid atmosphere (minimum temperature 60° F.). Shade from bright sunshine; repot as becomes necessary during summer. Control pests. You can scarcely expect success without a warm greenhouse.

How do you care for Lorraine (Christmas) Begonias after they are through blooming? They are usually discarded, because young plants develop into better specimens for following year. If you wish to grow on old plants, rest awhile by reducing water supply somewhat. In spring, cut partly back, repot, and start into growth again.

How can I make my angel-wing begonia bloom? Providing plant is growing well, it should bloom after it attains a reasonable size if it is not kept in too dark a place.

Why do my angel-wing begonias after a few days' growth dry up and lose the leaves? I keep them well watered and cool. Common causes of leaf dropping are too much or too little water, low temperatures, exposure to drafts, too dry atmosphere, and careless repotting. Minimum temperature should be 55° F.

What disease causes begonia leaves to turn yellow? This is usually not due to any organic disease but to the plants receiving a check to their growth due to dryness, too strong sunshine, arid atmosphere, or too low temperature.

Why do begonias bloom in hothouses and not after I get them home? I have one now, it grows just fine, but no flowers. Possibly too little light. Begonias need light shade from intense summer sun, but good light is necessary for flower production, especially in winter.

Begonias kept on the porch during the summer, brought in the house in the fall, dropped all their leaves. What can be the cause or causes? We have gas in the house.   Leaking gas may be the cause, but much more probably the dry air inside (especially after heat is turned on) is responsible. Install humidifiers. Stand plants on trays in moist gravel.

Will the fibrous-rooted begonias that grew at the New York World's Fair live through winter if covered with leaves?   Not in regions where freezing weather is experienced.

My potted, everblooming begonia blooms on one side branch only. What can I do with it? It is about 9 ins. tall, has 4 stalks full of foliage, smaller one coming from the bottom, so it should be bushy.   Needs good light to bloom well. Will stand more sunlight than any other begonia.

I have a begonia named Loma Alta that sends up huge bunches of blossoms but they always blast before opening. I keep them just moist. What causes this?   It may be due to keeping the plant *too* dry. Loma Alta makes a heavy foliage growth, and a healthy plant needs liberal supplies of moisture.

When a rex begonia droops, is it going into a rest period? It has just finished blossoming. Should I water it less often? When grown in the house, this often happens at the approach of winter. Reduce water supply (but keep soil somewhat moist). Repot, and water more when signs of new growth show in spring.

My rex begonia never seems to increase in size. As soon as a new leaf comes on, one turns yellow and dies. What is wrong? Wrong soil; too low temperature or too dry atmosphere. Soil should be humusy but porous; temperature not below 60° F. A humid atmosphere such as is provided by a terrarium suits these plants best.

PROPAGATION

Why do my begonia slips rot instead of root when I try to start them in water?   While some people report success with *some* varieties of begonias in water, a generally preferable method is to use moist sand (not sea sand) as a rooting medium. If water is used, add a few lumps of charcoal.

Can Calla Begonias be made to grow from slips, and how? (New York.)   Yes. You must be careful to select the greenest slips for cuttings. The white ones are devoid of chlorophyll and will not grow. The green ones produce white tips later. Root under glass dish.

When is the best time to take cuttings of double-flowered begonias? At the same time as cuttings of single-flowered varieties belonging to the same section would be taken, thus: of most fibrous-rooted and tuberous-rooted kinds in spring; of most winter-flowering hybrids in early winter.

How can rex begonias be propagated? May be increased by seed, division, or from leaf cuttings. Cuttings are best made from mature leaves in spring. Insert them in sand, or sand and peatmoss. Keep moist and shaded from direct sunlight. Young plants should develop in a few weeks.

How do you start new plants of a Christmas begonia? Most commonly from single leaves treated as cuttings and inserted in a bed of moist sand in December. They need 70° temperature and moist atmospheric conditions to succeed. Can also be grown from ordinary stem cuttings inserted in spring.

My Begonia sutherlandi has developed swellings or lumps on its stems. Can these be used to start new plants? Yes. If planted in the spring, these bulbous growths will develop into new plants.

Which is the best way to propagate the hardy Begonia evansiana? Collect the small bulblets that form so freely on the stems in late summer. Store them in a cool place for the winter, and plant them in boxes of light soil in spring. Also by division of old plants.

What precaution should be observed in sowing begonia seed? Use a light, woodsy soil mixture, finely sifted—upper layer through a piece of window screening. Water well *before* sowing. Scatter dustlike seed evenly, and press in lightly. Do not cover with soil. Cover pot with glass and place in dark—temperature 60° to 70° F.—until seed germinates. Never allow soil to become dry. Water by standing pot in dish so that moisture seeps up from below.

How may begonias be grown from seed? I have difficulties; they always damp off. Damping off is caused by a fungus that thrives when conditions for the seedlings are unfavorable. Avoid overwatering, too heavy shade, extreme fluctuation of temperature. Try using sterilized soil. Be sure soil is well drained. Water only on sunny days.

How should seedling begonias be transplanted? They are such tiny things. Prepare shallow boxes or pans by placing drainage material in bottom and filling with mixture of 1 part soil, 2 parts leafmold, 1 part sand sifted (the surface layer through window screening). Loosen seedlings and lift with roots intact (use wooden label with V-notch) and plant with leaves on surface, roots covered. Water with fine spray, or from below. Keep warm and shaded.

INSECTS AND DISEASES

See Section VIII.

What causes the younger leaves on begonias to crinkle and become hard or brittle?   Mites (microscopic insects) which suck the juices from the plant. Spray repeatedly with Black Leaf 40. Keep covered thoroughly with fine dusting sulphur.

My begonias fail to grow. Have been told they have root knot. What shall I use?   Root-knot nematode causes swellings on roots, and, finally, decay. Only control is to repropagate, throw out old plants and keep new ones growing in sterilized soil.

Little green plant lice are on my begonia plants. What shall I do?   Make a sudsy solution with Ivory soap; add 1 teaspoonful of Black Leaf 40 to a gallon. Invert plant, and dip foliage and stems so they are thoroughly wetted.

VARIETIES

What are varieties, names, and kinds of begonias, and their care, and when they bloom; also resting time?   This subject is much too extensive to discuss briefly. You will find *Begonias,* by Bessie Raymond Buxton (Hale, Cushman and Flint, 1939), a most helpful book.

Begonias: what kinds are best in the house?   A good selection of easy-growing kinds includes: *B. feasti* (beefsteak), *B. semperflorens* (wax), *B. argentea-guttata* (Trout), *B. coccinea* (angel-wing), *B. heracleifolia* (star), *B. scharffi* (*haageana*), President Carnot, and *B. fuchsioides.*

What are several varieties of begonias for winter blooming in house—hot-water heat?   *Feasti, manicata, heracleifolia, nitida, rosea-gigantea, Sunderbruchi, verschaffeltiana.*

What are Lorraine begonias?   Commonly known as Christmas begonias, they are the result of hybridizing *B. socotrana* and *B. dregei.* The first hybrid produced was named Gloire de Lorraine.

What is the name of the begonia with green-and-white, and some all-white, leaves; small red and deep pink flowers?   Often called Calla Begonia. It is *Begonia semperflorens* var. "Callalily."

Can you tell me the name of a hardy begonia? *Begonia evansiana*, a native of China, is the hardiest species. In a sheltered position it will live outdoors in New York. It comes in both pink- and white-flowered varieties.

CAMPANULA ISOPHYLLA

There is a plant common in Cape Cod homes, which is generally called Star-of-Bethlehem. This is not the same as the one that grows in our garden from a bulb. It is a larger plant with beautiful blue or white flowers. Can you give me some idea of the right name? This is *Campanula isophylla*, a native of Italy. It is a trailing plant with beautiful gray-green foliage; a winter bloomer. It can be purchased from florists.

How can Star-of-Bethlehem be grown in the house? See above. Grow in sandy soil that has humus added. Sunny window in winter; light shade in summer. Keep moderately moist in winter; water freely in summer. Feed with diluted fertilizer when in growth. Propagate by cuttings in spring.

CALCEOLARIA

How can I grow calceolarias from seed? If you propose to do this in an ordinary window, you have chosen a tough subject. Like cinerarias, the spotted and other hybrid calceolarias want coolness. Sow the fine seeds on the surface of level sandy soil in a pot in July or August; full shade and never dry; transplant the tiny seedlings to a flat and keep in a shaded cold frame. Pot later and keep in the frame till late fall, then move to a light place with a temperature around 40° to 45° F. at night. If temperature runs above 50° any time during the winter, failure is almost certain. Beware of aphids and white flies.

CINERARIA

Can cinerarias be grown in a south window in a home with vapor heat? Can they be carried through summer for flowering again the next season? Cinerarias are short-lived plants in a warm room. They are grown at 40° to 45° F. and never above 50° F. When through blooming, discard them, as they don't like summer weather.

How can I raise cinerarias from seeds? I used moist sand and covered with a glass, but one by one they died. As cinerarias have to be sown in July or August to get sizable plants for winter or early spring, damping off in hot weather is always a menace. Use very sandy soil and don't use glass cover. Stand the pan where it is shaded, and keep as cool as possible. Sow late in August or early September, to escape the hot days and nights. Cinerarias must at all times be grown cool, 40° to 45° F.

Will cinerarias bloom in a warm room? 70° to 80° F.?   No. If you can't give them a night temperature of 45° to 50° F., little more during day, don't try cinerarias either from seed or as blooming plants.

What causes cineraria leaves to curl and dry at edges? Probably too hot and dry an atmosphere; possibly plants are dry at the roots. Cinerarias don't last long in a hot, dry temperature; 45° F. at night is plenty. Aphids are prone to attack them.

How should cinerarias be cared for in the window garden? Cinerarias with their masses of purple, red, or rose-pink flowers and dark, heavy foliage can be purchased from a florist's ready for late fall and winter bloom. They like a cool but sunny window. Watch for aphids.

FUCHSIA

How are fuchsias handled as house plants?   Cuttings are rooted in spring, taken from old plants that have been started after a winter rest. If you keep them growing all year around in a warm room, you won't get flowers. They are spring and summer bloomers. Like full light but not full sun; rich soil and plenty of moisture and humidity when in growth.

Stable manure is usually advised for fuchsias, but this is hard to obtain. Is there any substitute?   Fuchsias, if grown in pots, require the standard potting mixture. (See Soil, this section.) If rotted manure is impossible, use leafmold or peatmoss with good loam, and add a little fertilizer. Feed like any other pot plant when in full growth.

What fuchsias will bloom indoors in winter?   *F. magellanica gracilis* is a winter bloomer. It will look well in a hanging basket, as it is a drooping, almost vinelike variety. The small flowers are ruby red. Most fuchsias are summer bloomers. By taking slips from larger plants in summer and having them well rooted by early winter, you may get bloom in late winter or very early spring. Or buy young blooming plants from a florist who has forced them.

I have a fuchsia that blossomed in May and June. What should I do so it will bloom during the winter months?   Fuchsias are not naturally winter bloomers. The winter is their resting season. (See other questions.)

Should fuchsias be given a rest period, or may they be kept in

bloom the year around? Fuchsias are not ever-blooming, and in winter old plants are best kept dry and cool until early spring, then cut back and new growth encouraged by warmth and more water.

How can I bring fuchsias through the winter? Old plants should be potted and rested in a cool cellar or room, and watered very little. Cut back in February or March and give warmer quarters, watering more when new shoots begin to appear. If you can't accommodate growing plants so early, keep practically dry and cool till April, then stand outdoors on warm days; indoors at night. Don't plant outside until all danger of frost is past.

How should a fuchsia be handled during its resting period in a house without a cellar or cold frame? Keep practically dry and as cool as possible during the winter months. Fuchsias will not stand freezing, yet they ought to be kept cool and dry. In a warm room and watered, they will continue growing, but the shoots will be too weak to flower later on.

What is the cause of buds and blossoms falling off fuchsia plant on window shelf indoors? Too dry an atmosphere, resulting in red spider; or white fly attack. Possibly either too wet or too dry at the root. Root injury always causes leaf drop. Spring and summer are the blooming seasons. Don't expect flowers in winter. The plants should be resting unless they are young plants. (See previous questions.)

Can fuchsias be wintered in cold frame? If the frame is absolutely frostproof and the fuchsias are kept dry and dark until March, they might survive. The so-called "hardy" variety Riccartoni is the only sort that will stand real frost.

GERANIUMS

Which kind of soil should be used for geraniums to get good flowers? A mellow, loamy soil (not a sandy soil) is best. It should be well drained and enriched with bone meal. Avoid excessive use of nitrogenous fertilizer.

Do geraniums like a rich soil? When grown in pots, a rich and rather heavy soil is best. In beds or borders too rich a soil induces rank growth at the expense of flowers.

What is the best fertilizer for geraniums? Plants in outdoor beds respond to bone meal or superphosphate and wood ashes. Avoid nitrogenous fertilizers unless soil is poor. Pot-grown plants appreciate cow manure, bone meal, or any complete fertilizer used in moderation.

What do you suggest feeding geraniums for Christmas blooming?   Providing you have a good winter-blooming variety, and have grown it specially for winter bloom, any good complete fertilizer that is moderately quick acting may be used after final pots are well filled with roots.

CULTURE

What must I do to start geraniums left to hang in cellar (root upward) when spring arrives?   Take them down, prune them back somewhat (cut back roots as well), and pot in sandy soil in pots just large enough to hold the roots. Give one good soaking and put in light, warm place. Avoid watering frequently until new growth is well started.

When is it safe to plant geraniums from window into open garden?   After all danger of frost has passed and ground has warmed up. About time lima beans are planted. Harden plants gradually before planting by standing them for few days in cold frame, on porch, or in sheltered place outdoors.

Should I break the soil and spread out roots of potted geraniums when I plant them in garden?   No, leave ball intact. Thoroughly soak it an hour before planting. Make hole plenty big enough, press soil firmly about ball; water well. Top of ball should be half inch below finished surface.

What window is best (in house) for geraniums?   The sunniest one, where a minimum temperature of 50° F. is maintained.

Should geraniums be always kept toward windows, one side always facing the window, or may they be moved? (Maryland.)   They may be moved if desired, but it is not advisable to change them around frequently.

How should one care for geraniums in the house? What about using milk on them? What size pots?   Do *not* use milk. Pots must be adjusted to size of plant. Avoid pots too large for plant. When pot is well filled with healthy roots, transfer to pot a size or two larger, using soil mixture suggested in first question on geraniums.

How shall I water my potted geraniums?   Watering must be adjusted to individual plant and environment. Aim to keep soil moist (but not wet and boglike) throughout. When water is given, saturate whole ball of soil. Sunshine, high temperature, breezy weather, vigorous growth all make more frequent watering necessary.

I have potted my garden geraniums. What procedure do I follow to keep them blooming in the house? Please give directions for watering, sunlight, clipping tops, and temperature. See other questions. Cut tops about halfway back at potting time. Give all available sunlight.

Can anything be done about correcting the growth habit of a peach-blossom geranium which is growing too tall and not sending out any side shoots below a distance of about 10 ins. from flower pot? Yes. You may "stop" the plant by pinching out the tips of the growing shoots, or, if necessary, you may prune the stems back to force new growth nearer pot.

Is it true if geraniums bloom continuously outdoors in the summer they seldom bloom freely in winter? Also, is the temperature of the room indoors important? Yes. All plants need a season of comparative rest. For the best winter bloom grow plants through summer in pots and pick off all flower buds until late fall. Give night temperature of 50° F.

How can I make my geraniums bloom through the winter? By preventing them from blooming in summer by picking off all flower buds. Also by keeping them in a light window. Some varieties are better winter bloomers than others.

Should geraniums be repotted, and how often? Mine are scrawny and do not blossom since being brought in from outdoors. Plants that have given a good display all summer can scarcely be expected to continue throughout winter. Rest them somewhat by keeping them drier, but not completely dry, until new growth begins in late winter.

How do you treat and store geranium plants through the winter? The best procedure is to cut the plants back part way and pot them a couple of weeks before killing frost may occur. Winter in a sunroom or window where temperature does not drop below 45° F. Water with care through winter.

Have geraniums in flower boxes now in the basement. Last summer they developed rather long stems and I want to cut them back this year. How shall I do it? I had these boxes in the unheated porch, but when the weather got too cold I put them in the basement for protection against frost. They lost all their leaves while in the porch (which I wanted to happen, to give them a rest over winter), but now in the basement they are producing small buds all over and it will not be long until they have new leaves. What shall I do?   Prune away ½ to ⅔ the length of each shoot. Repot into new soil, put in light place, and they will develop nicely by summer.

Can geraniums planted outside be successfully wintered by storing plants in peatmoss or similar material, or must they be potted?   They probably could be planted in peatmoss and sand, but potting in a sandy soil mixture would undoubtedly be surer and better.

Will geraniums keep all winter if pulled up by the root and kept in a cool fruit cellar? Have some beauties I would like to keep.   Yes, under the conditions you mention. Hang them up by the roots from the ceiling and pick off all leaves that decay.

What is best care for Ivyleaf Geranium? Mine becomes straggly and root-bound in spite of being cut back and continuously changed to larger crocks.   Perhaps your plant is so old that it would be wisest to start afresh from a cutting. When plants are well rooted, feed with liquid fertilizer at weekly or biweekly intervals. Pinch the tips out of growing shoots occasionally to induce branching.

What is the proper treatment of Ivy Geranium? Soil, exposure, watering, etc.?   Pot in rich, mellow soil that is well drained. Grow in full sun; light shade is desirable during hottest part of day in summer. Water to maintain soil always evenly moist, but not wet and stagnant.

What are conditions favorable to growth of the Martha Washington Geranium? Soil and moisture required?   Cool, airy, sunny conditions (minimum night temperature 45° F.). Porous, fertile soil with some lime added. Plenty of moisture when growing rapidly; little or none when resting.

How do I care for my Lady Washington Geranium that bloomed this summer?   After blooming period, gradually dry off, laying plants on their sides out of doors. In August prune back, shake old soil out of roots, pot into smallest possible container, water, and start into growth again.

Why do the leaves of my normally blooming geraniums turn brown and drop off?   Many possible causes: too dry atmosphere; lack of water; too much water; damage to roots when repotting; or too strong fertilizer or spray.

What causes brown edges on geranium leaves?   Probably wrong cultural conditions such as faulty soil, improper watering, or a parching atmosphere.

What causes my geranium leaves to turn pale green (almond-white) and not thrive? Have been recently repotted; long enough to be growing and thriving. Probably you are growing them with too little light. Low temperature could also be a factor. Try full sunshine and minimum temperature of 55° F.

Why do Ivy Geraniums always have some dead leaves during blossoming season? This seems a common complaint except with plants grown in a comparatively humid (and perhaps lightly shaded) greenhouse.

Will geraniums thrive inside in a window box when the house is heated by gas? Unless gas is escaping into room atmosphere, method of heating will make no difference. Good light, reasonable temperatures, proper soil, and good care are the factors that count.

What makes our geranium house plants thin and spindly instead of short, stocky plants as they are outside? Would having bottled-gas cookstove effect plants? Too high temperature, coupled with too little light. Pinching tips out of plants occasionally will help. Read other questions and answers on this subject.

My geraniums won't blossom. They are in a southeast window, the room temperature is between 75° to 80° F. most of the time. What is wrong? Temperature is much too high. Ideal temperature for geraniums is 50° to 60° F.

What causes buds of a geranium to turn brown and dry up? May be due to mechanical gas leakage; to general poor health of plant; to insufficient light; or to a very dry atmosphere.

What causes a geranium to have flowers of different colors? First red, and then pink? Plants sometimes "sport" or mutate. A red-flower geranium may produce a branch that bears pink flowers, and vice versa.

When I cut off pieces of my Rose Geranium and put them in a bunch of flowers, they start wilting almost at once. What can be done to prevent this? Very little. It will help to cut the geranium ahead of time and plunge it in cold water in a dark cool place for a few hours.

PROPAGATION

What is a good method for propagating geraniums? By cuttings. (Terminal pieces of stem 4 or 5 ins. long with lower leaves removed and bases cut cleanly across just beneath a joint.) Plant firmly in clean sand; keep shaded from direct sunshine and in a fairly moist atmosphere, at about 60° F.

What is the best way to start geraniums from cuttings? What kind of soil should be used, and how much water?   Start with good, clean cuttings made of shoots that are neither hard and woody nor yet very vigorous and watery. Plant in sand. Keep just moist (not sopping wet). When roots have formed, pot singly in small pots, using for this first potting a very sandy soil.

What is the recommended time for slipping Rose Geraniums? Cuttings will root any time, but the most favorable months are May, August, and September.

When is the right time to take cutting of geraniums so they will flower for Decoration Day?   August or September.

When should geraniums be started for spring outside boxes? From August to February, depending on size of plants needed. Early cuttings will finish in 5-in. pots; late cuttings in 3½- or 4-in. pots.

Why don't my geraniums bloom in the house before February? I usually start them from slips in August. They are very beautiful otherwise, with very large, thick, glossy leaves. The flowers are large and beautiful when they do bloom.   For early bloom propagate in May.

Is it better to root geraniums in water or in sand? What is the best time to root them for early blossoming?   Moist sand is best. Take cuttings early in September for late spring blooming; in May for winter blooming.

Before frost in October I take geranium clippings and plant them in sand in pots indoor for rooting. About 90 per cent eventually rot at the dirt line. What is wrong?   You will stand a greater chance of success if you take your cuttings in late August or early September. Keep the sand moist but not wet. (See Insects and Diseases of Geraniums.)

My geranium slips looked very healthy at first, but now leaves are turning yellow and dying. No gas in house, and plants in south window. What is the trouble?   Cuttings are losing water faster than they can take it up. Reduce the transpiration by shading from bright sun and by placing them in box covered with pane of glass. Allow small amount of ventilation.

When and how do I pot geranium slips rooted in sand?   As soon as roots are ½ to 1 in. long. Plant singly in small pots, using very sandy soil without fertilizer added. Do not press soil too firmly. Water well immediately; syringe for a few days.

Have an Apple Blossom Geranium and can never start a new

slip. When and how should I try?   May or August. Make cutting 4 or 5 joints long; cut with sharp knife below joint; remove lower leaves; plant firmly in moist sand; keep moist, shaded from strong sun, in a moist atmosphere at 60° F. or more.

How does one slip Martha Washington Geraniums?   Very much as any other geranium. The shoots that root with greatest ease are young ones produced after plants have been started into growth in late summer, but tips of older shoots may also be used.

How may geraniums be grown from seeds?   Sow seeds in spring in pots of light, sandy soil. Cover very lightly, keep moist (and shaded until seedlings appear) in temperature 60° F. If seed is good, it will soon germinate, and under favorable conditions, the transplanted seedlings make rapid growth.

Why don't my seedling geraniums bloom?   Possibly they are growing too vigorously because of too-rich soil. Too much shade also reduces blooming. Try keeping some plants in pots.

How long after geranium seed is planted may blooms be expected?   From 6 months to 1 year.

How can large geranium plant be divided into smaller plants? What fertilizer is recommended?   Geranium (*Pelargonium zonale*) plants do not lend themselves to this method of propagation. Increase stock by means of cuttings. Any commercial fertilizer may be used advantageously.

INSECTS AND DISEASES

See Section VIII.

I have an Ivy Geranium that is almost 3 ft. tall. It was a slip last spring; now the leaves are starting to curl down. What is the cause of this?   It may be due to a severe attack of aphids. Examine young shoots and under sides of leaves; if plant lice are found, spray with any good contact insecticide.

Have a pelargonium 6 years old; bloomed once with gorgeous red and brown blooms. It has never blossomed since. I've changed dirt and pots, started new slips, but none will bloom. White flies bother it all the time. What shall I do for it?   This is a Martha Washington variety. To control white flies, spray at weekly intervals (until trouble is cleared up) with a nicotine insecticide used according to manufacturer's directions. For cultural details, read answers to other inquiries.

Why do geranium cuttings rot while in the sand and turn black and die without rooting?   The fungous disease known as Black Leg causes these symptoms. The rot begins at base and works upward to leaves. Use clean flats and sand that has been thoroughly baked. Propagate from healthy plants only.

VARIETIES

There is a small-leafed geranium similar to Rose Geranium, with a most unusual and delightful emanation from the leaves. What is its name?   Perhaps you mean *Pelargonium citriodorum* (lemon-scented), *P*. Dr. Livingston (lemon-rose-scented), *P. denticulatum* (pine-scented), *P. fragrans* (nutmeg), *P. odoratissimum* (apple-scented), or *P. tomentosum* (peppermint-scented).

What varieties of geraniums are best for outdoor planting? How and when should they be propagated to bloom for Decoration Day? What soil and fertilizers should be used?   Beaute de Poitevine, S. A. Nutt, Red Fiat, Pink Fiat, Radio Red, and Ricard. By cuttings, rooted in sand bed in September. Good ordinary soil and any standard fertilizer is O.K.

I have seen a geranium on the market in both red and light pink. The green leaves have a white border around. What is the name of this geranium?   Silver-leaf S. A. Nutt (red-flowered), Madam Languth (pink).

GERBERA

Do gerberas or African-daisies, when brought indoors from the garden, get a rest period; or should they continue to show leaves?   Gerberas do best when kept growing during the winter at 55° F., as that is their real flowering season. They are not likely to prove good window plants at ordinary room temperatures.

HELIOTROPE

Is heliotrope a satisfactory house plant?   Heliotrope can only be made to bloom in winter by purchasing plants forced by the florist, or by starting cuttings in summer which are ready to bloom by late winter. To force winter bloom on mature plants, they must be kept pinched back and disbudded through the summer. Heliotrope must have a very sunny position in a cool window garden. Water moderately. Cut back long, sprawling branches occasionally. Watch for white fly (which see).

Can a heliotrope potted from the garden be kept over the winter to set out again in summer?   Yes. Cut back a bit and keep cool—not above 55° F. Cuttings can be rooted in February to make more plants to set out in late May.

Can heliotrope and lavender be treated in the same manner?
No. Lavender is a hardy plant and thrives outdoors the year
around. Heliotrope is tender, and is grown either from seed or
from cuttings. It is used either as a pot plant indoors or as a
bedding plant outdoors in summer.

IMPATIENS

**What varieties of patience-plant shall I get, and how should it
be cared for indoors?** The Latin name is *Impatiens. Impatiens sultani* has bright red, single blossoms. Hybrids of this
variety are white and pink; one has variegated foliage. *I. holsti*
is a stronger grower, with large scarlet flowers. *Impatiens* is a
willing house plant. Give plenty of water, but pour surplus from
saucer after soil is soaked. Prune in spring; root cuttings from
pruned branches. It blooms constantly through the winter. Use
standard potting mixture. (See Soil, this section.)

MARGUERITES

Are marguerites satisfactory as house plants? Yes. Purchase blooming plants from florist. They will do well in a sunny
window. Sink pots in garden bed in summer where they will do
almost equally well. For winter bloom, keep plants disbudded
through summer. New plants root readily from cuttings. Marguerites need ample water. Watch for aphids. Use standard
potting mixture. (See Soil, this section.)

MARICA

**Is the marica sometimes called Twelve Apostles? Does it make
a good house plant?** Yes, the maricas are sometimes given
this nickname because of the number of their irislike leaves,
which sometimes reach 12. *M. gracilis* is the smaller leaved of
the two generally grown, and has white and violet, irislike fleeting blossoms which appear at the tips of leaflike peduncles in late
winter. *M. northiana* has larger leaves and blooms about the same
time, having larger violet and white fragrant blossoms. It blooms
less freely than *M. gracilis. M. caerulea* has 4-in. violet-blue
flowers. New plants can be started from the peduncles, which
produce young plants after bloom. Maricas need sunshine and
warmth for early bloom. Sponge the glossy leaves to keep them
free from dust. Use standard potting mixture. (See Soil, this
section.)

**I have a Marica gracilis which grew lustily and increased
greatly in size. Why didn't it blossom?** Perhaps you kept it
too cool. At 50° to 60° F. bloom is considerably delayed. The
flowers should appear in late winter if plants are kept at a day

temperature of about 70° F. Pot-bound specimens seldom bloom well. Yours may need division; or discard the old plant and start new stock. (See previous question.)

Is it safe to divide old plants of marica?   Yes, they can be easily divided. Or start new plants from those which develop on blooming stalks.

How old does the Twelve Apostles have to be before it blooms? This plant (marica), if grown from a small offshoot, may take 2 to 3 years to reach blooming size. Put the plant outdoors in partial shade during the summer. Bring in before frost.

Does the Twelve Apostles require much sun and water? Marica presumably is meant. It can take its full share of sun and light in a window, but use care in watering at all times; placing outside in partial shade during the summer is desirable. It blooms in late winter or early spring, depending on the species.

What makes the tips of my marica leaves turn brown? Probably watered too much. This plant is related to the iris, and, while evergreen, it has its resting season. When the leaves go bad, the best thing to do is to repot in fresh soil (after cutting away dead roots) and give only enough water to prevent wilting until it becomes active again.

PANSIES

Will pansies bloom indoors in winter?   Seed must be sown in late July; seedlings transplanted to rich ground. If for pots or boxes, plant in September and bring inside before hard freezing. Unless you have a light, frost-free porch or big window with temperature not above 45° F., don't try. Rather plant in cold frame, lift, and pot in March, and you will get some flowers.

PRIMROSES

What primroses can I grow indoors in winter?   *P. sinensis* or Chinese Primrose, single or double. Can be purchased from a florist. Bears pink, magenta, or white blooms. Long blooming period. *P. malacoides,* or Fairy Primrose, has small, frothy violet blossoms throughout winter. *P. obconica,* with vigorous hairy leaves, has larger flowers. *P. grandiflora fimbriata* (Giant Fringed Primrose) has flowers more than an inch across in white, through pink to deep rose. Water daily, in the saucer. Keep in cool east window, with a dish of water near by to provide humidity. Use fibrous potting mixture. (See Soil, this section.)

What can I do to make my primrose bloom? It is about 3 years old.   Not knowing the kind of primrose, we can't advise.

There are several types grown in pots for winter and spring flowers in greenhouses, and dozens of hardy kinds that bloom outdoors in the spring and early summer if conditions are right. The greenhouse kinds are discarded after one season.

What conditions are best for primroses as house plants? How much water? How much light and sun? How much heat, and how cool at night? For *P. malacoides* and *P. sinensis*, not above 50° F. at night; even less is better. *P. obconica,* 50° to 55° F. at night. All like partial shade, ample water, but plenty of drainage in the pots. Soil should not be very acid.

What care does the Christmas-blooming primrose require? If you mean *P. obconica,* this is raised from seed sown in February or March, grown on in pots in moderate shade through the summer, and from fall on kept at 55° F. or so. Don't give too much water, yet never allow to wilt for lack of moisture at the roots. Discard the plants after blooming.

How can I propagate a Chinese Primrose? The Chinese Primrose (*P. sinensis*) is raised from seed each year. Choice double sorts that do not seed usually produce side growths which can be cut off with a knife and rooted.

STRELITZIA

How is Bird-of-paradise (strelitzia) handled in winter? Should I take it out of pot and plant in ground in summer? The strelitzia is a big subject for a house plant, needing a tub—since it won't bloom until of some size. In winter, give only a moderate amount of water; good rich soil with plenty of drainage; full light but no feeding while semi-dormant. Don't take out of pot or tub in summer, sink to rim, and feed regularly. Blooms generally in late summer and fall. Winter temperature, 45° to 50° F.

Whenever my Bird-of-paradise makes a new leaf the old one dies. Why doesn't it bloom? You won't get blooms until the plant has 10 or more healthy leaves. The dying leaves indicate something wrong at the roots. Either insufficient size pot, poor drainage, not enough water while in active growth during the summer, or too much water in winter when it should be semi-dormant.

ANNUALS AND BIENNIALS

Is it possible to raise annuals indoors in winter without the plants becoming stalky? You can germinate the seed but will not be able to grow them satisfactorily unless you have an abundance of light and a temperature not above 50° F. for most sorts. Still less chance to flower them. All the annuals florists grow in winter are kept at the above night temperature and no higher in the day except through sun heat.

Dwarf varieties of many garden annuals—such as marigold, ageratum, and zinnia—supply color for the indoor garden in late fall or late spring, if seed sowing is carefully timed.

ALYSSUM

Can I make alyssum bloom indoors?   Yes, if you have enough sun and a really cool window or sun porch. Sow the seeds in late summer in pots or boxes.

BROWALLIA

Is the browallia an annual? I potted mine in the fall and about January the leaves withered and it died.   *B. elata* is an annual for outdoor use. *B. speciosa* is a biennial or perennial, but not hardy. The variety known as Sapphire is sown in the fall, carried along in a greenhouse through the winter, and planted out in the spring; or sown in spring to flower indoors in winter.

Are browallias suited to the window garden?   Yes, they make most satisfactory house plants. The tubular flowers, rather like small petunias, are blue, violet, or white, and literally cover the plants through a long blooming season. They are easily grown biennials which form shrubby, compact plants. Purchase them in bloom from a florist, or grow them yourself from spring-sown seed.

FORGET-ME-NOT

Can forget-me-not be made to bloom indoors?   Yes. It needs a cool but humid atmosphere and, unlike most other annuals and biennials, can stand some shade, though not much indoors. Plant the seed in spring for the following winter's bloom. This is really a greenhouse subject for winter bloom, but with the right conditions you may have flowers.

LOBELIA

Is lobelia a plant which can be made to bloom indoors in winter? Yes, you can grow lobelia from seeds or cuttings to produce winter bloom. Since it does not need as much sun as many other flowering plants, you will have pretty good chance of success if the window is cool. There are many fine blue varieties, and White Gem is a pure white.

MORNINGGLORY

Can I have morningglories in my window garden? Yes, if you have a cool, sunny window. Plant seeds in individual pots in August. Transplant to larger pots as needed. Have strings ready near the glass to encourage the vines to climb. Heavenly Blue is the most beautiful variety. Pearly Gates is similar, but pure white.

NASTURTIUM

How can nasturtiums be grown indoors in winter? They must have a cool, sunny window or sun porch. Plant seeds in late summer in pots of soil without too much fertilizer. Or slip some of the summer bloomers in the garden, keeping them cut back to prevent bloom until winter. Of course black aphids will attack them indoors as well as out. Use some of the double fragrant varieties.

PETUNIA

How can I grow petunias in the house during the winter? I took a few in this fall and they wouldn't grow. Petunias are not winter bloomers, nor can they be classed as good house plants.

SNAPDRAGONS

Are snapdragons practical house plants? If you have a very cool sun porch or bay window (40° to 50° F. night temperature), you may be able to have blooming snapdragons (*Antirrhinum*) through the winter. Though these are perennial in the South, they are grown as annuals in the North. Buy budded plants from a florist, or grow your own from seed planted the previous spring. Select dwarf, rust-resistant varieties. Or you can start plants in summer for winter bloom by slipping those growing in the summer garden. Whether plants are started from seeds or slips, they should be kept pinched back to encourage winter bloom.

FOLIAGE PLANTS

GENERAL

What temperature is best for foliage plants indoors?   No one temperature is best for all. The majority grow well in night temperature 55° to 60° F. with a rise of 10° in the daytime permitted. For cooler rooms try English Ivy, Leopard-plant, Australian-silkoak, eucalyptus, aspidistra, Babystears, Pick-a-back plant, Strawberry-geranium, Spider-plant, and Norfolk-Island-pine.

Does it help to spray water on the leaves of foliage plants grown in the home?   Daily sprinklings with atomizer syringe benefit all plants having leathery leaves, such as rubber plants, palms, and pandanus. On the mornings of bright, sunny days syringe plants with thin or hairy leaves such as coleus or pilea.

Some people tell me to wash my foliage plants with milk, others to wipe the leaves with olive oil. Which is better?   Both are harmful, they merely result in an artificial gloss due to the oil or to the fat of the milk. When you sponge leaves, use lukewarm, soapy water.

My foliage plants indoors do well in summer, but in fall their leaves turn yellow and drop off. What is the cause?   When artificial heating is used, air becomes too dry for plants. Lack of atmospheric moisture is one cause of failure with house plants. Install humidifiers. Stand plants on shallow trays of sand or gravel kept moist.

Can you give a list of foliage house plants that can easily be raised from seed?   *Eucalyptus globulus* (Blue Gum), *Eucalyptus citriodora* (Lemon-scented Eucalyptus), *Grevillea robusta* (Australian-silkoak), coleus, *Asparagus sprengeri* and *Asparagus plumosus* (asparagus ferns), and *Cordyline indivisa* (*Dracaena indivisa*).

ARALIA

Is Aralia sieboldi a house plant?   An easy subject to grow in a light window where the temperature ranges between 55° and 65° F. Shade from bright summer sunshine is desirable. Water to keep soil always evenly moist but not waterlogged.

How can Aralia sieboldi be raised from seed?   The correct name is *Fatsia japonica*. Sow seed in pots of light, sandy soil in spring; cover seeds to own depth with sifted soil. Keep moist; temperature, 65° F. When an inch or two high, transplant to small pots of sandy soil. Grow in light window.

ASPARAGUS

What kind of soil does Asparagus plumosus like, acid or alkaline? More on acid than alkaline side. It likes a garden soil that has both peat and sand in it (2 parts soil, 1 part peat, 1 part sand); this should be enriched by ⅛ part of bulk of dried cow manure and a pint of bone meal.

What are asparagus "ferns"? Two are commonly grown: *A. plumosus,* with flat sprays of fine foliage, and *A. sprengeri,* with coarser and less regular leaves. These foliage plants are *not really ferns.* Both are subject to red spider, so spray once a week with cool water. Transplant once a year, or whenever pots become filled with roots. They like plenty of light and air. Water regularly and feed once a month. (See next question.)

What are the water requirements of Asparagus sprengeri? Is it the moisture or temperature conditions that turn foliage yellow? *A. sprengeri* likes adequate and regular watering once a day. Once or twice a month substitute liquid manure. Leaves turn yellow from lack of food, if plant is pot-bound, or if temperature is above or below 55° to 65° F.

How do I raise asparagus "ferns" from seed? Very easily. Soak seed in tepid water for 24 hrs. before sowing, then plant 1 in. apart and cover to a depth of ¼ in. in light, sandy soil, in a pot or pan. Keep moist, dark, and in temperature of 65° to 70° F.

ASPIDISTRA

What is the common name for Aspidistra lurida? Parlor palm and cast-iron plant are two common names for the aspidistra.

Why do the leaves of my aspidistra turn yellow? Yellowing leaves mean either red spider mites are sucking the life out of them, that you have watered too much or have exposed plant to extreme drought. If red spider is the trouble, spray or sponge the leaves with any good contact insecticide.

Does the aspidistra plant ever bloom? Old, well-established plants sometimes do. The flowers are relatively inconspicuous, being reddish-brown in color and borne at soil level.

Can aspidistra be increased in any other way than by division? No. In nature it may propagate by seed, but these do not seem to form in cultivation. Divide in spring and keep newly potted divisions in warm room and moist atmosphere until new roots become established.

AUSTRALIAN-SILKOAK

What kind of soil does Australian-silkoak (Grevillea robusta) like?   A sandy and rather peaty mixture that does not tend to become waterlogged. Very heavy soil is unsuited to this plant, particularly in its young stages.

AVOCADO

Should avocado seed be dried before attempting to root it in water? Mine have always formed a slimy coating in water and never rooted.   Do not use water; plant seed in a pot of porous soil; keep moist and in a temperature of 60° to 70° F.

BABYSTEARS

What is the plant called Babystears and how can I grow it in the house?   Babystears, or Creeping-nettle, is *Helxine soleirol,* a native of Corsica and Sardinia. It looks like a fine green moss; grows well in sandy soil, kept moist, in morning sun or very light shade. Easily propagated by pulling apart and setting pieces in soil.

BAY TREE

Are there several varieties of bay trees, and how should they be treated? Mine were given me as a gift. I am at a loss as to how to keep them growing.   There is only one true bay tree. It is not hardy in New York. It eventually grows to large size. Tubbed specimens are best wintered in a cool, light, frostproof cellar.

CAMPHOR

How can a camphor plant be raised?   The camphor tree, (*Cinnamomum camphora*) can be raised from cuttings under a bell glass with bottom heat and a sandy peat medium. But since it grows to tree size and needs a winter temperature of around 55° to 60° F., it is not particularly suitable as a house plant. Camphorosma is a group of small shrubs or herbs with camphorlike odor, some of which are grown in herb gardens. They are not hardy and have to be brought indoors in winter.

CHINESE EVERGREEN

What is the real name of Chinese Evergreen, so often grown indoors in water? What are its requirements?   *Aglaonema modestum* is a very satisfactory house plant for rooms with little sun. Grown in water to which a few small pieces of charcoal have been added to keep the water sweet, it behaves well in average living-room conditions.

COLEUS

Can I dig up coleus plants from the garden and put them into pots for winter decoration indoors? If plants are cut back at time of potting, they may grow into decorative specimens by late winter; but a much better plan is to take cuttings from outdoor plants in August, root them in sand, and pot up to provide young new plants for your indoor garden.

How can coleus be raised as house plants? Mine always become sickly. Coleus are raised from seed or cuttings but are not A-1 house plants. They like full light, temperature not above 55° F. in winter, and careful protection from mealy bugs.

Mealy bugs on my coleus are a constant source of trouble. What shall I do? Mealy bugs on coleus are difficult to eradicate because forceful syringing with water is apt to damage leaves. Try brushing them off with a soft camel's-hair brush dipped in soapy water or denatured alcohol.

CROTON

I have a croton (codiaeum), potted in fibrous loam, but while the plant in general does well, sometimes leaves wilt and drop. What causes this? If plant is growing outdoors, cool spells may be the cause. This plant loves heat and lots of it. Not a good house plant unless high humidity with heat is provided.

CRYPTANTHUS

What is a cryptanthus, and how should it be grown? It is a miniature bromeliad (pineapple relative) that is grown for the beauty of its stiff little leaves. It grows best in a terrarium or in a warm room where air is not too dry. Pot in sandy, humusy soil with charcoal added, or in orchid peat and leafmold mixed.

DUMB CANE

I have a dumb cane (dieffenbachia) in the house and the lower leaves turn yellow. What shall I do? Too low a temperature or lack of moisture in air are commonest causes of yellowing. Excessive dryness at root may be a contributing cause. This plant likes warmth, a moist atmosphere, shade from strongest sunshine, and a fair amount of moisture.

Why is dieffenbachia called dumb cane? Is it poisonous? Not poisonous, but, like its relative, the Jack-in-the-pulpit, it contains sharp crystals of oxalate of lime. If the stem is chewed, these pierce the tongue, causing it to swell with intense pain. Speech may be impossible for several days.

Can a "leggy" dieffenbachia be successfully air-layered? The plant is 30 ins. high?   Cut halfway through, slanting and upward. Insert a toothpick and bind with a large ball of sphagnum moss and keep constantly moist and warm. A thick stem may take a year before it is rooted enough to cut below moss and pot.

HOLLY

I have a dwarf holly plant in a pot. Can it be made to fruit indoors?   Holly is not a house plant, but some species are not hardy except in the South. Most hollies are unisexual and fruit is not possible unless both types (a male plant and a female plant) are grown near each other.

LEOPARD-PLANT

Is the Leopard-plant classed as a foliage or a flowering plant? Like most "foliage plants," *Ligularia kaempferi aureo-maculata* blooms (and the yellow flowers are quite attractive); it is grown primarily for the beauty of its large, rounded leaves, which are conspicuously spotted with yellow markings.

Under what conditions does the Leopard-plant grow best? How is it propagated?   It likes a rather cool room with full sun or partial shade. A freely drained soil, but enough water to keep it always moist. In summer plunge outdoors in a partially shaded position. Propagate by dividing up the old plant in spring.

MANGO

Am raising mango tree from seed. Do you think it will bear? No, it will not. The mango is a large tropical tree that sometimes attains a height of nearly 100 ft. Is only hardy in the most tropical parts of the United States. Fruits of seedling mangoes are very inferior to named varieties.

MARANTA

How should Maranta leuconeura and kerchoveana be cared for?   Marantas, grown chiefly for their unusual foliage, are semi-tropical plants which flourish in a warm greenhouse. However, the maranta does unusually well in farm kitchens where the range and steaming kettles provide the needed humidity. It is often called Prayer Plant because it folds its leaves at night. Keep warm and moist. Use fibrous potting mixture. (See Soil, this section.)

MONSTERA

What is the foliage plant, of climbing habit, with large, heart-shaped, cut leaves? You are probably referring to *Monstera deliciosa* (*Philodendron pertusum*), a very showy foliage plant which looks well in modern rooms and which can be grown in good light without direct sun. Though a climber, it grows rather slowly and is usually treated as a foliage plant, trained on cork bark.

NEPHTHYTIS AFZELI

What are the requirements of nephthytis indoors? Nephthytis is a tropical vinelike foliage plant which usually comes from the florist trained on cork bark. It does not need full sunlight and stands ordinary living-room conditions well. Trailing portions cut from the main plant do well grown on in water.

NORFOLK-ISLAND-PINE

How do we take care of Norfolk-Island-Pine during the summer? *Araucaria excelsa* makes a good but slow-growing pot plant. During the summer sink pot outside in light shade and syringe and water regularly. In winter it wants 55° to 60° F., and even light to keep it shapely. Spray regularly to prevent spider and mealy-bug attack.

I have had an araucaria house plant for the past 4 years. It is now 40 ins. high. The branches are starting to droop. Can you suggest the reason? It is natural for lower branches eventually to droop. If plant is wilting, you have either overwatered or given too much fertilizer with perhaps not enough light and too much heat. Stimulants are not called for when plants droop.

PALM

How shall I take care of date palm? (1) Temperature from 55° to 65° F.; (2) soil—ordinary loam, peatmoss, and sand, proportions 5–3–1; (3) watering—never completely dry but not too wet. Just moist at all times, soaking thoroughly and not again until surface feels firm; (4) exposure—never expose to full sunshine if grown as a pot plant.

Is there any special fertilizer or treatment to give palm trees and how often must they be watered? Palms need full shade and must never be dry, yet not constantly soaking wet. No feeding is needed until pots are full of root.

What possibility is there of growing palms? Palms are good house plants if given shade but full light and are not subjected to dry, hot rooms in winter.

PANDANUS (SCREWPINE)

How should I care for a pandanus plant?   Keep out of bright sunshine and use care in watering. It is easy to kill this plant with overwatering.

My pandanus leaves are turning yellow, especially at the tips. What is the cause?   A sure sign of root trouble; you probably have overwatered. Keep on dry side and don't use too large a pot. Don't expose to bright sunshine.

How should shoots from pandanus be rooted, and when? Cut off the suckers at base and insert in sandy soil. If you can place the pot in a box and cover with a sheet of glass, all the better. Do this in the spring, when growth is active.

PEPEROMIA

How can I grow the striped peperomia successfully? Peperomias require fairly warm, humid conditions and protection from direct sunshine. A humusy soil (well drained), kept uniformly moist, is desirable.

Rooted leaf cutting of Peperomia.

What causes small brown spots on the under side of peperomia leaves?   Spots on the under side suggest injury from thrips or other insects. Poor foliage generally is due either to sunburn, lack of moisture in the atmosphere, or too much water on the leaves.

My peperomia gets large, irregular brown spots on the back of the leaves. Can you tell me why and what to do?   Such spots or patches are usually an indication of disease brought about by atmospheric conditions. These plants do best in a terrarium or a shaded greenhouse. Keep out of the sun.

PICK-A-BACK

What is the Pick-a-back plant? *Tolmiea menziesi,* a native of our Pacific Northwest. It has the curious habit of producing young plantlets on its leaves from which new plants can be grown. It is an interesting, worth-while house plant.

The Pick-a-back plant (Tolmiea menziesi) *is one of the few which forms new plants on the growing leaves instead of by runners.*

How shall I care for the Pick-a-back plant? Grow in pots of light, rich soil. Keep quite moist at all times. Thrives in full sun or part shade. Although a hardy plant, it seems not to object to ordinary room temperature. Propagate by planting well-developed plantlets that are borne on mature leaves.

PINEAPPLE

What can I do with a pineapple plant that is nearly 2 years old and does not seem to grow any more? It stands nearly 8 ins. high now. Doesn't it flower? If a true pineapple, grown from the tuft of the fruit, flowers will not develop. If some other member of the bromeliad family, flowers are apt to be quite attractive. Don't overwater, and give full light. They are naturally slow growers.

What care is needed for the pineapple plant? The true pineapple needs plenty of warmth, light, and sun, and very careful watering, as it quickly resents very wet conditions at the root. Frequent feedings (2 a week) with liquid manure or fertilizer are of great help to a healthy plant.

POMEGRANATE (PUNICA)

Can pomegranates be grown from seed? Yes, they can, and if wanted merely as house plants are quite satisfactory. For fruit production (when they can be grown outdoors) named varieties are used, and these will not come true from seed.

How are pomegranates propagated? By hardwood cuttings planted in open nursery beds in February; by taking rooted shoots directly from base of plant; by layering; by green cuttings taken in summer.

POTHOS

What care is needed for Pothos aureus?   It likes shade, a uniformly moist (but not a boglike) soil, temperature of 60° to 70° F., and occasional sponging of leaves with lukewarm, soapy water. Correct name is *Scindapsus aureus*.

REDWOOD BURL

How long will a redwood burl last? Also can a sprout of it be rooted and grown as a pot plant?   A burl kept with its base in a shallow container of water lived and thrived for many years at the New York Botanical Garden. Sprouts cannot be rooted.

RUBBER PLANT

What care is needed in watering and feeding rubber trees grown as house plants?   *Ficus elastica*, the recognized rubber plant of early days, likes part shade and lots of room, as it eventually becomes very tall, rarely branching. Give plenty of water and food once a month when root-bound.

How does one encourage the rubber plant to branch out, rather than grow as a single upright stem?   *Ficus elastica* is not very responsive to cutting back, but if done after the plant has 6 or 8 leaves, removal of the point will induce 2 or 3 breaks. The natural habit is to grow single stemmed for many years before branching.

Can I cut back large rubber plant when the trunk is thick? *Ficus elastica,* if cut back, may die from the shock if it is treelike and has no lower leaves. The regular method of propagation is to slit the stem partly through, wrap with moss, and keep constantly moist. If your plant has a branch with ½-in. stem, you can so treat the branch, but if there are no branches and the trunk is really heavy, 1 in. or more, it's too large for air-layering.

What is the best way to reduce the height of a long-leaf rubber plant?   Make an upward cut halfway through the stem, insert a toothpick, and wrap with a ball of moss, keeping same damp until roots form. Do this in the spring. It should be ready for severance and potting in about 3 months. Lower part of plant will probably make 2 or 3 new shoots after a while.

What is the name of the rubber plant with leaves that widen out toward the tips? What culture does it need?   This is the Fiddle-leaved Fig (or rubber plant)—*Ficus lyrata,* or *pandurata.*

It requires the same general care as the common rubber plant—
Ficus elastica.

SAGO-PALM

I have a Sago-palm in a pot. It is about 20 years old, but I've
had it only 5 months. It isn't doing well since I brought it inside.
Can you suggest proper care? *Cycas revoluta* likes sunshine
with only moderate shade from strong summer sun. Avoid overwatering but never allow to dry out completely. In fall don't be
alarmed if the lower leaves turn brown and drop. It's natural for
them to go as new ones are produced.

SENSITIVEPLANT

How can I grow a Sensitiveplant in my sunny window?
Sow seeds of *Mimosa pudica* in pot of light soil in March.
Transplant seedlings into 2½-in. pot when second set of leaves is
well grown. Later pot into 4-in. pot. Grow in well-drained soil,
minimum temperature 60° F. Never permit to suffer from dryness.

SNAKE-PLANT

Under what conditions will sansevieria do best? Dry,
moderately warm rooms with full light. Water carefully once a
week. This is enough under ordinary conditions, as it is easily
killed by overwatering.

I can never get the sansevieria to grow and do well. Why?
Too much water and not enough light. This plant, when well
rooted, can go for weeks without water. Shade also is detri-
mental.

My sansevieria plant had flowers on it this summer. Is this
unusual? Not so unusual as is sometimes thought. Old, well-
established specimens are apt to bloom, and once they begin, they
repeat the performance year after year. The flowers are light
greenish, in feathery spikes, and are very fragrant.

How does one increase sansevieria? These are grown from
divisions of roots or rhizomes. Pieces of leaf planted in moist
sand will root and make plants, but if you so treat the variegated
sort, the young plants will come green leaved.

SPIDER-PLANT

Is the Spider-plant a house plant? Yes, it is a species of
chlorophytum (*C. variegatum*). It has green-and-white-striped
leaves and sends out long, slender stems which bear young plants
at their extremities.

STRAWBERRY-GERANIUM

What will encourage growth of Strawberry-geranium? Should it be kept on the dry side? In sun or shade? This is *Saxifraga sarmentosa,* which is almost hardy. Don't try to grow it in a hot, dry room, or it will become infested with red spider. Sun or shade, providing light is good. Moderate supplies of water. If you want runners bearing young plants to develop, grow it in a hanging basket or on a wall bracket.

UMBRELLA-PLANT

What conditions does the feathery green plant called Umbrella-plant require? *Cyperus alternifolius* is really a bog plant and needs a moist or wet soil. It does well if the pot is kept standing in a saucer of water; prefers plenty of sunshine.

How are young plants of the umbrella-plant raised? *Cyperus alternifolius* is easily raised from seeds sown in soil kept constantly moist. Another method of increase is to cut off the leafy top with about an inch of stem attached. When roots have formed, plant in pot of soil.

GIFT PLANTS

AZALEAS

What is the proper soil for azaleas and other ericaceous plants? It must be lime free, definitely acid, and well drained. The addition of liberal amounts of oak leafmold or peatmoss to the mixture is recommended. (See Soil, Acid Potting Mixture, this section.)

How shall I care for a tender azalea after blooming? Keep well watered, in full light, in a room at 50° F. If overlarge for pot, shift to one 1 in. larger, soaking soil well after repotting. Use acid potting mixture. Pot firmly but do not ram earth down hard.

Should I cut back my indoor azaleas, and when? No, merely pinch back any extra-long shoots, but don't prune in the usual way for shrubs or the plants may die. Azaleas make but short growths each year.

What care is needed for an azalea plant grown indoors? Pot azaleas should only be indoors during the winter and while in bloom. From mid-May on pot should be sunk in ground, with light shade, regular watering and spraying, pinching back of overlong growths. A level teaspoonful of ammonium sulfate in a gallon of water twice a month will keep the soil acid. Use a general fertilizer occasionally. Bring indoors before severe frost.

How should I treat my tender azalea after bringing indoors in autumn? Keep just moist, in a light, cool room at 40° F. until 4 weeks before you want full bloom, then bring into warm, sunny room, water plentifully. Give complete fertilizer until color shows on buds.

Should an azalea plant have a rest period during the winter? Yes. After being brought indoors before severe frost, a potted azalea must be kept cool (40° to 60° F.) and just moist until after Christmas. Experts can bloom them at Christmas, but the window gardener should not attempt it.

How can I tell whether my tender azalea is going to bloom? The buds should be well set when brought indoors in the fall.

What is the best way to force growth of evergreen azaleas? Why try to force growth? If outdoor hardy sorts aren't growing well, conditions are not right. Azaleas are slow growers and to force growth by overfeeding, too much shade, or other ways, would mean failure to set buds for next year's bloom.

An Easter azalea plant was put aside and forgotten after blooming until discovered in November, in dry, warm cellar. Is this plant dormant or really dead? An azalea so treated is dead—or it ought to be! Don't waste time on it. Azaleas after flowering need a cool place, moderate water, and good light before being sunk outdoors. The plants that are flowered in pots are practically evergreen and should never be bare of all leaves.

How are greenhouse azaleas propagated? The small-flowered Kurume sorts are easily rooted from cuttings, using the short shoots that come after blooming. Root in sandy soil in a box with a piece of glass on top. The Indica types of azaleas have to be grafted, entailing both skill and hotbed facilities.

I was presented with a fine azalea plant. Why has it shed all its leaves? You either let it get dry at the roots or the foliage became infested with red spider (which see). Both will cause defoliation, and, if complete, the plant cannot be revived.

I have an azalea which I purchased in a florist shop 2 years ago. Last year it bloomed beautifully. Now it is dying. Can you give me any help in the care of the plant? The soil is probably over-alkaline and of a dry nature. Frequent watering and an application every 6 weeks of a solution of 1 tablespoonful of aluminum sulfate to 1 gallon of water should help.

Should I plant outdoors a pink-flowered azalea purchased in a florist's shop? (Vermont.)   If your azalea is small flowered, it is a Kurume, and there's little chance of its surviving a winter outdoors. If large flowered, it is an Indica, and positively will winter kill. If you want garden azaleas, plant sorts listed as such. For correct care of your azalea, see previous questions.

I have a small-flowered and a large-flowered house azalea. Can you tell me what they are?   The small-flowered type is Kurume. The large-flowered is an Indica. There are many named varieties of each type.

CHRYSANTHEMUMS

How long can chrysanthemums be kept flowering indoors? Two weeks is average. Spraying daily with cool water will help to keep foliage fresh looking and prevent its turning brown and dry before the flowers fade. Keep in a cool location.

Are any of the potted chrysanthemums used for gift plants hardy enough to be transferred to the garden?   Yes, those that flower the end of September and early October are usually hardy varieties. The large-flowered kinds at Thanksgiving time are not.

Is there any way to save chrysanthemum plants sent in the fall from the florist? They don't winter over outside.   After blooming, cut stems down, store pot in cool, light cellar or shed. Propagate by cuttings or division in March. Keep potted on or plant in garden in April. Lift in September and bring into very cool sunroom or porch to bloom.

I received a beautiful chrysanthemum plant for Thanksgiving Day. What care should I give it now so that I will be able to keep it and plant it in the spring?   Remove from pot and plant in sheltered corner until spring. Cover lightly with leaves. Flowering at Thanksgiving, it will be too late for garden use but you might repot it in September and bring inside.

How can one best grow mums to bloom during months of November, December, and January? We have the severe cold of Lake Erie and a long winter. Could they be brought into the house when winter comes and so bloom during these months? (New York.)   Pinch plants well in early season. Pot from the garden in early October. Use late varieties. Give a sunny location in a cool room.

CYCLAMEN

Why does cyclamen always die a few days after it comes from

the florist?   The florist grew the plant in a moist atmosphere and temperature 40° to 50° F. Living-room conditions are too warm and dry; however, you should be able to keep the plant for a few weeks if you can find a window where its ideal requirements are more nearly met.

The leaves on the cyclamen I received for Christmas are turning yellow. What caused this?   Sudden change from greenhouse to dry, hot atmosphere of house is responsible. Cyclamen should be kept cool, well watered, and away from too much sunlight. An east or west window is best. At ordinary living-room temperature, watering twice daily may be needed.

How cold is it safe to have cyclamen when flowering, and when not flowering?   At 40° to 45° F. a plant in flower will be far happier and last much longer than in a room of 60° to 70° F. After blooming, gradually dry off and rest in the cellar, or in cold frame outdoors. Repot in July, and with luck you may get the corm to start again.

How shall I water cyclamen plants during their flowering period?   If cyclamens are kept cool enough—40° to 50° F.—they will not dry out quickly. If kept in a hot room, watering freely and frequently may prolong their lives for a week or two, though it will not take the place of a low temperature. Water from below, keeping soil moist but not soggy. (See following question.)

How long must you let a pot of cyclamen soak in a pan of water to wet it thoroughly?   If the water in pan is halfway up the pot and the soil is moderately dry, allow to soak 10 to 15 minutes, then stand in sink to drain off surplus.

Are cyclamens difficult as window garden plants?   Cyclamens are among the most difficult of all plants for the living room. Old bulbs that have blossomed can be dried off and kept dormant in a cool place until July, but it's a 50–50 chance to get them to start up strongly again.

Is it worth while to save cyclamen bulbs over? If so, what care should be given during rest period?   It can be done, but is not generally considered worth while.

Can one keep cyclamens for years, or do they die after they are a year or so old?   Cyclamens seldom are worth keeping after they flower, and it takes about 18 months to get a sizable plant from seed. Bulbs normally go dormant after blooming and frequently refuse to start up again in late summer, but experts carry them in active growth for 2 years. The wild species will live for 20 years or more, and bulbs as large as a plate have been found.

How can I make a cyclamen plant bloom the second year, having got it from a florist when in flower?   Cyclamens are not easy plants to keep over a second year, and even expert gardeners seldom attempt it. Gradually reduce water after flowers finish, but spray regularly to prevent mealy bug and mite attack. When leaves have died down, keep in cool place and quite dry. Shake out in July, and repot in fresh soil and lightly water and spray regularly. Give full light, but shade from sun. If the corms push up leaves freely, all's well; if only 2 or 3 leaves start, don't waste time on them.

How long should a cyclamen bloom?   Cyclamen should flower either in a greenhouse or under favorable home conditions from Christmas-time until March. Eight to 12 weeks is average. Remove faded blooms.

Should faded blooms be removed from cyclamen with a knife or scissors?   Neither. Get a firm grip on the stem of a dead flower or yellowed leaf and give a sharp pull. It comes out cleanly.

How is a cyclamen repotted?   Do not disturb earth about the corm more than is necessary. Place it, with adhering soil, in larger pot, using standard potting mixture. Top of corm should be well above soil level when potting is completed. After potting, soak from below.

I have heard that cyclamens are subject to mite. Can anything be done to prevent them?   Shredded tobacco stems scattered on soil surface, or napthalene flakes sprinkled in saucer of pot may ward off damage from mites.

How can one keep the leaves of cyclamens clean?   Dust can be sponged off, or water can be applied with bulb spray; but constant spraying with insecticide is necessary, otherwise mites and mealy bugs will ruin the plants.

How shall I slip a cyclamen?   Cyclamens cannot be "slipped," but experts sometimes have divided large bulbs in two. The only successful method of raising new plants is from seed, which comes true to color of parent plant, but it requires skill, good facilities, and patience for 18 months.

Can one grow cyclamens from seed? What soil and how long a time before blooming?   Seedlings are easy to start, if seed is sown thinly in July or August; but after that, troubles begin. If you can simulate greenhouse conditions for 18 months, and can keep the plants free of mites and other pests, you might succeed. Even florists usually procure their cyclamens from specialists. They like a compost of good loam, sand, rotted manure, and peatmoss; shade during the summer yet full light; careful watering; high humidity and frequent spraying; and in the fall and winter a temperature not above 55° F.

Why do my seedling cyclamens get only one leaf at a time? Some are over a year old. Cyclamens are specialists' plants, and it is almost too much to expect to grow them from seed in a window when lots of florists don't attempt to raise them, preferring to buy plants when 1 year old and carry on to the blooming stage.

GENISTA

Can anything be done with a genista after it has stopped blooming? Genistas (the greenhouse kinds) are strictly gift plants, not even good house plants for any length of time. They are not hardy outdoors in the vicinity of New York. Keep in a sunny window, water well, and see that there is circulation of air around them. In other words, don't crowd genistas in with a lot of other plants.

HYDRANGEA

Why did my hydrangea die the day after I received it as a gift? The hydrangea does *not* die that quickly. If leaves and flowers wilt, it is suffering from lack of water. Immerse the whole pot in a pail of water for 20 minutes. It will revive immediately.

How long should a hydrangea flower in the house? It should flower not less than 3 weeks. Keep it away from a hot, sunny window and radiators. Water *thoroughly* twice a day.

What care and treatment should be given pot hydrangeas? Florists' hydrangeas are propagated from cuttings in early spring grown on in 4-in. pots which are sunk in the open ground during the summer and well fed. Put into larger pots in September and place in a cold frame with sash but well ventilated. Bring inside before hard freezing and keep in cool cellar 40° F. till late December or January. Give just enough water to prevent drying, but leaves should fall off. Start in full light at 50° F.—never above 60° F. Give plenty of water at all times and lots of light. After blooming, cut back well and carry outside during summer if a large specimen is wanted the next season.

What must I do to make a pot hydrangea bloom in March or April? If you have only room facilities, don't expect to do what florists can't always manage. A hydrangea has to rest, dormant, in a cold cellar until late December. Start up at 50° F. and never above 60° F. Grow it cool, or you'll have a blind plant.

Will pot hydrangeas bloom again?   Yes. Cut back a bit and keep watered till safe to sink pot outdoors. Feed and water in full sun to encourage growth. Bring indoors before hard frost and induce rest by coolness and very little water. Start up again in January. Give full light but little water at first. Temperature never should be above 60° F.

Can my hydrangea be planted in the garden after it has stopped flowering?   Yes. After it has finished blooming, cut back stems about half their length, remove plant from pot, and plant in garden where it will have plenty of room. It will grow into a big, shrubby plant. Water well.

I would like to know something about hydrangeas. Are they hardy?   The florists' hydrangeas are hardy, but in areas where hard freezing occurs the wood is killed to the ground. If you have a variety that will bloom on the new wood, well and good. If not, and the wood is killed back, you'll never see any flowers. Such kinds have to be kept in pots and brought indoors and rested during the winter.

Twice I have purchased plants of Hydrangea Bluebird, and after potting, new shoots appeared, but in a week or two the plants died. The potting mixture had a pH of about 4.5. Temperature, watering, and light conditions apparently perfect. What was wrong?   If you bought actively growing young plants, why not in pots? Who told you to use such extremely acid soil? No variety comes truly blue unless the soil is neutral or on the acid side. Some sorts come blue more readily than others, but you undoubtedly overdid the acidity. Unless your soil is naturally alkaline, forget the pH stuff and use a good rich compost.

What element is it that makes the hydrangea flowers blue?   Acidity of soil causes blue flowers, but some varieties come blue more readily than others. Repeated watering with alum solution or aluminum sulfate (1 level teaspoon to 1 gal. of water) will cause blueness.

JERUSALEM-CHERRY

Why do leaves and berries fall off a Jerusalem-cherry soon after I receive it?   If your house is hot, Jerusalem-cherry will not survive. It likes a cool room (about 50° F.), plenty of water, and a location away from chills or drafts. Spraying the leaves daily may help. It is a poor house plant.

How shall I treat a Jerusalem-cherry after it has fruited? Unless you want to grow a big specimen, throw the plant away. Old plants can be cut back a little, kept on dry side until spring, then shifted into a larger pot and stood outdoors with slight shade during the summer. Give plenty of water and feed; bring indoors in September.

When shall seed of Jerusalem-cherries be sown for Christmas coloring? Sow seed in January or February. Grow on in pots and plant outdoors in late May. Lift carefully with ball in September, pot, and shade till established, then place in a bright window or greenhouse. Selected types can be raised from cuttings taken early in the year.

ORNAMENTAL PEPPER

How can ornamental peppers be kept small and full of blooms as you see them in the markets? Raise from seed annually and grow in full light. You can't expect plants grown in a window to equal those grown in a greenhouse, but pinching several will induce bushiness. Plant outside for the summer and pot up in August. Grow in temperature of 50° to 60° F.

POINSETTIA

Why do the leaves of a poinsettia turn yellow and drop continually? Poinsettias are heat lovers. They thrive outdoors in the summer but want a temperature of about 60° F. constantly after early September. If you can't give them high humidity with a temperature not much higher or lower than 60°, leaves will drop. Possibly plants became chilled or were in a draft.

Will my poinsettia bloom again? How should it be treated? Keep dry after it has bloomed and stand in cellar. Cut back halfway in May, and water. Give full light. Sink pot in ground outdoors in June, and keep watered and fed. Bring indoors end of August, and give sunny window and lots of water. Night temperature has to be 58° to 62° F., not lower or higher, or leaves will drop and it will not flower.

Will a poinsettia that has bloomed, bloom the next winter? For 2 years I have pruned mine and it grows beautifully green but does not bloom. Old plants will bloom the following year if conditions are right, but the plants grow large and will not tolerate severe pruning. If you don't give the right temperature— 60° F. from September on, with full sun, it will not flower.

I carried over a poinsettia last year and it made good growth but never bloomed. What was wrong?   One cause is keeping it near a light at night. The poinsettia is a "short-day" plant, and if placed in a room where the lights are on several hours every evening, it won't bloom.

I raised a poinsettia this summer in a pot in the yard and brought it in the house in October. Just as the buds for the blooms started, they dried up and fell off. I saw some fine web. Has some minute insect done the damage?   Bring indoors earlier if in your section it gets cool at night after August. The web suggests red spider. Regular spraying is needed to prevent this and mealy-bug attack.

Why do my poinsettias, cut back and nursed through the summer, have only a few petals to each flower?   Poinsettias will grow well outdoors during the summer, but if after late August you can't keep a steady temperature of 60° F., the leaves will drop, and if the temperature is 70° F. or more, poor or no flowers result.

After bringing in poinsettias from a summer in the garden (in September), how can one "hold them back" from blooming until about Christmastime?   Yours is an exceptional case. The trouble with most people is to get them to flower. Temperature should not be above 60° F. at night. Too high a temperature will cause premature, poorly developed blooms.

I brought some dormant poinsettias from California in May, planted them, and they grew; when cold weather came, I carefully potted them. Why did they wither and die?   Poinsettias in growth won't tolerate root disturbance.

If you cut poinsettias close to the soil, will they sprout again?   Poinsettias may be cut back 2/3 while quite dormant, but when actively growing no cutting back should be practiced unless the young shoots are to be rooted as cuttings.

When and how does one make cuttings from poinsettias and grow them into blooming plants?   After blooming, the plants are allowed to rest. Keep quite dry until May, then cut back and start in a warm temperature. The cuttings are taken off when 4 to 6 ins. long and rooted in sand between June and August— the latter date for small plants. They need a greenhouse to grow successfully.

Should poinsettia cuttings be started in part sand? What temperature is needed?   Short 4- to 6-in. cuttings will root either in plain sand or a sandy soil. Successful growers use bottom heat at 70° F. with high humidity. They can be rooted outdoors in June or July if in a closed box with glass on top.

ROSES

Are roses good house plants?   As a general rule, no. Some of the miniature ones, such as *Rosa rouletti,* Tom Thumb, or Pixie will do fairly well. The gift plants received at Eastertime will flower for about 2 weeks and then should go into the garden. While indoors, spray the foliage daily with tepid water and give the soil plenty of moisture.

Some of the buds failed to open on the rosebush I received at Eastertime. Can anything be done to prevent this if I get another next year?   Don't let the soil dry out, spray the foliage daily, and keep the plant in a sunny window, turning it around each day so that it will receive sun equally on all sides.

Are the climbing rosebushes hardy which I received in flower last Easter?   Yes. After they have finished blooming, prune off dead flowers, remove from pot, and plant in a sunny location in enriched soil.

SHRIMP-PLANT

What exposure does Shrimp-plant like?   Shrimp-plants like plenty of sun, so keep them in a sunny window. Do not keep too near a radiator, as they should not dry out. They need plenty of water. This is a fine house plant, untroubled by any insect pests.

What will I do with my Shrimp-plant when it gets tall and leggy?   Cut the plants back each spring and root cuttings for new plants to bring indoors in the fall. Cuttings will root easily, either in pots of sand or in a cold frame.

Can Shrimp-plant be wintered in a cold frame?   No, it is too soft and will die, even with protection. Even at a temperature of 45° shrimp-plant is unhappy. It grows best at 55° to 60° F.

Can you tell me the native habitat of Shrimp-plant and any legend or general information about the plant and its care? *Beloperone guttata* comes from tropical America. There are no legends, as it was practically unknown except to botanists up to 1905. Some of the species were discovered over 100 years ago.

SHRUBS

AZALEA. See Gift Plants.

CAMELLIA

How should a camellia plant be grown?   If in a pot, stand in light shade in open in summer. Bring in in September. Night temperature should be 50° F. It requires sun. Keep soil always moist, but not waterlogged. In spring, after blooming, repot or top-dress as necessary. Feed once a week when good growth is being made.

When should I pot my camellia and in what soil mixture? Never repot unless soil is obviously unsuitable or unless pots are crowded with roots. Do this as soon as flower buds have set. Soil should consist of good loam, leafmold, sharp sand, with some bone meal and dried cow manure added. After potting, spray frequently with clear water. Avoid overwatering.

What about pruning camellias?   Only prune sufficiently to keep plant shapely. Thin crowded plants by removing weak growths. Cut back any long, straggly shoots. Do this immediately after flowering. Remember flowering shoots for following year arise from base of flower; to cut back flowering shoots destroys following year's bloom.

How can the buds be kept from falling off a camellia plant? It was just loaded with buds when I took it in this fall and all but 3 fell off.   Indoor camellias ordinarily lose buds: (1) because the indoor temperature is too high and the atmosphere too dry; (2) lack of sufficient moisture; (3) lack of light.

Can a camellia be grown in the house? How old must it be to bloom?   Camellias are not satisfactory house plants unless, perhaps, you can keep them in a cool sunroom. In wintertime they are harmed by temperature higher than 50° to 60° F. Plants often bloom when quite young—3 or 4 years old.

Indoor camellia plant has conditions in my home similar to gardenias. Is this right? Is it a sun-loving plant? (New York.) Camellias need cooler growing conditions than the florists' gardenia. They enjoy sunshine and a free circulation of air. It is important that the soil be always reasonably moist.

Can one start camellias from a bud in the winter?   Not from a flower bud. Camellias are propagated by cuttings, grafting, and layering. July is a good time to take cuttings. (See Propagation—Section II.)

What are the best varieties of camellias for growing indoors? Alba Plena (white), Donkelaari (red and white), Sarah Frost (light red), Candidissima (white), Compt de Gomer (pink), Debutante (flesh pink).

CITRUS FRUITS

What sort of potting soil shall I use for citrus fruit trees grown as house plants? A standard potting mixture. (See Soil, this section.)

GRAPEFRUIT

Have a grapefruit tree grown from seed, now 10 years old, 8 to 10 ft. tall, in good condition. I plant it out of doors during the summer and in a wooden tub in the winter. Why has it never bloomed? Seedling grapefruits are capricious as to time of blooming, particularly when grown as house plants. In winter they should be grown in cool temperature, 40° to 50° F., and light, airy conditions.

LEMON

Can you give me information about indoor culture of dwarf Ponderosa Lemon trees? Type of soil, exposure, room temperature? Soil should be rich, rather coarse, and well drained. Expose to maximum sunshine. Night temperature should be 45° to 50° F. with a 5° to 15° rise permitted in daytime. Plunge plant (pot and all) in outdoor garden bed in summer.

Will a lemon tree planted from seed ever bloom without grafting? Is about 5 ft. tall, trunk diameter 1½ ins. It may bloom with age. Seedlings often take many years from time of seed sowing until they bear flowers.

What fertilizer could I use to feed a lemon tree? Any complete commercial fertilizer will be satisfactory. It is not necessary to select one having a particular analysis. Fertilizers of organic origin are to be preferred to non-organic materials.

ORANGE

What is the correct care for orange trees? Temperature and fertilizer? Can they be grown as other house plants with success? Essentially the same as for grapefruits and lemons. See replies to inquiries on these subjects. The plants grow well as house plants, but often they fail to bloom or develop fruits.

How can I treat an orange tree, as a house plant, to always have oranges on it? Don't expect the impossible. Oranges of all kinds, including the dwarf Otaheite (inedible sort), need lots of light and to be kept free of insect pests. Plant the pot outdoors in summer, as this may induce flowers to set fruit.

Why do blossoms on dwarf orange and lemon trees drop and bear no fruit?   Lack of light, or improper water relations within the plant (due to unsatisfactory environment) is probably responsible. Take care the plant is not kept too dry when flowers and fruits are developing.

Can a small orange tree, grown from a seed, be grafted to bear? If so, how?   Yes. The operation should be done in spring. A whip graft is probably best. For details read discussion on grafting, Section II.

What varieties of citrus fruits can be grown as pot plants? Ponderosa lemon, Otaheite orange (inedible), Satsuma and Kumquat orange.

CRAPEMYRTLE

Could a crapemyrtle be grown in a tub like an oleander? Outdoors in summer, indoors during the cold months?   Yes, very easily. Store it in wintertime in a frostproof place and at that season keep soil very nearly dry.

GARDENIA

Can gardenias be grown as house plants?   *Gardenia veitchi* (the one that blooms in winter and early spring) is not adapted for house culture. Much more suitable is the summer-flowering *Gardenia florida*.

What type soil do gardenias thrive best in—acid or alkaline? Acid, very definitely. A pH of 4.5 is generally considered best. Chlorosis (yellowing of the foliage) results from alkaline-soil conditions.

Can you recommend a good soil mixture for gardenias? Two parts mellow loam, 1 part peatmoss, ½ dried cow manure, ½ sharp sand. To this add a 4-in. pot of bone meal and a heaping tablespoonful of iron sulfate (copperas) to each bushel.

What kind of food should be given gardenias?   A 4–12–4 fertilizer is recommended. Particularly suitable are fertilizers that provide nitrogen in the form of ammonia such as tankage, dried blood, and sulfate of ammonia.

The gardenia that I received for Christmas had developed yellow leaves at the tips of the shoots. What is the trouble?   This is a deficiency of iron. To prevent as well as cure, apply ½ teaspoon of iron sulfate to the soil and water thoroughly. To keep the plant growing, apply ½ teaspoon of 4–12–4 or 5–10–5 every 6 weeks. Never apply lime.

When is the best time to repot my gardenia house plant? It appears pot-bound to me. Any time from April to August inclusive that the plants show evident need of this attention. The final pots should be filled with roots before winter begins.

When and how should gardenias be pruned? Pruning of the florists' *Gardenia veitchi* consists of "stopping" (pinching out the tips) growing shoots each time they attain a length of 6 ins. or so from spring to mid-August.

What causes gardenias to dry up? The leaves become brittle and drop off and the plant seems to be dead. I've had 3 plants do the same. Gardenias, and particularly the variety grown by florists for decorative purposes, need high atmospheric humidity. This cannot be provided in the house and is one of the major causes of failure.

What is the correct application of water to the gardenia? Because of varying environmental factors, no exact answer is possible to your question. *Gardenia veitchi* must never be subjected to dryness at the root. The Capejasmine (*Gardenia florida*) is kept rather on the dry side during winter.

Any helpful suggestions for gardenias in this climate? (Connecticut.) Only variety recommended if you have no greenhouse is *Gardenia florida*. Grow as tub plant, storing in winter in light cellar or sun porch at temperature of 45° to 50° F.; place outdoors, in sunny position, in May. Water freely and feed during summer. Bring in before killing frost. Keep much drier in winter.

I have a beautiful gardenia bush. In summer it bloomed. Now, indoors, the buds turn black and yellow at bottom and don't get larger. Why? It has loads of buds, but they never get to bloom. (New Jersey.) If your plant is *Gardenia florida* (Capejasmine), it should be wintered in a cool, light, frostproof place. Dwelling-house atmosphere is too dry for gardenias.

How would I treat a gardenia plant that was hit by frost or cold air in house? If severely damaged, it probably won't recover. If damage consists only of moderate injury to leaves, keep in warm place. Water with great care, so that soil is not kept in saturated condition, and lightly spray branches with atomizer 2 or 3 times daily.

I have 2 lovely gardenia plants, one with 17 buds and the other with 7. I also started 6 small plants. How can I produce large blooms like the florists do? The variety *veitchi* thrives only under expert care in carefully controlled greenhouses. You are probably growing *Gardenia florida,* which naturally has much smaller flowers.

Year-old gardenia plant has never bloomed. Would sinking the pot in ground outdoors in summer help?   Plunging outdoors is a satisfactory procedure with the Capejasmine (*Gardenia florida*). *Gardenia veitchi* is best grown in a greenhouse with high temperature and high atmospheric humidity.

How do you make gardenias bloom?   No simple method can be given. You must provide conditions that are to the plant's liking, so that it grows vigorously and ripens its wood satisfactorily. (Read replies to other inquiries about gardenias.)

I have a beautiful gardenia which I raised from a flower. It blooms almost constantly. I think it should rest more. What care should it have?   We know of no gardenia that blooms throughout the year. *Gardenia florida* (Capejasmine) blooms over a long summer period. It is rested by being kept cool and nearly dry in winter.

Can limbs be cut off a gardenia plant and rooted, and, if so, when is the best time?   Large branches that have become woody are not suitable material for propagation. Cuttings of the young terminal shoots that are firm but not hard and woody are started in winter and spring. (See following question.)

What is the most successful way to root gardenia cuttings? They are not easy to handle unless greenhouse facilities are available. Cuttings 3 or 4 nodes long are inserted in sand or sand and peatmoss from December to March. The sand is maintained at a temperature of 75° to 80° F. and the surrounding atmosphere 70°. A humid atmosphere is necessary.

What are the white, woolly insects that cluster on my gardenia? How to kill them?   Mealy bugs, one of the worst pests of this plant. Wash them off with a forceful stream of water, or with a sponge dipped in soapy water to which Black Leaf 40 is added at teaspoonful to a gallon.

Are there different kinds of gardenias?   Yes, those commonly grown by the florist, and unadaptable as house plants, include *veitchi,* Hadley, and Belmont. The only kind really useful to the home gardener is *Gardenia florida* (more correctly but more rarely called *G. jasminoides*).

HIBISCUS

How shall I care for hibiscus house plant?   Presumably you have the Chinese Hibiscus. If so, prune plant back hard in spring and repot in any good, well-drained soil. Spray lightly with water each sunny day. Keep soil moist but not waterlogged. Give full sunshine. In winter keep soil just moist in temperature about 50° F.

I have a Chinese Hibiscus growing in a pot, as the cold here would kill it if I planted it outside. What is the best plan for keeping it safe all winter?   Keep in a light cellar or sunroom where the temperature is not less than 40° F. nor more than 50° F. Give only sufficient water to prevent soil drying out completely.

HYDRANGEA. See Gift Plants.

LANTANA

How are lantanas handled to bloom in winter?   Buy small plants in summer and sink the pots in soil out of doors until autumn. Bring in before danger of frost. *Do not repot* at this time. Keep in a cool, sunny window or sun porch at not more than 60° F. Give water sparingly at first, then more water and liquid manure. They should start into fresh bloom in December or January. In spring, repot in standard potting mixture (see Soil, this section), and sink outdoors in garden bed. If winter bloom is desired a second year, keep summer bloom pinched back. It would be better, however, to buy new small plants for winter bloom. See next question for usual way of handling lantanas in winter.

I have a weeping lantana. When does it bloom?   Lantanas are naturally summer-to-fall bloomers. Must be brought indoors after September. Keep moderately dry and cool throughout winter. Cut back and give more water and warmth from March on; plant out in late May.

OLEANDER

How can oleanders be grown successfully in tubs?   Prune back old growths and top-dress in spring and increase temperature and water supply. Feed occasionally in growing season. Give full sun. After midsummer keep somewhat drier. Store in winter in light, cool, frostproof place and keep nearly dry. Spray to keep clean of scale and mealy bugs.

My oleanders look perfectly healthy, but never bloom. I keep them on a glass-enclosed porch in the winter and around an outdoor birdbath in summer. What else do they need?   This is often due to insufficient ripening of the wood. To induce ripening, make sure plant has ample light and air and rather dry conditions at the root after the season's growth is completed.

FERNS

SOIL AND FERTILIZER

What soil is recommended for indoor ferns?   Mix together 2 parts good loam, 2 parts leafmold, 1 part sand, ¼ part dried cow manure, ¼ part broken charcoal, and add ¾ of a pint of bone meal to each bushel.

What is the best fertilizer for ferns?   There are many good commercial preparations on the market now. Plant tablets, dry commercial fertilizers, or liquid commercial fertilizers are all satisfactory if used according to manufacturer's directions. Liquid manure is always good; some growers prefer sheep manure.

Do vitamin tablets for ferns really do much good?   No. Although many claims (supported by unscientific observations) have been made to this effect, both practical growers and scientists are now satisfied that green plants are able to manufacture all the vitamins they need for their own use.

PLANTING

Should house ferns have large, roomy pots or do they prefer to be pot-bound? How deep should plant be set in soil?   Most plants thrive in pots just large enough. Too-big containers allow overabundance of food and water, resulting in plant indigestion. Let crown of plant be level or just a little above soil level. Allow 1-in. space above soil to receive water.

Is good soil enough or is it necessary to provide additional drainage for ferns?   Although moist soil conditions are appreciated, drainage must be perfect for ferns. Soil should be porous, there should be an inch or more of cinders over broken crock in the bottom of the pot, and finally ferns should not stand in a saucer or jardiniere in which water has been allowed to collect.

How often should ferns be repotted?   Usually not oftener than once a year. Divide, if necessary, and always give them fresh soil. Young ferns that have filled their pots with roots by July may need a second potting but should not be divided.

When is the best time to divide and replant an old Boston-fern?   In spring, just as new growth is beginning. Select younger and stronger crowns from outside of the plant for replanting rather than old woody interior parts.

CARE

Are there any tricks to watering ferns? Soil should never be allowed to bake out nor be kept constantly soggy. Keep soil medium-moist and when water is given, soak ball of roots and soil thoroughly. Never apply water in a stream heavy enough to settle in heart of the plant. The best way is to immerse pot in pail or tub of water, then allow to drain before replacing in saucer.

Do ferns like plenty of sunlight? Ferns prefer light but not direct sunlight. In fact, too much sun may be the cause of a sickly, light-green appearance.

What window is best (in house) for ferns? An east, west, or north window, or any place within a room where they receive plenty of light but not direct sunlight.

CULTURE

Is there a general routine for keeping ferns looking bright and crisp? Dry leaves form on my ferns right away. Probably lack of moisture either in the soil or air. Water regularly and keep away from radiators, in temperature above 55° F. When buying a new fern, look for a young one that has not been growing in a greenhouse too long.

How should ferns be cared for in the city apartment? Use same procedure as care of ferns in a house. They do not like direct sun and want plenty of light; moisture in air and soil, warmth, and to be kept away from drafts. Choose only the thriftiest ferns for apartment conditions, such as Rabbitfoot, Holly, and Birdsnest.

Will it help my fern to cut off fronds that have turned brown at the tip or have been broken off? Cut off brown or damaged fronds. Ferns must have plenty of room, for fronds are easily damaged either from close contact with other plants or people brushing past them.

Should one cut the runners on ferns grown in the house? A friend told me to cut them off my fern, and it doesn't seem to be growing so well since I did it. By all means cut the runners off house ferns. They never develop into fronds and only take strength from the rest of the plant. Perhaps your fern needs repotting in fresh soil.

What special care should be given a house fern to produce luxuriant foliage? Mine has a tendency to turn yellow fre-

quently. Is it possible the pot is too small?   Yes, it is possible the pot is too small. (See previous questions.)

Will ferns do well in a Wardian case or terrarium?   Yes, many of them do better there than in the average living room. Pteris ferns are especially good for terrariums, the small rock ferns or polypodium, small Hollyferns, and possibly the Maidenhair.

Should ferns (house plants) be put outside during the summer?   Many ferns benefit from being plunged (planted nearly to the rims of the pots) in an outdoor bed of ashes in a shady spot during the hottest months.

What causes the fronds of ferns to turn brown and fall off? This may be due to people passing by and injuring tips. It may also be due to growing conditions: too small a pot, too low temperature, too hot or too dry atmosphere, lack of water in soil, poor drainage. Check up on conditions.

How can I save my fern, just ordinary house fern, after an overdose of tablet fertilizer?   Obviously, roots were burned from an overdose of fertilizer. Better charge it up to experience and start over with a new fern.

I left a fern in an unheated room and it froze. What can I do for it?   If only tops and not roots were frozen, tops should be cut off and roots repotted in fresh soil to encourage new top growth. If roots as well as tops were frozen, plant is a total loss.

BOSTON

What is the proper care for a Bostonfern?   Provide any good, well-drained soil, plenty of water, air, light (but not direct sunlight), and humidity in the atmosphere (steam-heated rooms are likely to be too dry). They love warmth and should never be where temperature drops below 55° F.

My Bostonfern does not send out sprouts, only long stems, and very few leaves. Should it get fertilizer in the form of cow manure?   Cut off long stems, or runners, which do not turn into fronds and only take strength from plant. If otherwise healthy, diluted liquid cow manure may be given once a month. (For other cultural directions, see previous questions.)

How should lace ferns be grown?   Probably you mean Whitman Fern, a sport of the Bostonfern. It needs essentially the same care as the common Bostonfern, but special care must be taken to keep any dead leaflets picked off and to prevent water lodging in the centers of the plants.

Mold is beginning to show around the topsoil of my fernery in which are several plants of the common Bostonfern. What does the soil need? Mold seems to indicate that the drainage is poor or that you are not providing sufficient ventilation. Are there drainage holes in the bottom of fernery and an inch of broken crock or cinders under soil? Better change soil and pay attention to drainage when repotting.

Why does a crossbred (Ostrich-Boston) fern revert back to Boston type? Your fern is a somewhat unstable "sport" from the Bostonfern. Such mutants often tend to revert to type. Unless the typical Bostonfern fronds are cut out, they will eventually displace the weaker-growing type.

HOLLYFERN

Is there such a plant as a Hollyfern? The Hollyfern is a cyrtomium. Its fronds are divided into small leaflets each one resembling a holly leaf in outline. It is one of the best ferns for the house and grows steadily. In summer, put it outdoors in a shady spot.

MAIDENHAIR

What are the best growing conditions in the house for the Maidenhairfern? Maidenhairfern is one of the most difficult to grow in the house. It likes a porous soil that contains plenty of humus, and more moisture in the air than is usually found in any house. A temperature of about 65° F. and shade from direct sunlight are necessary. A terrarium is most likely to provide the requisite conditions.

PTERIS

What is the best time to pot, and what is the best fertilizer for greenhouse pteris? Several varieties are available, all generally known as "table ferns." They grow rapidly under favorable conditions and should be repotted into the next size pot whenever their containers become filled with roots. Liquid manure or any good plant food, applied once a month to well-rooted specimens, is sufficient.

RABBITFOOT

How should Rabbitfootfern be cared for? Rabbitfootfern can stand higher temperature and drier air than any of the other house ferns. Should do well in the average living room. Keep it out of direct sunlight but see that it has plenty of light. Like all ferns, it needs a porous soil and plenty of moisture and should be kept away from drafts.

PROPAGATION

How are ferns propagated from the spores on the back of the leaves? The average person may find it difficult to do. Take a piece of soft brick and a clay saucer. Sterilize these by baking. Stand brick in saucer and wet thoroughly. Scatter spores over surface of brick. Keep a little water in saucer and cover with glass, leaving slight opening at bottom for ventilation. Keep in diffused light, temperature 60° to 70° F. First growth of fern looks like green scales.

Is it safe to divide fern plants? Yes, but not oftener than once a year. New crowns or heads which have sprung up around the original crown can be pulled or cut off gently and each piece potted in a pot of suitable size. Probably the original plant can go back into the same pot with fresh soil.

DISEASES AND PESTS

See Section VIII.

When ferns have black specks on the under side, is that fungi? If these black or brown specks appear in even lines or regular pattern on the under sides of the leaves, they contain the spores by which ferns reproduce themselves. They are not harmful to the plant.

My Swordfern has little black spots on stems. Is it a disease? If these black spots are on the stems, not on the back of the leaves, they are a scale insect. If it is a scale, half a teaspoon of kerosene to a quart of soapy water makes a good spray. Or purchase a whale-oil preparation and use according to directions. If there are only a few scales, hand pick them with a toothpick.

VARIETIES

What are the best ferns for indoor culture? Bostonfern (and its several variations), Hollyfern, Birdsnestfern, and pteris ferns. All of these will thrive in the average home if given reasonable attention.

Is Ostrich-plume-fern all right for the house? The native woods Ostrich Fern (*Pteretis struthiopteris*) is hardy and not suitable for indoor culture. If by Ostrich-plume-fern you mean one of the feathery Bostonfern types, it is a suitable house plant.

VINES

WHAT TO GROW

Will most vines do better in a conservatory than in the house?

Yes, if ideal conditions and care are given; yet remarkably good results are obtainable in the house with vines that are adapted to such conditions; this group is by no means a small one.

What kind of house plants grow long and trailing, in addition to ivy and philodendron? *Cissus antarctica* (Kangaroo-vine) is one of the best and longest growing; Grape-ivy, pothos, tradescantia (wanderingjew), and sweet potato.

What vines grow best in a light window? Can they be grown in water? Ivy, philodendron, and tradescantia are stand-bys to grow in water. They do not need sun. Pothos and nephthytis will grow in either water or soil. Grape-ivy and *Cissus antarctica* (Kangaroo-vine) do well in soil.

What are the names of vines that will grow in water in the house? In a light place: English Ivy, philodendron, tradescantia, pothos, nephthytis, passion vine, sweet potato. In sun: trailing coleus and *Zebrina pendula,* a large-leaved wanderingjew whose leaves are purple on the under side and silver-striped on the upper.

What vines are best for a city apartment? The thriftiest vines are philodendron, pothos, *Cissus antarctica,* with Grape-ivy a close runner-up.

What about growing vines indoors in water? Should the water be plain or are there solutions which should be added? Many vines grow satisfactorily in water—plain water plus small piece of charcoal to keep water sweet. Don't disturb roots by changing the water; simply add more as needed.

Is it safe to use foliage vines to frame the sides of a sunny south window used for other house plants? Yes, if the foliage vines are not kept in the direct sunlight of the window but are fastened or trained to the window frame facing in toward the room.

How should the leaves of vines be kept clean? Spray vigorously once a week with cool water on both the upper and the under sides of the leaves. This not only prevents insects but keeps the foliage fresh looking. Or sponge leaves with soapy water occasionally.

Can any vines be grown from seed for use indoors? Morningglory, especially the Japanese ones and Heavenly Blue; Black-eyed-susan-vine (*Thunbergia alata*), Cup-and-saucer-vine (*Cobaea scandens*), Canary-bird-vine (*Tropaeolum peregrinum*).

How should Boston-ivy be cared for in the house? True

Boston-ivy is *Parthenocissus tricuspidata*. This is a large-leaved vine which drops its leaves every autumn. It is an outdoor, not an indoor, vine.

CREEPING FIG

Can you suggest a creeping vine that will cling to a masonry wall behind a small pool in a sunroom?   The Creeping Fig (*Ficus pumila*) will suit your purpose. It is small leaved, intensely green, and makes a flat mat against the wall, up which it creeps. A variegated variety is also available.

ENGLISH IVY

How can hardy ivy be grown in the house?   Keep in cool, light place, away from radiators and direct sunlight. Spray foliage once a week with cold water to keep clean and free from dust and red spider. Keep soil moist; feed monthly with pinch of complete fertilizer. It also grows well in water.

Does an ivy require sunshine when grown indoors?   No. Ivy should not be in direct sun. It does need good light. North window preferable.

We have been unsuccessful in keeping ivy cuttings alive over the winter in the house in water. What is the proper method? Glass container best; be sure to have piece of charcoal in the water so that it will stay sweet and not have to be changed; add water as needed. A light but not sunny place is preferred.

My ivy, grown in water in the light, dries up and dies. How may this be remedied?   The location is either too sunny and hot, or the plant has red spider. Spray both sides of leaves vigorously with cool water once a week. Keep in a light but not sunny place.

What is the best method of starting indoor ivy?   Cuttings, rooted in water. Take tip ends of ivy, having at least 4 mature leaves. Remove 2 lower leaves and stand in water. Longer stems may be used but leaves must be removed from as much stem as is under water.

Why do the leaves of ivy turn yellow?   Too much sunshine perhaps, a too hot and dry atmosphere, or soil too dry.

My ivy (indoor) has a brown scale on its leaves. What causes this?   Brown scale is an insect. Most effective control is to sponge leaves and stems with soapy water to each gallon of which is added 1½ teaspoonfuls of Black Leaf 40. If necessary, use a soft toothbrush to remove scale from stems.

How can variegated ivy be grown successfully? Variegated ivies should be grown in north windows only, or in eastern exposures if shaded by larger plants. Good soil, moderate watering, and spraying of the foliage once a week to keep it clean are of basic importance.

I have a green-and-white variegated ivy. As the new leaves come out the old ones turn brown and die, beginning on one side. Why? Probably due to too much sun. Keep in a north window. Check other general factors: soil, watering, and cleanliness of foliage, for additional causes.

What are some unusual and hardy types of English Ivy for indoor culture? Baby Ivy (*Hedera helix minor*), two variations of Pittsburgh Ivy, Merion King and Little Beauty, *H. helix cordata* with rather large heart-shaped leaves, *H. helix palmata*, *H. helix digitata*, and *H. helix marginata*. Try local greenhouses for unusual types.

What are best kinds of English Ivy for indoor culture? The standard English Ivy (*Hedera helix*) and the Pittsburgh Ivy are the two thriftiest kinds. Many variations have been developed but their availability depends on local market.

GRAPE-IVY

I have a trailing house plant that looks like poison ivy. What is its name and of what country is it a native? *Cissus rhombifolia* (it used to be called *Vitis rhombifolia*). Its common name is Grape-ivy and it is a native of northern South America.

Is the Grape-ivy a satisfactory house plant? Yes, it is splendid and will thrive with any reasonable care in a warm room. It appreciates sunshine except for shade from the intensest of summer sunshine, a good rich soil, free drainage, adequate supplies of water, and feeding when pot-bound.

Is Grape-ivy a form of English Ivy? No. Grape-ivy is *Cissus rhombifolia*, which is quite different in appearance from English Ivy (*Hedera helix*). Its leaves are made of three leaflets while those of the English Ivy are merely lobed. It is less subject to insect pests than English Ivy and usually looks well longer.

GERMAN-IVY

I have seen German-ivy grown indoors in ferneries. Is this a difficult house plant? No, *Senecio scandens* does well in window boxes or fern stands, in full diffused light and without direct sun. Plant in standard potting mixture to which charcoal has been added to keep soil sweet. When growing well, water weekly with liquid manure. Cuttings root easily in moist sand.

KENILWORTH-IVY

Can I grow Kenilworth-ivy as an indoor vine?   Yes, this dainty little vine (*Cymbalaria muralis*) with its violet flowers and leaves tinted with red beneath, grows well in a sunny window if the atmosphere is not too dry. It requires standard potting soil. Often it will seed itself in the soil about the base of other pot plants.

KANGAROO-VINE

Does Kangaroo-vine (*Cissus antarctica*) make a good house plant?   Yes, this is one of the toughest and least temperamental of house vines. It does not object to living-room temperatures. New plants can be propagated from cuttings.

MYRTLE

Will myrtle grow indoors?   Yes, it will, but it must be sprayed, without fail, once a week with cool water to ward off red spider, its greatest handicap to growing well indoors. It does not like too warm a location. Myrtle will root and grow in water, or larger plants may be potted in soil.

PASSION-FLOWER

Would passion-flower grow in the house during the winter months? Should it be cut back before being brought in?   Passion-flower (*Passiflora*) makes an excellent winter house plant. It grows luxuriantly outdoors during summer and it may have to be cut back before being brought indoors. Train to a bamboo stake and put strings against the window up which it can climb. To encourage growth of vine, it *must* be provided with something on which to climb. Growth depends on height of trellis or string provided.

My passion vine, kept in a south window, grows well during winter but does not flower. Will anything encourage blossoms?   Early winter should be a season of comparative rest (temperature 55° F.; soil on dry side). In late winter increase temperature 15° to 20°; give more water. Repot if necessary, or, if not, feed every 2 or 3 weeks. Rest season is important.

How can you propagate the passion-flower?   By tip cuttings rooted in sand kept constantly moist or in water in a glass container. Keep in a light but not sunny window. When well rooted, pot up in a rich, humusy soil.

PHILODENDRON

What are cultural directions for philodendron? The philodendrons used as house plants are tolerant of warm rooms and some shade although they appreciate atmospheric moisture and sunlight. Give well-drained, humusy soil and avoid potting too frequently.

What is the proper method for growing philodendron? In water or soil? Philodendron grows well in either. If in water, keep a piece of charcoal in the container to keep water sweet. Do not change water but add to it as needed. If soil is more convenient, any good garden soil that is porous is all right. See that it is watered regularly.

How does one obtain a cutting of philodendron? By cutting off the tip ends or any side shoot. The piece cut off should have at least 4 leaves. Remove 2 bottom leaves so that the nodes from which the leaves grew can go under water. New roots will appear from these nodes. Sometimes cuttings can be selected with aerial roots already formed at nodes.

What can be done to make a philodendron branch and to prevent it from becoming stringy? As soon as distances between leaves start to get longer than normal, pinch off the ends of the vine. The plant will branch out and the severed pieces, if long enough, may be rooted in water to make new plants.

What should be done with philodendron when leaves become too small? It is probably growing in too dark or too cool a place. It does not need sun but plenty of light and a temperature of 60° to 70° F. If roots are healthy, give it a plant tablet, or feed with liquid manure or good complete fertilizer once a month.

How should philodendron vine be taken care of? The leaves seem to dry off. Do I water too much? Dying leaves are evidence of root injury or too dry atmospheric conditions. Never water a plant if the soil is really moist. Shake out your plant, and if roots are decayed, repot and water carefully. Don't use much fertilizer. Perhaps you have been overfeeding.

POTHOS

What kind of exposure does pothos like? Pothos will grow in either sunlight or good diffused light. Good for a south window as well as for an east or west one.

SWEET POTATO

How start a sweet potato vine in water?   Select a good-sized sweet potato and a glass container about 8 ins. deep and suitably wide. Thrust a toothpick in the middle of either side of the potato and let the toothpicks rest on the rim of the container. Keep water at a level so that the lower end of the potato is always covered.

WANDERINGJEW

What is the botanical name of the trailing indoor plant called Wanderingjew?   Two plants of very similar appearance go by this name. One, *Tradescantia fluminensis,* produces white flowers, leaves often variegated; the other, *Zebrina pendula,* flowers pink or red-purple, foliage striped above, purple beneath. Both are of the very simplest culture and will grow under similar conditions.

What is best time to put in slips of Wanderingjew?   They root readily at any time if planted about 2 ins. apart in pots of sandy soil. Stand pots in box with 1 in. sand or cinders in the bottom. Water well, cover with sheet of glass, and shade lightly from bright sunshine.

WAXPLANT

Could you tell me anything about the house plant known as "Parlor Plant"? It has thick waxy leaves and clusters of small, star-shaped waxy flowers.   From your description this is *Hoya carnosa,* or Waxplant. It is a native of southern China and Australia and is an old-time favorite. Botanically it is related to the milkweeds (*Asclepias*).

What kind of soil should be used for Hoya carnosa?   Soil rich in humus. One part good garden soil, 1 part coarse sand, 2 parts leafmold, with the addition of ⅛ part of bulk of dry cow manure and a pint of bone meal to each bushel.

Should Hoya carnosa have sunshine or shade, plenty of moisture, or kept on dry side?   It appreciates sunshine, good drainage, and plenty of moisture in spring, summer, and fall but should be kept drier and cooler (50° F. night, 60° to 65° F. day) in winter.

Why doesn't my Hoya carnosa (5 ft. long and 5 years old) bloom?   Although slow to flower, your plant is large enough to do so. Does it get plenty of sun and has it filled its pot with roots? Plant must be pot-bound to bloom well, hence avoid over-potting. A partial rest in wintertime is very beneficial.

CACTI

SOIL AND FERTILIZER

Are cacti in the house grown in all sand? Cactus plants can be kept alive and will grow in sand for long periods but thrive better and are more permanent if planted in a loose, porous soil mixture.

What is the proportion of sand to soil for cacti grown in the house? From ¼ to ½, depending upon how sandy the soil is that is used.

What soil do cacti require? Cacti form a large family and there are some differences in soil requirements of individual kinds. In general, a loose, porous soil, fertile but not over-rich in nitrogen, is desirable. Many species benefit from the addition of lime. (See Sandy Potting Mixture.)

What kind of soil for night-blooming cereus? The soil must be very porous, so that water drains through quickly, even when packed together. Mix good garden soil, sand, and broken brick until you get this result, then add 1/10 part in bulk dried cow manure and a pint of bone meal to each bushel.

Is there any fertilizer suitable for cactus plants? Cacti do not need much fertilizer. Bone meal, wood ashes, and very old cow manure that has been well dried may be used with discretion.

Can liquid manure be fed to potted cacti? Yes, and with benefit, but only if the plant is vigorous, is in active growth, and has filled its container with healthy roots. It should be well diluted. (See Liquid Manure.)

Should we start feeding cacti, and what month? Never feed cacti unless they are strong, vigorous plants that have filled their pots with healthy roots. Feed only during growing season (usually late spring and summer) and then sparingly.

POTTING

When should cacti be repotted? The repotting of healthy cacti that have filled their receptacles with roots should be done at the beginning of their growing season (in most cases from March to May). A plant that is planted in unsuitable soil and is consequently unhealthy may be carefully repotted at any time.

CULTURE

How can a cactus be made to bloom? The cactus family is a large one. Some kinds flower regularly and with ease while others are much more capricious. Study the individual plant, provide it with the best possible environment, and see that it has a period of rest immediately before its season of active growth.

What temperature must be held to keep cactus plants healthy? A minimum of 50° F. for plants grown indoors. Some few kinds are hardy outdoors even in the North.

What is the best method of watering cactus plants?   Submerge pots nearly to their rims and leave in that position until water entering drainage holes in bottom of the pots seeps through and wets surface soil.

Can you tell me something of the care of cacti so they will blossom? I have one that blossoms about July; last year the buds formed and then dried up.   You probably kept plant too dry. Pot-grown cacti require moderate amounts of water over the greater part of the year. Supply quite a generous quantity when growth or flowers are developing.

How often should cactus plants in small flowerpots be watered?   This depends largely upon prevailing weather and other environmental factors. In general, water often enough to prevent soil from ever drying out *completely,* yet soil should be allowed to become nearly dry before each watering.

How often should cacti in small pots be watered when they are in the house in wintertime?   In winter most cacti are resting and soil should be permitted to dry out almost completely before water is applied. The frequency with which this occurs varies with the individual plant and its environment.

How can succulents and cacti be kept thriving in an apartment with not much sun?   Grow them in a window where they will receive the maximum amount of light (even though this is not direct sunlight) possible. Attend carefully to watering, potting, cleaning, and other details.

Will cacti grow and bloom better if set outside in summer? Should they be left in pots or set directly in the ground?   If their indoor position is a sunny one and otherwise satisfactory, it makes little difference whether they are left indoors or are set outside. If set outside, they should remain in their pots.

How can cacti be carried successfully through the summer out of doors? We have a lath house. Would that be better than the rock garden?   Bury the pots nearly to their rims in a well-drained bed of soil or cinders located in a sunny position.

Why do my miniature cacti fail to grow?   Because the soil or other environmental factors are not to their liking. Read with care the answers given to other inquiries and be guided accordingly.

I have 2 cacti 6 ft. tall that have never blossomed. Why? Some cacti do not bloom until they are several years old. Resting plants by keeping them decidedly on dry side during winter often helps blooming, as also does exposure to full sunshine at all times.

Will the Peanut Cactus plant blossom? The Peanut Cactus (*Chamaecereus silvestri*) normally blooms from May to July. Its flowers are tubular, nearly 3 ins. long, and orange-scarlet in color.

How can a model cactus indoor garden be assembled and developed? Purchase 10 or 12 easy-to-grow kinds from a reliable dealer. Grow them separately in pots. Read about cacti. Join the Cactus and Succulent Society of America. Increase collection by exchange and purchase.

NIGHT-BLOOMING CEREUS

What will make a night-blooming cereus bloom and keep the buds from dropping off? Good cultural care, good light, suitable soil, proper temperature; plenty of water and feeding when growing, little water during resting period; freedom from scale and mealy bugs.

How should a large night-blooming cactus be cared for through the winter? Would it do all right in a dark cellar? It should be kept in a light place at all times. Providing the soil is kept nearly dry through the winter, it may be kept in a temperature of 40° to 45° F. At warmer temperatures, more water is needed.

Could a cereus plant be cut back? I had one given to me and it had been broken in many places, but this past summer it put out new growth. When is blooming time? Yes. Dust the cuts with finely powdered sulphur. Summer.

A night-blooming cereus started from a slip bloomed once when 2 yrs. old but hasn't had a flower since. It seems healthy enough and is growing well. What is wrong? Young plants bloom either irregularly or not at all, especially when growing vigorously. Your plant will probably bloom when it is older. Avoid overfeeding or overpotting.

How long does it take for a night-blooming cereus rooted from a cutting to bloom? This cannot be stated with any degree of precision. Usually several years.

One of two night-blooming cactus plants blooms profusely, the other has only 2 or 3 blooms. Why? Assuming plants are of

similar age and receiving similar care, this may be due to one
being a shy-blooming type. Such shy bloomers are familiar to
cactus fans.

When should a large night-blooming cereus be transplanted?
In April or May.

PROPAGATION

**I have two cactus plants that are night blooming, have a
cream-yellow, waxlike flower about 5 ins. in diameter. Can you
tell me the correct way of increasing these to make more plants?**
This is the night-blooming cereus. Cuttings of the stems, each a
foot or so long, taken in the summer and set in clean sand which
is kept moist, will soon form new roots.

How should cactus cuttings be made?   Most cacti root
readily from cuttings. Make cuttings spring or early summer.
After cutting, leave lying in sun for few days to dry cut surface,
then insert in sand bed. Keep sand just moist, atmosphere not
close and humid as recommended for cuttings of most plants.

**How should seedling cacti be grafted on larger or stronger
stock? Have raised many from seeds.**   Seedling cacti are not
usually grafted. Grafting is reserved for varieties that do not do
well on own roots. While a simple process, this can scarcely be
adequately described in a brief reply. (See Grafting—Section
II.)

How can I start cactus seed?   Plant seeds in pots filled ⅓
with "crocks" and ⅔ with very sandy soil that has had no fertilizer
added to it and that has been passed through ¼-in. screen. Sow
in spring. Cover seed to own depth. Keep soil moderately moist
at all times. Temperature should be 60° to 70° F.

How long does it take cactus seeds to come up?   From 1 to
2 weeks under favorable conditions.

DISEASE AND INSECTS

**How can I remove mealy bugs and scale insects from my cactus
plant?**   Mealy bugs are easily washed off with a forceful
stream of water. Scale can be removed by scrubbing gently with
a soft toothbrush dipped in Ivory soapsuds or in a pyrethrum
or rotenone insecticide.

CHRISTMAS CACTUS

What kind of soil is best suited to Christmas or Zygocactus?
Equal parts of turfy loam, leafmold, and coarse sand (not sea-
shore sand) together with a pint of bone meal and a quart of

wood ashes to each bushel is a good mixture. One tenth part by bulk of old dried cow manure may be added if loam is poor.

What fertilizer or procedure is used to blossom Christmas Cactus which has been grafted to Barbados gooseberry root stock? If healthy, use very diluted liquid cow manure monthly during growing season. Plunge plants in semi-shaded place outdoors June to September. Full sun indoors other times. Water moderately April–January. Keep nearly dry January–April.

How often should a Christmas Cactus be repotted? Ordinarily every two or three years, or whenever the pot is filled with roots and the soil appears to be worn out.

When should the Christmas Cactus be transplanted? In spring if the plant is healthy. A plant that is unhealthy because of poor root condition may be carefully repotted at any time.

Must the Christmas Cactus have sunshine to bloom? It needs full exposure to sunshine except from May to September; during this period shade from full intensity of strong sunlight.

How do I care for my Christmas Cactus after it blooms? Rest plant by keeping it nearly dry for 6 or 8 weeks. When new growth appears, repot or top-dress with fresh soil and water so that soil is kept fairly moist.

Why do Christmas Cactus leaves turn yellow and fall off indoors each winter and come out again on the porch in summer? Because the indoor atmosphere is too arid for these epiphytic plants. Attach humidifiers to radiators. Stand pots on trays of moist gravel or sand.

Why do leaves of Christmas Cactus turn yellow and eventually drop off? Two pots of same outdoors all summer; taken indoors September 15; one very healthy, the other in the above condition. May be due to poor root conditions. Take plant from pot, carefully remove old soil, and repot into fresh soil in pot just big enough to contain root mass.

What makes Christmas Cactus leaves turn yellow and grow very small? They do not grow broad as they should. They are planted in sandy soil. Soil is probably too poor. Try repotting into a richer (but still porous) mixture.

What care must I give to my Christmas Cactus so that the buds will not drop off? Out of 25 buds appearing on the plant about 7 or 8 develop into full-blooming flowers. Common causes of bud dropping are overwatering, exposure to cold drafts, a position too close to a hot radiator, and lack of sufficient potash in the soil. Syringe foliage frequently in autumn. Water plant sparingly. Feed a little liquid manure weekly.

I have a Christmas Cactus plant several years old, and it hasn't bloomed. Someone told me it must be a male plant. Are there male and female plants? How can you tell?   The Christmas Cactus bears male and female parts in the same flower, not upon separate plants.

What can I do to have my Christmas Cactus bloom at Christmastime instead of in March?   Outside a greenhouse such regulation not possible. Varieties, however, differ on blooming time. Can you get a slip from a plant known to bloom near Christmas? Withhold water entirely in October and during that month keep in a cool place, then bring to sunny window at temperature of 65° to 70° F. Water very moderately. Feed with liquid manure.

Why does Christmas Cactus send out tiny hair roots at each leaf joint?   This is quite a natural phenomenon and occurs particularly if the plants are grown in a moist atmosphere.

How can a Christmas Cactus be started from an old plant? By stem cuttings planted firmly in moist sand in spring. By grafting on to pereskia, cereus, or other suitable stock in early summer. (See Grafting—Section II.)

What is the botanical name of the Christmas Cactus? *Zygocactus truncatus*. It used to be called *Epiphyllum truncatum*. It is a native of southern Brazil.

ORCHID CACTUS (EPIPHYLLUMS)

What is a good potting mixture for an orchid cactus or epiphyllum?   This needs a moister and richer soil than desert types of cacti. Two parts loam, 2 parts leafmold, 1 part sharp sand, and ½ part dried rotted manure plus a pint of bone meal to each bushel should be about right.

Would like some information on the orchid cactus. Does it like sun or shade, sandy or rich soil?   Epiphyllums enjoy moister soil and a moister atmosphere than most cacti. The soil should be rich in humus but porous. Shade from strong summer sunshine is needed.

What is best fertilizer for epiphyllums?   Dilute liquid cow manure and bone meal.

What time of the year does the orchid cactus bloom? Will it freeze in winter?   The epiphyllums or orchid cacti bloom from April to July ordinarily. They are natives of the warmer parts of North, Central, and South America and are not adapted for outdoor culture where freezing weather is experienced.

What is the trouble when a night-blooming orchid cactus sets many buds which turn brown and wither when no larger than peas? The plant is well watered and sprayed with water after the buds appear. Lack of potash in the soil is said to cause buds to drop. Overwatering will also bring this about.

What is the reason my epiphyllums grow but seldom bloom? To bloom satisfactorily they must be given a rest each year. This is done by keeping them as dry as possible (without permitting the leaf-like stems to shrivel) for a period of 8 to 10 weeks during the winter.

SUCCULENTS

SOIL AND CULTURE

People speak of cacti and succulents. What is the difference? A cactus is any plant belonging to the botanical family Cactaceae. A succulent is any plant of a fleshy character adapted to conserve water and store same in its tissues. Nearly all cacti are succulents, but not all succulents are cacti. Century-plant, aloe, air-plant, stapelia, and many others are succulents that belong to families other than Cactaceae.

Do succulents need the same kind of soil as cacti? In the main, yes, but succulents that are not cacti form a much more diverse group than those that are, and, in consequence, their specific needs tend to vary more. Good, sharp soil drainage is of primary importance.

In what kind of soil should succulents be planted? This varies to some extent with the individual needs of the large number of species that comprise this group. It *must* be porous but should not, as beginners often think, be nearly all sand. The admixture of coarse cinders of finely broken brick is helpful. Many species appreciate lime.

Do succulents need a resting season? Yes, all do. As they come from many different parts of the world, their seasons of rest vary. Thus most South African succulents grow in our winter and should be rested in summer, while species that are native to lands north of the equator commonly rest in our winter. When resting, keep cooler and drier than when growing.

BOWIEA

How can bowiea be grown?   *Bowiea volubilis,* or, more correctly, *Schizobasopsis volubilis,* is a South African with large onionlike bulbs from which is formed a tall, delicate, green vinelike growth. Pot in porous soil with only base of bulb buried. Give sunny window. Keep soil moist when green growth is in evidence; dry at other times. Goes many years without repotting.

BROMELIA

What is the correct care for bromelias?   Bromelias, of which there are many species, are relatives of the pineapple. Treat like most other succulent plants—sandy soil with leafmold, plenty of drainage in the pot, and careful watering. They like partial shade and a winter temperature of 55° to 60° F. They flower at various times.

BRYOPHYLLUM

How can I make a bryophyllum or air-plant bloom?   Good culture that has as its object the rapid production of a large, vigorous plant. It needs a rather warm temperature (60° to 70° F.), plenty of sun, rich but quite porous soil, rather ample supplies of water, and feeding when it has filled a 6-in. pot full of roots. Low temperatures, too dry soil, and lack of light prevent blooming.

What is the name of the house plant that produces many little plants along the edges of its fleshy leaves?   Several species of kalanchoe (bryophyllum) possess this habit. They are easily propagated from the plantlets.

What is the botanical name for the airplane plant?   We find no reference in literature to this name. Could you mean the air-plant, *Kalanchoe* (*Bryophyllum*) *pinnata?*

CRASSULA

What could cause a crassula (jade-plant) to drop most of its leaves?   Too much water or possibly very extreme drought. This succulent plant should be treated like a cactus—plenty of drainage in the pot but water enough to prevent shriveling. The exact frequency of watering depends upon the size and condition of plant as well as upon the weather and position in house.

What can be done to encourage a jade-tree (crassula) to bloom? Kept it in good health for 10 or 15 years?   The jade-tree does not normally bloom until it is many years old. Younger specimens sometimes bloom if pot-bound. (See next question.)

I have a so-called "rubber plant" about 10 years old; it bloomed 2 years in succession, the last time 3 years ago, and not since. Why?   Your plant is probably the so-called Japanese Rubber, *Crassula argentea;* its failure to flower regularly is probably due to giving it too much water, so that it never rests. This plant is a succulent and needs to be kept on the dry side in late summer and early fall.

A friend has given me a plant of Crassula multicava. Is it a good house plant?   One of the best for a sunny window where temperature is about 50° at night and 60° to 65° F. during the day. It blooms freely in early spring. The flowers are delicate pink and very dainty. Give a porous soil. Propagate by cuttings in the spring.

CROWN-OF-THORNS

How can I keep my Crown-of-thorns (Euphorbia splendens) green? The leaves come on and drop off. It just refuses to bloom in the house.   Probably you are keeping the plant too dry. It cannot produce leaves and flowers without a constant supply of moisture during its growing season.

Does Crown-of-thorns require a dry soil?   Soil should be exceedingly porous and well drained but should be kept moist whenever leaves are present on stems. When leaves fall off, keep soil nearly dry until new growth begins.

Which plant food is best for Crown-of-thorns?   Avoid the excessive use of fertilizer. A vigorous plant with a strong, healthy root system will respond to small amounts of any complete fertilizer applied during its active growing season.

What window should a Crown-of-thorns plant stand in? Why do the buds blast?   The sunniest possible. Bud blasting may be due to extreme dryness, gross overwatering, or low temperature. Ordinarily temperature should not go below 45° F.

Is the Crown-of-thorns a constant bloomer?   Yes, if kept in good growing condition, it will bloom much of the year. (See previous questions for culture.)

KALANCHOE

What is the proper soil and care for successful blooming of the Kalanchoe blossfeldiana?   Soil should be moderately rich and quite porous. Grow in full sun. Propagate by cuttings in spring. Repot plants as roots fill pots. Water fairly freely when in active growth, and feed gently when final pots are root-filled.

Why do the leaves fall from my Kalanchoe coccinea, but it still blossoms? The leaves fall after I bring it in the house in the fall. This is due to sudden change of environment and particularly to the drier indoor air. Transfer plant to house at least two weeks before heat is turned on. Keep soil fairly moist, and on bright mornings spray foliage with clear water from atomizer syringe.

LITTLE-PICKLES

Can you tell me something about the plant called "Little-Pickles"? This is *Othonna crassifolia*, native of South Africa. A trailing plant with tiny green, sausage-shaped leaves and small, yellow daisy flowers. Excellent for a hanging pot or basket. Grow in cool, sunny window. Keep soil on dry side. Propagates very readily from cuttings.

LIVING ROCKS

How should living rocks (lithops) be treated? Plant closely together in shallow pans filled with exceedingly porous soil. Tops of plants should be well above soil level. Surface pans with gravel or small stones. Water freely October to May. Keep nearly dry at other times. Shade lightly from bright summer sun. Grow in temperature of 50° to 60° F.

SEDUMS

How can healthy small potted sedums be kept growing? Grow them in the sunniest window in a room where temperature is not excessive. Pot them in a porous, well-drained soil and keep moderately moist at all times. Sedums are easy to grow.

STAPELIA

I can never get stapelia to grow and do well. Why? They are sometimes rather tricky. They need an open, porous soil, rather more water than is commonly accorded cacti, and a light shade during summer. They should be kept nearly dormant in winter.

Concerning stapelias: mine are rested, kept fairly dry in summer, and form buds in late August or early September. Buds wilt, however, without maturing. How should they be treated? Perhaps you keep them too dry in summer. Usual practice is to rest by keeping nearly dry in winter and to water moderately and encourage growth in summer.

TYPES AND VARIETIES

What are some of the most interesting succulents, other than cacti, for the window garden? The list is vast. You might try euphorbias, echeverias, stapelias, haworthias, gasterias, kleinias, cotyledons, crassulas, kalanchoes, and some of the South African rock plants (lithops). *Succulents for the Amateur,* by Scott Haselton (Abbey Garden Press, 1939), is a good book on this subject.

BULBS, HARDY, FOR FORCING

IRIS

Can Wedgewood Iris be grown successfully in the house in winter? If you have a cool room (50° to 55° F.), plant the largest size bulbs in 6- or 8-in. pots; give full light and sun; keep free of aphis and don't disturb the roots. This iris may flower, but it really needs greenhouse or outdoor culture. Don't use small bulbs for indoors, as they won't bloom.

LILIES

Will regular garden lilies bloom indoors? The Regal Lily is a good pot plant but rather tall. Potted in late fall and given 55° to 60° F., with full light, it will flower in April or early May. Other hardy lilies are not likely to do well under room conditions.

Can Easter Lilies be raised in the house? If a bright, warm sun porch or conservatory is available, Easter Lilies can be grown successfully.

What is proper time to pot Easter Lilies for growing in house? Date depends on variety. Bermuda or *harrisi* Lily should be planted September 1 to October 1; Creole Lily, October 1 to November 1; Croft Lily, October 1 to November 1.

How can Easter Lilies be made to bloom in time for Easter? Starting temperature should be 50° to 60° F. After rooting, minimum night temperature, 65° to 70° F.; day temperature, 75° F. When plants are 3 to 4 ins. high, move to lower temperature (60°) for 14 days, then to high temperatures. Water frequently.

LILY-OF-THE-VALLEY

Can I make lily-of-the-valley bloom indoors? Yes. Order large, cold-storage pips sold for forcing. Plant in moist fiber, leaving tops exposed. Place at once in sunny window and give plenty of water.

DUTCH BULBS

What spring-flowering bulbs can be forced in pots of soil for winter bloom? Daffodils (suggested varieties): February

Gold, Odorus Orange Queen, Golden Sceptre, Pearly Queen, Alasnam, King Alfred, Croesus, Diana Kasner, Cheerfulness. Tulips: Fred Moore, Tea Rose, Mr. Van Tubergen, Le Reve, De Wet; Species: *Clusiana* and *Kaufmanniana*. Minor Bulbs: Grape-hyacinth, crocus, snowdrop, chionodoxa, scilla, lily-of-the-valley; Dutch hyacinths.

Daffodils (and other spring-flowering bulbs) grown for winter bloom are planted in pots, pans, or flats, and then stored in cold, dark place (such as a bed made against north wall of house) for several weeks to make roots before being brought indoors.

How are hardy (spring-flowering) bulbs forced for winter bloom? In late October pot up in crocked bulb pans in standard potting mixture (see Soil, this section), 3 to 7 to a pot, according to size of bulbs. Tips of bulbs should be level with the surface of soil in pot. Soak well from below. Bury in trench outdoors or in empty cold frame, placing pots on 2-in. layer cinders or small stones covered with 1-in. layer peatmoss or humus. Pack damp peatmoss or dead leaves around and over pots 1 in. deep and mulch above with leaves, salt hay, or soil. Or store in cold, dark cellar where freezing occurs. Leave to freeze and root for at least 6 weeks, then bring in as desired for succession of bloom. Place first in half light at 40° to 50° F., with little water. Bring gradually to sunlight, warmth, and plentiful watering. When flower stalks appear, give complete fertilizer. When blooms open, remove from full sun.

Do you water daffodils or tulips which are potted and kept in a cold cellar for later forcing? After bulbs are potted they should be thoroughly soaked. If conditions are right (i.e., if there is proper humidity in the cellar), they will not require additional watering. However, if pots dry out, they must be watered.

In how many days will tulips bloom after they are taken out

of the cold-storage pit? They will bloom in 5 to 8 weeks, depending on earliness of variety and temperature.

FORCING BULBS FOR INDOOR BLOOM

Bulbs are placed, close together but not touching, in bulb pan, and covered with soil.
Bulb pans are placed in frame or trench and covered with leaves or litter.
After a period of several weeks to allow roots to form, they are brought indoors to make foliage growth and eventually to flower.

Can we plant tulip bulbs in indoor pots to bloom at Easter? How and where? Yes. See previous questions.

What care is given to spring-flowering bulbs forced for winter bloom after they have bloomed?   Foliage is ripened as in garden, being kept green as long as possible. As spring comes, pots can be sunk outdoors until foliage matures. When leaves turn yellow and dry off, remove bulbs and store. In fall, plant outdoors for garden bloom. If more bulbs are to be forced, use fresh stock from bulb grower or from garden.

BULBS, TENDER, FOR FORCING

In what sort of soil should tender bulbs be forced?   Light, well-drained, and fertile. Avoid use of *fresh* manure. (See Soil, Fibrous Potting Mixture, this Section.)

AGAPANTHUS

What is proper care for an agapanthus both winter and summer?   In winter, rest. Keep nearly dry in temperature 45° F. In spring, increase water supply and temperature. In summer, stand outside in sunny position and water and feed freely. Repot in spring only when growths become crowded.

How deep should lily-of-the-nile (agapanthus) be planted in pots to take into basement for winter?   The tuberous root stocks should be planted just beneath the soil surface, so that the crown of the plant is practically at the surface.

How can I make agapanthus bloom? It grows.   Perhaps you do not rest it enough in the winter. At that time it should be stored in a cool (40° to 45° F.), light place and should be watered only often enough to keep foliage from wilting.

AMARYLLIS (HIPPEASTRUM)

Are amaryllis bulbs planted inside or out? If out, should they be dug out for winter? When do they bloom? (Ohio.)   Plant in pots indoors, leaving upper half of bulb sticking out of soil. They bloom from January to April, but the same bulb does not produce bloom over this entire period.

What soil should be used for amaryllis?   Heavy loam, enriched with bone flour (1 pt. per bu.) and well-rotted or commercial cow manure (2 qts. per bu.).

How shall I plant an amaryllis bulb?   Select a pot just large enough to hold bulb, comfortably surrounded by soil. Pot up in potting mixture indicated in previous question, with top half of bulb exposed. Water well from below after potting.

When do I plant an amaryllis bulb? I planted it last year—no blooms. Plant new bulbs December to March.

Should amaryllis bulbs be kept in the dark until rooted? This is not necessary. A temperature of 60° to 70° F. and just sufficient moisture to keep the soil damp (all the way through) is needed.

How can amaryllis bulbs be kept from year to year? Keep plant growing by watering and feeding during season when leaves are developing or present. When leaves die down, keep dry. Re-pot every third or fourth year; top-dress at beginning of growing period other years. (See answers to other inquiries.)

How shall I top-dress a potted amaryllis? By scraping off the top inch of soil in the pot without disturbing the bulb and substituting good garden loam containing a complete fertilizer.

Is there some fertilizer that I may feed amaryllis to produce better and more blooms? When the plants are growing, and providing the pots are well filled with roots, use liquid manure (which see) or any good complete house-plant fertilizer.

What is the trick of raising amaryllis in the house? Make sure that it is rested in fall and early winter. Water freely, feed and otherwise encourage growth when leaves are growing. Plunge outdoors in shaded spot during summer. When potting, do not bury bulb more than halfway in soil.

How long do you leave amaryllis bulb in dry dirt before applying water? From time leaves yellow and die away until the first signs of new growth can be seen sprouting out of top of the bulb.

How long should amaryllis bulbs be dried off? I want mine to bloom in March. Individuals vary greatly. Some are nearly evergreen; others die down quite early in the fall. Six or 8 weeks would perhaps be a minimum.

When should I start to water amaryllis bulbs to have them bloom in January or February? They are now in a cool, dark room in pots. Pick out bulbs that went to rest early. Examine carefully in December, and if you can find any showing tips of flower buds out of top of bulb, start these up by watering and placing in temperature of 70° to 75° F.

Last Easter I bought an amaryllis. Left it outdoors without watering until September, when I brought it indoors and started to water it again. To date no sign of any growth. What is wrong with it? You dried it off too soon. It should be encouraged to grow as vigorously as possible through the summer to build up bulb and following year's bloom.

In what window should amaryllis be kept—south or east? Either exposure should be satisfactory. They need as much sunlight as possible during winter and spring, and light shade during the summer.

Have some fine hybrid amaryllis bulbs which bloomed the first year; now—in spite of following directions for resting, feeding, etc.—I get no more blooms though the bulbs are growing well with big leaves. Have had bulbs 2 years. What is the trouble? Amaryllis bought and flowered first year often fail to bloom second year. Their energy is used to establish a new root system. As good foliage has developed, your plants should bloom from third year on.

Why don't hybrid amaryllis bulbs brought home from Florida bloom? I have about 3 doz. bulbs and all bloomed before we got them. It may be that they have not established themselves yet. This may take a year. (Read other replies on this subject.)

How is the best way to grow amaryllis bulbs to a really large size? Mine seldom reach 3 ins. in diameter. Good cultivation over a period of years is the answer. This implies potting, watering, feeding, resting when required, suitable soil, temperature, and light conditions, as well as maintaining the plants free from pests. (See previous questions.)

Is bulb fiber as good as soil for growing an amaryllis bulb? No. To grow these successfully so that they will last from year to year nourishment is needed, and this is not contained in bulb fiber.

Is it unusual for an amaryllis to bloom in December? It was kept in a warm basement and manure water was used. No, it is not particularly unusual, although most bulbs produce their flowers later in the winter.

Do amaryllis often bloom more than once a year? Mine bloomed 3 times this year. The amaryllis (*Hippeastrum*) does not bloom more than once a season. Strong bulbs will sometimes produce more than one flower scape, however. If your plant blooms every 3 or 4 months, it is something other than *Hippeastrum*. There are many bulbs of the amaryllis family (*Amaryllidaceae*) with varying characteristics.

How may a fine hybrid amaryllis (hippeastrum) be propagated vegetatively to make a rapid increase in the stock of bulbs? By cutting bulb into segments, each containing small part of basal ring. These pieces are planted in sand and peatmoss and placed where bottom heat of 70° F. is available. Keep just moist and shaded and new bulblets should arise in few weeks.

I have amaryllis hybrids, from seed, already as big as marbles, but they have stopped growing. Should the bulb be nearly out of the soil? What fertilizer should be used and how often? What soil? Bulbs of young amaryllis naturally grow out of soil. They will cease growing for a period in late summer. Use bone meal in soil, which should be a medium porous loam. Feed when in active growth with liquid manure (which see) or other organic fertilizer.

ARUM PALAESTINUM

What is the plant history of the Black Lily-of-the-Nile? *Arum palaestinum,* also called the black calla, is native of Palestine, a relative of our common skunk cabbage, of the tropical anthurium, and of the white calla lily. First discovered by the Genevan botanist M. Boissier near Jerusalem.

What can I do to make a black calla come into bloom? Have tried, but to no avail. Perhaps your tuber is too small and will bloom when older. Grow it in rich soil, keep moist and in light position during summer. Dry off completely during winter.

BRUNSVIGIA

How can brunsvigias be grown as house plants? They are often shy bloomers and plants will sometimes live for years without producing flowers. Pot bulbs in rich, sandy soil. Grow in sunny position. Water freely and feed when in active growth. Keep quite dry from time leaves die down until signs of renewed growth begin to show.

CALADIUM

How can I preserve fancy caladium tubers from season to season? My tubers deteriorate more and more each season, till finally there are none left. Apparently your growing conditions are unsatisfactory. These plants are gross feeders, and to build up a good tuber for succeeding year, a rich humusy soil, adequate supplies of moisture, and summer feeding are necessary.

What is the most dependable fertilizer for potted caladiums? Organic fertilizers are best. Bone meal and dried cow manure at potting time, followed by feeding with dried blood and liquid cow manure during growing season, are recommended.

Will caladium grow well in jardinieres with hole in bottom for drainage? Why do leaves wither quickly? Can soil be too wet?

If properly cared for, they will. Withering of leaves could be due to excessive water. While they appreciate moist soil, a waterlogged condition is fatal.

Is it possible to keep the Fancy-leaved Caladium in the window garden all winter, or does it have to be stored in sand to rest?   Yes, providing the temperature is maintained at not less than 60° F. and the soil in which it has been growing is kept quite dry.

After getting caladium bulbs to start, leaves are small, but stems of leaves are abnormally long; growing in parlor window which gets some sun during day. What causes this?   This is usually true of the first few leaves. If the condition persists, it is probably because of lack of sufficient light.

When should Fancy-leaved Caladiums be started indoors in spring?   From March to June, depending upon facilities available and upon when the plants are wanted to be at their best. A temperature of 70° to 80° F. is needed for starting caladiums.

I have a Fancy-leaved Caladium. It grew rapidly at first, but the leaves drop off as soon as they get a good size; now there are but 2 new ones coming on. What shall I do?   In all probability this is due to a too-dry atmosphere. Perhaps you start the plants too early for house cultivation. Tubers planted in May will give better results.

I was told to cut my caladium down when it started to droop. Did I do right? Should I keep the roots damp while stored? No. Growth should not be checked suddenly at the first sign of the plant going to rest in the fall. A gradual drying-off process should precede final dormancy. Keep tubers dry in storage.

How should a caladium which has finished blooming in the house be treated?   As soon as plant begins to lose foliage in fall, gradually reduce frequency of watering. When all leaves have gone, withhold water completely and store pots containing bulbs in dry place, at a temperature 60° to 70° F.

How can you divide caladium bulbs?   In spring cut well-developed tubers into sections, each containing a portion of the apex. Dust cut surfaces with powdered sulphur. Plant in mixture of sand and peatmoss. Temperature should be 70° F.

CALLALILY

What kind of soil grows callalily best?   They like a moist soil that is well supplied with humus and plant food.

How should callalily bulbs be cared for after blooming?
Keep feeding the plants (good organic fertilizer) and encourage
strong growth until July, then gradually dry off and rest until
September. Repot and start into growth at this time.

Should a callalily be given a rest period? If so, when? A
rest period is very desirable. Dry plants off in July and August,
beginning by gradually reducing the water supply and finally
turning the pots on their sides, so that the roots are kept dry for
5 or 6 weeks.

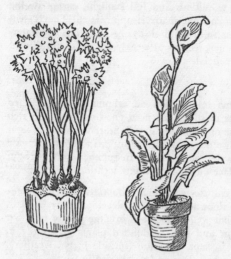

*Two satisfactory
house plants: the
quick-growing but
short-lived Paper-
white Narcissus,
and the slower-
growing but long-
blooming calla.*

**My white callalily forms a bud but never matures. Can you
tell me why?** This may happen if you are growing the plants
in insufficient light; also if you have diseased tubers that do not
produce a good, healthy root system.

**I have a white callalily 5 years old which never has blossomed.
What is the reason?** This plant needs rich soil, ample moisture during growing season, at temperature of 50° to 60° F.,
feeding when in active growth, and a definite rest period during
late summer.

**After blooming time is over in summer my calla (Richardia
albo-maculata) forms bunches that look like seeds. Could they
be planted?** Seeds of this plant are clustered together after
the manner of those of the skunk cabbage. Sow when ripe in pots
of light humusy soil and keep moist, at temperature of 60° F.

CLIVIA

Can clivias be grown as window plants?   Yes. Stand potted plants outdoors in summer; feed and water regularly. Bring indoors before frost and give a light window. Water enough to prevent shriveling, as the plant is evergreen. When buds push up, give more water.

I have had a clivia 6 years which bloomed only when I bought it. Are there any secrets of how to make it bloom?   Clivias need cool growing conditions and full sunlight, except during summer months, when light shade is appreciated. They resent disturbance at roots. Soil should always be moist but not waterlogged. During summer, feeding at weekly intervals with diluted liquid manure is beneficial.

CRINUM

Can you give me information on crinum lilies?   When grown in large pots or tubs, they need good drainage and rich soil. Plant with base of bulb deep in soil. Store in winter in light place, at temperature of 50° F., water little. In spring, increase temperature and water more freely. In summer, water freely; feed generously; place outdoors in sunny location.

What is proper culture for Crinum fimbriatulum (Milk-and-Wine Lily)?   Mine does not bloom but develops many bulblets. Plant in very rich but well-drained soil in large pots or tubs. Set bulbs deeply. Water and feed established plants generously in summer and grow in sunny position (outside in hot weather). Keep in cool, frostproof place and nearly dry in winter.

FREESIAS

When is the best time to start freesias in the house and how should they be taken care of?   Plant bulbs in September in fertile, porous soil. Space 1½ ins. apart. Put in cool place. Give little water at first, more as growth develops. Place in a cool, sunny window when tops are 1 to 2 ins. high. Avoid overwatering. Feed lightly when flower buds appear.

How can I have a succession of freesia bloom in my window garden?   Plant bulbs at 2-week intervals from September to November; 3 months are needed from planting to flowering.

Freesias planted in pots grew well but did not bloom. Why?   After planting, freesias need a period in a cool, frostproof light place to develop root growth. When growth starts, the temperature should be 40° to 50° F. at night, with a 5° or 10° rise in daytime.

My freesias last year were more beautiful than all expectations, exceeding those at the Philadelphia Flower Show. This year I took advised care of them, and they are spindly and small-leaved; used fertilizer this year but not last. This has happened before. Why? I bought giant-size bulbs. It is advisable to buy new bulbs each year. Quality of bloom depends largely upon cultivation bulbs receive *previous* year. In house or small greenhouse it is difficult to provide ideal conditions for bulb development.

Why are my freesia leaves turning yellow? They are 8 to 9 ins. high. Overwatering will quickly cause freesia leaves to turn yellow. Lack of sufficient light or extreme dryness of the soil will cause a similar condition.

My freesias are growing spindly without blossoming and are drying up. Why? Temperature too high. Atmosphere too dry and possibly lack of sufficient sunlight.

How should freesias that bloom in the house be cared for to have bulbs for another year? Mine will bloom about Christmas time. If brought into bloom as early as Christmas, it may be difficult to provide conditions that will insure good bulbs for following year. Water and feed and keep growing in sunny, cool position until foliage fades, then gradually dry off.

How are freesia bulbs stored through their summer rest period? Either in the pots of soil in which they were grown (soil kept dry, pots on sides in cellar or shed), or shaken from soil and kept in cotton bags in cool, dry place.

I've grown freesias from bulbs and have lots of little bulblets. Will they produce? They are planted now. They will not bloom while very small, but if grown under good conditions they should soon make blooming-size stock.

Can freesias be grown successfully in the garden? This can be done only in the warmer sections of the country. They cannot be handled as summer-flowering bulbs.

GLOXINIA

What soil mixture should gloxinia bulbs have for best growth? Should gloxinias be watered from the top or bottom? A loose, humusy soil. Adding to the mixture flaky leafmold, very old rotted manure, sharp sand, and broken charcoal is helpful. They can be watered from top to bottom providing the soil is thoroughly wetted through and no water is splashed on the leaves.

What are cultural requirements for the gloxinia, from bulb planting to maturity, and back to rest again?   Put tubers in pots just large enough to hold them, in light, humusy soil, February or March. Keep just moist in temperature of 70° F., increasing water supply as growth develops. Pot on into 5- or 6-in. pots when first pots are filled with roots. Feed liquid manure or complete fertilizer biweekly when in full growth. Shade from sun. Dry off gradually after flowering.

Will you please tell me if gloxinias grow best in a shady or sunny place?   Shade from anything but weak early-morning and late-afternoon sunlight is necessary.

May I have some information about gloxinias? Do you water them and bring them to the window or in the sun right away, or do you wait and let them set awhile before bringing them into the sun? Flowers never developed from the buds mine had last year.   Probably you gave them too much sun. (See answers to two previous questions.)

What is correct temperature for gloxinias? How should watering be done?   During the growing season a minimum temperature of 60° F. (rising to 70° in daytime) is satisfactory. Watering should be done with caution until a good growth of leaves has developed, then it may be given more freely.

Why do my gloxinia buds turn brown and die?   The blasting of the buds may be due to an infestation of mites, but more probably the air is too dry. A moist, but not stagnant, atmosphere and freedom from draft provide congenial conditions.

Why do my gloxinias grow tall and lanky? Those I have seen at florist shops are bushy.   This may be due to too little light. They need shade from bright sun, but good light otherwise.

Why do gloxinia leaves curl and look limp? I drop no water on the leaves.   You probably are either keeping the soil too dry or you have watered it so much that the roots have rotted off. Gloxinia leaves normally die down after flowering.

Why have my gloxinias, potted last February, failed to bloom?   It is impossible to give a specific answer without knowing more of how well plants grew, and under what conditions. They were started at the right time. (Read replies to other inquiries on gloxinias.)

What is proper care for gloxinias after they bloom?   Shortly after blooming is over, begin to reduce the moisture supply by increasing the intervals between applications. As leaves die down, intensify this drying-off process; finally store plants (leaving bulbs in the soil) in a dry place at a temperature of 45° to 50° F.

Should gloxinias be dried off every year after flowering? Left in the pots and stored?   Yes. (See previous question.)

When can I take my gloxinia out of storage and start it growing?   From mid-February to end of March. Should it show signs of activity (new leaves appearing), it should be potted and started without delay.

What is the proper blooming season for gloxinias?   Under greenhouse conditions, with skilled cultivation, they may be brought to bloom at almost any time. However, they are naturally summer and early-fall bloomers, and it is easiest to have them in flower at those seasons.

Which gives the better satisfaction in starting a new gloxinia, to plant a leaf after it has rooted in water, or to plant the unrooted leaf in soil immediately?   The best plan is to root the leaf cuttings in moist sand or sand mixed with leafmold or peatmoss.

How and when does one start new gloxinia plants from their leaves? Are mature or immature better?   Leaf cuttings consist of partly matured, medium-sized leaves with some of the apex portion cut away. They are taken in early summer and planted in sand and leafmold, or sand and peatmoss, in a warm propagating bed. Keep only just moist until new tubers form.

In starting gloxinias from leaf cutting, what is done after you have a tuber and roots formed? Mine don't seem to start.   If cuttings are started late in the season, the young tubers are rested through the winter and started up in the spring. Even with early summer-rooted cuttings, a period often elapses between formation of the roots and tuber and development of leaves.

What is the best method of starting gloxinia from seed?   Sow in January or February in very sandy, humusy soil that has been finely sifted. The seed is exceedingly small and should not be covered with soil, but firmly pressed into the surface. Keep evenly moist at all times in a temperature of 70° F. Shade seedlings and transplant as soon as large enough to handle.

HAEMANTHUS

Can the Bloodlily, native of South Africa, be started in the house in the winter and set out in the spring, then taken in the house again and repeat the same culture again?   Haemanthuses should not be taken out of their pots and set in garden.

If desired, pots could be plunged to their rims in bed of ashes outdoors (in light shade) during hottest months.

HYACINTH

I have seen hyacinths forced in winter in dishes of fiber or pebbles. What kind are they, and how should they be handled? These are the delicate, fragrant Roman hyacinths. Bulbs are delivered from the seed house in August, and if they are planted immediately and left for 10 days or 2 weeks in the dark, then brought to a cool, sunny window, they will be in bloom by Christmas. General planting and care the same as for tender narcissi.

Left: bulb pan removed from pre-rooting storage, ready to be brought indoors. Right: paper cap, open at top, used during early growth to induce formation of longer flower stems of certain bulbs, especially hyacinths.

HYDROSME RIVIERI

What is the Sacred Lily-of-India?   This name is applied to *Hydrosme* (*Amorphophallus*) *rivieri*—a relative of the callalily. It is a native of Cochin-China. In spring large tubers produce a tall, dark-colored, foetid, calla-like bloom; in summer, a single, stout leaf of umbrella shape finely divided into many leaflets.

Have been given a Sacred Lily-of-India, supposed to bloom black. Looks like a large potato. What is name and how do I care for it?   *Hydrosme rivieri.* Grow it in pot of loose humusy soil, or plant it out in garden in summer. Leaf is produced in summer; flower in spring. In fall dig up and keep dry until following spring. Flower is exceedingly curious.

What is correct culture for a Snake-palm or Sacred Lily-of-India?   Snake-palm is a common name applied to *Hydrosme* (*Amorphophallus*) *rivieri*. Plant large tuber in pot of fertile soil. Water when young leaf appears, and increase supplies as growth develops. Keep quite dry during resting season. Plant may be set outdoors in summer.

HYMENOCALLIS

How must I plant hymenocallis bulb outdoors? Can it also be forced indoors during the winter? Most species are not suited for outdoor cultivation except in extreme South. A nearly related plant (ismene) may be planted outdoors for summer bloom. Hymenocallis may be grown as a house plant. Winter-blooming kinds are *speciosa* and *caribaea*.

IXIA

How can ixias be grown? I cannot make them live. Bulbs start, then die off. Treat exactly like freesias. Pot in early fall, spacing bulbs about 2 ins. apart. Water carefully at first, more freely afterward. Grow in cool, light position (night temperature 45° F.). Dry off gradually after flowering. Avoid overwatering and high temperatures.

NARCISSI

What tender narcissi are usually grown as house plants in fiber or pebbles for winter bloom? Is culture the same for all? Paperwhites, pure white, fragrant; Soleil d'Or, golden yellow, fragrant; *tazetta orientalis* or Chinese Sacred Lily, two shades of yellow, fragrant. Yes, all are forced in the same way.

How can I grow tender narcissi as house plants? Buy bulbs from a reliable house so that you will know that they have been well grown. Plant in moist bulb fiber, or place in dishes of moist pebbles to which bits of charcoal have been added. Place for 2 weeks in a cool, dark closet or cellar until growth starts. As roots develop, bring to more light. Keep cool. When foliage growth begins to develop, place in *cool*, sunny window.

I bought narcissus bulbs. The directions say plant on 1 inch of gravel and fill around with garden soil. I always plant these in stones. The soil is to be kept very wet. Do you think this better than stones? Growing in stones is just as satisfactory if not more so than the method described.

I started some Paperwhite Narcissi the first of November, now they are about 3 ins. high. How long before I should bring them into the light and a warmer temperature? They should be brought into growing temperature immediately.

When narcissus bulbs are planted in the house, is there any way to keep them from getting so awful tall? My present ones are now 30 in. high. These are undoubtedly being grown at too high temperature. Best daytime temperature is 70° to 75° F.

night temperature 60° to 65° F. The lower the temperature, the shorter and more satisfactory will be the plants.

Why do my narcissus bulbs have only leaves and not flowers (bulbs grown indoors in water)?   If bulbs are good quality, failure is most often caused by excessively high temperature.

My Paperwhite Narcissi, growing in pebbles in a cool cellar, grow tall and fall over before blooming. Why?   They must have been planted too early and kept in a dark place too long. They must have full light to mature.

I planted 18 Paperwhite Narcissus bulbs indoors in light soil. The bulbs were bought at 2 different places. I had a fine forest of foliage, but only one small bloom; why? I kept them in the dark 4 or 5 weeks, then in a sunny window.   Excessively high temperature was the probable cause of this failure. Best planting date for Paperwhite is from October 15 to November 15. Two weeks in cool dark for rooting is sufficient.

What procedure should be used in keeping Paperwhite Narcissus bulbs for the next season?   It is impractical to keep Paperwhite Narcissus over from year to year.

How do you restore bulbs of Paperwhite Narcissus after forcing indoors? (Pennsylvania.)   These bulbs cannot be restored in Pennsylvania. They are tender bulbs, and outdoor planting revivification cannot be practiced in your section.

Can the Paperwhite Narcissi bulbs grown in water in the house be made to blossom again out of doors? (Washington.)   If your section of Washington has a mild winter such as is found near Orting, Washington, these bulbs will produce blossoms again after the second year.

Do Paperwhite Narcissi, kept in the house, ever develop seeds that are worth planting? I have 2 that seem to be developing seeds.   It is not worth while to save the seeds.

Is it possible to get bloom from Chinese Sacred Lily (*Narcissus tazetta orientalis*) and similar bulbs for house bloom, if stored after foliage matures and planted following fall?   No, it is not possible. Polyanthus narcissi do not bloom the second year after forcing.

What does this mean—Chinese Sacred Lilies, price 14–15 cm per M $37.50?   Cm means centimeters. Per M means per thousand. A centimeter is the international measure for bulbs. This is usually used in the wholesale trade.

ORNITHOGALUM

Have carefully followed directions for Ornithogalum aureum with poor results. Only one bulb out of 4 in the same pot has started and that has blossomed low. What is the trouble? This species needs considerably more warmth and moister conditions than most ornithogalums. A temperature of 60° F. at night and 65° to 70° F. in daytime is not too much.

OXALIS

How should I care for oxalis? I have several different kinds. Tender oxalis are potted in September, 3 or 4 bulbs in a 4-in. pot or bulb pan in porous, fertile soil. Water carefully at first; more freely as growth develops. Repot into 5-in. pot when 4 ins. is filled with roots. When blooming is over, gradually reduce water and keep quite dry through summer. Grow in temperature of 60° F.

Why can't I grow oxalis successfully in the house? Because the environment is not likely to be suitable. They need plenty of sunlight, ample water during growing season, none during dormant period, a loose, porous soil, and a temperature of 55° to 65° F.

How do you store, and where is the best place to plant, oxalis bulbs? During dormant season leave bulbs in soil in pots, keep dry, and store in cellar or shed. They may be grown in pots or in hanging baskets in greenhouse, sunroom, or sunny window.

Why do my oxalis bloom for only a short time in my window garden? Oxalis have a definite season of bloom. Unlike some geraniums, begonias, and fuchsias they do not produce flowers over a period of months.

Why don't my oxalis bloom? Have one in east and west window. Possibly lack of sufficient light. These plants need full exposure to sunshine for good results. Overcrowding, or an unsuitable soil may be contributory causes.

RANUNCULUS

My ranunculus is drying leaf by leaf; it's in the north window. What is the cause? Probably too warm and dry. This bulbous plant must be grown indoors in cool (night temperature 45° F.), moist conditions for best results. A cool sun porch would afford right conditions.

VALOTTA PURPUREA

What can you tell me about Valotta purpurea? The Scarborough-lily is a tender evergreen bulb. It needs rich, porous soil. Repotting is resented and should be resorted to only when absolutely necessary. Never let soil become dry. Grow in full sun and feed plants vigorously.

VELTHEIMIA VIRIDIFOLIA

What sort of soil (pH) is best for Veltheimia viridifolia?   It thrives well in a soil that is about neutral providing it is porous and well drained.

Does the Veltheimia viridifolia bulb ever send more than 1 bloom up at a time?   Ordinarily, it produces a single raceme consisting of many individual flowers.

Plant Troubles and Their Control

INTRODUCTION

BY CYNTHIA WESTCOTT

DISEASES AND PESTS have taken their toll of food crops and ornamental plants since the beginning of history; often they have influenced the course of world events. Rust, for instance, is known to have been blighting wheat for more than two thousand years; the ancient Romans found it so important that they held a yearly festival and offered sacrifices to the rust gods for the protection of their grainfields.

Another rust disease is credited with keeping the British confirmed tea drinkers, for after practically all the Ceylon coffee trees were destroyed by rust the plantations were turned over to the growing of tea. The world's coffee production became centered in Brazil, and it was the Americans who took over coffee as their favorite beverage.

Potato blight, another fungous disease, produced the Irish famine of 1845, so disastrous that it caused mass emigration from Ireland and changed British political policy away from self-sufficiency to Free Trade. Even today, in the United States, that same fungus does untold damage in a bad blight year. In 1942, when there was a serious epidemic of late blight, growers who had not sprayed their potatoes found them almost a total loss. Many did not even bother to dig them.

American grapes introduced into France for hybridization experiments brought with them a few phylloxera, and these plant lice in the short space of 10 years (from 1865 to 1875) nearly wrecked the wine industry. Two and a half million acres of vines were affected.

In 1868 there escaped from the laboratory of a scientist at Medford, Massachusetts, a few caterpillars which had been imported for experiments in breeding silkworms. The gypsy moth now costs the state of Massachusetts about a million dollars a year.

Shipments of broom corn from Italy or Hungary, about 1908, brought in the European corn borer, now familiar to everyone who has grown or eaten sweet corn, and one of our most serious insect pests. Corn plants in Connecticut, in 1940, had an average of 3 to 5 borers apiece.

Every schoolboy has heard how the Japanese beetle arrived in New Jersey from Japan, sometime prior to its discovery in 1916, in soil around the roots of nursery stock; and every Eastern schoolboy has doubtless collected his quota of beetles at a nickel a quart.

Relatively recent is the Dutch elm disease, established about 1930 by means of bark beetles, some of which came in from Europe in elm burls imported for furniture veneer and others in the wood of crates used for shipping dishes. Although the full story has yet to be written, the eradication campaign, temporarily slowed up by the war, has already meant the loss of more than 60,000 fine elms.

Even more recent, probably with most of its story in the future, is the white-fringed beetle, a native of South America first noted in Florida in 1936 and now a menace to peanuts, cotton, yams, and other plants in several Southern states.

And so plant life goes on, from one generation to the next, with disease and pest control a continuing problem and not something that has suddenly descended upon us in the twentieth century. Increased transportation facilities and more crowded living may mean a few more pests in our suburban gardens, and perhaps one or two new ones unknown to our fathers, but the chief reason we hear so much more about pests nowadays is because, with improvement in methods of control, our standards are so much higher. We are no longer satisfied with a wormy apple or a half-rotten vegetable.

By now you are probably asking, "What has all this to do with my small home garden? Pest control is chiefly for the government and commercial growers, isn't it? If I am satisfied to grow some for the bugs and some for me, isn't that my own business?"

The amateur gardener may feel justified in asking this question. The answer is: "Unfortunately, no!"

Diseases aren't kept in place by a scarlet-fever sign, nor does a boundary fence or hedge mean anything to a beetle. Your neighbor suffers by your neglect. So do you! When rust first came to Ceylon it did not kill the coffee trees immediately: it merely weakened them a little and meant a smaller crop. The growers were satisfied with a little less than perfection and had scarcely begun to worry when they woke up one day to find themselves out of business. If you ignore pests in your home garden year after year, your crops will get progressively leaner. On the other hand, it doesn't help to get hysterically alarmed about pests and diseases. They are as natural as weeds, and control is merely another garden operation, like weeding or cultivating. It may require a little more intelligence and forethought, but it will probably take far less time and energy than other garden operations.

Importance of Diagnosis

In plant medicine, as in human medicine, diagnosis is 9/10 of cure. You must know what is wrong with your plant before you can select the right control measure. The wrong medicine, or even unnecessary medicine, may do more harm than good.

Some diseases and pests are readily recognized by layman gardeners; others are extraordinarily difficult even for a specialist to identify. If you are in doubt, do nothing until you get advice from some competent person. (Your neighbor is usually not qualified, even though his advice is profuse and free.) The most reliable source of advice is your county agent or your State Experiment Station. It is far better to send a specimen than a description, and to send a whole plant if possible, for the trouble you think is in the leaf may originate in the stem or roots. Diseased material travels best flattened out between layers of newspaper. Don't send live insects about the country, for they may escape and establish themselves in some hitherto-uninfested area. Insects may be quickly killed by dropping them into a cyanide collecting jar or into a jar of kerosene.

In making your own diagnosis, check the obvious things first. *The name of the plant is of primary importance.* Some insects and diseases are promiscuous, attacking a wide variety of plants; but others are highly selective, attacking only the members of a certain family, or even genus, so that the name of the host plant may mean almost immediate identification.

Consider also the time of year. A webby mass in a tree in the spring probably means tent caterpillars; in late summer it indicates fall webworms. An elm leaf perforated in May is probably chewed by a cankerworm; in June, by the elm-leaf beetle; in July, by the Japanese beetle. These dates are for New Jersey, where the writer lives. If you live in Florida, or California, or Maine, your dates, as well as your pests, may be quite different. That is one reason for you to keep in close touch with the information put out by your own State Experiment Station.

Diagnosis is a process of elimination. After knowing the plant that is being attacked and the time of year, look at the foliage. Holes in leaves are probably the work of some chewing insect, although there are one or two diseases that cause shot holes.

Disease is the term applied to the abnormal condition that comes from the work of bacteria, fungi, viruses, one or two higher plants, or unfavorable environmental conditions.

Injury is the term applied to havoc caused by insects. The different chewing insects make their own patterns in the leaves. When all the leaves of a single twig or branch are chewed off down to the midrib, or, as in the case of pine, the needles are chewed down to the fascicles, then sawfly larvae may be responsible. Flea beetles make tiny round perforations; weevils produce rather typical angular openings; beetle larvae (grubs) more often "skeletonize" leaves, chewing everything but the epidermis and veins.

If the leaf is yellowish, or stippled white, or gray, the loss of color may be due to sucking insects. You may see them, or their cast skins, or brownish eggs, or excrement, on the underside of the foliage. Yellowed leaves that are cobwebby or mealy underneath indicate red spider, while whitish streaks spell thrips. If there is no sign of insects, the yellowed leaf may be a symptom of malnutrition, perhaps lack of nitrogen, or unavailable iron. Leaves curled up, or cupped down, may harbor aphids; deformed leaves may be due to the cyclamen mite; blotches or tunnels, to leaf miners; round or conical protrusions, to aphids, midges, or gall wasps.

Leaf spots with definite outlines and filled with numerous minute dark pimples are of fungous origin; smooth spots are usually symptoms of a bacterial disease. Fungi may produce irregular blotches on a leaf, but if the black specks or pimples are missing, the blotches may be sunscald or windburn—the result of cells collapsing when water could not get up from the roots fast enough to replace that evaporated from the leaves. Spray injury also produces leaf spots. When phlox leaves die progressively up the stem, it very likely is due to some unbalanced water relation; but if chrysanthemum leaves die in the same fashion, it may be due to drought, leaf-spot fungus, a wilt fungus in the soil, or to leaf nematodes, the latter being more probable with Korean varieties. Reddish pustules on a leaf say rust; a white felty growth, mildew; and dark soot, a mold living on aphis honeydew.

A dark lesion, or canker, on a stem indicates a fungous disease; a sawdustlike protrusion is the sign of a borer; but a gummy substance exuding on a peach tree may be caused either by the peach-tree borer or the brown-rot fungus.

Wilt—the partial collapse and dying back of a plant—may result from any one of many causes: high temperature, lack of moisture, root injury from too-close cultivation, too-strong fertilizer, a soil fungus which invades the vascular system, or one which causes a crown or stem rot, large grubs, or microscopic nematodes working on the roots. Rots may follow physiological disturbances, and then millipedes and other small animals feast on the disintegrating tissues. *Determine, if you can, the primary cause, and don't worry about the secondary effects.*

It all sounds enormously complicated, but with a little practice you learn to recognize at a glance the signs and symptoms of common pests and diseases, just as you recognize your acquaintances when you pass them on the street. You don't stop to analyze why that is Mrs. Smith; you just know that it is. With a little more training you'll be noticing signs in spite of yourself and walking along the street muttering, "The lace bugs have certainly made Mrs. Smith's azalea look sick; I wonder why Mrs. Jones never sprays her junipers for scale; Mr. Brown's corn smut is a public menace. If the Board of Health makes me cut down my ragweed they ought to make him burn up his smut boils."

Types of Control

Having, so far as possible, diagnosed your plant trouble, how are you going to control it? There are four main avenues of approach: immunization, exclusion, eradication, and protection— and sometimes it takes all four.

1—Immunization means the development, by hybridization or selection, of varieties which are resistant to certain diseases. One hundred per cent resistance, or total immunity, is impossible, but if you can buy varieties reasonably resistant to the diseases most prevalent in your locality, that is the first, and easiest, control method to attempt. Some seed catalogues list resistant varieties, and your State Experiment Station will help you out with suggestions. Many resistant vegetable varieties are listed in United States Department of Agriculture *Leaflet 203*, which you may obtain for five cents from the Superintendent of Documents, Washington, D.C.

There is a theory, widely held by gardeners, that vigorous plants are more resistant to diseases and pests. This is more often due to coincidence rather than to any true relationship between lack of vigor and susceptibility. The same cultural practices which produce a vigorous plant often check the spread of pests. Red spiders flourish and plants languish in close quarters where there is little air circulation. Proper pruning and feeding of elm trees check the spread of Dutch elm disease only indirectly by reducing weak or dead wood in which the bark beetle, disseminator of the fungus, lays its eggs. Some fungi, weak parasites, can enter plants only through wounds, and thrive on decaying tissue, but other parasites, such as rusts, smuts, and mildews, can operate only on a vigorous plant. In corn-breeding experiments it has been found the hybrids of high vigor are more susceptible to smut than those of low vigor; but since vigor is more important than smut resistance, we must continue to control this fungus by eradication methods.

Japanese beetles definitely prefer young, succulent leaves to old and wilting ones, and you never find Mexican bean beetles waiting until plants are weakened before they move in!

There are some rather hazy theories about plant nutrition as a factor in disease resistance, but we have not yet gone very far along this line. No matter how well plants are cultivated and fed, one still cannot ignore their insects and diseases. The sooner this fact is recognized, the sooner the gardener will get over having nightmares about pests and learn to take them in his stride. He cannot have a garden without planting seeds; he cannot continue to have a garden, year after year, unless pest control becomes a routine operation.

2—*Exclusion* is practiced by counties, states, and countries by means of quarantine laws and regulations, backed up by careful inspections. You can apply the same principle to your garden by looking at every plant, whether acquired by gift or purchase, with a suspicious eye before allowing entry. If you insist on acquiring a diseased plant, either disinfect it or put it in an isolation hospital far removed from your healthy plants.

Buy certified seed when you can. That means that government inspectors looked at the seed plants in the field and certified them as being free from specific diseases. Treating seed with hot water or a disinfectant is another exclusion measure. Farmers through their co-operatives have been able to obtain treated seed more readily than the home gardener, but there is a present movement to encourage seed dealers to disinfect seeds sold in small packets. If you ask for treated seed often enough, you may get it.

3—*Eradication,* of course, means the destruction of a pest after it gets established in an area. It includes soil sterilization to kill soil fungi or nematodes, or treating the soil with lead arsenate to kill grubs; or putting carbon disulphide into an ant nest, or breaking off a tent caterpillar egg mass or wiping out the nest. It means getting after Japanese beetles with traps, or picking them off into a can of kerosene, or putting milky-disease bacteria on their trail. It may mean taking up an entire plant and its surrounding soil (as in crown rot), or cutting off a branch of apple or pear that has fire blight. It means removing and burning rose leaves infected with black spot; cleaning up peach or plum "mummies" (wizened, dried-up fruits), or maggot-riddled apples; or spading under or burning up all vegetable refuse after harvest.

Remains of any diseased plants should be carefully burned.

Eradication may mean crop rotation to starve out the insect or disease, or cleaning up additional weed hosts, or eliminating some plant which is an "alternate host" and so a necessary factor in the life cycle of a certain disease. Eradication measures were applied long before people understood the nature of the plant disease. The first barberry eradication law was passed in France in 1660, when it was noticed that wheat rust flourished when barberries grew near by. Nowadays we eradicate cedars to prevent the apple-rust fungus from completing its cycle, and take out black currants to save pines from blister rust.

To sum it up, eradication is really garden sanitation, the removal of all factors injurious to plant health. *It is probably the most important control method available to the home gardener.*

4—Protection involves the spraying and dusting of plants to kill or to keep away insects or diseases. (Some dormant spraying, however, is more properly an eradication measure.) When chemicals are applied in a wet mist, we call it "spraying"; and when they are applied as a dry powder, the operation is known as "dusting." There are many arguments as to the relative advantages of dusting and spraying; but each has its place, even in the small garden. The lazy gardener will use his small dust gun more often than his sprayer, which should be—though it seldom is—thoroughly cleaned after each use.

A spray or dust used against insects is called an "insecticide," and one against bacteria and fungi a "fungicide." In addition there are "fumigants" and "disinfectants," "attractants" and "repellents"; as well as materials to make the sprays spread and stick.

Sometimes one chemical serves two purposes. Lime-sulphur is used both as a fungicide and a dormant spray for scale insects. Sulphur dust is equally effective against mildew and red spider. Bordeaux mixture—a copper fungicide—sometimes serves as a repellent for insects.

In the home garden dusting, in many instances, is more convenient than spraying for the control of pests or diseases.

Insecticides are generally divided into *stomach poisons* (such as lead or calcium arsenate or cryolite) for chewing insects; and *contact sprays,* like nicotine sulfate, pyrethrum, or rotenone) for sucking insects; but the latter will often control the chewing insect as well.

Insecticides and fungicides are sold under more than nine hundred different trade names, all variations in one way or another, based on a relatively small number of chemicals. The trade name is unimportant except as it indicates a reliable manufacturer; *it is important to read the label on each package and know you are using the right chemical at the right dilution for your particular purpose.* These chemicals are listed in the following pages with formulae for the small garden and cautions as to use. The possibility of spray injury is ever present. Some plants are at all times allergic to certain chemicals; others can stand them Jf it is not too warm, or too cold. There is grave danger of injury when two incompatible chemicals are mixed together.

It is not possible to cure all garden troubles with one general spray any more than one kind of pill will cure all human ills, from a sprained ankle to cancer. Sometimes, however, sprays or dusts may be combined to take care of both insects and diseases of certain kinds. Such combination sprays or dusts may be purchased under trade names or, occasionally, mixed at home.

The timeliness of the application is most important. Fungicides should be applied *before* rains, so that a protective coating will be present when the fungous spore or the bacterium starts to grow in the presence of moisture. For fungous diseases, spraying should start *well before the disease is expected,* and should be continued, at whatever intervals are needed, to keep it in check. For rose black spot in New Jersey that means weekly treatments from early May until the end of October; but July 1 to September 1 usually covers the spraying period for late blight of potatoes. The adult Japanese beetle is with us from mid-June to mid-September, but for the boxwood leaf miner there is only a 10-day period in May, during which the flies are laying their eggs, when spraying will have any effect.

Know your insects and know your diseases, and don't waste your money and your patience by spraying too early or too late, or with any material but the right one.

ALPHABETICAL LIST OF INSECTS, DISEASES, AND CONTROLS

ANTS

What can be done about ants in the garden? Ants are undesirable in the garden not so much because of their feeding but because they loosen soil around roots, causing plants to wilt and die, and they cart around and nurse aphids and mealy bugs for their honeydew. They may be fought either by distributing poisons to be carried back to the nest or by applying boiling water or fumigants to the nests.

How can you get rid of red ants that like to be on the roots of marigolds and many other flowers? If you cannot find the nests or if they are so close to the plants you hesitate to use fumigants, then use poison ant baits. There are a great many on the market, most of them in special containers ready for use. Thallium sulfate and sodium arsenite are the chief ingredients of ant poisons. Both are extremely poisonous to humans so that a special container is necessary. To make a small quantity of ant syrup, boil 1 pt. of water with ½ teaspoon sodium arsenite (or ¼ teaspoon for Argentine ants), cool, and stir in 1 lb. sugar.

How can I rid my perennial flower beds of great colonies of big black ants, which destroy everything in areas of 3 to 4 ft.? Fumigate the nest with calcium cyanide granules; make holes with a pointed stick down into the nest to a depth of 8 ins.; pour in the granules and cover hole immediately with soil; or open holes and pour 1 teaspoon carbon disulphide into a small nest and 1 tablespoon into each of several holes in a large nest; or punch holes over nest and pour in a few crystals of paradichlorbenzene.

How can you exterminate the large red ant leaf eater, stripping the bushes clean? (Texas.) The leaf-cutting ant does not eat the leaves but carries them to its nest where it chops them up in pieces as a medium on which to grow the fungi it uses for food. Spraying the foliage with lead arsenate might have some deterrent effect, but fumigating the nest is surer. Ordinarily the injury by this ant is more interesting than serious.

How can I get rid of ½-in. long black ants that live inside trunk of my English Walnut tree? Entrance is narrow fissure 18 ins. long. Have tried filling with cement but they burrow around.   This is the carpenter ant, which seldom works through living bark but can enter through a wound in a tree and play havoc in the interior. Easiest method would be fumigation with cyanogas if you can close up the fissure. Or paint the interior of the tree with a sweetened solution of sodium arsenite. You can probably buy a prepared ant bait which has a base of sodium arsenite.

APHIDS (PLANT LICE)

What year-round program would you suggest for aphids? Aphids are soft-bodied sucking insects controlled by contact insecticides; in general spray for them when you see the first few individuals. They are more numerous at certain seasons of the year, the time varying with the host plant, so that spraying is generally spasmodic rather than regular. Often an aphicide may be included in a spray put on for other purposes.

What should I use to destroy plant lice?   Nicotine sulfate, 1 to 1½ teaspoons, and 1 cubic inch of laundry soap or 2 level tablespoons of flakes to 1 gal. of water is the most widely used and successful spray for aphids, but any contact spray or dust is satisfactory (pyrethrum, rotenone, or nicotine dust), provided the insects are hit.

Can you kill aphids in the dormant stage?   The dormant spray applied to fruit trees often kills aphid eggs, and applied to evergreens takes care of the fluffy white bark aphids on pine and the spruce-gall aphid. Some of the shade-tree aphids will be reduced by dormant spraying, but such a spray would not be used unless needed for scale insects.

Can anything be done to destroy the white aphids which feed on roots of plants?   Nicotine sulfate and soap solution, or nicotine sulfate alone, when used at 1½ teaspoons a gal. and poured into a depression around the plant stem, is helpful. Tobacco dust may also be worked into the soil. Root aphids are usually tended by ants, so that ant-control operations should also be started.

ARMADILLOS

How do I get rid of the armadillos that root up my garden at night? (Florida.)   Armadillos are as difficult as rabbits to control. The best method is a fence of 2-ft. chicken wire around the garden, otherwise shooting, if permitted, or trapping in rabbit traps put across their paths. They cannot be readily poisoned.

ARMY WORM

What is the dark-green, white-striped worm, similar to a cutworm, which attacks grasses, corn, and grain crops, feeding at night and hiding under clods, stones, or leaves during the day? Army worm. Controlled by scattering poison bait in late afternoon. (See Cutworms.)

Army Worm: attacks corn, grain, and grass. Dark green, white stripes; feeds at night.

ARMILLARIA ROOT ROT

What is the fungous disease, especially prevalent in California, which kills trees, shrubs, and other woody plants, being most destructive on lands recently cleared of oak?   It may be recognized by the white mycelial threads or fans, black shoe-string strands extending through the soil, and honey-colored toadstools that grow near the base of the trunk. Remove dead trees and shrubs, taking out all roots. Rhododendrons and azaleas may sometimes be saved by exposing crowns and main roots for a season. Avoid planting in areas of high-moisture content. Disinfect soil where diseased plants have been taken out with carbon disulphide. Inject 45 c.c. into holes 8 to 9 ins. deep and staggered 18 ins. apart.

ARSENICAL SPRAYS AND DUSTS

See Lead Arsenate; Calcium Arsenate.

ASIATIC BEETLE

How do you identify the Asiatic beetle? (New York.)   There are 2: the Asiatic beetle (*Anomala orientalis*) and the Asiatic garden beetle (*Aserica castanea*). They both are the size and shape of Japanese beetles and work on grass roots in the white grub stage. The adult Asiatic beetle varies in color from light brown to black, with or without mottled marking. It is sometimes found feeding on roses and other flowers but does not do much damage there. The garden beetle is a smooth copper brown, and has been described as an animated coffee bean. It stays in the ground during the day and feeds on foliage, bangs against windows, and flies into cars at night. The larvae injure grass roots and some vegetables. The adults injure leaves of asters, zinnias, and other low ornamentals and carrots, parsnips, turnips, beets, and pepper tops.

How do you combat the Asiatic beetle? (New Jersey.) Grub-proof lawns and spray foliage of ornamentals with arsenate of lead. Lime may act as a deterrent on food plants. (See Grub-proofing; also Japanese Beetle.)

Are castor bean plants a protection from Asiatic beetle? (Connecticut.)   Their efficacy has been greatly overrated. Entomologists claim tests in cages show that the foliage is practically nontoxic and they cannot be used as trap plants in the field because beetles do not go to the castor bean before their favorite food plants have been exhausted.

Last summer I found hundreds of young Asiatic beetles in a semi-dormant state around my garden plants. I grub-proofed the lawn with arsenate of lead. How do they hibernate? Will my garden be eaten up next summer? (Massachusetts.)   They will hibernate in the soil under the grass roots of your neighbor's lawn, and the beetles may fly to feed on your plants next summer. However, treatment should reduce the infestation.

Is it possible the Asiatic beetles came from the roses and destroyed the bent grass in large spots? (Iowa.)   The Asiatic beetle is not prevalent in Iowa. Lawn may have been injured by white grubs or chinch bugs or the fungous disease called brown patch, and your rose pest is probably the rose chafer. (See Rose.)

What should I use for the Asiatic beetle? (California.) Nothing. According to statistics the Asiatic beetle is not a problem in California.

BAGWORM

How do you destroy bagworms? (Georgia.)   This pest, generally distributed in the East, is more severe in the South. Hibernation is in the egg stage in the female bags, made from interwoven twigs and leaves. The young hatch late in spring, spin their own bags, and immediately start feeding on evergreen and deciduous trees. Control by picking off and burning bags in late winter and by a heavy arsenate-of-lead spray when feeding starts. Use 4 tablespoons arsenate of lead to 1 gal. water.

BARIUM FLUOSILICATE

What are the uses of barium fluosilicate?   A fluorine compound of especial value in the control of blister beetles, strawberry-leaf rollers, and sometimes flea beetles. Mix 1 part with 3 of flour, talc or sulphur, and apply as a dust. Usually sold under the trade name of Dutox.

BEETLES

What are real "beetles"?   Members of the insect order Coleoptera, with chewing mouth parts and hardened front wings forming convex shields. Except for a few beneficial types, such as ground and lady beetles, they are injurious both in their grub or larval stage and as adults. They are controlled by stomach poisons used in the ground (see Grub-proofing) or on the foliage.

Do beetles ever come through closed windows into the house in winter?   They get in through very small cracks and crevices around the windows. Lady beetles are very frequent house visitors in winter while elm-leaf beetles enter houses in late summer to hibernate.

BENEFICIAL INSECTS

What bugs are harmful and which are harmless in the garden? (Ohio.)   The harmful bugs are discussed under the different host plants. Of the harmless or helpful ones lady beetles, ground beetles, and praying mantes are most often seen in the home garden, although sometimes, if you look closely at a group of aphids, you will see a sluglike creature, larva of the syrphus fly, working among them.

BICHLORIDE OF MERCURY (MERCURIC CHLORIDE; CORROSIVE SUBLIMATE)

What is bichloride of mercury?   A general disinfectant and virulent poison, to be used with caution. Of value in gardens for treating limited soil areas, where diseased plants have been removed, for some seed, rhizome, or corm treatments, and for disinfecting roots. Usual dilution is 1 to 1,000, or 1 7-grain tablet to a pint of water. Mix only in glass or enamel container.

Can corrosive sublimate be used around the roots of perennials in the fall to discourage fungous blights of various sorts?   It is not a good idea to use any chemical as a general soil treatment around growing plants, but if 1 or 2 plants have been infected with some root or crown rot, then the area involved, including soil around near-by plants, may be treated. Treatment should be made immediately and not left until fall. The bichloride will check spreading mycelium but will not always kill the hard sclerotia or resting bodies. Great care should be exercised in removing diseased plants.

BIOLOGICAL CONTROL

What is biological control?   The control of plant or animal pests by other living organisms. Notable examples include the work of the Australian lady beetle on the cottony cushion scale, ground beetles on gypsy moths and predacious wasps, and the bacterial milky disease on Japanese beetles. Biological control can never completely exterminate a pest and usually must be supplemented by mechanical measures.

Is there any biological control for codling moth? (Illinois.) Yes, birds and many insects work on the codling moth, but they have never been able to reduce it below the point of commercial damage. Other control methods must be used.

BIRDS

What is the best way to keep birds from eating vegetable seeds?   Farmers' supply places sometimes sell a crow repellent for treating seeds, but some say that crows often work down a whole row of corn, hoping to find a kernel that is not treated and palatable.

Is there any known object besides old-fashioned scarecrows that will keep birds out of the strawberry patch?   Cover the strawberries with coarse cheesecloth or netting.

Can you tell me anything that will poison sparrows?   The baits used for cutworms and slugs sometimes kill birds by mistake. Do not put it out for sparrows; you may kill desirable birds also. Use a sparrow trap or a gun.

BLISTER BEETLES

What are those long bugs that attack Irish potatoes and gardens? (North Dakota.)   Blister beetles. They are common in most states, feeding on vegetables and many ornamentals, especially asters and Japanese anemones. They are as much as ¾ in. long, plain black, or black with gray margins, or yellow or gray stripes, or brown or gray.

Blister Beetle: attacks asters, anemones, potatoes, and many other plants.

What is the best insecticide for blister beetles? They are hard to kill, but the consensus of opinion seems to be that fluosilicates do the best job, either barium fluosilicate or cryolite mixed with 3 parts flour or talc. A calcium arsenate and lime dust is also effective, and mixtures of pyrethrum and rotenone fairly successful. Knocking the beetles off into a jar of kerosene or driving them away with a tree branch are helpful measures.

BORDEAUX MIXTURE

What is Bordeaux mixture? A fungicide of great value in the control of plant diseases. The regulation formula is 4–4–50, meaning 4 parts copper sulfate, 4 lbs. hydrated lime to 50 gals. of water, but for many ornamental plants a weaker solution is needed. Bordeaux mixture may be purchased in dry powder form to be mixed with water at the time of spraying, or it may be made at home by keeping on hand 2 stock solutions, one made by dissolving 1 lb. copper sulfate crystals in 1 gal. of water, and the other by dissolving 1 lb. lime in 1 gal. of water. Dilute only at the time of use, the amount of water determining strength of Bordeaux; never put 2 stock solutions together, but add the water to lime solution and then stir in copper sulfate solution. For a 4–4–50 mixture use 1 part of each stock solution to 10½ parts water; 3–8–50, 1 part to 14⅔ parts water; 2–2–50, 1 part to 23 parts water.

Please define 3–5–50 Bordeaux mixture or any such combination of figures. What do they stand for? They are a kind of shorthand to describe strength of spray. The first figure is for the copper, the second for lime, and the last water; in this case it means 3 lbs. copper sulfate and 5 lbs. lime to 50 gals. of water. Ordinarily lime and copper are used in equal amounts, as 4–4–50 or 3–3–50, but sometimes lime is increased to avoid injury to specific crops.

What can you substitute for Bordeaux mixture when you do not have an agitating sprayer? Will Kopper Queen act the same?

(Oregon.)   There are several metallic copper sprays which may be used to replace Bordeaux mixture and they are safer when lime is undesirable. Kopper Queen is one of these, but you should get specific instructions from your county agent or Experiment Station.

What amount of Bordeaux mixture should be used per gallon of water?   Directions come on the package, usually 8 to 12 tablespoons of prepared dry Bordeaux powder to 1 gal. of water. For most ornamental spraying about half this amount is safer, less conspicuous, and equally effective.

BORERS

How can borers be prevented from doing their deadly work? Borers are caterpillars or grubs, larvae of moths or beetles, that work in woody or herbaceous stems. Some, like the European corn borer or common stalk borer, are best prevented by cutting down weed hosts and burning old stalks at end of the season. Twigs infested with borers should be cut out and burned, but when the borer is in a woody trunk, such as rhododendron or lilac, it may be fumigated by squirting in some nicotine paste, sold as Bortox or Borerkil, or by injecting a few drops of carbon disulphide with a machine oilcan, and then plugging the hole with putty or gum. Newly set trees should be protected from borers by wrapping trunks with kraft crepe paper wound spirally from crown to the first branch.

BOX-ELDER BUG

What will destroy box-elder bugs? They infest the trees and eat my fruits and flowers. The young is red and the adult dark gray, with a red border. (Arizona.)   Since they are sucking insects, nicotine sulfate and soap or other contact insecticide may control them on the plants, but to prevent their swarming into the house, avoid planting the pistillate tree near by, for the eggs are laid on the fruits.

BUG

What is a bug, horticulturally speaking?   A term used by the layman to denote any insect but by the scientist to mean a sucking insect of the order Hemiptera, which means half-winged. The basal half of the fore wing is stiffened and the other half membranous. They often have an offensive odor. True bugs include stink bugs, lace bugs, plant bugs, and chinch bugs.

What can I do to kill sucking bugs?   Use a contact insecticide, which see. (See also Insects.)

CALCIUM ARSENATE

How is calcium arsenate used? A stomach poison somewhat safer to use on vegetable foliage than lead arsenate but poisonous to humans and not to be used on edible plant parts near harvesttime. As a dust, calcium arsenate is diluted with 3 to 19 parts of lime or gypsum, according to the pest to be controlled. As a spray, the usual formula is 1 tablespoon calcium arsenate and 2 tablespoons hydrated lime to 1 gal. of water.

CARBON DISULPHIDE

What is carbon disulphide and what are its uses? A useful fumigant but *very inflammable*. It is heavier than air; when used in fumigating beans for weevils, place it at the top of the container. By means of a force or plunger-type machine oilcan it may be conveniently applied to borer holes, which must be plugged to prevent gas from escaping, or into holes in ant nests in garden or lawns. It is used to disinfect the soil when root-knot nematodes or various fungous rots are a problem.

CATS

How can cats be kept out of the garden? (Massachusetts.) They can't, very well. Aside from a small city garden, where numerous cats may congregate, they do little damage to the garden itself, but of course they are enormously destructive to birds. They often are a great help to the gardener in the control of rabbits, mice, and moles.

CENTIPEDE

In digging I see quite a few slender orange-and-brown insects about 2 ins. long, that run fast and want to be in the dark, look like thousand-legged brown or tan miniature snakes. Are they injurious to plants? (Kentucky.) These are probably centipedes, meaning hundred-legged, although literally they have about 15 pairs of legs. They are usually beneficial in the garden, preying on other insects, but the larger ones may inflict painful bites on humans.

What is the color of a centipede in infancy? (New York.) The true centipede is yellow to brown, like the adult, but the garden centipede, so-called, but really a symphyllid, is small and white. This creature injures plants and has become an important pest in greenhouses and truck fields in some states.

CHINCH BUGS

How do you guard against chinch bugs? (Ohio.) Chinch

bugs are very small black-and-white sucking insects, red when young, which injure corn and small grains for the farmer and lawns for the homeowner. In hot, dry seasons large brown patches in lawns are very commonly chinch-bug injury. A 1 per cent rotenone dust, applied in June and again in August, is the most effective lawn treatment, but at the present time tobacco dust must be substituted. Growing soybeans between the corn rows will shade the base so that the chinch bugs will avoid the corn (they do not touch soybeans or any plant outside the grass family). They may be trapped as they migrate from small grains to corn by a barrier line of crude creosote.

Chinch Bug: small black-and-white sucking insect destructive to lawns.

CHLOROPICRIN

What is chloropicrin?   Tear gas, a soil fumigant usually sold as Larvacide. It is excellent for the control of weed seeds, nematodes, various soil insects, and some soil fungi, and may be purchased in a special dispenser with full directions for dosage. It should be used in a loose, moist soil, at a temperature above 60° F., and the gas should be held in the area by flooding with water or covering with impervious paper. It is deadly to living plants and should not be used within several feet of them.

COMPOST

Is there a way of combating insects and diseases by treating the compost heap and using it where plants are to be grown? The compost itself may be treated to insure against its being pest-ridden, but it will confer no immunity to the plants in the garden bed.

What is the danger of carrying over fungi and insect pests in compost?   There is some danger, and that is why we recommend burning plant material known to be diseased or likely to harbor insects. If doubtful plant debris is included in the compost, it may be treated with chloropicrin before use.

CONTACT INSECTICIDE

What is meant by a "contact insecticide"?   A material used to kill insects by direct contact due to interference with the respiratory system. Used chiefly for sucking insects not amenable to stomach poisons, but contact sprays will usually kill those chewing insects that are actually hit with the chemical. Oils, nicotine sulfate, pyrethrum, or rotenone are most used as contact poisons. Sometimes the killing is quick, as with pyrethrum or nicotine, sometimes it takes 24 to 48 hours, as with rotenone.

CRAWFISH

I am having considerable trouble with crawfish digging up my lawn. How do you exterminate them? (North Carolina.)   Use ¼ pint commercial coal-tar creosote emulsion in 3 gals. of water, and apply ½ cupful in each hole, or else 2 tablespoons carbon disulphide poured in each hole and covered with soil.

CROWN ROT

What will prevent crown rot?   Crown rot is a disease causing sudden wilting of plants from a rotting at the crown or soil line. In the North *Sclerotium delphinii* and in the South *Sclerotium rolfsii* are the causative fungi. There is no real prevention, except to put healthy plants in a new location. The fungus may live for several years in the soil in the form of reddish-tan sclerotia, which resemble mustard seeds. Therefore it is important to take out all surrounding soil when the diseased plant is removed. Unless soil can be dug out for 1 ft. deep and 2 ft. or more in area and replaced with fresh, bichloride of mercury or Semesan should be poured over the earth and crowns of near-by plants.

CUBE

What is cube?   One of the plants used as a source of rotenone. It is grown in South America and is being imported as shipping conditions permit.

CUTWORMS

How shall a poison bait that will kill cutworms be mixed? There are many formulae, but the following is a simple mixture. Thoroughly mix 1 tablespoon Paris green or white arsenic with 1 qt. of bran. Put 2 tablespoons molasses or syrup in 1 pint of water and moisten the bran until it is crumbly. Scatter bait thinly in late afternoon.

How about a remedy for cutworms that is not injurious to birds, animals, or children?   Any poison bait left where young children or pets can reach it is dangerous. Scientists say there is little proof that songbirds are killed by cutworm bait, but gardeners often have sad experiences blamed on poison bait. The safest measure is a paper collar around each seedling as it is set out, 1 in. below the ground and about 2 ins. above.

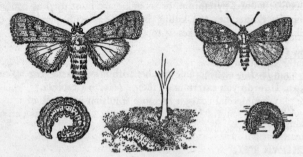

Cutworms: attack young cabbage and tomato plants and other seedling vegetables and flowers. Left, Greasy Cutworm; right, Dark-sided Cutworm.

Do cutworms stay in the soil in some form over winter? (New Jersey.)   Usually cutworms winter as small larvae in cells in the soil, or under trash or in clumps of grass, although sometimes they winter as adult moths or as pupae. In spring the larvae feed, usually cutting off seedlings at the surface of the ground, and change to the adult stage in summer. Plowing at that time will prevent egg laying on broken land.

Is Snarol an effective poison bait for cutworms?   It has a good reputation. No one remedy is 100 per cent effective in all situations.

CRYOLITE

Is cryolite an effective insecticide?   Sodium fluoaluminate, sold as Kryocide, natural cryolite, and as Alorco Cryolite, the synthetic form, is less poisonous to humans than the arsenicals. It is a stomach poison of especial value in control of blister beetles, cucumber beetles, and flea beetles, and may be used on beans up to the time the pods form. As a dust it is mixed with 1 to 3 parts of flour, talc or sulphur, but *never with lime*. For spraying use 2 tablespoons to 1 gal. of water.

DAMPING OFF

What would cause seedlings in flats to sort of rot at the stems just at the top of the soil?   This is known as damping off—a disease caused by any one of several soil fungi. There are two types, pre-emergence damping off when the sprouted seeds rot in the soil, and post-emergence damping off, when the young seedlings wilt and fall over. For growing in flats either soil or seeds may be treated, but seed treatment is more practical for sowing directly in the garden.

What is the safest preparation for soil treatment to prevent damping off in seed flats? Formaldehyde, perhaps. Dilute 2½ tablespoons commercial formaldehyde with 6 times as much water and sprinkle over a bushel of soil, mixing thoroughly. Wait 24 hours before planting, and water well immediately after planting.

When starting seeds in the house in boxes, what is the safest thing to use to prevent damping off? The formaldehyde treatment outlined above would be all right but not so convenient for small lots of seeds as dusting the seeds themselves with appropriate chemicals. (See Seed Treatment.)

DERRIS

What is derris? One of the plants used as a source of rotenone. It was imported from the Far East and the supply is largely limited to the amount in this country before Pearl Harbor.

DIABROTICA BEETLES

What do you do about the 12-spotted beetles? They ruin all the late blooms—roses, gerberas, carnations, chrysanthemums. (California.) These are the 12-spotted cucumber beetles, Diabroticas, very common in your state. They are hard to kill, but dusting with one of the fluosilicates, cryolite or Dutox, or with pyrethrum, would be helpful.

DOGS

What are your views and advice on the dog-nuisance question? Owners should be willing to keep their dogs restrained and, when walking them on leash, should keep them curbed rather than allowed to ruin lawns and shrubs near the sidewalk. For advice I can only refer you to the letter symposium recently conducted by O. M. Scott and Sons Co., in *Lawn Care*. Moth balls around shrubs and BB guns in action seemed to get most votes. A barberry hedge and a few chopped twigs of barberry scattered about was one idea that might work. Wire shrub guards are usually quite successful. There are many dog-repellent sprays on the market but they all have a fleeting effect.

DORMANT SPRAYING

What is a dormant spray?   A spray applied while plants are dormant, which means sleeping, that is, while deciduous trees are bare and before evergreens have started into new life. At this time the plant can stand a stronger spray than during the growing season, and a strong spray is needed to get hard-shelled insects like scales.

When and how should the dormant spray be applied to trees and bushes? (Illinois.)   The safest time is toward the end of dormant season, just before new growth starts. In Illinois that might mean the end of March for lilacs and early April for evergreens. For dormant spraying the home gardener usually has a choice of lime-sulphur, either the commercial liquid or a dry mix, or an oil spray, either a miscible oil or an oil emulsion. The liquid lime sulphur is preferable and should be diluted with 7 to 9 parts of water. It is safe, but unpleasant to use, impossible near painted surfaces because of the indelible stain, and leaves an objectionable residue on evergreens. Miscible oils, colorless oils which mix readily with water to form a white liquid, are sold under many trade names. Most manufacturers suggest a 1 to 16 dilution for deciduous trees and 1 to 25 or 30 for evergreens. Oil sprays may be injurious unless they are used on a bright, clear day with the temperature well above 45° F. Do not use on beech, black walnut, butternut, Japanese or sugar maple, or magnolia. Do not use on such evergreens as retinospora, cryptomeria, Douglasfir, true firs, hemlock, Japanese Umbrella Pine, or yew.

DUSTER

What is a garden duster?   Machine for applying insecticides or fungicides in dry dust form. For the small garden choose a dust gun, ranging in size from 1 pt. to 2 qts. capacity. Choose one with an extension rod and a flange which will allow you to stand up while using the duster and yet drive the dust from the bottom of the plant up through it. For the larger garden a bellows or a rotary duster will save much energy in operation.

DUSTING

What is "dusting" as used in the garden?   The application of a fungicide or insecticide in dry powder form.

How do you know how much garden dust to use? Tried a dust gun which didn't cover the leaves sufficiently without extreme labor and when tossed out by hand seemed too much. Many plants wilted. I used sulphur and rotenone. (Virginia.)   Apply only as much dust as will cover the plants with a thin, even coating. This can be done only with some sort of duster. If yours was too hard to work, it either was the wrong type for the number of plants or else needed adjusting. Coverage of the underside of the leaves is most important and can be done only with the right apparatus, never by throwing it on. Your method of application together with the sulphur in your dust would account for the plants wilting. Sulphur may be injurious to any plant in hot weather, but vegetables are particularly sensitive. Beans occasionally require sulphur, but cucurbits should never have it.

Do you dust plants when they are wet with dew or when they are dry? There is always an argument on this question, but if ornamental plants are dusted when they are wet, the cure will be far worse than the disease. When copper-lime dust is used in place of Bordeaux mixture for vegetables, it should be used when the plants are wet with dew to make the proper membranous coverage over the leaf.

DUTOX

What is Dutox? See Barium Fluosilicate.

EARTHWORMS

It seems as though I have 10,000 or more saboteurs on my lawn, night crawlers, that tear the devil out of it. Is there any solution for their extermination? Yes, you may treat the lawn with bichloride of mercury, at the rate of 2 ozs. in 50 gals. of water sprinkled over 1,000 sq. ft. Water the lawn well afterward. If arsenate of lead has been used in grub-proofing, that will suffice for earthworms also.

Do angleworms feed on and destroy peony, iris, and other tubers? I have dug them up and found worms imbedded in them and nothing left but the outer shell. Your peony probably succumbed to Botrytis blight and the iris to borer and rot. Earthworms do not feed on living plant tissue.

When garden worms are found in flower pots, do they feed on the roots of the plant? No. Worms in pots are chiefly a nuisance because they clog up the drainage holes. Watering with lime water will get rid of them.

EARWIGS

Is there anything possible on this earth to exterminate earwigs? (California.) Earwigs, beetlelike creatures with their "jaws" on the wrong end, are poisoned with the standard bran bait used for cutworms or a special earwig bait containing oil.

To make the latter, mix 3 lbs. bran with ¼ lb. sodium fluosilicate and then moisten with 1 cup fish oil.

How can the small home gardener combat the European earwig? (New York.)   In New York State he usually does not have to. Earwigs appear occasionally in the East but are chiefly Western pests. The bait given above will cover 2,000 sq. ft. The formula can be reduced to make a smaller amount.

FALL WEBWORM

What is the difference, if any, between the fall webworm and the fall cankerworm?   The fall webworm forms weblike nests in trees in August and September, somewhat like the nests of tent caterpillars. The caterpillars are yellow or green, about 1 in. long and hairy. Control by wiping out with rags dipped in kerosene; by spraying with lead arsenate; or by dousing the webs with nicotine sulfate solution. Fall cankerworms, prevalent early in the spring (usually May), are yellowish or green, and "inch" along, and for this reason are sometimes called inch-worms or measuring-worms. The female fall cankerworms lay their eggs in the fall, so it is a good practice to use tree Tanglefoot around trees in September to catch them as they climb upward. The best complete control is to spray the trees each spring with arsenate of lead.

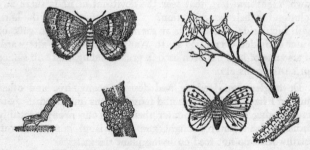

Fall Cankerworm (left) and Fall Webworm.

FLEA BEETLES

What about flea beetles? (Florida.)   Flea beetles, that get their name from their habit of quickly springing several inches when disturbed, are small oval beetles which chew tiny shot holes in the foliage of most garden crops. Two species in Florida are most troublesome on beets, cabbage, and tomatoes. In the North potatoes and seedling tomatoes, peppers, eggplants, and crucifers are almost sure to be riddled by flea beetles early in the season. Dusting with cryolite or a 1 to 8 mixture of calcium arsenate and hydrated lime, will control flea beetles, and spraying with Bordeaux mixture will repel them. Weeds and other debris around the garden should be burned to destroy winter hiding places.

FORMALDEHYDE (FORMALIN)

What is formaldehyde? A useful soil disinfectant. (See also Soil Sterilization.)

Is it safe to use a weak solution of formaldehyde (1 to 50) on a seed bed that has been planted, but seed not germinated, to curb damping-off fungus? (West Virginia.) This is not a weak solution of formaldehyde; it is the standard strength for drenching *fallow* soil, which will probably have to air out at least a week before planting. It would not be safe to use after the seed is planted. (See Damping Off for the formaldehyde method of treating soil for flats, and see Seed Treatment for ways to prevent damping off in garden soil.)

What concentration of formaldehyde will kill insects and larvae without destroying foliage on seedlings? None. Formaldehyde is never to be used around living plants. If you must disinfect the soil, the plants will have to be moved out for a couple of weeks, and since you do not want to set infested or infected plants back in treated soil, you have to start a new batch of seedlings. So try some other method of controlling your insects.

FUNGI

What are fungi? Members of the Thallophytes or lowest plant group. Lacking the power of manufacturing their own plant food, they live as saprophytes on decaying plant tissue or as parasites on living higher plants. They are characterized by a vegetative stage, consisting of fungous threads or mycelium and fruiting bodies which contain the reproductive organs. Some fungi are readily recognized at a glance: mildew with its white weft of mycelium growing over a leaf; rust, which produces reddish dusty spore pustules, and smut with its masses of black spores; some can be differentiated only by microscopic examination.

What do you do for white fungus? (California.) Such a question is too indefinite. A white fungus may be the coating of mildew on a leaf, it may be the white weft of mycelium at the base of plants in crown rot or Southern blight, or it may be the fans of white mycelium peculiar to the Armillaria root rot, prevalent on woody shrubs in California. Then there is downy mildew and many other possibilities.

What do you recommend as treatment for mustard-seed fungus? (Missouri.)   This question is almost as brief as the one above, but it can be answered definitely because there is only one fungus, *Sclerotium rolfsii,* that would be present in Missouri, known as the mustard-seed fungus. It causes the disease known as Southern rot or blight or crown rot and gets its name from the reddish sclerotia which look like mustard seed. (For control see Crown Rot.)

FUNGICIDE

What is a fungicide?   A material used to eradicate bacteria and fungi in soil or on seeds, or, more commonly, used as a protectant to cover susceptible plant parts before the disease organisms arrive. Most fungicides are compounds of either copper or sulphur.

GOPHERS

What is the best way to poison California pocket gophers? There are many species of pocket gophers (ground rats) found in California, Oregon, and Washington. There are special gopher traps on the market, but poisoned carrot bait is simpler. Cut 1 qt. of fresh carrots into pieces 1½ ins. long and ½ in. square and dust over 1/16 oz. powdered strychnine alkaloid. Open the runways at intervals with a pipe probe and insert the pieces of bait. Use care in handling. This bait is extremely poisonous.

GRASSHOPPERS

We were almost ruined by a grasshopper wave last summer. I scattered poison bait. Is there anything else one can do? (Washington.)   You can plow sod land where grasshoppers have laid their eggs. Poison bait, to be effective, must be put out for the young hoppers and broadcast early in the morning of a warm, sunny day. The bait formula given under cutworms is all right for grasshoppers but will be somewhat more effective if a sprinkling of salt and part of a chopped-up orange or lemon is added to it.

GROUND BEETLES

Have found several June bugs in the ground this fall. Are they harmful? (New York.)   You would not be apt to find June beetles in the ground. You probably found ground beetles, black or brown or iridescent large beetles with very prominent jaws that live in the ground or under stones. These are beneficial insects, feeding on cankerworms and other pests, and should not be disturbed.

GRUB-PROOFING

How do you kill grubs in the soil? Lawns may be treated with lead arsenate, 10 lbs. mixed with a bushel of soil, and spread evenly over 1,000 sq. ft. and well watered in. The treatment is equally good for larvae of Japanese or Asiatic beetles or for white grubs, larvae of June beetles.

Is there a safe chemical that can be worked into the vegetable garden for grub-proofing it? No, it is better not to put any chemical in the soil. Arsenate of lead may stunt some plants, and, if a very heavy dose has been used, may be taken up to some extent in the edible portion. Spading the vegetable garden and leaving it rough over winter will kill some of the grubs, and birds will do their share.

GRUBWORMS

See White Grubs.

HARLEQUIN BUG

How do you get rid of Harlequin bugs? (Kansas.) This brilliantly colored red or yellow and black or blue bug causes the leaves of horse-radish, mustard, cabbage, and related crops to curl and turn brown. It lays clusters of black-banded eggs that look like barrels. Hand-picking before egg laying and removal of eggs are the best control. Nicotine dust will kill the young nymphs, or a pyrethrum dust may be tried. Destroy all old plant parts.

INFORMATION

What we need is plenty of information on pests. We find some that are different from Eastern states. Are they pests or beneficial? (California.) Your own State Experiment Station is set up to give you exactly that knowledge. Not many gardeners realize what a wealth of information, applicable directly to their own state, may be obtained for the price of a penny post card requesting certain bulletins or circulars. In your particular case you can write to the College of Agriculture, Berkeley, California, and ask for a list of publications. You will find there such very useful bulletins as *Insects and Other Pests Attacking Agricultural Crops, Diseases of Flowers and Other Ornamentals, Diseases of Truck Crops, Diseases of Fruits and Nuts,* and many others. With the emphasis now on vegetable gardening practically every state has concise information ready for the home gardener as well as the farmer. Ask for it.

INSECTICIDE

What is an insecticide?   A substance that kills insects by poisoning, suffocation, or paralysis. Insecticides are used as stomach poisons, contact poisons, fumigants. They sometimes act as repellents. Lead and calcium arsenates and cryolite are stomach poisons; nicotine sulfate and oil sprays are contact poisons; while pyrethrum and rotenone act in both ways. Carbon disulphide is a typical fumigant and Bordeaux mixture is often used as a repellent.

INSECTS

Just what are insects?   Members of the animal group Arthropoda, meaning jointed legs. True insects, of the class Hexapoda, meaning 6-legged, are characterized by always having 3 pairs of legs and 2 pairs of wings in the adult form, except for flies, which have but 1 pair. The body is composed of head, thorax, and abdomen. Along the abdomen are small holes, spiracles, which form the breathing apparatus. Contact poisons work through their action on the spiracles. Chewing insects have jaws and bite holes in plant tissue, and hence can be controlled by spreading a stomach poison in advance of the insect. Sucking insects cannot bite but obtain their food through a beak which pierces the plant epidermis to get at the sap. Since they cannot be injured by stomach poisons, contact sprays are necessary.

JAPANESE BEETLES

What are effective ways to eliminate Japanese beetles? (New York.)   Chemical treatment of soil (grub-proofing) in lawn areas; biological control by distribution of natural parasites, especially the milky-disease bacteria; spraying foliage during the flying season; hand-picking; trapping in special beetle traps.

How and when do you fight the Japanese beetle—a month-by-month schedule? (Pennsylvania.)   Grub-proofing (which see) is done either in May or September, and one treatment should last for 3 years. Summer spraying normally starts at the very end of June and may have to be continued until the end of September on plants like roses, although beetles often stop feeding on vines in late August. If shade trees are sprayed with lead arsenate at the end of June, one spraying will normally give protection for the season. With shrubs, vines, and flowering plants the number of applications depends on the rapidity with which new growth is formed. Roses and ampelopsis require a spray weekly to keep the new growth covered.

Will arsenate of lead injure grass roots in a lawn? Not if it is used at standard strength, 10 lbs. per 1,000 sq. ft. and mixed with soil so that it can be spread evenly. Water it in well. Do not apply in the heat of summer, but in late spring or early fall.

Is there any control, other than arsenate of lead, for Japanese beetle grubs in lawns? Yes. The spore dust of Milky White Disease—a natural enemy of the beetles—is the best means of controlling and eliminating this pest, and it is now available commercially. Directions for use are printed on the packages.

In order to destroy Japanese beetle grubs I put a quantity of arsenate of lead in cold frame, thereby destroying the soil vegetation. How can I remedy this condition? Take out the soil and put in fresh. Arsenate of lead is often injurious to plants and should never be used for vegetables because of the danger of the roots taking up some of the poison. If you have no soil free from grubs, you can treat a batch with chloropicrin (which see) before using it.

Is there anything I can do to the soil in flower beds? The beetles destroy hollyhocks, cannas, petunias, roses, and geraniums. (New Jersey.) Soil treatment for flowers is unwise; lead arsenate will often cause stunting. For flowers, the most effective control is picking off the beetles; for roses, cutting the buds when they show color and enjoying them in the house. Pyrethrum sprays, now scarce for use on flowers, will paralyze or kill beetles without disfiguring blooms, but in general you have to rely on lead arsenate in a spray or dust to take care of the foliage and hand-picking the beetles into a jar of kerosene.

Can you tell me something to get rid of Japanese beetles? I have tried traps and they seem to attract them. That is exactly the purpose of a trap: it is painted bright yellow and baited with geraniol just to attract the beetles. Unfortunately, the trap attracts more beetles than get caught in it, so that the near-by plants serve as beetle food and suffer proportionately.

What is the best method of exterminating Japanese beetles before they are hatched? Only by picking off or trapping (in *yellow* traps) the adults before they can lay their eggs in the grass. The eggs will hatch into grubs even if the soil has been treated with lead arsenate, but if the poison is in the soil, the grubs will gradually die, as they feed on grass roots.

Is it possible to recognize the Japanese beetle in the daytime? How can you fight the Japanese beetle on rosebushes? (Louisiana.) In Louisiana you probably will not have to fight Japanese beetles on rosebushes. If and when you do, lead arsenate either in sulphur dust or a combination spray will keep the foliage reasonably whole, but to save the flowers you should cut the buds and let them open indoors. The beetle is readily recognized. It works in the daytime and prefers hot sunshine. It is about ½ in. long, shiny metallic green with bronze wing covers and tufts of white hairs protruding from under the wing covers. It is a very handsome beetle.

What do you do with Japanese beetles? (California.) Nothing in California. It's not your problem yet. (But see preceding questions.)

What is the most effective repellent of the Japanese beetle? (Connecticut.)   Rotenone, probably. Most of the special Japanese-beetle sprays have a derris base, sometimes with rosin as a sticker. During wartime the legal use of rotenone is exceedingly limited. Hydrated lime will serve as a repellent on grapes and lead arsenate will serve as both repellent and stomach poison on ornamentals.

How should green-colored arsenate of lead be prepared for use on roses and grapevines?   The green or coated lead arsenate spray is no longer in favor; experiments showed it to be much less effective. Green sulphur dust containing 10 per cent lead arsenate may be purchased under the name of Pomo-green. Do not use arsenate of lead, green or white, on grapes. By the time beetles are numerous the fruit has already formed.

Is DX effective against Japanese beetles?   Yes. For shade-tree spraying it is usually used with arsenate of lead, reducing the amount needed and so making a less objectional residue on the trees.

Can I check Japanese beetles with castor-oil beans?   Probably not. (See Asiatic Beetle.)

Does fall spading help exterminate the Japanese beetle? Yes, especially if you take the trouble to destroy or throw out to the birds the grubs you turn up. Birds, by the way, are great allies. The holes you see in the lawn in late summer are where the robins, starlings, and other birds have gone in after the grubs. The starlings are given the most credit for eating the hard beetles, but some other birds work at them. In my garden brown thrashers will pick a beetle off a rosebush and then whack it down onto the cement path to soften it up for eating.

Is the Japanese-beetle nuisance likely to abate soon? Does severe cold tend to kill them? (Connecticut.)   The menace will abate but never cease. The beetles stay wherever they have become established, but their numbers diminish after 4 or 5 years at peak abundance. Natural enemies and man-made control methods take effect. Any newly introduced insect does more damage than a long-established pest. Beetles will probably take their place with tent caterpillars and cankerworms as nuisances to be expected each season but not to be unduly excited about. The grubs go so far down in the soil severe winter cold has little effect.

Do Japanese beetles bother geraniums?   They are attracted to them; indeed it is geranium bait used in traps, but there is some evidence that beetles are killed by eating certain varieties of geraniums.

Which plant is easy to cultivate, free bloomer until frost, and free as possible from Japanese beetles? (Connecticut.)   Phlox and the Heavenly Blue morningglory answer your requirements. Roses, marigolds, and zinnias are favored food plants; delphiniums are not much bothered by beetles, but they are not easy to grow. Blue eupatorium will contrast with your phlox and give you color until frost. It has few insects; if it blights, you can always remove a plant and have plenty left. To replace marigolds, try Orange Flare cosmos. It has almost no pests and diseases and grows with no effort at all. Scatter the seeds broadcast in any odd corner; rake them in lightly. With no more attention they bloom from early July to November.

Japanese Beetle. Injury to silk on corn causes poorly filled ears.

Which vegetables would be least affected by Japanese beetles? Most vegetables are little affected by Japanese beetles. They are extremely fond of soybeans and sometimes appear on snap and lima beans; they injure the silk of corn; they are numerous on, but seldom injurious to, asparagus foliage, and they often play havoc with rhubarb leaves.

JUNE BEETLE

What is a June beetle?   See White Grubs.

KEROSENE EMULSION

Can you give me government formula for kerosene emulsion to be used to kill aphids on flowers and vegetables?   I can give you a formula from Dr. Dodge of the New York Botanical Garden. To make a stock solution heat 2 pts. kerosene in a hot-water bath (not over a fire) to 150° F. Dissolve 1 oz. good laundry soap in 1 pt. hot water. Pour the kerosene gradually into the soap solution, stirring vigorously for 5 minutes, or until a smooth emulsion is formed. When cold, this should be a smooth jelly. If there is any separation of kerosene and water, the emulsion is unsafe for plants. Use 1 part stock solution to 65 parts water to control aphids, mealy bugs, and white flies. Some plants may be injured by this spray and all should have the kerosene washed off later.

LACE BUGS

How do you kill lace bugs? (Iowa.)   Lace bugs, small bugs with lacelike wings that work on the underside of leaves, sucking out the sap so that the upper surface becomes a stippled white, gray, or yellow, are readily killed by any contact insecticide applied with a good spreader and sufficient pressure. Nicotine sulfate and soap solution is good in your state, but in the South a white oil is more often recommended.

LEAD ARSENATE

What is lead arsenate?   A widely used stomach poison, extremely valuable for spraying ornamentals and for some food plants like apples. Because of the residue problem, lead arsenate being the most poisonous of the arsenicals, and because it burns some tender foliage, it is of less value in the control of vegetable pests. The strength of the solution varies with the pest to be controlled, but for normal spraying 2 level tablespoons per gallon is about the right proportion. It should be used with sticker, either casein, or some trade-marked preparation, or ordinary household flour. As a dust it may be mixed with 4 to 5 parts of hydrated lime but it is more often added to sulphur to make a combination insecticide-fungicide dust. One part lead arsenate to 9 parts of sulphur, or 1 part lead, 1 lime, and 8 sulphur are the usual combinations. Lead arsenate may be added to Bordeaux mixture or lime-sulphur sprays, but it should never be used with soap.

Have a pet cat. What spray will take the place of arsenate of

lead on garden flowers and vines? **Have Japanese beetles.**
There is no need to change from arsenate of lead on the cat's
account, and this is the best choice for flowers and vines. In my
10 years of doctoring other people's gardens with lead arsenate
there has never yet been a case of harming pets. Dogs and cats
like to follow around when you are spraying and kittens want to
play with the nozzle, but if you shut them in the house during
the actual mixing and application of the spray, there is no problem with the residue on the plants. Of course you do not want to
leave a pail of lead arsenate standing where a dog or cat might
mistake it for milk. Mix up your spray and dispose safely of
what is left in your spray tank and you will have no trouble.

Is it harmful to put lemon oil on plants? If you mean the
furniture polish that goes by that name, yes, but there is a tried-
and-true insecticide sold for years for use on house plants and
that is safe when used according to directions.

LIME-SULPHUR

What is lime-sulphur? A fungicide, often acting as an insecticide also. Particularly valuable in dormant spraying for the
control of fungous diseases and scale insects, but also useful as a
summer spray to control apple scab and other diseases, boxwood
canker, red mites on fruit trees, spider mites on evergreens.
Liquid lime-sulphur is used at a 1 to 7 or 1 to 9 dilution as a dormant spray and 1 to 40 or 1 to 50 as a summer spray. It stains
paint and leaves an objectionable residue, but is relatively safe. Do
no use it within one month of using oil.

MAGGOTS

What causes ground maggots and how can they be got rid of?
(Maryland.) Maggots are legless white larvae of flies that
lay their eggs in plants near where the stem meets the ground
or in crevices in the soil. The cabbage maggot is the one most
bothersome to the home gardener. For control see Cabbage.

MEALY BUGS

What are the fuzzy white bugs on my house plants? Mealy
bugs, sucking insects closely related to scales; flattened, oval,
with short projections from the body, and often looking like
bits of cotton fluff because of the eggs carried by the females in
a cottony sac. Mealy bugs are especial pests of house and greenhouse plants, and in the South on such outdoor plants as gardenias, azaleas, citrus fruits. In the North, Taxus is often heavily
infested, and the Comstock mealy bug is a coming apple pest.

What is the life history of the mealy bug? How does it travel

etc.?   The female mealy bug deposits her eggs in a cottony waxy sac attached to the rear end of her body. When she has laid 400 to 600 eggs, the sac is left at the axils of branching stems or leaves and the female dies. The eggs hatch in about 10 days, and the flattened, oval, yellow young crawl over the plants, sucking the sap, and soon a waxy covering is exuded from their bodies. They are sluggish and do not move much. The males transform into small, active 2-winged flies to mate with the females and then die. Mealy bugs are disseminated by ants and by moving about infested plants.

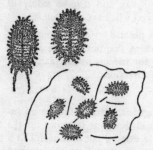

Mealy Bug; attacks many house plants; the small, soft bugs are covered with a cottonlike fluff.

How can I rid a small greenhouse of mealy bugs?   If the greenhouse is not attached to the dwelling, frequent fumigation with calcium cyanide (Cyanogas) will kill young mealy bugs. Plants may also be sprayed with or dipped into a solution of 1 lb. of soap to 3 gals. of water, but this must be washed off within 2 hours to prevent burning. Spraying with Greenhouse Volck, a white emulsion, is probably the easiest solution, provided manufacturer's directions are rigidly followed and the spray washed off several hours later. Volck may be temporarily scarce due to the war and the old reliable nicotine sulfate and soap spray have to substitute. (See Control of Ants.)

What is the best method of getting rid of mealy bugs and how long does it take? (California.)   First wash off your plants with a strong spray from the hose, then use a white oil emulsion, such as Volck, at the rate of ½ cupful to 3 gals. of water and 3 teaspoons of nicotine sulfate. It may be necessary to spray 2 or 3 times at weekly intervals to clean up an infestation. Be sure the soil is moist and that the plants are not suffering from lack of water before using an oil spray.

What will destroy mealy bugs in the soil? (Ohio.)   Remove soil from around the roots and pour in some of the spray just described.

Can window boxes once infested with mealy bugs be used again? (Connecticut.)   There is no reason why not, if the soil is cleaned out and the box thoroughly washed with strong soap and water.

We are plagued with mealy bugs on our flower and vegetable plants. Can you recommend a safe spray so as not to harm the plant or poison the vegetables? (Pennsylvania.)   I cannot believe that mealy bugs in an outdoor garden would be that much of a pest in Pennsylvania, although I have occasionally seen coral-bells and yew with bad cases of mealy bugs in this region. Perhaps you have root aphids. (See Aphids.)

MICE AND RATS

How can you keep rats from eating plants in a city garden where, because of lack of co-operation from neighbors, it is impossible to get rid of all of them? (Maryland.)   Poison put out for the rats would probably get a pet cat or dog, and even traps would have to be used cautiously to avoid maiming a pet. When the house plants on my window were mysteriously chewed I could not believe it was a rat until I caught it in the act one night. It was killed in a trap baited with sunflower seed. Red squill obtainable from county agents is a poison deadly to rats and relatively harmless to pets.

What can be used in winter mulch to discourage mice? (New Jersey.)   Snap-back mousetraps can be put in the mice paths under the mulch, or poison bait may be safely used, since it is under cover. A very simple bait is 1/16 oz. strychnine dissolved in 1 pt. boiling water and poured over as much oatmeal (about 2 lbs.) as it will wet. Mix well. Put it out, a teaspoon at a place, under shelter of mulch or brush or boards or in a wide-mouthed jar.

What is a sure cure for moles and field mice? (Connecticut.) Set snap traps for the mice in the mole runways. (See also Moles.)

MILDEW

What makes mildew on plants? (Texas.)   A fungus, of the type they call an obligate parasite because it must get its food from living plants. When the wind carries a spore (little seed) to a leaf and the moisture conditions are right, the spore sends out a germ tube that grows into white threads, mycelium, which branch over the leaf in a soft, white, felty coating. This fungus does not grow inside the plant but sends little suckers, haustoria, into the sap. In a few days chains of spores are built up from the mycelium which gives the powdery effect. Later black fruiting bodies with the sexual or overwintering spores are formed. Because it is on the surface, mildew is more readily controlled than many other fungi and may even be eradicated after the first signs of it appear.

How may one control mildew? (Minnesota.)   Sulphur is a specific for mildew, and the easiest way to apply it is in dust form, but sulphur or copper sprays may be used.

MILLIPEDES

What is the best way to rid a garden of the dark-brown, hardshelled, spiral variety of worm which eats root vegetables? (Massachusetts.)   This is a millipede. The name literally means thousand-legged, but the number falls far short of that, although this animal comes in many segments and there are 2 pairs of legs on each segment (the centipede has only 1 pair to each segment). Ordinarily millipedes in the garden act more as scavengers than as a direct cause of injury, but they do some feeding on potatoes and other root vegetables. The only control measures known are trapping them with baits used for wireworms or with poison bait recommended for sowbugs. (See Wireworms; Sowbugs.)

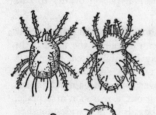

Red Spider: very tiny; makes fine webbing on under sides of leaves.

MITES

What kind of spray is used to kill or cure possible mites? (New York.)   There are 3 kinds of mites apt to be troublesome in the garden: red spiders, spruce mites, and cyclamen mites. Red spider is a good term because mites do belong to the spider group, characterized by 8 legs rather than the 6 of true insects, for all their almost microscopic size. Red spiders and spruce mites make a fine web underneath the leaves or between needles, and their sucking turns foliage yellow or needles rusty brown. They are best controlled by breaking the webs with a strong stream of water and then dusting with sulphur. The cyclamen mite stunts and deforms plants, especially delphiniums, and causes blackened buds that never develop. Control with rotenone spray with nicotine sulfate, alternated with sulphur dust. Destroy seriously infected plants.

MOLE CRICKET

How do you get rid of cricket moles? (Florida.) Mole crickets are dark-brown burrowing insects, about 1¼ ins. long, with front legs enlarged for tunneling. They come out at night to feed and are destructive because they eat the vegetative parts of seedlings as well as disturb the roots. Sulphur acts as a deterrent in planting seed. For poison bait use a mixture of 1 oz. of Paris green to 1½ lbs. cottonseed meal moistened with syrup. Or use a grasshopper bait, replacing the bran with poultry egg mash.

MOLES

How do I get rid of moles? This is a very popular question. It was sent in by 91 gardeners in 32 different states. It is unfortunate that moles, which really do a lot of good in the world by eating white grubs and other insects, should also have the bad habit of making unsightly ridges and mounds in lawns and of disturbing the roots of flowers and vegetables by their tunnels. Actual feeding on plants is probably done by mice which use the mole runs. (See following questions.)

Do moles eat bulbs? That is a moot question. The gardener says "yes" and the scientist says "very unlikely."

How do you get rid of moles without traps or poison? (Pennsylvania.) There is not much left except patrolling the ridges and watching for movements indicating the mole is at work and then killing it with a spade or a fork. A dog after a mole is disastrous, but cats may catch moles without any extra damage to the garden. One cat of my acquaintance (not my own, which always turn out lazy) had an unbroken record of a mole a day. Flooding the mole runs with water in the spring is said to drown young moles and mice.

What is the best method of controlling moles? (Oregon.) Trapping. Fish and Wildlife Service in Oregon and Washington report negative results with poison baits and cyanide dust but success with traps correctly set. They also say that the skin of the Oregon mole, if properly prepared, may be sold for enough to pay for the time and trouble. Traps should not be set in the shallow runways but in the deeper main highways. Two types of traps may be used, the scissors, or the diamond-jaw. Both depend on a trigger, sprung when the mole follows its natural instinct of burrowing through an obstruction of loose earth placed in the runway. Use a strong trowel to set the trap in the runway, aligning it so the jaws of the scissors trap straddle the course or the choker trap encircles it. Pack the earth firmly under the trigger, so the mole cannot work through without springing it. In gravel soil the choker works best. Skin the mole by slitting from chin to tail, peeling out the body, and cutting off tail and legs. Pin flat on boards in an oval shape and dry thoroughly in the shade. The Oregon mole is superior to the European mole and should sell for a fair price.

What will eradicate Townsend moles? (California.)   These are Oregon moles. (See previous question.)

Can one ever get rid of moles? (Iowa.)   Maybe, with persistence, but you don't want to get rid of those that are not actually injuring your garden. Think of your white-grub problem in Iowa. The loop or choker trap has been found to be very effective in Iowa soil.

How do you combat moles? (New York.)   New York State has 3 different moles. The naked-tail mole does much of the damage to lawns and golf courses on Long Island and in the lower Hudson Valley. In central and western New York the star-nosed and the hairy-tail moles are working. The star-nosed throws up earth in a mound similar to a gopher mound, but the other two make the familiar ridges. Use mole traps for these, but snap-back mousetraps for the star-nosed variety.

What are the best ways, supplementing traps, to discourage moles? (New York.)   Calcium cyanide may possibly be effective in April and May when the young are in the nest. Or open the runways at intervals with a sharp stick and drop in a teaspoon of lye, paradichlorbenzene, or naphthalene. Some report success with trade-marked materials such as Mole-Nots. Trapping remains the most effective method.

MOTHS

What is the difference between moths and butterflies?   Both are adults of caterpillars, often called worms. Moths are night fliers and structure of antennae is different.

I have a small golden moth infesting shrubs and grass and when I use the hose they fly up in great numbers. No one seems to know what they are or has noticed them. They last from June or July to September. What are they? (New York.)   They are probably the crambid moth, adults of sod webworms. Webworms are not a major lawn pest in New York as they are in California and some other states, but sometimes the larva, a fat caterpillar which lives in a silk-lined nest, injures the grass roots. Kerosene emulsion has been recommended but is rather a nuisance for the home gardener to prepare. Pyrethrum sprays are satisfactory, or sprays containing dichlorethyl ether. Grub-proofing with lead arsenate works very well. In your particular case the larvae of your moths may not be doing enough damage to bother about.

Gypsy Moth: attacks trees, and, occasionally, vegetables. Caterpillars, 2 in. long with conspicuous blue and red markings.

NICOTINE SULFATE

What is nicotine sulfate? Usually purchased as Black Leaf 40. An extremely useful contact insecticide. It is poisonous but is readily washed off, and so may be safely used on vegetables and fruits to within a short time of harvest. It is used ordinarily in a soapy solution but it may be added to Bordeaux mixture, lead arsenate, lime-sulphur, or oil sprays. The dosage varies according to the insect to be controlled. A normal solution (1 to 800 dilution) is made with 1 teaspoon nicotine sulfate and 1 oz. soap (1 cu. in. laundry soap) per gal. of water. For more resistant insects the dosage is increased to 1½ to 2 teaspoons per gal. Ordinarily nicotine sulfate may be used without injury to plants, but caution is needed on a very hot day in the garden or in an enclosed greenhouse that is too warm.

NICOTINE DUST

How is nicotine dust used? Used instead of a spray in some situations. To make a small quantity of dust pour 1 oz. (2 tablespoons) nicotine sulfate into 1 qt. of lime in a can containing 4 or 5 stones the size of marbles. Close the lid tightly and shake or roll slowly for several minutes. Do not have the container more than half full. Use the dust freshly mixed.

NEMATODES

What are nematodes and in what manner does soil become in-

fested? (**Georgia.**)   Nematodes are roundworms or eelworms, too small to see with the naked eye, that live in moist soil, in decaying organic matter, or as parasites in living plant tissues. They can travel only a short distance in the soil by themselves but are spread by surface water, by moving infested soil from place to place, and, very commonly, by local transfer and shipment of infested plants. Nematodes are more serious in sandy soils in Southern states, or in California. In the North they may live over the winter in perennials, but cannot survive free in the soil or in annuals.

How do you recognize the presence of nematodes? (Texas.) There are 3 types of nematodes apt to bother the home gardener: the stem and the bulb nematode, which produces discolored streaks or rings in narcissus bulbs and stunted phlox with distorted crinkled leaves; the leaf nematode, which turns the lower leaves of chrysanthemums brown; and the root-knot nematode, which would be your chief problem in Texas. This infests about 900 different plants, causing stunting and often death. When diseased plants are pulled up, round or irregular swellings or galls are found on the roots. The root-knot nematode infests beans, peas, and other legumes, and the galls should not be confused with the nodules formed by beneficial nitrogen-fixing bacteria.

How can root-knot nematodes be destroyed without killing shrubbery and perennials in infested beds? (California.)   You cannot treat the soil to kill nematodes without killing all living plants as well. California Agricultural Experiment Station *Circular 330* gives a list of plants that are most important hosts of the root-knot nematode and a list of plants reported resistant. Aside from grains and grasses, generally conceded to be nematode resistant, the list is short: sweet potato for a vegetable; apricot, avocado, citrus, date, and some varieties of cherries, plums, and peaches for fruits; and evening primrose, gaillardia, lupine, marigold, Michaelmas daisy, rudbeckia, and zinnia for ornamentals.

What is the latest information on combating nematodes in the Southern garden? (Texas.)   Rotating plantings with resistant-grain crops or treating the soil with carbon disulphide or chloropicrin (Larvacide). Carbon disulphide is exceedingly inflammable, although relatively inexpensive, and chloropicrin has become almost standard in the past 10 years. As a nemacide it is used at the rate of about 10 lbs. per 1,000 sq. ft. Injections are made with a special dispenser, using about 2½ c.c. injected 5 to 6 ins. deep at about 1-ft. intervals. Complete directions come with the material. It is not so effective if the area is not covered with impervious paper or flooded with water after treatment. As for crop rotation, it has been found that if cotton is rotated with alfalfa, nematodes are kept to insignificant numbers, so perhaps growing alfalfa in between vegetable crops would help. Growing most susceptible crops in winter, when the nemas are not so active, is also a partial solution.

Is there a quick, economical method of ridding garden soil of root-knot nematode? (Georgia.) Carbon disulphide is cheaper than chloropicrin and gives good results in a sandy soil. Use 1 to 2 ozs. per hole, and make the holes 6 to 9 ins. deep, 18 ins. apart, in staggered rows. Cover after treating for a couple of days and then air out at least a week before planting. There is always danger of fire or explosion in working with carbon disulphide. Another possibility is to divide your garden and in half of it grow such partly immune crops as onions, parsnips, strawberries, and turnips, and then the next year change about. Or give up half of it after taking off a spring crop and plant to *Crotalaria spectabilis* in rows 3 ft. apart. Cultivate frequently to keep it free from all weeds that might harbor nematodes. This may practically starve out the nematodes in one summer and the next year you can do the other half.

What about hot-water treatment for plants infested with nematodes? Normally this is best left to the commercial grower. Bulbs take a pre-soaking at 70° F., a pre-cooking, and then a 4-hour treatment at exactly 110° to 111.5° F., with formaldehyde added to prevent basal rot. Treating peonies infested with root-knot nematodes, in hot water held at 120° F. for 30 minutes, may be possible for the amateur gardener but not unless he has an accurate thermometer and a very steady source of heat.

OIL SPRAYS

Where can miscible oil be bought in New York City area? At any seed store and in most hardware stores. Ask for a dormant oil spray (almost all those sold to small gardeners are of the miscible type—an oil that mixes readily with water). Miscible oils are procured under such trade names as Scale-O, Scale-Oil, Scalecide, etc. (See Dormant Spraying.)

PRAYING MANTIS

Can you tell me about praying mantis? I am planning to purchase an egg case next spring. (Illinois.) If the praying mantis is not naturally present in your neighborhood, it might not pay to spend much for an egg case, for these ferocious-looking beneficial insects are not commonly found much north of 40° latitude. The mantis belongs to the grasshopper family. It is very long and thin, with prominent eyes and enormous front legs used for preying on other insects but often held up in a praying attitude. The baby mantes look just like the adults, except for lack of wings. Their cannibalistic instincts are so well developed they often eat one another. Do not let the egg masses hatch in the house, for heat brings them out in the winter and there is no way to feed the young mantes until they can survive out of doors.

I have hundreds of praying mantes in my garden. What do the egg cases look like? I find so many tentlike formations. (Kansas.) The egg cases are a sort of dingy cream or yellow in color, shaped something like a round hatbox, but not especially regular, about 1 in. across, and made of a frothy gummy substance which hardens in that same frothy texture. They are usually attached to twigs of trees or shrubs.

PYRETHRUM

What is pyrethrum? A contact insecticide obtained from the pyrethrum plant, mostly grown in Africa. It is especially effective against aphids and soft-bodied insects, but it will kill whatever chewing insects it hits. It is useful for spraying flowers where a stain would be objectionable, but the available supply does not warrant its free use on ornamentals. Most of the pyrethrum sent into the country is processed into insect bombs and sent out to the armed forces stationed in the tropics. For use on the Mexican bean beetle, impregnated pyrethrum dusts are more efficient. Thiocyanates are now added to some pyrethrum mixtures.

RABBITS

Now that fencing material is on the priority list, how can rabbits be kept out of the garden? (Pennsylvania.) Some sort of fence is still the best solution. If you cannot get the poultry wire ordinarily recommended, a picket fence may be substituted, or a low concrete wall built. The expense of either of these would be justified if the vegetable garden is to be permanent, and would look better than a wire fence even it were obtainable. A temporary expedient sometimes used is a fence of 18-in. roofing paper. Properly braced between the corners, this works well for the first part of the season but after many rains is apt to sag enough to let in the rabbits. There are reports that a row of child's windmills, or glass bottles stuck in the ground neck down, will act as a fence in scaring rabbits away.

Will dried blood sprinkled around roots of beans or other vegetables prevent rabbits from eating them? (New Jersey.) Dried blood has long been listed as an effective rabbit repellent, as well as being good for the garden. It may be difficult to obtain during the war, and gardeners report that it is not always effective.

What is a good rabbit repellent? (Illinois.) The New Jersey Fish and Game Commissioners has listed 9 repellents for harassed gardeners: 1, dust plants, when damp, with powdered lime; 2, dust liberally with dusting sulphur (some vegetables do not take kindly to sulphur); 3, sprinkle plants with red pepper; 4, spray with a solution of 3 ozs. Epsom salts in 1 gal. water; 5, spray with 1 teaspoon Lysol in 1 gal. water; 6, spray with 2 teaspoons Black Leaf 40 in 1 gal. soapy water; 7, spray with solution of common brown laundry soap; 8, spray with 1 oz. tartar emetic and 3 ozs. sugar in 1 gal. of water; 9, sprinkle naphthalene flakes between rows of plants.

How can you keep rabbits from eating young soybeans? That is the $64 question. Soybeans are often used to keep rabbits away from other plants. They work that way in my garden, and I still get a lusty crop of soybeans. Formerly I credited moth balls with repelling the rabbits just enough to give the soybeans a fighting chance, but I visited a garden last summer where the rabbits had not allowed one soybean plant out of hundreds to get above 6 ins. high and the moth balls were so thick the garden looked white. Now I have come to the conclusion that it is my neighbors' cats, hunting young rabbits, that keep the population down to reasonable proportions.

How can we prevent rabbits from eating our shrubs and evergreens? We have sprayed with copper sulfate, which is a waste of time. (Illinois.) Most repellents do not remain effective long enough. A box trap placed under shrubs in the winter and early spring when food is scarce may catch many rabbits. Rabbits are protected in some areas, and you would probably have to make arrangements with the game warden. With rabbits such a menace to gardens, a permit may sometimes be obtained for shooting them from the Fish and Game Commission, but one still has to get permission to shoot from the local police, and that is often denied in thickly settled suburban areas.

Is there any repellent which can be put on trunks of trees and shrubs? Commercial preparations have a temporary effect. One may be made at home by melting 5 parts resin and stirring in 1 part linseed oil. Apply it to the bark with a brush while warm but not hot. This may be toxic to peaches and sweet cherries and should be used with some caution on other fruits. Grafting wax would be a safe repellent.

Rabbits have chewed the bark completely from the trunk of a young flowering crab planted this spring. Can anything be done to save the tree? (New Jersey.)   You might try bridge grafting (which see), which has worked successfully for apple trees girdled by rabbits and mice. Unless you are acquainted with this art, it would be better to have the work done by a tree expert, and that might cost as much as a new tree. Next time, if you can possibly get the wire, protect your tree with a cylinder of close-mesh woven wire, 18 ins. wide, sunk into the ground a few inches and held away from the trunk with stakes. Sometimes prunings left on the ground around the trees and bushes will feed the rabbits enough to keep them from injuring the trunks. (See page 1170.)

RED SPIDER

What is red spider?   See Mites.

ROTENONE

What is rotenone?   The principal insecticidal constituent in roots of derris, timbo, cube, or lonchocarpus. It acts as a stomach and contact poison for insects, kills fish and cold-blooded animals, but is not injurious to man except as a throat irritant. It leaves no poisonous residue on the plant. Rotenone formerly was obtained from the Far East and is now coming in from South America. Lonchocarpus is being established there to provide a new source of rotenone. Rotenone dust before the war was used in a 1 per cent dilution, or derris analyzing 4 per cent rotenone was used for spraying. At the present time dust mixtures have been cut to 0.5 per cent to make the supply last.

RUST

What is a good spray for rust? (California.)   That depends on whether or not you have true rust, a fungus that manifests itself in erumpent reddish-brown or reddish-orange pustules of spores, or, in the case of cedar and apple rust, in long, gelatinous spore horns. Sulphur is the best fungicide for the control of rust. For ornamental plants it is most easily applied as a dust. Very often gardeners speak of "rust" when they merely mean a reddish discoloration of the tissue, which might be due to a variety of causes but never to the true rust fungus.

SCALE INSECTS

What is life history of scale? What plants are attacked? What are treatments?   Do you mean indoors or out? There are many different scale insects, but 2 general types. Those found in gardens in New York would be mostly of the armored-scale type, that is, after they finish the young crawling stage a hard, separable shell is formed on their bodies and they stop moving around. In this group is the oyster-shell scale on lilacs, scurfy scale on apples, rose scale on roses, euonymus scale on euonymus and bittersweet, juniper scale, pine-needle scale, and many others. This group is controlled by spraying before growth starts in the spring (see Dormant Spraying) and sometimes for the young scales in midsummer. The second group includes the soft or tortoise scales, represented in a Northern garden by maple and magnolia scales but more often seen on house plants, where they have to be scrubbed off or sprayed with nicotine or a white oil. (See House Plants.)

How do you get rid of cottony cushion scale on trees? (Texas.) Ask your State Experiment Station where you can get a colony of Australian lady beetles. In California they may be secured from the Citrus Experiment Station at Riverside.

SEED TREATMENT

Should seeds be treated before planting? Yes, the application of a chemical protectant is insurance against damping off, either in the seed flat or the garden row, and in addition it may prevent some diseases due to organisms carried on the outside of the seed.

What chemicals are used for seed treatment? Red or yellow copper oxide, usually sold as Cuprocide; zinc oxide; Semesan, an organic mercury; and Spergon and Arasan, synthetic materials.

Can you buy one dust and treat all kinds of seeds? Not very successfully; there is a marked difference in response of seeds to chemicals. Red copper oxide, for instance, is apt to be injurious to seed of cabbage and other crucifers, while Spergon is particularly effective for peas. Possibilities are: Semesan for celery; cabbage and other crucifers; Semesan, Jr., for corn; Spergon: peas, beans, lima beans, lettuce; Cuprocide: beets, carrots, celery, eggplants, peppers, spinach, tomatoes, cucumbers, melons, squash, and pumpkins; zinc oxide: lettuce, cabbage, spinach; Arasan: onions, tomatoes, and beans.

How do you dust the seeds? Is it injurious to use too much of the protectant? Using too much dust may be decidedly injurious, causing stunting or preventing germination entirely. The usual rule is 1 teaspoon per pound for small seeds and ½ teaspoon for larger seeds like cucumber and squash. For a small packet of seeds use about as much as can be held on the tip of a knife. Put seeds and dust together in a glass jar, shake until each seed is faintly coated, and then dump out onto a strainer so that all excess dust can be shaken off.

What about the organisms carried inside the seeds?   They cannot be killed with external dusts. They must be soaked in hot water or bichloride of mercury—a treatment usually not given unless the disease organism is presumably present. Tie seeds loosely in cheesecloth bags and keep the temperature of the water constant: 122° F., 25 minutes for cabbage, 15 minutes for other crucifers; tomato seed, 25 minutes; 118° F., 30 minutes for celery. Seed potatoes are treated in 1 to 1,000 bichloride of mercury 1½ hours, but seeds only 10 to 15 minutes, after which they are washed to prevent injury.

SLUGS AND SNAILS

What is a certain positive method of ridding your garden of slugs? (California.)   Is there ever anything "certain positive" about gardening? Metaldehyde as the active principal in slug baits was tried out first in California and was so successful there that it has become more or less standard for the rest of the country. Many of the baits sold under trade names contain metaldehyde, which exerts a fatal attraction on slugs, and then, when they come close enough to touch it, liquefies them. The bait is put out in small piles, about the size of a silver dollar, and should be covered in some fashion to protect it from the weather, birds, and pests.

How can I best rid my grounds of the soft-bodied slug? (Vermont.)   Use a combination of methods—poison bait, sprinkling lime or salt in the slug paths, dusting plants with fluosilicates or nicotine dust or lead arsenate, or dusting ground and plants with dry Bordeaux mixture as a repellent, trapping slugs by putting out shingles at night and destroying the catch in the morning. In the long run the most effective method is to keep your garden so cleaned up that slugs will have no daytime hiding places. Cleaning irises in late fall deprives slugs of a favorite winter home.

What is best method for combating slugs? We use lime but it whitens shrubs. They attack cherry trees, purple-leaf plum, and flowering quince. (Utah.)   Put your lime on the ground in a circle, enclosing the tree trunk. Try spraying the slugs at night with a spray of ¼ to ½ lb. alum per gallon water. Try metaldehyde baits.

Will a boardwalk in a garden be the cause of an exceptionally large number of slugs?   It would provide the protected hiding place favored by slugs, but it should also prove a help in getting rid of them, for poison baits put under the boardwalk would not endanger children, pets, or birds.

What is the best way to destroy slugs and snails without risk of poisoning birds or pets? (Ohio.) If poison baits are put out under little jar covers or pieces of board, there is little danger to pets, but to play absolutely safe, resort to lime on the ground, cleaning up plant debris, hand-picking, and probably spraying or dusting plants as outlined above. For hollyhocks I have found that lead arsenate added to the dust used to control rust will take care of slugs sufficiently. There is practically no danger to pets when a poison is used on plants.

Are hard-shell snails or big, fat, soft ones harmful or beneficial in the garden? Have roses, iris, lilies, etc. (Pennsylvania.) They are not exactly beneficial. Roses will be little bothered by true slugs in Pennsylvania, but they have their special brand of false slugs or sawfly larvae. (See Rose.) Any plant with leaves close to the ground like iris or lily will be apt to have light-colored areas in the leaf where the slugs have eaten everything but the epidermis.

What do you do about snails? (California.) Snails are just slugs (soft molluscs) with a shell. Use poison baits in spring and summer in rainy weather or when there are fogs at night. Either metaldehyde slug bait or a mixture of 1 part calcium arsenate and 16 parts wheat bran may be used. Hand-picking is always successful. Lime around trees will act as a barrier to prevent snails from climbing the trunk in destructive numbers.

How can I rid my plants of snails? (Texas.) Another bait, listed by a group of Southern nurserymen and entomologists, contains 1 qt. dry bran, ½ oz. Paris green, ½ cup molasses, and ½ cup water.

SOIL STERILIZATION

Isn't there some way to get the soil in such a healthy condition that insects and diseases will not bother a plant? Disease organisms in the soil may be killed by soil sterilization, but there is no known way to render plants immune to attacks by fungi or insects. There are a few instances where fertilizing is somewhat linked up with resistance; there is little exact knowledge along this line.

How do you sterilize soil? The usual aim is not a complete destruction of all living organisms but a partial sterilization which will control harmful organisms. Heat is one of the best means, but there are difficulties. Steam is excellent but practical only for the commercial greenhouse operator; hot water can be used, but it is apt to puddle the soil; baking is used for small quantities, but there may be toxic materials liberated; this may be true also when electricity is used. Formaldehyde is most useful for treating small lots of soil to prevent damping off of seedlings. Formaldehyde dust is used, but the liquid sprinkle method seems more generally satisfactory. For each 20 × 14 × 2 and ¾ in. flat of soil use 1 tablespoon formalin diluted with 6 tablespoons water. Sprinkle it over the soil and mix thoroughly. Let stand 12 to 24 hours; *after* the seeds are sown, water immediately.

How do you treat soil in the garden?   It is rather an expensive procedure recommended only for the control of specific organisms when crop rotation is not feasible. Formaldehyde is usually used for root-rot fungi. Dilute 1 part commercial formalin with 50 parts water and apply ½ gal. to each sq. ft. of soil. Cover for 1 to 2 days with burlap, paper, or boards. Spade to air out the gas and wait about 2 weeks before planting. Chloropicrin (Larvacide) is used against nematodes, weed seeds, and certain fungi in the soil, at the rate of 1 lb. to 140 sq. ft. The soil should be in a loose, moist condition and the temperature 60° to 85° F. The fumes are very injurious, and treatment must not be carried on near living plants. After the chloropicrin is injected into holes 6 to 8 ins. deep and about 15 ins. apart, the holes should be closed and the soil flooded with water, or else covered with impervious paper. Carbon disulphide may also be used for soil treatment against fungi, nematodes, ants, termites, and other insects. It is cheaper than chloropicrin, but highly inflammable. Directions for use are given under Specific Diseases and Pests. Bichloride of mercury may be used fairly safely around living plants, but it has a rather temporary effect.

SOOTY MOLD

I have had trouble in my greenhouse with a black sooty substance forming on the leaves. It is hard to wash off. **What is it and how prevent it from forming? (Wisconsin.)**   This is a black fungous growth, called sooty mold, but the fungus is not parasitic on the plant; it is merely growing in insect honeydew that drops on the leaves; in your case very likely from white flies, but on outdoor shrubs very often from aphids. There is not much hope of washing it off. You can prevent it by spraying to control your insect population.

SOWBUGS

How do you destroy hog bugs? **The bug is flat and fairly round, hard legs along the side. (Virginia.)**   They are usually called sowbugs, probably named for female hogs because of their shape. But they are sometimes called pill bugs because of their tendency to roll up into little balls. Sowbugs are not true insects but crustacea, related to crayfish. They are grayish in color, segmented, with 7 pairs of legs about ½ in. long. They hide at the base of plants under clods of earth or manure. A sweetened bait is used to destroy them. One formula calls for 1 qt. bran, ½ oz. Paris green, ½ cup molasses, and ½ cup water. The poisoned bran is placed around in small piles. If the bait is used outdoors, it should be covered to protect birds and pets.

What is the specific for sowbugs? In greenhouses or in dry periods outdoors a sugar bait seems to work best for sowbugs, a simple formula of 1 oz. Paris green to 9 ozs. sugar. This is mixed dry and put on small wooden or tin plates throughout the beds.

Do sowbugs eat seed in flats? I am not certain about the seed itself, but they injure the seedlings by feeding on the roots and tender growth.

SPITTLE BUGS

What causes the white frothy substance that looks like white foam to come on plants? This is the spittle bug, so named because the young nymphs have the habit of secreting a quantity of frothy material between molts. The adults leave the "spit" protection and look something like leaf hoppers, but because of their bulging eyes are often called froghoppers. In Michigan the pine spittle insect may be injurious to pines and other conifers by sucking the sap. Occasionally young trees are killed. Use contact insecticides at double the strength recommended for aphids, and apply the spray with great pressure.

What can I do to rid my plants of insect in a sort of frame? Have heard it called spit bug. Various species of spittle bugs may occasionally injure garden plants. In New Jersey several years ago a devastating attack on strawberries was repulsed with derris dust. Any fairly potent contact insecticide applied with enough pressure to penetrate the protective froth should be satisfactory. Spittle bugs do get around. They have been several times reported from penthouse gardens high over New York City.

SPRAYERS

What are garden sprayers? Machines to apply liquid insecticides or fungicides to plants in a fine mist. Sprayers vary from pint- or quart-size atomizers useful for house plants to huge power apparatus that will spray tall trees with 500-lbs. pressure. For the average garden a cylindrical compressed-air sprayer or a knapsack sprayer of 3- to 4-gal. capacity that fits on the back will be sufficient. For small trees and shrubs a bucket or barrel sprayer that holds 12 gals. and is mounted on a small truck to move around the garden will be most convenient. Motor-driven estate sprayers are also available. Copper is at a premium now, but if a copper sprayer rather than a galvanized one can be procured it will be worth the extra price in longer life. No sprayer is better than the care given it. Rinse thoroughly immediately after use and occasionally take it apart for cleaning. Strain all spray mixtures into the tank through cheesecloth to prevent clogging. Extra parts can often be obtained from manufacturers or distributors to keep old sprayers in operation.

Is any single spray, such as the cartridge type, sufficient for all average conditions?   Generally speaking, the cartridge spray does not give so complete control as spraying with a portable sprayer, although it has its uses in some gardens. For one single piece of apparatus, useful for shrubs and small trees as well as flowers and vegetables, the bucket pump, of the Paragon type, is most useful, but this requires two people to operate it to best advantage. The compressed-air sprayer, if it is provided with an extension rod and swivel nozzle, will do a comprehensive job in most gardens.

SPRAY MATERIALS

Spraying charts are usually given for the large farmer, not the back-yard gardener. Will you furnish a simplified spraying chart where a gardener requires only a pint or a quart at most? So far as possible the directions in this section are given in small quantities, usually 1 gallon. One pint, or even a quart, will not go very far, even in a back-yard garden. Moreover, anyone capable of filling out income-tax blanks should be able to do a little arithmetic on garden sprays. Remember that there are 3 teaspoons in 1 tablespoon, 16 tablespoons in 1 cup, or 8 liquid ozs., 4 cups in a quart, and 4 qts. in a gallon. Buy a set of kitchen measuring spoons and a glass cup marked off in ounces. When the recipe calls for 1 teaspoon per gallon and you need only a quart, use the tiny ¼ teaspoon measure.

What can I use on vegetables that is harmless to people or dogs and will kill the chewing bugs?   Rotenone. Cryolite is also relatively safe, as compared with arsenical sprays, and may be used until the edible parts are noticeable.

What are the main spray materials to have on hand? I understand some of these sprays are the same, only going under different names.   You understand correctly. Insecticides and fungicides are sold under 900 different trade names, but basically they depend on nicotine, lead, calcium, or magnesium arsenate, pyrethrum, rotenone, fluosilicates, oils for action against insects, and copper or sulphur for fungicides. Always read the label on your proprietary mixture and know what you are buying. Only the plants you grow and the diseases and pests you have can determine how many different materials are required in your garden. Theoretically, 1 fungicide, 1 stomach poison, and 1 contact insecticide would see you through, but not all fungi react to copper or to sulphur, and not all insects can be controlled by rule.

Isn't there some one spray I could use for all the garden ills to which the far South is heir? (Louisiana.) Unfortunately, no, but garden Volck comes close to taking care of some of the most important Southern pests. For help in your state read Dr. Eddy's column, "Bug News," in *Home Gardening,* published at New Orleans. Send to the Department of Entomology, Louisiana Experiment Station, for *Insect Pest Control Service Leaflet No. 31.* It is excellent.

Would you suggest how to plan a spray schedule for a perennial border? It would take more than the space I am allowed here, but I wrote a book telling you when and how to spray your ornamentals. *Consult The Plant Doctor,* Stokes, 1940.

SULPHUR

How is sulphur used in the garden? A valuable fungicide with many uses but especially in the control of rust and mildew, and also of some value as an insecticide in the control of red spiders and other mites. In the home garden, sulphur is usually used in dust form, and it may be safely combined with lead or calcium arsenate, rotenone, or cryolite. Wettable sulphurs are available to use as liquid sprays. In very hot weather sulphur should be used cautiously, for it is apt to burn the plants. It is incompatible with oil and should not be used within 30 days of an oil spray.

Is there a green dusting sulphur available for the amateur gardener? Yes, one may be purchased under the name of Pomo-green. Personally I do not find the green color of enough benefit to justify the extra expense. It is less conspicuous, but any that falls to the ground shows up more than the ordinary yellow sulphur. The green dye does, however, slightly increase the fungicidal value.

SQUIRRELS

How do I get rid of chipmunks? (Massachusetts.) It has

been said, although I cannot prove it personally, that chipmunks are unsuspicious creatures readily caught in snap-back traps baited with a nut, pumpkin seed, or berry, and placed near their burrows. These ground squirrels eat some slugs and insects and should not be destroyed without reason. Bulbs may be planted in wire baskets to protect them.

Our corn patch was neatly devastated, a dozen ears per night, by some animal that shucked as it ate. Is it likely to have been squirrels? How can we combat such an unseen adversary? (Connecticut.)   It may have been woodchucks or squirrels, although they are bold enough to eat in the daytime, and in New Jersey this past season we had authenticated cases of raccoons destroying corn. There is not much solution except to plant enough for you and the animals too. In my garden they are satisfied with the outside row. (See Corn.)

How do you get rid of gray squirrels? (Virginia.)   Get permission to shoot them, which is easier said than done in many communities.

How do you prevent squirrels from monopolizing feeding stations? (New York.)   If the feeding station is hung from a horizontal wire, metal guards may be placed either side; or if the feeding station is on top of a post, a guard may be placed underneath; but if the station is anywhere within leaping distance of a tree, the guard is useless.

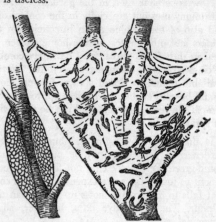

Tent Caterpillar forms grayish-white tent-like nests in early spring; left, egg mass on winter twig.

TENT CATERPILLAR

How can I control the tent caterpillar which attacks wild-cherry and apple trees in the spring?   As soon as the webs form, while worms are still very small, wipe them out of the crotches of branches with a pointed stick or a swab dipped in kerosene. If webs must be destroyed after the caterpillars are well developed, do so in early morning or after sunset when they have returned to web for warmth. A preventive control is to cut off and burn the twigs bearing egg masses which can be seen after the leaves have dropped in autumn or winter.

TERMITES

How can anyone treat their ground to get rid of white ants or termites which get into all woody roots and ruin plants? (Kentucky.)   Use lead arsenate in topsoil as for grub-proofing. Use sap pine stakes beside plants, pull them occasionally; destroy termites with hot water. Treat soil with Lethane or Loro (thiocyanate sprays) 1 teaspoon in 1 qt. water. Swarming will indicate location of a colony, which can be drenched with kerosene.

Where termites are in cordwood, 50 feet from a brick house, is there danger that they will get started in the house itself? (Maryland.)   Not unless there is any woodwork on the building in direct contact with the ground. If there is, a metal shield can be inserted.

TEXAS ROOT ROT

Has there been anything found to control root rot? (Texas.) Texas root rot, also called cotton or Phymatotrichum root rot, is probably the chief problem in gardening in certain parts of Texas, Arizona, and New Mexico. The fungus *Phymatotrichum omnivorum* is a native soil inhabitant in semi-arid regions of low humidity, high temperature, and alkalinity. It attacks 1,700 plant species. The monocotyledons are immune, so you can grow palms, irises, lilies, gladioli, and bulbs without trouble. During the period of summer rains dense circular mats of fungus mycelium appear on the surface of the soil, at first white, later tan and powdery. Plants turn yellow and die rapidly. Sometimes a tree can be saved at the first sign of wilting by applying ammonium sulfate, 1 lb. to 10 sq. ft., in a basin around the tree and letting water run in until the soil is wet 4 ft. deep. Garden soil may also be treated with ammonium sulfate, but if there are no shrubs within 20 ft., the fallow soil may be treated with formaldehyde (1 to 70 dilution, 1 gal. applied per foot) or with carbon disulphide (2 to 5 ozs. per hole, in holes 18 ins. apart and 6 to 12 ins. deep).

WITCHES'-BROOMS

What are witches'-brooms and their cause? (Massachusetts.)

Broomlike excessive development of twigs in response to an irritation caused by insects, fungi, or some virus. Hackberry is a notable example with often hundreds of brooms, each a mass of stubby twigs arising from a swelling at the base of a branch, on a single tree. A gall mite and a powdery-mildew fungus seem to be jointly responsible for this deformation. There is no control in this case, but cutting out the brooms improves appearance.

WHITE GRUBS

This spring I plowed and planted land that had not been farmed for 25 years; grubworms killed potatoes, cabbage, etc. What was reason? (Illinois.)   Grubworms are white grubs in your area, soft-bodied white worms with brown heads, curved bodies ½ to 1 in. long. They look like Japanese beetle grubs but are a little larger. They damage lawns in the same way and are much more injurious to root vegetables than are the grubs we suffer from in the East. As you continue to garden your land, the injury should get less. It is most serious in areas neglected for a long time. White grubs are larvae of June beetles. There is a 3-year cycle, the grubs staying in the ground 2 years and the large brown beetles flying the third year and eating tree foliage. Injury from the worms is greatest the year after beetle flight.

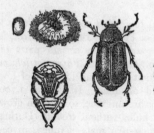

White Grub: large, soft white grub with brown head—larva of the June beetle; attacks roots of grass and other plants.

How shall I rid my soil of grubworms? (Texas.)   Prevent trouble, if possible, by not planting garden crops on sod land, or land grown up to weeds and grass the preceding year. If such land must be used, plow in the fall, or spade, and keep the ground free of weeds by working it frequently. Legume crops will suffer less than corn or potatoes. Lawns may be treated with lead arsenate (see Grub-proofing), but this is not advisable for garden soil.

WIREWORMS

I have a pest in the soil about the thickness of a darning needle, light brown, very tough; have to cut off the head to kill

it; ¾ to 1½ ins. long; seems to live in the roots. **Is it harmful to plants? (Indiana.)**   You have described a wireworm, a chewing insect which feeds underground on germinating seeds and underground roots, stems, and tubers. Potatoes, beets, beans, cabbage, carrots, corn, lettuce, onions, turnips, and other vegetables may be injured. Damage is worse on poorly drained soil or on land that has been in grass sod. The adult stage of the wireworm is a gray, brown, or black click beetle, an amusing creature that clicks itself right side up when it falls on its back.

What is the best method for exterminating wireworms? (New Jersey.)   If newly broken sod must be used, plow it thoroughly and then stir it once a week for 6 weeks in the fall preceding spring planting. Improve drainage. To help control wireworms, with a growing crop put vegetable baits—a hollowed-out potato or pieces of carrot in the soil near the plants and take them up periodically and destroy the worms.

WOODCHUCKS

How do you get rid of woodchucks?   The United States Fish and Wildlife Service has developed a special woodchuck cartridge, which may be obtained through county agents. When lighted according to directions and placed in a den mouth, this will diffuse a lethal gas through the den.

How prevent woodchucks from eating strawberries?   A fence is the only sure protection, except a dog.

What can I do about woodchucks that eat my garden plants? Watch for them early morning and late afternoon and shoot them. Find the holes and poison them with cyanogas.

How is cyanogas used to kill woodchucks?   A woodchuck usually has at least two openings to his home. Close these up with heavy stones and soil to keep gas fumes in. Put about 3 ozs. of cyanogas into one opening and then close. This is an extremely fatal poison, so handle carefully. The fumes are given off when the crystals are in contact with moist soil. The gas is heavier than air, so it settles into the burrow.

ORNAMENTALS

ACONITE

Why do monkshood leaves and stems die? Cure? Bulbs look healthy. (Connecticut.)   If the vessels are black when you cut across the stem, dying leaves are probably due to verticillium wilt, results of a soil fungus affecting the vascular system. No cure. Plant healthy roots in new or sterilized soil.

Can one prevent yellowing of leaves or complete defoliation of aconitum before blooming? (Ohio.)   Since this is presumably the same verticillium wilt, nothing will prevent the disease except starting over with new roots in fresh soil.

Is there any other cause of blight of aconitum, except verticillium? (New Jersey.)   Yes, sometimes the crown-rot fungus so destructive to delphinium attacks aconitum. In this case you usually see white threads or seedlike bodies on the soil, and the plant may topple over at the crown. Remove plant and surrounding soil. Disinfect area with bichloride of mercury.

Why do the flower buds of my aconitum turn black and not open? (New Jersey.)   The cyclamen mite affects aconitum as it does delphinium. Remove infested portions and spray frequently with rotenone, when it is available for ornamentals, or nicotine sulfate and soap as a second choice.

AGERATUM

What do you do for white flies on ageratum?   The white flies usually come along when you get your plants from the greenhouse in the spring and cause minute white spotting of the foliage all summer, getting worse toward fall. Frequent spraying with nicotine sulfate and soap, hitting the under side of the leaves, is helpful.

How can I keep mooly aphids or milk cows from my blue ageratum? I lose the plants each year. (Missouri.)   "Mooly" is evidently mistyped for woolly, but the pun is too good to lose. Ants keep root aphids herded together so they can feed on the honeydew (milk) excreted. Make a shallow depression around each plant and pour in nicotine sulfate and soap solution. (See also Ants, for their control.)

AFRICAN-VIOLET

How can I get rid of the mealy bugs on my African-violet? It is difficult, because spraying injures the foliage. Watch for the first signs of these white woolly sucking insects and remove them with a small brush dipped in alcohol. Touch only the bug, not the leaf. Avoid a too-hot, dry atmosphere.

How rid my African-violet of a small insect that weaves a white web all over it?   It is probably a mealy bug, and if the infestation is that bad you'd better burn the plant and start with a healthy one.

Is there a remedy for lice on African-violet plants? You probably refer to mealy bugs, for ordinary aphids are not so common on this plant. Constant vigilance is the remedy; pick off the first bit of cotton fluff you see, or touch each insect with a small swab of cotton on a matchstick (or a very small paint-brush) dipped in alcohol.

What causes a moldlike covering over the topsoil of house plants, particularly African-violets? Insufficient aeration. Cultivate the soil occasionally with the tines of an old fork. Too much water compacts the soil and encourages the moldy surface growth. You may need to repot with a fresh mixture.

ALYSSUM

Why does Basket of Gold Alyssum die? Possibly because of wet feet. Good soil drainage is necessary; the foliage should be kept dry. This plant thrives on walls and other dry locations.

AMARYLLIS

Can mealy bugs be removed from scales of amaryllis bulb? Have tried alcohol sprays and enclosing pot in bag with napthalene flakes, but still mealy bugs. Be wary about alcohol *sprays*. You can remove bugs with a tiny cotton swab on a tooth-pick dipped in alcohol. Or try scrubbing bulb and base of leaves with a rag dipped in nicotine sulfate and soap. Exposure to napthalene fumes may be dangerous to growing bulb.

What is the grub that gets into amaryllis bulbs? Probably larval form of greater or lesser narcissus bulb flies. Grub of the greater fly may be up to ¾ in. long, the lesser up to ½ in. Commercial growers often treat bulbs with hot water, but there is nothing for the home grower to do after the injury is noted.

Why do amaryllis leaves turn yellow and die? They do not dry up but have something like wet rot. If the rot is wet, it may be bacterial soft rot following work of bulb-fly larvae. If the bulb is not sound, do not save it for another year. Burn it.

AMARCRINUM

How do I get rid of thrips on Amarcrinum howardii and Urginea maritima? Have sprayed with nicotine and dusted with sulphur. Sulphur is probably useless. Nicotine sulfate re-quires 1 oz. soap per gallon to be effective, and the addition of 2 tablespoonfuls kerosene per gallon may help. Or you might try the tartar-emetic spray described under gladiolus.

ANEMONE

How can one protect anemones from the blister beetle?
Only by constant vigilance when the beetles appear in midsummer. Sodium or barium fluosilicate dusts are said to give best control. The latter may be purchased as Dutox. Combination pyrethrum-rotenone sprays are also helpful, as is hand-picking of the beetles. Lead arsenate gives some control. (See Blister Beetle.)

ARBORVITAE

What is the best solution to use on arborvitae when the branches become a rusty color? (Illinois.)   The rusty color is often due to spruce mite, similar to red spider. The most potent spray is a miscible oil, applied before new growth starts in the spring. (See Dormant Spraying.) During the growing season, forceful spraying with water, dusting with sulphur, or spraying with glue (½ lb. dissolved in warm water and diluted to 3⅓ gals.) are all useful methods.

What might be the cause of arborvitae turning brown and dying? (Mississippi.)   If the whole tree dies, it may be from prolonged injury from spruce mites, but the browning and dying of inner leaves are a natural shedding. Dying of the tips of the branches, twig blight, is a fungous disease, calling for cutting off and burning of infected portions.

How do you destroy little red bugs that suck the sap from arborvitae? (Arkansas.)   You may mean the arborvitae aphid, a very small, hairy, amber-brown plant louse. Apply a good contact spray, such as nicotine sulfate and soap, with as much pressure as possible, for these aphids are covered with a powdery film which makes them hard to kill.

Why do the tips of arborvitae twigs turn white? (Connecticut.)
This is the work of a leaf miner, which winters in the leaves and emerges as a moth to lay eggs in June. Spraying with lead arsenate, with nicotine sulfate added, in early July helps to kill larvae as they enter the base of the leaves.

ASPIDISTRA

What causes the white-looking fungus or scale or whatever it can be called on aspidistra leaves? How can it be cured? (Louisiana.)   There is a fungous disease, anthracnose, characterized by white spots with brown margins. Spraying is seldom necessary or profitable. There is also a brown scale listed on aspidistra. Perhaps you refer to mealy bugs. (See House Plants, this section, for control.)

ASTER, CHINA

Will paper collars adequately protect transplants, aster particularly, from grubworms? (Oregon.)   Collars will protect against cutworms (fat caterpillars which cut off plant stems near the surface). Collars offer no protection against the white grubs, larvae of June beetles, which stay in the soil and feed on roots of garden plants.

After being full-grown and flowering plants, asters dried up and died. What was the cause? (New York.)   Aster wilt, a disease caused by a soil fungus, a species of fusarium, which grows into the roots and affects the vascular or water-conducting system of the plant. Young plants may be infected and not show symptoms until flowering, as in this case.

Why do some asters thrive until they are 7 to 8 ins. tall, then turn brown, rusty, and die? I can't find anything at the roots or on the tops. (Idaho.)   This is an earlier manifestation of the same aster wilt. Infection often takes place at transplanting, with the leaves drying and dying somewhat later. Plant wilt-resistant seed, many varieties of which are now on the market.

When asters have blighted, how long a time must elapse before they can be safely grown in the same ground? (Illinois.)   No one knows exactly how long the fusarium wilt fungus lives in the soil, but it is several years.

What can I do to prevent root rot in my aster bed? I plant wilt-resistant seed, disinfected with Semesan, without the desired results. (Illinois.)   Certain soils are so infested with the wilt fungus that a certain percentage of "wilt-resistant" plants will succumb, the situation being worse in wet seasons. Try sterilizing the soil in the seedbed with formaldehyde and transplanting seedlings to a fresh location. (See Soil Sterilization.)

Is there anything to sterilize the ground for infected aster plants? It is a large space. (Wisconsin.)   It will scarcely pay to treat a large space. For a small area try a formaldehyde drench, spading the soil, and then saturating with a solution of 1 gal. commercial formalin diluted with 50 gals. of water. Apply ½ to 1 gal. per sq. ft. of soil, cover with paper or canvas for 24 hours, and then air out for 2 weeks before planting.

What causes some asters to open greenish white instead of coloring up? (California.)   Aster yellows, a virus disease transmitted from diseased to healthy plants by leaf hoppers. The leaves lose their chlorophyll and turn yellow, while the blossoms turn green. Plants are usually stunted. This is the most serious aster disease and occurs throughout the United States.

How can I prevent aster yellows?   Only by preventing insect transmission. Remove diseased plants immediately, so there will be no source of infection. Spray frequently with contact insecticides to kill leaf hoppers. Commercial growers protect asters by growing them in cloth houses made of cheesecloth or tobacco cloth with 22 meshes to the inch.

How can I get rid of the small root lice that suck life out of aster and other annuals? (Illinois.)   Make a shallow depression around each plant and pour in the same nicotine sulfate and soap solution used for spraying above-ground aphids. It also helps to work a handful of tobacco dust into the soil as each seedling is set out.

What treatment will reduce damage to asters by the tarnished plant bug. (Kansas.)   This small, light and dark brown sucking insect is hard to control. It is very active, occurs on many kinds of plants, stinging the flower buds and spotting the leaves, and has several generations a season. Contact insecticides will kill those insects it hits, and sulphur dust is suggested as a repellent. Derris (rotenone) dust is effective. Cleaning up all trash and weeds will make hibernation difficult for the bug.

What is the control of the common black beetle on asters? (Michigan.)   You probably mean the long, slim blister beetle, which is very destructive to asters. Dust with Dutox, or sodium fluosilicate, or spray with cryolite. (See Blister Beetle.)

AZALEAS

What is azalea flower-spot disease? (Louisiana.)   A relatively recent fungous disease which has spread from South Carolina through the Gulf states since 1931 and has been reported from California. Pinhead spots on the flowers enlarge to brownish blotches and the flowers collapse in about 3 days. Black resting bodies form in the petals and winter in the fallen leaves. The indica varieties are especially susceptible.

How do you control azalea flower-spot?   Spraying has little permanent effect and injures the bloom. The best "cure" is prevention by placing a barrier between the fungus sending up its little spores from the soil and the petals. A thick mulch of Spanishmoss fiber has been quite effective. After blooming, clean up and burn the old contaminated mulch, and put on a new mulch for the summer, adding 4 to 5 ins. additional material when the buds break in January. Asphalt paper mulch proved effective in experiments at Louisiana State University.

What are cause and treatment of moldlike white threads and general decline of azalea plants? (California.)   Azaleas in California are subject to attack by the oak-root rot fungus (*Armillaria mellea*). Besides the white threads (*mycelium*) the fungus has shoestringlike black strands which go through the soil and produce honey-colored toadstools. Increase vigor of plants by feeding; remove some of the soil from crowns and roots; avoid too-high soil moisture content. Treat soil known to be infested with carbon disulphide 2 months before planting new azaleas. Inject 45 c.c. to a depth of 6 to 9 ins. at staggered 2-ft. intervals.

My azalea buds blight before they open. Why? (Ohio.) There is a fungus which blasts terminal flower buds in the summer so they do not bloom the following year and sometimes kills leaf buds and twigs. Prune out and destroy all diseased material. Spray with Bordeaux mixture after blossoming.

What bores holes in my Azalea mollis? It goes in near the ground and comes out at top of branches? (New Jersey.) (New York.)   Probably the azalea borer, but this starts at the top and works down. The beetle lays its eggs near the tip and the young larva enters near a leaf node and bores down through the twig into the crown. Cut off dead and dying tips; inject nicotine paste into holes showing sawdust.

My azalea plants (outdoor) have been attacked by lace bugs. How can I get rid of them? (New Jersey.)   Spray with nicotine sulfate or other contact insecticide when the young nymphs hatch, usually in early June. There are 2 or 3 broods of the azalea lace bug, and spraying may need to be repeated at 3-week intervals throughout the summer. Cover under surface of leaves very thoroughly. The sucking of lace bugs turns the leaves of evergreen azaleas coffee-colored and those of deciduous varieties whitish.

What kills black aphids on azaleas? (New Jersey.)   Aphids are not ordinarily so common on azaleas as on other hosts, but they may be killed with the usual nicotine sulfate and soap spray, or any other contact insecticide.

When and with what do I spray azaleas for red spider and other pests? (West Virginia.)   For the South, spraying with a white oil emulsion, such as Volck, is most often recommended. Use ½ cup Volck and 3 teaspoons nicotine sulfate (Black Leaf 40) to 3 gals. of water. Spray just after blooming and again in late May or early June to control lace bug, thrips, mealy bugs, and mites (red spiders).

What causes leaves to drop on a webby string from an azalea house plant? Is dry sulphur good for this?   Probably the work of red spiders. Water is more important than sulphur. If the plants are bathed frequently, or treated with a fine mist spray from an atomizer, and kept under sufficiently humid conditions, red spiders will never have a chance to cause this much damage. After the plant has been thoroughly washed and dried, dry sulphur may be dusted on. Or you can use the Volck spray mentioned in the previous answer for outdoor azaleas. But *never* use oil and sulphur together, or within 30 days of using either one.

BEGONIA

What makes the leaves of begonia turn brown on the edge and get lifeless?   Perhaps unfavorable environment and perhaps injury from leaf nematodes, which cause irregular brown blotches, enlarging until the leaf curls up and drops. Prune off and burn infested portions; do not let leaves of 2 plants touch; water from below instead of wetting the foliage. The nematodes will be killed if potted plants are submerged in hot water held at 115° to 118° F. for 3 minutes, but this may cause injury and is more for the florist than the home grower.

Dry spots form on leaves of begonias until they are almost eaten up. What are cause and treatment?   Possibly sunscald, possibly the leaf nematode just discussed.

I have a Calla Begonia, healthy a month ago, now with leaves withering and tops of new branches falling off. Why? (Wisconsin.)   This is probably due to unfavorable environmental conditions rather than any specific organism. The Callalily Begonia is conceded to be difficult. Cool, moist air, fairly dry soil, and watering from the saucer only are recommended.

When my tuberous begonia was budded to bloom, the leaves, then the stalk, turned brown and dropped. What was the trouble? (Nebraska.)   It is hard to be sure without personal inspection, but there is a soil fungus, pythium, which causes a stem rot and may produce a soft rot and collapse of the crown and stalk. Avoid crowding of plants. Do not replant in infected soil without sterilizing.

A tuberous begonia rotted after a promising start. It wasn't overwatered. What could we have done wrong? (Ohio.)   Tuberous begonias are sometimes attacked by larvae of the black vine weevil, which destroy the roots so that the plants wilt and die. If the white grubs are found in the soil one recommendation is to take out the plants and kill larvae by pouring 1 tablespoon benzene into the hole in the ground and tamping the earth firmly.

What blight or insect attacks tuberous begonias to keep them from developing properly? (New York.) Insufficient light may be responsible, even though these are shade-loving plants. The cyclamen mite or possibly thrips may cause deformation. Frequent spraying with nicotine sulfate and soap before blooming may be of some benefit.

What spray shall I use for plant lice on a Lorraine Begonia? Nicotine sulfate and soap before flowering; pyrethrum while in bloom.

What is the tiny white or transparent worm which gets in the stalks and roots of begonias? It is probably only a scavenger worm feeding on tissues rotting from some other cause; possibly a fungous stem rot. If the plant is this far decayed, you should start over with a healthy plant in fresh soil.

What causes a sticky sediment on my begonia? It is honeydew, secreted by sucking insects, aphids, mealy bugs, or white flies.

BIRCH

How can white birches be protected against a small worm that gets between the layers of the leaves? (New York.) This is the birch-leaf miner, which causes a brown blotch on the outer half of the leaf. The worm is the larval stage of a black sawfly. Spray with nicotine sulfate and soap (or use lead arsenate instead of soap) about June 1.

How can I stop insects from eating leaves of cut-leaf birch? (New York.) The birch aphid sucks sap from leaves of cut-leaved birch and may be controlled with nicotine sulfate and soap spray. Cankerworms chew holes in birch leaves in May. Spray with arsenate of lead.

How can I eliminate bronze birch borer from a weeping birch? (New York.) The flat-headed, light-colored grubs, ½ to 1 in. long, make winding galleries underneath the bark; the adult beetles feed on foliage. Trees growing under adverse conditions may die. Spray with lead arsenate in June to control beetles, and see that trees are well fed and watered.

BITTERSWEET

What is the treatment for scale on Oriental Bittersweet?

The euonymus scale often covers bittersweet vines with a heavy infestation of slim white male scales, and darker, rounder females. Spray before growth starts with a miscible oil, at a 1 to 16 dilution, adding 1 teaspoon nicotine sulfate to each gallon. Spray again in summer, when your scales hatch, with a white oil, such as Volck, usually at a 1 to 50 dilution, with nicotine sulfate added, on a not too-hot day.

BOXWOOD

What is good for boxwood with white scale? The leaves are dying on most of bush and spreading to others. (D.C.) Oyster-shell scale may infest boxwood, but it is dark brown or gray in color. You may refer to nectria canker, a serious fungous disease which kills the leaves and twigs and produces pinkish-white spore pustules on the backs of the leaves and on the stems.

How do you control boxwood canker? (New Jersey.) Chiefly by sanitary measures: cleaning out old leaves and dead twigs twice a year and getting rid of all material that can hold moisture. Never water boxwood so that the foliage is wet for long periods. After cleaning, spray with lime sulphur, 1 to 50 dilution, directing the spray into the interior of the bush.

What should I do for my young boxwood, dying by degrees? (North Carolina.) Probably the canker disease just discussed is responsible. This is somewhat more prevalent farther North, but it is sometimes serious in your state. Clean out; spray; avoid prolonged wetting of foliage.

What treatment will keep boxwood leaves from turning brown? (Delaware.) Winter injury, nectria canker, serious infestations of scale, or leaf miners will all cause brown, unhealthy foliage. Winter protection and sanitary measures are most important.

What about the orange flies that come on boxwood in May? (Connecticut.) These are the adults of the boxwood leaf miner, a very serious insect pest which can only be fought in the brief 10 days to 2 weeks when the flies have emerged from the leaf blisters and are laying their eggs. Start spraying with 1 part molasses to 5 parts water, plus 1½ teaspoons nicotine sulfate per gallon when the blisters get little windows and the orange maggots inside have black eyes. Repeat as often as necessary to keep foliage sticky during the flying period.

What shall I do for red spider on boxwood bushes? (Tennessee.) Spider mites turn the leaves a light, unhealthy color. Dusting with sulphur, spraying with pyrethrum, or spraying with a summer white oil, as recommended under azaleas, should be successful.

BROWALLIA

How do you treat the black-spotty disease that infects foliage of browallia? (Mississippi.)   Smut has been reported on this host, and would make black sooty masses over the leaves. The best thing to do would be to remove smutted leaves and burn them. However, you may merely be having sooty mold growing in insect honeydew, in which case you use contact sprays for the insects.

BULBS

What formulas have been used with known success in combating fungous diseases of newly planted bulbs?   The most successful formula is to plant clean, healthy bulbs. Look them over carefully and discard any that show signs of black sclerotia. Look for these small, flat, hard bodies under the outer scales. Soaking for 2 hours in a 1 to 1,000 solution of bichloride of mercury may kill fungi, but it is better to discard diseased bulbs. Plant in a new location or in treated soil if you have been previously troubled with much disease.

How can ants be destroyed which occur in clumps of bulbs? (Alabama.)   A new recommendation for ants is to punch holes a few inches deep, pour in a few crystals of paradichlorbenzene, and fill up with soil again. Too strong a dose too close to the bulbs might injure them. (See also Ants.)

What are the minute white worms found in and around rotting bulbs? Do they cause the decay or are they scavengers, cleaning up? (Minnesota.)   They are scavengers, doing their appointed job. Don't worry about them, but do hunt for the primary cause of rotting.

CACTI

What shall I do for white furry web spots on small spiny cactus?   The spots are doubtless mealy bugs, which may be removed with a toothpick, or small brush, by washing off with water applied as a fine spray; by spraying with pyrethrum or, using caution, with a white oil emulsion like Volck. (See House Plants.)

How do you combat mealy bugs on cacti too spiny to use a brush on?   It should be possible to get a fine-pointed brush dipped in pyrethrum solution or nicotine down in between the spines. As a last resort spray with a white oil, such as greenhouse Volck, following manufacturer's directions for dilution. Spray in shade and follow with a spray of pure water after several hours. Cacti may be injured by oil.

How do you cure cactus scab?   Maybe you refer to a corky spot due to unfavorable conditions, often prevented by increasing light and decreasing humidity, but perhaps you are describing scale. Remove scale with a brush dipped in pyrethrum solution or scrape off with a small piece of wood.

What causes pricklypear cactus to get a white fungus or mold on it, and what can be done to prevent it? (Texas.)   A white mold is rather improbable on cactus. You may be describing mealy bugs; or possibly one of the scale insects common on Pricklypear Cactus. (See previous questions for control.)

My Christmas Cactus is covered with a web, and large pieces drop off. How can I prevent this?   The web is probably produced by red spiders, which flourish in a dry atmosphere. The Christmas Cactus does not need to be kept as dry as other cacti, and should be frequently syringed with water to keep spider mites in check. Try also spraying with nicotine sulfate or pyrethrum.

How can I use sulphur on cactus with mildew?   True mildew, a white powdery coating, would not be common on cactus. Perhaps you have a rot encouraged by overwatering. Cut out the diseased portions and dust the cut surfaces with powdered sulphur.

What is the cause of cactus plants dying off at the base? Probably too much water. Cacti are very subject to rot caused by fungi which flourish in the presence of moisture. Infection often starts through wounds, which should be avoided so far as possible.

How do you overcome silver and brown rust on cactus? This "rust" is more likely due to unfavorable light conditions than to a fungus. Increasing the light and decreasing the humidity may help.

CALADIUM

Worms have appeared in the caladium plant and all the brightly colored leaves have withered and died. What can be done?   Probably nothing at this stage. Worms in the soil can be flushed out with lime water, but they do no damage except to clog the drainage holes. It sounds as if the plants had either been drowned with the roots in too soggy soil, or else had dried out.

CALENDULA

Is there something that will kill black bugs on calendula? (Minnesota.) Nicotine sulfate and soap spray applied thoroughly and often should clear up the black aphids which are practically inevitable on calendula.

CALLA

What can I do for tiny black bugs on my calla? Strong soapsuds seem to do no good. Add ¼ teaspoon nicotine sulfate (Black Leaf 40) to each quart of soapsuds. Repeat the spray at intervals.

Why didn't the flower on callalily I raised bloom? Had beautiful bud, but did not open. There are only two diseases of callalilies: a root rot which may prevent flowering, and a slimy, soft rot which starts in the rhizome, and spreads up into the flower stalk. Your plant may have been infected with the root-rot fungus, or some physiological condition may have prevented blooming. In either case, it would pay to start over with a fresh rhizome next year.

CAMELLIA

What do you do when camellias have root lice? (North Carolina.) If you are sure the trouble is root aphids and not from the root-knot nematode, a weevil grub, or other pest, scoop the soil away from the trunk somewhat and pour in a solution of nicotine sulfate and soap. There are also root mealy bugs. If they or root lice get too serious you have to take up the plant, wash off the roots carefully, and replant in fresh soil.

I have a camellia that has small spots on leaves, pinhead size, leaves are light green, sick looking. Growing in a tub in hothouse. What can I do for it? (Texas.) The soil may be wrong; or the plant may be in too strong sun or improperly watered, but the light spots indicate the tea scale working on the under side of the leaves. This is a white cottony scale, the most serious pest of camellias. Spray with Volck at a 1 to 50 dilution, with the plants shaded from the sun. Several hours later spray again with pure water. Two treatments may be necessary to clean up a heavily infested plant.

CAMPANULA

Why don't I have success with campanulas? They rot away. Have a dry soil. (Delaware.) There are 2 soil fungi which may cause crown or stem rot under moist conditions, but your trouble may be physiological and due to insufficient water. Try another location and improve the soil with organic matter such as leafmold or peatmoss.

CANDYTUFT

What is the cause of candytuft turning white? Looks like mildew and is dying. (North Carolina.)   A white rust is common on candytuft and other members of the crucifer family. White pustules appear on under side of leaves, which turn pale. Burn diseased plants or plant parts and clean up cruciferous weeds, such as wild mustard. Spraying with Bordeaux mixture may help.

CANTERBURYBELLS

What can be done to prevent canterburybells from rotting just before blooming? (Ohio.)   Possibly growing plants in a new location, or disinfecting the soil with formaldehyde, perhaps merely by improving soil texture. Might be due to winter injury.

CARNATION

What causes me to lose my clove pink? Foliage turns brown in center of clump and spreads until entire bed is dead. (Tennessee.)   It may be a fungous stem rot, partially controlled by spraying with Bordeaux mixture. Try healthy cuttings or plant in a new location. They need a very well-drained soil.

Is there any pest that will cut carnations off at the joints? (Montana.)   Cutworms, possibly. Try a poison bran mash on the soil at nightfall, or spray with lead arsenate. A fungus, called branch rot, may girdle the nodes, or joints, and cause death of the branch. Remove infected parts.

What do you recommend for baby snails that feed on carnation buds? (California.)   Hand-picking or a poison bait of 1 part calcium arsenate to 16 parts wheat bran. In New Jersey I can prevent slug damage on hollyhocks by dusting with sulphur-lead arsenate dust. It might work for snails on carnations.

My greenhouse carnations wilt and dry up. What shall I do to produce strong, healthy plants? (Rhode Island.)   Several soil fungi cause wilts or stem rot, being more prevalent at high temperatures and in wet soils. Steam sterilize your greenhouse soil and bring in only healthy plants. (See also Soil Sterilization.)

What is wrong with my hardy carnations? I get them started and they bloom until August, then droop and die. (Iowa.)   Are there rusty pustules on the under side of leaves and do the leaves turn pale? If so, try sulphur dust to control rust. More likely soil fungi are to blame. Try a new location. Perhaps your carnations merely dry out and require more organic matter in the soil.

CEDAR

Do windbreaks of Maryland pines or cedar trees harbor diseases which may be transmitted to fruit trees near by? (D.C.) Pines are not dangerous to orchard trees, although I am not sure what you mean by Maryland pine. Redcedar harbors the cedar-apple rust fungus. Brown galls put out orange spore horns in the spring, and infective material is carried to apples as much as a mile or more away, although the amount of infection is roughly proportional to distance. In some apple regions cedars are prohibited by law.

Some of the cedars in my hedge are developing brown patches; I suspect red spider. Can you prescribe a remedy? (Georgia.) It is very likely red spider. Try forceful spraying with nicotine sulfate and soap, or dusting with sulphur, or occasional drenching with a strong stream of water from the hose. (See also Juniper.)

CHINESELANTERN

What type of insecticide will kill the striped beetles which ruin our Chineselanterns? They resemble cucumber bugs but are much hardier. (Minnesota.)   They probably are striped cucumber beetles which are certainly hardy, but should be killed by spraying the plants with lead arsenate, or cryolite. If you want to grow cucumbers you'd better get rid of the Chineselanterns entirely, because the beetles carry a virus disease, mosaic, from one host to the other.

A yellow-and-black bug lays eggs, hatching a slimy, sucking bug. What will destroy these? (Michigan.)   If your "bug" is spotted, it is the tortoise beetle; if striped, it is the cucumber beetle. (See above.) The "slimy" bugs are the larvae, or immature beetles. Those of the tortoise beetle carry their excreta in a pack upon their backs. Spray with lead arsenate, or cryolite.

CHRYSANTHEMUM

What causes the leaves of an outdoor chrysanthemum to curl up and turn brown?   This question, in one form or another, was asked most frequently of all the pest questions. Verticillium, or fusarium wilts, septoria leaf spot, or improper water relations, will all turn foliage brown, but in 9 cases out of 10 leaf nematodes are to blame.

What are leaf nematodes, and how do they work?   They are eelworms—microscopic animals which live in the soil and in wet weather swim up the stems of chrysanthemums and enter the leaves through the stomata—small mouthlike openings in the leaves. Infection begins with a yellowish-brown discoloration bounded by the larger veins, so that the discolored area is usually pie-shaped. Later the entire leaf turns brown and brittle, and may fall.

How may leaf nematodes be controlled?   First, by removing and burning seriously infested plants; next, by cutting off and burning all chrysanthemum tops after blooming. Make cuttings or divisions only from healthy plants or clumps, and either plant in a new location or sterilize the soil with formaldehyde or chloropicrin.

Will spraying control leaf nematodes?   Not entirely, but it will help. Frequent spraying with nicotine sulfate as a contact insecticide, combined with Bordeaux mixture as a repellent, is recommended.

What about the hot-water treatment for nematodes?   A drastic treatment, to be used only for especially valuable varieties that cannot readily be replaced. Cut back stems after blooming, clean off roots, and immerse in hot water at exactly 120° F. for ½ hour. Replant in sterilized soil.

How do nematodes spread from one plant to another?   If the leaves touch, they can swim across in wet weather. They can also be carried by the gardener on hands, tools, or clothing. Do not cultivate or handle the plants when they are wet with rain or dew.

Some of my chrysanthemums have dried leaves halfway up the plant; others were all right. Why? (New York.)   Some varieties are much more resistant to nematode injury than others. Ask your dealer for varieties that will withstand nematodes. The Korean chrysanthemums are notoriously susceptible.

Early in summer my mum plants start turning yellow on lower leaves. The leaves turn brown and crisp. This moves up stem until entire plant is dead. Roots show no growth since planting. What should I do? (Utah.)   This may be nematode injury, but in your state it is likely to be verticillium wilt. Start fresh with healthy plants in a new location or in sterilized soil.

How do you prevent the lower leaves on tender mums from spotting and shriveling? (Ohio.)   If your trouble starts as definite black spots, rather than brown wedges, you probably are dealing with a fungous disease, septoria leaf spot, which is quite readily controlled by spraying with Bordeaux mixture and picking off infected leaves. If the spotting is white and powdery, it is due to the mildew fungus, and you should dust with sulphur.

What causes my mums to get black and wilted at the lower part of the plants? (New Jersey.)   If you are sure it is a black wilting it may be due to a leaf-spot fungus, or a soil fungus. If the color is brown, it is probably the work of leaf nematodes. (See answers to above questions.)

Will the fungus Sclerotium delphinii, which caused crown rot among the hybrid delphiniums, be likely to affect chrysanthemums planted in that bed next spring?   Infection is possible, since this fungus is known to occur on almost every garden plant, but the disease is far more prevalent on delphiniums. Play safe and treat the soil with formaldehyde or chloropicrin this fall or very early next spring. (See Soil Sterilization.)

What do you advocate for exterminating dodder on chrysanthemum plants? (Pennsylvania.)   This charming parasite seems to be increasing as a garden pest. Once a plant is entwined with the orange tendrils, there is no remedy except breaking off and burning the parasitized plant parts before the white dodder flowers set and drop their seed for another year.

What insect causes mums to open only partially? (Illinois.) If the foliage is not brown and crisp, suggesting leaf nematode injury, it may be the gall midge, which lives in little conical projections of the leaves and flowers. Pick off and burn infested plant parts. Spraying with nicotine sulfate and soap will help some, but not much. A fungous disease, ray blight, also deforms flowers.

What shall I spray with to kill those little black bugs that get on chrysanthemums? (Missouri.)   These are aphids, almost inevitable on chrysanthemum tips in late summer, and sometimes all summer. They are readily killed with any contact insecticide, such as nicotine sulfate and soap. Spray often enough to protect the new growth.

I have a chrysanthemum plant with black insects creeping on it. If I cut the branches down, will it be all right to put it out in the garden in the spring? (D.C.)   Yes, you may safely move your infested plant to the garden. Aphids are readily killed with any contact insecticide. (See previous question.)

Each year my indoor chrysanthemum gets covered with little green bugs. How can I get rid of these pests?   The green bugs are undoubtedly aphids, or plant lice. Spray with nicotine sulfate and soap if they get numerous, but pure water will help in prevention. Wash the foliage frequently, or apply a fine mist from an atomizer.

What can I do to prevent root aphids? (New Jersey.)   Scoop out the soil from a shallow depression around each stem and pour in about a cupful of nicotine sulfate solution, 1½ teaspoons per gallon of water. Control ants.

What poison can be used in a cold frame for a small green caterpillar which eats young leaves? (New Jersey.)   Spray with lead arsenate without injury to the foliage; keep the glass sash off until the spray has thoroughly dried.

What is the little bug like a ladybug that eats the flowers of Astrid mums every fall? (Texas.)   If the "bug" is green with black spots, it is the spotted cucumber beetle, known in your section as the diabolical diabrotica because it is so fond of so many garden flowers.

How do you eliminate diabrotica beetles?   Control is difficult because sprays discolor the flowers. Pyrethrum or rotenone would be best, but if these are scarce, cryolite is a possibility, preferably used in dust form. As a last resort spray or dust with lead arsenate.

What treatment shall I use for insects that eat centers of chrysanthemums? (Missouri.)   Probably these are the 12-spotted cucumber (diabrotica) beetles discussed above.

What are the flying, hard-shelled, rather beetlelike bugs that attack some chrysanthemums during the blooming season? (Indiana.)   Black-spotted green beetles are diabroticas; long, black beetles are blister beetles. For the latter try dusting with Dutox, trade name for barium fluosilicate. (See Blister Beetles.)

What do you do for a small beetle, yellow with black spots, that eats beans and chrysanthemum flowers? (New York.)   The Mexican bean beetle is not ordinarily a chrysanthemum pest, but when it has devoured all the bean foliage in sight it may seek other fields. Try spraying or dusting chrysanthemums with lead arsenate.

What can one use to keep grasshoppers from eating buds? (Kentucky.)   Poison bran mash, as used for cutworms, is the recommended control for grasshoppers; but probably it would be easier to spray the chrysanthemums with lead arsenate after the buds form but before they flower.

What is treatment for gall on garden chrysanthemums and disposition of infected plants? (New York.)   Assuming this is the bacterial crown gall which appears at the base of the plant, and not the gall midge, there is nothing to do for infected plants except to remove and burn them.

Is the soil liable to harbor crown gall infection the succeeding year?   Yes, the bacteria may live for some time in the soil. Plant in a new location or sterilize the soil.

What is the gall midge?   A fly, which lays its eggs in foliage and buds, where the larvae stimulate the formation of small conical galls. This is primarily a greenhouse pest, controlled by nicotine fumigation at night, but sometimes attacks outdoor plants. Spray repeatedly with nicotine sulfate. It is usually easier to remove infested chrysanthemums.

About July something attacked my chrysanthemums; they broke off about 3 ins. from ground, leaving piles of what looked like white ant eggs. What caused this? (Ohio.)   The stalk borer was probably responsible, the "ant eggs" being frass excreted by the caterpillar inside the stem. When you see borer injury, it is too late to help the plant. Cleaning up weeds is best prevention.

What is the round black worm around roots of shasta daisies? (New Jersey.)   Likely a millipede feeding on roots rotting from some other cause; perhaps a fungous stem rot. Remove and burn the diseased plant if the roots are destroyed.

How shall I exterminate termites in beds? (Texas.)   Put some carbon disulphide in a machine oilcan and inject a few drops at intervals into the soil around the plants.

CITRUS

How shall I care for scale on dwarf citrus fruits in the house? Spray with nicotine sulfate and soap or lemon oil. If scale persists, try a white oil such as Volck. (See House Plants for special precautions.)

My grapefruit tree has become infested since being taken in from garden. Same pest on cacti. What is it?   The infestation is probably mealy bugs, which flourish on cacti. Use the same treatment as for scale.

What is the cause and cure of syrup substance on leaves of dwarf lemon and orange?   The sticky material is a honeydew secreted by sucking insects, probably mealy bugs in this case, although possibly scale insects, white flies, or aphids. (For control see previous two questions; also House Plants.)

CLEMATIS

In late fall what attacks Clematus paniculata, which has flourished like a green bay tree? Hordes of beetles practically denude the vines overnight. (Georgia.)   These are probably blister beetles. Dusting with barium fluosilicate (Dutox) will be most satisfactory. (See also Blister Beetles.)

How can I kill blister bugs that eat vines in summer? (Louisiana.)   Blister beetles are more prevalent on clematis in the South than in the North. They are hard to kill, but spraying or dusting with a fluosilicate, such as Dutox, may be effective. If available, a combination rotenone-pyrethrum spray or dust will help. Knock off the beetles into a can of kerosene.

My Clematis jackmani climbers, after getting several feet high, wilt unexpectedly. If dry stem rot causes this, what can be done? (Wisconsin.)   It sounds like stem rot. After the fungus has girdled the stem so that the vine wilts suddenly, nothing can be done. Spraying or dusting with sulphur through the season may aid in prevention. Start cuttings from healthy plants.

COLEUS

Are mealy bugs on coleus caused by too much or too little watering?   Mealy bugs, like most sucking insects, thrive in a dry atmosphere, but too little water cannot "cause" them. Also if the plants are unhealthy from a waterlogged soil they may succumb more readily to mealy-bug injury. Spray at the first sign of bugs.

What is one to do to get rid of the soft white fungous scale on coleus? I scrape it off, but this is not drastic enough.   It is neither a fungus nor a scale you describe, but mealy bugs again. Spray with nicotine sulfate and soap, and if that does not work try greenhouse Volck, following manufacturer's directions exactly. (See House Plants.)

What causes blistered or puckered leaves?   It sounds like the work of the cyclamen mite, which attacks so many greenhouse plants. (See Cyclamen.)

What can I do to stop a white moldy rot on coleus, kept as a house plant?   There is no white mold on coleus, but you may have a combination of white woolly mealy bugs, very common on this plant, and a black rot, called "black leg" because it rots the stalks at the base. For the mealy bugs see House Plants; for the rot, destroy infected plants; pot new ones with fresh soil.

What causes white fungous growth? Changed from glazed to

clay pot, but growth persists.   Changing the pot won't affect mealy bugs on the foliage. Spray and spray again until you clean them up. (See answers to previous questions.)

COLUMBINE

How can one keep the roots of aquilegia from becoming infested with worms? (Minnesota.)   The worms are probably millipedes, and usually they swarm around when a plant is weakened or dead from other causes, either disease or unfavorable cultural conditions.

What makes hybrid columbines pass out in a perennial bed where everything else is happy? (Pennsylvania.)   Hybrid columbines, like hybrid delphiniums, are usually short-lived, but sudden passing out may be due to crown rot, a fungous disease; or to the columbine borer.

What remedy will prevent crown rot? (Alabama.)   Crown rot in Alabama is caused by *Sclerotium rolfsii,* a fungus that is generally prevalent in the soil and kept viable because it can attack so many different plants. Soil sterilization is difficult and not too satisfactory. Remove infected plants as soon as noticed and pour a 1 to 1,000 solution of bichloride of mercury over the area.

What about the columbine borer?   This is a salmon-colored caterpillar that works in the crown of the plant. All you can do is pull up and burn the victim and in the fall destroy all waste grass, weeds, and other debris which might harbor borer eggs over the winter.

The leaves of our columbine have little silvery-white lines all over them. Could you tell me the cause? (Rhode Island.)   These are the serpentine tunnels of the columbine leaf miner. The larvae work inside the leaf and a small fly emerges to lay eggs for the next generation.

What is the cure for white line discolorations in leaves? (Illinois.)   There is no cure, but picking off and burning all infested leaves as soon as noticed and cultivating the ground around the plants in fall and early spring will help prevent further infestations. Spraying with nicotine sulfate and soap may help.

What shall I do for plants turning brown because of a certain type of spider that gets on them? (Florida.)   If this is red spider (the tiny mite which makes webs on the under side of the leaves), try sulphur dust, but not when the temperature is so high (above 90° F.) that the sulphur will burn the foliage.

COSMOS

What is the cause of annual cosmos turning brown and dying? (Nebraska.)   It may be a bacterial wilt, but more likely a fungus stem blight. A grayish lesion girdles the stem and all parts above die. Spraying is of little value. Remove infected plants when noticed, and pull up and burn all tops after blooming.

CRAPEMYRTLE

How is mildew on crapemyrtle controlled? (Alabama.) Either by a dormant spray of 1 to 8 lime sulphur when the buds start swelling; or by spraying with wettable sulphur, or a copper spray, after growth starts. It is important to spray early; otherwise the white fungus will stunt the buds.

What spray formula will destroy white fly covering my crapemyrtles, causing smut? (Louisiana.)   The smut is a fungous, sooty mold growing in the honeydew secreted by the white flies. Spray after blooming with a white oil, such as Volck, 4 tablespoons, plus 3 teaspoons nicotine sulfate, to 3 gals. of water, but not within 30 days of using sulphur to control mildew.

CRABAPPLE

Why do the leaves of a Bechtel's Crab curl up and drop in summer? (New Jersey, Illinois.)   Bechtel's Crab is peculiarly susceptible to the cedar and apple rust, a disease even more prevalent in the Middle West than in New Jersey. Spores are carried from the cedar galls in the spring and the resulting infection of orange spots on the crabapple leaves shows up in midsummer. Defoliation follows heavy infection.

How do you prevent rust?   Never plant cedars and crabapples together. It is preferable not to have them on the same property, but at least get a windbreaker of a house or trees between the two as a barrier to windborne spores. Remove cedar galls in winter and early spring. Spray crabapples with colloidal sulphur when leaves come out, and every 10 days until July.

I have sprayed my Malus floribunda but it is always full of aphids. What can I do? (Michigan.)   Try spraying with a miscible oil just before the buds break. (See Dormant Spraying.) If aphids appear during growing season, spray with nicotine sulfate and soap; or add the nicotine to any lead arsenate spray without the soap.

What treatment shall I give small flowering crab? No new growth, leaves shrivel, fuzzy white substance appears at crotches and twig intersections. (Rhode Island.) The fuzzy white substances are woolly aphids, controlled by spraying thoroughly with nicotine sulfate and soap. The tree is apparently dying from other causes—improper planting or some soil trouble.

What solution should be painted on trunks of young flowering crab trees in March to prevent green worms from climbing up and depositing their eggs? (Illinois.) None. No chemical should be applied directly to the trunk. If you have time and money to burn, apply a band of balsam wool and cover with Tanglefoot. This will prevent cankerworm moths from climbing the crabapples, but will not stop young worms from dropping onto crabapples from near-by shade trees. Spray with lead arsenate in May in any case, for the trunk treatment reduces infestation not more than 10 per cent.

CROCUS

Is there any method of preventing squirrels from eating crocus bulbs? (Massachusetts.) Plant the bulbs in wire baskets, which may be purchased for this purpose, or made at home from ½-in. wire mesh. A few napthalene flakes may act as repellent, but too many will injure the bulbs with their fumes.

CYCLAMEN

What causes a cyclamen to become soft and die? I watered mine carefully through the bottom of the pot, but it died within 2 weeks. It sounds like bacterial soft rot, usually serious only when plants are too wet, or shaded, or not well ventilated. Your plant may have been infected when it came from the greenhouse.

What would cause a cyclamen to wilt suddenly and the bulb to rot? Probably the bacterial soft rot suggested in the previous question. Possibly a fungous disease called stunt, although here the dying is usually gradual.

What is cyclamen mite, and how does it affect the plants? This mite is a microscopic spider, white to pale brown in color, that infests many varieties of ornamental plants causing puckering, curling, or other deformation of the leaves, and flower buds to become blackened and distorted. If plants are kept close together the mites can crawl from one to another. They can also be spread by hands, tools, clothing.

How do you control cyclamen mite? Once you get an infested plant in the home, it is best to discard it to save other house plants. Greenhouse operators should clean up their stock by the hot-water treatment, submerging the plants for 15 minutes at 110° F. Pick off all deformed leaves at once.

DAHLIA

What causes dahlia roots to rot? (Florida.)   Any one of several fungous or bacterial diseases. With verticillium wilt the lower leaves gradually lose their color, the roots are decayed, and the stem shows black streaks when cut across. With stem rot and soft bacterial rot, wilting is rather sudden.

How are the wilt diseases of dahlias cured?   There is no cure. All you can do is remove infected plants immediately and plant healthy tubers in a new location, or sterilize soil with formaldehyde or chloropicrin.

When the tubers rot, is the soil too damp? (New York.)   A heavy, wet soil encourages stem rot and bacterial wilt, but the organisms have to be present. Improving drainage and lightening the soil with sand or coal ashes will help.

There is a little brown worm about ½ in. long that eats my dahlia roots. How should I treat ground before I plant? (Ohio.) It is probably a millipede feasting on tissues rotting from one of the wilt diseases just discussed. (See previous questions.)

When I dig my dahlias in the fall, the tubers are almost always rotted away. Why are gray-blackish insects present? (New York.) Doubtless millipedes again. They look brown to some, grayish to others. They are hard, with many legs, usually coiled into a circle, and almost always scavengers feeding on rotting tissue.

My bulbs are drying up and some show rot all through. How do you prevent this? (New York.)   Botrytis, fusarium, and other fungi and bacteria may cause storage rots. Use care in digging to avoid wounds, store only well-matured tubers, avoid any frost damage, and keep at 40° F. in sand that is only very slightly moist. Too much moisture will increase rotting. Dusting tubers with sulphur before storage may help.

How is corrosive sublimate used to keep bulbs from rotting? (Missouri.)   Wash the tubers to remove soil and then soak in a 1 to 1,000 solution of corrosive sublimate (2 tablets to 1 qt. of water) for 30 minutes. Dry thoroughly before storing.

Some dahlia leaves have bright yellow mottling; is that mosaic, and what can be done? (Montana.)   The mottling is a typical symptom of mosaic, a virus disease carried from one plant to another by aphids. There is usually dwarfing or stunting. Control aphids with contact sprays, and remove and burn infected plants.

What are the chief causes for dahlia "stunt"? (Illinois.) Either mosaic or the feeding of sucking insects, often leaf hoppers, but sometimes thrips or plant bugs. Stunted dahlias are short and bushy with an excessive number of side branches. Leaf hoppers cause the margins of the leaves to turn yellow, then brown and brittle—a condition known as hopper burn.

How do you control stunt caused by insects? Spray once a week with nicotine sulfate and soap, beginning early in the season and covering under side of leaves thoroughly. Bordeaux mixture will serve as a repellent for leaf hoppers but is too unsightly for general use in the ornamental garden.

After plants are stunted, are the tubers good the following year? (New Jersey.) Yes, if the stunting was due to leaf hoppers and the tubers appear sound. But if the stunting was due to mosaic, a virus disease, the tubers should not be used.

What is the trouble with my dahlias, which start out grandly but then shrivel up, get curled leaves, and produce buds that do not open? (Illinois.) Probably stunt, due either to mosaic or insect feeding. (See preceding answers.)

My miniature dahlia is full of buds, but they rot. What is the matter? (Ohio.) It may be gray mold, the same type of botrytis blight that affects peony buds. Remove all diseased buds and spray with Bordeaux mixture. Burn all plant tops in the fall.

How can I prevent mildew? (Pennsylvania.) Dust foliage with sulphur, especially in late summer.

If dahlias mildew badly at the end of the season, will the tubers be injured? (California.) Probably not, but mildew is a serious disease on the West coast, and dahlias should be sprayed or dusted with some sulphur fungicide.

Is the borer which attacks dahlia stalks the corn borer? (New Jersey.) Yes, if the borers are flesh-colored when young, later turning smoky or reddish. If the caterpillar is brown, striped with white, it is the common stalk borer, also prevalent on corn, but using giant ragweed as its favorite food plant.

What can I do to prevent borers? (Illinois.) Clean up and burn stalks of all herbaceous plants in the fall. Include the weeds, for many of these harbor borers over winter. Spray stalks with nicotine sulfate (2 teaspoons per gallon) and soap once a week. A rotenone spray (when it is allowed again for ornamentals) will be more effective.

How do you prevent the little black flies from biting or stinging buds so they only partially open? (Vermont.) The tarnished plant bug is brownish rather than black, but it stings and blackens the buds. Control is difficult. Keep down the weeds and spray frequently with nicotine sulfate, or dust with sulphur.

European Corn Borer: adult, yellowish brown; larva, pink. Frequently attacks dahlias.

Last summer I found a lot of black bugs and some ladybugs on my blooms. The petals had holes in them. Were the little black bugs to blame? (Texas.)   The black bugs were probably aphids or plant lice, controllable by spraying with nicotine sulfate and soap. If the "ladybugs" were green instead of red, they were diabrotica or cucumber beetles and responsible for the holes. (See Chrysanthemum.)

What can I do about aphids on roots? Have tried ground tobacco. (Wisconsin.)   Tobacco dust in the ground should help, but pouring a solution of nicotine sulfate and soap in a shallow depression made around each dahlia stem will be a more potent remedy.

This year grasshoppers ate our dahlia blooms. Is there any way to prevent this? (Mississippi.)   A poison bran bait scattered on the ground is the usual recommendation, but this is poisonous to birds and pets. Spray or dust the flowers with lead arsenate or other stomach poison if the residue is not too objectionable. Keep down weeds. (See also Grasshoppers.)

How do you rid dahlias of snails? (Michigan.)   A poison bait, made of 1 part calcium arsenate to 16 parts wheat bran, with enough water added to make a moist mash, scattered around plants, is said to be satisfactory in controlling snails in California, where they are a constant pest. Or try one of the newer metaldehyde slug baits, obtainable under commercial trade names such as Metameal or Snarol. (See also Slugs.)

How can I eliminate red spider? (California).   Dust with fine sulphur, covering the under side of the leaves particularly.

Do thrips ever attack dahlia? How may they be protected? (Iowa.)   They may infest the flowers, turning the petals whitish. Regular spraying with nicotine sulfate and soap for the control of leaf hoppers may discourage infestation by thrips. Spray flowers with rotenone, or try tartar emetic. (See Gladiolus.)

How do I exterminate termites? (Texas.)   Inject a few drops of carbon disulphide into the soil at intervals around the plants. Close up the holes to keep the gas in the soil. (See also Termites.)

DAPHNE

The leaves of my daphne are turning yellow. Why? (California.)   This may be chlorosis, due to an alkaline soil which makes iron unavailable. Spray leaves with 2 teaspoons ferrous sulfate and ¼ teaspoon glue in a quart of water. Or treat the soil with a mixture of iron and aluminum sulfate. (See Chlorosis.) Your *Daphne odora* may also be dying from Armillaria root rot, which see.

DELPHINIUM

Last summer I lost a great number of my delphiniums. A creamy, seedy substance formed around the plants, making the roots rot off. Later it spread to the phlox and buddleia. What is it? (Ohio.)   This is a good description of crown rot, caused by the fungus *Sclerotium delphinii* (in the South called by *S. rolfsii*). White fungous threads, mycelium, form at the base of the stalk and spread over the ground. Seedlike bodies, sclerotia, are also formed, often in great numbers. The roots are attacked so that the plant is readily pulled up. This fungus attacks more than 100 species of ornamentals, and readily spreads to other plants in wet weather.

How shall I grow delphinium when the plants rot off at the ground and the earth turns white and rust color? (Kansas.) Another phase of crown rot. The sclerotia which are at first cream-colored turn reddish or rusty as they mature, and there may be so many crowded together at the base of the plant that it seems as if the earth itself had changed color.

How shall I keep delphinium from getting crown rot; how stop its spread to other plants? (Illinois.)   Stopping the spread immediately is very important. Dig up an infected plant as soon as noticed, using a shovel so as to get all the surrounding soil harboring the sclerotia. If you pull up the plant and leave the sclerotia behind, they may live for months or years ready to infect other plants. Wrap the diseased specimen and soil in several thicknesses of newspaper and hurry it to the bonfire.

Will bichloride of mercury 1 to 1,000 cure crown rot, or does the plant have to be destroyed? When is the best time to apply? (Massachusetts.)   Usually it is not possible to save the plant already infected, but try to save neighboring plants by pouring 1 to 2 qts. of the solution into the space from which the diseased plant was removed and over the crowns of near-by plants. Sometimes a lightly infected specimen can be saved. Apply whenever the disease is noted.

Does the bichloride of mercury permanently sterilize the ground, or is crown rot likely to appear another year?   You may expect crown rot every year in the same place. The bichloride apparently kills the mycelium but has no permanent effect on any sclerotia left behind in the soil. The disease reappears at the first sign of warm, humid weather. It is a good idea to remove soil over an area of 2 ft. across and 1 ft. deep, and replace with fresh earth.

Is there any other chemical to prevent crown rot? I have tried napthalene flakes. (Iowa.)   Napthalene is somewhat effective in stopping the spread of the white mycelium, but it cannot be relied on to kill the sclerotia. Sulphur dust will likewise check the mycelial growth. The permanent remedy is to sterilize the soil, when all plants have been removed, with formaldehyde or chloropicrin. (See Soil Sterilization.)

Can delphiniums be replanted after sterilizing soil in bed where others died of sclerotium rot? (New Jersey.)   Yes, if you use formaldehyde or chloropicrin according to directions and wait until all odor has disappeared from the soil before replanting—usually about 2 weeks. Naturally, put back only healthy plants. The treatment is not guaranteed; a new location is preferable.

What makes delphinium get a mildewed appearance and what can be done to prevent it? (New York.)   This is powdery mildew, a fungus appearing as a white coating on the leaves. In the East it is seldom serious before late summer. Dust with sulphur, or use one of the combination sprays with copper as a fungicide.

Is it possible to prevent mildew? (Illinois, Minnesota, Colorado.)   The mildew problem seems to increase in importance as one goes West, until a climax is reached in California. However, many of the new hybrid strains are fairly resistant to mildew, and dusting or spraying with sulphur or spraying with Bordeaux mixture gives reasonable control. There is no "prevention" except cleaning up and burning all old plant material.

Why do delphiniums mildew so badly? (California.)   It's your famous California climate, which seems to encourage mildew on delphinium, roses, and other plants. But cheer up, troubles even up, and Easterners have to fight black spot and cyclamen mite as much as you do mildew. Try to get California strains of delphinium more or less resistant to mildew, and dust with sulphur.

How do I prevent rust and white mold? (Wisconsin.)   The white mold is mildew. (See answers to previous questions.) True rust is not very common on delphinium. Discolored patches on the leaves may be due to the broad mite or the leaf miner (which see).

How do you control black spot?   This bacterial disease appears as tarry black spots on the leaves. It is not serious except in wet seasons, when it may be controlled by spraying with Bordeaux mixture. In a normal season picking off infected leaves and cleaning up old stalks in autumn are sufficient.

How should dry Bordeaux mixture be diluted for spraying delphiniums when they come up in the spring? (Pennsylvania.) Use about half the strength recommended on the package, which usually gives directions for a potato spray. If your brand calls for 8 to 12 tablespoons per gallon, use 4 to 6, adding 2 tablespoons flour to the dry powder before stirring the water in very slowly. Strain through cheesecloth into the sprayer and use *immediately*.

Is there a remedy when the leaves curl and plants fail to bloom? Those that do bloom have green blossoms. (Utah.) This is a virus disease, probably aster yellows. There is no cure except taking out infected plants as soon as noticed and spraying with contact insecticides to control the leaf hoppers, the insect carriers of the virus. Such diseases are common in the Northwest.

Why do my delphiniums grow large and thrifty, have one blooming period, and then get a black rot? (Ohio.)   There are various delphinium rots besides sclerotium crown rot, caused by at least 2 bacteria and several fungi. Rotting is usually worse in wet weather and with succulent tissue. Some growers feel that the act of cutting down the old stalks after blooming spreads the rot organisms.

What causes the yellowing of leaves on hybrids? When the plants were treated with nitrate of soda every 10 days, they took on a healthy green again. (Illinois.)   You answered your own question: evidently your plants lacked nitrogen. But be careful about applying too much. Getting too succulent a growth will mean more rot diseases.

Why do my delphiniums turn yellow and dry? (Indiana.)
Possibly due to fusarium wilt, this fungus being common in soils
in the Middle West. There is usually a progressive yellowing of
leaves from the base upward. But the yellowing may also be due
to crown rot, lack of nitrogen, lack of water, or intense heat.
Try a new location.

**What causes delphinium buds to become black and wadded
up? (Indiana.)**   The cyclamen mite, a light-colored spider
mite too small to see with the naked eye, and a very serious pest
on delphiniums. It deforms the leaves, blackens the flower buds,
usually preventing bloom, and stunts the plant.

**What can be done to overcome cyclamen mite on delphinium?
(Wisconsin.)**   The treatment most generally approved is
spraying thoroughly with rotenone, often alternating with sulphur dust. If rotenone is not available, nicotine sulfate and soap
may be substituted with fair success. Start spraying very early in
the spring. Pick off deformed parts; discard severely infested
plants.

Do coal ashes help in the control of mites?   Some growers
believe that a 2-in. layer of sifted coal ashes put on for the winter
and left on for the shoots to come through in the spring aids in
cutting down mite infestation.

**What should be done for brown spots on under side of leaves
of delphinium? (Illinois.)**   If these spots are rather glassy in
appearance, they are due to the broad mite, which is not so
harmful as the cyclamen mite and more readily controlled with
sulphur dust.

What causes blighted areas in the leaves?   The larvae of
leaf miners feed inside the leaves, which collapse and turn brown
over rather large areas, usually near the points. Remove and
burn infested leaves. Spraying with nicotine sulfate and soap
may help.

Why are there red lice during blooming time? (Michigan.)
Why any calamity? These are the same aphids so prevalent on
annual larkspur. Spray thoroughly and frequently with nicotine
sulfate and soap.

**Why do my young delphiniums get little red bugs and finally
die? (Illinois.)**   These are aphids, plant lice. If you spray
with nicotine or other contact insecticide when they first appear,
they will not get so numerous they will cause death. Your young
delphiniums may die from other causes.

I have tried sulphur dust for the little red lice. How can I pre-

vent them? (Michigan.) Sulphur dust will be of little benefit. You need nicotine sulfate and soap, or a pyrethrum spray.

My delphiniums always get orange lice on the under side of the leaves. When shall I start watching for them and what shall I do? (Michigan.) These aphids usually get serious toward midsummer, but sometimes appear in spring. When the leaves start cupping downward, looking like umbrellas, you always know red aphids are underneath. Use a spray rod with an angle nozzle so you can cover the under side of the leaves.

My delphinium leaves get infested with tiny red insects. Are they red spiders? (New York.) Probably they are red aphids. Red spiders are almost too small to see with the naked eye and form a mealy cobweb on the under side of the leaves. If you really have the spider mites and not aphids, sulphur dust will work.

DOGWOOD

What can be done for bark borers on dogwood trees? (New Jersey.) Twig borers can be taken care of by cutting below the infested portion, but bark borers are best prevented by wrapping newly transplanted trees in kraft crepe paper, extending from the crown up to the first branches. Leave on 2 years. After infestation borers may be surgically removed, but it is not always possible to save the tree.

I had 2 flowering dogwoods which I planted; 1 died, bark blistered, chipping off easily. Can the other tree be saved? (Ohio.) A crown canker disease might have that effect but I do not know of its occurring in Ohio. It may have been bark borers. (See previous question.) If you cut out all borers in remaining tree, wrap the trunk, and feed and water it; it may live.

Dogwood, pussy willow, other shrubs, and roses have some disease; are covered with scales of shell-like nature; trees finally die. What is the remedy? (Maryland.) All these plants are subject to attack by scale insects, but they are of different types. Dogwood can have round scurfy scale or cottony cushion scale, white fluff under brown shell. Spray with miscible oil in spring before growth starts. (See Dormant Spraying.)

ELM

What is best to use for yellow striped bugs on Chinese elms in July? Little result from Red Arrow or Black Flag. (Ohio.) This is the elm-leaf beetle, a chewing insect little affected by a contact insecticide like Red Arrow. Have your trees sprayed with lead arsenate in June.

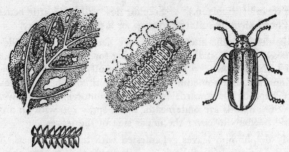

Elm Leaf Beetle: distinct yellow stripes; larvae black.

What spring care can be given to an elm which gets covered with small worms causing the leaves to turn brown and fall in midsummer? (New Jersey.)   Cankerworms chew foliage in May, but in June the dark, dragon-shaped larvae of the elm-leaf beetle skeletonize the leaves, causing the browning and defoliation. Two lead arsenate sprays are best, the first after the leaves come out in May and the second in early June; otherwise, plan one treatment in late May. Power spraying by a tree expert is required.

What is a practical insecticide for Chinese elms? Affliction is a black caterpillar worm which attacks foliage. (New Jersey.) This is the larval stage of the elm-leaf beetle, the most serious pest of elms, but readily controlled by power spraying with lead arsenate.

What is the scale infecting the bark of my Chinese elms? (New York.)   Elm scurfy scale and 2 or 3 other scale insects may appear on elm bark, causing death of branches and occasionally of young trees. Use a dormant spray before growth starts, such as a miscible oil at 1 to 16 dilution. (See also Dormant Spraying.)

Why did the elm tree give off a black secretion so that the lily bed under it looks like a city garden? (New Hampshire.)   The secretion was colorless honeydew from aphids on the elm, but when it dropped onto the lily leaves a black fungus grew in it. (See Sooty Mold.) There is no control except spraying the elm for aphids and the expense may not be warranted.

The leaves of the 5-year-old elm in our vegetable garden turn yellow and fall off in August. (Ohio.)   The elm-leaf beetle may be the cause, or the Dutch elm disease, or cephalosporium wilt, or a new virus disease, common in Ohio, called pholem necrosis. Call in a tree expert for diagnosis, or send specimens of twigs to your Experiment Station at Wooster.

What is the Dutch elm disease? A wilt disease, first reported in Ohio in 1930 and in New Jersey in 1933. It is transmitted by bark beetles which came in from Europe on elm burls imported for furniture veneer, wood for dish crates, etc. Wilting is followed by yellowing, curling, and dropping of leaves. When the twigs are cut across, the vessels are black, but this is also true of cephalosporium and verticillium wilts, so that laboratory cultures are needed for a true diagnosis. So far there is no real control except destruction of infected trees to prevent spread. Keeping trees healthy by proper feeding and watering and pruning reduce infestation of the dark beetle carriers, which lay their eggs only in weakened or dead tissue.

What causes Chinese elm trees to bleed so long after pruning? Mine have been discharging for two years. (Illinois.) Elms are subject to a condition known as slime flux, which means a continuous exudation from wounds due to positive pressure in the sap. Often this bleeding flux has an alcoholic odor and attracts insects.

What will dry up sap flowing from borer hole wound? (Oklahoma.) It is slime flux. Sometimes it helps to drill a hole below the bleeding wound into the heartwood and insert a drainpipe. This carries the flux out beyond the tree trunk and gives the wound a chance to heal.

EVERGREENS

Is there any spray with an odor which will keep the dogs off my evergreens? (Tennessee.) There are on the market many dog repellents with such descriptive names as Dawg-gone, Dogz-off, Dogsix, Scram, Anti-Dog, Marvel Dust. Black Leaf 40 is supposed to be a dog repellent, but whenever I spray with this nicotine sulfate the dogs persist in following me all around the garden.

Is there anything else I can do to keep dogs off evergreens? The repellent sprays have but a fleeting effect. (Wisconsin.) Lasting and inconspicuous are the wire shrubbery guards, placed 3 or 4 around each shrub. If they are unavailable and you can spare some wire coat hangers, borrow some wire cutters and make your own guards. File one end to a point, make a right-angle bend so that the point sticks out from the tree, and put the other end in the ground.

Is it advisable to use a dormant spray of miscible oil for pines

and junipers? **What concentration of Scale-Oil or Scale-O?**
Yes, if you have a serious infestation of scale insects. Spray only
on a bright day, before new growth starts, with the temperature
about 45° F., and follow manufacturer's directions for dilution,
usually 1 to 30 or 1 to 35 for evergreens. Oil sprays should not be
used every year but only when definitely needed.

**Should evergreens have a dormant spray in early spring for
red spider? (New York.)**   Yes, if the infestation was serious
the preceding year; otherwise, rely on sulphur dust and syringing
with the hose during the growing season. If you use a dormant
oil spray, wait 30 days before applying any form of sulphur.

**What is the most effective control measure for bagworms on
evergreens? (Illinois.)**   Pick off the bags whenever you see
them during the winter. Spray with lead arsenate when the
young worms start feeding, probably in late May. (See Bagworms.)

**What is the best treatment for gall on evergreens? (New
York.)**   Depends on the evergreen. If cedar, then cut out the
rust gall before the spore horns develop; if spruce, spray to kill
the gall aphids before new growth starts, using a nicotine-soap
or nicotine-oil spray. Cut out the galls on blue spruce in early
summer. (See also Spruce.)

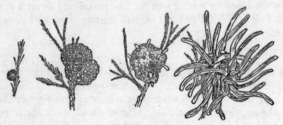

Stages in the development of rust galls on cedar.

**What can I put on to prevent grasshoppers? They are destroy-
ing the evergreens around a new home. (Ohio.)**   Grasshoppers
occasionally are destructive to evergreens. The best control is
a poison bran bait. (See Grasshoppers.)

**The inside of my evergreens are brown with needles fallen off,
but the outside looks all right. Could this be caused by grasshoppers in them all the time? (Maryland.)**   Possibly (see
Grasshoppers), or perhaps it is due to red-spider injury. If the
browning occurs in late summer and fall, it is merely natural
maturing of the needles. The individual leaves of evergreens do

not stay on forever, but ripen and drop as any other tree. The new outer leaves stay green while the older inside foliage is lost each year.

What feeding procedure should be followed to revive dying evergreens? (Illinois.)   Feeding may kill them off more quickly, just like giving a large meal to a person with high fever. Have the cause of the dying evergreen diagnosed by an expert before you try to revive it by feeding.

EUONYMUS

Why do the stems of my Euonymus radicans, 15 years old, growing on cement garage, become white? (Massachusetts.) Your vine is completely covered with the euonymus scale. Look closely and you will see thin white sticks, the male scales, and brownish oval females. When the young scales hatch, they are yellowish and crawl slowly about, but the adults are motionless. Scale is always worse on a vine attached to a wall.

Oyster-shell scale, one of the most common pests on fruit trees, is controlled by spraying with a miscible oil spray; that is, one which will readily mix with water.

How shall I check or prevent euonymus scale?   Use a dormant spray, miscible oil at a 1 to 16 dilution, in spring before growth starts; in summer, when young scales hatch, apply a white oil, such as Volck, at a 1 to 50 dilution, adding 1 teaspoon nicotine sulfate per gallon. Temperature must be above 45° F. for spring spraying and below 85° F. for summer application of oil. Try to get the spray in back of the vine, close to the wall.

What is a satisfactory treatment for blight of evergreen shrub euonymus? (Virginia.)   You probably have euonymus scale, treatment for which is given in previous question. Sometimes, in the South and West, euonymus foliage is covered with the white coating of the mildew fungus. A sulphur spray or dust will control this, but it must not be used within 30 days of an oil spray.

FERNS

What is wrong with a fern when it gets minute white specks all over it? Also brown ones which are larger? The white ones can be moved but the brown ones are tight.   A perfect description of the fern scale. The white bodies are male scales, and those that move are young ones; the brown pear-shaped objects are female scales, which stay put. A severe infestation ruins the fern.

I have used Black Leaf 40 and soap without success for the fern scales. What shall I try now?   Try spraying with lemon oil or Volck, following directions carefully, and washing off with a pure water spray several hours later. Remove badly infested fronds.

Fern is covered with brown spots and a sticky substance on back of leaves. Friend insists these are not spores but living creatures. However, spots don't move. What are they?   Probably the soft brown scale or the smooth brown hemispherical scale common on ferns. The sticky substance is honeydew. If you can't get rid of them with a brush dipped in soapsuds, try lemon oil or Volck.

What should you do for moldy-looking spots on ferns?   Your spots are likely mealy bugs. (See House Plants.)

What is the most effective treatment for white lice on ferns? Do you mean white flies, those tiny mothlike creatures? (See House Plants.)

My maidenhairfern gets brown places in the leaves; cause and cure?   Nematode injury is a possibility; this may cause brownish areas in leaves, although more often they are black bands. Remove and burn infested leaves.

I have a staghorn fern attacked by worms each year; they eat foliage at night, hide in ground in day. What will kill the worm and not affect the fern? (Florida.)   This is the Florida fern caterpillar, pale green changing to black, which feeds at night, and may strip a fern in a day or two. Dusting with pyrethrum powder, or a pyrethrum spray, will probably be more effective than lead arsenate and less harmful to the fern.

What laces fern leaves? We can find no insect to cause it. (Kansas.)   Possibly the Florida fern caterpillar, with its nocturnal habits, has come to Kansas. (See previous question.)

Will Bordeaux hurt Boston ferns?   A weak 2–2–50 solution of Bordeaux mixture should be fairly safe. It is sometimes recom-

mended to control the rhizoctonia damping-off disease which
may rot the lower fronds of Boston ferns.

What causes rust on sword fern? (Washington.)   Rust is a
fungous disease somewhat common on outdoor ferns. In the
Northwest there are 8 fern rusts which have fir as an alternate
host, causing white blisters on the fir needles. Ferns and firs
should not be grown close together.

FIR

The lower branches of several fir trees are dying. Is this usual
in this type of evergreen? (New Jersey.)   There is usually a
definite reason when branches die, even though it may be unfavorable location, crowding, or injury from red spiders. Lower
branches of firs are occasionally infected with a fungous needle-
and-twig blight. Prune out and burn infected parts.

**Four beautiful Douglasfirs have died on our property this past
year. Is it caused by an insect between bark and wood and will
it spread to more trees? (Washington.)**   Firs in the Northwest may succumb to various rust diseases and to the dwarf
mistletoe. Bark beetles are also a possibility. The latter will spread
to other trees if infested dead wood is left unburned. Call in a
tree expert for exact diagnosis.

FUCHSIA

**How can small white flies infesting fuchsias be controlled?
(California.)**   White flies seem to be inevitable on fuchsia,
whether it be a greenhouse plant or grown outdoors as in California. The important thing is to spray for the nymph stage, when
the white flies look like pale-greenish scales. Start with nicotine
sulfate and soap; switch over to an oil spray (Volck) as a last
resort.

**Black spots appear on under side of fuchsia leaves which turn
yellow. Cause and remedy?**   There is a rust which comes in
brown spots on under side of leaves, but yellowing of leaves is
probably due to sucking by white flies and the black spots are
insect eggs or excrement. (For control see previous question.)

What causes root rot in fuchsia? (Kansas.)   Probably a
waterlogged soil, although a verticillium wilt has been reported
from fuchsias growing outdoors in California.

GAILLARDIA

How can I keep grubs out of the stems of gaillardias?   Your
grubs may be larvae of the common stalk borer, with the best

control depending on cleaning up all weeds and woody stems in autumn. Frequent spraying with nicotine sulfate may partly repel borers. (See also Dahlia.)

GARDENIA

What is the best insecticide for the mealy bugs on gardenias? Probably a white oil, such as Volck, with nicotine added, if used with due precaution. (See Mealy Bugs.)

My gardenia has a little white speck that looks like mold, but when you mash it, it is alive. What is it?   The specks are mealy bugs. Clean up the first you see, before the infestation gets serious.

How do you get rid of lice on gardenias?   You probably mean mealy bugs, which see. If you refer to aphids, spray with nicotine sulfate and soap.

My Capejasmine, which grows outdoors, had some sort of insect eat a fringe around the leaves, but I never can find the insect. What can I spray with? (North Carolina.)   It may have been some sort of weevil with nocturnal habits. Spray the foliage with lead arsenate.

How should I rid my gardenia plant of beetles? (New Jersey.) Depends on kind of beetles. Fuller's rose weevil, a gray-brown snout beetle, is sometimes reported on gardenia. It feeds at night. Spray with lead arsenate.

GERANIUM

Is there any way to prevent geranium stalk rot? Some of mine rot each winter, but I do not think they are too wet.   Stem rot is usually associated with poor drainage or excessive watering. Start with cuttings from healthy plants placed in fresh or sterilized sand.

About a third of my geranium slips have shriveled at the ground, turned black, and died. What is the cause?   Either a fungus or a bacterial stem rot. Take cuttings from healthy plants and place in clean new sand. Keep slips on dry side.

What spray should be used to kill the tiny white insects on under part of leaves of a rose geranium?   These are white flies, hard to kill when they get to the moth stage. Spray with nicotine sulfate and soap, using 1½ teaspoons Black Leaf 40 and 2 ozs. soap per gallon. Next day wash off excess soap.

My choicest pelargoniums have green bugs. How can I get rid of these pests?   Spray with nicotine sulfate and soap for aphids.

After pruning geraniums and using a 45 per cent angle the stems turn black and rot back for 4 or 5 inches. What can be done? (California.)   Try frequent pinching back instead of occasional heavy pruning. When you prune, do it close to a node and disinfect your knife between cuts in 5 per cent formalin, or denatured alcohol.

GLADIOLUS

How do I recognize thrips on my glads? (Wisconsin.)   The gladiolus thrips is a small slender insect, 1/16 in. long and only as wide as a small needle. When young, it is yellow, but changes to black as an adult. It feeds by rasping petals and leaf surface. It is hard to find because it hides under the leaf sheaths and inside the flowers.

What causes gladioli to fleck or get speckled and the foliage to turn whitish? (Wisconsin.)   These are typical results of thrips injury. Infested spikes may fail to bloom, or the flowers may be spotted, or they may dry and shrivel.

Does the planting of onions near the gladioli increase the possibility of thrips on the gladiolus? (Illinois.)   No, the onion thrip is a different species.

What is the best spray for gladioli to avoid the difficulty caused by thrips? (New York.)   In the past few years tartar emetic and brown sugar have been recommended most frequently. Amounts have varied widely, but the formula can be reduced to 1 oz. tartar emetic and 2 ozs. (¼ cup) brown sugar to 3 gals. of water, and still get effective control.

What is to take the place of brown sugar in tartar-emetic sprays for gladiolus thrips?   The brown sugar for 3 gals. of spray may be replaced by 2½ ozs. honey or 2⅛ ozs. sorghum.

What may be used as a substitute for tartar emetic, rotenone, or derris as an insecticide for gladiolus thrips on growing plants next summer? The above 3 items are becoming scarcer. (Ohio.)   Rotenone, the active principle in derris, is now banned on ornamentals, but to date tartar emetic has been available in small quantities. Recent experiments show that 2 teaspoons nicotine sulfate and 1 cup corn syrup per gallon of water is even more effective than tartar emetic. The corn syrup can probably be reduced considerably and still give results, but if molasses is used with nicotine, there is poor control.

How high should gladiolus plants be before you start spraying and how often after the first time? (Wisconsin.)   Start when the plants are not more than 6 ins. high and repeat weekly for about 6 weeks, or until flowering.

Why do my glads bloom only partially? Only 2 or 3 of the lower flowers open. Should the bulbs be left in the ground all winter? (Oklahoma.)   Thrips are probably to blame. Take up the corms and treat them with naphthalene flakes. Make sure also all old tops and debris are burned in the fall, for thrips may live through an Oklahoma winter. Plant in a new location if possible.

Is it harmful to next year's plants to leave thrip-infested gladiolus bulbs in ground during winter? (New York.)   In New York, thrips would presumably be killed out over the winter, but the corms might harbor various fungous diseases. Why not clean up?

Will it be safe to plant new gladiolus bulbs in the same ground affected by thrips this past summer? (Minnesota.)   I think you can rely on a Minnesota winter being cold enough to kill out the thrips.

If in storing my gladiolus bulbs I keep the temperature near 40° F. from December 1 to March 1, will I be free of thrips? No, you will need to treat the bulbs in storage, or else dip them before planting, or both.

I am using naphthalene flakes on my gladiolus bulbs this winter to check thrips. Will you tell me when, how long, and how much to use?   The safest time for treating is when the corms first go into storage. Place in paper bags and add 1 oz. flakes for each 100 corms; close the bags. Leave only 2 to 3 weeks, then remove from bags, screen off excess flakes, and store as usual.

I lost almost 1,000 glads this last season. My husband refuses to use naphthalene flakes, as he says they injure the bulbs. How about this?   If the treatment lasts under 4 weeks, is given early in the season, and directions are followed as to amounts, there should be little injury. Too much naphthalene too long will be injurious.

Does it injure gladiolus bulbs to remain in naphthalene flakes longer than 3 weeks?   Three weeks is the prescribed time. Some think that if the right amount is used there is no harm in waiting until it all evaporates, but ordinarily a month should be the limit for treatment.

Is there any other way to control thrips? (Michigan.) Bulbs may be dipped before planting in 1 to 1,000 solution of bichloride of mercury for 4 hours if the husks are removed. Treating for 20 to 30 minutes with hot water held at 115° to 120° F. is also said to be satisfactory.

Would carbon disulphide be good for thrips on glad bulbs, and how strong would you use it? (Massachusetts.)   Carbon disulphide emulsion has been used by some commercial growers to control mealy bugs on corms, but it is rather dangerous for the amateur. You'd better stick to napthalene flakes.

I have to store my gladioli, tigridia and zephyranthes, side by side in the fruit closet. Should they all be fumigated with napthalene flakes? (Michigan.)   The gladiolus thrips does infest tigridia, its near relative, but I can find no reports in the literature as to dosage and possible injury. You will have to experiment for yourself to see how much napthalene may safely be used. So far as I know the gladiolus thrip has not been reported on zephyranthes.

Is Semesan good for treating glad bulbs in spring before planting?   It is used to control scab, a bacterial disease, and sometimes thrips. Soak for 7 hours in a 1 per cent solution.

I have heard that soaking bulbs for thrip will delay blooming for 2 weeks. Is it true? (Wisconsin.)   Disinfectants frequently have a slight retarding effect on growth and bloom; the length of delay varies with circumstances.

If glad bulbs are put in napthalene flakes for a month this fall, do they need treating before planting in spring to kill thrips?   Dipping before planting as well as fumigation is a double precaution and will take care of scab as well as thrips.

Are there any cultural practices which aid in the control of thrips?   Digging early in the fall, before the corms are quite mature, and cutting off and burning the tops before the thrips can work down into the corms will help.

When bulbs are taken from ground there appears a brown scale or spot. Is this a disease, and what steps may be taken? (Virginia.)   This is probably scab, a bacterial disease which shows as circular black depressions with a raised margin. Clean off husks before planting in the spring. Discard corms where the scab has gone through to the corm itself and treat the rest in 1 to 1,000 bichloride of mercury for 2 hours, or else for 5 minutes in calomel, 1 oz. to 1 gal. of water.

The tips of the leaves start turning brown, and this continues down the stem until the plant dies and bulbs rot. What will correct this? (Indiana.)   This may be scab, although usually there are definite spots on the leaves. It may also be dry rot, a fungous disease which turns the leaves yellow and produces dark sunken lesions on the corms and root decay. Discard all spotted corms, treat before planting, and, if possible, practice a 4-year rotation, that is, do not replant gladioli in infested soil inside 4 years.

How do you treat gladiolus bulbs for fusarium yellows? (Indiana.)   You can't entirely prevent yellows by corm treatment. The fungus lives in the soil and is widely distributed throughout the Middle West. Some varieties are more resistant than others. Wait at least 4 years before replanting gladioli on diseased soil. Use only corms that bear cormels; treat as for scab.

If space is limited and you must replant gladiolus bulbs in the same place, is there any way of inoculating the soil against disease and thrips? (Mississippi.)   You can't inoculate it, but you can disinfect a small area with formaldehyde or chloropicrin. (See Soil Sterilization.)

GLOXINIA

What causes gloxinia buds to blast when nicely started? Sometimes a gray mold fungus, botrytis, of the same genus that causes peony buds to blast. Usually poor ventilation and excessive humidity are contributing causes. Remove all diseased parts as soon as noticed.

GOLDENGLOW

My goldenglow was eaten up this year by beetles, light green with black spots. What were they? (Kansas.)   These were diabrotica, or spotted cucumber beetles, very hard to kill. Try a fluosilicate dust, such as Dutox, or a cryolite dust. Lead arsenate spray may help.

GOURDS

How can I keep insects from ruining fancy gourds? (Georgia.) Gourds are afflicted by the same pests and diseases as cucumbers. A combination spray of Bordeaux mixture, or yellow copper oxide, with lead arsenate and nicotine sulfate, should take care of wilt, borers, cucumber beetles, aphids, and white flies more or less successfully. Start spraying when the plants are small and repeat at 10-day to 2-week intervals. For chewing insects alone cryolite may be used as a spray or dust. Wipe the gourds with a dis-infectant to prevent spotting after harvest.

GUM

Is there anything I can do to prevent the beetles from taking to the gum tree? (Maryland.)   Do you mean Japanese beetles? Have your tree sprayed with lead arsenate in June.

HACKBERRY

How can leaf galls in hackberry trees be eradicated? (Colorado.)   These galls are caused by plant lice. Spray with 3 teaspoons nicotine sulfate, 2 ozs. soap, and 3½ ozs. molasses per gallon of water.

HAWTHORN

With what shall red hawthorns be sprayed when red cedars surround them? (New York.)   Spray several times during May with wettable sulphur or Bordeaux mixture.

What should I do about a sort of mildew which turns the leaves on my English hawthorn yellow and causes them to fall in midsummer? (Iowa.)   The orange rust will cause defoliation, and so will a fungous leaf spot, to be controlled by spraying with Bordeaux mixture in May. If you have true mildew, a white coating on the leaves and buds, spray with 1 to 50 lime sulphur before the buds open and after the petals have fallen.

What is the remedy for the lesser borer in the trunk of Paul's Scarlet Hawthorn?   I am not sure which borer you mean. If it is one that brings sawdust to the mouth of holes, you can gas it with a few drops of carbon disulphide, sealing up the hole with putty or gum. If it is the flat-headed borer, keep your tree growing vigorously, paint pruning scars and other wounds, and perhaps try a repellent wash on the trunk—whitewash with lime sulphur added for a strong odor.

HELENIUM

What shall I do for white grubs in roots of helenium? (Michigan.)   There is not much you can do for plants where the roots are already eaten off. White grubs are usually worse in land recently taken over from sod. Perhaps you can transplant your heleniums to a bed that has been in cultivation for a long time. Spading a bed and leaving it rough over the winter will kill some grubs. You can work lead arsenate into the soil, but this is apt to injure ornamental plants.

What about the black "bugs" on helenium? (New Jersey.) The chief offenders are small black snout beetles, which start chewing the young shoots in early spring and often keep working until flowering. Frequent spraying with lead arsenate or other stomach poison keeps them fairly well in check. Later in the summer black aphids may appear. You can add nicotine to the lead arsenate spray or use a separate application of nicotine sulfate and soap.

HEMLOCK

Hemlock branches turned brown and died until 4 or 5 had to be cut off. What can be the cause? (Tennessee.)   It might be red-spider injury, or a fungous blight. You can dust with sulphur for the former; for the latter you can only cut out and burn infected limbs.

HIBISCUS

What makes the leaves on Chinese hibiscus dry up and fall off? (Wyoming.)   It is hard to say. There is a fungous blight, a stem rot, and a leaf spot which might have such symptoms, but your trouble is more likely one of water relations—either too dry soil or one waterlogged from overwatering.

The buds on my hibiscus formed but before blossoming turned brown and dropped off. Why? (Maine.)   If you had a spell of rainy weather, it might have been botrytis blight, gray mold, which possibly might have been prevented by spraying with Bordeaux mixture.

HICKORY

What spray will kill the grubs that get in hickory nuts? (Ohio.) These are the larvae of the hickory-nut weevil in all probability. Spraying has not been recommended for the control of this pest. The larvae leave the nuts in the late fall and pass the winter in the soil, and it has been suggested that harvesting early and fumigating with carbon disulphide would kill the grubs and so prevent them from producing weevils for another year. However, this is probably not feasible for the homeowner with 1 or 2 hickory trees.

HOLLYHOCK

What is the cause of the rusting, yellowing, and dropping of foliage of hollyhocks? (Maine.)   Rust is due to the rust fungus, which produces its spores in little reddish pustules on the under side of the leaves. Yellow areas appear on the upper surface, and with a bad case of rust the leaves turn yellow, wither, and may fall off. There are usually rust lesions on the stem as well as on the leaves.

Is there any way to prevent rust on hollyhocks? (Connecticut.) Remove and burn infected leaves as soon as noticed, and burn all old stalks and leaves in the fall. Dust with sulphur, starting in early spring, being careful to cover the under surface of the leaves.

I used dusting sulphur early on my hollyhocks but was unable to get more. What else could be used in place of it? (Maine.) Bordeaux mixture might be used but it would be a poor second choice. Sulphur will keep, so one can order it early, and keep a supply on hand.

I sprayed my hollyhocks from the beginning with Evergreen. Why didn't it stop the rust? (Maine.)   There is no reason why it should, as Evergreen is a contact insecticide meant for the control of sucking insects. It might have some effect on red spiders, which turn hollyhock leaves yellow, but it would do nothing for the rust fungus.

Hollyhocks in different sections rot out. Why? I've put road ashes, lime, peatmoss in, as section is damp. (New Jersey.) Haven't you any well-drained place that has ordinary good garden soil? Any self-respecting plant might rot in such a mixture. Sand is the only thing you haven't tried, and that might work. Don't forget that hollyhocks are biennials. They die naturally after blooming.

HONEYSUCKLE

How can I exterminate aphids on honeysuckle? (Kentucky.) It is rather difficult, for the aphids congregate on the young shoots in great numbers and dwarf the leaves. Even the flower buds may be injured. Spray frequently with nicotine sulfate and soap; start when you see the first few aphids, and not the first few hundreds.

HOSTA

My hosta last fall looked lacelike, the leaves were so badly eaten. What is the cause and what shall I do? (Ohio.)   Slugs will have this effect on hosta leaves. A metaldehyde bait is recommended (see Slugs) but I prefer to dust the foliage with sulphur-lead arsenate dust.

HOUSE PLANTS

What are the white plant lice that look like cotton that come on house plants?   These are mealy bugs, sucking insects like aphids. They are prevalent in greenhouses and on many house plants—coleus, croton, cactus, crassula, gardenia, poinsettia, rubber plant, and many others. A severe infestation is evidence of neglect.

What can be done to rid house plants of woolly aphis? These are mealy bugs. It is easier to prevent them than get rid of them. Keep your plants frequently syringed or washed, in a not-too-hot or dry atmosphere. Remove the first bit of white fluff you see with a tiny cotton swab wrapped around a toothpick and dipped in alcohol (omit the alcohol for cactus).

How do you rid house plants of the white mealy bug that leaves a sticky substance on the leaves? The sticky substance is honeydew, secreted by various sucking insects. If mealy bugs get started despite picking them off, spray with ½ teaspoon nicotine sulfate and ½ oz. soap in 1 qt. of water. If this does not clean them up, use a white oil emulsion, such as Greenhouse Volck, following manufacturer's directions as to dilution, usually 1 to 50. Have the plants somewhat shaded from the sun and rinse with pure water several hours later.

Should house plants with mealy bugs be repotted after control? It is not necessary if you got control; if you did not, repotting would do no good. Of course repot your plants if their growth requires it.

Do you know a home remedy good for plant lice? Just ordinary soap and water will do, but nicotine sulfate (Black Leaf 40) is not very expensive and is more efficient. Use ¼ teaspoon nicotine and ¼ oz. soap (1 level tablespoon granulated soap) to 1 qt. of water. Aphids are not hard to kill if they are sprayed frequently.

My house plants show a brown scale and a sticky substance. Can the scale be avoided by treating the sticky substance? It's the other way around. You treat the scale and then it can no longer secrete the honeydew. Wash scales off in very strong nicotine sulfate and soap solution, scrubbing them off with a brush, and then spray with normal-strength nicotine spray, as given for aphids. Use Volck for stubborn cases.

We are bothered with very small white bugs that suck the under side of leaves; when the plant is shaken, they fly off and settle back again. What are they? These are white flies. Spray the plants in the morning, before the flies get active, with nicotine sulfate and soap, hitting the under side of the leaves.

What can you use to get rid of the little white maggots in the soil? These are fly maggots, often present in soil with much humus or plants fed with organic fertilizers. Water the plants with a solution of nicotine sulfate without the soap. Or the soil may be baked before using for potting.

What causes the small black flies on house plants, similar to fruit flies?   These breed from the maggots or eggs that came in with the potting soil. Some recommend watering the soil with lime water as for earthworms, or working in tobacco dust, or watering in any contact insecticide.

Is there any way to keep red spiders off my indoor plants, other than constantly washing them off under running water? A frequent bath is the best way to keep red spiders in check. Any contact spray, nicotine sulfate and soap, or pyrethrum, or rotenone, or dusting with fine sulphur, will help fight spider mites.

How do you get rid of red spider in the greenhouse?   Frequent syringing with pure water is helpful and this may be followed with a sulphur dust. However, too much syringing in a greenhouse is often accompanied by increased plant disease, in which case one of the thiocyanate sprays such as Lethane or Loro would be more satisfactory.

A small insect inhabiting greenhouse looks like a crab, spins web from leaf to leaf. Have tried dusting and force of plain water. What shall I use?   Probably some species of spider, harmless to plants.

Can insects, scale, etc., be controlled in a small greenhouse by fumigating only?   You will probably have to supplement with some spraying. Nicotine fumigation is effective against aphids and does fairly well for thrips, but is not so good for white fly and scale. Cyanide fumigation will kill aphids, most thrips, young scale, and many mealy bugs. There are many precautions, for the safety both of the plants and the operator, that must be observed. Get very exact information from your State Experiment Station.

How can the home gardener make a fumigating cabinet and how much cyanogas do you use in it?   United States Department of Agriculture *Farmers' Bulletin 1362* includes working drawings of a fumigation box. The dosage of cyanogas will vary according to the plants you want to fumigate and the exact size of your box. It is all rather complicated for the average home gardener; but apply to your State Experiment Station for more help with your specific problems.

Is there a way to destroy angleworms in a potted plant? Dust the surface of the soil with hydrated lime and water it in, or else water the plants with lime water. Earthworms do no damage in themselves, but they clog up the drainage hole.

Having trouble with soil nematodes in my house-plant soil.

Can you recommend a procedure to be used on a small scale?
Your potting soil may be fumigated with chloropicrin, tear gas,
sold as Larvacide, and available in small quantities with complete directions for use. (See also Soil Sterilization.)

**What is the yellowish-brown scale which forms on top of soil
in pots?**   An indication that your soil needs cultivating and a
little oxygen allowed to get into it. Scratch it up with the tines of
an old fork.

**My jade-plant, peperomia, and some others have a rust on
the under side of the leaves. What is it?**   Probably not an
organic disease so much as a reaction to environment, possibly
too much water and not enough oxygen in the soil.

What causes powdery mildew to appear on house plants?
This is a fungous growth that usually comes only when plants
are kept in a too-moist atmosphere—something that seldom happens with house plants. Dusting sulphur will control it.

**What will destroy or prevent wiggle-tails, or mosquitoes, in
water garden or pots in the house without injuring the plants?**
Try spraying with pyrethrum, if you can get it.

HYDRANGEA

**What shall I use on my hydrangeas to prevent brown spots
on the leaves? (Texas.)**   To control leaf spot, spray with
Bordeaux mixture or dust with sulphur. Remove and burn infected leaves.

**What solution should be used for mildew on hydrangeas, or
should the soil be treated? (Texas.)**   Treating the soil won't
do any good for mildew. Dust with fine dusting sulphur, or spray
with Bordeaux mixture. Sometimes spraying with potassium sul-
phide has been recommended for the Southwest.

IMPATIENS

**Why do my impatiens plants get a sticky substance on them?
They have something like grains of sugar, especially variety
sultani.**   These grains of sugar are honeydew secreted either
by scale insects or aphids or else nymphs of white flies. (See
House Plants.)

IRIS

Some of my iris rhizomes are rotting. Although the shell
seems dry, the inside, if opened before destruction is complete,
is wet and slimy. What is this? (New York.)   This is a perfect
description of bacterial soft rot. You put your thumb on a sup-

posedly firm shell only to have it sink into slimy, vile-smelling goo. The rot may start in the leaves, following punctures by young borers, and there is often a water-soaked appearance to the leaves.

What can I do to overcome soft rot in iris? (New York.) In the first place, take control measures against the borer (see below). Next, remove and destroy immediately any rotting rhizomes. Dig them out with surrounding soil and disinfect your trowel. If the rot gets very bad over a whole bed, plan on treating all the rhizomes at the time of division, right after flowering. Take up the clumps, separate the rhizomes, cut out all soft tissue, cut leaves back to 6-in. fans and immerse rhizome and fan for 30 minutes in 1 to 1,000 solution of bichloride of mercury or for 1 hour in a Semesan solution, 1 oz. to 3 gals. of water. Work on newspapers so all debris can be gathered up and burned. Leave treated plants out in the sun for a day or two before replanting.

Is there any way I can clean up infested iris without relocating it? (New York.) After you have treated it in the disinfectant you can pour the solution into the iris bed and be fairly safe in replanting. There is less danger of rot if the upper surface of the rhizome is kept exposed to the sun rather than covered with soil.

Will applying hydrated lime to our soil prevent the dying out and disappearance of bearded iris? (Georgia.) No. Iris is said to like lime, but so do the bacteria that cause soft rot. If the soil is slightly acid, it will deter the bacteria responsible for the disappearance of your iris.

How do you destroy the borer which attacks iris, cosmos, calendula, etc.? (Illinois.) It is not the same borer. The iris borer, a fat, flesh-colored caterpillar with a dark head, specializes in iris. In cosmos it is probably the stalk borer. Sanitary measures are most important in getting rid of iris borers. If you are dividing the iris and treating for soft rot, do it early while the borer is still in the stalk and before it has eaten out the rhizome; in any case, before it has left the rhizome and pupated in the soil. The moth lays its eggs on old leaves and debris during the fall. Sometime in October or November, after a killing frost, clean up and burn all this old material, leaving only a clean fan of new leaves. In the spring cut out infested leaves, or kill the borer in place by squeezing the leaf in your fingers.

Have you found an effective means of controlling the iris borer? An arsenic spray doesn't do much good. (Pennsylvania.) Sanitation is more important than spraying, but 2 or 3 applications of lead arsenate, with a little fish oil added as a spreader, or wheat flour as a sticker, are said to give some control. You have to start early in the spring, to get the borers before they actually enter the leaves.

What ate long holes or skeletonized my vesper iris seedlings during the summer? (New York.)   My guess is that slugs were at work, but a zebra caterpillar also chews iris leaves. Spray or dust with lead arsenate.

Does anyone but me know anything about the little round iris-wrecking beetle? Have fought it for years but never found it mentioned. (Connecticut.)   A small, round, flat, dark weevil is said to eat iris pods and sometimes the petals. Try spraying with arsenate of lead.

How can you lick thrips in iris? Does dark, rainy weather foster their growth? (Minnesota.)   Thrips are especially disastrous to Japanese iris, but bearded iris may also be infested. Nicotine sulfate and soap forcibly sprayed into the leaf bases will give about as good control as anything. You can also try tartar emetic as recommended under gladiolus. Thrips are usually more numerous in hot, dry weather.

What is the meaning of brown spots on iris leaves? (Texas.)   This is a fungous leaf-spot disease, usually fairly well controlled by cleaning up all old leaves in the fall, but occasionally requiring 2 or 3 applications of Bordeaux mixture during the summer.

Why do iris leaves turn brown and dry during July and August? (Wyoming.)   Crown or rhizome rot fungi may be the cause, or perhaps merely overcrowding and lack of water. If there are any signs of gray mold, or white fungous threads with seedlike bodies, remove and destroy infected rhizomes. Sterilize the area with bichloride of mercury or Semesan.

Why do my iris blooms last only 1 or 2 days and die? (Oregon.)   The life span of a single iris flower is only a day or two; that's the way it is made. But if you mean that after 1 or 2 flowers come out your whole stalk withers and dies, that may be some fungous disease working at the crown, or possibly a very serious infestation of thrips.

My beautiful iris garden is being ruined by root-knot nematodes. What can I do? (Arkansas.)   The root-knot nematode is one of the worst Southern problems since it cannot be killed by winter cold nor readily starved because it attacks so many kinds of garden plants. If you have any land that has not been growing nematode-susceptible plants, you can start a new iris garden there. You'll have to start with new rhizomes also. If you must use the same location, you can take out the iris and grow a cereal crop for a year or two which will starve out the nematodes, or you can disinfect the soil with chloropicrin. (See Nematodes; Soil Sterilization.)

IVY

What can be done to keep red spider from killing house ivy? Give it a weekly bath. Water is the very best deterrent for spider mites, and if the foliage is washed frequently the creatures will never get started. If, however, the leaves are yellow and cobwebby, dip the vines in a nicotine sulfate and soap or pyrethrum solution.

My ivy gets a brown (looks like a flaxseed) sucking insect on it. I have tried repeatedly to eliminate it. What is it? If it is brown and thin, it is evidently the soft brown scale, and not the white oleander scale which is equally common on ivy. Frequent spraying with nicotine sulfate and soap when the young are hatching and the scales are vulnerable is supposed to keep them under control. If this does not work, try an oil spray, such as Volck.

How do I get rid of the tiny brown slugs on the leaves of an ivy plant? These are probably scale. (See previous question.) The best way to keep the plant free from them is to note the first one that appears and wipe it off with a soapy rag.

My English Ivy was infested with scale in September; picked off most of it and then noticed a sticky clear fluid oozing from the leaves. Is it from the scale? Yes, honeydew secreted by the insect. You will have to spray to clean it up.

My Germanivy is defoliated by a minute black insect. What is it and how can I make it feel very unwelcome? It is a black aphid, very common on ivy. Spraying with, or dipping in, a solution of nicotine sulfate and soap will make this plant louse unwelcome. So will the weekly bath that keeps red spider in check.

What makes ivy plants wilt and the leaves turn yellow? Red spider, usually encouraged by too dry an atmosphere, will cause leaves to turn yellow, but a bacterial disease, encouraged by too-high humidity and too-high temperatures, will also cause yellowing of leaves and sometimes their wilting if there are bacterial lesions on the petioles. This disease would be far more common in a greenhouse than in the dry air of the average home.

What causes new leaves on grapeivy to dry and drop? Grapeivy is susceptible to a fungous leaf spot and die back, which may kill the young leaves. Spraying with Bordeaux mixture will control it. More probably your grapeivy does not like its soil conditions. The new leaves will dry if the soil is either too wet or too dry.

JAPANESE CHERRY

Why did my two Japanese cherries die after the fourth blooming year? (Illinois.)   It sounds as if they might have had a harmful spray. An oil spray too strong, or applied when it is too cold, can kill ornamental trees.

JUNIPER

What spray shall I use for juniper scale? (Pennsylvania.) If your bushes are not too close to any painted surface, spray with 1 to 9 dilution of lime sulphur before the new growth starts, about the first week in April in Pennsylvania. If your junipers are close to the house, this spray will discolor the paint and you should use a miscible oil. (See Dormant Spraying; also Evergreens.)

How can I keep bagworms off junipers? Does spraying do any good? (New York.)   Yes. Spray with lead arsenate when the young worms begin moving around with their bags and chewing, usually late May. Pick off bags and burn during fall and winter. (See Bagworms.)

How can I get rid of all the red spiders in my juniper? (Idaho.)   Forceful spraying with nicotine sulfate and soap, repeated several times, may work. Or dust with fine dusting sulphur. Dormant spraying with a miscible oil may be necessary, but oil sprays sometimes injure junipers. (See Arborvitae for formula for a glue spray sometimes recommended.)

What causes my pyramid juniper to be slowly dying; needles turn yellow-brown and drop off? Mate on other side of doorstep is just fine. (Wisconsin.)   It may be red spider, and a juniper near a wall, in a very hot position with little circulation of air, is far more susceptible to injury. The upright junipers very often get brown and unsightly in a few years, no matter what control measures are used.

LARKSPUR

What is good to kill little yellow lice on larkspur? (Arkansas.) Spray frequently with nicotine sulfate and soap.

Why does my larkspur turn yellow, soft at base, and rot? (South Carolina.)   This is probably crown rot, or Southern rot (due to *Sclerotium rolfsii*). Remove infected plants and soil. (See Delphinium.)

Why do my annual larkspur plants turn yellow and die just before or after first blooms appear? (Massachusetts.) This may also be crown rot (due in Massachusetts to *Sclerotium delphini*). The fungus starts working in warm, humid weather which may coincide with blooming time of the larkspurs. (See Delphinium for control.)

LAUREL

What shall I do for laurel blight, when the leaves are spotted and burned followed by slow death? (New Jersey.) You probably have two distinct troubles. The spotting is not often serious on mountain laurel, but when the shrubs are brought in from the woods and stay in shady places under the drip of trees, the leaf spot may become unsightly, in which case it may be controlled by spraying with Bordeaux mixture. The burning is probably winter burn and sunscald, due to drying effect of winter wind and sun. Death may be due to neither the leaf spot nor the sunscald but to some unfavorable soil condition.

LAWN

How can I prevent neighbor's dogs from tearing up the grounds to get at moles aside from getting rid of the moles? Why not attempt getting rid of the moles that attract the dogs? Dogs are a nuisance, but there is nothing except a fence and a gate tightly latched to keep them off a lawn. Even in suburbs, where dogs are kept on leash, their owners usually walk them on the lawn side of the sidewalk rather than curb them.

How can I get rid of moles in the lawn? We have tried traps, the pitchfork, castor beans, cyanide gas, Mol-o-gen, and we still have the moles. (Ohio.) Traps have to be set with great care. A few chemicals you haven't tried are carbon disulphide, paradichlorbenzene, strychnine poison bait. (See Moles.)

Can chinch bugs be controlled by applying tobacco dust around the edges of the lawn? (Massachusetts.) No. You have to cover the entire area very thoroughly. Rotenone dust is preferable to tobacco dust but its use is not permitted on lawns now. Apply 25 lbs. tobacco dust per 1,000 sq. ft. and work it in thoroughly. Make 1 application in June, and 2, about 10 days apart, in August for the second brood.

What caused white, slimy mildew spots on my lawn under red oak trees? (New Jersey.) There are several fungous diseases of turf, most common being large brown patch, dollar spot, or small brown patch, and spot blight of pythium disease. The latter may be your particular trouble. It occurs in warm, humid weather and where the air is stagnant, as it might be under an oak tree. Control has not been well worked out, but bichloride of mercury or Semesan will probably check its spread. Avoid overwatering. Avoid also, in humid weather, letting the clippings remain on the grass.

What causes the half-circle formation of toadstools, killing the grass, and what can we do to correct it? (Washington.)   This is a fairy ring of mushrooms rather common in lawns. The fungous mycelium starts in one spot and spreads in a circle, sending up the fruiting bodies at intervals. Various chemicals are recommended: 4 ozs. iron sulfate to 1 gal. water; 1 oz. potassium permanganate to 4 gals. of water; or 1 to 1,000 bichloride of mercury dilution. Cut grass close for several feet around the rings and wet the ground thoroughly.

LILAC

What can be done to stop oyster-shell scale on a lilac hedge? (Massachusetts.)   If the hedge is away from any painted surface, spray with lime sulphur, 1 to 8 dilution, in the spring before new growth starts. In Massachusetts this would be the end of March. Miscible oil, 1 to 16 dilution, may also be used and is preferable if the bushes are close to a house.

I have a gray scale on lilacs; have used lime sulphur. What spray do you suggest? (Ohio.)   Perhaps you have the round, scurfy scale, less amenable to lime sulphur than the oyster-shell scale. Use a miscible oil spray, such as Scale-O, or Scalecide, at a 1 to 16 dilution, before the buds break but on a clear day with the temperature above 45° F.

I sprayed my lilac bushes in early spring with Scalecide, but in spite of this I see a white scalelike lice on the branches. (New York.)   One dormant spraying does not always clean up an infestation of scale. When the young hatch in the summer (your white scalelike lice), spray with nicotine sulfate and soap.

The bark of my lilac has cracked and breaks off, and I have found something like eggs on the ground. Do I have to cut out the infested shoot? (New York.)   Yes, cut it out and burn it. If the bark is breaking off, the shoot will not live and meanwhile you can burn up the borer. The eggs on the ground are frass, or excrement, which the borer has pushed out of the holes. If the bark is sound and the branches look healthy, you can gas the borer by injecting a few drops of carbon disulphide from a machine oilcan and plugging the hole with gum or putty. Or you can squeeze in some nicotine paste, sold as Bortox, and need not plug up the hole.

What moth, beetle, or other insect is responsible for the borer in lilacs? (New Jersey.)   The adult of the lilac borer, an inch-long white grub, is a wasp; the adult of another borer common in lilacs, a cream-colored larva with black spots, is the leopard moth, white with black markings. To control either borer, use carbon disulphide or nicotine paste in the holes, or cut out and burn all infested branches.

How can I keep borers from getting into my lilacs? (Iowa.) There are various repellent washes for the trunk and branches but there are none sure to be safe under all conditions. Watch for the first sign of borer work, usually a hole with sawdust coming out, and treat immediately. (See answers to the two previous questions.)

How can I prevent lilac leaves from becoming mildewed during the summer? (Indiana.)   The mildew, or white powdery coating over the leaves, comes from a fungus which grows over the outside of the leaves and so can be readily killed by dusting with fine sulphur. Mildew usually appears in late summer. It is unsightly but has little permanent deleterious effect.

How do you rid lilacs of microsphaera? (Connecticut.) *Microsphaera alni* is the scientific name of the powdery mildew fungus. Sulphur dust will eradicate it.

What shall I do for an insect that rolls up lilac leaves, leaving eggs and web? Eventually the leaf is eaten through in this spot and the leaves are scalloped, but I think this is done by another insect. (Washington.)   Probably 2 phases of the same insect, the lilac leaf roller, which is reported in the Puget Sound region. Spray with nicotine sulfate and soap to kill the young larvae, or with lead arsenate before the leaves are rolled.

What causes the foliage to turn brown and die shortly after blooming?   Any one of several blight or leaf-spot fungi, a bacterial blight, a wilt from verticillium fungus in the soil, a graft blight due to grafting on privet stock, too much fertilizer, or not enough water.

Why did large lilac bushes develop black and brown spots on the leaves and fall off?   Probably a fungous disease. Prune out blighted twigs and spray with Bordeaux mixture.

LILY

What causes lily buds to have brown spots on them? (Illinois.)
Presumably botrytis blight, a fungous disease, which produces
oval, orange, or reddish-brown spots on the foliage, a bud blight,
and sometimes stem lesions. The disease is more prevalent in rainy
weather.

**Can you spray the growing lilies with something to bring them
through the blossoming period? (New York.)**   Spraying with
Bordeaux mixture every 2 weeks, starting in early spring, should
control botrytis blight sufficiently to obtain normal flowering.
Pick off and burn each spotted leaf.

**Just how does the lily-disease mosaic look on the foliage? (New
York.)**   The leaves of infected plants are patterned with light
and dark-green mottled areas, varying with the species. Mottling
is accompanied by stunting, and leaves may die, from the base
upward, prematurely.

**I have some formosanum giant white lilies grown from seed.
After a few years the blooms twist and go completely bad. Is
there anything I can do to correct this trouble?**   Mosaic will
distort the flowers. It is not seed-transmitted, but the melon (or
cotton) aphid carries the virus from other diseased lilies to your
healthy seedlings. There is no control except ruthlessly roguing
out all diseased plants so the aphids cannot feed on them.

**How do you tell the difference between mosaic and chlorosis
in lilies? (California.)**   Mosaic, the virus disease, shows up as
a mottled green-and-yellow effect, while chlorosis, a physiological
disease, often appearing in lilies grown with too much lime in
heavy soil, is a yellowing of the entire leaf, except near the veins.
Spraying with 0.5 per cent solution of ferrous sulfate will often
bring back green color.

**My lilies were a complete failure last year. Leaves on gold-
banded and pink-spotted varieties became yellow and twisted and
the bud died. Can you advise procedures for next year?**   This
may have been basal rot, due to a fungus, fusarium, which came
to you in diseased bulbs. The lower leaves turn yellow and the
plants seldom come to flowering. In buying new bulbs make sure
they are healthy. It is said that some control is obtained by immersing diseased bulbs in formalin diluted 1 to 50.

**Why do lily bulbs turn yellow and die after growing a few
inches? Some never come through the ground. (Iowa.)**   This
may be bulb rot from diseased bulbs, or stump rot, caused by

phytopthora living in the soil and attacking the new growth as it emerges from the soil. Spraying with Bordeaux mixture will help in the latter case.

What would you suggest is wrong with our regal lilies which grow well, with firm stalks and buds, and then suddenly topple over with the stem withering halfway? (Minnesota.)   There is a disease called limber neck, which seems to be due to unfavorable physiological conditions, but no one knows very much about it, or how to prevent it.

Why have my Madonna lilies grown smaller and poorer in quality? They have small white insects on bulbs when dug up. If these insects are very, very small, they are bulb mites, and doubtless responsible for your lilies getting poorer. Destroy infected bulbs; plant new ones in another place in a well-drained soil. If your insects are larger, they may be root aphids, and you may be able to kill them with a solution of nicotine sulfate and soap.

What can I use to keep bugs off the lily blossoms? (Illinois.) There are several species of aphids which infest lilies, one of which, the cotton aphid, carries the mosaic virus. In addition to aphids on the buds, the leaves, especially in late summer, are very often completely covered with these plant lice. Spray with nicotine sulfate and soap, or a pyrethrum spray, repeating as needed.

How can one protect Madonna lilies from a worm that hollows out the stem? (Indiana.)   This is the common stem or stalk borer that attacks many garden plants. Clean up the weeds round about and burn in the fall any plant tops suspected of harboring borers. It may be possible to save a lily in bloom by slitting the stem and killing the borer with a knife, or injecting some nicotine paste.

How can I keep moles away from lilies?   Plant bulbs in wire baskets, or use poison bait. (See Moles.)

LOCUST

I have noticed large bulges in the bark of our flowering locust. Is this a disease? What do you suggest as a remedy? (Connecticut.)   The swellings are caused by the locust borer, a devastating pest not readily controlled. The larvae live in the wood, and the adult, black, yellow-marked beetles come out in September to feed on goldenrod and lay their eggs in crevices in the locust bark. If the tree is painted with a mixture of 9 parts Tanglefoot and 1 part 50 per cent sodium arsenate solution it will kill all the beetles that come in contact with it.

LUPINE

What causes a large, healthy Russell lupine plant to die late in August? (Washington.)   It may have been a fungous stem, crown or root rot, but it may also have been unfavorable soil conditions. Russell lupines have often been short-lived in this country. Some think a rather peaty soil, well supplied with organic matter and phosphorus, and testing *p*H 5.5 to 6.0, works best for lupines.

Can anything be done to Russell lupines to prevent aphids? I have sprayed with everything. (Massachusetts.)   You can't exactly prevent aphids, but you should be able to kill the first few before they multiply with any contact insecticide, either pyrethrum or nicotine sulfate and soap.

MAGNOLIA

My beautiful small magnolia seems to have scale. Is this usual? Sprayed with lime sulphur last spring. Correct? How strong? Large blackish magnolia scales are not unusual. A dormant lime-sulphur spray at 1 to 8 dilution should have gotten the scales, but it is an unpleasant spray to use. Try a miscible oil at a 1 to 16 dilution. (See Dormant Spraying.)

MAPLE

Last spring after getting its foliage in full my Norway maple began to die out in the small branches, finally getting so thin you could see through it. What caused this? (Virginia.)   Verticillium wilt, a serious fungous disease of maples, works that way, with the sudden dying of a branch. There will be green streaks, later turning black, in the sapwood. Maples sometimes recover from mild cases of wilt if the infected branches are promptly pruned out. Often, however, the tree must be removed and destroyed as quickly as possible, getting out the roots also. Plant another kind of tree in that location.

My Silver Maple tree is all eaten up by worms. What can be done? (New York.)   If it is the green-striped maple worm, a caterpillar 1½ ins. long with dark and yellow-green stripes alternating down the back, spray with lead arsenate when the caterpillars are young, probably in June. The forest tent caterpillar, blue-black with white diamonds, chews in May, and hence requires an earlier spray.

What insect works on the leaves of hard maple trees? (Illinois.) The green-striped maple worm and caterpillars of the tussock moth are reported feeding on foliage of hard maples in the Middle West.

Can you tell me how best to control maple aphids? (Massachusetts.) The Norway maple aphid, a large, greenish plant louse, not only wrinkles the leaves but drops its sticky honeydew on cars parked underneath. If you can afford it, have the tree sprayed with nicotine sulfate and soap. A tree expert with a power sprayer will be needed for large trees.

Our Japanese maple drops its leaves about the end of July; they seem to dry up. We give it plenty of water. What is the trouble? (Ohio.) It is possible to give it too much water. Aphids sometimes get so numerous the leaves curl and dry. This maple must be sprayed cautiously, for it is susceptible to spray injury which may cause the leaves to burn or fall. Nicotine sulfate and soap may be used on a not-too-hot day.

Why do the leaves of my Japanese maple get rust spots on them and roll up and fall off? (New York). This may be sunscald, or perhaps spray injury. (See answer to previous question.)

Is the spray used for leaf curl on peach trees injurious to dwarf red maples? (Oregon.) It depends on what was in the peach spray. Very often an oil for scale is combined with Bordeaux mixture for leaf curl and in that case it might be injurious, some maples being susceptible to oil injury.

I have a bug or a germ which splits the maple tree limbs. (Ohio.) There are several maple borers, the work of any one of which would so weaken the tree that branches might be split off. The callus borer is marked by swellings and abnormal growths.

What do you do for borers? (New York.) If they are in the branches of small limbs, cut out the infested parts and burn. Borers in larger limbs may sometimes be killed by inserting a wire, or gassed by injecting carbon disulphide or a nicotine paste.

Last season we had trouble with worms under the bark of young maples, causing excessive bleeding. Is there anything we can do to prevent their appearance this season? (Ohio.) In Ohio newly set maples are prey to the fly-headed borer. Trunks should be wrapped from ground to first branches with Kraft crepe paper, or a good grade of wrapping paper. It may not be too late to wrap for another year. Repellent washes do little good.

Do maple trees normally require a yearly spraying? (New Hampshire.)   One treatment with arsenate of lead after the leaves are well out will give protection against chewing insects such as the green-striped maple worm, but in some seasons of light infestation you may not absolutely require it. A *yearly* dormant spray is not necessary on maples, and oil sprays may even be injurious.

MARIGOLD

What insect, triangular in form, spotted brown or gray, stings top of marigolds before buds appear so they are flat and empty? (New York.)   The tarnished plant bug works on marigolds. It is oval in shape, mottled brown in color, and stings the buds of many flowers. It is a sucking insect, sometimes subdued by nicotine or sulphur dust but very hard to control. Remove all near-by weeds.

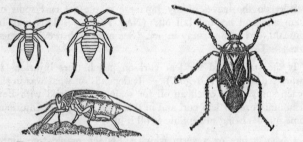

Tarnished Plant Bug: attacks marigolds and many other garden flowers. Triangular, spotted brown or gray.

Why do my dwarf marigolds turn brown and dry up after blossoming well for a month? It is not lack of water. (New York.) Perhaps you cultivate too close to them, perhaps it is a fungous stem or collar rot or wilt. If the latter, you must remove diseased plants and either sterilize soil or use another location for your next planting.

MATRIMONYVINE

What causes greenish warts on leaves of matrimonyvines? I cannot see the insects. (Illinois.)   This is a leaf gall caused by an insect you can't see because it is inside the gall. It is a mite anyway, and almost too small to see. You can't do anything about it except remove and burn infested leaves.

MONKEYPUZZLE TREE

Do you know anything to do to a monkey tree whose branches

are turning and dropping? (Virginia.)   The lower branches of the monkeypuzzle tree may be attacked by a fungous blight. All you can do is remove and burn dying wood.

MOUNTAIN-ASH

How can I combat worms on my mountain-ash trees? They completely strip the foliage. (New York.)   This is the worst of the wormlike larvae of the mountain-ash sawfly which works a couple of weeks ahead of the Japanese beetle. Spray with lead arsenate in late May and get ahead of the worms. If they are already working, add nicotine sulfate to your arsenate spray.

MYOSOTIS

Stems of Myosotis palustris turned black from soil toward tips. What caused this? (New York.)   A wilt due to a fungus, probably sclerotinia, in the soil. All you can do is remove infected plants, digging out all surrounding soil and filling the hole with fresh soil from another location.

NARCISSUS

What can I do to save my narcissus from destruction by a large, short grub, which eats the centers of the bulbs? (Idaho.)   This is the larva, yellow-white and about ¾ in. long, of the narcissus bulb fly, which resembles a bumblebee and lays her eggs at the base of the leaves or in the neck of the bulbs. When the bulbs are taken up, infested ones will be of lighter weight and softer. Burn those seriously infested.

Is there any specific spray for the control of the narcissus fly? Napthalene flakes are not satisfactory. (Washington.)   No, there is no spray nor any satisfactory treatment for the bulbs except immersion in hot water 110° to 115° F. for 2½ hours, but this is more suited to the commercial grower than the small gardener. Large bulbs may require 4 to 5 hours treatment, with the temperature held constant over that long period. It is easier to burn all infested bulbs and purchase more.

My daffodil bulbs, which have been in the ground for several years, are now being destroyed by maggots. Someone gave us a lot of tankage. Would that be the cause? (New York.)   The maggots are probably the larvae of the lesser bulb fly—yellowish-gray, wrinkled, about ½ in. long. There are usually several to a bulb, as opposed to the narcissus bulb fly, where there is usually one. The life history and control are about the same. The tankage did not bring your maggots but might provide a favorable medium for them, since they are not confined to living tissue. (See previous question.)

If Von Sion Narcissi come up green and yellow, instead of their original beautiful yellow, is the soil, fertilizer, or what to blame? (Georgia.)   This particular narcissus often loses its original character after growing out in gardens a year or two, but if the leaves were streaked with yellow along with the streaking of the flowers, you probably have mosaic, a virus disease, and the diseased individuals should be rogued out.

Why do my double white daffis, just before opening, turn brown and black? Have tried lime, shallow and deep planting, and moist places. (New York.)   These late-flowering double narcissi frequently blast before flowering. Lack of continuous moisture and hot weather have been blamed. Be careful of too much lime.

When bulbs are started growing in the house, in darkness, what causes mold to occur on them?   The mold may be one of the storage rots coming to you with the bulbs. Inspect bulbs before starting and discard any with mold. A piece of charcoal in the water will keep molds from the outside under control.

What causes buds to blast just before coming into bloom? Planted in water and pebbles.   Some say the flower buds will blast if the water falls below the level of the shortest roots at any time during the growing period.

What do Paperwhites and Soleil d'Or, planted indoors in sand, peatmoss, and gravel mixture, cease growing and wither without blooming?   Did you start them too early in the fall? They need a dormant period to flower well. It is possible the bulbs had been treated for bulb flies or nematodes and somewhat injured. Why not try the simple pebble-and-water method for Paperwhites rather than your peatmoss mixture?

NASTURTIUM

How do you control black aphids on nasturtiums? (New York.)   By using nicotine sulfate and soap or other contact spray frequently, faithfully, and usually frantically. These aphids are very hard to kill. Use an angle nozzle to reach the under side of the leaves; start spraying early and continue through the season. Sometimes it seems simpler either to ignore the aphids and yellowing leaves or omit nasturtiums.

What can I do to keep the plant lice formed by black ants off nasturtiums? (Michigan.)   These black aphids (technically they are bean aphids) are not "formed" by the ants and they may appear quite independently of them, but often they are herded about by the ants, who feed on the honeydew secreted by the aphids. (For control see answer to the previous question.)

What do you use for cutworms? (Michigan.) Since paper collars are rather impractical for nasturtiums, you will probably have to resort to a poison bait. (See Cutworms.)

OAK

My large oak is infested with borers. All summer small branches were falling off the tree and each branch had a large brownish worm. What can I do? (Connecticut.) This worm, the grub stage of a beetle, is known as the oak-twig pruner because it cuts off the branches. Since the larvae winter in the fallen branches, your job is to clean up all these and burn them.

What can I do to put new life in an oak tree which was struck by lightning? (Maryland.) If possible have a tree expert go over it to note extent of damage, remove shattered limbs, and apply a wound dressing. Feed with a rapidly available fertilizer. Valuable trees may be equipped with lightning protectors—a very good form of insurance.

This fall there were loads of little white bugs clinging to the bark of our oak tree. Later they seemed to have disappeared. We are worried about the tree, which has not responded to treatment. (Kansas.) These could have been the young stage of scale insects, several of which infest oak, or, if they were fluffy white bits, some sort of woolly aphid or else woolly flata, rather common on many trees in late summer and causing no particular damage. The poor health of your tree may be due to borers, or to scale. Have it examined by a reputable tree expert.

OLEANDER

How can I keep my oleanders free from insects? Soap solution and nicotine seems to have little effect. Nicotine sulfate and soap is supposed to control the young, motile stage of the oleander, cottony cushion, and hemispherical scales, but for adult scales and mealy bugs you may need an oil spray. (See House Plants.)

PALM

The soil of my potted palm seems to have many small insects like soil lice, not worms or nematodes. Do they hurt the roots and how can I destroy them? They sound like root aphids. Out of doors root aphids can be killed by making a depression around the plants and pouring in nicotine sulfate and soap. Experiments with poinsettia in pots gave control of the aphids by loosening the

earth and submerging pot and earth ball in a solution of 3 teaspoons Black Leaf 40 and 1 oz. soap per gallon of water, heated
to 110° F. before use.

**Little white spots form on the leaves of my palm. They can
be washed off but reappear. What shall I do to prevent this?**
The spots are probably mealy bugs, possibly one of the many
species of scale. Keep the leaves syringed frequently and keep
bait around to control ants, for they often carry around young
insects. If nicotine sulfate and soap does not give control, try
Volck. (See House Plants.)

PANSY

**What can be used to prevent rabbits from eating pansies?
(Ohio.)**   Probably a wire fence around the pansy bed is the
best method. If that is impossible, try moth balls or some other
of the many repellents suggested under Rabbits.

**How shall I get rid of cutworms? Have tried Snarol and moth
balls without success. (Massachusetts.)**   Snarol should be
fairly effective, but moth balls would be of little use. For formulae
for home-made poison baits, see Cutworms. Dusting the plants
with 1 part arsenate of lead to 9 of sulphur or talc might help.

**What is the white moth, similar to the cabbage moth, that lays
its eggs on pansies? These hatch into small black hairless caterpillars that eat foliage and stems; during the day they lie on the
ground, climbing up the plants at night. Lead arsenate seems to
help somewhat; rotenone and pyrethrum not at all. (Washington.)**   You have described the sluglike larva of the violet
sawfly, the adult of which is a four-winged black fly; so the moth
you mention must be something else. Lead arsenate is by far the
best control for dealing with false slugs or sawfly larvae.

**What is it that eats leaves and flowers of pansies? Have found
one mahogany-colored worm with short hairs. (North Carolina.)**
The woolly bear caterpillar comes close to your description. It
has a brown body, black at each end, and clipped hairs. It eats
all kinds of garden plants. Spray or dust with lead arsenate or
other stomach poison.

**How do you prevent pansy plants raised indoors from getting
infested with lice?**   Keep them syringed frequently. Spray
with a contact insecticide when necessary. Nicotine sulfate and
soap used when the temperature is high may cause injury, the
genus Viola being somewhat susceptible. Spray with pyrethrum.

What can I do for ants? (Iowa.)   Find the nest and inject
carbon disulphide or paradichlorbenzene crystals. (See Ants.)

PECAN

What should I spray pecan trees with, and when? (Texas.)
A suggested spray schedule lists a dormant oil spray for scale, and 4 applications of Bordeaux mixture for scab, starting when the nuts set and repeating at 3-week intervals. Add nicotine sulfate for aphids and lead arsenate for caterpillars and leaf-case bearers. Clean up and burn old hulls and infested nuts to control shuck-worm and nut weevils. Consult United States Department of Agriculture *Farmers' Bulletin 1654* and your State Experiment Station.

What caused my trees to shed the pecans before they matured? (Louisiana.)   Pecan scab, a fungous disease, causes the nuts to dry up and fall. Control by spraying with 3–4–50 Bordeaux mixture. In buying new trees, choose resistant varieties such as Stuart, Frotcher, Moneymaker, and Success.

PENTSTEMON

Why didn't my Garnet Pentstemon bloom? Tips of branches blighted and turned black instead of forming buds. (Texas.)
Crown rot, caused in Texas by *Sclerotium rolfsii,* is common on pentstemon and would blight the buds; but generally the whole plant would wilt. (See Crown Rot.) Pentstemon likes a well-drained but not dry soil, and dies out in a year or two if kept in full sun.

Tips of buds are webbed together and a small worm bores down center of stalks. What shall I do to prevent this? (Indiana.)
The tobacco bud worm reported on some garden plants is probably the pest you have. Spray thoroughly with lead arsenate as the buds form. With the hydrangea leaf-tyer, also a bud worm, the leaves may be opened and the worm killed before it injures the flower buds.

PEONY

What causes peony buds to blight? (Michigan.)   A disease called botrytis blight, caused by *Botrytis paeoniae* and *B. cinerea,* and widely distributed across the United States. Young buds turn brown or black and fail to develop; irregular brown to black areas show on the leaves, and black pimples (sclerotia) form at the base of the stalks.

Why do stalks wilt and fall over? (Wisconsin.)   Another symptom of Botrytis blight. If the old stalks are left in the ground, the sclerotia will produce spores in the spring to infect the young shoots coming up. In wet weather the shoots turn

black and rot at the base, often being covered with a gray mold.
If the weather is dry early in the season, the disease may not
show up until the bud stage.

Why do peonies have brown spots on the petals? (Virginia.)
Usually because of Botrytis blight. The rain splashes spores from
infected buds to opening blossoms and everywhere a spore starts
to germinate there is a brown spot on the petals. However,
browning may also be due to thrips injury. (See Thrips.)

Is bud rot curable? (Wisconsin.)   Not curable, but often
preventable. In the fall cut down and burn all peony tops, so the
sclerotia cannot overwinter. With a sharp knife cut each stalk
just below soil level. Never use the tops for mulching. Spray
several times in the spring with Bordeaux mixture, starting when
the reddish new shoots can first be seen poking through the
ground.

**Why does the foliage turn black after blooming period? (Ten-
nessee.)**   It may, in a wet season, be due to Botrytis blight.
Every infected bud or leaf should be cut off and every infected
shoot carefully pulled up to prevent spread of the fungus. Black-
ening may also be due to stem rot, a fungous disease characterized by blighted foliage, white film areas (mycelium) on the
stem, and large black sclerotia in the pith.

What can be done for stem rot?   Remove the infected
shoots very carefully so as not to drop out any of the sclerotia,
which are formed loosely in the pith and fall out of the stalks.
Burn.

What would cause roots to rot? (Montana.)   Possibly botrytis blight or stem rot; or sometimes a downy mildew which
causes a wet rot of the crown. It may help to sprinkle a solution
of Semesan or bichloride of mercury over the soil. Peonies should
not be planted in too-wet soil; if it is heavy clay, lighten it with
coal ashes. Never leave manure on as a mulch so the shoots have
to push up through it.

**What insects or worms eat out the insides of roots? (New
York.)**   Worms are probably millipedes feasting on tissue dying from some rot disease. They are not apt to be injurious to
healthy roots. Eelworms, or root nematodes, may infest peonies
and cause galls on the roots, but these worms are too small to be
seen with the naked eye.

**Is it natural for peonies to die during August? Should they be
cut back at this time? (Wisconsin.)**   No, they should retain

foliage all summer and not be cut back until late September or early October—just before frost. Your peonies may be afflicted with one of the diseases discussed above.

The foliage on my peonies turns a light color and looks blistered. What is wrong? What is the remedy? (Colorado.)   Apparently a physiological disease called measles or edema and associated in some way with too much soil moisture or atmospheric humidity. There is no practical remedy known.

How can I control rose chafers on peonies? (Massachusetts.) There is no very satisfactory answer to this universal question. Pick off as many as you can and spray with rotenone or pyrethrum. If it is any comfort to you, when the Japanese beetles get worse in Massachusetts, the rose chafers will diminish.

Should one discourage the big black ants that come on buds? (Pennsylvania.)   They do no damage of themselves, merely feed on the sweet substance exuded from the peony buds. Some authorities think they carry botrytis spores around with them, so that it may be wise to spray the plants with nicotine sulfate and soap.

PETUNIA

We are bothered with slugs and sowbugs eating petunia stems. Used bran bait which killed birds, but didn't kill pests. Is there something safer to use? (Michigan.)   If you use poison bait, put it out in the evening, and place under boards so birds cannot get at it. Spraying with lead arsenate or dusting with sulphur-lead arsenate will deter slugs and not harm birds. (See Slugs; Sowbugs.)

Petunias in my flower boxes dry up and don't bloom well near the end of the season. What is the trouble? (Ohio.)   It may be purely cultural difficulties—not enough water or poor soil conditions in the crowded box; but it may also be due to one or two fungi causing basal or root rots. Next time be sure to use fresh soil, and try treating the seed before planting. (See Seed Treatment.)

By the end of June insects start to eat petunia leaves in my window boxes. What kind of spray should I use, and how often? (Illinois.)   Use a stomach poison as a spray. Lead arsenate dust is also effective, but it discolors foliage. If you have Tri-ogen on hand for roses, try that; the lead arsenate in this combination spray leaves a much less conspicuous residue. Spray often enough to keep the new growth covered.

PHLOX

What is the cause of phlox foliage drying up from the roots to the bloom? (Colorado, Kansas, Illinois, Michigan, Minnesota, Missouri, Ohio, Pennsylvania, Washington, Wisconsin.)   This question is almost as universal as the one about chrysanthemum foliage turning brown, and there is no real answer. It is evidently a physiological disease and not one caused by any specific organism. It may be due to a checking of the food and water movement at the point of union between current and old growth.

Is there any remedy for phlox blight?   A liberal supply of water and cutting diseased stems back to sound wood may help. Fungous leaf spots may accompany the blight; these can be checked by spraying with Bordeaux mixture.

What is the best remedy for rust? (Maryland.)   There is no rust common on phlox, gardeners all over the country notwithstanding. The reddish discoloration of the leaves termed "rust" is merely one phase of the leaf blight discussed in the two previous questions. (For a definition of the fungous disease see Rust.)

When our perennial phlox is in full bloom a stalk or two in a clump suddenly shows green wilted leaves, and in a day or two entire plant may be dead. What is the cause? (West Virginia.) This may be the leaf blight discussed above, or death may be due to the fungous crown rot or Southern blight. (See Crown Rot.)

How is mildew prevented? (New York, Texas.)   Dust the foliage with fine sulphur, being careful to cover the under surface. Except for phlox variety Miss Lingard, mildew on phlox in New York does not start much before July, so that treatment may be delayed until then. In Texas start when the foliage is well out. Phlox that is crowded or shaded is more subject to mildew. Copper sprays also will control it.

Can phlox be sprayed with dusting sulphur when blooming? (Massachusetts.)   You can't ever "spray" with a dust. Spraying is the application of chemicals in liquid form; dusting, the application of finely divided dry materials. If you are careful to dust the foliage from underneath, and not down onto the flowers from above, there will be little injury to the bloom. Sulphur, however, does fade bright colors.

What can be done to prevent phlox from turning yellow before blooming? (Virginia.)   If the foliage is really yellow (and not brown, as in leaf blight), red spiders are probably to blame. These can be seen in mealy webs on the under side of the leaves. Sulphur dust is the standard control measure but does not work too well. Frequent syringing with water, or spraying with contact insecticides, may be necessary. (See Red Spider.)

A small, soft-bodied insect, orange with black stripes, attacks my phlox. Nothing seems to control it, and I have never been able to find out what it is. What is it? (Indiana.)   Probably the phlox bug, a sucking insect with reddish or orange margins on the wings and a black stripe on the back. Kill the nymphs by spraying with nicotine sulfate and soap, and repel them by dusting foliage with tobacco dust, or, preferably, with rotenone.

What shall I do for a striped flying beetle? (Virginia.) Striped cucumber beetles attack flowers. Spray or dust with lead arsenate, cryolite, or one of the fluosilicates.

PHOTINIA

Please tell me what causes scale on photinia, and what to do for it? (Texas.)   Scale is a sucking insect. Usually, when adult, it is covered with a shell and attached to the plant, although the young scales may move around. In Texas you can control scale by spraying with a summer oil (such as Volck) and nicotine when the young scales are crawling. Lace bugs are more common on photinia than scale, and can be controlled either with the nicotine-oil spray or with nicotine sulfate and soap. (See Scale Insects; Lace Bugs.)

PINE

Have white scale on mugho pine. What is the proper treatment? (Iowa.)   Preferably lime sulphur, 1 to 9 dilution, applied in spring before new growth starts. If the pine is near a house, substitute miscible oil at a 1 to 50 dilution with 1 teaspoon nicotine sulfate per gallon. Or spray with nicotine sulfate and soap when the young scales are in the crawling stage. Pines may be injured by oil sprays. (See Dormant Spraying.)

How can I save Scotch pines that have an insect or worm in the buds? (Michigan.)   The worm is the grub of the European pine-shoot moth; it emerges as a reddish, white-marked adult sometime in June. The easiest method of control on small trees is to break off and burn the infested shoots (readily told by light color, or crooked bend, or mass of resin) before the moth comes out to lay her eggs. If the trees are too large, spray, about the middle of June and in early July, with lead arsenate and nicotine sulfate.

Is there any control for the worm that starts boring through

the new growth of pines, killing the trees, if not found in time? (New York.)   This may be the pine-shoot moth; but more likely is the white-pine weevil, the grub of which mines into and kills the leader of the tree. Cut out the infested shoot below the grub; remove some of the laterals, and tie up one to replace the leader.

Why are the needles chewed off my pine twigs, leaving only a brush of new growth at the tip? (New Jersey.)   This is the work of a recently introduced sawfly which is rapidly becoming a very serious pest of pines in New Jersey. The larvae hatch from scalelike eggs on the needles in late April or the beginning of May. They work in groups and clean up one branch before moving to the next; but they feed only on the old growth, not the young needles. Spray with lead arsenate at the first sign of feeding. The addition of nicotine sulfate gives quicker results. There are many sawfly species working on pines in the spring and summer. One type webs the needles together. Spray at the first sign of feeding.

What insect works on white pine, boring small holes in the trunk? What is the treatment to save the tree? (Minnesota.) There are several bark beetles which make such holes. Treatment is difficult, and a badly infested tree should be cut and burned to prevent beetles migrating to other pines. Newly transplanted trees should have the trunks wrapped. Keep the trees fed and watered properly. (See Borers.)

What can I do to save my trees from the pine beetle? (Louisiana.)   The Southern pine beetle is distinguished by making pitch tubes at the base of the tree. It leaves no sawdust cast behind, as does the bark beetle, but produces a gummy exudation. Kill the beetles in the burrows, and spray the trunk with a strong solution of arsenate of lead. Treat all pines near by. Keep the trees well fed and watered, for this beetle works in weakened hosts.

How may pines be cleared of bagworms? (West Virginia.) Cut off all the "bags" you can reach. Spray with arsenate of lead when the young worms start feeding. (See Bagworms.)

What is best for red spider? (Ohio.)   There is no "best" for red spider. If your trees are small, it will be easiest to dust them with sulphur, alternating with frequent syringing with the hose. (See Red Spider.)

What is the best way to get rid of white-pine rust? (Michigan.) Destroy all currants and gooseberries within 900 ft. of the pines, as these serve as alternate hosts for the white-pine blister rust, probably the most important disease of this tree.

PLUM, ORNAMENTAL

I have a Prunus pissardi which loses its leaves every summer. What causes this? How can it be corrected? (Pennsylvania.) Perhaps it was sprayed for the Japanese beetle, so prevalent on this host. *Prunus pissardi* objects strenuously to many spray materials, dropping its leaves at the first treatment. Rotenone dust will control the beetles without injuring the foliage. This tree often drops its leaves in unfavorable weather even when no spray has been used.

Plum Curculio: a small, gray, humpbacked snout beetle.

POINSETTIA

What can be done for mealy bugs on poinsettias?   Remove them singly with a toothpick, spray with nicotine sulfate and soap, or with Greenhouse Volck, if the pest still persists. (See House Plants; Mealy Bugs.)

POPLAR

What control is possible for a bug or beetle that works on the leaves of our Lombardy poplars? (Indiana.)   If it is a yellowish beetle with black stripes or spots, and the grubs skeletonize the leaves, it is the cottonwood or poplar-leaf beetle at work. Control by spraying with lead arsenate in May.

A scale is forming on the trunk of our Lombardy poplar. Any cure? (Indiana.)   The oyster-shell scale is common on poplar. Spray while dormant with a miscible oil, or with lime sulphur. (See Dormant Spraying.)

PRIVET

What is the best spray for a brown scale our privet hedge gets every summer? (California.)   Spray with a summer oil (such as Volck) and nicotine when the young are crawling. You may need to repeat spray once or twice during the summer. Use a 1 to 50 dilution, with 1 teaspoon nicotine sulfate per gallon added.

PYRACANTHA

What causes the leaves of pyracantha to turn rusty brown and the berries to fall? (Texas.)   Pyracantha is subject to fire blight, a bacterial disease which will suddenly kill back branches. Cut diseased branches out. (See Fire Blight.) If the leaves are merely discolored and not dead, lace bugs may be sucking underneath. If so, spray with any contact insecticide.

My pyracantha has a weblike substance, with twigs and leaves in meshes on the limbs. What shall I do? (Arkansas.)   Probably red spiders are at work. A strong spray from the hose every few days will keep them down. Spray with wettable sulphur, or dust with fine sulphur dust.

RHODODENDRON

How can an amateur detect, and either prevent or destroy, rhododendron borers? (Pennsylvania.)   It is hard to prevent them, but you can detect them by the sawdust (insect frass) protruding from holes in the trunk or branches; and they can be killed by squirting in nicotine paste, sold as Bortox or Borerkil.

What can be done for lace bugs? (New Jersey.)   Yellowed or speckled white leaves, with brownish bits of excreta on the under side, are sure signs of lace-bug injury. Spray with nicotine sulfate and soap or other contact insecticide when the young bugs hatch (usually late May or early June), and repeat in 2 weeks.

How can we get rid of red aphids on rhododendrons? (New York.)   Are you sure you have aphids? They are most unusual on rhododendrons. The best rule for aphids on any shrub is to spray with nicotine sulfate and soap.

What is the cause of a black film on leaves? (New Jersey.)   It is a fungus, sooty mold growing in the honeydew dropped by aphids working on the leaves of some tree overhead or near by. There is little you can do for the rhododendrons, except scrubbing the film off. Having the trees sprayed for aphids is usually expensive. Tulip trees are the worst offenders.

How do I get rid of the pest that eats the margins of the leaves? (Oregon.)   Any of several night feeders may do this, but the most important is the black vine weevil. Work lead arsenate into the soil around the plants, 2 lbs. per 100 sq. ft., and spray the foliage with lead arsenate.

My rhododendrons have a dry curling blight on the leaves. They eventually drop off. I have sprayed with rotenone, without

control. What shall I use? (Massachusetts.)   This may be a fungous blight or canker, but it is more likely the effect of winter wind and sun. Spraying will not help in either case. Watering the rhododendrons thoroughly in the fall and providing some sort of windbreak over the winter will be most helpful.

The leaves have dried up and turned brown. What can I do? (California.)   This can't be winter injury, as in Massachusetts, but it could be summer burning; or injury at the roots from the black vine weevil; or borer injury; or an attack of armillaria root rot. You'll have to call in some local expert for a real diagnosis, although it seems a little late to save your shrub.

What is the cause of large black spots on leaves? Adjacent plant that gets more sun is healthy. (California.)   Sooty mold on the surface, or fungous leaf spots, which would be more likely to occur on a plant in the shade. It is probably not serious, and picking off infected leaves is sufficient control.

ROSE

The leaves of my roses have black spots. What is the cause? (New Jersey.)   The causative agent is a fungus, *Diplocarpon rosae*, which grows into the leaf and forms the black spots by its dark mycelial threads just under the cuticle. In a few days little black pimples show up in the spots. These are the fungous fruiting bodies ready to discharge their spores, which are carried by rain or wind, by gardeners on hands, tools, or clothing, or even by beetles, to a healthy leaf. There they start another cycle if given 6 hours of continuous moisture for germination.

The leaves turn yellow and all drop off before the summer is over. Why?   That's the way black spot works, first spotted leaves, then loss of color, and finally defoliation. There may also be lesions on the stems. Roses often put out a second set of leaves and lose these, too, thus weakening the plant so that it may not live through a hard winter.

What is an easy way to control black spot? (Nebraska.) There is none. A control program means applying a dormant spray in early spring and a summer spray or dust *weekly*, from the time the leaves come out until late frosts in the fall. It also means picking off and burning all infected leaves as soon as the spots appear.

What is an effective early spring treatment to kill the spots that may still be present on the canes? (New York.)   A dormant spray of lime sulphur, 1 to 9 dilution, just as soon as the roses are uncovered and pruned in the spring.

Does sulphur really control black spot? If so, how should it be applied, on the foliage or on the ground around the bushes? (Michigan.)   It works very well, if used faithfully. It will do no good on the ground. Get a good dust gun and cover the plant with a fine film of dust, working from underneath and making sure the lowest leaves are coated.

Is there a better remedy for prevention and cure of black spot than Massey dust (9 parts sulphur and 1 part arsenate of lead)? In spite of faithful use my roses develop spots by the end of the season. (Kansas.)   Massey dust will give about as much protection as anything else. There are various 3-in-1 sprays and dusts on the market which are fairly satisfactory. Despite the best of care, black spot is apt to show up by the end of the season. For encouragement, compare your roses with those of your neighbor who has done no dusting.

Does Tri-ogen used as a spray give as good protection from black spot and mildew as Massey dust? (D.C.)   It always has for me. I like it because it controls sucking and chewing insects also, in one operation, and leaves somewhat less noticeable residue on the foliage than sulphur. Also it is safer to use in hot weather, although in cold weather the copper in the spray may spot certain varieties.

Is it harmful to pick off all leaves when all are infected? Yes, it probably is. Theoretically, you pick off every infected leaf, but this means starting early in the season and taking only an occasional one. If you wait until there is 100 per cent infection, the shock to the plant of sudden and total defoliation would be great. Pick off the worst leaves, remove all those fallen to the ground, and resolve to do better next year.

To control black spot, would it be wise to destroy all plants now in the garden, and plant new stock? (West Virginia.) No; you are more than likely to get black spot with your new plants from a nursery. Buy whatever new plants you like, but do not destroy the old for this reason. Merely start your spraying program with the dormant spray.

To destroy black spot, would it help to remove 2 or 3 ins. of topsoil, then sprinkle sulphur and put on new topsoil?   This would remove some inoculum, old leaves rotting into the soil, but it might also injure some of the rose roots. Sulphur in the soil would not help much and might make the soil too acid. A mulch of peatmoss has been suggested as a barrier between spores in the soil and the developing new leaves.

Is there any way to sterilize the ground in a rose bed to prevent

a recurrence of black spot? (Ohio.)   No; and even if you could, the next new plant you bought would bring it back to your garden.

If rose leaves turn yellow and fall off with no sign of spot, is this black spot? (Pennsylvania.)   Usually it is not. Leaves may turn yellow from too much moisture in the soil in early spring, or from drought in summer.

Can cow manure cause black spot? (Virginia.)   No.

Where no winter protection is required, what can be done through the winter to guard against black spot? (Maryland.) You might put on the 1 to 9 lime-sulphur spray in December, after the plants are dormant, and repeat in early March before growth starts. Remove and burn infected leaves.

Black spot has been unusually bad this year in spite of constant dusting with sulphur. Why? (Michigan.)   The way the material is applied and the timing of the treatment before rains are important in control, but some seasons black spot flourishes in late summer despite the most careful control measures.

I am allergic to sulphur. Is there a substitute to take its place for black spot? What is the best all-around spray? (Texas.) Tri-ogen has been used successfully in Texas as an all-around spray, and it has a copper rather than a sulphur base. There are probably other combination sprays locally available to you which do not use sulphur.

Does cold weather freeze out black spot? (Indiana.)   It kills the summer spores, but not the mycelium living in leaves fallen to the ground, or the special winter spores. In some states, probably including Indiana, the mycelium in lesions on the canes lives through the winter and produces summer spores again the next season.

Should roses be treated with Massey dust or other preparation before being covered with a mound of earth for the winter? (New York.)   A late treatment of sulphur dust will have little effect; it would take lime sulphur at dormant strength, and in New York roses are seldom sufficiently dormant when time comes to hill them up in November.

What causes mildew? (Utah.)   The mildew fungus, which sends its white, felty, mycelial threads branching over the leaf or flower buds and gets its food by little rootlike suckers extending into the plant sap. The powdery effect comes from chains of summer spores growing upright from the mycelium. These spores are readily detached and carried by wind or rain to healthy leaves.

What was wrong with my Improved Lafayette polyanthas this summer? The calyx was swollen and white, leaves wrinkled, stems white, bloom scanty. Is there danger of this spreading to a bed of hybrid teas? (Ohio.)   Mildew will deform the buds, curl the leaves, and cover everything with a white coating. Ordinarily mildew is severe on certain ramblers and polyanthas in May and June, and may affect hybrid teas in late summer. If your hybrid teas are regularly sprayed with a fungicide throughout the summer, you need not unduly fear infection from the polyanthas.

Why does one of my climbing roses always have mildew, even the shoots as they come through the ground? (Missouri.)   Some varieties are more susceptible than others. Either change your roses for others more resistant to mildew in your locality, or make up your mind to keep them faithfully sprayed or dusted.

Can you tell me how to prevent blue mold from forming on my Dorothy Perkins rose arbor? I have cut back, every spring and fall, and sprayed, but it persists. (North Carolina.)   Mildew is most persistent on Dorothy Perkins. Cutting back shoots will do no good. The spores will come on the wind from somewhere. Start treating as soon as the leaves appear, and keep it up at least once a week through flowering, and occasionally thereafter. If it is a large arbor, you can probably get better coverage with a liquid spray than with a dust from a small dust gun.

What is the best treatment for white mold on climbers? (Massachusetts.)   Whatever is expedient. Sulphur, applied as a dust or a spray, is the specific for controlling mildew, but copper materials are also useful. Since copper occasionally causes injury in cold weather, and since to control mildew on climbers you need to start soon after the leaves come out, sulphur is probably safer in Massachusetts. If you have a dust gun large enough to give coverage of your climbers, then dust with fine sulphur; otherwise spray with a wettable sulphur, following manufacturer's directions. Tri-ogen will give excellent control on varieties that do not object to the copper applied at May temperatures in your state. In June you will have little injury.

What causes mildew on Else Poulsen? I still have Tri-ogen. What other spray could I use? To what extent does mildew injure plants? (Iowa.)   Else Poulsen is not subject to mildew in New Jersey gardens. Try sulphur dust if Tri-ogen is unsatisfactory for you. Mildew will cause curling and dropping of the leaves, imperfect flowers, and, in a bad infestation, injury to the stems.

What kind of spray is effective against mold on buds? (California.)   In California you have a very special problem with mildew, and although sulphur dust is often recommended, spraying is sometimes more effective. Your Experiment Station suggests a combination of 1¼ ozs. lime-sulphur solution, 2 ozs. wettable sulphur, and 1 teaspoon nicotine sulfate per gallon, to control diseases and aphids.

How does one treat roses that build up big rust spots, like dust, on the stems of bush and buds, which finally kill the plant. (Michigan.)   These dusty pustules are made up of spores of the rust fungus; they are orange early in the season, later turning dark brown. Clean up all fallen leaves; treat with dormant lime sulphur in the spring; and dust weekly with sulphur through the growing season.

What can be used to rid bushes of yellow fungous growth? (Wisconsin.)   This also is rust, which attacks the canes as well as the foliage. Prune out infected canes and follow directions given above. Rust is prevalent in the Middle West, but is seldom seen in the East except sometimes north of Albany and Boston.

Foliage of rambler rose is spoiled during summer by brown spot on leaves. Spray controls this on later leaves, but the early leaves are infected while plant is blooming and spraying then spoils the appearance of the plants. What is the trouble? (Illinois.)   There are several fungous leaf spots, in addition to black spot, which may occur on roses; but control would be the same. Tri-ogen is inconspicuous on roses and may be used during blooming.

What is the best treatment for brown canker? (Ohio.)   The very best treatment is to refuse to plant in your garden any rose that comes to you with its canes covered with little white spots with reddish margins. Next best is to remove all cankered canes at spring pruning, following this with the dormant lime-sulphur spray. Any treatment for black spot will reduce canker infection during the summer.

Some of my bush roses and climbers have long canes which turn brown at the ends, and eventually the entire cane dies. Why? (Illinois.)   Probably due to a canker which has girdled the base of the cane and cut off the water and food supply. Clean out infected canes at pruning. Use the dormant lime-sulphur spray.

What causes roses, when cut back, to start getting brown on the stems, and this brown to travel down until the whole stem is dead? (Florida.)   Canker fungi often follow pruning cuts, unless these cuts are clean and sharp and made close to an eye, and on a slant, so water will not stand on the tissue. If you have much trouble, disinfect your pruning shears between cuts.

What is an effective control for peduncle necrosis, a disease quite prevalent here, chiefly in red varieties? (Illinois.)   Peduncle necrosis, a drooping of the flower pedicle and a reddish lesion on the upper part, seems to be some physiological disease, for which no control is known. Possibly a feeding program can be developed to get these roses to hold their heads up. It is interesting that the disease has been reported on Radiance, ordinarily considered foolproof.

What causes the leaves to turn a pale yellowish-green, and what will prevent this? (Florida.)   Red spiders will do this, but in Florida the trouble is probably too alkaline a soil, making iron unavailable. The soil can be treated with ferrous sulfate, but it will be better to acidify the soil by adding sulphur. Send a soil sample to your State Experiment Station and ask for directions.

Why do my climbing roses turn black toward the stalk during the fall? (New York.)   If roses are fed in late summer with an excess of nitrogen, so there is much succulent growth, this will turn black and soft at the first touch of frost.

I sprayed regularly with Black Leaf 40, but some of the leaves turned brown and dropped off. Used well-rotted cow manure and Vigoro as a fertilizer. (Illinois.)   Defoliation could have been from black spot, Black Leaf 40 having no effect as a fungicide; but more probably the browning and leaf fall were due to too much attention in hot weather—a combination of spray and fertilizer injury. Apply commercial fertilizers only in small amounts, to a moist soil, and water in well afterward. Spray with nicotine only when the temperature is moderate.

Will lime-sulphur spray help roses? (New Jersey.)   Very much when used as a 1 to 9 dormant spray, just after pruning in the spring. It controls scale and "burns out" overwintered cane lesions of black spot. It is not ordinarily used for a summer spray on roses.

What dormant spray is good for roses? (Washington.)   Use the 1 to 9 lime-sulphur spray, if applied immediately after pruning—which will probably be sometime in midwinter in Washington. You may also use a 5-5-50 Bordeaux mixture which will take care of diseases, but not do much for scale.

What will kill scale on wood of climbing roses? (Pennsylvania.) If the bushes are not against the side of a garage or a house with light paint, give the dormant 1 to 9 lime-sulphur spray. If staining painted woodwork must be avoided, substitute a miscible oil. (See Dormant Spraying.) But, in my experience, this is a poor substitute for lime sulphur on roses.

How do you kill the green licelike "beasties"? (Pennsylvania.) The "beasties" are plant lice, or aphids, sucking insects readily killed by thorough application of any contact insecticide; nicotine sulfate (Black Leaf 40) and soap solution is very effective.

What are the little green bugs that cover rose stems? (Pennsylvania.) More aphids. Both the pink and the green potato aphids are common on roses. They prefer new growth, either succulent new leaves, or stems and buds.

How early should one start spraying to get rid of aphids? (Michigan.) Fairly early in the spring. Since a contact insecticide is required, wait until the first few start working. Ordinarily cool, rainy weather in the spring and the cooler weather toward fall encourage aphids, and they are not so numerous in midsummer. However, in New York this past summer there was an extraordinarily vicious plague of aphids in an unprecedentedly dry August. One cannot predict insect invasions accurately, but must be prepared to cope with them immediately.

How can roses (indoors) be freed of a small black insect pest? I have tried nicotine to no purpose. Add soap to a nicotine sulfate solution and it should take care of aphids. Try scrubbing them off with a soapy rag and then spraying the entire plant. It may be black fly. (See House Plants.)

My rose garden is located near 2 old apple trees. Spraying with Tri-ogen twice weekly proved ineffective against a plague of white flies in September and October. What should I use? (Connecticut.) These white flies are apple leaf hoppers, whose late summer brood is often difficult to control. It would be better not to use Tri-ogen more than once a week. Try an alternate spray of nicotine sulfate and soap, directing your spray underneath the leaves. The stippled white leaves are unsightly, but there is no lasting injury from this late brood of leaf hoppers. The early brood comes in May and is more readily controlled with weekly sprays of Tri-ogen.

What is the best control of red spider on leaves? (California.) Probably the lime-sulphur spray suggested for mildew on California roses. In the East, either sulphur dust, or the contact insecticide included in a combination spray—plus an occasional washing with the hose—will keep red spiders in check. They are most serious in enclosed gardens or on roses under overhangs where there is little air circulation.

When buds open you can see numerous very minute white insects running along at the bottom of the petals. What kind of disease is this? (New Jersey.)   It is not a disease. The insects are thrips, usually the flower thrips, but sometimes onion or greenhouse thrips. They are rasping-sucking insects and injure the flowers rather than the foliage.

What makes my roses turn brown? Just before they open the outside leaf is brown and dry, but if I take off the leaf the bud will open. (Wisconsin.)   Thrips very often cause roses to "ball" in this way. Sometimes the bud will open normally, and sometimes all the petals turn brown.

How are thrips on roses controlled? (New York.)   Sometimes frequent spraying with nicotine sulfate and soap gives fair control. Tartar emetic as used for gladiolus is also recommended. (See Gladiolus.) Thrips injury is usually worse in a dry season. After a wet spring there is seldom a serious infestation of thrips in June.

I dug up some bushes this fall which had not thrived and found small white particles on the roots. What caused this? (New York.)   If the particles were alive, you could have soaked the roots in a nicotine sulfate and soap solution, then poured the solution into the soil and replanted, for they may have been root aphids. If the particles were a fungous growth, it would be too late to save the plants.

What is the trouble when the new shoots die on the end and the buds dry and fall off when the size of small peas? (Pennsylvania.)   The rose midge is to blame. The adult is a yellow-brown minute fly which lays her eggs in the leaf and flower buds; these hatch and the maggots burrow into the new growth, causing the result you describe. When each maggot reaches maturity (indicated by the orange color), it drops to the ground, where it pupates just beneath the surface, and produces another midge. In warm weather the whole life cycle takes only 10 to 12 days, so there are many generations in a season.

What is the control for rose midge? (Indiana.)   It is difficult to control. A rather heavy mulch of tobacco dust, frequent spraying with nicotine sulfate and soap, and removal of all infested tips will reduce the infestation. Lavogen, a proprietary compound, is now offered as a soil fumigant for midge.

How can I get rid of big insects on Paul's Scarlet? They eat up every plant. These bugs work in pairs by the hundred. They fly. (New York.)   You describe the rose chafer, sometimes called rose bug, which is a long-bodied, long-legged tan or grayish, rather soft beetle. They are often found in pairs, mating. They feed on the flowers and are a destructive pest for about 6 weeks in late May and June. Their numbers diminish with the advent of Japanese beetles.

Rose Chafer or Rose Bug: brown beetle attacking many garden flowers.

How may one eliminate the rose chafer? (Rhode Island.) It is not easy; hand-picking is really the best control. A spray, 1 oz. (4 level tablespoons) lead arsenate, ⅓ cup molasses to 1 gal. of water will partially control the beetles but will not look very well on the flowers. Tri-ogen used as a general rose spray gives fair control of rose chafers.

Japanese Beetle (left) and Asiatic Beetle.

What is the best way to save roses from the Jap beetle? How much insecticide and when to use it? (New York.)   The lead arsenate in any combination spray or dust will keep rose foliage reasonably free from chewing by beetles. Pick them off the flowers. Beetles become numerous by the end of June, and continue into September. To protect the new leaves, which the beetles prefer, a weekly treatment is required.

Japanese beetles destroy buds. Should the buds be cut off

shortly after they are formed, or would it be more beneficial to the stalk to leave the buds on? (Pennsylvania.)   The plant does not care whether or not the buds remain; all it wants is plenty of green leaves to make more food. Leave the buds on until they show color, then cut them and enjoy them in the house. Cut in the morning, or the beetle will get them before you do. Cut off fading, full-blown flowers, which attract beetles. When cutting, make a clean slanting cut just above an eye—as if you were spring pruning; it saves lots of canker trouble.

What is the Asiatic beetle? What color, how can it be recognized and found? (Illinois.)   It resembles the Japanese beetle in size and shape, but is duller in color, which varies—either light-brown, purplish-black, or mottled. The Asiatic garden beetle (another species) is copper-brown and feeds only at night. Both beetles are most dangerous in the grub stage, feeding on grass roots, and both are chiefly pests of the Atlantic seaboard.

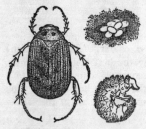

Asiatic Beetle: feeds at night; attacks asters, zinnias, carrots, beets, peppers, and other plants. Grubs injure grass roots and vegetables.

What can I do about the Asiatic beetle which chews up my rose? (Michigan.)   Are you sure you have the Asiatic beetle? This one and its cousin the Asiatic garden beetle are chiefly distributed along the Atlantic seaboard and are not primarily pests of roses. Perhaps you have rose chafers, or the rose curculio.

Is the Asiatic beetle the same as Fuller's rose beetle? (Oregon.) No, Fuller's rose weevil is a small gray snout beetle with grayish patches. It is also a pest of citrus trees on the West coast. Spray with arsenate of lead, and pick off by hand.

How do I get rid of green beetles with black spots on them? They get inside roses and ruin all blooms. (Texas.)   These are the Diabrotica or 12-spotted cucumber beetles. If they are not controlled by the lead arsenate in your regular schedule, try a fluosilicate dust, such as Dutox. Rotenone sprays or dusts are helpful.

Last year a little green worm (coiled) ate all the leaves off my roses. I used Black Leaf 40. (Minnesota.)   This is the coiled rose worm, controlled by spraying with lead arsenate and by cleaning up all decayed wood and pithy stems in which the insect can hibernate over winter.

Why do the leaves turn brown early in summer? Find green worms on under side; spraying does not seem to help. (Michigan.)   These are rose slugs, not true slugs but sawfly larvae, which skeletonize the leaves, eating out everything but the veins, and so cause the browning. Slugs work in the early spring, starting almost as soon as the leaves come out, occasionally in midsummer, and often have a late summer brood.

I used Black Leaf 40 for green worms but they weren't all killed. (Minnesota.)   Rose slugs are chewing insects to be controlled with a stomach poison. Black Leaf 40 is a contact spray which would kill only those slugs it happened to hit. The lead arsenate in Massey dust, or in Tri-ogen, gives almost perfect control if treatment is started early in the season and the *under side* of the leaves get covered.

What kind of a pest eats holes in the leaves and buds? (Missouri.)   Perhaps the rose curculio, a red beetle with a black snout. Eggs are laid and larvae develop in the buds and young fruits, so pick off and burn all dried buds. Spray with lead arsenate.

I have observed wasps chewing the edges of my rose leaves. Should I try to poison them? (Wisconsin.)   This is the leaf-cutter bee taking circles from the leaf to roll into a cylinder for a nest and then coming back to cut a larger circle which fits the top exactly. I am always so intrigued by the seeming intelligence of this insect—which really does little harm—I never want to poison it; but it will probably succumb to arsenate of lead on the leaf.

In pruning my roses I found branches dry and dead inside, and a small black beetle. What will exterminate this insect? (Oklahoma.)   This is the rose cane borer or stem girdler. All that can be done is remove and burn infested shoots, cutting below the borer. Fall pruning sometimes encourages the insect. If you leave long canes in the fall and the borer works near the top, you can cut out the injured wood in the spring without any real damage to the bush.

What will kill ants around bushes and not kill the rose plants? (Missouri.)   You can flood them out with water and kill them elsewhere. Probably carbon disulphide injected into an ant nest a little away from the rose roots would not injure the rose. (See Ants for more suggestions.)

How can I keep moles from eating our rosebushes? (Montana.) The eating is probably done by mice in the mole runs, but the tunnels may disturb the roots. (See Moles; Mice.)

How can I prevent rabbits from destroying my rosebushes? (Pennsylvania.)   If you don't like the looks of a fence, or cannot get the materials, there are various chemicals which have an evanescent effect. Moth balls work for me, but I think they are helped along by the neighbors' cats. (See Rabbits.)

What is the best all-purpose spray for hybrid tea roses? I am not adept at diagnosing pests and diseases. How frequently should it be used? (New York.)   Tri-ogen is probably the most widely used all-purpose spray. It has some faults but fewer than some other combinations. Use it according to directions for single strength, *never double strength*. Start about the first of May, continue to mid-October, every 7 to 9 days.

What is the most practical, inexpensive, all-around spray or dust for my rose garden of 500 bushes grown for commercial purposes? (Mississippi.)   The commercial growers in Texas use a combination of 90 per cent dusting sulphur and 10 per cent Tennessee copper. Probably you could use lead arsenate with this. Write to Dr. E. W. Lyle, Texas Agricultural Experiment Station, Substation No. 2, Tyler, Texas, for further information.

RUBBER PLANT

What is the cause of rust eating leaves of rubber plants? There is a fungous disease, anthracnose, which appears as a scorching and tip burn of the leaves, and has little rose-colored spore pustules; there is a true scorching from dry air in a too-hot hothouse; and there is a red scale. Pick off spotted leaves; do not let drops of water stand on the leaves; keep the house cool, atmosphere humid. Spray for scale with a contact insecticide.

SEDUM

What makes sedum rot off on top of the ground? (New York.) Sedum is subject to both crown rot and stem rot, two fungous diseases. Remove diseased plant and surrounding soil and fill in the hole with fresh gritty soil before replanting; give perfect drainage.

SNAPDRAGON

Small brown dots appear on the under side of leaves of my snapdragons. Is this rust? (Louisiana.)   Yes, the rust pustules are chocolate brown and show on the under side of the leaves.

How can I control and kill snapdragon rust? (West Virginia.)

It can't be killed, but dusting with sulphur will help prevent new infections. By far the easiest way to control this disease is to purchase rust-resistant varieties.

What causes snapdragon to wilt and die? (Texas.) In Texas, Southern blight, cotton root rot, verticillium wilt, stem rot, and some others. Remove and burn diseased plants and try to replant in a new location.

SPRUCE

What is an effective remedy against spruce gall? (New York.) Spruce galls are caused by aphids. The one that causes the elongation and swelling of the tips of blue spruce has fir as an alternate host. When new growth starts, the aphids work at the base of the leaves, causing each cell to become enlarged and the whole gall to look something like a small pineapple. The best control is to remove and burn the galls before they open and free the new aphids in midsummer.

What kind of spray shall I use for spruce gall, and when is the proper time to spray? (New York.) For Norway Spruce, where the galls are located at the base of the twigs, rather than at the tips where they are easily cut out, spray with nicotine sulfate and soap in the summer after galls open to expose the aphids; spray in the spring, just before new growth starts, with a 1 to 30 miscible oil, with 1 teaspoon nicotine sulfate added per gallon. With the blue spruce, if it was impossible to cut off all the galls while they were closed, give this tree the dormant spray, also being very cautious as to temperature. The oil spray will remove the bloom on the needles temporarily. (See Dormant Spraying.)

Why do needles of a Black Hills Spruce turn brown and fall off? (Illinois.) All spruces are subject to infestation by spider mites (like red spiders), which suck the sap from the needles, turning them grayish, and later brown, and often causing defoliation. A dormant spray of 1 to 30 miscible oil or a summer spray of colloidal sulphur have been recommended. (See Mites; Red Spider.)

What causes the needles of our Norway Spruces to turn brown and fall next to the trunk? Have found a small moth hidden in the branches. (Illinois.) There are several small moths the larvae of which mine in the leaves of spruces, feeding on them and webbing them together. Ordinarily they are not serious and the browning of the inner needles may be natural ripening. Spray with lead arsenate if necessary to control the larvae.

What diseases get on Koster Blue Spruce? Should they be sprayed?   The most serious disease is a canker or die back of the lower limbs, which is not amenable to sprays. Cut out and burn the diseased branches. Rust may sometimes attack spruce but is not important in ornamental plantings. In general you do not need to spray spruce for disease control, but occasionally for gall aphids and spider mites. (See above questions.)

A blue spruce suddenly drops all its needles with no apparent cause. Would you suggest a spray? (New York.)   No, never spray unless you have "apparent cause." A tree in that condition might be made sicker with a spray. It sounds like a drouth reaction, but it could be too heavy, wet soil, or escaping gas, or too strong a spray or some other environmental cause.

Borers in my spruce trees cause white encrustations on the trunks. What spray should I use, and when? (Illinois.)   If these are bark beetles, there is no spray that will help, and seriously infested trees should be cut and burned before the beetles escape to other spruces. Ask a tree expert to diagnose the trouble.

STOCK

Why can't I raise good-looking stocks? Mine are always spindly and buggy. Even when I spray them they are small and sickly. (California.)   Stocks in California suffer from several diseases. Young seedlings get a bacterial wilt, controlled by immersing seed in hot water held at 127° F. for 10 minutes, and planting in a new location. A fungous crown rot appears on overwatered, poorly drained soil; mosaic stunts the plants. Remove infected plants and spray to control aphids with nicotine sulfate or pyrethrum.

What can be done to control stem rot? (Arizona.)   Stem and root rot are caused by a soil fungus which yellows the lower leaves, girdles the stem, causing wilting, and rots the roots. Since the fungus spreads for several feet through the soil away from the plant, it is not removed by taking up diseased plants and surrounding soil. Sterilize the soil (see Soil Sterilization) or plant in a new location.

SWEETPEA

How do you control mildew on sweetpea? (Washington.) Dust frequently with fine dusting sulphur, starting before mildew usually appears. This may be combined with nicotine dust to control aphids.

Will treating soil prevent green lice on sweetpeas? (Wis-

consin.)   No. You must spray for aphids during the growing season, using pyrethrum or rotenone or nicotine sulfate and soap, up to blooming time.

Will treating soil prevent blighting of sweetpeas? (Wisconsin.) It will help in the control of various root rot diseases which cause wilting or blighting of the plants. (See Soil Sterilization.) Treating seed is a further precaution—1 minute in 95 per cent alcohol and 20 minutes in 1 to 1,000 bichloride of mercury.

What causes sweetpeas to wilt just below the flower buds, then the whole plant turns greenish white and dies? (Connecticut.) A fungous disease called anthracnose and common on outdoor sweetpeas has this effect. The fungus also causes a disease of apples and lives over winter in cankered limbs and mummied apples as well as on sweetpea pods and seed and soil debris. Burn all plant refuse in the fall. Plant only those seeds which appear sound and plump. If you save your own seed, use only those from healthy seed pods.

Why do my sweetpeas develop a curled and puckered appearance? I plant on new ground each year, treat seed with Nitragin, give plenty of moisture. (Idaho.) This is probably mosaic, carried from plant to plant by aphids. Virus diseases are common in the Northwest and there is nothing you can do except try to control aphids by sprays or nicotine dust and to remove infected plants promptly.

SWEETWILLIAM

What causes sweetwilliams to rot and turn yellow? I do not overwater them. (California.) A stem rot caused by a soil fungus, usually most destructive during warm, rainy periods, which you don't often have in California. Change the location if you can; use a light soil; avoid wounding the stems in cultivating.

SYCAMORE

What causes sycamore leaves to turn yellow and drop all summer long? (Missouri.) The most common cause is the fungous disease known as anthracnose, scorch, or leaf-and-twig blight, but this usually appears as brown areas on the leaves and is serious chiefly following a wet spring. It is controlled by spraying 2 or 3 times with Bordeaux mixture in the spring, and by cleaning up all infested leaves in summer. Yellowing and leaf fall may be due to hot, dry weather rather than disease.

TIGRIDIA

What treatment should be given tigridia bulbs which, when lifted from the border, are found to be covered with aphids? (New Jersey.)   This is probably the tulip-bulb aphid, which commonly infests gladioli, a relative of tigridia. For gladioli the napthalene treatment for thrips works for the aphids; also a 2-hour soaking in warm nicotine sulfate and soap solution. You will have to experiment to see if either treatment injures tigridia.

TULIPS

What causes tulip blossoms to blister? Is it a disease? Botrytis blight causes brown or water-soaked spots on the petals, which might be called blisters. This is a fungous disease, very contagious, often known as gray mold or tulip fire. The spores are carried by the wind and rain from infected leaves or blossoms to healthy ones. Small black sclerotia are formed on leaves and petals rotting into the soil, and on the bulbs, and serve to carry the fungus over the winter. Spray with weak Bordeaux mixture in early spring.

Can the bulbs of diseased tulips be dug up and treated and used again? (Maine.)   If the blighted blossoms are picked off immediately, and if all blossoms are cut off as they start to fade; if diseased leaves are removed when seen, and all leaves are cut off at ground level as soon as they ripen, the fungus may never get down to the bulb, and it is safe to leave it in the ground. If the bulbs are dug, it is better to discard any showing sclerotia than to treat them. If healthy new bulbs are to be planted in old infested soil, then the soil should be treated. (See Soil Sterilization.) If tulips are seriously diseased early in the season, the bulb is also infected, and should be taken up and destroyed immediately without waiting for normal digging time.

Why did my last year's tulips grow headless stalks? (New York.)   Botrytis blight often causes blind buds. These usually come when the bulb itself was diseased in the ground, and not as the result of secondary infection from plants near by.

Last spring most of my bulbs failed to grow; those that did were sickly looking. Was this due to not covering the bulbs, or disease? I planted large, healthy bulbs. (Minnesota.)   It probably was disease. If you planted deep enough, there was no need to cover. You either had botrytis blight from sclerotia in soil, or on the bulbs under the husk so you did not see them, or else they had gray bulb rot. The latter also is a sclerotial disease; it is more often characterized by large numbers of tulips failing to come up than is the botrytis disease, which is characterized by a weak growth above the ground. Plant new bulbs in another location, and make sure there are no black bodies either on the surface of the bulb or under its outer covering.

Why do white or yellow varieties seem not to be affected by the virus disease which causes "breaking" of the colors? (New York.)   The breaking is a depigmentation, and if there is no color pigment in the flower, or very little, it cannot "break." However, there is now known to be another virus which adds color to light-colored varieties.

How can I prevent my bulbs from being eaten by very small insects? (Missouri.)   These are probably bulb mites, very small, yellowish-white spiders. A heavy infestation will pulverize the inside of a bulb. Discard all such bulbs; dip the rest in nicotine sulfate, 2 teaspoons per gallon, for 10 minutes, and replant in another location, or in sterilized soil.

What are the thin white worms, ½ in. long, that eat bulbs in the ground? (Illinois.)   These are probably scavenger worms, feeding on bulbs rotting from some other cause. Seek for the original culprit.

What treatment do you recommend for the earth of beds where ground aphids are present? (New Jersey.)   Soak it with nicotine sulfate and soap solution, and work in tobacco dust.

How do you keep lice off tulips when starting an indoor garden?   Soak infested bulbs in warm nicotine sulfate and soap solution for an hour or two. If aphids appear on foliage, spray with nicotine.

Do moles eat tulip bulbs? (Washington.)   Moles are supposed to be carnivorous, living on grubs and other animal life. Usually the mole makes the run to the tulip bed and mice follow along to do the actual eating. (See Moles; Mice.)

TULIP TREE

How can I save a tulip tree that shows signs of fungous growth on the south side? (New Jersey.)   Consult a tree expert. If fungi are growing out from the trunk, it is a sign of internal decay.

Each year a blight on leaves of young tulips is temporarily stopped by a Bordeaux mixture. Why does it reappear after 2 weeks? (Illinois.)   Leaves of young tulip trees often turn yellow and fall due to hot, dry weather, but there are a few fungous leaf spots which may cause blotches in the leaves. Ordinarily, spraying is not necessary, and the best control is to clean up all infected leaves.

Can anything be done for a tulip tree, about 10 years old, badly infested with oyster-shell scale? (New Jersey.)   This may not be oyster-shell scale. There is a special tulip scale, oval, brown, ⅓ in. across, that is far more common and injurious on this tree. A miscible oil, 1 to 16 dilution, applied in early spring, should control it. (See Dormant Spraying.)

TRUMPET VINE

What do you use for green lice on trumpet plant? (Pennsylvania.)   Spray with nicotine sulfate and soap, starting early, before the leaves curl.

What can be done about leaves curling up on the trumpet vine, caused, I think, by red spider? (Pennsylvania.)   If the leaves are curled, it is more likely that aphids are at work. Red spiders are more apt to turn the leaves yellow and mealy. Spray with nicotine or any other contact insecticide.

VIBURNUM

What treatment should be used on common viburnum to discourage pests which cause the leaves to curl? (Illinois.)   This is the snowball aphid, and it starts curling the leaves almost as soon as they unfold. The books all say that spraying with nicotine sulfate and soap frequently, starting when the buds first break, will control this pest, but I have never been able to. Spraying and picking off curled leaves reduce the damage but do not entirely prevent it. One suggestion: dipping the ends of the twigs in the nicotine solution might be worth trying when you have the time. Usually after you fight the aphid for a few years you either ignore it or plant another variety of viburnum.

When a snowball tree, or any other shrub, is diseased, can one get it back to a normal, healthy condition, or must it be replaced? (Minnesota.)   That all depends on the disease, or the pest. The common snowball will curl up with aphids every season. You would have to select a different variety.

Bush of Viburnum carlesi has a deposit of rough white along the stems. Is it mealy bug? What can I do to save the bush? (New Hampshire.)   Probably not. Many woody shrubs in late summer are attacked by lightning leaf hoppers, whose young leave flocculent white masses over the twigs. There seems to be no permanent injury. Spray with nicotine sulfate and soap and don't worry.

Each summer black spot comes on the leaves of my **Viburnum carlesi and they drop off. What preventive? (Kentucky.)** There is a bacterial leaf spot listed for viburnum, but this may not be your trouble in Kentucky. Spraying with Bordeaux mixture is recommended, but in New Jersey I find *Viburnum carlesi* objecting to copper, the spray injury being worse than any disease. Try picking off and burning infected leaves and cleaning up fallen leaves.

VIOLET

What can be done to protect violets against caterpillars? (Louisiana.) Pick the caterpillars off by hand so far as possible. Dust with arsenate of lead.

WALNUT

I have an English Walnut that makes a new growth every spring and then the leaves drop off, and it is bare the rest of the summer. What causes this? (Pennsylvania.) It may be a leaf-spot disease, but more likely uncongenial surroundings. The English Walnut is exceedingly particular as to soil requirements, being intolerant of wet soils but requiring very deep, fertile soil with no excess of alkali.

WILLOW

The beautiful willow on my lawn, which has reached gigantic proportions, keeps losing its leaves as a result of bugs. It seems a shame to cut down the tree. Is there something I could spray on the bark and branches within my reach? (Long Island.) It would not help to cut the tree down. These are doubtless willow beetles. Have your tree sprayed once a year, in late May or early June, with lead arsenate. There are plenty of commercial tree-men with adequate apparatus on Long Island; it will cost far less for spraying than to have the tree cut down.

What can I do about the millions of dark red lice that get on our large weeping willow—midsummer to frost? It is impossible to use the yard for laundry. (Ohio.) Have your tree sprayed with nicotine sulfate or other contact insecticide by a tree expert with power apparatus.

Will whitewashing a willow keep tree borers from attacking it? (Illinois.) It probably would have little effect. Wrapping the trunk with wrapping paper or kraft crepe paper will keep borers out, but is usually done only the first 2 years after transplanting. Some repellent washes are effective but might be dangerous applied by an amateur. Better get the advice of a reliable treeman in your vicinity.

Is there any relation between scale insects and borers on pussy willow? What is the prevention? (Pennsylvania.)   No relation that I know of. Spray for scale with a miscible oil. (See Dormant Spraying.) Borer repellents are rather injurious. Inject nicotine paste into borer holes if you see fresh sawdust. Cut down seriously infested trees and start over. Pussy willows grow fast.

YEW

Are all insects injurious to yews controlled by applying arsenic to the surrounding ground? (Pennsylvania.)   No. Arsenate of lead, at the rate of 3 lbs. per 100 sq. ft. of soil, is used chiefly to kill the grubs of the black vine weevil, which is probably its most injurious insect pest. Yew is also subject to attacks by scale insects and mealy bugs, which are controlled by spraying foliage with strong nicotine sulfate and soap, or a summer oil and nicotine.

YUCCA

What are the soft-bodied insects which infest yucca? What spray for control? (North Carolina.)   Aphids are soft-bodied insects infesting yucca, but mealy bugs—soft white creatures—are more likely to be the trouble. Spray forcefully with nicotine sulfate and soap. Repeat as necessary.

ZINNIA

What is the cause of the white, powderlike discoloration on zinnias? (New Jersey.)   This is powdery mildew, a fungous disease, which usually appears toward the end of the season and is chiefly of importance because of the unsightly foliage. Dust with fine dusting sulphur.

What makes the leaves of zinnias curl up from the sides? (Vermont.)   Mildew sometimes has this effect. Or it may be a water relation.

Have been troubled by rust. What will stop it? Could it start from narrow strip of brush and small trees adjoining garden? (Massachusetts.)   There is no rust common on zinnias, but there is a bacterial, and also a fungous, leaf spot which may cause reddish discoloration of the leaves in late summer. It is not usually serious, and although it might be prevented by spraying with Bordeaux mixture, the cure would be as bad as the disease. You need not fear the strip of brush as far as "rust" is concerned, but if the weeds flourish, too, it would be a source of insect pests.

The roots of zinnias planted in open ground are covered with aphids; the plants withered after they had grown a few inches. How can we get rid of them? (Rhode Island.)   You can try making a shallow depression around each plant and pouring in a solution of nicotine sulfate and soap; but if your soil is so badly infested, it would be better to plant more zinnias in another location. (See also Soil Sterilization.)

What should be used to get rid of tarnished plant bugs? Have tried many sprays without success. (New York.)   Sprays are not much good for this pest; frequent applications of nicotine sulfate spray or nicotine dust or even sulphur dust might help. The first and most important step is getting rid of the weeds that harbor this plant bug.

This year zinnias have been badly infested with stem borers, but there were no marks or sawdust visible on outside. Cannot find material telling life cycle or control. Can you supply? (California.)   These probably are the common stalk borers, although they are listed as general only east of the Rockies. They winter as eggs on weeds and old stalks, so that the chief control measure is getting rid of these. (See also Borers.)

VEGETABLES

ASPARAGUS

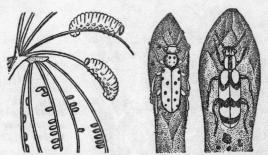

Asparagus Beetles: attack asparagus shoots; grubs eat foliage; center, Twelve-spotted Asparagus Beetle.

Will rust-resistant asparagus always escape the disease?   Not entirely. The Mary and Martha Washington varieties are reasonably rust resistant, but in some seasons in certain areas the red-and-black pustules show up on the leaves and stems, with yellowing of the tops. In that case dust with sulphur 3 times at 2-week intervals after cutting season. Burn old tops.

Is there a spray or remedy of any kind for asparagus beetle?
(Oregon.)   This red, blue, and yellow beetle is chiefly controlled by clean cutting during the harvest season, although an
occasional dusting with rotenone may be needed. After the cutting
season dust with 1 part calcium arsenate mixed with 3 parts
hydrated lime.

What about the Japanese beetle on asparagus? (New Jersey.)
The Japanese beetle may appear in swarms on asparagus foliage
in midsummer, but the injury is rarely sufficient to call for treatment.

BEAN

What is the chewing insect, colored yellow with black spots,
shaped a little like the ladybug but longer? (Texas.)   Either
the Mexican bean beetle or the bean leaf beetle. The former looks
more like a ladybug with its 16 small black spots, but it is larger,
more convex, and coppery-yellow in color. Its yellow larvae are
also found on the leaves. The bean leaf beetle is prevalent in
Southern states. It is about the size of a ladybug, red to yellow in
color, with 6 black spots and a black band around the wing covers.
Its larva is a white grub which feeds on the stem and roots *below*
the soil line. Both beetles are controlled by the same treatment.
The yellow-green spotted cucumber beetle also feeds on bean
foliage in Texas, and this, too, looks like a ladybug.

*Mexican Bean
Beetle: coppery yel-
low, sixteen black
spots; both adults
and spiny, dirty yel-
low larvae feed on
under sides of
leaves.*

All known insecticides failed to destroy a ½-in. long yellow
creeper on beans—looks like a caterpillar. What is it? (Massachusetts.)   Probably larvae of Mexican bean beetles, which are
fat, soft, covered with black-tipped spines, and something under

½ in. long. They succumb to rotenone dust in this stage. The larvae are easier to kill than the adult beetles.

Are little pests that look like a yellow bur on green beans the bean beetle? (Ohio.) Yes. That is a very good description of the larvae of Mexican bean beetle.

What are the time cycles of the Mexican bean beetle? With a succession of string beans I notice some plantings suffer more than others. (New York.) You are right. Beans planted in June in New York will mature in July between the two broods of beetles. The first beetles appear in May, when the early beans come up, feed for a week, lay their eggs in orange-yellow clusters on the under side of the leaves. The larvae hatch in another week, feed for 2 to 5 weeks, pupate on the leaves, and in 1 more week produce the adults which feed and lay eggs for the second generation. This is usually much more destructive than the first, untreated bean foliage being completely riddled during August and September.

How long a season has the bean beetle? (Virginia.) About as long as the beans are growing. In Virginia the Mexican bean beetle will probably have 3 broods a season.

What is the cheapest and most effective way to destroy bean beetles without harming the plants? (New York.) Spray or dust with calcium arsenate or cryolite up to the time flowers form, then change to rotenone, preferably in dust form for ease of application and coverage. In the small garden it would be better to use rotenone from the beginning. Never use lead arsenate, even before blooming, for this burns the foliage.

Will rotenone powder, used as a spray, control the Mexican bean beetle if applied frequently, starting a week after beans have come up? (New York.) Before the war, derris powder, analyzing 4 per cent rotenone, could be used as a spray, but the wartime rotenone dust is only 0.5 per cent rotenone and should be used straight as a dust. There are, however, proprietary rotenone sprays available. By watching the life cycle, described above, and treating only when larvae or beetles are present, much time and material may be saved. It is important to begin early, to get the overwintered beetles as they lay their eggs and the first larvae before they can produce more beetles.

Will turpentine in water sprayed on the soil where beans are to be planted keep away the bean beetle? No. You must spray or dust the foliage.

Is daily picking of the bean beetles and eggs the easiest way to

control them? (**Virginia.**)   An occasional dusting will be a lot easier than daily picking off, unless there are very, very few beans. Combine the two methods, picking off as many as you can whenever you have time. Each female removed before egg laying, or each cluster of eggs burned up, means fewer beetles for the next brood.

Is there anything other than spraying, dusting, and hand-picking to control the Mexican bean beetle? (New York.)   Yes, sanitary measures at the end of the season are very important. Clean up and burn all plant debris, or else spade or plow it under deeply, and clean up all weeds and trash around garden so there will be no hiding place for the overwintering females.

Is there anything to be done about such pests as bean beetles and cutworms during the winter? (Indiana.)   Fall plowing or spading and keeping the garden clean during the winter will certainly help to discourage both of these pests.

What can I do for the little bugs that come on lima beans? (Maryland.)   The Mexican bean beetle is as destructive to lima beans as it is to string beans. Use the same control measures.

What will destroy the Japanese beetle on string beans? (Massachusetts.)   Rotenone dust or spray, as recommended for Mexican bean beetle, will also take care of Japanese beetles.

How can I kill or prevent small green bugs with black dots on back which eat bean foliage? Was afraid to spray on account of poisoning the vegetable. (California.)   These are diabrotica, or 12-spotted cucumber beetles. You may safely spray with either rotenone or pyrethrum. The latter may be better for this particular beetle.

My string beans had little greenish bugs all over the plants all season. What are these? How can I get rid of them? (New York.) The regular bean aphid is black; the pea aphid is green and sometimes attacks other legumes. A greenish leaf hopper sometimes infests beans. Nicotine sulfate and soap spray should keep any of these under control and may be applied almost to picking time, if the pods are washed carefully. Or rely on the rotenone used for beetle control.

What shall I use, and when, for very tiny white flies that rise in a cloud from string beans? (California.)   It is doubtful that white flies on beans are injurious enough to warrant control measures. They may be sprayed with nicotine sulfate and soap, but this poison, although readily washed off, is not desirable on beans close to picking. Pyrethrum is safe.

How does the bug called a weevil get into beans? (Massachusetts.)   Eggs are laid on the pods while the beans are in the garden; these hatch into grubs which burrow through the pod into the bean. There they change into the small, dull gray adult weevils with reddish legs. Several broods may be produced in storage, ruining the beans for either seed or food.

The beans I raised last summer have little holes from which have come little beetles. What treatment should the vines have to prevent them? (Maine.)   These are the bean weevils (weevil being merely the name given to a beetle with a little snout). There is no treatment for the vines except to clean them up and burn them. The beans have to be treated after harvest. (See next question.)

How can I protect the beans from weevils during storage? There are several methods: (1) Fumigate with carbon disulphide. Place seeds in a box or container, such as a garbage can, that can be closed tightly; pour carbon disulphide (*very inflammable*) into saucer, 3 tablespoons for each 10 cu. ft., and keep closed 24 to 36 hours. (2) Spread out in pans and heat dry in the oven at 130° to 140° F. for 1 hour (some say 30 minutes). (3) Suspend seeds in cloth bag in kettle of cold water and heat to 140° F. Dry quickly. (4) Shake beans thoroughly in a container, with 1 pt. of lime to each qt. of beans.

Does treatment injure the beans for food or seed?   It should not, if directions are followed, although the heat or lime treatments might be preferred to carbon disulphide for food beans. The excess lime can be shaken off in a strainer and then the beans washed.

Last year my pole beans did poorly and when I pulled them up there were a lot of very small bugs on the roots. What were they? (Massachusetts.)   Root aphids, in all probability. Push the soil away slightly from around each stem and pour in a cupful of nicotine sulfate solution, 1½ teaspoons to 1 gal. of water.

I had some fine Kentucky Wonder beans, but after a while the leaves turned brown and the beans stopped growing. What caused this? (Massachusetts.)   This might have been the root aphids just mentioned; or perhaps dry root rot, caused by a fungus which lives several years in the soil, necessitating a long rotation; or rust. (See below.) It could have been heavy, wet soil without the fungus. In our town, in an "experience meeting" at the end of this past season, we learned that pole beans did extremely well in the plots that were almost pure ashes, and hence well drained, and very poorly at the other end of town, where the soil was heavy clay.

Last summer I was bothered with "rust spots" on my green beans, varying from skin deep to the center of the pod. What was the trouble? (North Carolina.)   Not true rust but a fungous disease called anthracnose or pod spot, which shows as round sunken spots with dark borders and pinkish spore pustules in the center. Anthracnose cannot be "cured" but it may be prevented by planting seed from healthy pods, or else seed grown in the West where the disease is not a problem. Avoid working with beans when they are wet, as this spreads the spores from diseased to healthy plants. Resistant varieties are chiefly of the shell-bean type.

What causes blight on leaf of green beans? (Ohio.)   If there are small angular lesions and black veins, this blight is anthracnose; your State Experiment Station lists Livingston's Pencil Pod Wax, Keeney's Rustless Golden Wax, Longfellow, Black Valentine, or Hopkins' Earliest Red Valentine as worth trying for resistance to anthracnose. If the blighting shows up as irregular light-green wilting patches on leaves and irregular blotches on pods, it is bacterial blight.

How is bacterial blight controlled? (Ohio.)   Use disease-free seed, either from healthy pods or Western grown. Do not work with wet plants. Varieties Refugee 1,000 to 1, Refugee Wax, or Late Stringless Green Refugee are more or less resistant snap beans. For dry beans choose Michigan Robust Pea, Perry Marrow, Yellow Eye, or Scotia.

What is the treatment for rust which comes about mid-season on pole beans? (Massachusetts.)   True rust is a fungous disease which shows as reddish powdery pustules on the leaves. In Massachusetts it is generally serious only on pole beans, where it causes early death of the vines. The rust winters over on dead plants and on stakes. Destroy vines after harvest, and next year use new poles or soak the old in formaldehyde (1 to 100 dilution), and keep them wet overnight by covering. Kentucky Wonder, U.S. No. 3, and U.S. No. 4 are resistant to some forms of rust.

How can rust spots be eliminated on green and yellow beans? (Illinois.)   If you have true rust, and not anthracnose (see above) varieties like Hodson Long Pod, Wisconsin Refugee, Improved Rust-proof Golden Wax, and Black Valentine may be rust resistant in your section of the country. You cannot eliminate rust once it shows up in the planting.

What is the treatment for mosaic on green snap beans? (Washington.)   There is no treatment. The virus usually comes in with the seed. Rogue out plants with mottled light and dark green leaves. Choose resistant varieties like Refugee, U.S. No. 5, Idaho Refugee, and Wisconsin Refugee. In Washington, curly-top, another virus disease, may affect beans. Rogue out dwarfed plants with puckered leaves.

Why do my string beans mildew? (California.)   Powdery mildew is a fungous disease very prevalent in California. It usually attacks beans in cloudy weather or toward autumn. Dust with sulphur. The Refugee beans listed above as resistant to mosaic are also resistant to mildew.

Does mildew come on string beans because of soil or atmospheric conditions? (California.)   This is not a soil fungus; the spores are carried by the wind. For some reason the California atmosphere is peculiarly conducive to mildew, not only on beans but many other vegetables and ornamentals.

BEET

How are leaf miners kept out of beet tops? (New York.) There is no spray that will prevent maggots from working inside the beet leaves, turning the tissues brown. Pick off infested leaves and destroy the wild host, lambsquarters. Incidentally, lambsquarters when young is a perfectly delicious vegetable, preferred by many to spinach, so a good way to destroy it is to cook it for dinner.

What about beet webworms?   There are several species of caterpillars which eat the leaves and web them together. Dust with calcium arsenate dust and remove weeds like lambsquarters.

Should beet seed be treated before planting to prevent damping off?   Definitely. The rough beet seed may carry spores of several disease organisms. Copper oxide is very effective for beets. (See Seed Treatment.)

What causes spots that resemble warts on beets?   The same organism that produces potato scab. Do not grow beets on land that has grown scabby potatoes. If the soil is alkaline, make it slightly acid with sulphur, and avoid any alkaline agents such as lime and manure. Use a cover crop of rye to replace the manure.

How can I keep beets and spinach from blighting? Our soil is slightly alkaline. (Washington.)   In Washington blight probably means curly-top, a virus disease that used to be called Western yellow blight, characterized by yellowing, stunting, and death. The virus is transmitted by the beet leaf hopper, so that insect control with contact insecticides is important. There is little else you can do except rogue out diseased plants immediately and keep down weed hosts. Soil acidity is *not* a factor, as it is in scab.

Is leaf spot on beets prevented by spraying?   Spraying with Bordeaux mixture may prevent the round, red-bordered spots from getting numerous, but in the small garden picking off spotted leaves is ordinarily sufficient control.

BROCCOLI

How can I keep aphids off Italian Broccoli? (Oregon.) Spray or dust with nicotine until the heads form, then treat with pyrethrum if necessary. Often the aphids cluster on a single head or leaf which may be removed and burned. If aphids are numerous on a head cut for eating, separate into flowerettes and soak in strong salt water. The aphids will float out and can be poured off. Then rinse the broccoli well in pure water before cooking.

How are root maggots and worms controlled?   See Cabbage. Broccoli is a member of the cabbage family, and while it is free from many cabbage diseases, it has its share of aphids, root maggots, and worms eating the foliage and flower heads. Use rotenone or pyrethrum rather than arsenates or cryolite.

BRUSSELS SPROUTS

What is the best control for worms and aphids on Brussels sprouts?   Rotenone dust is allowed for worms on Brussels sprouts and will keep the aphids down to some extent. Or they may be sprayed or dusted with nicotine. (See also Broccoli.)

CABBAGE

Is there any way to prevent white maggots from attacking the roots of cabbage plants? (Wisconsin.)   When a young cabbage wilts and, upon being pulled up, discloses white maggots working on the underground stem and roots, it is too late for control. There are several ways of preventing maggot injury. Cheesecloth over the seedbed, or a tar-paper disk placed around each plant when it is set out prevents the fly from laying her eggs; dusting seedlings with calomel, or soaking the ground with bichloride of mercury, kills the maggots as they hatch.

How are tar-paper disks, for control of root maggots, applied? Cut a 4-in. square, or circle; make a hole in the center with a spike, and make a cut from the outer edge to the hole, so you can get the paper around the stem. (Or ready-made disks can be bought.) Work gently, so as not to bruise the young seedling.

The disk should stay flat on the ground and fit snugly around the stem.

Cabbage Root Maggot. Eggs of this pest are laid on stems, near ground level, in early spring.

Cabbage Worm: adult white or yellow butterfly; worms, green.

What is the calomel treatment for seedlings? The ground may be dusted, after the plants are set, with a 10 to 80 calomel-lime mixture, but it is easier to treat them before setting. Mix 5 ozs. calomel with 2 ozs. cornstarch and put in a salt shaker. Lay the plants on a smooth surface, moisten stems, shake on the dust, then turn the plants over and treat the other side of the stems.

How do you treat seedlings set out in the garden with bichloride of mercury? Dissolve 2 tablets in 1 qt. of water (1 to 1,000 solution) and pour ½ cupful around stem of each plant. *Caution:* this is a virulent poison, and also corrosive; mix in a glass jar; keep away from children and pets.

What is the best way to control the black flea beetle on small cabbage plants? (Virginia.) These small but very active beetles do considerable damage to young plants, often riddling the leaves with tiny shot holes. Before the cabbage heads form it is safe to dust with cryolite (1 part to 3 of flour or talc), or with calcium arsenate (1 part to 4 of lime), or to use either one as a spray. (See Cryolite; Calcium Arsenate.)

What can be used to keep worms from eating cabbages? Until the heads are the size of baseballs it is safe to dust or spray with calcium arsenate or cryolite, as recommended for flea beetles above. After that spray or dust with rotenone or pyrethrum; or resort to hand-picking.

What can be substituted as a spray or dust to kill cabbage worms when rotenone is not available? Is there any treatment that will not poison such food plants? Poisons may be used up to time heads form without danger of harmful residues. After that, use pyrethrum.

Is there more than one type of cabbage worm? There are 3. The true cabbage worm, green caterpillar of the common white or yellow butterfly; the cabbage looper, a striped pale-green worm that moves like an inchworm and changes into a brownish-gray moth; and a small, greenish caterpillar that is the larva of the diamondback moth. All these are controlled in the same way.

Will sulphur keep the worms from eating young cabbage plants? (California.) In certain experiments sulphur dust has prevented chewing by the tent caterpillar. It would be worth trying on cabbages, but do not expect too much from it. It seems to work chiefly on young larvae.

Is lump lime good to destroy cabbage worms, and those little dark worms which hold themselves in ring shape? (Maine.) Lime is used to control cabbage clubroot, if your soil is acid, but would have no effect on cabbage worms. The little dark worms are millipedes (which see) and not very injurious.

How can I control blue aphids on cabbage? (California.) By a nicotine-soap spray, or nicotine dust, which may be used almost to harvesttime if the heads are washed carefully. Pyrethrum used for worms will also control aphids.

What treatment is best to kill grasshoppers that attack garden vegetables such as cabbage and broccoli? (California.) Scatter poison bait thinly in the morning, being very sure that none of the bait touches any edible plant parts. (See Grasshoppers.)

The leaves of my cabbage plants turned yellow and the cabbage died. Is anything wrong with the soil? (Wisconsin.) This is cabbage yellows, caused by a soil fungus—a species of Fusarium—very common in your state. Either plant in a new location or grow resistant varieties such as Jersey Queen, Marion Market, All Head Select or Improved Globe, Wisconsin All-Seasons, Wisconsin Ballhead, Wisconsin Hollander No. 8, or Red Hollander.

In order to grow cabbage, do I have to buy yellows-resistant seed? (New York.) It may not be necessary in New York.

The disease is not so prevalent as in the Middle West, and if you have no previous record of cabbages dying or yellows on your soil, you need not worry much.

For years I have had trouble with cabbage plants. Just before ready to head up the leaves turn yellow and drop off. The plant dies. There is no evidence of insect pests. (Delaware.) Your soil is apparently well inoculated with the "yellows" or fusarium wilt fungus. Plant resistant varieties.

What causes cabbages to rot off the stalk? (Iowa.) Black rot or blight, a bacterial disease, is one cause. The plants are stunted, leaves turn yellow to brown, shrivel and drop off, or the head may decay and fall off in a slimy mass. The vascular ring in the stem and the leaf veins are black. Use clean seed, or disinfect with hot water (see Seed Treatment); plant in disease-free soil; remove and burn diseased plants; clean up all cabbage refuse.

What causes the tops of the cabbage leaves to turn black, sometimes running through entire head? (Wisconsin.) Either the black rot just discussed or a fungous disease called blackleg. There are dark areas with black dots on stems and leaves. If the stem is girdled near the ground line, the plants wilt and die. Use cabbage seed grown near Puget Sound, where disease is rare, or treat with hot water. Practice sanitary measures given above and a 4-year rotation.

What is the best remedy for preventing clubroot in cabbage and cauliflower? (Michigan.) Clubroot is the name of a disease which causes grossly enlarged and malformed roots and stunted, sickly plants. If the disease has been present previously, treat the soil with fresh hydrated lime, 10 lbs. to 100 sq. ft., and rake it in shortly before planting.

What is the cure for cabbage wilt—curled tips of leaves, whitish color? (California.) This may be powdery mildew, with the fungus growing over the leaves and causing the white color. If so, you can dust with sulphur. If it is a chlorosis (an actual loss of color in the leaf tissue), then perhaps some chemical is lacking for good nutrition, or your soil is too alkaline.

My copper-oxide-treated cabbage seed would not grow; some other plant varieties are critically impaired in seedling growth. Why? (New Hampshire.) No one knows exactly why, but members of the cabbage family are sensitive to copper and are often injured by treating seed with copper oxide. If a damping-off treatment is required in addition to hot water, use Semesan or zinc oxide. (See Seed Treatment.)

CARROT

We have trouble with maggots in the carrots. Can you give any help in controlling this pest? (Washington.)   Your Experiment Station suggests that in western Washington early carrots be planted so they can be harvested by July 15, and in small blocks, so they can be screened and the rust fly prevented from laying her eggs. Do not plant late carrots before June 1. For late carrots crude napthalene flakes may be applied to the soil weekly, from July 20 up to one month of harvest.

Please advise me about the small worms which make burrows in carrots. Are they wireworms? (Oregon.)   Probably these are the maggots of the carrot rust fly discussed in the previous question. Control measures for Washington should also apply for Oregon.

What grub or bug eats tunnels through the sides of carrots? (Iowa.)   In Iowa the carrot grub, which looks like the common white grub and eats pieces out of the carrots, and the rust-fly maggots, which make rust-colored tunnels, are the chief insect pests. Control both pests by dusting the ground along the row, as soon as the seed is planted, with calomel (1 part to 25 of gypsum, talc or lime); or by spraying with 2 ozs. Calomel to 5 gals. of water. Rotating is helpful.

Can carrot worms be avoided by harvesting early or by adding lime to the soil? (Michigan.)   By planting in June the first brood of the rust fly can be avoided, and harvesting can be done before the second brood. Lime is sometimes recommended to drive away the carrot beetle but should not be used unless your soil requires it. Napthalene flakes will do a better job for the maggots. (See above.)

What are the insects which look like blue lice and infest my carrot roots? How can I get rid of them? (New York.)   These are root aphids (plant lice); they look bluish because of a powdery coating. If the infestation is bad enough to require control, pour nicotine sulfate, 1½ teaspoons per gallon of water, around the stems after loosening the soil.

How do I keep ants from putting plant lice on carrot roots? (New York.)   Find the nest if you can and inject carbon disulphide or paradichlorbenzene crystals, or use ant bait. (See Ants.)

How can I keep my carrot crop from rotting in the garden? (Arizona.)   Your carrots either have Southern blight (see

Crown Rot) or else bacterial soft rot, a bacterial disease that more often appears in storage, but occasionally in the garden. The fungi and bacteria are in the soil, so you must plant in a new location or treat the soil. (See Soil Sterilization.)

Is there a foliage disease of carrots? (New Jersey.)   There is a leaf blight which produces spots on the leaves, after which they turn brown and die, but it is not ordinarily serious enough in the home garden to require more than cleaning up old tops. If necessary, spray with Bordeaux mixture.

CAULIFLOWER

How are cauliflower troubles controlled?   Treat seed and practice same sanitary measures as recommended for cabbage. Never use calcium arsenate or other arsenicals on cauliflower, but rely on rotenone or pyrethrum. Occasionally there is a bacterial or fungous spot on the heads; for this there is no practical control.

CELERY

Is blight on celery in seed or soil? (Indiana.)   Both. There are 3 blights, early and late blight caused by fungi, and a bacterial blight. The organisms are carried over in celery refuse in the garden and on the seed. Practice a 3-year rotation and either use seed that is 2 years old or treat it with formaldehyde (1 part to 240 parts water) for 15 minutes, after pre-soaking for 30 minutes in lukewarm water, or in bichloride of mercury, 1 to 1,000 solution, for 10 minutes.

How can celery blight be prevented? (Pennsylvania.)   Spray with Bordeaux mixture at weekly intervals in the seedbed; and at 7- to 10-day intervals after setting out in the garden. Blight is worse in a wet season and is spread by working with plants when they are wet.

Our celery is injured by slugs; is there any remedy? (Pennsylvania.)   Clean up hiding places such as loose boards and old plant debris; sprinkle lime on the ground, or use a poison bait. (See Slugs.)

How can I get rid of beetlelike bugs in celery plants? (Pennsylvania.)   These are tarnished plant bugs and very difficult to get rid of. Clean up weeds and try pyrethrum dusts or sprays, sulphur, or nicotine.

COLLARDS

How may one overcome insects on collards? (Alabama.) Rotenone or pyrethrum sprays or dusts will take care of cabbage worms and aphids, or nicotine sprays may be used for the latter if the greens are thoroughly washed. Pick off harlequin bugs—the brilliant red or yellow, black-and-blue sucking insects.

CORN

How can one tell when corn has been stung by the corn-borer moth? (New York.) The yellow-brown moth of the European corn borer lays its eggs in groups of 20 or more on the *under* side of the leaves, and the larvae, tiny, flesh-colored borers, tunnel their way into the stalk, leaf stems, and ears. Their presence is shown by tassels bending over or broken; fine sawdustlike castings on the leaves; small holes in the stalks, often with protruding borings.

When should table corn be planted to avoid the borer? (Michigan.) There are 2 broods of the European corn borer. Extra early corn will be injured by the first, and very late corn will be attacked by the second brood. Corn planted between the middle of May and the first of June will mature chiefly between the broods and thus escape much injury.

What is the latest on the control of corn borer? (Vermont.) That the treatments for the borer must be related to growth stages of the corn. Give the first dusting when tassels can be seen on half the plants by looking down into the tops. Dust into the tassel whorl, and give more treatments at 5-day intervals. Dual-fixed nicotine dust has proved most satisfactory in borer control. Rotenone dust is also used, but it will not give complete control.

How else can one fight the borer? The corn borer feeds on more than 200 kinds of plants and winters, in the larval stage, in old herbaceous stems. It is extremely important to clean up in the fall not only old cornstalks and stubble, but to burn dahlia and gladiolus tops, and to clean up weeds, especially pigweed and smartweed.

Is the common stalk borer injurious to corn? Yes, especially at the edge of the corn patch near weeds, or where wasteland has been recently turned into garden. The young caterpillars are brown, white-striped, turning grayish as they increase in size. The moths lay their eggs in September on giant ragweed and many other weeds. Cleaning up is the only known control measure.

Can worms in sweet corn be avoided? (Washington.) The corn earworm is more widely distributed than the corn borer, and the caterpillars are large, brown to green in color, and striped. The moths lay their eggs chiefly on the corn silk, and the young larvae feed on that and the tip of the ear. Standard control is the injection of ¼ teaspoon (15 to 20 drops) of mineral oil (preferably containing pyrethrum extract) into the tip of each ear immediately after the silk has wilted, or about 5 days after it appears. *Application before wilting may prevent pollination,* and thus cause poorly filled out ears. Some recommend cutting off the silk to remove the eggs.

Corn Earworm: large brown to green worm, with distinct striping. (See Corn Borer, page 1072.)

I have read of a dust to sprinkle on the corn silk to keep out borers. What is it? (Ohio.)   Partial control of the corn earworm may be obtained by dusting the silk with a mixture of equal parts of calcium arsenate and sulphur.

Can anything be done about Japanese beetles on sweet corn? (New Jersey.)   They congregate on the silk, which may be dusted with hydrated lime. If rotenone dust is used for the European corn borer, it will partially control Japanese beetles. Handpicking is always effective.

How can squirrels be kept from eating corn? (Indiana.) Squirrels, and occasionally raccoons, are very destructive pests of corn, and there is little to be done except shoot them, which is not permitted in many localities. In my garden the corn was planted in a square block this past season. The squirrels started to eat on the outside row, and when this was left to them they ignored the rest of the corn patch.

How eliminate smut from sweet corn? (New York.)   The only control measure is to cut off and burn the large smut boil— from ear, tassel or stalk—before it opens to discharge the black spores which will infect other corn. Avoid the use of manure likely to be infested, and burn up stalks after harvest. Spraying is not helpful and there are no resistant varieties.

Is there any other important corn disease? (New Jersey.) Bacterial, or Stewart's, wilt may be serious after a mild winter. There are discolored streaks in the leaves, and young plants wilt and die. The bacteria are spread by corn flea beetles. Many of the new hybrid varieties are resistant to this disease.

CUCUMBER

What measures can be taken against striped cucumber beetles? They seem almost impossible to destroy. (Illinois.) They are hard to control, but there are many ways to fight these green, black-striped beetles: 1. Remove weed hosts, especially Chinese-lantern plants. 2. Protect young seedlings with hotkaps or cheese-cloth tents. 3. Plant extra seeds in the hills, and discard the most injured seedlings. 4. As soon as the ground cracks over the seed-lings, start dusting with cryolite, or a 1 to 15 calcium arsenate-gypsum dust; or rotenone, nicotine dust, or pyrethrum. Repeat treatments as often as needed to keep plants covered with dust.

Striped Cucumber Beetle attacks cu-cumbers, melons, and squash; green with black stripes; larvae attack roots.

What causes bugs in the roots of cucumber plants? (Pennsyl-vania.) The larvae of the spotted cucumber beetle works on the roots of many plants and is known as the Southern corn rootworm. The beetle, green with 12 black spots, is controlled like the striped cucumber beetle. The spotted beetle also attacks many ornamental plants, where it is known as diabrotica beetle. "Bugs" may also be root aphids (which see).

A worm eats our pickle cucumbers. Is there a remedy? (Illi-nois.) The white or green pickle worm is especially destruc-tive in Southern states but is occasionally found as far north as Illinois. It bores into the ripening fruits. The dusts listed for the striped cucumber beetle should be helpful. Destroy all old vines.

What is the control for the large, flat, gray beetle which attacks cucumber, pumpkin, squash, and melon vines? I have used moth balls in the hills with the seed and it seemed to work. Was it by accident? (Arkansas.) Probably, although the moth balls might have some repellent effect on the squash bug. (See Squash for more details.)

How rid cucumber vines of lice? (Texas.) The melon aphid is very destructive to all cucurbits, causing leaves to curl, wilt, and brown; it attacks many other plants, including lilies, to which it carries mosaic. Spray with nicotine sulfate and soap, using 1½ teaspoons Black Leaf 40 per gallon; or dust with nicotine dust, being careful to get underneath the leaves. If rotenone or pyrethrum is being used for beetles, it will help control aphids.

How are white flies on cucumbers killed? (New York.)   The treatments for aphids (see previous question) should subdue them. They are often abundant on cucurbits, but of minor importance.

What pest or disease causes cucumber to wither, runner by runner, until the plant dies and semi-mature fruit shrivels up? (New York.)   It is either the squash vine borer (see Squash) or wilt. The latter is a bacterial disease, very prevalent, disseminated by spotted and striped cucumber beetles, which carry the bacteria in their digestive tracts over the winter and deposit them in droppings on the leaves as they feed. The young vines may be sprayed with Bordeaux mixture, or, better, dusted with a mixture of 4 to 5 per cent metallic copper, 7 per cent arsenate, plus flour or talc. If such a prepared dust is not available in your regular seed store, inquire at a Farmer's Co-operative, or ask your county agent.

My pickles show mosaic. What can I do about that? (Michigan.)   Control the weeds, such as burweed, milkweed, catnip, pokeberry, and groundcherry, which harbor the virus; control the melon aphids and cucumber beetles, which carry the virus from the weeds to the cucumbers. For a slicing cucumber plant Shamrock.

My cucumber leaves look rusty and yellow. What causes this? (Massachusetts.)   Bacteria produce angular leaf spots and fungus brownish circles. Treat seed with 1 to 1,000 solution of bichloride of mercury for 5 minutes, rinse, and dry. Spray foliage with 2–2–50 Bordeaux mixture; or dust with copper dust, especially latter part of season. Clean up and burn all old vines.

EGGPLANT

How can one get an eggplant that does not die of wilt? (Alabama.)   You have to set healthy plants grown from clean seed in soil that has not grown eggplant for 4 years. Eggplant wilt—also called foot rot, blight, leaf spot, and wilt from its various symptoms—is so severe in the South that clean seed is rarely found. So treat it with bichloride of mercury (1 tablet to a pint of water) for 10 minutes; then rinse in running water and dry thoroughly. Tie seed in cheesecloth bag before immersion. After drying, treat seed with copper oxide. (See Seed Treatment.) Spray plants, starting in the seedbed, with 1½–1½–50 Bordeaux mixture every 10 days.

What makes eggplants wilt? (New Jersey.)   In New Jersey it is probably verticillium, which stunts the plants and turns the leaves yellow. The plant wilts in the heat of the day and the vessels are dark if the stem is cut. Use a long rotation which does not include tomatoes, potatoes, or raspberries. The fungus can live in the soil a long time.

LETTUCE

Why did my head lettuce rot after it was transplanted from the greenhouse? It was covered with a grayish fuzz. (New York.) This was botrytis blight, or gray mold disease, which infects seedlings if they are kept too wet in the greenhouse, and shows up as bottom rot. Remove plants carefully with surrounding soil, and soak the soil with 1 lb. copper sulfate dissolved in 7 gals. of water. Sterilize the soil used for flats in greenhouse or cold frame. A similar rot, but starting from the top down, is called "drop," and is controlled in the same way.

MELON

How do you exterminate the small yellow chewing insect with black stripes known as the cantaloupe bug? (Texas.)   The striped cucumber beetle frequently congregates on melon fruit. (See Cucumber for control.)

What insect kills my cantaloupes almost overnight? It is same color as leaves, small, egg-shaped, and the leaves scald and brown. (Missouri.)   The melon aphid almost fits your description. (See Cucumber for control.)

Can root rot on melon vines be prevented? (Vermont.)   Fusarium wilt, a soil fungus, causes the plants to become stunted and yellowed. Long rotations reduce the amount of wilt.

My muskmelons did well up to ripening, then wilted and died. Why? (Michigan.)   Perhaps the fusarium wilt just discussed; or cucumber wilt (see Cucumber); or the squash vine borer. (See Squash.)

ONION

Is there a practical method (for small garden) for keeping onions raised from seed free from the onion maggot? (New York.)   Treat the seed with calomel before planting (2 parts calomel to 1 part seed); or moisten soil at base of plants with 1 to 1,000 solution of bichloride of mercury. Use shallow planting. Onions may also be sprayed with Bordeaux mixture, plus lubricating oil, but this is not so convenient for the small garden.

What causes onions to rot? Seemingly a worm or bug bores

through stalk. (Wisconsin.) This is the onion maggot discussed above. When damaged onions are put in storage, they decay and cause surrounding bulbs to rot.

I pulled and stored my onions and found that majority are going bad. Why? (Pennsylvania.) Fungi following after maggot injury are responsible. Onions should be stored only where there is free air circulation, either in a string bag, or else with the tops left on and braided into chains to hang up on the wall. The latter method is easy and very successful, and you can always cut off just the size onion you want without rummaging through a bag.

What is the best means of control for onion thrip? (Connecticut.) It is very difficult to control this small sucking insect which rasps the leaves and turns them whitish. Early planting is said to be helpful, for most thrips are present after July 1. Spray with 1 oz. tartar emetic and 2 ozs. brown sugar to 3 gals. of water; or with nicotine sulfate; or dust with nicotine.

Can cutworms be prevented from injuring young growing onions? (New York.) Paper collars are impractical; so use poison bait if cutworms are too numerous to destroy by handpicking. Take care in spreading the bait that it does not come in contact with the onions. (See Cutworms.)

What is the black powdery mass on leaves and bulbs? Onion smut, a fungous disease. The easiest way to avoid it is to grow onions from sets, because they can be infected only in the young seedling stage. In growing from seed, start in a clean, new seedbed and transplant; or else, after sowing the seed, but before covering, sprinkle it with a formaldehyde solution (1 tablespoon to 1 gal. of water).

PEA

How are damping off and root rots on peas prevented? (Connecticut.) Early planting helps get peas started before the root-rot fungi can get in their work; but treating with Spergon (which see) helps prevent root rot as well as damping off. Avoid heavy, low, and poorly drained soils. Use a 3- to 5-year rotation.

How can I control the pale-green plant lice that suck the sap from the vines? The pea aphis is very difficult to control, but rotenone dust is helpful. In warm weather a nicotine spray or dust will be fairly effective.

How can moles be prevented from destroying green peas? I have read that moles eat only worms. If so, what becomes of the pea seed? (Washington.) Gardeners are frequently skeptical about the biologist's statement that moles live on animal life. If the mole tunnel disturbs the pea roots, various root-rot fungi might destroy the pea seed. (See Moles for control, if any.)

PEPPER

What should be used to kill lice on pepper plants? (Nebraska.) Nicotine sulfate and soap should be safe if the fruits are care-fully washed; but pyrethrum or rotenone may be substituted as non-poisonous materials. In general, peppers have the same pests as potatoes, and control measures are the same.

Why do my peppers turn brown and fall off as soon as they are formed? (Connecticut.)   This is probably due to weather, which in Connecticut in 1943 caused not only blossom and fruit drop of many plants, but a blossom-end rot of the fruits after they were formed. (See Squash; Tomato.)

POTATO

How prevent potato leaves from curling and turning brown, and the vine dying before the tubers are full grown? (New York.) This is late blight, the most destructive disease of potatoes. Plant only healthy tubers, and start spraying with Bordeaux mixture when the plants are 6 ins. high; repeat every 10 to 14 days until the plants stop growing.

What can be done for potato blight? I have been told that the remedy is more expensive than it is worth in a small patch. (Michigan.)   It may cost more to spray than to buy potatoes, if you count the time used. That is why they are not usually recommended for small back-yard gardens. Early potatoes can be dug before blight gets much of a start. Untreated late po-tatoes may survive in a very dry summer, but in a wet season unsprayed late potatoes may not be worth digging.

How can the home gardener, with no power-spray equipment, prevent late potato blight? (Massachusetts.)   Spraying is pref-erable, and may be done with a 3-gal. compressed-air sprayer, but dusting may be substituted, using a 20 to 80 copper-lime dust, probably procurable where farmers buy their supplies in your vicinity.

When should blighted potatoes be dug? (Massachusetts.)   If the vines are severely infected, dig as early as possible before the fungus gets down to rot the tubers.

Is there any treatment of the soil to prevent potato rot? (Con-necticut.)   No, it would not pay or help much to chemically treat soil for potatoes, and the best seed treatment is to make sure they are sound when cut for planting. The practice of hilling potatoes is in a sense a helpful soil treatment because it interposes more of a barrier between the fungous spores developing on the leaves and the tubers below.

What is the cause of scab on potatoes? (Vermont.) A common soil organism closely related to bacteria, *Actinomyces scabies* by name. It is unable to grow in an acid soil, but as the soil becomes increasingly alkaline scab injury increases, varying from slight russeting to greatly roughened scabby areas on the tubers.

What can be done for potatoes that get rough, scabby hides? We put plenty of cow manure on. Do we use it too green, or too much, or too often; or is it the weather? We used to have lovely potatoes. (Kansas.) You use it too much and too often for soil infested with scab organism. Manure has an alkaline effect, like lime and wood ashes, and the more alkaline the soil the better *Actinomyces* likes it.

What can be done with soil that produces scabby potatoes? (New York.) Get your *p*H (soil acidity) down to around 5.4. Adding flowers of sulphur will increase acidity. The amount needed varies with the original *p*H, but might run around 10 lbs. per 1,000 sq. ft., or 300 to 400 lbs. per acre.

The Government puts out some kind of solution for potato seed. What is it? (New York.) State Experiment Stations or county agents may arrange co-operative seed treatments for farmers but I doubt if the Government gives out any such material. To control scab and rhizoctonia, uncut potatoes may be soaked in 1 to 1,000 solution of bichloride of mercury for 90 minutes just before planting; or in yellow oxide of mercury for 1 minute. The back-yard gardener would do better to make sure he is using clean, sound potatoes for seed and omit the treatment.

Potato Bug. Both the orange-and-black-striped adults and the fat, copper-colored larvae, destroy foliage.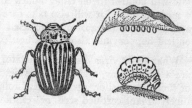

How are potato bugs controlled? (New York.) Add a tablespoon of calcium arsenate, or lead arsenate, to each gallon of Bordeaux mixture, to take care of these large orange-yellow, black-striped beetles and their enormous humpbacked, reddish larvae. This is the famous Colorado potato beetle.

How do you control the old-fashioned black potato bug?
(Ohio.)   Blister beetles are hard to kill. Hand-picking is excellent. Fluosilicates, either cryolite or Dutox, are probably the most effective chemicals; but if calcium arsenate is being used for the Colorado potato beetle, that may suffice.

How shall I exterminate long-bodied gray or brown beetles that clean out potato patch in one night? (Nebraska.)   These, too, are blister beetles. They may be plain black, or striped, or margined, or brown or gray, but, in any color, they have voracious appetites. (See previous question; also Blister Beetles.)

We were warned that if we planted potatoes in soil where nothing had recently been grown they would be wormy. Why?
(Ohio.)   White grubs and wireworms are usually prevalent in sod land, and when this land is prepared for a garden the worms remain until their life cycle is completed. Potatoes planted in newly broken sod land are very apt to have brown tunnels going through the tubers. If new land must be used, plant potatoes as late as possible. (See Wireworms.)

Last year my potatoes were scabby from wireworms. How can I raise clean potatoes in the same ground another season? (Ohio.)
After one year of cultivation you may have fewer wireworms, but it would be safer to try a crop of clover to starve out the wireworms before planting potatoes again. Digging potatoes early (before the wireworms injure the tubers much), and plowing or digging the land in midsummer, and keeping it cultivated until frost, will help get rid of them for the following year.

Why do the edges of potato leaves get brown before the late blight season? (New Jersey.)   This is a condition called hopperburn, due to the sucking of many leaf hoppers. Nicotine sulfate will control them, either added to Bordeaux mixture, or as a separate spray; it will also take care of pink and green potato aphids. The Bordeaux mixture itself has some repellent effect on leaf hoppers and also on flea beetles.

What about virus diseases of potato? (New Jersey.)   There are a great many, and the names describe the symptoms. Some of these are "yellow dwarf," "leaf roll," "mosaic," and "spindle tuber." Plant certified seed, or resistant varieties, and rogue out any plant that seems to be infected.

Some of our potatoes had a layerlike black moss inside them. What caused it? (Virginia.)   There are many causes of tuber discoloration: late blight and other fungous diseases, some bacterial and virus diseases, and a physiological disease called black heart. Your trouble may be the latter, and it comes from too great heat and lack of oxygen. If the potatoes stay out in bright sun after digging, or if the storage place gets too hot, black heart may develop.

PUMPKIN

How can cucumber beetles on pumpkins be controlled success-fully? (Illinois.)   Any of the treatments discussed under cucumber should be satisfactory on pumpkin. Since the residue on pumpkin is not a problem, calcium arsenate can be used as well as rotenone.

How can the pumpkin vine borer be kept from entering vines as they are beginning to set fruit? (West Virginia.)   For the control of the squash vine borer, and also squash bugs on pumpkin, see Squash.

RADISH

What control is there for the light-green worm, like a cater-pillar, that eats leaves of radish? (New Jersey.)   This is prob-ably the larva of the diamondback moth. (See Cabbage for con-trol.)

Is it safe to eat radishes grown in soil treated with corrosive sublimate to eliminate wormy root crops? (Pennsylvania.) Since the radish is eaten so soon after planting, soil treatment with corrosive sublimate is undesirable. For a small planting of radishes covering with cheesecloth to keep the maggot fly from laying her eggs is practical and safe.

Why are my radishes small with a black spot up the middle? There is a disease called black root of radish, caused by a fungus, but there is not much known in the line of control. Try a dif-ferent location, and the Red Globe type.

RHUBARB

Why does rhubarb rot? (Virginia.)   Phytopthora foot, or crown rot, causes sunken spots at the base of the leaf stalks and a rot and wilting which progress from stalk to stalk until the whole plant dies. Dig out and burn diseased plants, being careful not to scatter infected soil. Disinfect the location with 1 to 50 formaldehyde. Plant only healthy roots.

What are the insects that bore holes in rhubarb stalks? (Pennsylvania.)   Rhubarb curculios. Pick them off, because sprays do not seem to control. They are black-snout beetles which puncture stems and cause black spots. Destroy dockweed near rhubarb.

SQUASH

Is there any treatment for Hubbard squash, for worms that burrow inside stem?   The squash vine borer is a white grub or caterpillar that works inside the vine, causing wilting beyond the point of attack, which is indicated by yellow excrement outside. Cut out the borer at this point and mound loose soil over the wound so the vine will put out new roots. Dust plants with rotenone or cryolite; burn vines as soon as crop is harvested.

Is there any way of exterminating the rather hard-shelled sucking insect, with repugnant odor, which attacks squash plants first, then others? (Texas.)   This is the squash bug, sometimes called stink bug, which is distributed all over the United States. The adults are brownish black, ⅔ in. long; they hide under the leaves and suck the sap, causing the vines to wilt. They attack all vine crops, but prefer squash. They are hard to kill, but the young nymphs are partially controlled with nicotine or pyrethrum sprays or dusts. Hand-pick the adults, or trap them under boards. Destroy all old vines in fall.

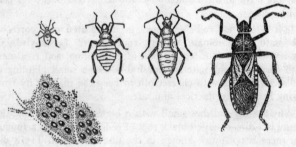

Squash Bug: large, rusty black, lively beetle, destructive at all stages, hatching from orange-colored eggs on under sides of leaves; attacks squash and pumpkins.

What causes summer squash buds to drop off? (Connecticut.) Chiefly unfavorable weather conditions. The dry summer of 1943, following a wet spring, in Connecticut caused much blossom rot. However, the male and female flowers are separate on squash plants, and the male flowers of course drop off without setting fruit.

Why can't I raise crookneck squash? Something attacks the roots and prevents fruits from maturing. (Michigan.)   It may be a water relation rather than an organism at the roots. Blossom-end rot is common in squash, causing the small squash to wither at the blossom, which is followed by secondary rot fungi. This disease is thought due to an insufficient or uneven water supply.

What caused about 8 out of 10 straight-necked squash to rot shortly after setting? (Connecticut.) The weather, and resultant dry soil, caused this blossom-end rot. (See previous question.)

Is Black Leaf 40 effective as a control for squash vine borer? It is recommended for vine-type winter squash, such as the several Hubbard varieties. In spraying, particular care is taken to drench the base of vines and surrounding soil. Application should be repeated at least twice a week, for 3 or 4 weeks, starting about July 1. Arsenate of lead is also suggested, at intervals of a week to 10 days.

TOMATO

What is the cause of blossom-end rot, which looks more like a fungous disease than a rot? It covers from ¼ to ½ of the fruit, is gray-black and quite firm. (Oregon.) Blossom-end rot does look like a fungous disease, and it is probably the most common tomato disease across the country, but it seems to be due to disturbed or uneven water relations. When the plant is growing rapidly in moist weather, and a dry spell follows, water is lost from the tissues faster than it can be taken up by the roots. The blossom end of the fruits, being farthest away from the roots, loses water first and the cells collapse and turn black.

What will prevent tomatoes rotting at the blossom end just before ripening? (Illinois.) Maintain an even water supply. A deeply prepared soil well supplied with organic matter helps; but plants that receive too-heavy applications of nitrogenous fertilizers, particularly manure, are more subject to this rot. A balanced fertilizer high in superphosphate and available calcium decreases susceptibility. Calcium nitrate is good to use as the source of nitrogen. Although blossom-end rot usually shows up in periods of drought, it may appear when the soil has received so much rainfall that the small roots are killed for lack of aeration.

What causes rot inside perfectly good-looking tomatoes? (Connecticut.) Probably the same type of weather and soil conditions that cause the blossom-end rot discussed above.

Is tomato wilt carried on the seed, or does it remain in the soil? (Mississippi.) Both. Primarily a soil organism, the wilt fungus may be carried on the seed. If doubtful seed is to be planted in clean soil, it should be treated before planting, but it is much wiser to use seed from healthy plants.

What is the cause of blight on tomatoes that begins at bottom of plant and works up? Leaves curl, fruit develops but does not come to completion, plant dies slowly. (Pennsylvania.)   This is probably fusarium wilt, caused by a fungus that lives in the soil. At first the leaves roll up and wilt in the middle of the day, later there is a permanent wilting, yellow leaves, and death.

If tomato plants all succumbed to the wilt in damp season last year, will they do so again this year when planted on the same ground? (Connecticut.)   If you plant susceptible varieties, they are very likely to, for the fungus lives several years in the soil. Rotation or soil sterilization is necessary; also cleaning up all tomato refuse.

My tomatoes wither and stop bearing about the first of August. What are wilt-resistant varieties? (Tennessee.)   Marglobe, Pritchard, Rutgers, Pan American, Break-o-day, Louisiana Gulf State, and Prairiana are reasonably resistant to fusarium wilt.

What are the causes and cure for the mosaic disease of tomatoes? (Pennsylvania.)   The cause of mottled dark and light-green misshapen leaves is a virus. The only cure is prevention: destroying diseased plants as soon as noticed and also weed hosts, and controlling insect carriers.

What are the weed hosts of mosaic?   Groundcherry, horse-nettle, jimsonweed, and nightshade are the most important. Tomatoes should also be grown as far away as possible from tobacco, petunias, and potatoes, for the same virus may be present in these plants.

Can tobacco dust or nicotine spray be used safely on tomato plants? I think I read somewhere that a virus disease results. (New Jersey.)   The tomato mosaic virus is carried in ground tobacco, so that one should not smoke while working with tomatoes, nor use tobacco dust. However, nicotine sulfate used as a spray apparently does not carry the infective principle, and nicotine dust made from nicotine sulfate mixed with lime would also be safe. The gardener can carry the virus from plant to plant on his hands, which should be washed frequently with soapy water while working with tomatoes.

What can we do to overcome brown specks on our tomatoes? Will lime overcome this? (New Hampshire.)   Brown spots on the leaves and sunken black spots on stems and fruit may be due to early blight caused by a fungus (Alternaria). It is better to use sprays without lime, because this causes blossoms to drop off (lime in the soil is a perfectly good recommendation). Instead of spraying with Bordeaux mixture, use yellow cuprous oxide (Cuprocide) at 1 level tablespoon per gallon; or some other fixed copper spray, starting when the first fruits set, and repeating at 10- to 14-day intervals.

What causes anthracnose on tomatoes? What is remedy? (Indiana.) Anthracnose is a fruit spot rather common in the central states. The spots are dark, sunken, with concentric markings and pinkish spore pustules in the center. The fungus lives in the soil, so that a 4-year rotation should be practiced. Avoid poorly drained soil, and fertilize properly. Pick all ripe fruit frequently.

My tomatoes had an earthy flavor and were mushy. Was it the variety, or soil conditions? August was a wet month. (New York.) The rainy weather may have caused growth cracks in which one of the mold fungi grew to produce the mushiness and the flavor, which should not be charged against the variety. Staked tomatoes suffer less in a wet season. Keep tomatoes picked frequently, and remove and burn all soft and rotting fruit.

What is the best formula to prevent rust on tomatoes in southern Florida? The "rust" is probably sunscald; there is no true rust common on tomatoes. Keep as much foliage as possible on the plants, so that the fruits are not exposed to the sun in hot, dry weather. Verticillium and other wilts that cause loss of lower foliage increase sunscald. A very light covering of straw over fruit clusters may reduce this disease.

Are there many diseases that attack tomatoes? United States Department of Agriculture *Farmers' Bulletin 1934*, published in 1943, lists 38 diseases (exclusive of insect pests) which may be important in one part of the country or another. There are many leaf and fruit spots, wilts, and blights; Southern states have to contend with nematode root knot and Southern blight, while virus diseases, curly-top, and spotted wilt are prevalent in the Northwest. Consult your State Experiment Station if you need help. Despite diseases, tomatoes are an easy and prolific crop for the home gardener.

What is the easiest way to circumvent cutworms on tomatoes? A paper collar put around each seedling as it is being transplanted. (See Cutworms.)

What causes little holes in the leaves of tomato seedlings? (New Jersey.) Flea beetles. They may riddle the foliage if not controlled and seriously injure the young plants. Spraying with Bordeaux mixture will repel them. Dust with rotenone dust if available. (See Flea Beetles.)

How can I get rid of the huge green caterpillars on tomatoes? (New York.) The large tomato hornworm is best controlled by picking off by hand. Or dust with calcium arsenate before fruits set. If the caterpillar is in the fruits, it is the corn earworm, also called tomato fruitworm. Destroy infested fruits as soon as discovered. A bait of 1 part cryolite or Dutox mixed with 10 parts corn meal gives some relief when scattered over plants.

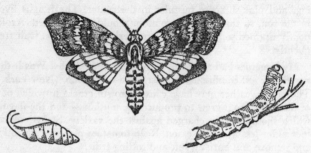

Tomato Hornworm: a rather fierce-looking, very large and nervous green worm; attacks tomatoes, and sometimes egg-plants, peppers, and potatoes.

What is the pest on tomato leaves in August that looks like salt on the leaves and later turns into tiny flies? (Wyoming.) Your grains of salt are the nymphs of white flies, common on tomatoes in late summer, but not particularly injurious. Nicotine sprays or pyrethrum or rotenone dusts may control them. (See White Flies.)

How get rid of the yellow bug on tomato plants that looks like a ladybug? (New York.) The Mexican bean beetle occasionally wanders over to tomato plants but ordinarily does not require treatment there. (See Beans.)

A green bug, with shield-shape marking, stings and ruins our tomatoes. Is there a remedy? (Texas.) This is the green stink bug, a close relative to the squash bug. The nymphs are greenish with black markings and the adults green or brown; they suck the sap of tomatoes, peas. beans, and other plants. Dust with pyrethrum or 3 per cent nicotine when the young bugs first appear, and repeat as needed. Also hand-pick.

Is there a way to get rid of the worm that enters the stalks of tomatoes in bloom so that the plant dies or breaks over? (Mis-

souri.) Getting rid of the weeds round about is the best and practically only way of getting rid of the common stalk borer. You may be able to kill the borer with nicotine paste before the plant dies. (See Borers.)

TURNIP

What can be done about maggots in turnips? See Cabbage for directions.

Is it safe to eat turnips grown in soil treated with corrosive sublimate for wormy root crops? This is an old-and-tried recommendation, and apparently is not dangerous. The turnips are eaten so long after the application that no poisonous residue is taken in by the turnip root.

Why do yellow turnips rot in the ground? (New York.) Sometimes bacterial soft rot follows along with the maggots, especially in a wet season, and if the plants are crowded together in the row. Thin your turnips early, and space widely. See that the rows are far enough apart. Remove all diseased turnips immediately.

FRUITS—GENERAL

What is the least equipment, in size and expense, needed by an amateur to spray 12 fruit trees? (New Jersey.) It all depends on the size of the trees. If they are very young a dust gun or a 3-gal. compressed-air sprayer might do the job for a while. For permanent spraying you should have a 12-gal. bucket sprayer, either of the Paragon type or one that has an agitator. It will come with a small truck for wheeling around and should cost around $25. Extra extension rods are available so you can get a spray up into a moderate-sized fruit tree. For a very large tree it may be necessary to hire someone with power equipment.

Three-gallon compressed-air sprayer, knapsack type, is convenient for spraying small fruit trees.

For back-yard fruit trees, what sprayings are really necessary? (Mississippi.) That depends on the back yard, but ordinarily a calyx spray, when most of the petals have fallen, and a foliage spray 10 days to 2 weeks later are most indispensable. (See also discussions under the different fruit hosts.)

When should fruit trees be sprayed, just before or after the bloom opens? (Mississippi.)   It depends on the fruit and the pests you want to control. In general, sprays are not applied when fruits are in full bloom for fear of preventing pollination. The farmer usually applies what is called a pink spray on apples, just before blooms open; but the amateur can often wait until the calyx spray, when most of the petals have fallen.

What is the best simple spray for fruit trees? (Michigan.) There is no one single spray that will take care of all fruit trees. Ask for help from your Experiment Station in revising a farmer's spray schedule to fit your needs. (See Spraying Calendar, Michigan State College, *Extension Bulletin 154.*)

What is the best spray material for fruit trees and when is the proper time to spray trees in Oklahoma?   Your best help is "Orchard Spray Calendar," *Circular 168,* from the Oklahoma A. and M. College Extension Service. Dormant spraying in Oklahoma may be with either 1 to 8 lime sulphur or a miscible oil applied before leaves come out when temperature is above 60° F. Wettable sulphur is favored as a summer fungicide above Bordeaux mixture or lime sulphur. (See also discussion under individual fruits below.)

What is advisable to use as a general spray for apple, cherry, and plum trees, also grapes? (Illinois.)   It is not possible to mix up one spray mixture and apply it to all kinds of fruits at the same time, although sometimes the pome fruits, such as pear and apple, may be sprayed together and sometimes sprays for stone fruits, peach, plum, cherry, may be combined. Grapes take a distinctly different schedule. For treatment see below under the separate hosts. Also send to the Illinois Agricultural Experiment Station, at Urbana, and ask for *Circular 492,* "Directions for Spraying Fruits in Illinois." There you will see that not only the kind of fruit makes a difference but also where you live in Illinois. Ask also for *Circular 524,* "Growing Fruits for Home Use."

When is the best time for dormant spray of fruit trees? What spray to use? Can this spray be the same for apples, peaches, plums, and cherries? (New York.)   The dormant spray is best applied after the buds have begun to swell but before they show green at the tip. Probably you could safely use a 1 to 9 dilution of lime sulphur on all these fruits, or even an oil spray, but you will get much better results if the spray is directed at specific pests for each kind of fruit and timed for these. Send for Cornell *Extension Bulletin 473,* "Spray and Dust Schedules for Protecting Orchard Crops from Diseases and Insects." (See also discussion below under different hosts.)

How and when should fruit trees too small to have fruit or blossoms be sprayed? Bulletins tell about pre-blossom sprays, etc., but with no older trees around how are you to know when to spray? (New York.) Having no fruit, you do not have to use all the different sprays, for they are chiefly intended to provide sound fruit. *If* scale is present, put on a dormant spray; later you can spray foliage to control cankerworms, Japanese beetles, aphids, etc., if these insects appear and are injurious.

Do you know what will kill rose chafers without killing fruit trees and bushes, which they attack so furiously in June we get no fruit? (Michigan.) Your Experiment Station (*Extension Bulletin 154*) says that rose chafers attack in the vicinity of sandy quackgrass sod. They are difficult to control, and you must be on the alert to spray immediately they appear. A repellent spray of lime may be used in some cases, but some fruits will be killed by repeated applications of lime. Three tablespoons lead arsenate and 2½ tablespoons molasses per gallon may be added to Bordeaux mixture when spraying for black rot of grapes, but this treatment will injure other fruits. On other small fruits 10 per cent pyrethrum dust may be effective.

What is the best method to deal with Japanese beetles in a young orchard? (D.C.) If the trees have not come into bearing, foliage may be protected with lead arsenate sprays, being careful to use lime with it on stone fruits. On trees where a poisonous residue on fruit must be avoided, spray with ½ oz. aluminum sulfate and 3 ozs. hydrated lime to 1 gal. of water.

How can I get rid of lice on my fruit trees? (Minnesota.) Add 1 to 2 teaspoons nicotine sulfate to a gallon of spray mixed up for other purposes. Nicotine should be especially added to a delayed dormant spray to control aphids.

Mice or rabbits gnaw the bark of my young fruit trees. What shall I do? (New York.) Mechanical protectors such as wood veneer, paper, cloth, or ¼-in. galvanized wire are most satisfactory in protecting young trees from injury. The wire is best if you can get it. Keep it away from the trunk except at the top of the wrap.

Is there any repellent I can put around young fruit trees to keep the deer and rabbits from eating the new leaves next spring?

Various repellents have been tried with success in some cases and no success in others. The most successful has been asafetida. Use the "gum in mass" size, about as large as golf balls, one in a cotton bag hung on each small tree 3 or 4 ft. from the ground. For larger trees, use more bags. The bags are of thin material, like tobacco sacks, or they may be made of cheesecloth. In dry weather, the material will harden in 5 to 6 weeks, and will need to be replaced. Napthalene flakes have been effective in some places—2 heaping tablespoonfuls to a bag, 1 bag to a small tree, 3 bags to a tree 5 or 6 years old. In dry weather the filling lasts about 2 months. During an average season, refill about 4 times.

Cylinders of woven wire protect young fruit trees from winter injury by rabbits and other rodents.

APPLE

How can I get 1 or 2 large apple trees effectively sprayed without spending more money than the fruit is worth? Local sprayers charge me $2.50 per spraying and decline to use anything except lead arsenate. (Massachusetts.) You cannot expect to get 1 or 2 fruit trees sprayed without its costing you much more than the fruit itself is worth. You have to balance the account by considering apples also as ornamentals and think of the fun you have picking your own fruit. The charge of $2.50 is moderate when it must cover time of 2 men, cost of materials, transportation of a special trip for only 1 or 2 trees, and the seasonal nature of the work. To save money you must do the spraying yourself, which would not have much effect on a large tree, or else resign yourself to wormy apples. A surprising amount of pies and applesauce come from unsprayed apples. My own unsprayed tree provided 7 families this summer with all the applesauce they could can for winter. If trees are not sprayed, it is very important to clean up all dropped apples every week.

How many sprayings of apple trees are indispensable for reasonably satisfactory fruit in the home garden? When we have our trees sprayed 5 times it is much cheaper to buy apples. (Ohio.) Five sprays are supposed to be the minimum for sound fruit: dormant, cluster bud, calyx, and first and second codling-moth sprays, but often the dormant spray may be omitted if there are no scale insects, and possibly one or two others. The calyx spray, when 90 per cent of the petals have fallen, and the first codling-moth spray, 17 days after calyx, are probably most useful in providing reasonably clean fruits. Use a 1 to 50 dilution of lime sulphur (5 tablespoons per gallon) and 2 tablespoons lead arsenate per gallon.

About how many gallons of spray should be used to cover a 5-year apple tree and a 10-year full growth—for dormant and full-leaf sprays? (New York.)   A foliage spray for a 5-year-old apple requires 1 to 2 gals.; 10-year-old, 4 to 5 gals.; 25-year-old, 12 to 15 gals. A dormant spray might take about half as much.

Can old apple trees which bear many infected apples ever grow sound fruit? (New York.)   Yes, with a definite spraying program combined with rigid sanitary measures.

What is the easiest and best way to spray a few apple trees infested with codling moth? (Massachusetts.)   There is no easy way, but in Massachusetts the calyx and second cover sprays are most important.

Codling Moth: the worst apple pest; also attacks other fruits. The larvae, pinkish-white caterpillars ¾ in. long, tunnel through fruits.

What is a practical control of curculio on apples in the small garden? (Massachusetts.)   Calyx and first cover sprays are most important in controlling curculio. (See schedule below.) Gather and destroy dropped fruit every week.

My McIntosh apples this year were covered with black spots ⅛ to ¼ in. in diameter. Trees were sprayed. Can you identify it and suggest a remedy? Seems to be a local infection. (Massachusetts.)   McIntosh apples are very susceptible to scab, a fungous disease more prevalent following a wet spring. It is controlled by lime-sulphur or wettable sulphur sprays which must be perfectly timed. (See spray schedule below.)

A spray schedule for Massachusetts adapted from Massachusetts State College Extension Leaflet 100D is as follows:

Delayed Dormant—Desirable spray if red mite or San Jose scale is present. Miscible oil or oil emulsion according to manufacturer's recommendations.

Pre-Pink—Desirable on McIntosh and other susceptible varieties to control scab. Five level tablespoons wettable sulphur or dry lime sulphur and 2½ tablespoons lead arsenate to 1 gal. water.

Pink Spray—Important for scab-susceptible varieties. Same mixture as pre-pink but add 1¼ teaspoons nicotine sulfate for aphids.

Calyx Spray—*Important* to control scab, codling moth, curculio. When 90 per cent petals have fallen, apply 5 tablespoons wettable sulphur or dry lime sulphur and 3½ tablespoons lead arsenate to 1 gal. water.

First Cover Spray after Calyx—Important to control curculio, leaf hoppers, and scab. Apply when temperature reaches 75° F. 5 or more days after calyx spray, using 5 tablespoons wettable sulphur, 3½ tablespoons lead arsenate, with 1¼ teaspoons each of nicotine sulfate and raw linseed oil per gallon water.

Second Cover Spray—*Important* to control codling moth, scab, and sometimes curculio. Apply 7 to 10 days after first cover spray, using same materials as first cover, but omitting nicotine sulfate and linseed oil.

Third Cover—*Important* for apple maggot and scab. About July 10, when maggot flies appear, apply 5 tablespoons wettable sulphur and 2½ tablespoons lead arsenate to 1 gal. water.

Fourth Cover—*Important* for apple maggot and codling moth. Apply about July 25 to prevent maggot (railroad worm) tunnels. Same as for third cover.

What sprays should be used on an uncared-for apple orchard in New Jersey?   You will probably need the 5 sprays listed in New Jersey *Extension Bulletin 228*. 1. *Delayed dormant,* beginning when buds show silvery until leaves stick out ¼ in. To control scale, aphids, scab, 1½ cups liquid lime sulphur and 2 teaspoons nicotine sulfate to 1 gal. water. 2. *Pink* (when fruit buds show color), 6 tablespoons liquid lime sulphur and 1 tablespoon lead arsenate to 1 gal. water. 3. *Calyx* (directly after petals fall, before calyx closes), for codling moth, curculio, scab, use wettable sulphur according to manufacturer's directions, or 5 tablespoons lime sulphur and 1 tablespoon lead arsenate to 1 gal. water. 4. *Ten days after petal fall,* for curculio, scab, and caterpillars, same as 3. 5. *Three to 4 weeks after petal fall,* for codling moth and scab, same as 3.

What causes brown spots through the interior of apples and what will prevent this? (New Jersey.)   Probably the apple maggot, a slender white worm which feeds within the pulp and carries with it germs of a soft rot. The adult is a small black-and-white fly. The maggot winters in the soil as a small seedlike pupa; the flies come out in summer, usually in July. The 2 sprays listed as third and fourth cover in the Massachusetts spray schedule above should work in New Jersey but check with the New Jersey Agricultural College concerning the proper time to apply them. Cleaning up every rotten, dropped apple is very important in preventing more maggot trouble for another year.

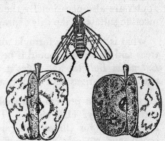

Apple Maggot. Small black-and-white fly is the parent of this well-known pest.

How can I reclaim apple trees whose fruit is always badly infested with railroad worms, or I suppose codling moth? (Vermont.)   Railroad worms are apple maggots (see preceding question) and quite different from codling-moth larvae, which are larger, ¾ in. long, pinkish white with brown heads. The larvae winter in cocoons in the crotches and under bark of trees. The moths emerge to lay their eggs in warm, dry weather about a week after the petals have fallen. The newly hatched caterpillars enter through the calyx cup of the fruit, unless a poison spray is in place. Later-hatched caterpillars enter the fruit through the side. After 3 to 4 weeks inside the apple the larva burrows through a mass of excrement from the surface and crawls down the branches for a suitable place for a cocoon. In addition to spraying, scraping the bark on the trunk up to 10 ft. during the winter will be very helpful in reducing codling-moth infestation. Chemically treated bands on scraped trees will collect larvae and prevent damage.

I have heard that dinitro-cresolate (sodium salt) is used for the control of codling moth on apple trees. Can you tell me how and when this is used? (New Jersey.)   Oil- or water-soluble nitro compounds are added to oil dormant sprays to control aphids, bud moths, and scale insects. I do not know of their use for codling moth. A sodium salt of dinitro-cresol is sold as Elgetol and should be used according to manufacturer's directions. It is water soluble and may be used as a dormant spray by itself or added to a 2 per cent lubricating oil emulsion.

I spray my 1 apple tree 4 times as prescribed in all manuals, but recently the apples have brown spots throughout and are sort of knotty and misshapen. Why? (New York.) Probably the result of apple maggot. You need a summer spray in addition, about June 25 to July 1, which is a combined codling-moth cover spray and first apple-maggot spray. A second spray for maggots should go on about July 10 to 15. The misshapen, knotty apples are also occasionally the result of redbug punctures. Add nicotine sulfate to the calyx spray if redbugs appear.

What is the proper formula and ingredients for spraying apple trees and how often should it be done? (New York.) Cornell *Extension Bulletin 473* gives a detailed schedule and formulae with modifications according to the pests you have in New York.

How do you prevent the apples from falling off the tree and getting wormy? (Illinois.) The 3 codling-moth sprays listed as minimum for Illinois are calyx, 17 days after calyx for first brood, and 9 weeks after calyx for the second brood. Amounts of lead arsenate to use are given in spray schedule for Massachusetts. (See also University of Illinois *Circular 524,* "Growing Fruits for Home Use.")

When and how often should I spray old Baldwin apple tree which bore very wormy apples this year? (New Hampshire.) Ask for University of New Hampshire *Extension Circular 252* for a complete spray schedule. For codling moth and railroad worms the calyx, first cover, and third cover (about July 7) are most important. (See Massachusetts schedule above for formulae.) Pick up all dropped apples.

My apple trees are young but will soon need a spray. What can I use that will not be injurious to the bees. (Iowa.) Any insecticide may be injurious to bees; that is why spraying schedules call for treatment before the blossoms open or after almost all the petals have fallen.

My apple trees have scaly bark and faulty apples. What should they be sprayed with and when? (Tennessee.) Consult University of Tennessee *Extension Publication 184* for a schedule, which calls for dormant spraying with lime sulphur before February 1; lime sulphur and lead arsenate in the pink bud stage 10 days after petal fall and again 10 days to 2 weeks later.

I've had scale on an apple tree for more than a year. Will a dormant spray used next spring be effective to save this tree?

(**Illinois.**)   It should be. Unless there is an extreme infestation, scale insects will not kill a tree very quickly. Use a 3 per cent oil emulsion, or 1 to 16 miscible oil.

How can I raise apple trees without having them destroyed by borers? (New York.)   Wrap the young trees when they are set out in kraft crepe paper, starting several inches below the ground and going up to the lowest branch. Remove in August and rewrap in a few weeks for a second year. Wire wraps later will keep out rabbits and mice and check borer infestation. Commercial repellent paints may be purchased that are partially satisfactory in borer control.

What should be done to borers deep in an apple tree? (New York.)   Poke in a flexible wire where you see sawdust protruding from the bark and try to kill them in place. Borers nearer the outside may be cut out with a knife.

What is the best method to remove fungus from an apple tree? This runs from ground for about 4 ft. up. (New York.)   If you mean a greenish moss on the trunk, that is of no consequence, but if you mean a collection of shelf fungi, they are indications of a heart rot inside the tree, which may or may not be worth saving by cavity treatment.

How do cedar evergreens harm apple trees? (Minnesota.) Because they form the alternate host for the cedar-apple rust. Spores are carried from the cedar galls in spring to infect young apples and foliage, which will show rusty spots in midsummer. Sulphur sprays for apple scab will often control rust. (See also Cedar.)

Blight on apple trees. Cause and cure? (Illinois.)   You doubtless refer to the bacterial disease known as fire blight, which kills back branches and blights blossoms so they appear burned by fire, and produces cankers on twigs or main trunk. Cutting out infected portions well below the visibly blighted area is most important, and so is breaking out blighted fruit spurs. If the disease is serious, apply a special full-bloom spray of 1–3–50 Bordeaux mixture. This spray must not contain any arsenicals for fear of poisoning the bees and preventing pollination.

What causes apples to rot on the tree and dry up? Is it a fungous disease or insects? What kind of spray should I use? (Illinois.)   It sounds like black rot, a fungous disease characterized by mummied fruits and by frog-eye spots on leaves as well as a bark canker. Either lime sulphur or wettable sulphur

in the regular spray schedule for apple scab should take care
of black rot, provided all mummied and rotting fruits are cleaned
up and burned. In southern Illinois another fruit rot, called bitter rot, may be prevalent. This requires summer spraying with
Bordeau mixture. See University of Illinois *Circular 492*, "Spraying Fruits in Illinois."

**How can I get rid of woolly mildew on an apple tree? (Wash-
ington.)**   Cut out mildewed twigs at the time of pruning.
Spray with 1 to 100 lime sulphur or wettable sulphur in the
cluster-bud and calyx stage and again 2 weeks after petal-fall
stages. If a regular schedule for scab is being carried on, powdery
mildew will be taken care of.

**Is there anything that can be sprayed into ground while tree
is in blossom to prevent Winesap apples from ripening with
specks and rottenness at core? (Maryland.)**   Elgetol has been
used to spray on the ground to eradicate the apple-scab fungus,
but this would not be the cause of rottenness at the core. Rot
and specks may be due to apple maggots, controllable by summer fruit spraying. Corky brown specks through the fruit sometimes come from lack of boron in the soil. In that case you can
apply powdered borax, $\frac{1}{4}$ to 1 lb., depending on age of tree.
The larger amount is not safe on tree under 25 years old. Apply
it like fertilizer. One dose will last 3 years.

**What is the cause and remedy of brown bitter spots in apples?
(Wisconsin.)**   Either the bitter rot or boron deficiency previously discussed or a disease called bitter pit, due to some disturbed water relation with no very definite remedy.

**What causes peculiar greenish sections in the flesh of some
apples? (Connecticut.)**   Climate, variety, water relations
seem to have something to do with this physiological condition
called water core; maintain an even supply of water; maintain
proper balance between root and top by pruning; pick fruit at
proper maturity.

APRICOT

**What can be done against wormy apricots? A tiny worm starts
eating around the stone and destroys fruit. (Michigan.)**   This
is the plum curculio, common also on apple, peach, and cherry.
It is controlled by lead-arsenate sprays and a stringent cleaning-
up campaign. (See Plum.)

**May lead arsenate be used on apricot trees without injury to
foliage? If so, in what strength solution? (Virginia.)**   Lead
arsenate is used with lime on all stone fruits to prevent injury.

In 1 gal. water use 1½ tablespoons lead arsenate and 3 of spray lime and usually 3 of wettable sulphur. This spray may be used for petal fall, or for calyx, and again 3 weeks later, after which lead arsenate should not be used in the home-garden fruit.

My apricot trees turn yellow and the fruit loses all its flavor. Is this a condition of the soil? (Utah.)   Quite probably in Utah it is a chlorosis due to too-alkaline soil, corrected by applying barnyard manure and equal parts of iron and aluminum sulfate, using 1 lb. of mixture to each inch of diameter of the trunk. Apply beneath the branch spread, either in water solution or in holes 12 to 18 ins. deep. Yellowing may also be symptoms of a virus disease. Consult your Experiment Station.

BLACKBERRY

How do you get rid of red rust in Alfred blackberry? It acts like fungi but does not yield to sulphur; very contagious. (Missouri.)   It is a fungus, officially named orange rust of blackberry. It lives all through the interior of the plant and cannot be controlled by fungicides as other rusts. Remove diseased plants, getting out all roots, before the contagion spreads further.

BLUEBERRY

Why do my blueberry bushes have little pieces of wood, which look like worms, on the ground near the roots? (Massachusetts.)   It sounds like frass (excrement) from a borer working in the stem. If you can find the hole, inject some nicotine paste, Bortox.

CHERRY

When is the proper time to spray ox-heart cherry to get better fruit and prevent insects? (New Jersey.)   The following spray schedule for cherries is adapted from New Jersey Agricultural Experiment Station *Extension Bulletin 228*. 1. *Before the buds swell,* to control scales and fungous diseases, 1½ cups liquid lime sulphur to 1 gal. water. 2. When *husks split* from small fruits, to control curculio, brown rot, leaf spot, wettable sulphur as recommended by manufacturer, 1 tablespoon lead arsenate, 5 tablespoons lime to 1 gal. water. 3. *Ten days after 2,* same as 2. 4. *When fruit first shows color,* for leaf spot, 6 tablespoons lime sulphur to 1 gal. water. 5. *Immediately after fruit is picked,* same as 4. Spray materials used to control maggots caused by cherry fruit flies are not safe in the home garden because of poisonous arsenical residue. Clean up all dropped fruit.

After my cherry tree blossoms the leaves curl up with aphids.

When and with what will I spray? (New York.)   A dormant spray of Elgetol or other dinitro compound (see apple) helps to control cherry aphids. When the aphids first appear and before the young leaves curl, spray thoroughly with nicotine sulfate and soap, repeating as necessary. Small trees may be dusted with nicotine dust.

How can I prevent rot of cherries on trees? (Illinois.)   The lime-sulphur in the spray schedule given above is intended to take care of brown rot, but wettable sulphur may be substituted according to manufacturer's directions.

What causes cherry leaves to turn yellow in midsummer and drop off? What spray do you recommend? (Wisconsin.)   This is a fungous leaf spot, controlled by the lime-sulphur in the preceding spray schedule. Proprietary low-soluble copper compounds may be substituted, but you should apply to your Experiment Station for safe brands and specific directions.

What will kill worms which feed on the roots of cherry trees until trees are killed? Will it be safe to plant another tree in this ground the following spring? (Michigan.)   I am not sure whether you mean the peach-tree borer which works on the trunk under the soil surface, or the larvae of white grubs. Keeping the ground plowed and cultivated before replanting will help get rid of the latter. The peach-tree borer stays under the bark rather than the soil; replanting in the same spot would probably be fairly safe. (See Peach.)

CURRANT AND GOOSEBERRY

Is gooseberry or any other berry harmful to pine trees? (New Jersey.)   Gooseberries and currants are alternate hosts for the white-pine blister rust. Where this disease is prevalent they should be removed whenever they are found within 900 ft. of white pines. Black currants are particularly susceptible to blister rust and should not be grown at all in rust areas.

Is there a disease-resistant currant? (Connecticut.)   Variety Viking is said to be resistant to white-pine blister rust.

What causes red blotches on Red Lake currant? (North Dakota.)   Large reddish blotches on leaves of currants frequently indicate aphids working on the under side. If there are rusty patches on the under side of leaves, it may be white-pine blister rust.

How can I rid currant bushes of aphids? (Illinois.)   Add 2 teaspoons nicotine sulfate per gallon of water to any spray applied as soon as the foliage is developed, or put on a separate spray of nicotine sulfate and soap. Direct spray toward under side of leaves.

What is the best insecticide for worms in gooseberries and currants? (Washington.) The currant fruit fly is a serious pest of currants and gooseberries in western Washington. White maggots feed inside the berry, causing the fruit to turn red and drop. One treatment recommended is the use of bait sprays to kill the flies before they deposit their eggs on the fruit. Use 2 ozs. lead arsenate and 1 qt. syrup to 3 gals. water; apply within a week of first fly emergence and repeat weekly until an arsenical spray is no longer safe on the ripening fruits. Another recommendation is to spray with Bordeaux mixture about 10 days before blossoms open, then 3 sprays, or dusts, of rotenone, at 10-day intervals, starting 10 days after blossoming.

What is best to use on gooseberry bushes affected with leaf-chewing worms? (Indiana.) A combination spray of Bordeaux mixture with 1 tablespoon lead arsenate and 2 teaspoons nicotine sulfate per gallon water applied as soon as the foliage is well developed will take care of the currant worm (your "leaf-chewing" worm) as well as aphis, leaf spot, and mildews. After the fruits develop, hand-pick the worms or dust with hellebore or rotenone.

What causes leaves to turn brown early part of summer? (New York.) If there are dark spots on leaves and later defoliation, it is a fungous leaf spot controlled by spraying with Bordeaux mixture. If the whole shoot blights, it is caused by an internal fungus. There is nothing to do but cut infected canes at ground level.

GRAPE

What is the proper spray to use for black rot on grapes? (Ohio.) Black rot causes more loss than any other grape disease. The berries turn purple prematurely and change to hard, black, shriveled mummies. Spray with Bordeaux mixture when new shoots are ½ in. long and again when they are 8 to 12 ins. long; spray after blossom fall and repeat at 2-week intervals if disease has been serious in other years.

What causes grapes to drop before ripe? (Pennsylvania.) Frequently the grape berry moth, which may destroy 60 to 90 per cent of fruit on an unsprayed vine. Add 2½ tablespoons lead arsenate to the Bordeaux mixture spray applied just after petal fall, and again 10 to 14 days later.

What do you do to keep Japanese beetle off grapevines? (Michigan.)   Until the use of rotenone was barred for wartime, the special Japanese beetle sprays were very effective if applied at least once a week. For the duration a heavy coating of lime will repel some of the beetles.

How do you control rose bugs on grapes? (Massachusetts.) Cultivate the soil around the vines thoroughly in May and early June. Spray with 4 tablespoons lead arsenate and 3 tablespoons molasses to 1 gal. water as soon as the beetles appear; repeat weekly if necessary.

My grapevine is troubled with a small insect or fly early and a small bug or hopper in midseason. What spray? (Wisconsin.) The early "fly" is probably a flea beetle, which will be repelled by the Bordeaux mixture used for black rot and poisoned by the lead arsenate added for berry moths. Leaf hoppers are sucking insects very injurious to grapes during the summer. Use nicotine sulfate, 1½ teaspoons per gal. of water, adding soap. Apply late June and early July.

How do you control mildew on grapes? (Michigan.)   A weak Bordeaux mixture spray should be effective.

PEACH

What is this white worm I find in the bark of my young fruit trees at the earth line? He buries himself in a jellylike mass. How can I keep him outside looking in only? (New Jersey.) This is the peach-tree borer, responsible for the death of many peach trees. The white, brown-headed worms, larvae of black-and-yellow wasplike moths, live in the bark from 8 to 10 ins. above the soil to 3 to 4 ins. below the surface. Control depends not exactly on keeping the worm outside but on gassing it under the bark before it does much damage.

Is there anything we can do for the peach-tree borer besides spraying? (Ohio.)   You cannot spray to control the borer, but you can fumigate it in early fall after the young worms have hatched and are under the bark. The standard material is para-dichlorbenzene. The crystals are placed carefully in a ring around the trunk, not closer than 1 in. nor further than 2 ins. from the crown. The dosage must be very exact: 1 oz. for trees 6 or more years old, ¾ oz. for 5-year-old trees, and ½ oz. for 4-year-old trees. No treatment should be given peaches set out less than 3 years. Before placing the crystals remove all grass, weeds, and debris from around the tree and immediately afterward mound up with additional soil, being careful not to disturb the crystals. The time of treatment varies according to the state, usually September for New York and up to November 1 for the South. The soil temperature should not be much lower than 60° F. for effective results. After several weeks the mound of soil should be leveled off.

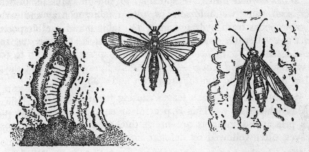

Peach Borer: a fat white grub, burrowing into peach trees at ground line.

How do you get rid of the worms that make gum at roots of peach trees? (Indiana.) If trees are less than 3 years old, or there are only 1 or 2, you can go after worms with a knife or a wire, a process known as worming. Another treatment, and one that is replacing paradichlorbenzene in some states, is ethylene dichloride emulsion, which is not limited by soil temperature. In very small dosages it may also be used on young trees. The emulsion has dosage directions which must be followed exactly. Although it has given very favorable results in many places, other localities have reported injury. Ask your own State Experiment Station for advice.

What other than a borer will cause peach trees to lose sap at the trunk, and the tips of the branches to be coated with a gummy substance? (Pennsylvania.) The gum is one manifestation of brown rot, controlled with sulphur sprays or dusts and also by cutting out diseased twigs and branches and destroying all infected fruit or old mummies.

Shortly before time for peaches to ripen they rot on tree and dry up, still hanging in December. Is there danger of next season's crop being affected? If so, what treatment? (Pennsylvania.) There is very much danger of brown-rot infection from these mummied fruits on the tree or others which have fallen to the ground. Pick them all and burn them. Follow a spray schedule. (See Plum; also schedule below.)

What is the spraying program for peach trees? (Massachusetts.)   Massachusetts State College suggests: 1. *Fall Dormant* —after leaves drop to control leaf curl, using 1 to 15 lime-sulphur or Bordeaux mixture. 2. *Pink*—when blossoms show pink, to control brown rot, using wettable sulphur or sulphur dust. 3. *Shuck*—when husks are splitting, to control curculio, brown rot, scab, using wettable sulphur, plus 1 tablespoon zinc sulfate, 2 tablespoons fresh hydrated lime, 1½ tablespoons lead arsenate to 1 gal. water. Or dust with 70 parts sulphur, 20 of lime, and 10 lead arsenate. *First Cover*—same as shuck sprays, applied 7 to 10 days later. *Second Cover*—same as Pink Spray, applied 14 days after first cover, to control brown rot and scab.

Red blotches on peach leaves causing them to curl up. Why? (Massachusetts.)   This is peach-leaf curl, a fungous disease. Its principal symptoms are much thickened distortions of the leaves, often followed by defoliation.

What is the best way to control peach-leaf curl? (Washington.)   Spray any time during the dormant season with 1 to 15 lime-sulphur solution, or 12 tablespoons dry lime-sulphur per gallon of water, or commercial Bordeaux powder diluted as recommended by the manufacturer.

Some insect I have never seen cuts a thin slice in skin of each peach, from which oozes a colorless syrup. What is it? (Massachusetts.)   The cuts are made by the plum curculio, a snout beetle. (See Plum; also spray schedule above.)

Oriental peach moth is attacking 2-year-old peach trees; 3 different varieties. What remedy should be used? (Ohio.) This small gray moth with chocolate markings lays her eggs in the leaves; the young worms bore in the twigs, later generations attacking fruit. Peaches that ripen early, like Elbertas, are not much injured. Control by spray is difficult and not very effective. Peach-borer treatments kill some moths, as do cleaning up fruit mummies and weeds and early cultivation of soil.

Green tips of my peach trees died back all last summer; little white worms inside shoots; told it was caused by tarnished plant bug; any control? (Indiana.)   Tarnished plant bugs do sting peach twigs and turn them black. There is little control except to destroy weeds and sometimes dust with sulphur. I think, however, since there were worms in the twigs it was the Oriental fruit moth; this kills back the twigs also. (See previous question.)

What to do for yellows in young peach trees? (Alabama.) Yellows may be due to a virus or to an alkaline soil. Ask your county agent for diagnosis and help.

Why do our peach seeds split, causing the peach to rot? What remedy? (Washington.)   There is a physiological disease called split pit which results in rotting embryos and a gummosis of the fruit. The cause and remedy are not exactly clear, but the symptoms are more pronounced on Phillip's Cling variety and in years of a light crop. It is suggested that thinning be delayed 5 weeks after pits start to harden.

What new spray is used to prevent dropping of premature fruits such as peaches? (Ohio.)   Hormone sprays are used to prevent premature dropping of some fruits, usually apples. One such spray is sold under the name of Fruitone.

PEAR

What is the cause of fire blight in pear and apple trees? (Iowa.)   Bacteria cause the disease but there are contributing factors. The more vigorous a tree the more susceptible it is to fire blight because the bacteria prefer succulent tissue. Do not overfertilize (fall feeding is safer than spring), do not prune heavily, and do not cultivate around the trees. Some varieties, like Kieffer, are more or less immune.

Will spraying a pear tree while dormant check fire blight? There is no way to have all the diseased parts pruned out without ruining the tree. (New Mexico.)   You will lose the tree anyway, if you do not have the diseased parts cut out, perhaps even if you do. The fire-blight bacteria are not on the outside, to be killed there by a spray, but are working down inside the twigs in the vascular system. Cut out *below* the infected portion of twigs and scrape away all dead wood from cankers on main trunks and large limbs. Paint these wounds with Bordeaux paint, made by stirring raw linseed oil into dry powder. In the spring the bacteria ooze out from dead twigs and cankers in little droplets which attract the bees. The bees, flying from blossom to blossom, carry around the bacteria and cause new infection. From blighted blossom clusters the bacteria work down inside the twigs into main branches. Spraying with 1–3–50 Bordeaux mixture when the blooms are open helps prevent this new infection. Break out all blighted blossom clusters.

Why did a few branches on my young pear tree die after fruit was hanging on? (Pennsylvania.)   Probably fire blight. It may have been secondary infection from twigs or fruit blighted in primary early-spring infection.

Is there any practical remedy for curing fire blight on pear foliage? (Connecticut.)   No. If you see blighted foliage, you must cut the whole branch out 6 ins. or more below the part that looks burned or blighted.

Is there anything that will cure pear blight? I had 4 dwarf trees; when the first one had it, I cut it down; the others all have it now. (Illinois.)   You cannot "cure" fire blight by any method. All you can do is to clean up infected parts and spray to prevent reinfection through the blossoms. Were you very careful to disinfect your tools after cutting down the diseased tree before working on the others?

I planted some pear trees in 20-ft. square space of apple trees. Am told it will give the blight. Would you leave them, take them out, or use some spray to prevent it? (Indiana.)   Pears are much more susceptible to fire blight than apples, and if blight is in your neighborhood, which is more than likely, they will probably acquire the disease first, after which bees may carry it to your apple trees; your pruning shears will carry it unless you disinfect them between cuts. Formalin at a 1 to 20 dilution makes a good disinfectant. If you leave your pears where they are, plan on a blossom spray as described above.

What may I spray on a pear tree to kill a snail-like insect that kills the foliage? (Ohio.)   This is the pear slug, whose slimy dark green to orange larvae skeletonize the leaves before they turn into sawfly adults. If pears are getting the regular apple-spray schedule, slugs will be controlled, or a separate spray of lead arsenate (1½ tablespoons to 1 gal. water) may be applied as soon as young slugs are noticed.

How can I get rid of the pear and plum leaf slugs? (California.)   The pear slug attacks pear, plum, and cherry. It may be killed by any kind of finely ground dust, but 1 to 2 per cent nicotine dust is preferable. It may also be killed by regular basic lead-arsenate sprays. But to avoid poisonous residue on fruit the arsenate sprays should be used in California either in early spring or after harvest.

How can I get rid of bugs on the pear tree—little worms eating the leaves? (New York.)   See two previous questions for treatment of pear slug.

Will you please give me information about pear psylla? (Massachusetts.)   The pear psylla is the most serious pest of pears in the Northeast and has been recently reported from Washington and Idaho. The adult psyllids are only 1/10 in. long, reddish-brown with rooflike transparent wings. They live over winter under the bark and in orchard debris, emerging in early spring to lay eggs in cracks in the bark and on the buds; eggs hatch into yellow nymphs which suck sap from leaf and fruit stems and leaves. To control, spray with miscible oil or oil emulsion before growth starts, as for scale. Lime sulphur 1 to 9 dilution, applied very thoroughly, will also prevent eggs hatching.

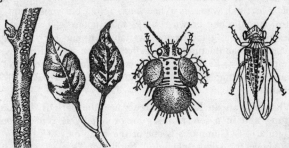

Pear Psylla. The adult (right) is a reddish-brown fly with transparent wings.

About the first of August the leaves of my young dwarf pear turned black and fell off. What caused this? (Maryland.) The pear psylla, whose sucking causes defoliation. The black discoloration was due to a sooty mold, growing in honeydew surrounding the psylla nymphs. A summer spray of weak Bordeaux mixture and nicotine sulfate is sometimes helpful if the psylla were not cleaned up by a dormant spray.

Is it proper to spray in winter a pear tree which was covered with a sort of mildew during the summer, or wait until spring? (Maryland.) If you mean a true mildew, i.e., a white coating on the leaves, summer sulphur sprays or dusts will control it, but more likely you refer to the blighted effect produced by pear psylla. (See above.)

PLUM

A fungus gathers on our plums each year and the fruit rots on the tree as soon as it starts to ripen. Why? (Michigan.) This is brown rot of stone fruits, a fungous disease very common on peaches, plums, and cherries and sometimes injurious to apples as well. In early spring spores are sent up from cup-shaped fruiting bodies growing out of old mummied fruits in the soil. The spores infect young fruits, producing a grayish mold. These are summer spores which are splashed by rain or carried by wind to infect other ripening fruits. Diseased fruits wrinkle and either hang on the trees or drop to the ground as "mummies."

Will you please tell me how to spray plum trees so that fruit will not rot and drop before ripening? (Illinois.)   Sulphur sprays or dusts are usually used to control brown rot. The following schedule may be used for plums: 1. *Dormant*—before the buds swell, to control scales and black knot, 1½ cups lime sulphur in 1 gal. water. 2. When *husks split* from young fruit, to control curculio and brown rot, 1½ tablespoons lead arsenate, 3 tablespoons lime, 3 tablespoons wettable sulphur (or as recommended by manufacturer) per gallon. 3. *Ten days* after No. 2, same mixture. 4. *Every 10 to 14 days* after No. 3, if brown rot is serious, use wettable sulphur and lime as in No. 2 but no lead arsenate.

What do you do for plum tree when the bark is dark and splitting and in a few places gum or a jelly is running out? (**Virginia.**)   Gummosis is one of the symptoms of brown rot. (See above for spray schedule.) Sanitation is even more important than spraying. Every mummied fruit fallen to the ground or left on the tree should be removed and burned.

How early do you spray plum trees? (Michigan.)   If there is scale, especially San Jose scale, use a dormant spray, either lime sulphur or oil, although this is needed only in occasional years. You can put on a pre-blossom or cluster-bud spray of wettable sulphur and lead arsenate, but for the home garden the calyx or husk-split stage may be early enough to start spraying.

What is the chemical that is put around plum trees to prevent curculio? (**Florida.**)   The curculio, a small, gray, humpbacked snout beetle is the cause of wormy plums. I do not know of any chemical for the soil, but keeping it well cultivated to destroy pupae and larvae in their earth cells and picking up and burning all dropped fruits are very important in controlling this serious pest. The lead arsenate in the spray schedule given above is for the curculio.

What is the best spray for plums that will not be injurious to small apiary in orchard? (Iowa.)   The spray schedule is so adjusted that there will be no poison on the open flowers when the bees go after nectar. (See above.)

QUINCE

When and with what material should quince trees be sprayed? (**New York.**)   A spray schedule for New York State calls for a dormant oil spray if lecanium scale is present, a pink spray of 1 to 40 lime sulphur, a calyx spray of lime sulphur with 2 tablespoons lead arsenate, 5 tablespoons lime to gallon of water to control leaf blight, leaf spot, codling moth, and Oriental fruit moth. Repeat calyx spray at 2-week intervals until there is danger of arsenical residue.

RASPBERRY

What are the various diseases that attack black raspberries? How can they be controlled? (Ohio.) Virus diseases—green mosaic, yellow mosaic, leaf curl, streak. Fungous diseases— verticillium wilt, orange rust, anthracnose, cane blight, spur blight, powdery mildew, leaf spot, bacterial crown gall. Most of these are controlled by sanitary measures: removing infected plants or plant parts. Many raspberry diseases are distributed in planting stock. A dormant spray of lime-sulphur and pre-blossom and after-blossom sprays of Bordeaux mixture will help control anthracnose and cane blight.

During the bearing season we noticed overnight a bush or two stricken as if with heavy frost or a blowtorch, then turning black and drying up. We could find no insects. What caused this? (Michigan.) This is cane blight, caused by a fungus which frequently enters through insect wounds. Remove and burn blighted parts immediately, destroy fruiting canes after harvest; avoid sites with poor air and soil drainage; control weeds; spray with lime sulphur, when buds show silver, for a dormant spray, and with 2-4-50 Bordeaux mixture 1 week before, again immediately after blossoming, and again after harvest.

How do I control orange rust on boysenberries? (New York.) Orange rust is a systemic disease, that is, the rust fungus is found throughout the whole plant, and not just on the leaves. Infected plants never recover; there is no control by spraying. Pull out diseased plants by the roots and burn before the rusty spores are shed to infect near-by brambles.

How can I rid my boysenberry vines of mildew? I used dry sulphur for 3 months but some of the runners died and the vines are all white. (Washington.) Try spraying with summer-strength lime sulphur or with wettable sulphur with a sticker. Consult your county agent for the best spray for your locality.

How can I get rid of crown gall without having to throw away all of my berry bushes? (Illinois.) You can't get rid of it. Even if you pull up these bushes, the bacteria will live in the soil for some years. Get healthy bushes and plant in a new location. Never bring in diseased stock from a nursery; refuse plants showing any signs of enlargements or galls.

What about insects on raspberries? (Wyoming.) Raspberry pests in Wyoming includes aphids, false chinch bug, fruitworms, grasshoppers, leaf hoppers, leaf slugs, legume bugs, mites, scales, strawberry leaf roller, and root weevil. Your county agent will help you work out a schedule for control of pests most destructive in your garden.

Some insect cuts rings about ¼ in. apart on my red raspberry canes and deposits its eggs between. What is the insect and its control? (Ohio.)   This is the raspberry cane borer. The adult is a black-and-yellow beetle who deposits her eggs in new growth after first encircling the stem with 2 rows of punctures. The girdled tips wilt, and unless they are cut out the young borers work down the canes. Cut and burn all infested portions; cut out old canes after harvest.

Do red raspberries have little worms in the caps? (Ohio.) Yes, these are the grubs of the raspberry fruitworm. The adult is a light-brown beetle that feeds and lays eggs on blossoms. Dust with 85 to 15 hydrated lime-lead arsenate dust as the blossom clusters are forming, repeat in 10 days.

Is there anything that can be grown to attract Japanese beetles away from raspberry bushes? (New Jersey.)   They exert such a potent attraction I doubt if even soybeans would entice them away. Pick your raspberries early in the morning and before beetles are active and keep bushes dusted with lime.

STRAWBERRY

How can you keep birds out of strawberry beds? (Illinois.) Cover the beds with tobacco cloth or cheesecloth.

What is the strawberry weevil? (New York.)   The strawberry weevil is a dark, reddish-brown to black, small-snout beetle. It hibernates in rubbish in hedgerows and perhaps under the mulch in strawberry beds. It lays an egg in an unopened bud and causes it to fall by cutting the pedicel. The grub feeds on pollen and pupates inside the bud, going into hibernation in midsummer. Dust with 80 to 20 hydrated lime-calcium arsenate dust in early May when the buds are first cut off and again 7 to 10 days later. Dust with pyrethrum or rotenone, if available, after fruits start to form.

What causes strawberries to wilt and die just when in fruit? Roots turn yellow, brittle, and rot. (Wisconsin.)   White grubs working on the roots will cause strawberries to wilt. These are most serious in land turned over from sod but may linger in soil in cultivation. They may be kept from injuring strawberries by putting a mixture of 1 part lead arsenate in 20 parts sand around the roots as each plant is set, using 1½ ozs. of the mixture per plant. If no grubs are present, it may be a fungous root rot, in which case new plants should be set in fresh soil.

How may I keep white grubs from destroying roots of new strawberry plants? (Missouri.)   Set out in a mixture of lead arsenate and sand. (See previous question.)

What is the small black beetle that attacks our strawberries? (Illinois.)   There are several beetle possibilities on strawberries. This one may be the adult of one of the strawberry root weevils. The grubs feed on the roots; later the weevils feed on the plants at night. A special weevil bait, sold as Go-West, may be scattered around the plants after harvest.

How do you deal with strawberry leaf roller? (Iowa.)   This is a small greenish caterpillar which draws the leaflet together with a silken thread, feeds inside, and causes it to turn brown and die. Spray with lead arsenate in early spring before larvae begin to fold the leaves. Rotenone dust may be used after fruits form. Burn leaves after crop is harvested.

Why do my strawberries turn white and the plants die? (Wyoming.)   Chlorosis either from a virus disease or too-alkaline soil. Send a specimen and a soil sample to your Experiment Station.

SECTION IX

Regional Garden Problems

(Arranged by States)

INTRODUCTION

BY R. S. LEMMON

AMONG the thousands of questions which had to be sorted and organized in the preparation of this volume, there were many that dealt with problems quite local in character.

To the editors it has seemed best to retain this material, so far as possible, for the value to many readers of its local application. The most practical way to do this seemed to be to arrange the questions by states.

Climatic and soil conditions, of course, do not follow state lines. Even within state boundaries such conditions may vary to a very great degree. Altitude, the direction of prevailing winds, the proximity of large bodies of water—all these and many other factors enter into the picture.

However, a certain amount of generalization based on the broad factors of latitude, topography, and the prevailing movements of large bodies of air can properly be applied to the climate of any given state. The relation of this fact to the growing of plants in any particular section of the country is obvious.

The residents of different states will find in these pages much information that will be of use to them. But may we emphasize again, wherever some particular local problem is involved, the importance of consultation with some local authority, such as one's county agent, or State Agricultural College or Experiment Station. The locations of the latter are given on page 1407. Local seedmen or nurserymen are also convenient, and usually reliable, sources of information.

ALABAMA

What do you consider good group plantings of PERENNIALS and ANNUALS, separately and mixed? Daylilies and angelonia; physostegia and shastadaisies; violets and zephyranthes; verbena and bouncing bet. For color combinations of annuals blended to taste try pink larkspur faced down with deep-blue petunias; lupines edged with pansies. The possibilities are limitless.

What FLOWERS can we grow to send to shut-ins during winter months? Pansies in little grape or strawberry boxes. Freesias, Paperwhite Narcissus bulbs in small bowls of pebbles, wanderingjew in attractive little pots, and many different kinds of easy-to-grow but much-appreciated succulents.

What APPLE can be raised in Alabama as a successful commercial venture? In extreme northern Alabama, Delicious, Black Twig, Jonathan, McIntosh, and several other varieties of apples should grow successfully.

When is the best time to set out AZALEAS and in what type of soil, for best results in this section? It is the custom, but not essential, to move azaleas when they are in full bloom. Balled plants should be moved carefully into beds that have been prepared with rotted leaves, rotted wood, and aluminum sulfate, and that are entirely free from lime. Be sure to set the plants at exactly the same level they grew in the nursery, and water well.

I am told that my AZALEAS and CAMELLIAS will do better if I pile oak leaves around them. Is this true? Yes. These plants succeed much better under a mulch than they do with clean cultivation. Oak leaves are excellent when applied about 4 ins. thick. As the leaves decompose and the mulch becomes more shallow, pile on more leaves to keep the blanket up to the original thickness. A mulch retains moisture, prevents extremes of temperature, and discourages weeds.

What are some of the best BULBS for fall planting on the Gulf Coast? Calla, cooperia, hemerocallis, hybrid amaryllis, iris species (native), leucojum, lilium, morea, narcissus, and zephyranthes.

Will AZALEAMUMS succeed in the Birmingham area? Yes, these popular garden perennials do well in this locality.

What can I do for the powdery mildew on my CRAPE-MYRTLE? At first signs spray with lime-sulphur solution and repeat after a week or so. Sometimes dusting with dusting grade sulphur will do as well, but it must be carefully applied after each rain until the mildew is under control.

Are any DAYLILIES evergreen in southern Alabama? Yes, many of the choice new hybrids are evergreen and are, therefore, of much value in the winter garden effect.

What sprays are recommended for various scales and insects common to FRUIT trees, and when should they be applied in middle Georgia? Lime-sulphur spray, obtainable from your seed store, is applied as a dormant spray in December to February. A light oil emulsion can be used as a summer spray.

Can FUCHSIA plants be left in ground outdoors during winter in the South? In certain sections and in certain well-protected places fuchsias may be grown as garden perennials. If they are growing in the ground, they will be much hardier, of course, than if they are plunged in their pots. As potted plants they are quite likely to freeze.

When should GLADIOLUS be planted in Montgomery, Alabama? February or March, so that newly emerging flower scapes will miss the late frosts.

When should Bermuda GRASS seed be planted? Sow in early spring if it can be watered; during the summer rains; or in early autumn if winter rye grass is not going to be used. When the grass shows definitely green, make a light application of a nitrogenous fertilizer and water in well. These feedings may be repeated at 4- or 5-week intervals during growing weather.

If GRASS (Bermuda or Centipede) grows around the base of camellias or azaleas, does it hurt them? It is better to maintain circles free of grass around the bushes. A mulch of peatmoss, bugasse, or leafmold placed on ground surface is very beneficial.

How can I eradicate Nut GRASS? Nut Grass is very difficult to eradicate in the lower South, but trials have shown that it can be discouraged to a marked degree if it is possible to grow a heavy cover of cowpeas on the plot for several summers after the annuals or bulbs have been lifted. Use Brabham or some other variety resistant to root knot, and sow the seeds as early in summer as the garden is vacant. Fertilize the cowpeas well and turn them under in October.

What HERBS are most suitable for southern Alabama? For fall: anise, chives, Winter Savory, sage, and dill. For spring: Sweet Basil, Summer Savory, Sweet Fennel, coriander, thyme, and Sweet Marjoram.

Can we make Nada IRIS bloom in this locality? As both parents like a moist, rich soil and a shady location, there should be no reason why Nada will not grow well if these conditions are furnished.

What are cultural requirements for Japanese IRISES in this state? Japanese irises prefer a moisture-retentive soil of slightly acid reaction. The roots may be planted after flowering, or during the autumn and winter. Applications of a plant food in March, May, and July should take care of nutritional needs; a mulch is highly desirable.

What is the best fertilizer for NANDINAS? I have strong, healthy plants, but the berries dry up and fall off before they turn red. Any good commercial fertilizer mixture should suit nandinas. An application in January, hoed or spaded in, and another in June to mature the new growth, should be adequate under normal garden conditions. Nandina berries will color best in the full sun; they may be destroyed by very low temperatures.

Can ORANGES be grown along the Gulf in Alabama and Mississippi? Yes. Satsuma Oranges are dwarf citrus trees that belong to the kid-glove group. These are quite hardy, and when budded on hardy trifoliate stock will produce excellent early oranges along the upper Gulf coast.

What is the proper method for growing PANSIES from seed in the South? Pansies are cool-weather annuals and the seeds will not germinate well in the warm weather of early autumn. Seeds sown after the weather turns cool in October or early November germinate well and give flowering plants in April and May. Sometimes germination in warm weather can be hastened by placing a small seed flat, properly prepared, in the refrigerator for a week or so.

Will PEONIES grow well in Alabama? Was told that they grow best near salt water. We are quite inland. Peonies are temperate-zone plants and in many parts of the lower South will not succeed. It is not the proximity of salt water that assures success with peonies, but a combination of soil and a long, cold winter without warm breaks that will guarantee a complete dormancy in the peony crown.

Why are RHODODENDRONS practically failures in the lower South, where soil conditions appear to be ideal, as azaleas and the white dogwood grow and bloom luxuriously? In the South there is not a sufficiently long or sufficiently severe winter season for rhododendrons. Soil conditions may be ideal but climatic conditions are definitely not right for these plants.

What ROCK GARDEN PLANTS will grow in partial shade in central Alabama? Most rock gardens are exposed to full sun, and the usual list of plants for rock gardens include few shade-loving species. There are many, however, which do excellently in partial shade. You could make a fine collection from the wildflowers of your locality. Deep pockets of earth may be prepared for hardy ferns, to be used as a dominant green note. Besides wild flowers you could add sweet violets, periwinkles, English Ivy, lily-of-the-valley, ladyslipper orchids, and practically all of the columbines. For taller specimens try hydrangeas, Flowering Dogwood, spicebush, sweetshrub (Calycanthus), and the small native evergreens and azaleas. Many other plants grow fairly well in partial shade but do not bloom so freely as in sunnier locations.

What about planting ROSES deeper than usual in the South? In this locality tests have showed that it is much better to set roses at exactly the same depth that they grew in the nursery.

When should bush ROSES be pruned in central Alabama? In February or in March, just before growth commences. Head the canes back to 4 or 5 good strong eyes, leaving 4 or 5 good canes if you can. It is usually suggested that the pruning cuts be made about ½ in. above a strong eye that points away from the center of the plant.

I have been told I cannot grow TULIPS on account of the winter temperatures here. Is this true? Yes. Tulips cannot be successfully grown in the deep South. They require several months of cold weather and a cool spring to develop normally.

ARIZONA

What are the characteristics of the SOILS of Arizona, Colorado, and New Mexico? The whole Southwest region has, except for the mountain areas, but little forests or other vegetation to provide humus. Hence, in general, the soil, whether sand, silt, clay, or *Caliche,* requires the addition of much humus. The compost pile is very necessary here. Peatmoss, rotted strawy manure, any decayed vegetation is useful. One successful gardener in central New Mexico began with a half acre of *Caliche*—shale clay. She first put on a heavy layer of dairy manure, had a team plow and harrow this. Next came 20 bales of peatmoss. A surface mulch of peatmoss and manure each fall with constant additions from the compost pile keeps her garden growing and blooming with a lushness unbelievable when one sees the surrounding soil and vegetation. The lack of humidity in the air, as well as low rainfall, makes much watering necessary. Incorporation into the soil of generous amounts of humus helps it to retain moisture and so reduces labor of watering.

What are the best FLOWERING plants to stand Arizona desert heat? Perennials that flower early, followed by annuals that can stand heat and dry air. Native plants should be most satisfactory. Such early perennials as dwarf phlox; dianthus, iris, euphorbia, oenothera. Annuals: verbena, zinnia, marigold, mesembryanthemum, mirabilis, petunia, portulaca, salvia, *Xanthisma texanum* (Star of Texas), venidium, xeranthemum.

What kind of FLOWERS can be planted in the fall in high altitude (7,000 ft.) where it is very cold? Fall planting of perennials is more successful in this climate if done early—even before the first killing frost. Plant shrubs and roses either fall or early spring. For fall planting: lilies, narcissus, peonies, pyrethrum, iris, campanulas, tulips, phlox, dianthus, dictamnus, heliopsis. Hybrid tea roses can be planted, if covered during the winter. Polyantha and floribunda roses should be quite satisfactory, and will give a long season's bloom and require little or no winter protection. Among the sturdiest are: Else Poulsen, Improved Lafayette, Kirsten Poulsen, Gloria Mundi, World's Fair. Climbing roses are more difficult, since in your climate they require protection from winter sun. Some of the hardiest are: American Pillar, Silver Moon, Tausendschon, Dr. W. Van Fleet, Paul's Scarlet Climber.

Can you advise me as to a good CLIMBER, either annual or perennial? I live in a hot, dry climate, and the season is long. Perennial climbers: *Bignonia radicans* (trumpetvine), *Clematis texensis, Lonicera heckrotti, Pueraria thunbergiana* (Kudzuvine). On north exposure: *Euonymus radicans vegetus, Ficus pumila*. Annual climbers: Cardinalclimber, Canaryclimber, morningglory, moonflower, *Solanum jasminoides*.

When is the best time to plant CHRYSANTHEMUMS in Arizona? Spring. Even late-spring transplanting brings earlier and more profuse bloom than if the plants are left undisturbed.

Can wild "INDIAN PAINTBRUSH" be transplanted and if so, how and when? Indian Paintbrush (*Castilleja collina*) is partially a parasite. To transplant successfully its host must be transplanted with it. *Chrysothamnus* (rabbitbrush) is one host of *Castilleja collina*. Transplant any time when ground is sufficiently moist to make a ball. They move easily in full bloom if kept well watered. Dig a trench around the plant, then lift it with a ball or clump not less than 1 ft. in diameter, taking with it any other plants contained in the ball.

Can I grow LILIUM bakerianum in Arizona?   *Lilium bakerianum* is listed among the difficult ones. Since it is a stem-rooting species, bulbs should be planted about 3 times their own depth. To prevent drying, as well as alternate freezing and thawing, a mulch is necessary. In its western China home it grows on steep, loamy slopes among shrubs and grasses.

When is the proper time to plant LILY bulbs in our Southern country?   Time to plant lily bulbs is determined by time of dormancy of the bulbs rather than by climate of their new home. *Lilium candidum* is planted in August and September. Top growth begins immediately. Plant lilies whose bulbs mature later, in September to November, such as: *Lilium regale, tenuifolium (pumilum), concolor, henryi, humboldti, tigrinum, croceum, umbellatum.*

What climbing ROSE will do the best here?   All the climbing forms of hybrid perpetuals and hybrid teas should do well. Some that are grown successfully in the Southwest are: Paul's Scarlet Climber, Silver Moon, Climbing Dainty Bess, Climbing Hadley, Climbing Talisman, American Pillar, Gardenia, and Mme. Gregoire Staechelin. Protection from winter sun may be necessary on a southern exposure. Spruce branches or cornstalks may be woven into rose trellis, or roses, support and all, may be laid on ground and covered.

ARKANSAS

Will DELPHINIUM and Oriental poppies grow in this part of the country?   Yes. *Delphinium belladonna, D. bellamosum* and the Chinese Delphinium are more likely to prosper than some of the fancy hybrids.

What flowers can I plant in a COCO-GRASS-infested area?   Few plants have the persistence of these stoloniferous grasses. Any that have, are little short of weeds themselves. Some that may fight their way are: Bishops goutweed (*Aegopodium variegatum*), Kenilworth Ivy, buttercup, Ageratum Little Gem, strawberry, and Moneywort (*Lysimachia nummularia*).

Can I put POINSETTIA plants outdoors in summer?   They can be put out during warm weather, in a spot with sunshine, but sheltered from strong winds. Be sure to bring them in in the fall before night temperatures drop below 55° to 60° F.

What is a good yellow ROSE that will bloom monthly?
Golden Dawn and Soeur Therese.

Are Marechal Niel ROSES out of style? In a way, yes.
They are still grown in the South, but newer varieties of yellow
climbers are often grown now, whereas Marechal Niel once had
the field to itself. In the North it is not hardy.

CALIFORNIA

SOIL AND FERTILIZER

What can I mix with adobe ground to make a garden?
Two very good materials to mix with adobe soil are decomposed
granite and bean straw. A 3-in. layer of granite, dug in deeply,
followed by a deeper layer of bean straw, also dug in deeply, will
help greatly. Decomposition of the straw should be permitted to
advance well before planting is done. This treatment will not improve drainage, for adobe is generally too deep.

What kind of fertilizer is best for adobe soil? The best
fertilizer for any soil is organic, either dairy, horse, or chicken
manure. In addition use a complete commercial fertilizer. Acid
phosphate will overcome the general lack of phosphate in California soil.

What is the treatment for hard, black soil, near Los Angeles?
Soil conditioners and fertilizers have already been discussed. (See
Section I.) The most important consideration of all is in respect
to water. First, don't ever work adobe soil when it is wet, for it
will cake and harden, and be put out of condition for a long
time. Second, do not overirrigate, for it drains poorly. Check the
soil to see how deeply it has dried, and aim to irrigate just enough
to moisten the soil to that depth. Cultivate as soon as the soil
surface is dry.

How can adobe soil be made to produce? See previous
questions. Alkalinity must also be considered. If plants look
yellow and stunted, there may be an alkaline condition. Soil sulphur or ferrous sulfate, at the rate of 2 lbs. per 100 sq. ft., will
reduce the alkalinity. More or less may be used yearly, after the
first application is made as a test. Normally, abode soil produces
heavily.

**It is cold and often foggy here, and this seems to slow plant
growth down. Would an extra amount of fertilizer give plants
beneficial warmth?** Commercial fertilizers will not supply

any warmth to the soil. However, nitrogen fertilizer will stimulate growth if the soil is not too cold, and phosphorus and potash may be used to hasten maturity.

We had to import soil for our garden, but now it is worn out. Can it be improved?   The lack of humus in most California soils is the cause. The imported soil may have had some, but the thin layer was stripped very soon. Soils wear out from lack of humus. Addition of bean straw, manures, or peatmoss would have helped maintain the purchased soil.

What can be done with soil spoiled by the oil from pods, leaves, and bark of eucalyptus trees?   First clean off all debris, then turn the soil as deeply as possible. Permit rains and heavy waterings to leach out the toxic oils. After lying fallow over winter, the soil should be in fair condition. Constant raking must be practiced to keep off the debris.

My soil is light, has no clay subsoil, and requires too much water. How can I use less?   The problem is not one of using less so much as of *losing* less. Add as much humus as possible. Cultivate as soon as the surface is dry. In irrigating, do not wet the soil too deeply for annuals, vegetables, or shallow-rooted plants, for the water will drain away. Trees and shrubs should be irrigated deeply and seldom, to encourage deep rooting.

What is a good book on soils and fertilizers for California? Some of the very best information on the subject is to be found in bulletins of the State Agricultural College, at Berkeley, California.

PLANNING AND ENVIRONMENT

Can one make an attractive garden with perennials alone? It often seems like less work to grow perennials, but if results are desired, they involve about as much work as annuals. One should start off with a good shrub background, not too tall, to add to the appearance and break the wind. Then select perennials that are proven in your region. Select them for durability, successive blooming dates, and reasonably clean habit. Interplant with bulbs like lilies, muscaris (grapehyacinths), watsonias, callas, narcissi, and others that grow for several years without lifting.

What are the best flowers for winter, spring, summer, and fall? This could make a long list, but here are some good ones: Spring: sweetpeas, freesias, narcissi, tulips, snapdragons. Summer: watsonias, dahlias, gladioli, marigolds, and zinnias. Fall: asters and chrysanthemums. Winter: sweetpeas, calendulas, snapdragons, and stocks.

Could you give a list of small perennials like geum and sweet-william? Such a list would include shastadaisies, *Heuchera sanguinea, Moraea bicolor,* trollius, platycodon, coreopsis, *Oenothera speciosa,* callas, physostegia, and, above all, *Aster frikarti.*

What are some good border flowers or plants, not over 12 ins. high? Annuals which might answer the purpose are lobelia, ageratum, *Tagetes pumila,* sweet alyssum, and *Phlox drummondi.* Perennials could be sunroses, *Chrysanthemum mawi, Nierembergia hippomanica,* coralbells, and gazania.

What flowers will grow in pots in the sun all day? The reason most plants fail under these conditions is the rapid drying of the soil. Geraniums and petunias do the best, although portulaca is often used. They all need plenty of water under the circumstances.

What plants will hold adobe soil on hillsides? Nothing surpasses *Mesembryanthemum edule* for this purpose; but other good ones would be *M. floribunda,* honeysuckle, creeping lantana, Mermaid Rose, and St. Augustinegrass.

What are good plants for adobe soil, especially in the sun? As a general rule, the same plants will grow in adobe as in any other soil, but the difficulty caused by poor drainage eliminates some. The doubtful type of plant would include choiseya, cistus, caesalpinia, helianthemum, leptospermum, and others known for their love of dry conditions.

What flowers or shrubs would do well on the west side of the house where the temperature sometimes reaches 140° F.? In such hot, dry spots one must go in for heat-loving plants. Leptospermum, oleander, lantana, bougainvillea, cistus species, plumbago, *Cotoneaster parnayi,* diosma, felicia, helianthemum, leucophyllum, *Pittosporum tobira, Viburnum suspensum* and *V. tinus,* all should do well. For annuals, marigolds, petunias, portulacas, and sunroses will give summer color.

What low perennial may be planted in the shady strip between drive and house? *Fragaria chiloensis* would be a happy choice. It is a creeper with bright-green foliage and bright-red fruits. *Campanula mayi* or *Saxifraga crassifolia* would give some color, but would grow 12 ins. to 15 ins. tall. *Ajuga repens* would also do very well.

What can be grown under eucalyptus trees? The heavy demand for food and water by the eucalyptus and the toxic effect of its leaves and bark make trouble for most plants. Grass, heavily fed and watered, is satisfactory, for debris can be easily raked off.

English Ivy is often used as a ground cover, but hand-picking of debris is necessary.

My house faces southwest, and the northeast corner gets little sun. What plants would do well there?   This is an ideal spot for some of the shrubs that do not like full sun, especially camellias, azaleas, gardenias, Star Jasmines, fuchsias, *Daphne odora,* hydrangeas, eranthemums, ginger-lilies, English Holly, and nandina.

What flowers or vines will grow on the north side of our house, where it is shady all the time?   There are many plants that grow well in the shade, the degree of shade being a limiting factor. Camellias, fuchsias, begonias, violets, ferns, *Saxifraga crassifolia* all do well up to a certain amount of shade. If very dense, use ferns, aucuba, sarcococca, and aspidistra.

We live under oaks, and find violets, iris, ferns, coleus, and begonias growing fine. What would do well in sunny spots in such soil?   In sunny spots near oaks most plants should thrive. If coleus and begonias overwinter, it would indicate a frost-free area, so try primulas, cinerarias, calceolarias, and cyclamen for winter. In the shade, try azaleas and camellias, for they should do well. In summer, avoid rank-growing annuals, but try the rest.

What climber would grow on the wall of a summerhouse facing the ocean near Los Angeles?   Few climbers compare with *Bignonia cherere* as a vine under such circumstances. If the large-leaved type is used, it has beautiful foliage every day of the year, and for most of the year it produces huge red trumpets of bloom. It does not object to the salt breezes. It will need a trellis till it has something to hold on to.

What vine similar to trumpetvine can I put on the north side of my house?   The trumpetvine itself, *Bignonia cherere,* does very well on the north, as will also *Bignonia violacea, Thunbergia grandiflora,* and *Distictis lactiflora,* all of lavender and blue shades. *Tecomaria capensis,* even more vivid than the trumpetvine, does well too. None of these like heavy shade, but normal conditions on the north are satisfactory. All are equally hardy.

LAWN

How can I grow a beautiful dichondra lawn?   The soil should be well enriched and perfectly graded. The plants are purchased in flats. They are divided with a knife into 2-in. or 3-in. squares. Planted about a foot apart, and well watered, these will soon spread. Frequent feedings with a balanced commercial fertilizer and plenty of water are needed to keep the lawn green. It should be cut 3 or 4 times a year. The fussy care which it requires is fast stopping the fad for this type of lawn.

What time of year is the best for starting a lawn in southern California? A lawn may be started at any time, but the best time is fall—September or October. This will establish the plants well before heavy rains and give a good turf before the summer's heat.

What is the best lawn seed to use? There is much discussion about this, but most people like blue grass, generally in a mixture of Meadow Fescue and redtop. Perennial Rye Grass must be renewed every few years. By all means buy the very best seed obtainable from a good seed house.

How much seed should be used? Oversowing of seed gives poor results, for the plants crowd themselves out. Six lbs. of blue grass per 1,000 sq. ft. is plenty, and 8 lbs. of Perennial Rye Grass.

My lawn is shady, and very damp and soggy. Should I reseed bare spots? Some means should be used to drain the soil better, for the lawn will never do well under such conditions. Regrading may do the trick; or drain tile may have to be used. There are some good shady grass mixtures on the market.

How do you renovate an old lawn infested with "devilgrass"? It can hardly be eliminated, for a tiny piece of root starts a new plant. The customary procedure is to hire a nurseryman to run a renovator over the lawn several times and rake out the roots as well as possible. This gives the new sowing a chance to fight the "devilgrass" (Bermuda Grass), though it will succumb again sooner or later.

How is a lawn of sagina moss made? *Sagina subulata* is not a moss, but a flowering plant. It is used as a shady ground cover. It must have light soil and good drainage. It may be planted at any time of the year, but preferably in spring. Flats may be purchased at some nurseries, and the plants are divided and planted quite closely. It has a serious failing in that it turns yellow in spots and must be replanted, but it is fairly permanent.

How can I get rid of the worm that causes small piles of mud all over my lawn? Add 1 lb. corrosive sublimate to 1 gal. of boiling water, and allow it to cool 1 hour. Then dilute with 4 gals. of cold water. Use 2½ pints of this solution with 50 gals. of water, and water the lawn copiously with a sprinkling can. This is very poisonous, so use care. Then sweep up the worms and remove them. If the lawn is small, this formula may be cut down, as long as the same proportions are kept.

HEDGES

What shrubs would make a good flowering hedge?   The list would be almost limitless in southern California, but some of the best would be abelias, white and red, *Cassia splendida, Plumbago capensis, Chalcis exotica, Choiseya ternata, Cotoneaster parnayi, Grewia caffra,* feijoa, pyracantha, *Solanum rantonetti, Viburnum suspensum* and *V. tinus,* and lantana. Properly cared for, a hedge of varicolored hibiscus may be beautiful. Oleanders, with pruning, work out well, especially the variety Mrs. Roeding.

How is a flowering hedge best planted?   Except for hibiscus, the plants mentioned could be planted from containers at any time. (Hibiscus should be well established before winter.) Allow plenty of room for each plant to develop into a good specimen. Drop a line, and stake out the center of each hole along it. Dig generous holes and add plenty of manure. In the rear, leave a good irrigation ditch. By all means carry on a program of pruning, so the hedge does not become an eyesore.

What are good plants for green hedges?   This would depend on the size required. For a very low hedge, nothing surpasses *Buxus japonica. Myrtus compacta* and *Ligustrum henryi* also make good low hedges. For a moderate-sized hedge, (up to 5 ft.) the Wax-Leaf Privet is unsurpassed. Boxwood is fine anywhere up to this height. For the tall hedge, *Pittosporum undulatum* outdoes any other. In hot, dry areas, *Ligustrum japonicum* is a tough, tall hedge.

Our Dwarf Eucalyptus windbreak blew over in a storm. What could we use that would be sturdier?   *Eucalyptus globulus compacta* is so shallow-rooted that it blows over easily. One good substitute is *E. cornuta lehmanni.* Another would be *E. sideroxylon rosea,* if it were topped out at about 20 ft. *Pittosporum undulatum* also makes a good windbreak if it need not be high.

SHRUBS

What shrubs may be planted in southern California in January and February?   Since most shrubs are grown in containers here, they may be planted at any time. Very tender plants, such as bougainvillea and hibiscus, are best planted later. In addition, roses and other deciduous shrubs are best planted while dormant. These are sold as "bare-root" plants.

What are some shrubs that would make good foundation plants?   Such a list should be made up of plants which will not cover the windows in a few years. Some good ones for sun are *Convolvulus cneorum, Correa speciosa, Juniperus tamariscifolia,*

Turraea obtusifolia—all of which grow very low. *Choiseya ternata, Murraya exotica, Viburnum suspensum, Myrsine africana, Myrtus compacta, Ligustrum indicum, Abelia floribunda, Diosma reevesi,* Gardenia Mystery, *Pittosporum tobira*—all of which grow to moderate size, and can be kept down easily by pruning.

Will you name some shrubs that are quick to grow and easy to care for around a new home? This is really the worst thing to do in California, as quick-growing shrubs around the house in 3 or 4 years make a jungle and a mess. Be patient, and a permanent effect may be obtained by using slower-growing, more durable material.

My shrubs and trees grow too fast. How can this be prevented? Overwatering and overfeeding cause too rank a growth. Do not use fertilizer for several years, and water just enough to keep plants from wilting.

TREES

What are some good evergreen trees for a small home in the Los Angeles area? The evergreen elm, *Ulmus parvifolia sempervirens,* tops the list. *Pittosporum undulatum* and *P. rhombifolium* give beautiful fruits, as well as being good foliage trees. *Jacaranda acutifolia,* nearly evergreen, has a mass of blue flowers in the spring. *Calodendrum capense,* a mass of pink flowers in summer, is a good tree. *Magnolia grandiflora* is everyone's favorite. For certain types of homes, olive trees have a fine character.

What kind of tree do you suggest putting in a front yard only 40 ft. wide? One of the finest trees is the evergreen elm, *Ulmus parvifolia sempervirens.* Care must be used in its purchase, for seedling forms vary too much. The best nurseries grow only from cuttings taken from fine trees.

What fruits are most likely to do well on the Pacific coast? There is no fruit that does not do well somewhere on the coast, except very tropical types. In the North, all the deciduous fruits, like apple, cherry, and plum, do very well. Further south, the evergreen fruit area begins, and citrus, avocados, and other subtropicals do well.

How do you cure curly leaf on trees? First investigate for the presence of aphids. Most so-called curly leaf is the result of these plant lice. They are easily controlled by a spray of nicotine sulfate, 1 to 300. If this is not the cause, it may be the curly-leaf virus, and in such a case immediately eradicate the diseased plant, for there is no cure, and it is contagious.

Where can one obtain information on tropical ornamentals?
Not many truly tropical plants thrive in southern California,
where subtropicals are the rule. Tropicals generally demand a
moist climate, with never any frost. They like light, moisture-
retentive soils. They desire at least partial shade. Obviously, lath
houses and conservatories are the answers. If attempts are to be
made to grow them, contact one of the large nurseries in southern
California which specialize in exotic material, and the State
Agricultural Experiment Station.

LATH HOUSE

**Would you please make suggestions for growing plants in a
lath house?**   On the whole, the plants that like shade prefer a
light soil containing leafmold, which provides good drainage. This
is often given by building raised beds and filling with prepared
soil. Careful attention must be given to watering, but the results
are worth while. Feeding should be done with cottonseed meal or
an acid fertilizer. Do not grow heavy vines on the lath.

What plants are grown in lath houses?   Camellias, fuchsias,
and begonias are raised by every lath-house owner. Other desirable subjects are gloxinias, streptocarpus, achimenes, caladiums, anthuriums, cyclamen, stephanotis, *Hoya carnosa,* and
sarcococca. Many orchids also do very well.

**What evergreen vine may I use over my lath house that will
not freeze easily?**   *Gelsemium sempervirens* is a good vine if
the temperature does not drop below 15° F. It has a light growth
that will not be too dense for the plants beneath, and in late
winter, is a mass of yellow bloom. It is very clean, and has re-
freshingly green foliage all year.

INDIVIDUAL PLANTS

Why doesn't my ALMOND tree bear?   A single tree never
bears; 2 varieties must be planted together to get pollinization.
Good combinations are Nonpareil and Ne Plus Ultra, or Ne Plus
Ultra and I. X. L.

**I have an ARBUTUS unedo which blooms but does not
set fruit. Why?**   Some arbutus do not bear well. It would be
well to investigate its environment before deciding that it is a
poor type. They like good drainage. They do not like to be
exposed to hot, dry winds; nor do they like an alkaline soil. If
conditions are favorable and the tree is healthy, then the seedling
is evidently a poor type.

I have an AVOCADO tree 8 years old. Why do the blooms

fall? There may be many factors. The tree may be still immature. Drainage may be poor. Overwatering or feeding before the fruits set may have forced off the bloom. Oil sprays are sometimes given at the wrong time, before the fruit is set.

My seedling AVOCADO has fruit. Will it be good? There is a chance that it will be good. All the good varieties were once seedlings. For new plantings, seedlings are not worth the gamble, when there are such fine varieties as Fuerte, Puebla, Nabal, Ryan, and others.

Should I destroy a seedling AVOCADO with black fruit, growing 8 ft. from another avocado? One tree or the other would be best removed, for the tops spread wide, and you would end up with 2 poor trees. The black fruit is typical of many fine kinds of avocados.

What time of the year should AVOCADOS be picked? Avocados are picked at any time of the year, depending on the varieties planted. For home use, they are best allowed to ripen on the trees. An avocado becomes somewhat soft when ripe.

Can AZALEAS be grown in southern California? Azaleas do beautifully with proper care. They should never be planted in full sun. A large amount of peatmoss should be mixed in the soil. Drainage must be perfect, and in heavy soils this means raising the plant above surrounding soil. During summer, water heavily, and feed generously with cottonseed meal or other acid fertilizer.

How may I encourage BANANAS to ripen in the Los Angeles area? First, types that fruit in this area should be purchased. Plant in a rich, well-drained spot that is protected from hot, dry winds. Keep the plant growing in healthy condition and fruit should ripen.

Is there any special care for BIRD-OF-PARADISE? Should it be pruned or divided? If you have it outdoors in your California garden, let it grow as it wants. Don't remove any but dead foliage, and don't divide before the foliage dies. Feed and water plentifully during summer.

How are BLACKBERRIES grown in California? Blackberries grow fairly well here, in heavy loam. Young plants are set out in early spring, about 3 ft. apart. The first growth is pinched when a few feet tall, to encourage branches which bear the fruit the next year. Each year canes that have fruited are cut out after harvesting. A mulch of manure in the spring and copious watering in the growing season are desirable.

Can BLUEBERRIES be grown in California? There are some places where they should grow well, but they seldom do. If you have a moist climate and cool winters, write to an Eastern nursery specializing in the new types, and try its recommendations.

What is the best care of BOXWOOD? Boxwood is a very easily grown plant. It likes a fertile soil, with plenty of organic fertilizer. It must never be allowed to become dry, for it will start to shed foliage. Frequent prunings or shearings will keep it dense. Be on the lookout for red spider, which mottles the foliage, and for scale. There are many sprays for red spider on the market, and scale is controlled by a 1½ per cent or 2 per cent oil spray in June or July.

How are BOYSENBERRIES grown? Plant in early spring, at least 5 ft. apart. Allow the vines to grow on the ground. Be generous with water and manure. Early the next spring tie the vines on trellises. As the berries start ripening, cut out new growth. After harvesting, cut off the vines which bore the fruit, and allow new growths to grow on the ground. These should be tied up early the following spring. Plenty of manure in the spring and plenty of water in the summer will produce tremendous crops.

In the West, should ranunculus BULBS be lifted after flowering? Yes; when they are dormant, they resent the water given other plants. When the foliage is yellowed and dry, they are ready for digging. Seedling-grown ranunculus give far superior bloom, but are troublesome to start.

What is the proper care for CALLAS in California? Callas are almost weeds here, except in bad frost areas. They enjoy a partial shade, but it is not necessary. They like a very rich soil and plenty of water and manure. They do not need a rest period. They may be divided at any time, but early fall is best.

Could you suggest a tree similar to the Deodar CEDAR? There are a number of fine coniferous trees for southern California. The Atlas Cedar and its blue variety the Canary Pine, the Aleppo Pine, the Stone Pine, the Monterey Pine, the Coast Redwood, and the California Incense Cedar, all do well in most sections.

When should CHRYSANTHEMUMS be planted, and how? New plants may be set out in the spring. They usually come in flats, and are planted about 12 ins. apart to the same depth they were growing. They enjoy a rich soil and reasonably generous watering. Pinch several times in summer to encourage branching and strong stems. Divide yearly, after blooming.

CITRUS FRUITS

We water our CITRUS trees by trenches and daily sprinkling. Is this too much?   Citrus trees do not need much water when once established. Overwatering forces growth at the expense of fruit, and may kill the tree. A tree several years planted need not be watered more than once a month. This will encourage deep rooting.

How old must a seedling citrus tree be before it bears fruit? This would be extremely variable, but a guess would be between 4 and 8 years. Seedlings are seldom worth growing.

Why does a young lemon tree produce hard lemons?   The first fruit of citrus trees often has a very thick rind. If the tree is a seedling, there is a good chance that it is a hard type. Citrus is one fruit that responds to good care. The Sunkist standard is maintained by rigid adherence to best cultural methods. These methods may be obtained from your local county agent.

I have a lemon that is losing its leaves. Why?   A very heavy crop of fruit often will strip a lemon of most of its foliage. Overwatering in poorly drained soil may cause the same result, but the poor health of the tree will be obvious. Less water and a feeding of commercial citrus food in the spring should bring it back. Lemon trees require very little water.

When should lemons be planted?   Lemons and other citrus and evergreen fruits are best planted in a well-worked soil in spring when cold weather is over and before summer's heat. A stake should be provided immediately, and some kind of shade on the south side to prevent sunburn on the trunk. Watering should be liberal the first year.

How are Meyer Lemons and dwarf limes grown?   There are no true dwarf limes, though the Rangpur is somewhat small. Lemons are quite hardy; limes definitely not. Where each can be grown, requirements are the same. Good drainage is essential. They want plenty of water when young, much less as they mature. Light feeding in spring is beneficial.

How can one tell the difference between young oranges and lemons?   The best way is to note the foliage. The lemon has much paler foliage than the orange, if the orange has been growing well. It sometimes is very difficult, except for an expert.

How does one apply lime around orange trees?   Lime is sprinkled on the soil rather heavily, as far out as the branches spread. It is cultivated in a few inches. Irrigation then carries it evenly through the soil. Ground limestone is the best form for amateurs.

What do you spray oranges with?   Under normal conditions, oranges are sprayed in summer with a miscible oil, usually a 2 per cent solution of light medium. This will kill red spider, scale, aphids, etc. It should never be applied when the temperature is above 90° F. in the shade. A perfect coverage is essential.

How do you prune COTONEASTERS to get good berries? Cotoneasters fruit on 1-year-old wood. After the berries fall, the wood on which they were borne should be cut back about 6 ins. from the ground. New growths for the following year's berries will spring freely from the stubs. Never be afraid to cut the sprays for decoration, for this can become a part of the pruning, if the stems are cut back to about 6 ins.

My COTONEASTERS, though faithfully watered and fertilized for over a year, have had no berries. Could they be "duds"?   Cotoneasters have perfect flowers, and are never "duds." Probably too much shade, too much water, too immature, or pruning off the flowering wood would be the difficulty. Since they are almost foolproof, patience will probably reward you with their showy berries. (See previous question.)

My CYPRESS tree yellows, then browns. It seems to be dying. Why?   This is a disease called Coryneum canker and has no permanent cure. Cutting out the first cankers to appear will retard the disease; as will a spray of 5–5–50 Bordeaux. Monterey Cypress is the most frequent victim. Forbes' Cypress seems resistant.

What special culture is needed for TREEFERNS?   The treefern, *Alsophila australis,* is not a temperamental plant, but it must be treated as a fern. It likes shade, leafmold, perfect drainage, and must never be allowed to dry out, even for an hour. During spring and summer it likes feedings of dried blood or liquid dairy manure.

How often should FIGS and PEACHES be watered?   The texture of the soil decides this. Sandy soils need more water; heavy soils, less. During the growing season, deciduous fruits require a moist soil. Watering every 2 weeks in sandy soil might not be too much. On the other hand, 2 or 3 good soakings might suffice in adobe soil.

What kind of soil and care do FUCHSIAS require?   They like protection from hot sun; the north and east sides of the house are good. If possible, provide a light, well-drained soil.

They must never suffer from lack of moisture. Regular monthly feedings of acid fertilizers are appreciated, the best being cotton-seed meal. This feeding should be started in March and continued until September.

How should FUCHSIAS be pruned when in the ground? In February or March, cut back hard, leaving only a little of the previous season's growth. The best plants are obtained if the new growth is pinched when about 6 or 8 ins. long, thus making the plant bushy.

How are potted FUCHSIAS cared for? Fuchsias are generally grown in 6-in. pots as rapidly as growth permits, and then shifted into 8-in. pots. If feeding is carried out, every 2 years should be often enough to shift plants to larger pots. During the growing season they should be watered heavily and food applied monthly. Each February or March they should be pruned hard.

How often should GERBERAS be divided? Do they require fertilizer? Gerberas are plants which really demand rich, well-drained soil. They particularly like organic fertilizer. Divide every 3 or 4 years in the early fall. They are subject to aphids, so spray with nicotine sulfate.

In California should GLADIOLUS bulbs be lifted? Yes. They multiply fast, and need separation, also to be kept dry when dormant. They can best be treated for thrips when out of the ground. After digging they should be kept in a sack for about 2 weeks with napthalene flakes, to kill thrips, then removed, and the napthalene screened off. Store in a cool, dry place.

When should we prune GRAPES set out last spring? There are 2 types of grapes in respect to pruning. Tokays, muscats, Ribier, and Zinfandel all require hard pruning. Pruning the first winter is to restrict the plant to 1 stem to form the trunk. It should be the most vigorous branch and should be cut back to 2 eyes. (See Grape.)

What is the difference between Strawberry and Pineapple GUAVAS? Though both belong to the myrtle family, they are different genera. The Strawberry Guava is *Psidium lucidum;* this and its variety The Yellow make 2 fine fruits and very attractive plants with light-green, glossy foliage. The Pineapple Guava (*Feijoa sellowiana*) has very pleasant fruit, excellent for jam, and is a beautiful large shrub with silvery foliage and bright-red flowers. Both are well worth growing for fruit and ornament.

I am interested in a small HERB garden. Can you suggest some herbs for it? Herbs do well in southern California, especially in light soils. They like poor soil and little water. Plant in early spring, and some yield will be had the same summer. The plants should be renewed every 3 or 4 years. A good list would include Sweet Basil, thyme, Sweet Marjoram, savory (both winter and summer types), tarragon, sage, rosemary, and some annuals such as caraway.

Why is it some people have such bad luck with English HOLLY in California?   English Holly is grown to perfection in California, but it will not thrive in the full blazing sun in summer. A slight shade must be provided.

What planting and care for IRIS in adobe soil?   Irises are exceedingly easy to grow. The only precaution to take in adobe soil is not to plant too deeply. Barely cover the rhizomes, and do not water heavily. Every third year clumps should be dug, saving only the new, strong rhizomes. Except in interior hot areas, this is best done in June or July. In the hot areas, September is better. Feeding in spring and fairly generous watering until they flower will insure good bloom.

How shall I care for JASMINE vines?   The two common jasmine vines in southern California are *Jasminum grandiflorum* and *J. Mesnyi* (*primulinum*). The former needs a sunny location, a rich soil, and plenty of irrigation, for it is most beautiful when the foliage is good at the time of flower, in summer. The latter needs sun, but too much water or fertility just adds to the rank growth which makes it disliked by many.

How should JASMINES be pruned?   True jasmines grow so abundantly that they should be severely pruned in winter. Old stems should be cut out at the ground each year, as the bloom is much finer on young growth. The bad reputation of the yellow jasmine is due to its excessive growth, but it can be kept in bounds and attractive by regular pruning.

What LILACS would bloom here in Los Angeles County?   Eastern lilacs are unsatisfactory, suffering either from excessive heat or mildew. The lilac that does very well is the Persian Lilac, *Syringa persica laciniata*. It has lavender flowers in the spring that are fine for cutting, and the plant is of graceful habit.

When should Regal LILIES be planted in California?   Regal Lilies should be planted as soon as they are on the market, in August or September. They like full sun and rich soil, but resent poor drainage, or fertilizer touching the bulbs.

Does LILY-OF-THE-VALLEY do well in the California coastal region?   There are a number of nice plantings here. They need shade and a light soil.

Can MANGOES be grown in southern California?   They can and are grown in frost-free areas. They need plenty of water, and the soil should be constantly mulched.

What would be a good covering under OAK TREES? Three very good ground covers would be the evergreen ornamental strawberry (*Fragraria chiloensis*), bugle weed (*Ajuga reptens*), and English Ivy (*Hedera helix*).

How are OLEANDERS pruned to keep them vigorous and flowering freely?   After the plant is several years old, old stems, as soon as they are done flowering, are cut off almost to the ground. No plant suckers more freely, so do not be afraid of harsh cutting.

Can PAPAYAS be grown in California?   Only in a few sections, which never have frost. They are difficult to pollinize, and several trees must be planted. Though they are delicious, and have been fruited, they are a gamble.

How are flowering PEACHES pruned?   These plants have an unhappy life in the southern California area, because most people fail to cut them hard enough. They need the stimulus of hard pruning. They should be cut back each year after flowering, leaving only about 6 ins. of growth of the previous year. If done right after blooming, there will be plenty of time for the plant to send out and mature strong growth for next year's bloom.

Is the PEONY plant a shrub? Will it grow in southern California?   Though there is a shrubby type, most peonies are herbaceous, dying to the ground in winter. In southern California they grow well in only a few favored locations. The long, hot summer is too much for them. They are not a good choice.

What should I do to have success with perennial PHLOX? Hardy phlox grows well in southern California, but it takes clean, healthy stock, planted in rich soil, with some little protection from the afternoon sun. They should be divided, in the fall, every few years. Flower heads should be removed immediately after fading.

What is the culture for NORFOLK-ISLAND-PINE in order to get rapid development?   This plant is not a rapid grower even in California. If your section is not subject to hard frost, treat like any other tree. It will not make more than 1 or 2 tiers a year.

How are dwarf POMEGRANATES grown?   Dwarf pomegranates are grown chiefly for their decorative bloom. They require little care. Like most deciduous plants, they enjoy plenty of food and water during the growing season. Thinning out occasionally in winter encourages better bloom. Do not allow fruit to mature on the plant. There are some new types which are really showy.

How should a Santa Rosa PLUM be pruned?   Pruning fruit trees is a long subject, well covered by bulletins obtainable from your county agent. Training should be started the first year and practiced every winter. (See Plums.)

How should PYRACANTHAS be pruned?   Pyracanthas and cotoneasters have the same habits, and should be pruned much alike. After the plant is several years old, each berry-producing branch should be cut back to within about 6 ins. of the trunk; each year thereafter the producing branches to within 6 ins. of their bases. They should never be sheared, for it will result in a top-heavy plant. The time for pruning is when the berries fall or dry.

ROSES

When should roses be planted?   Roses are best planted in the dormant season, from about December 15 to May 1. They are sold without any soil then. A far more vigorous plant will result than from one bought out of a container. For good results, buy only Grade 1.

How should roses be planted?   Holes generous enough to receive the roots without cramping should be dug. Depth depends on type of soil, for in sandy soil the bud graft should be covered; in adobe, it should be exposed. Mix a shovel of dairy manure in the bottom, then hold the plant at the required depth and pull in a little soil, and work it around the roots with the fingers. Gradually fill the hole, packing the soil around the roots. Water thoroughly.

How should roses be fertilized?   A liberal dressing of dairy manure in early spring and again in June, with light applications of commercial fertilizer, monthly, between April and August, will keep roses growing and blooming.

When should rosebushes be pruned?   In southern California, roses try to be everblooming. This is not in the best interest of the plants. Water should be withheld after September, and the plants allowed to become dormant. Then, in December, a severe pruning is in order, every other year. Reserve only 3 or 4 stout canes, and reduce these to about ⅓ their length. Proper cutting of buds and dead blooms, leaving only about 3 eyes below the cut, will take care of most of the pruning in the intervening 2 years.

How should Climbing Etoile de Hollande be pruned? This and other climbing hybrid teas are not vigorous as a rule. If several year-old canes are cut back to a foot or so from the ground, new, strong breaks will result. In picking the blooms, cut long stems. They really appreciate a rest period, forced by withholding water after September.

How should a Belle of Portugal rose be pruned? Belle of Portugal is one of the most vigorous plants that grow. Pruning is mostly a matter of cutting it back to decent limits. Old heavy canes may be cut back hard, but the growth that is forced is so vigorous it is difficult to handle. One thing certain is that no matter how severe the pruning, little permanent harm can be done.

How should Paul's Scarlet Climber be pruned? This rose and other climbers of its type differ from the hybrid teas in that wood of the previous season is required for bloom. They are best pruned after blooming. Old canes should be cut down low. The new canes may be shortened, and lateral growths restricted to 2 or 3 eyes. At this time, tying and training are best done.

What is the method of, and time for, pruning roses? They are generally pruned by cutting off buds and dead blooms. If these are cut so that only 2 or 3 eyes are left on each cane, and all weak and crossing growths are removed, little more will be needed. Any heavier pruning that seems required should be done in December and January.

How should I care for roses in tubs on a patio? Roses may be well grown in large tubs, if feeding and watering are properly done. During winter, cease feeding, and hold down water. In the spring a top-dressing of manure will be appreciated. Thereafter, feed monthly with commercial fertilizer.

When are rose cuttings taken in California? Most roses are budded, for their own roots are weak. Understock roses are grown from hardwood cuttings inserted in the field in winter. Greenwood cuttings may be rooted at almost any time.

What are the best roses for southern California? With any rose list, people near the coast must check for mildew resistance, while those in the hot valleys must check for heat resistance. Some favorites are President Hoover, Hadley, Autumn, Talisman, Dainty Bess, Etoile de Hollande, Mrs. E. P. Thom, Mrs. Sam McGredy, McGredy's Ivory, Scarlet, Picture, Los Angeles, K. A. Victoria, Joanna Hill, Victoria Harrington, and Eclipse.

How many years before SAPOTAS and CHERIMOYAS bear

fruit? Are 2 trees necessary for cross-pollination?   Seedling sapotas take 7 to 8 years, budded stock takes 4 to 5 years. Seedling cherimoyas bear in 4 or 5 years; budded stock takes 2 or 3 years. Two trees are not necessary in either case, but some growers recommend hand pollination of cherimoyas for greater yield.

What is the proper culture for SCHIZANTHUS and WALL-FLOWER?   Neither plant is difficult to grow. Seed is sown from July to September. There may be difficulty with seed during the hot months, so the later date may be the more convenient. When a few inches high, the seedlings should be moved to the spot in the garden where they are to grow. Shade them for a few days, till they take hold. Neither seems too fussy about soil outdoors.

When are STRAWBERRIES planted, and what is their care? Strawberries in California may be set in the fall. They must have a well-worked soil with good drainage, and are planted on raised beds about 2 ft. wide, with a shallow irrigation trench. They need copious water during summer, for they are shallow rooting. They are generally left several years without replanting. A feeding of manure or a complete fertilizer in the spring is advisable.

What are TANGELOS?   Tangelos are fruits resulting from crossing the grapefruit and tangerine. The old name of grapefruit was pomelo, hence the name "Tangelo." They grow the same as oranges, requiring identical care, and produce delicious, tangy fruits in winter. Several varieties are on the market which have fruiting periods from November till early summer.

Can THEA sinensis be safely planted outdoors in southern California?   The true tea plant is frequently found in southern California, making a very attractive shrub. In adobe soil, plant it a little above the soil level. In sandy soils, plenty of water is necessary. Plant it in full sun. Acid fertilizer is most appreciated in spring.

What VEGETABLES may be planted in January and February?   Among the many vegetables planted in southern California in winter are cabbage, broccoli, spinach, kohlrabi, beets, turnips, carrots, and onions. Parsley also may be planted for flavoring. In some areas, more favored by good drainage and mild climate, peas and squash (under hotkaps) may be planted at this time.

How are VIOLETS seeded or planted, and do they do well in southern California?   Violets do very well in California. They want a light soil and some shade. Though they must be divided every few years, they will become permanent if cared for. Try the huge type, "Royal Robe."

I have VIOLETS planted around an oak, growing and blossoming freely, but the whole plant heaves out. Why?   Violets in California have this habit, and undoubtedly to a greater degree when leaves falling on them force them to grow upward for light. They should be divided every few years and replanted firmly, for they will lose vigor if growing too much on the surface.

How should WALNUTS be watered?   Walnuts are irrigated more or less frequently, depending on the soil. Sandy soil may require monthly irrigation during the growing season, while adobe would need but 1 watering. Some experts claim an irrigation about 2 weeks before harvest makes shucking easier. If trees are grafted on black walnut stock, overwatering encourages black root rot.

COLORADO

Our springs are dry and late in Colorado. Can you give me a list of ANNUALS which can be planted in the fall?   Larkspur, California Poppy, calendula, echium, bartonia; in short, all of the hardy annuals. The catch is that Colorado winters are so dry, cold, and sunny that it is difficult to keep the young seedlings moist. A mulch of hay helps.

We live northeast of Colorado Springs, altitude 7,500 ft.; I cannot get ANNUALS to grow more than 6 ins. high. Can it be the soil or cool weather?   Cosmos and morningglories do well. Since these annuals thrive this high in other parts of your region, your trouble may be poor soil, alkali soil, or perhaps late planting. Zinnias enjoy rich soil and full sunshine.

How do you take care of BOYSENBERRY bushes over winter in Colorado?   Remove the canes from supports; lay them flat and cover with straw, cornstalks, or spruce branches. It is advisable to spray first with lime sulphur, or aluminum sulfate, to make them less attractive to mice.

We irrigate our land in Colorado. I have a bare bank that I wish to cover with some drought-resistant GROUND COVER; it will have to depend on rain for moisture. What shall I use?   *Sedum stoloniferum* can "take it," making a year-round cover. "Erosion Net" (sold by seed houses), or burlap, helps to hold the new surface if bank is steep.

What treatment should be given MONKSHOOD aconitum?

In any except subalpine regions in Colorado aconitum would resent open sunshine and consequent dryness. Try changing to shade, or semi-shade, and deep, rich, peaty soil.

What can I do to raise PANSIES successfully in southern Colorado?   Sow seeds in prepared seedbed early in September. Keep moist and mulch when ground begins to freeze. Next May transplant to permanent bed of good loam enriched with rotted manure and peatmoss, in open sun. *Keep seed pods picked.*

What are the best, showiest, and easiest grown PERENNIALS for late summer blooming in this climate?   *Anemone japonica,* anthemis, chrysanthemums, especially the "Cheyenne" strain, *Clematis davidiana,* eupatorium, helenium, *Heliopsis pitcheriana,* monarda, perennial asters, *Phlox decussata, Physostegia virginiana, Plumbago larpentae* (Ceratostigma), rudbeckia hybrids, *Salvia argentea, S. Pratensis.*

What PERENNIAL, preferably a foliage plant, would make the best low-growing border for my garden in eastern Colorado? *Cerastium tomentosum* (kept within bounds), *Festuca glauca, Euphorbia myrsinites*—all 3 have silver-gray foliage. *Teucrium chamaedrys,* kept shorn, makes a neat green, miniature hedge, suggestive of boxwood edging.

Tea ROSES bloom prolifically in this climate but are hard to keep from freezing out during the winter months. How would you advise to mulch and protect for winter?   Prune down to 6 or 8 ins. in autumn, mound up soil or peatmoss around each plant. Cover with a layer of any open material that will shade from sun and permit air circulation, such as spruce or fir branches, or straw held down with wire.

Can you give some information on spring versus fall planting of ROSES, shrubs, and trees in Denver, a mile above sea level? In such regions of dry, sunny cold winters the difficulties of watering and protecting newly planted woody material make spring planting preferable.

How can I grow SWEETPEAS successfully in southern Colorado?   In autumn, dig a trench 12 ins. wide and 12 to 18 ins. deep. In the bottom put a 6-in. layer of dairy manure. Fill with good, rich, friable loam. Early the following March add a dash of bone meal and sow seed.

FLORIDA

When is the best time to transplant AMARYLLIS?   Root action commences in late September or early October. The bulbs should be lifted, divided, and reset, therefore, in the early autumn. Bone meal or other alkaline plant food is good for these bulbs.

What is the best type of soil for BLACKBERRIES in Florida? A sandy loam soil that has a relatively high organic content is best suited for the bramble fruits. A heavy hammock type is ideal, particularly if there is a constant water table 2 or 3 ft. below the surface. A slightly acid soil is considered best.

How are CALADIUMS of the fancy-leaved varieties used to beautify the house and lawn? Plant the tubers in a partly shaded position that is sheltered from strong winds. The soil should contain an abundance of humus and should be reasonably moist at all times. Feeding with liquid fertilizer during season of active growth is very beneficial.

What is the correct culture for CALLAS in northern Florida? Callas are tropical bulbous plants easily injured by frost. The roots are usually received in November, and they can be planted at once in a rich, acid, mucky mixture in large pots or urns. These containers may be plunged under trees and taken indoors when frost is forecast. They may be held in a dormant state until danger of frost has passed in March, and then planted in a rich acid bed out of doors.

I am confused by descriptions in CITRUS catalogues. What are some of the best varieties for our garden near Orlando? Orange: Hamlin and Lue Gim Gong Pineapple; grapefruit: Foster, Duncan, and Marsh; grapefruit hybrids: Eustis Limequat, Sampson Tangelo. Sour orange is the best understock, and many nurseries in your vicinity will be able to furnish first-class 2-year-old trees in these varieties budded on sour orange trees.

What is frenching and bronzing of CITRUS fruits, and how cured? Frenching is the result of a zinc deficiency, and is corrected by adding zinc sulfate to the sprays. Bronzing results when there is insufficient magnesium available to orange trees. Dolomite in judicious amounts will usually correct a bronzed condition. Epsom salts and a potassium—magnesium sulfate will also correct the deficiency.

What causes pineapple ORANGES to split open before ripe, and how is this prevented? Usually thought to be caused by a deficiency of copper. Small amounts of copper sulfate (bluestone) will tend to ameliorate the condition.

What are the brown dots on the under sides of ORANGE leaves? Round brown dots with reddish centers are Florida red scale. This pest can be controlled with an oil emulsion spray, used according to the directions on the package.

What are some of the best CLIMBERS for central Florida? Bougainvilleas in their several attractive colors, the very colorful flamevine, herald trumpet—a rampant tropical creeper, Queens wreath, with its gorgeous purple blossoms, the Quisqualis, the luxuriant coralvine, the fast-growing skyflower, and the fragrant Confederate Jasmine, and several other vining jasmines, are among the most popular of Florida's many vines.

What about COLUMBINES for central Florida? Although columbines are native to extreme western Florida, they do not grow readily in the peninsula. They can be flowered, however, with good culture. Get plants from the North and set them in a partially shaded place in November, feeding them a balanced plant food every 2 or 3 weeks as they grow. They need an abundance of water and must not have too much root competition for water or nutrients.

When should DAHLIAS be planted in southern Florida? For spring and summer bloom plant the roots in January or February; for autumn bloom arrange to have roots held in cold storage and delivered in late August or early September.

How may good DAHLIAS be grown in central Florida? The roots are procured in February or March, and are planted about 5 ins. deep, in garden beds that have been enriched with compost and a commercial fertilizer. Drive a stout stake by the stem end of the root and tie the plant every 8 ins. or so as it grows. Feed liberally every 3 or 4 weeks. Dust with sulphur at the first signs of red spider.

How can I have autumn DAHLIAS in central Florida? Arrange to have cold-storage roots delivered in August or early September. Set the roots in good soil about 5 ins. deep; water and feed liberally as the plants grow. These roots will be difficult to carry over in Florida, so it is suggested that you treat these as annuals starting over each autumn.

Will DIMORPHOTHECA ecklonis grow in northern Florida? This perennial woody plant will probably grow during the spring as an annual. If you purchase the young plants in February and grow them for spring bloom, they will probably succeed. Certainly this species is very rare in Florida gardens at present.

Can I increase my very beautiful FLAME-OF-THE-WOODS? Yes, use softwood tip cuttings in June or July and insert them in clean white sand in a new box. Place cheesecloth over the box;

set in on the north side of the house, and daily sprinkle with a fine spray. The cuttings should root in 4 or 5 weeks.

Will FOXGLOVES grow in northern Florida? Possibly in the extreme western end these perennials will succeed, but they are certain to be a disappointment in most parts of this state. Like many other perennials, they need a long, cold winter for inducing an unbroken dormancy.

What varieties of FRUIT—apples, peaches, and pears—will grow in Florida? Apples are not satisfactory even in extreme western Florida, although some merit is claimed for the Helm apple there. The Chinese Sand or Pineapple Pear is the only one that withstands the ravages of pear blight well enough to warrant planting in Florida. Jewel, Waldos, Honey, and Angel peaches grow very well and fruit fairly well most years in northern Florida if they are properly sprayed and pruned.

How shall I fertilize, water, and care for lawn of Centipede GRASS? Centipede Grass is one of the best lawn materials for the light, sandy soils of Florida. An application of a balanced fertilizer, at the rate of 20 lbs. per 1,000 sq. ft., in March, another in June or July, should suffice. Water the fertilizer in as soon as applied, and irrigate often enough to keep the grass leaves from curling and turning gray-green. Frequent mowing is necessary for a good Centipede turf. During the growing season, the mower must be used at least once each week.

Will HELIOPHILAS grow in northern Florida? Yes, these South African annuals should do well if the seeds are sown in flats in January, the seedlings grown in a not-too-moist soil, and the plants set out in March.

What can I do to have IRISES from Kentucky bloom in Florida? Nothing! Excepting in extreme western Florida bearded irises are not successful. The light, sandy soils and lack of sustained low winter temperatures do not suit these favorites of temperate gardens. Why not use native Southern species that do succeed so beautifully?

When should I fertilize my LAWN? Early in March apply a mixed plant food that is high in nitrogen; then again when the rains start in June make a second application.

At what rate should I apply a 5–7–5 mixed fertilizer to my LAWN? About 20 to 30 lbs. per 1,000 sq. ft. constitutes an adequate feeding.

Can old-fashioned LILACS be raised as far south as Jacksonville? No, the light, sandy acid soils and lack of a real dor-

mant season do not suit these popular temperate garden plants
and they are certain to be disappointing.

**When should a MULBERRY tree be pruned to be sure of a
good crop in Florida?**   Mulberry trees should be pruned directly after they have finished fruiting in the spring.

What is the best time to plant NASTURTIUMS in Florida?
Nasturtiums must be grown in autumn in order to mature blossoms before frost; or in spring, by sowing after last frost for
blooming before hot weather sets in and kills the plants.

When should my OLEANDERS be cut back?   Just after
flowering. If they are to be kept from getting very large, root
prune them at this time by driving a spade deep in a circle about
2 or 3 ft. from the plant.

**Is PEAT from local bogs good for us to use on our gardens?
We can no longer buy peatmoss at the seed store.**   Local peat
is excellent if it comes from an inland bog. Be very certain that
you do not buy muck from a tidal marsh, however, as this saline
material will kill plants.

**Can PEONIES be grown successfully in the central part of
Florida?**   Peonies are a complete failure in peninsular Florida.
The light, sandy soil and the lack of continuously cold winter
to assure complete dormancy combine to defeat our best attempts
to make Southerners out of these temperate garden favorites.

**How far back should ROSES be trimmed, and what time of
the year is best?**   Bush roses should be pruned, in January or
February, to 4 or 5 strong eyes on each of 4 or 5 canes. Make the
pruning cuts about ½ in. above a strong eye that points away from
the center of plant. Climbing roses may be pruned at same time,
using a renewal system to remove all of the canes more than 1 or
2 years old. Blossoms on climbers are borne from spurs on 1-year
canes.

**I want to use old-fashioned ROSES. Which ones will do best
with least care?**   The old French Rose grows well. Among our
most dependable old roses are: Louis Philippe, Safrano, Duchesse
de Brabant, Marie van Houtte, Minnie Francis, and Mme. Lombard. Plants of these varieties will thrive in your Southern garden long after plants of cutting varieties have succumbed. Several Texas nurseries are specializing in these old sorts.

When is the best time of year to set ROSE bushes?   Roses
planted in December and early January will have time to make
good root growth before top growth is started by the warm days

of early spring. The earliest possible planting is considered best for Florida.

Will Centaurea moschata (SWEETSULTAN) grow in northern Florida? Yes, very excellent sweetsultans have been grown and sold in this section. Sow seeds in a flat in October or November. Transplant seedlings to well-enriched beds in midwinter. Plants should blossom in April and May. Red spiders must be forestalled with sulphur dust or frequent syringing during dry periods.

Will VIOLAS succeed here? Yes, these miniature pansies do very well if plants are bought from a Northern specialist in November and planted at once to grow through the cool winter.

What is culture for WATSONIAS in northern Florida? Watsonias, like gladioli, may be planted in February in northern Florida. Set the corms about 3 ins. deep in beds that have been enriched with compost and a commercial plant food. The blossoms should be produced in April and May.

Will the WILLOW OAK grow in Florida? Yes, the Willow Oak (*Quercus phellos*) is native to northern Florida and will succeed as a fast-growing, desirable tree as far South as the central part of the peninsula.

Will the WEEPING WILLOW grow successfully in Florida? It will grow in heavy soils close to watercourses in northern Florida, but it will not grow so well as it does farther North, nor can it be considered nearly so beautiful here as in the temperate states.

GEORGIA

What grows most satisfactorily in partial shade in this section, other than azaleas and camellias? Oakleaf Hydrangea (*H. quercifolia*), St.' Johnswort (*Hypericum*), heavenly-bamboo (*Nandina domestica*), stewartia, cydonia and illicium, are all excellent shrubs for the shady garden.

What is best position and soil for AMARYLLIS? Amaryllis grown outdoors in the South does well in a sunny or lightly shaded position in a well-drained, fertile soil that is neutral or very slightly acid.

What are cultural needs of hybrid AMARYLLIS? Apply balanced fertilizer immediately after blooming; water well through dry periods during growing season. In fall mulch with half-rotted leaves to which is added some bone meal and cow manure.

The tops of my AMARYLLIS are green the year around. Some of the outer leaves turn yellow and soft, but they do not yellow like other bulbs. When should they be dug?   They should be dug in late fall. If the foliage has not completely died down (and this does not happen with all amaryllis), it may be artificially ripened off by drying in a sunny, airy place.

About 20 months ago I planted some AMARYLLIS seeds, the plants from which have been green ever since, without blooming. What time of year should they be given a rest period? How? The best results are obtained if seedling amaryllis are grown on without rest until after they produce their first blooms. This is usually in from 18 to 36 months from time of sowing.

My Fancy-leaved CALADIUMS die down in the fall. What shall I do with them?   In November lift them; cut off the few remaining leaves; pack in peat, dry sand, or sawdust, and store the container in a frost-free place until spring.

What causes the black scum on my CAPEJASMINE bush, and how can I prevent it?   This sooty mold on gardenia leaves follows the attacks of whitefly and can be corrected and prevented by occasional applications of an oil emulsion spray. One application in September, another 2 or 3 weeks later, and possibly a third during midwinter should prevent this condition. Your seed house will have oil sprays put up in small cans for your convenience.

I have read that DAFFODILS of the North have longer stems than those of the South. What can I add to the soil to make my daffodils have longer stems?   In all probability the climate is responsible for the shorter daffodil stems, and even though your bulbs are adequately fed, there will be a tendency to shorter stems.

When do you plant DAHLIAS in Georgia?   In March and April. If the emerging tips are nipped by the latest spring frosts, no great damage will be done; but it is best to plan your planting so that there will be no frost damage.

When is the best time to transplant DOGWOODS, redbuds, and other trees from the woods?   December through February, while the trees are dormant and without leaves. Remember that transplanting is a surgical operation and that extreme care must be exercised to keep the roots covered and the trees protected from sun and wind during transport. Cut back moderately the lateral branches, plant at the same depth they formerly grew, and wrap the trunks with burlap or muslin as protection against sunscald and borers. Use trees under 8 ft. in height rather than larger ones.

What is the best method of protecting GERBERAS from cold? If gerbera plants are killed to the ground, you may cover the crowns with a light mulch of pine straw or oak leaves. If you are in the southern part of the state and wish to keep the plants from being killed on cold nights, cover with a heavy blanket of Spanish moss, uncovering after danger of severe cold has passed.

How are GERBERAS cared for? Gerberas are not particular as to soil type, provided it is well fortified with plant food and plants have enough water. They will be benefited by a good mulch of oak leaves, peat, or similar organic material.

Should I use fertilizer when I plant my GLADIOLUS? Balanced commercial fertilizer can be scattered in the bottom of the 4-in. deep planting furrow and lightly cultivated in. Then set out the corms.

How can I grow GOURDS in a hot, dry location? If it is too hot and dry for gourds to thrive in your part of Georgia, I think you would have to get an early start with them and allow them to mature in midsummer. However, gourds should thrive in most sections of Georgia.

How are HERBS grown in Georgia? Herbs may be grown exactly as you would grow garden vegetables, in the same soil and with the same fertilizer, care, and watering.

What HERBS are best for middle and south Georgia? For fall planting: anise, chives, Winter Savory, sage, and dill. For spring planting: Sweet Basil, Summer Savory, Sweet Fennel, coriander, thyme, and Sweet Marjoram.

What varieties of tall, preferably fragrant, IRISES are suitable for Southern climate? Which are the best red ones? Purissima, Frieda Mohr, Happy Days, Los Angeles, Golden Treasure, Destiny, Pale Moonlight, Shining Waters, and Sandalwood are all excellent tall varieties in the popular price range that have proved to be good in the Macon, Georgia, area. The best near reds are Ethel Peckham and the Red Douglas.

What is the IVY that is so effectively used around the huge oaks in the Tallahassee and Thomasville area? This is the Algerian Ivy (*Hedera canariensis*), a relative of the English Ivy. It is considered one of the very best ground covers for spots where grass will not grow.

Can I make a good LAWN in a wooded area? On the land

spread a layer of cow manure, compost, rotted oak leaves, together with some balanced commercial fertilizer. Spade or plow this deeply; rake level; plant. In October or November sow Italian Rye Grass for a winter effect until warm weather, then plant sprigs of St. Augustinegrass in rows about 12 ins. apart. Always water well, as growing grass needs a great deal of moisture.

What is best grass for a wooded LAWN?   Italian Rye in winter if there is partial protection from fallen pine needles. Charlestongrass is satisfactory in summer after it is well established. In southern Georgia, St. Augustinegrass is excellent for shady locations.

Why do NANDINA berries drop?   They will not drop if there has been good pollination at flowering time. If there is rain when the blossoms open, the pollen will be washed away, and there will be either no set, or a poor one.

When is the proper time to plant NANDINA berries? How long does it take for them to come up?   Nandina berries may be sown when they are red, or as they begin to fall from the plant. Germination is slow, and the plantlets will probably not appear until the following spring or summer.

What can I use in place of PANSIES during the heat of the summer?   Torenia (wishbone-flower) is an excellent substitute for pansies that will grow during summer months. Sow seeds in flats in April or May, and transplant to garden when the pansies come out.

Will PEONIES do well in this climate? Would you advise early, midseason, or late varieties?   None will succeed south of Atlanta. Use only tried early varieties in north Georgia.

How can we get PERENNIAL flower seed to come up in August and September, when, in this section, it is so hot and dry? Germination will be poor at this season. Hold the seeds until later in the autumn for best results.

Will perennial POPPIES grow year after year in this locality? Possibly they will succeed in extreme north Georgia; from Macon southward they are a failure.

ROSES

Can roses be grown in the Far South in sandy soil?   The sandy soils, and warm winters, and the prevalence of disease make rose growing difficult in the Far South. Large wholesale nurseries in eastern Texas have brought the price of roses to very low levels in recent years and many successful gardeners grow roses frankly as annuals. The plants are bought in the fall, planted well in very rich beds, and forced for blooms during the following spring. In summer they are usually discarded as worthless.

When should climbing roses be pruned? November to January in Georgia a renewal system is used, old canes are cut low down, leaving this year's and last year's shoots only. Climbing roses flower from spurs that are borne on last year's canes. Old wood is not floriferous.

What is the name of the hardy red rose that grows so freely here? There is also a light blush pink that seems to thrive without any care. The red rose is Louis Philippe, sometimes called the "cracker rose." The light, shell pink is probably Marie van Houtte. Safrano, Minnie Francis, and Duchesse de Brabant are also old-fashioned roses that will grow for many years in Southern gardens.

When is the best time to transplant the RED SPIDERLILY? This flower, *Nerine sarniensis* (often misnamed *Lycoris radiata*), is best transplanted in July or early August.

Will you give suggestions as to planting of SHRUBBERY around small residences in vicinity of Atlanta? Plants that are evergreen, slow growing, hardy, and resistant to drought would include azalea, camellia, podocarpus, box, Japanese Holly, Chinese Holly, boxthorn, cotoneaster, pyracantha, primrose, jasmine, Wax or Glossy Privet (*Ligustrum lucidum*), and abelia. These are all suitable for foundation planting.

When shall I prune SHRUBS that were injured by frost? It is more tidy to cut the shrubs back as soon as the injured parts turn brown, repeating later if inspection shows that the injury extends farther than your first pruning.

Can you suggest pink- and blue-flowering SHRUBS and flowers for my town garden, and yellow, orange, and white for my country place? For town garden: camellia, rose, azalea, deutzia, weigela—all pink; buddleia, plumbago, althea, vitex— all blue. For the country: yellow—hypericum, thryallis, tithonia, forsythia; orange—primrose, jasmine, *Alyssum saxatile, Rosa hugonis;* white—gardenia, philadelphus, camellia, rose, althea, ligustrum, azalea.

Can TULIP bulbs in South be grown and increased for a number of years, as are narcissi? They are not satisfactory for naturalizing. Certain varieties of tulips in sections of the upper South can be naturalized. In the lower South tulips of certain varieties must be placed in cold storage for 2 or 3 months and planted in December.

How can I grow large TULIPS in north Georgia?   In extreme north Georgia use only varieties that are recommended; plant in well-enriched beds. (See Tulips.)

Will VERBENAS act as perennials in the lower South? Yes, they may be grown from cuttings, plants then lifted and divided and reset in winter, for spring bloom. Red spiders must be controlled in hot, dry weather with sulphur dust, or by syringing with hose.

IDAHO

What perennial DAISIES, other than white ones, would you suggest for Idaho, elevation about 3,500?   Any of the earlier Michaelmas daisies (hardy asters) should be suitable. Try Adorable, Harrington's Pink, Redrover, or Gayborder Supreme. Aster Frikarti is more like a daisy, and very lovely. Northland daisies (hardy chrysanthemums) are beautiful and are very satisfactory where the season is long enough. They bloom in early autumn.

What are the names of some HEDGES which will stay green all year in this climate? Would a wild shrub (pachistima) do? Probably none except your native evergreens. Spruce and cedar make lovely hedges and can be kept clipped down. Pachistima might be suitable if it grows high enough. It is very difficult to transplant.

Can you give a list of low-growing (not to exceed 12 ins.) PERENNIAL flowers that will provide bloom from early spring to late fall? They would be in sun, no shade.   *Anemone pulsatilla; Campanula carpatica, C. pusilla;* heuchera, various; *Phlox subulata; Gypsophila repens, Iberis semperflorens; Thymus serpyllum; Saponaria ocymoides; Penstemon crandalli, P. caespitosus, P. humulis;* alyssum, arabis; aubretia; lewisia; antennaria; helianthemum; dianthus, various; sempervivum; *Nepeta mussini, Veronica spuria; Melampodium cinereum; Malvastrum coccineum; Linum flavum* and *L. alpinum; Oenothera caespitosa, O. lavendulaefolia,* and *O. missouriensis; Ceratostigma plumbaginoides;* iris, dwarf varieties; *Abronia fragrans; Physaria didymocarpa; Teucrium chamaedrys.*

What causes red RASPBERRY blight in an irrigated country? If the blight referred to is the yellowing of the leaves, it is usually caused by too-wet subsoils, especially heavy or clay soils. Install underground drainage or plant in lighter, better-drained soils.

I live in an area having neutral to slightly alkaline soil, at an altitude of 4,250 ft. It is irrigated country, so water does not have to be conserved. There are many plants that will not do well, either because of the short growing season, or because of water about the roots. Can you name some SHRUBS, besides lilacs, bridalwreath, and snowballs, that might thrive? The following shrubs are suggested for trial: Highbush Cranberry (*Viburnum opulus*); *Spiraea arguta*, or *S. thunbergi*; Austrian Copper Rose; River Birch (*Betula fontinalis*). Trees: weeping willow; Soft Maple or Silver Maple; birch; and possibly sycamore. Evergreens: Blue or Black-hill Spruce; and possibly *Juniperus scopulorum* and *J. pfitzeriana*.

Would gardenia, azalea, roses, and rhododendron SHRUBS do well in the mountains of Idaho, elevation about 3,500 ft.? Gardenias and azaleas are usually grown in a greenhouse. Azaleas and rhododendrons require a very acid soil, and for this reason will not thrive in any of our Western soils. Roses should grow well in Idaho if protected in winter by a heavy mulch, or by mounding up with earth.

Can the TRUMPETVINE be grown where there are zero winters? Yes, it must have winter enough to cause it to lose its leaves and to give it several weeks' rest. Trumpetvine should grow in Idaho.

ILLINOIS

What are the best 4 or 5 APPLE trees for the Midwest, for the small home garden? A good list (which pleases the one making the list only, since tastes in apples differ) might include Melba for an early; Anoka or Joan or Beacon for fall; and Cortland, Jonathan, and Northwestern Greening for winter. Best way to pick apples is to try the fruit and see what you like.

Why don't I have any success with ASTERS? Is it the climate here in north Illinois? No, your difficulty (if by asters you mean the so-called annual aster grown from seed) is probably due to disease, either aster wilt or aster yellows. The answer to wilt is to use wilt-resistant varieties. The answer to yellows is not so easy. Commercial men grow them under cloth, to keep off the aphids which carry disease from plant to plant. Something of the same effect can be had by growing them between taller plants not too tempting to aphids (in the vegetable garden between rows of corn, or in the flower garden placed among the taller stalks of dahlias), but this is not always too successful. Insect control helps, but not much.

What pruning is required on AZALEAS in the Middle West?
Only enough to keep them shapely. Such pruning as is required
should be done immediately after blooming. Careless use of the
pruning shears can destroy bloom for 2 or 3 years.

How can I control orange rust in my BLACKBERRIES?
Eliminate wild brambles from the locality; remove diseased plants
in the patch, including roots, as soon as the disease appears in
early spring; plant a resistant variety such as Eldorado.

**Can BLUEBERRIES be raised successfully in northwestern
Illinois?**   Yes, provided you will acidify the soil properly. (See
Blueberry.)

**Can BLUEBERRIES be successfully raised in eastern central
Illinois?**   Yes, provided good culture and soil acidification receive careful attention.

What is a sweet CHERRY for central Illinois?   Black Tartarian is most universally successful, but it is necessary to have 2
or more trees, as they are self-sterile, and sour cherry pollen does
not fertilize them.

**Can large CHRYSANTHEMUMS be grown in garden in
Chicago during usual season?**   Eugene A. Wander, Avalanch,
and King Midas, all fairly large-flowered, do well. Suggest a visit
to the hardy mum exhibits at the University of Chicago display
grounds.

**Can you suggest some small pompon MUMS that will bloom
not later than October 1, and that are hardy in this climate?**
Try Early Bronze pompon or the more recent September Bronze.
Also the brilliant yellow, September Gold.

**Will CRAPEMYRTLE live through the winter in the latitude
of Chicago?**   No, even the so-called hardy type will kill out.

**In what localities is the new lawn plant, DICHONDRA
REPENS, hardy? I have seen it in California and Texas. Is it
hardy in Illinois?**   *Dichondra repens* (Ponyfoot) would not
be hardy in Illinois. In the South it may have possibilities
although it generally has been included among the lawn pests.

What is proper care for wintering perennial DIGITALIS?
If possible, handle in cold frames, with the glass on, covered with
mats to shut out winter sun. Lacking this, use umbrellalike cover-
ings that allow the air to get in, but not water and sun. It is a
tricky species to grow in Illinois.

**What plants will provide the most cutting FLOWERS to be
grown in a small yard in Chicago?**   Among the annuals, per-

haps more blooms can be cut from marigolds and zinnias than from any others in this class. Petunias are excellent because they provide low edgings in the garden picture yet yield satisfactory flowers for cutting too.

For people who do not like the ever-present FOUNDATION PLANTINGS of evergreens, what do you consider the best substitute for my locality, near Chicago? It would have to be something that will do at least reasonably well in good deal of shade. A neat, healthy, clean shrub that will grow in shade is a problem, but *Euonymus alatus compactus* comes pretty close to filling the job. With clean, dark-green foliage and striking autumn color, it is a highly desirable semi-formal shrub.

I have a home on Lake Michigan, and have plenty of sand in front down to the lake; what would you suggest for a GROUND COVERING of character?   If in shade, and if you can get plenty of leafmold, this sounds like a perfect spot for the bearberry (*Arctostaphylos uva-ursi*). There is no shrub, vine, or subshrub that will do well in sun on pure sand, at least to the point where it can be considered a ground cover.

Where can we secure information on extra-fine eating GRAPES that will grow in this locality? (Winnetka.)   The New York Fruit Testing Association, Geneva, New York, or your local State Experiment Station, Urbana, Illinois, will give you the information you want, if your local seedsman cannot supply it.

Which are the varieties of HERBS most practical for growing in this latitude? How should the seedbed be prepared for best results in herb production?   Perennials: sage, thyme, chives, mint. Annuals: Sweet Basil, dill. These are the easiest to grow, but since taste is such a personal thing, the only criterion is, after all, what you like.

How far North will KERRIA JAPONICA grow?   Into southern Wisconsin.

Have trouble in growing perennial LUPINE. Is there any special treatment?   Yes. They are legumes and must have the special inoculating bacteria to form the nodules they require in order to extract nitrogen from the air. Also, while they require calcium, they need more iron than most legumes. The trick is to keep them at a pH of about 5.9 to 6.8, where by juggling iron and calcium you can give them what they want. A tricky species, and definitely not for the amateur, except where peculiar soil conditions prevail.

What MAGNOLIAS are suitable for Northern climes?

Only two magnolias are commonly grown in Illinois, the Saucer Magnolia (*M. soulangeana*) and the Star Magnolia (*M. stellata*).

What pruning is required on MAGNOLIAS in the Middle West?   In the Middle West, the problem is to get them to make adequate growth, not to cut out any excess wood. Throw away the pruning shears and you'll have better luck. Only if branches are badly placed or broken should they be touched.

How far North will NECTARINES bear?   While they will bear in Illinois, they are so subject to curculio damage that they are seldom successful there.

Can I be sure of a crop if I plant Southern paper-shell PECANS in Illinois?   Not as a general rule. Even in southern Illinois, the Stuart, one of the hardiest Southern varieties, seldom matures its kernels. The good Northern varieties succeed best south of central Illinois. Try the Major, Posey, Indiana, and Green River. Plant more than one variety for cross-pollination.

How far North will PECAN nuts grow?   Southern Illinois is about the Northern limit of the pecan.

What is the best time to plant PEONIES in southern Illinois? Specialists in this area try to plant as close to September 15 as possible.

Is it necessary to mulch such PERENNIALS as delphiniums, phlox, or Crimson King Carnation in this latitude?   They are better for a mulch if it is not too dense and soggy. Think of a mulch for these plants as protecting the ground from winter sun, not as a blanket of insulation to shut out all cold. Make it airy but shady. Allow the breeze to blow through.

Why can't we keep PERENNIALS over winter? We cover them for the winter months.   Probably killed with loving kindness: a dense covering of leaves or other compact material will smother rather than protect plants. Use light, airy mulches, but apply *after* the ground freezes, not before. Remove early in spring (say about March 15 in the Chicago area) to avoid damaging spring growth.

I have a RHODODENDRON in a 15-in. pot. Can this be planted in the garden and safely left outside all winter? I live in a suburb near Chicago.   Probably not. Most of the forcing types of rhododendrons are not winter hardy in Chicago.

Should ROSES be planted in full sunshine or in part shade? Either: some of the delicate pinks and the types of red that "blue" in sunshine are better for light shade at midday. But that doesn't mean you can grow roses in the shade of maples or dense oaks.

Can ROSES be hilled up 6 or 8 ins. with dirt before ground has frozen and before their leaves have fallen? I always wait for leaves to fall and wood ripen; then the ground freezes suddenly and I don't get them covered. Juggling with the right time to cover roses is one of those things that make gardening interesting (and confusing). The leaves must be off before they are covered, which means after a good sharp freeze, but usually we have a warm spell after such a freeze which allows for pulling the earth around the plant. If you have only a few plants, you might try the old trick of saving a few bushels of unfrozen earth in the cellar and applying this after the wood has ripened.

What bush ROSES are best suited for Chicago region? All hybrid perpetual roses are suited to Chicago; in fact, are much more so than the more favored hybrid teas. With hybrid perpetuals, choose any that strike your fancy: they're all hardy.

What climbing ROSES may be left on fence or trellis all winter with little protection? The old rambler types (which bloom on new wood) survive this sort of treatment, even though their condition horrifies the meticulous rosarian. The dead wood can be cut out in spring, or the old shoots removed in fall. However, be prepared for the white mildew that attacks practically all roses of the rambler type.

How far North will SPICEBUSH grow? The spicebush (*Benzoin aestivale*) makes satisfactory growth as far North as southern Wisconsin.

Are there any STRAWBERRY varieties resistant to the new red stele root-rot disease? Yes, the Aberdeen and Pathfinder varieties are resistant. Promising seedlings, originated by the United States Department of Agriculture and State Experiment Stations, are being tested in different sections of the country before being released to the trade.

How can I succeed in growing everbearing STRAWBERRIES? It is not easy to grow these fruits well, especially during the heat of summer. They require very fertile soil of good texture and a continuous supply of water throughout the season. Ground should be mulched lightly to keep berries clean. A protective winter mulch is also necessary. Rockhill (Wayzata) is one of the best varieties. (See Strawberry.)

Is it possible to transplant the SWEETGUM TREE in central Illinois? I have been unable to do so successfully. Yes, but get a nursery-grown tree with fine, fibrous roots. And be sure you plant it in rich, deep land. It won't grow in dry soil.

Is the BIRCH family bothered with borers in central Illinois? The birch borer makes this beautiful tree all but impossible to grow in central Illinois. By the time the pest is discovered, the damage is done, and there is no preventive treatment.

Can espalier or DWARF FRUIT TREES be grown in Illinois? Yes, but do not expect too much from them. The training of fruit trees in special shapes was originated in Europe, so that they could be planted along stone walls where the heat would help ripen the fruit. In the Middle West, the problem is too much heat, not too little. Use espaliers for special ornamental effects, not where fruit in quantity is the object.

How late (in the fall) can FRUIT TREES be planted in central Illinois? Planting can go on all winter long provided good cultural practices are followed, but March or April should be equally satisfactory. It is a question of convenience and comfort, not of the thermometer, which ends the fall-planting season.

What are the best FRUIT and NUT TREES for the average yard in this region? The best sure-fire fruit trees for Illinois are apples, crabapples, and sour cherries. Native walnuts are about the only nut trees that are really reliable, and these must have light, loamy soil and good drainage.

Will a tree WISTERIA grow in Chicago climate? Yes, provided its other requirements are met. Grows in almost any soil; thrives best in deep, rich loam that does not get too dry.

Are there any WILDFLOWERS that can be grown in northern Illinois, which can be developed from seed? Most wildflowers depend on seed for their continuation. Many are perennials and require as much care as other perennial seeds. Some possibilities are: *Aquilegia canadensis,* many violets, goldenrod, Allegheny Foamflower, Butterflyweed, wild asters, Dutchman's-breeches, annual phlox.

INDIANA

Can you tell me how to grow DELPHINIUM in Indiana? Delphiniums come from cold regions and resent hot summers. To coax them into good behavior give them a deeply prepared friable loam and under each plant put a 4-in. layer of peatmoss. Cut flower stems off before they begin to seed.

What are the most desirable FLOWERS to plant in a rock

garden in northern Indiana?   Arenaria, various; *Androsace carinata* and *A. sarmentosa; Antirrhinum glutinosum; Campanula pusilla* and *muralis;* dwarf iris in variety; *Thalictrum alpinum; Melampodium cinereum; Physaria didymocarpa; Phlox subulata, P. douglasi,* and *P. multiflora,* aubretia; arabis; alyssum, perennial; *Aquilegia alpina;* heuchera, various; lewisias; draba; primula, various; *Tiarella cordifolia; Hypericum reptans; Dianthus alpinus* and *P. neglectus;* Fern, *Woodsia scopulina; Iberis sempervirens;* dwarf penstemons; *Veronica rupestris; Gypsophila repens; Tunica saxifraga;* thymes, various; *Viola nuttalli; Saponaria ocymoides.*

Can Smyrna FIG plants winter in the back yard in this section of Indiana?   Definitely not; but figs can be grown in tubs and carried over in a cool cellar (between freezing and 40° above) and set out again in early May. These will *not* be the Smyrna fig (which requires a special wasp for pollination) but the type which can be pollinated by American insects.

Is there an American HOLLY to use in climates such as Indiana in order to have enough berries to be attractive in winter?   You can't grow holly such as you see on Christmas cards. The deciduous species that will grow in Indiana are *not* very hollylike.

Can PECANS, ENGLISH WALNUTS, and FILBERTS be successfully grown? What types are best?   Only in the southern end of Indiana are pecans and English walnuts likely to succeed. Filberts can be grown over most of the state.

What kind of PEACH trees would be best for Indiana climates?   Practically any varieties in commerce are successful in your state.

What is the best time to plant ROSES in southern and northern Indiana? Should plants be 1, 2, or 3 years old? Either late fall or early-spring planting is satisfactory for roses of any age.

When is the best time to set out monthly blooming ROSES? Either late fall or early-spring planting should prove satisfactory. Which is the better depends upon what kind of a winter or summer follows planting—something no one can foretell.

Which are 2 of the best red everblooming tea ROSES particularly adapted for Indiana?   The 2 which have given widest satisfaction in your state are Crimson Glory and the old Gruss an Teplitz. Much depends upon what your definition of "best" is. One of these is sensationally beautiful; the other is a dependable producer of thousands of mediocre blooms.

What types of roses are preferable for this climate? Any but the tender noisette and tea roses. J. H. Hill, the McGredys, polyanthas, hybrid teas, climbers, pillars, and Briars are better than hybrid perpetuals in Indiana.

What are the most desirable SHRUBS and EVERGREENS to plant in a rock garden? *Juniperus horizontalis, J. horizontalis douglasi,* and *J. horizontalis plumosa; Mahonia repens; Ceanothus fendleri; Arctostaphylos uva-ursi; Pachystima canbyi; Euonymus radicans kewensis; Daphne mezereum* and *D. cneorum; Yucca glauca; Cotoneaster horizontalis; Cotoneaster adpressa.*

What kinds of plants, shrubs or evergreens, to place on north and west side of house facing east and located on southwest side of 2 streets? Select enough of 1 variety on each side to give continuity. Large shrubs of coarse texture are suitable near a big old shingle structure; while smaller, neater ones of fine texture are better for colonial or stucco.

What summer- and fall-blooming SHRUBS, especially evergreens, are particularly suitable for this locality? Soil is sandy loam. There are practically no evergreen shrubs which would have good flowers during the summer and fall in this locality. Most evergreen shrubs bloom in the spring.

When is the best time to put out STRAWBERRY plants in this locality, and what variety do you recommend? Late March or early April if you can get them into the ground. Four new varieties that give general satisfaction in Indiana are Dorsett, Fairfax, Catskill, and the everbearer Gem.

IOWA

Has the Massachusetts BAYBERRY ever been grown in Midwestern gardens? Yes, but not successfully. It requires acid soil and a moist, cool atmosphere—conditions which cannot easily be supplied in Iowa.

Can BLUEBERRIES be grown successfully in central Iowa on our Tama loam? Yes, provided rules for cultivation and acidifying the soil are observed. (See Blueberry.)

What are some of the best hardy CHRYSANTHEMUMS for the central part of Iowa? Dean Kay, Dean Ladd, My Lady, Eugene A. Wander, September Bronze, September Gold.

What CHRYSANTHEMUMS will bloom before freezing in northeast Iowa? Most of them freeze here in September before blooming. Some seasons early varieties in full flower get caught while those in bud escape. Try varieties dated to flower in late September, such as September Bronze, September Gold, and Algonquin. Avoid white and light pinks, as these are more susceptible to frost injury.

Are Flowering DOGWOODS hardy in south Iowa? Yes, although flower buds are usually killed in severe winters.

Is it possible to grow American HOLLY (Ilex opaca) in northern Iowa? No, it is not winter hardy in Iowa.

What could we plant on bare ground that would be LAWN enough for our 15-month-old son to play on by June? It needn't be a permanent lawn. This is a question to make a lawn man cringe, since the only answer is to recommend planting either of the 2 species he particularly hates: timothy or oats. Both will cover the ground with a rough, haylike coating which can be mowed, but neither is really satisfactory. The only other possibility, Italian Ryegrass, can't take the punishment that even a 15-month-old will give it.

Can I grow flowering MAGNOLIAS here in Iowa? *Magnolia soulangeana* and *M. stellata* do well on any rich, loamy soil well supplied with humus, but would probably need watering during summer droughts. Wrapping in burlap when small will protect buds from winter killing, but when the plant attains tree size, you will have to be reconciled to losing bloom about every third spring.

Will NECTARINE trees survive southeast Iowa winters? No.

What NUT TREES are hardy as far North as central Iowa? Butternut, black walnut, and hickory. Central Iowa is the Northern limit of all three.

Will the PASSION FLOWER (Passiflora) live out of doors in southeast Iowa? *Passiflora incarnata*, the Wild Passionflower, will survive in Iowa, but is not the exotic tropical beauty one might imagine from its name. The more showy species will not survive.

Are there varieties of PEACH and of APRICOT hardy in central Iowa? Specialists in Iowa have been working on the peach problem for years, but have not been able to offer a solution. In the case of apricots, however, the Hansen Manchurian hybrids, and those from the Dominion Experiment Station at Morden, Manitoba, can stand temperatures as low as 40° below zero.

What kinds of PEACH and PEAR trees are most adaptable to Iowa?   No reliably hardy peaches can be recommended. Pear varieties that will withstand severe exposure are Parker, Bantam, Tait, Dropmore, Pioneer, Ming, and Patten (the latter originated in Iowa).

What is a good low-growing PERENNIAL for the north side of a house?   If you mean the dense shade north of a house, where no sunshine ever falls, no showy perennial will grow. If the shade is only moderately dense, with sunshine sifting through the foliage of trees, you might try *Phlox divaricata canadensis, Vinca minor,* dwarf irises, *Dicentra eximia,* dwarf columbines, *Campanula carpatica,* or various primulas.

Is there a red RASPBERRY suited to this Middle West climate, for the home garden, that will bear the first year?   Latham and Chief are two varieties that have been successful over a wide range of the Middle West, but neither should be allowed to bear the first year, nor should any other variety be allowed to do so.

My black RASPBERRIES dried up on the plants this summer. The canes are weak and all pitted with gray spots. What can I do about this condition?   Your plants are infected with the common and serious disease known as anthracnose. Cut out the canes most badly infected; feed the plants with a straw-manure mulch or complete fertilizer in early spring; spray the canes carefully with either Bordeaux mixture or lime sulphur at least twice a year, especially when the leaves are unfolding, and just before the blooms open. (See Section VIII.)

Can ROSES and SHRUBBERY be successfully planted in the fall in northern Iowa?   Yes, provided the normal precautions are taken. Fall planting is much preferred to late-spring planting.

I understand the climbing Dr. Van Fleet ROSE should not be pruned. How should it be grown in northern Iowa? Must one take it down each fall? Or is there a real hardy rose that could take its place?   Dr. Van Fleet needs pruning to keep it in bounds and to cut out old, unproductive wood. But remember that it blooms on 2-year-old wood, and if all the old growth is cut away, you get no bloom. Protect in winter by laying down and covering with earth. Few climbers are more hardy than Dr. Van Fleet.

When is the best time to transplant STRAWBERRIES in Iowa? I see some transplanted in fall and some in spring.   As early in spring as the soil can be planted and worked is best. Only pot-grown plants have much chance to succeed if planted in late spring.

Should TRITOMA be stored for winter? Yes, dig the clump with dirt adhering to the roots and store in a cool (from 33° to 40° F.) cellar until late April.

Is VITEX hardy in this part of Iowa? Have tried to grow it and it winter kills. It is not hardy outdoors without very heavy protection; or by means of cutting back, taking up the clumps of roots, and wintering in a cold frame.

Are Carpathian WALNUT trees hardy in Iowa? No records are available, but they have survived severe weather in central Wisconsin. The Wisconsin State Horticultural Society, Madison, 6, Wisconsin, can probably give you the information you want.

Is the lovely low-growing YEW suitable to our Iowa climate? Practically all of the low-growing varieties of the Japanese Yew are fully winter hardy in your locality, provided drainage is good and suitable cultural practices are followed. Protect from harsh, drying winter winds.

KANSAS

I wish to plant a harvest APPLE tree (one that bears during our harvest in June) which will give me fruit in the shortest length of time. Is it possible to plant one to bear in a year or two, and what species would be best for this locality—a hot and usually dry section? One cannot usually expect an apple tree to bear much fruit until it is several years old. Write to your Department of Horticulture in the College of Agriculture at Manhattan, Kansas, for apple varieties recommended for your locality.

As a boy I spent many hours grubbing BUCKBRUSH. Recently I ordered some plants from a Minnesota nursery including one called Coralberry, and it turned out to be buckbrush. Did I get fleeced or do people really plant this bush? Coralberry (*Symphoricarpos vulgaris*) and buckbrush are the same thing, and it is an entirely respectable plant—away from its own home.

Should CHERRY trees be pruned each year to get larger fruit and better yield? If so, when? Cherry trees do not usually stand severe pruning. In early spring remove diseased wood and broken branches, and thin out crowding and crossing branches.

I have a good GRAPEVINE. How can I get more plants,

just like it?   Most native grapes are propagated easily by cuttings. In early spring cut several of the best 1-year-old canes into pieces about 15 ins. long with 2 or more buds on each piece. Plant these in good soil, with at least 1 good bud above ground. With good care many of these cuttings will root and grow. The best plants may be reset in a permanent location the following spring.

We seeded a new LAWN early this spring and have a good stand of grass. Should it be mowed, or left to grow this year? It can be mowed, but not shorter than 2 ins. Don't let it get real long before you mow, as it will suffer from such a major operation.

Should grass clippings be raked off the LAWN?   Don't rake off the clippings unless they are very heavy and likely to smother the grass. If they are raked off, use them for the compost heap, and spread over the lawn after they are rotted.

We have been told that we should cut our GRASS high. How high is "high"?   Leaving 2 to 3 ins. is a high cut.

How can we raise good LUPINES?   Lupines are cool-season plants and consequently are not suited to your locality.

ROSES

Why do monthly ROSES grow tall instead of bushy? Shade will draw up the plants somewhat. If the canes are very long and don't produce blooms, they are probably coming from the understock on which the monthly rose was budded. Canes of this kind should be cut out.

I have hybrid tea ROSES I wish to transplant in the spring. When should this be done?   Transplant as early as the soil can be worked. Prune the tops back, leaving only 3 or 4 ins. Take up a good ball of soil with each plant. (See Roses.)

A polyantha ROSE planted last spring did not have a bud on it all summer. What is the cause of its failing to bloom?   Polyanthas normally bloom freely the first season. Possibly the polyantha top died and the understock on which it was budded came up, and did not bloom. If the plant is producing long, straggly canes, it would be better to replace it.

What is the best winter protection for ROSES in western Kansas?   Hill soil up around the plants approximately 8 ins. Wait until the ground is frozen, and then add straw or similar material several inches deep, so that all of the soil mounds and the level soil between plants are mulched.

How heavily shall I prune ROSES in the fall that were put out in the spring?   Don't prune your roses in the fall. Wait until spring, and then prune out the wood that has been winter killed. (See Roses.)

What everblooming ROSES will do well in this part of Kansas?   Betty Uprichard, Condesa de Sastago, Crimson Glory, Editor McFarland, Golden Dawn, Good News, Margaret McGredy, Mme. Cochet-Cochet, Mrs. Sam McGredy, Radiance, Red Radiance, Soeur Therese.

What climbing ROSE would be best for the arch over a garden gate?   Paul's Scarlet Climber (scarlet); Mary Wallace (pink); Silver Moon (white). But they all need winter protection.

KENTUCKY

At what depth should FREESIA bulbs be planted? What month should they be planted?   Freesias should be planted heavy end down, with the tips barely below soil level. A good test for depth is to be able to feel the bulb tops without being able to see them. September is the best planting month for freesias.

How can one get rid of BERMUDA GRASS in this section? If it gets a start on either lawn or farm land nothing else will grow.   Where vegetables or flowers are planted Bermuda Grass must be constantly dug out until entirely eradicated. Several chemical preparations, such as Atlacide, Hammond's Weed Killer, and Dupont Weed Killer, used according to directions, will eradicate this.

How may rural families raise their own HERBS? What type of soil is suitable?   Practically all of the kitchen herbs may be grown in the open garden. Frequently home gardeners set off a special spot for these so that they may grow undisturbed year after year. They are not particular as to soil, but naturally respond to extra fertilization and initial preparation. Most catalogues now list special collections of kitchen herbs, both in seeds and in established plants.

How can I get PANSIES started in winter?   Pansies may be started in a cold frame or hotbed, or in flats in the house during winter. They cannot be successfully started from seeds outdoors after late summer or early fall. The plants themselves will be fairly hardy in your locality after becoming established, but winter-planted seeds outdoors would not germinate until the following spring.

Is it possible to have healthy perennial PHLOX plants in this vicinity, where we have very humid, hot summers? What soil conditions are suitable to them? Ohio Valley has the above summer conditions, and freezing and thawing for 5 months in winter. Perennial phlox may be grown in your section as successfully as anywhere else. They are entirely hardy and like good, rich soil. With established plantings, fertilizer may be put on top of the ground during winter. A mulch on the surface of the soil during the hot months of summer will keep the reflected heat from burning the lower foliage; watering should be done by laying the hose on the ground; soaking the soil but not sprinkling the leaves.

What is the proper culture for TRITOMA? Tritoma ("redhotpoker plant") should go through the winter safely, without extra protection. It is wise, however, to cut the foliage down after the first frost and cover the area with 6 or 8 ins. of leaf-mold or other mulch. Tritomas are not particular as to soil, but an occasional fertilization will produce larger blooms. Seeds may be planted in early spring or in a cold frame in fall. The usual method of propagation is from divisions of the old plants taken up in early fall and replanted promptly.

LOUISIANA

How can CHRYSANTHEMUMS be grown in northeastern Louisiana? Garden chrysanthemums are started from tip cuttings rooted in sand in April and set into beds of fertilized soil when they have become well rooted. If divisions of the old clumps are used, the plants will have a great deal of leaf spot, and so cuttings are much to be preferred.

What is proper time to trim CRAPEMYRTLE in northern Louisiana? When the leaves fall in the autumn. Crapemyrtle flowers on the current year's wood, so pruning must be done *before* growth starts, never after.

What are the best flowering EVERGREENS to plant in vicinity of New Orleans? Among the choicest evergreens for this area are the many beautiful varieties of azaleas and camellias. The tea of commerce is a very beautiful flowering evergreen shrub, as are also illicium, bananashrub, the poinsettia, and (in sheltered locations) that queen of flowering shrubs, the hibiscus.

What care and culture do GERBERAS require? If you can get fresh seeds these will germinate well in about 2 weeks; if not, buy divisions of old plants, set them at the same depth at which they grew previously in beds that have been made rich by spading in compost. Use a mulch of oak leaves to cover the soil around the plants, and apply a balanced plant food in January and June—watering well, of course, during all dry periods.

Should one take up GLADIOLUS bulbs every year? Yes, it is by far the best practice to lift gladiolus corms every year, just after the foliage turns yellow. The tops are cut off, the mother corms are discarded, and the new corms are stored in shallow boxes in a cool, shaded place.

Is CENTIPEDE GRASS successful as a lawn grass in the deep South? It is being advertised quite a bit here. Yes, this is undoubtedly one of the finest grasses for this section, particularly for light, sandy soils and dry areas. The sprigs or runners are stuck into well-prepared soil after the rains have begun in early summer, and a good lawn should result before cold weather. Be sure to have the apical end *up* when you plant the runners.

Should CALLALILIES be left in ground all winter? Mine did not bloom, but leaves are still green. Planted them last February or March. In semi-tropical sections of Louisiana, callas may be left in the ground all the year round. The soil must be acid, mucky, retentive of moisture, and free from too much competition from the roots of large shrubs and trees.

When is the best time to move SPIDERLILIES? White Spiderlily (hymenocallis) in early spring. Red Spiderlily (lycoris), July or early August.

In Louisiana should PEONY roots be dug up in winter, stored, and replanted in spring? The practice is sometimes followed in warm climates. The clumps are dug about the first of December and placed in *cold* storage where the temperature is held at about 35° F. In the early spring the clumps are replanted. Since the method is not entirely satisfactory, it is best to choose another type of plant which is better adapted to the warm climate.

Name several varieties of PEONIES (double) that grow and bloom well in the South. When is the time to plant them? Peonies are not happy in most parts of Louisiana. The winters are too mild to assure complete, long dormancy for the crowns of the peony clumps, and any attempt to grow these temperate perennials will only result in disappointment.

Which ROSES thrive best in the Louisiana soil and climate? Many of the true tea roses, such as Safrano, Marie van Houtte, Minnie Francis, Duchess de Brabant, and Louis Philippe will survive for many years. It is best to grow the modern cutting varieties as annuals, renewing a part or all of your rose bed each autumn.

How late can ROSE bushes be planted in central Louisiana? What is best fertilizer to use? Early planting is recommended, and December to February is considered the best period. However, the latest possible date would be about April 1. Cow manure is difficult to surpass as a plant food; commercial mixtures are excellent, either in conjunction with it, or alone if manure cannot be obtained.

What is proper care for ROSES and best time to plant in southern Louisiana? Roses should be set between December and February, the earlier the better, so that the root systems may become well established before the top starts to grow in the warm weather of spring. Have the beds fertilized in advance, plant at the same depth as they grew in the nursery, and water in well. Be sure that the plants never suffer from drought, and feed every 4 weeks during growing weather.

What is the best way to keep SNAPDRAGONS over winter in Louisiana? Young plants (less than 1 year old) should carry through the winter in the open ground without special preparation, if the drainage and other conditions are normally good.

MICHIGAN

Our BOYSENBERRIES winter kill every year. Why? Boysenberry canes are not winter hardy at low temperatures, or where exposed to harsh winds and winter sunshine. Lay down the canes and cover with earth, removing covering in spring toward the first of April.

Can you give us some information on the growing of CAMELLIAS outside, in climate similar to that around Detroit, Michigan? The camellia cannot ordinarily be grown outdoors in climates severer than that of Virginia. In very sheltered locations it may survive in the vicinity of Washington, D.C.

Will CHRYSANTHEMUMS winter safely in northern Michigan, near Petoskey? Yes, with protection. A blanket of evergreen branches intermingled with leaves would be the best covering. Apply when soil is slightly frozen. Soil should be well drained.

How late is it safe to plant CROCUS, hyacinth bulbs, and other early spring-blooming bulbs in southern Michigan?

Crocus, scilla, and hyacinth bulbs can be planted safely as late as sound unshriveled bulbs are available, although earlier planting is preferable. Tulips, on the other hand, should not go in until about the middle of October. While most experts condemn late planting of narcissi, I have planted these December 1 with good results by setting them 6 ins. deep—over the *top* of the bulb. They bloom late, but with perfect flowers.

Can you suggest EVERGREENS suitable for this climate? *Juniperus chinensis, J. pfitzeriana, J. monosperma, J. scopularum, J. horizontalis, J. sabina tamariscifolia; Picea canadensis albertiana* and *P. pungens; Pinus aristata, P. montana mughus, P. nigra, P. ponderosa, P. strobus,* and *P. sylvestris; Taxus canadensis; Thuyas; Tsugas; Abies lasicarpa* and *A. concolor; Pseudotsuga taxifolia; rhododendron* in variety.

Can you give me information on the raising of FOXGLOVE (Digitalis purpurea)? Plant seed in late May in shaded cold frame. When fall rains start, put on glass to protect from excess moisture. Cover plants with marsh hay or evergreen boughs after the first freeze, and replace the glass. Transplant into permanent situation (light shade and loose, loamy soil, with plenty of humus) toward the end of April or the first of May.

What varieties of FRUITS—strawberries, grapes, raspberries, blueberries, and peaches—are best suited to the highlands 40 miles south of Mackinaw Strait in Michigan (Otsego County)? Strawberries—Dunlap, Blakemore, Mastodon (everbearing); grapes—Fredonia, Seedless Concord, Golden Muscat; blueberries —Jersey, Harding; raspberry (red)—Indian Summer and Sunrise; raspberry (black)—Major Blackcap and Cumberland Blackcap.

Can the GUM trees Liquidambar and Nyssa sylvatica be grown in central or northern Michigan? *Nyssa sylvatica* (Sourgum or Blackgum) is not considered hardy in central Michigan. It is difficult to transplant, unless nursery-grown stock is used. It likes low, damp soil with plenty of humus. Hardly worth trying in this region. Liquidambar (Sweetgum) is hardy over most of the lower peninsula of Michigan, provided conditions are right. This is the Northern limit of its range. Must have deep, rich, moist soil, and stand free from all shade. Neither species would attain full stature in Michigan.

Will you please give me, as nearly complete as possible, a list of HERBS which will thrive in this vicinity? Annual: basil, borage, parsley, Summer Savory, anise, burnet, caraway, coriander, dill, marjoram. Perennial: balm, catnip, chives, fennel, chamomile, horehound, lavender, mint, pennyroyal, rue, sage, thyme, and yarrow.

Can HIBISCUS (rosa-sinensis) be grown in Michigan?   No, it is a tropical and will tolerate no frost whatever.

Will ILEX crenata nummularia be hardy in Grosse Pointe (Detroit), Michigan?   The Japanese Holly is not considered reliably hardy north of the Ohio River, though it sometimes survives a hundred miles north of there in well-sheltered spots. Not a good bet for Michigan.

Can Virginia HOLLY be grown in the Northern States? No; it is not hardy in the North. Grows in protected spots in Massachusetts, but Michigan winters would be too hard on it.

Is there any shrub HOLLY, 5 to 10 ft. high, that is reliably hardy in southern Michigan?   The word "reliably" is the pinch. You probably mean an evergreen holly that is 100 per cent hardy and looks like the pictures on the Christmas cards. And the answer to that is "No." There are three deciduous hollies, all of which have attractive winter berries: *Ilex glabra* (Inkberry), *I. laevigata* (Smooth Winterberry), and *I. verticillata* (Black Alder.

Will LOGANBERRIES survive here? Planted a few roots 2 years ago, and one bush is alive yet but does not bear.   Loganberries seldom survive Michigan winters. Boysenberries, which are root-hardy, are similar, but need cane protection. They are superior in flavor and more productive.

Which are the best NUT trees to plant in Michigan?   Black walnut, hickory, and butternut. If you are near any of the Great Lakes, toward the southern part of the state, the hazels or filberts may do well for you.

Can Alberta PEARS be raised successfully in lower Michigan? Do you mean the Elberta peach? The southwestern corner of Michigan is one of the world's great peach sections. On the other hand, if the newer Canadian hybrid pears (like Tait-Dropmore and Pioneer, or the Chinese Sand-pears grown in Canada) are meant, the answer is also "Yes." However, these pears are a compromise between hardiness and quality, and ought to be dropped from consideration for high-quality sorts that will do well in Michigan, such as the new Cayuga, or old favorites like Bartlett and Seckel.

Can perennial PHLOX be transplanted in the early spring in Michigan?   Yes, this is the preferred time. Move as soon as ground can be worked.

What PLANTS are best for Michigan climate? Only the hardier types. Would suggest investigating the large number of species and varieties being grown in the Nichols Arboretum of the University of Michigan, Ann Arbor, Michigan.

What low-growing ROCK GARDEN perennials are hardy in northern Michigan—30° to 40° F. below zero in winter? *Actinella acaulis; Androsace sarmentosa; Anemone blanda* and *A. aephyra;* Aethionema, *various; Callirhoe involucrata; Gypsophila repens; Campanula muralis; Hypericum reptans; Iberis sempervirens; arenaria, various; Armeria laucheana;* aubretia; *Campanula pusilla; Dianthus alpinus; Heuchera sanguinea; Iris pumila; Linum alpinum; Aquilegia saximontana* and *A. alpina;* primula, various; *Phlox subulata, P. multiflora,* and *P. andicola; Penstemon caespitosus, P. crandalli* and *P. alpinus; Physaria didymocarpa; Saponaria ocymoides; Papaver alpinum; Veronica rupestris.*

Is it possible to grow RHODODENDRONS successfully in Detroit, Michigan? Yes, but this is no tyro's job. Careful preparation of the soil is essential. Protection from *winter* sun and wind are particularly important. The best trick is to plant on the north side of a building or dense hedge, so that on June 21 the sun just touches the base of the stem. Then as the sun recedes to the south in winter the shade of the building will protect the plant from sun. In exposed locations, protection, such as burlap or wrapping in straw, will still be needed. Above all, don't neglect watering, even during the winter. And see that the soil remains acid.

When is the best time to set out hybrid tea ROSES in southeastern Michigan? There is no "best" time, since we cannot tell in advance what the weather will be. Plant as early as possible in spring, or as late as possible in fall. Many commercial growers and landscapers set out stocks during thaws in December and January. In fall planting, covering is necessary. Sometimes good pot-grown plants (7-in. to 8-in. pots) are available for late-spring and early-summer planting.

Is fall planting of hybrid tea ROSES considered safe in Michigan, in the area of Grand Rapids? If done *late* enough, fall planting is usually better than spring planting. Protection by hilling up is necessary.

Why can't ROSES in central Michigan be pruned in autumn? They can; but there is not much point in doing so, since the branches will have to be cut back to live buds in spring anyway, and the unpruned branches help hold snow, which is a good mulch, in place.

What are the hardiest varieties of climbing ROSES? Is CLEMATIS hardy in northern Michigan?   No climbing roses are winter hardy in Michigan. All need protection afforded by laying them down and covering with earth. Most of the clematis species are hardy, with proper culture.

Will SAGE grow from seed in Michigan?   Yes, but results are slower than from divisions, and variation can be expected. Better plant an improved variety, like Holt's Mammoth, from divisions.

What SHRUB or evergreen can you recommend for planting on north side of house where soil is dry?   Your native *Cornus stolonifera,* the Red Osier Dogwood, is a highly desirable and hardy shrub for just such a situation. Pfitzer's Juniper is a desirable evergreen subject, but may need some watering to become established.

MINNESOTA

Will you please name several of the spring-flowering BULBS, other than tulips and narcissus, that we can grow here in southern Minnesota?   Chionodoxa (glory-of-the-snow), crocus, galanthus (snowdrops), muscari (grapehyacinth), ornithogalum (Star-of-Bethlehem), scilla (squill).

How can I protect CANTERBURYBELLS for winter? They can be wintered satisfactorily in a cold frame. If this is not available, use a light straw mulch on the ground around plants and under leaves. Then place a thick layer of lightweight brush over the bed, and cover this with straw or marsh hay. The brush is necessary to keep straw from smothering the green leaves that remain all winter.

Will you give the name of a good CHERRY-PLUM tree which is suited to the climate in central Minnesota?   The list of hardy varieties includes Oka, Sapa, and Zumbra. The Compass variety is an excellent pollinizer for the above.

I want to plant some CURRANTS. What is a good variety? There are several excellent varieties including the old Perfection and the new Red Lake. These are hardy in your state. In some localities, however, planting is restricted because of danger from the spread of the white-pine blister rust. Consult your State Nursery Inspection Service at St. Paul.

We grow some DOGWOODS here, but not the beautiful large-flowering kind. Do you think that we could? The Flowering Dogwood of the South and East is not hardy in your section.

Our little EVERGREEN trees don't look quite right, and we have been told that they have red spiders. Is there a cure? See Section VIII.

What is the best time to prune EVERGREENS like junipers and arborvitae? Prune lightly in the spring just as soon as the new growth begins to show. Evergreens make rapid growth right after that and will soon hide the cut ends or stubs.

We have extremely cold winters here. Last year the temperature went to 36° below before we had any snow. I have never seen a FORSYTHIA this far North. Would one survive our winters? Some of the hardier forsythias may survive, but the flower buds are winter killed when exposed to such low temperatures.

Is it possible to grow FOXGLOVE 6 to 8 ft. tall in Minnesota? It would certainly be very unusual. Half that height would be average.

What kind of FRUIT trees are best adapted for growing in Polk County, Wisconsin? Write to the Department of Horticulture, Wisconsin College of Agriculture, Madison, Wisconsin, for their list of fruits recommended for planting in that locality.

Can GLADIOLUS bulbs be left in the ground if heavily mulched and well drained? I recently read an article where it was claimed that they were being successfully wintered that way, even here in Minnesota. Yes. Cover with a 12-in. mulch of manure or straw after ground freezes. Usually considered better and easier to dig, store, and replant.

How can I raise Golden Muscat GRAPES in southern Minnesota? This variety is not recommended for general planting so far North. Possibly the plant could be protected from winter injury if entirely covered with straw; however, the growing season might not be sufficiently long for good crops to mature.

Is it necessary to give winter cover to GRAPEVINES here in southern Minnesota? Most of the standard grape varieties must be protected during winter. The varieties Alpha and Beta are usually winter hardy if the wood is well matured before cold weather.

My arborvitae HEDGE is almost 7 ft. tall, and I would like to have it just about 3 ft. Can it be cut back to that height?

No. Evergreens like this should not be pruned back beyond the green, actively growing shoots. They do not renew themselves from old hardwood as deciduous shrubs do.

Even the hardiest privet HEDGES kill back here in the winter. What would you suggest for clipped hedge about 6 ft. tall? *Lonicera bella albida,* the White Belle Honeysuckle.

When should PANSIES be planted out in the garden?   Pansies if grown in a cold frame over winter will not be injured by the frosts and light freezing of early spring. Plant them in the garden as early as the soil can be worked.

When and how is PANSY seed sown?   Sow the seed about mid-July in a seedbed well loosened up with leafmold. When the seedlings are large enough, transplant to a coldframe, using a similar soil, where they are kept over winter.

Do you know the name of a good PEAR suited to the climate of central Minnesota?   The Minnesota State Fruit Breeding Farm has originated several new and promising pear varieties. The Bantam and Patten Number 5 are now recommended for trial. These 2 varieties planted together help, through cross-pollination, to insure heavier crops.

We have read about mixing PEATMOSS with soil to make it acid. There is a lot of peatmoss near here. Could we use it? Not all peatmoss is acid. The only way to be sure is to have it tested. It can be used as humus in your soil, however, whether acid or not.

How deep should PEONIES be set?   Cover peonies with about 2 ins. of soil.

Will you give a list of hardy PERENNIALS for central Minnesota?   Coreopsis, gaillardia, peonies, iris, delphinium, hosta, aquilegia, shastadaisy, thalictrum, dictamnus, hardy asters, hemerocallis, hardy chrysanthemums, phlox, veronica.

What PERENNIALS would form a good backbone for a northern Minnesota garden where frost comes early and winter killing is a problem?   Coreopsis, gaillardia, peony, iris, delphinium, aquilegia, shastadaisy, veronica.

What kind of PERENNIAL plants can I grow in southern Minnesota?   Coreopsis, gaillardia, peonies, iris, delphinium, aquilegia, hosta, shastadaisy, thalictrum, dictamnus, hardy asters, hardy chrysanthemums, phlox, statice, veronica and euphorbia.

Will black RASPBERRIES do well in this part of the country? Black raspberries are doubtfully hardy in the extreme North.

When is it best to plant ROSES, fall or spring? It is safer to plant roses in the early spring. If fall planted, they must be very well protected against severe winter temperatures.

What is the best way to protect a TREE ROSE during the winter in Minnesota? Dig up the plant carefully so as not to injure roots. Lay it in a long trench and carefully work soil around and over it. Cover with at least 6 ins. of soil. After the ground freezes 1 or 2 ins., cover with several ins. of straw.

How much of hybrid tea ROSE tops should you prune off in the fall? Don't prune in the fall. After they are uncovered in the spring, cut back to good, sound, live wood.

We have sandy soil and 40° below zero in the winter. Can I raise climbing ROSES? Yes, if given good winter protection. Take the canes off their support in fall and tie them together to make one long bundle. Lay this bundle flat on the ground and completely cover with soil. Have 2 or 3 ins. of soil over all canes. Mulch over the soil with several ins. of straw.

What causes climbing ROSES, after being uncovered in spring, to die back to within 2 ft. of the ground? The buds are alive, yet the canes die back. The canes are wrapped with marsh hay and waterproof paper. If there is a section near the base where canes are exposed or poorly protected, canes will be killed from that point to their tips. Also canker, a fungous disease, may girdle the canes, producing similar results.

What fruit-bearing SHRUBS are hardy enough for our Northern climate? Korean Cherry, Juneberry, elderberry, American Highbush Cranberry, and some of the flowering quinces are hardy, especially in favorable situations.

Which of the cultivated varieties of WALNUT are hardy enough to be planted in central Minnesota? The named varieties are not always winter hardy in central Minnesota. Even in southern Minnesota the Thomas, Ohio, and Ten Eyck, standard varieties, are recommended only for trial.

MISSISSIPPI

When is the best time to set out new CHRYSANTHEMUM plants? Rooted cuttings of chrysanthemums should be set out in the garden in May or June. It is better to use cuttings than divisions from the old clumps, as in this way you will avoid carrying over infection of the leaf-spotting disease. Choose an overcast afternoon, water the plantlets in well, and shade them for a day or two.

How can RAINLILIES be made to bloom and thrive in the delta section of Mississippi?   These little flowers (*Cooperia*) of the west wind usually succeed quite well in this section. With sufficient moisture, fertilizer, and freedom from severe competition they should bloom profusely during the summer months.

How deep should GLADIOLUS corms be planted?   In light, sandy soils of the lower South it is best to set gladiolus corms 3 to 4 ins. deep. Thus they will have better moisture and will not topple over when in bloom.

What GRASS is best suited for the Gulf coast?   There are several excellent lawn grasses for this section. For shade, under trees—St. Augustine. Poor soil, not much shade—Centipede. Full sun, good soil—Bermuda. Good soil, lots of moisture—Carpet Grass.

Could I trim a GARDENIA bush to shape? Would it bloom? When should it be cut?   If you have *Gardenia florida* (Cape-jasmine) prune, if necessary, just when growth begins in spring, by thinning out crowded shoots and cutting back straggly branches. (See Pruning *Gardenia veitchi*.)

Tell me why my white SPIDERLILIES will not bloom even though the foliage develops? They have been in the ground several years.   Too much shade. Lack of plant food (they are gross feeders and respond well to fertilizing), or lack of moisture during growing season.

Will the LOQUAT or "Oriental plum" grow in the lower cotton belt?   Yes, the loquat is a most ornamental evergreen tree, hardy in the Gulf coast region. Ordinarily it bears large annual crops of delicious yellow fruits that are esteemed as fresh fruit and for pies, tarts, and conserve.

Can NANDINA be grown from cuttings?   Attempts to grow nandina from cuttings will be disappointing, in spite of the best possible care. Propagate these shrubs by sowing ripened seeds in a flat. Care for them until the following summer, when germination should be complete.

When is the best time to plant ROSES on the Gulf coast?   Between December and February. Early planting is much to be preferred, as the root systems will then have time to become well established before top growth is forced out by the warm weather of spring.

What is the best soil for growing ROSES? A sandy loam or delta soil that is fairly high in organic matter, retentive of moisture, and well fortified with readily available nutrients.

Give me list of the best climbing ROSES, everblooming. Yellow Banksiae, Belle of Portugal, Silver Moon, Paul's Scarlet, Reve d'Or, Climbing Dainty Bess, and many of the new patented varieties.

Is the old-fashioned MOSS ROSE obtainable? Where? You will find the Moss Rose listed in many general catalogues, and by most specialists in roses.

MISSOURI

I would like to know when to plant bulbs of AMARYLLIS formosissima, also known as Jacobean Lily, in Missouri. Early spring, or should I wait until May? What kind of soil and fertilization? Plant after danger of hard frosts has passed. It will thrive on a variety of soils but prefers a medium loam. Soil should be highly fertile; very old manure and liberal supplies of bone meal are good.

What ANNUAL can I plant that will bloom all summer in a north bed that gets sun early morning and late afternoon? Annuals are notorious sun lovers. A few that will condescend to grow without full sunshine are: godetia, lobelia, nicotiana, *Centaurea imperialis* (Sweet Sultan), clarkia, California Poppy; *Cynoglossum amabile* (Chinese Forget-me-not). (These last two may be sown in fall.)

What care should I give perennial ASTERS set out in the fall? A light mulch of straw, hay, or dry leaves over winter is all they need. Remove mulch before growth starts early in spring.

What AZALEAS will grow well in Jackson, Missouri? *Azalea mollis* hybrids; *Azalea calendulacea; A. nudiflora, A. mucronata, A. obtusa,* var. *amoenum.*

A YOUNGBERRY plant we bought in Oregon never has borne fruit. Is it our climate, or soil? Is at least 10 years old. Probably the climate. Some plants from the Northwest do not produce normal growth in Missouri.

What sweet CHERRIES are hardy and satisfactory in the Middle West? Sweet cherries are not a reliable crop in the Midwest. They lack hardiness, both as to heat and to cold. They are also troubled considerably by insects and diseases. Sour cherries and Duke hybrids are more adapted to this region. Varieties of sweet cherries which should do well are Napoleon, Black Tartarian, Bing, Windsor.

What would be the best type of living CHRISTMAS TREE for us?   Colorado Blue Spruce or Red Cedar.

How can one grow large CHRYSANTHEMUMS outdoors in Missouri?   Most large-flowering commercial or greenhouse mums do well outdoors in Missouri. Grow just 3 or 4 stems on each plant. Remove all side buds, letting the top bud only flower. *Plenty* of water and culture is essential.

What shrubs and flowers would be good for a CITY GARDEN in this state?   Shrubs: *Cotoneaster divaricata* and *C. acutifolia; Deutzia lemoinei; Kerria japonica;* Philadelphus, various; *Spiraea prunifolia; Virburnum carlesi.* Perennials: tulips; narcissi; ornithogalum; phlox, early varieties; Oriental poppy; dianthus; lupine; pyrethrum; linum; gaillardia; dictamnus; *Lilium croceum, L. tigrinum, L. superbum, L. umbellatum;* anchusa; chrysanthemum; aster (Michaelmas daisy). Annuals: calendula; marigold; petunia; verbena; *Phlox drummondi;* gypsophila; larkspur; dimorphotheca; zinnia; calliopsis; *Mirabilis jalapa* (Four-o'clock); *Bartonia aurea.*

I have a SHASTADAISY from Idaho. Its flowers there were very large, but mine are smaller. Does Missouri climate have something to do with it?   Climate is not to blame. Shastadaisies need full sun, fertile loam soil, a good supply of water during the growing season, and a light mulch of straw or leaves over winter.

Can we raise DELPHINIUMS in the Midwest successfully? Set out strong plants in spring. A deep, fertile loam soil is required. Add a generous amount of ground limestone if the soil is acid. Full exposure to the sun and constant moisture at the roots during the growing season are essential. Cultivate frequently, and provide good drainage to prevent winter injury. A light mulch of straw or hay over winter may be beneficial.

What hardy FERNS will succeed in Missouri, and how are they grown?   Ferns like a cool, shady exposure (north). Any soil that contains a good supply of leafmold or peat, and constant moisture, will be satisfactory. Plant ferns in fall before the ground freezes. Collect native species from your vicinity or purchase from a local grower.

What kind of HERBS can we raise here?   Anise, caraway, chervil, chives, coriander, dill, fennel, tarragon, lavender, sage, Lemon Balm, rosemary, spearmint, Summer Savory, Sweet Basil, thyme, Sweet Marjoram. Culture of medicinal herbs on a commercial scale requires considerable experience, and should not be attempted by the novice.

Can LAVENDER be grown in Missouri? Where can a "start" be obtained? How is it cured (as used in sachet bags)? Yes, lavender can be grown in Missouri. Plants may be obtained from most nurseries. Hang small bunches of the flowers and leaves in a warm room or shed where they will dry quickly. They can be put in sachet bags, etc., as soon as dry.

Is it possible to grow MAGNOLIA grandiflora in the vicinity of St. Louis, Missouri? What soil does it prefer? Yes; but St. Louis is about the Northern limit for this tree; consequently growth is slow and mature specimens relatively small. A southern exposure with a north to northwest windbreak is most favorable. Grows best in a fertile clay loam soil. Flowers appear in July.

What culture for hardy PHLOX in Missouri? Give full sun, fertile loam soil containing a good supply of organic matter, adequate drainage to prevent winter injury, frequent cultivation, and irrigation during a dry growing season. Transplanting or dividing may be necessary after the plants have grown in one spot for 3 or 4 years.

What is the proper winter protection for RHODODENDRONS and azaleas in Missouri? A 6- to 10-in. mulch of dry leaves, preferably oak leaves. Rhododendrons exposed to direct sun during winter should have a burlap or lath screen to prevent the leaves from "burning" or turning brown.

Can tree ROSES be grown in central Missouri? Plant in spring in fertile clay loam soil well supplied with humus. Cut back the top growth or "head" to 3 or 4 eyes, and tie the main stem firmly to a strong stake. Full sun and a constant supply of moisture are necessary. For winter protection, loosen roots on one side, bend the plant over, cover top with soil and a heavy straw mulch, firs wrapping main stem with burlap or paper. Uncover early in spring before growth starts.

What is the best time to plant ROSES and when is the best time to prune? Set out roses in the fall, if the plants are dormant; otherwise wait until early spring. Prune hybrid teas in early spring. Climbing roses are pruned after they flower.

Why do my ROSE bushes grow so tall, and have very few leaves? Any of the following might be the cause: too much shade; suckers from seedling stock at base of grafted plant; black spot, defoliating plants; excess nitrogen in the soil.

How much should a Hercules climbing ROSE be pruned each year (flowers 5 ins. in diameter—now 2 years old)? Also Blaze? Depends on type of trellis and effect desired. For extensive coverage remove only the dead wood and a few of the oldest canes each year. Drastic pruning results in few flowers until the plant gets re-established. Both of these climbers bloom best on two-year-old canes.

What flowers would be best for a SHADY GARDEN, with some sun in afternoon? Anchusa, balsam, bleedingheart, spring-flowering bulbs, campanula, columbine, ferns, forget-me-not, fuchsia, eupatorium, godetia, daylily, lobelia, mertensia, primula, lily-of-the-valley, plantainlily, tuberous-rooted begonia, thalictrum, tradescantia, vinca, violets.

Is it good or bad to cover STRAWBERRIES with straw or leaves during the winter, in Missouri? A straw mulch is recommended, especially for young plants just getting established. Leaves are all right if they are not permitted to remain excessively wet, pack down, and thus smother out the plants.

How should URCEOLINA miniata be cared for in order to have it bloom? This rare Andean bulb will probably not be hardy in Missouri. Suggest growing it in a pot of light but rich soil in a sunny greenhouse or window. Rest by keeping quite dry after leaves die away in winter. Repot in spring as growth begins.

Are there any large-flowered white or yellow VIOLETS which will grow well in Midwest climate? *Viola blanda* (white), *Viola hastata* (yellow), *Viola rotundifolia* (yellow). Violets need light shade, friable soil containing lots of leafmold, and extra water during dry weather. Protect them with a light mulch of leaves or straw over winter.

MONTANA

What FLOWERS which grow here have attractive seed pods, or blooms, that may be used for winter bouquets? Echinops (Globethistle); eryngium (Sea-holly); asclepias (milkweed); yucca; *Martynia proboscidea* (Devilsclaws); *Clematis orientalis; Koelreuteria paniculata.*

What are some good shade-tolerant FLOWERS for north of house and under trees in this climate? *Anchusa myosotidi-*

flora; aconite; *Aster sub-coerulea;* lily-of-the-valley; bleeding-heart; hosta; mertensia; myosotis; primula; *Phlox divaricata* and *P. carolina; Campanula carpatica* and *C. rotundifolia;* bloodroot; trollius; thalictrum; violet; *Epimedium niveum.*

Our GLADIOLUS bulbs seem to "run out." Is this because of the short season? Possibly the season is too short to mature the new corms. Rich, deeply prepared soil and sufficient moisture at roots to keep them growing vigorously in open sunny location, protected from wind, should help to produce better corms.

What HEDGE is best suited to this climate? To form a neat shorn hedge, Amur River Privet. For an informal taller hedge, Persian Lilac, *Rosa hugonis, Rosa rubrifolia,* and Chinese Elm.

Is the Moutan Tree PEONY adapted to the northern Rocky Mountain region? Peony Moutan may be grown in Montana if altitude is not more than about 4,000 ft. above sea level. It grows with coaxing, in Denver, Colorado, at 5,280 ft. altitude. Drying of the stems by winter wind and sun seems to be the difficulty.

Could you suggest PERENNIALS for cold climate and short growing season, at elevation of 5,700 ft.? Peony; iris; *Phlox subulata, P. divaricata, P. decussata; Trollius europaeus; Mertensia virginica;* campanula; pyrethrum; *Papaver orientale, P. nudicaule;* primula; delphinium; rudbeckia hybrids; *Centaurea macrocephala; Physostegia virginiana; Clematis integrifolia, C. recta, C. grandiflora;* Monarda Cambridge Scarlet.

Twenty-five years ago we had wonderful SWEETPEAS in Northwest Montana. Now rust or blight gets them. What can be done? See Section VIII. Where days are hot and nights cool, do all artificial watering as infrequently as practical, but always thoroughly, and always before noon. Try the new spring-flowering type.

NEBRASKA

Will you list some ANNUALS that bloom most of the summer and can endure the heat and drought of Nebraska? Zinnia, marigold, petunia, portulaca, annual gaillardia, *Vinca rosea, Anchusa capensis,* annual phlox, scabiosa, cosmos.

Is BOXWOOD out of the question in this locality? Boxwood is not hardy under your conditions.

What is the best way to protect the BOYSENBERRY, as it

winter kills here?   Allow the new canes to lie on the ground as they grow. Cover them with clean straw to a depth of 3 ins. in late fall. Remove the mulch in spring just before the buds on the canes start to grow, then lift up and tie the canes to a support.

Why did a hard November freeze kill CHINESE ELM and still not affect other trees in Nebraska?   Most of the other shade trees used in your section go into a state of dormancy without the help of moderately cold weather in early fall. The Chinese Elm apparently requires some cold weather to harden it off before it becomes dormant and is able to stand a hard freeze.

We have some EVERGREENS planted against the front of the house. Do you advise mulching the ground there for winter? Yes, a loose mulch of peatmoss, leafmold, or some similar material helps to conserve soil moisture and prevents too-deep freezing.

What annual HERBS may be grown in Nebraska?   Sweet Basil is easily propagated from seed and very easy to grow. It makes a dense, bushy growth about 24 ins. high. Lemon Balm is propagated from seed and is also easily grown. (See Herbs.)

Will you name 3 perennial HERBS that may be grown in Nebraska, and give their uses?   Chives are onionlike plants having small stems which are cut several times during the year and used as flavoring or as garnishing. Sage is the most commonly grown perennial herb. Its principal use is in the flavoring of sausage, in dressings for poultry or rabbit, and as sage tea. Lavender is a member of the mint family used as a natural perfume in silks and linens.

My tulips and narcissi do well, but my HYACINTHS always fail. Is there any special care they should have?   Your experience appears to be typical. Hyacinths don't seem to be adapted to your section of the country.

I know that IRIS should be moved in summer, but if it is necessary, can they be transplanted in early fall?   Yes; though it is beyond the recommended planting season.

What LILIES can we grow most easily here?   The Tiger Lily, Regal Lily, and the Orangecup Lily (*Lilium elegans*) are the most adaptable.

There are several gardens in town that have spotted orange LILIES. The flowers are close together and face upward. Can you tell me what they are?   This is *Lilium elegans* (also sometimes listed as *Lilium umbellatum*). The common name is Orangecup Lily.

What PERENNIALS can we grow that will stand heat and drought?   Iris, perennial sweetpea, veronica, lythrum, euphorbia, statice, gypsophila, hardy asters, liatris, physostegia.

When do you advise planting hybrid tea ROSES?   Early spring is safer than fall planting in your section. If you plant early, just as soon as the ground can be worked in spring, the plants will come along as rapidly as fall-planted stock.

Must I hill up soil around hybrid tea ROSES for the winter? This makes good winter protection. After the ground freezes, add a mulch of some loose, light material.

On what date should I hill soil around my hybrid tea ROSES? About mid-October. It should be done just before the first hard freeze. If not done before the ground freezes, you will have trouble handling the soil.

What is the best kind of winter protection for ROSES in this section?   Hill plants 10 to 12 ins. high. Fill holes so left with leaves or straw and cover plants completely. Climbers should be hilled and branches bent down and covered completely with soil and mulch.

Will you tell me what to do after I uncover my hybrid tea ROSES?   Hybrid tea roses should be pruned after they are uncovered in the spring. Cut back to good, sound, live wood. Ordinarily that leaves canes of 6 ins. or less in length.

I know nothing about hybrid tea ROSES, but wish to have a rose garden. Will you advise me about a dozen good varieties to start with?   Betty Uprichard, Condesa de Sastago, Crimson Glory, Editor McFarland, Golden Dawn, Good News, Margaret McGredy, Mme. Cochet-Cochet, Mrs. Sam McGredy, Radiance, Red Radiance, Soeur Therese.

When is the best time to plant TREES, spring or fall? Spring planting is safer than fall planting. Planting should be done *very* early to get the most good from spring moisture.

NEVADA

Are there any AZALEAS hardy enough for this climate? Last winter the coldest was 16° below zero but temperatures sometimes go to 37° below zero.   Azaleas require very acid soils and refuse to grow in soils that contain lime. Most Western soils are filled with lime and for this reason azaleas will not thrive. It is doubtful if they would survive 37° below even if the soil is suitable.

When should one set out FRUIT trees?   Plant in Nevada in early spring after severe cold is over but before the buds start to swell; latter part of March or first part of April, depending on the altitude.

Should ROSE bushes be trimmed back to 8 ins. in vicinity of Reno, Nevada?   All roses except the shrub roses should be cut back to 8 ins., or even less, in early spring. Flowers come on the new growth and too much old wood will produce small and inferior flowers.

NEW MEXICO

How long should DAHLIAS be kept out of the ground before planting again?   Only until climatic conditions permit replanting.

What are the best bush FRUITS and when should they be planted?   Raspberry, loganberry, boysenberry, strawberry, and grape. Plant in spring in the North; fall or spring in central New Mexico and South.

What are the best tree FRUITS to plant in this climate? In the higher-altitude regions of northern New Mexico: apple, crab, pear, plum, and cherry. Toward the South, and in lower altitudes: peach, apricot, cherry, pear, fig, persimmon.

What is best lawn GRASS to plant in western New Mexico? In high-altitude regions of northern New Mexico, Kentucky Blue Grass. Central and southern: Bermuda Grass.

Is there any GRASS that will stay green the year around? In regions with sufficiently cool summers, yet not too extremely cold winters, Kentucky Blue Grass keeps green all winter if well watered.

When would you make a LAWN in New Mexico?   March to June in the North; September to November in the South.

How can a LAWN be kept in good growing condition? First by providing a surface, at least 4 ins. deep, of good loam containing adequate humus on which to seed or plant the grass. In the dry air of the Southwest, lawns keep in better growing condition when given a mulch in November of 50 per cent peatmoss and 50 per cent sheep manure pulverized and raked in, followed by watering as needed to keep roots moist.

How often should GRASS be mowed here? A little, secluded, intimate lawn should be kept shorn more frequently and closely than is necessary for a large expanse. In general, lawns in New Mexico are better mown not too frequently or too closely, since the slightly longer grass helps provide shade and so prevents surface drying.

What fertilizer should I use for a LAWN? Before seeding, apply a balanced fertilizer. To keep a lawn growing at its maximum vigor, give an application of ammonium sulfate in June, substituting in alternate years a balanced commercial fertilizer.

How often should I water my LAWN? In New Mexico, lawns need watering as frequently and as thoroughly, both summer and winter, as is necessary to keep the grass roots moist at all times. This is true of even the higher-altitude regions, except where snow covers the ground most of the winter.

When is the best time to plant ROSES in New Mexico? Spring in the North; fall or early spring in the South.

What winter protection do ROSES need? In the North prune hybrid teas back to 6 ins.; mound the plants up with soil, compost, or peatmoss; cover with spruce branches or cornstalks. In the center and South no winter protection is necessary. No protection is necessary for shrub roses or polyanthas anywhere below 7,000 ft. altitude. Above that they are hardly worth the necessary coddling.

When is winter protection necessary for ROSES? Winter protecting of hybrid teas and climbers may be done after the surface inch or two of ground freezes.

What hardy tea ROSES are continual bloomers here? Almost all hybrid teas thrive and bloom where the altitude does not exceed 6,500 ft. Some that are especially successful, nonfading in bright sunshine, are all the varieties; McGredy; Better Times; Amelia Earhart; Christopher Stone; Condesa de Sastago; Dainty Bess; Edith Nellie Perkins; Editor McFarland; Etoile de Hollande; Radiance; Caledonia; Joanna Hill.

Will you name some shrub ROSES for northern New Mexico? *Rosa hugonis; R. setigera; R. rubrifolia; R. rugosa Agnes; R. rugosa Pink Grootendorst; R. rugosa Max Graf.* For central and southern New Mexico all of the above and probably any and all species.

What climbing ROSES are suitable for New Mexico? Any and all climbers revel in the sun of southern New Mexico. Some that bloom most profusely are Gardenia; Silver Moon; Paul's Scarlet Climber; Climbing Hadley; Climbing Talisman; Climbing Dainty Bess. In higher altitudes the choice is more limited and climbers require protection from winter sun.

What are the best STRAWBERRY plants to grow and when should they be planted?   Everbearing Strawberry: Mastodon, Rockhill (non-runner). One-crop varieties: Senator Dunlap, Fairfax. They should be planted any time except midwinter. June transplants of Mastodon bear well the following September.

I IRRIGATE with water from a ditch, using trenches and rows for my garden. Will you give suggestions for arrangements of flowers in garden?   Since ditching necessitates rows, regimentation of plants is difficult to avoid. Three possible combinations of plants suitable for your conditions might include:

Heliopsis, Lemoine's Star	Delphinium hybrids	*Helenium autumnale rubrum*
Aster, Robert Parker		*Salvia pratensis*
Aster, Mt. Everest		Iris, Golden Hind
Aster, Beechwood Challenger	Monarda, Salmon Rose	Aster Harrington's Pink
Phlox, R. P. Struthers		*Clematis recta grandiflora*
	Chrysanthemum, Algonquin	Chrysanthemum, Algonquin
Phlox, Africa	Phlox, Africa	Chrysanthemum, Early Bronze
Phlox, Snowcap		Monarda, Cambridge Scarlet
Zinnia, Yellow Chrysanthemum, Mars	Zinnia, Old Rose	Zinnia, Salmon Rose
		Lavatera, Loveliness
Dictamnus rosea	Iris, Blue Triumph	Scabiosa, Isaac House hybrids
Chrysanthemum, Santa Claus	Phlox, Jules Sandeau	
Echium, Blue Bedder		
Petunia, Elks Pride		
Petunia, Salmon Supreme		

In lower altitudes and in southern New Mexico use fewer perennials and more annuals for continuity of summer bloom.

NORTH AND SOUTH CAROLINA

Will gardenias and CAMELLIAS grow out of doors in this part of North Carolina?   Both would remain alive outdoors but it is doubtful whether you would ever have any blooms. The gardenia will stand temperatures as low as 20° to 24°, but anything lower than this kills the plant back to the roots. Both must have wood at least a year old on which to bloom. Your best chance would be to grow them as tub or box plants, keeping them indoors and well watered during the severer months of winter.

How often should CAMELLIAS planted in boxes be watered during the winter months in a greenhouse? What are best plans for building a greenhouse 12 × 20 ft. especially for camellias? Often enough to keep soil always moist but never waterlogged. When water is applied, give enough to saturate whole body of soil. Build greenhouse where it receives full sunshine and with ample ventilation *both* at top and sides. Provide heating system to keep night temperature 50°.

What good varieties (double) of CAMELLIA japonica can be planted outside in South Carolina? *Alba plena, Candidissima,* Sarah Frost, *Chandleri elegans,* Comte de Gomer, Lady Marion, and Stiles Perfection.

Please give some hints on pruning or shearing EVERGREENS. Also, what is the proper time? I live in western North Carolina. Evergreens are not pruned in the general sense of that word. They may be clipped or sheared any time during the growing season, beginning in spring, just as new growth starts. This encourages bushier, more compact growth, but any late-fall or winter shearing would increase the danger of winter killing.

What is the best GRASS to sow in a yard where there is lots of shade? One of the shady spot mixtures, containing about 60 per cent blue grass, mixed with a little Domestic Rye Grass. Fertilize and water 2 or 3 times heavily in shaded areas where tree roots compete with the grass for nourishment and moisture.

What is the proper fertilizer to use on NANDINA to produce maximum number of berries? Old rotted cow manure and bone meal. It needs a well-drained position and generous amounts of water in dry weather. (See next question.)

Why doesn't my NANDINA have berries after having bloomed? Rainfall influences production of berries. Cross-pollination from one plant to another is necessary. Plant in groups for this reason. There is a chemical preparation sold under the name of Fruitone-B which may be sprayed on the blossoms of nandinas, hollies, and many other plants. This usually produces heavier crops of fruits or berries. Try this on your nandinas next spring.

Do you trim NANDINA plants? If so, when?   Pruning is usually unnecessary. If, however, they are too large for the space you want them to occupy, the entire plant may be trimmed back; or the older, heavier shoots may be cut clear back to the ground. During winter or very early spring new shoots will appear from the roots.

Will PANSY seeds planted December 1 bloom the following spring?   If planted in a cold frame or hotbed the first of December the plants will be large enough to set out in the open in early spring and will start to bloom almost immediately. Planted in the open ground the first of December seeds will not germinate until spring, and would be several weeks coming into bloom.

Do PEONIES in South Carolina require partial shade or full sun to best stand our hot summers?   Peonies will stand partial shade in temperate gardens, but do well only in the extreme northwestern corner of South Carolina. They require a long, cold winter to induce complete and unbroken dormancy, and are a disappointment in most parts of the cotton belt.

What hardy PERENNIALS can be depended upon for summer bloom in the mountain region of western North Carolina? You may almost take your choice from perennials listed in dealers' catalogues. The writer has seen practically all well-known and many unusual perennials flourishing in the western mountain section of your state. Pick the ones which appeal to you most, and plant them with full assurance that they will succeed for you there.

Will you please give information about the growing of all plants, especially ROSES, in this locality? Most articles are written for the states north of us or south of us, or the western part of the country.   You live in a latitude where all annuals grow rapidly and where practically every variety of perennial plant will do well. Only the doubtfully hardy ones need any winter protection and your main handicap in growing hybrid tea roses would be the false springs and late freezes which occur almost every year. When roses go dormant in early winter, hill soil up around them to a depth of about 6 ins.; prune bushes half-way back, and do not give any other protection. Your section is ideal for growing climbing roses and floribundas. The same rules for fertilization and spraying apply there as in every other part of the country.

Are there any ROSES which will grow on a fairly windy shore (eastern exposure) in eastern North Carolina? The soil is well

drained, good sand-humus mixture. You might not be able to succeed so well with hybrid tea roses as growers in other sections, but hardy climbers and floribundas adapt themselves perfectly to your locality, soil, and climatic conditions. A few of the older, more reliable hybrid tea roses are satisfactory if not given too much winter protection. This causes them to make premature growth in spring which frequently is killed back by late freezes.

Can you recommend quick-growing, medium-sized SHADE TREES for lawns in this area? The fastest growing are Chinese Elm, Box Elder, and weeping willow, but they are not among the most desirable or longest lived. Tulip-poplar, Sweetgum, and your native maple grow fast enough, and are among the best of the permanent shade trees for your locality. Native evergreens do well if moved when small.

What are all the odd and unusual fruiting SHRUBS and TREES, semi-tropical and otherwise, which would grow and fruit in eastern North Carolina? All kinds of barberries, cotoneaster, dogwood (both tree and bush forms), euonymus, hollies, honeysuckles, privets, and viburnums will give a varied display in fall and winter. Many shrub roses also bear attractively colored hips. The callicarpas have lilac and violet fruits; snowberries and coralberries bear profusely, as do the various types of eleagnus which have orange and silvery fruits. Among the trees nothing is prettier than your native hawthorn, wild plum, magnolia, and mountain ash. Several North Carolina nurseries list most hardy trees and shrubs.

When should I plant SWEETPEAS in South Carolina? Sow the early-flowering or later kinds in November. Protect with litter during severe spells. The early sorts should bloom in May, the late sorts 2 or 3 weeks later.

NORTH AND SOUTH DAKOTA

How deep should I plant DAFFODILS? Do they need any special winter protection? Cover bulbs with 5 or 6 ins. of soil when planting. They can be protected with a loose mulch of straw or coarse hay. The mulch goes on after the ground is frozen.

When is the best time to sow KENTUCKY BLUE GRASS seed? In early spring or in late summer.

How can one grow and winter Regal LILIES in North Dakota? Plant in fall or early spring, in well-drained soil.

The top of the bulb should have about 8 ins. of soil above it when planted. Mulch with 2 to 4 ins. of straw after the ground freezes in the fall.

Where can hybrid NUT seed or trees be obtained for trial in this locality (northern Great Plains)?   Contact the United States Department of Agriculture at Beltsville, Maryland; your State Experiment Station at Fargo, North Dakota; the Experiment Station at Morden, Manitoba, and the secretary of the Northern Nut Growers' Association at Geneva, New York.

Can PEONIES be planted this spring or must we wait until fall?   Fall is the better time to plant peonies, and you will be just as far ahead if planting is done then.

When is the best time to plant PERENNIALS in our cold country?   Early spring. Good-sized clumps of the hardier sorts may be planted about the first of September, and if properly mulched will winter well.

Are there any climbing ROSES that will winter here without protection?   The old variety, Queen of the Prairie, might, but modern sorts listed in most catalogues need good protection.

Will Texas ROSES winter kill in South Dakota?   No tea or hybrid tea rose will winter successfully in South Dakota without covering with a heavy mulch or earth. Some shrub roses like Austrian Copper or *R. setigera* should winter without protection. There is no reason why roses grown in Texas, if they have been properly handled, should be less hardy than those grown in other sections.

What is the best time to dig TULIP bulbs in North Dakota? Two or 3 weeks after foliage matures, dig the bulbs and leave stems and foliage attached. Spread them out in shallow trays and store in a dry, cool place. The tops can be removed and bulbs cleaned up in late summer.

How soon should TULIPS be replanted? They were dug in early summer and have been stored under the back porch. Replant these bulbs soon after mid-September.

OHIO

What is the best type of soil for growing APPLES in central Ohio? What cover crop would you recommend while the trees are small?   Central Ohio is largely a silty clay loam. Make sure the soil is well drained. Sow soybeans in early June and plow under in September. Then sow Rye Grass as cover crop if soil is not to be kept cultivated.

Can GERBERAS be wintered over in Sandusky, Ohio? How are the roots stored? If by "wintering over" outdoor culture is meant, this is theoretically possible, except that a mulch heavy enough to protect the plant will probably smother it. Gerberas can be lifted after a sharp frost has killed leaves, with dirt adhering to the roots, and stored in a cool place (above freezing, but must not go above 40° F.) covered with damp sand or peat to retain moisture. Examine during winter and sprinkle if needed. Plant out again in spring when apples bloom.

Have you any suggestions for growing HERBS for condiments in Ohio? All of the annual and most of the perennial herbs can be grown in Ohio. In general a rather poor sandy soil in full sunshine is their preference. (See Herbs.) For fuller detail, with their uses, see *Gardening with Herbs* and *Gardening for Good Eating* by Helen M. Fox.

Will you please give me a list of some HERBS that will grow here? Annuals: chervil, coriander, caraway, dill, fennel, Summer Savory. Perennials: basil, burnet, chives, hyssop, marjoram, mint, sage, sorrel, tarragon, Winter Savory.

What are the best climbing ROSES for northern Ohio (especially yellow)? Two good yellow climbers are Primrose and the newer Doubloons. Neither, however, is winter hardy: both will need protection.

What is the best ROSE collection to plant in this part of the country? Plant the collection offered by your favorite seed house or rose specialist. They select varieties that are reasonably sure to satisfy anyone who grows them.

What is the proper time to plant hardy SHRUBS and PEREN-NIALS in northern Ohio in the spring? Crapemyrtle, catalogues state, is hardy north of Virginia, with protection. What kind of protection is meant? Plant any time before the leaf buds begin to open. "Protection" means some kind of burlap wrapping or screen, as of pine boughs, to protect it from winter winds.

How and when should I plant everbearing STRAWBERRIES in central Ohio? Plant as early in spring as plants are available and soil can be prepared. Avoid newly turned sod because of danger of grub damage. Any good loam will grow strawberries; even lighter sandy soils if fertilized. (See Strawberries.)

OKLAHOMA

Can you give me pointers on how to grow the garlandflower (DAPHNE)?   Daphne is propagated by cuttings and layers. *Daphne cneorum* seems to need a green finger. It will tolerate much sunshine, also partial shade; resents acid soil, likes a little lime; a friable soil, and a rock at its back.

How can I succeed with DELPHINIUM in Oklahoma? Delphiniums are cool-climate plants and dislike heat. Deeply prepared, friable, sandy loam will help content them. A layer of peatmoss under their roots may even make them smile.

What FLOWERS, if any, can be grown as borders to shrubbery in a shady lawn?   Chiefly early flowers that do their growing before trees are in leaf: *Anchusa myosotidiflora;* bleedingheart; columbines; daylilies; Himalayan daisy; lily (*croceum,* Regal, Madonna, Tiger); narcissus; Oriental poppies; Phlox *divaricata; Plumbago* (*ceratostigma*) *larpentae;* primulas; *Trollius europaeus;* tulips.

What FLOWERS that are good honey producers will grow in an Oklahoma garden?   Willow, linden, apple, plum and pear trees. Crocus, nepeta, clovers, Michaelmas daisies, and monarda (Beebalm).

Can you give a list of FRUIT trees, berries and small fruits that do the best in this climate?   Strawberry; boysenberry; dewberry; plums: Japanese varieties and Greengage; cherry, early varieties; peach; apricot; apple; crab, and pear.

When shall I plant GLADIOLI in Oklahoma?   First planting between March 1 and 15. Successive plantings every fortnight till mid-May.

Will you tell me how to get rid of BERMUDA GRASS? Grasses are difficult to eradicate, since their narrow leaves do not succumb to poison sprays. An airtight covering of heavy building paper or old linoleum is effective, also persistent hoeing of grass blades as they appear. No plant survives long when smothered or sheared above ground in its growing season.

What would be the best grass for a LAWN that will grow under trees and will stand dry weather?   Shady lawn mixture if it is to be sprinkled or irrigated; otherwise, Buffalo Grass; or if too shady for this, a ground cover such as *Vinca minor.*

Our LAWN is barren of Bermuda Grass in shade of trees and where their tiny roots come to the surface. Will you recommend

a grass or ground vine that will overcome this and withstand the hot winds of Oklahoma? *Vinca minor* is a presentable ground cover, tolerant of shade, heat, and dryness.

How shall we care for PEONIES in the South? Peonies do not like a hot climate. Give them deeply prepared rich soil with a layer of peatmoss below their roots. Plant with the eyes 2½ ins. below the surface of the ground. For larger blooms remove all side flower buds.

What varieties of PEONIES shall we plant? Some of the older varieties stand Southern climate best: Karl Rosenfield, Auguste Dessert, Claire Dubois, Festiva Maxima, Duchess De-nemours, Couronne d'Or.

What PERENNIALS will do well in partial shade, and in full shade? If shade is caused by trees, enrich the soil and add leafmold or peatmoss. Aconitum; anemones, several varieties; *Anchusa myosotidiflora**; columbine; Bleedingheart; Hosta*; Ladyslipper; *Lilium concolor, L. philadelphicum, L. croceum;* lily-of-the-valley; *Mertensia virginica*; Phlox divaricata; Plumbago (ceratostigma) larpentiae*;* Primula*; pulsatilla; Bloodroot*; *Vinca minor*;* violets*; *Uvularia bellidifolia.*

What PERENNIALS will give color from spring to frost? Continuous bloom spring till frost is possible from a succession of different varieties such as spring-flowering bulbs; mertensia; *Clematis davidiana;* peonies; irises; dictamus; *Phlox divaricata, P. subulata, P. carolina ovata,* and *P. decussata; Campanula carpatica, C. persicifolia; Nepeta mussini;* eupatorium; monarda; chrysanthemums.

Will you please give suggestion for HARDY FLOWERING PLANTS for central Oklahoma climate? Perennials: *Anthemis tinctoria;* chrysanthemums; dictamus; heleniums; *Heliopsis pitcheriana;* hemerocallis (Daylilies); *Iris pumila* varieties, *I. tectorum,* I. tall-bearded; monardas: Cambridge, Scarlet, and Salmon-pink; *Phlox divaricata, P. subulata,* and the sturdier varieties of *decussata;* scabiosa.

What PERENNIALS grow best on north side of house in Oklahoma? Ferns, columbine, *Phlox divaricata, P. carolina ovata, Trollius europaeus, Anchusa myosotidiflora,* primulas, campanula, bleedingheart, *Uvularia bellidifolia.*

Will you give some information on ROSE culture and protection in the Southwest? Roses in the Southwest need a

*These will grow in full shade.

deep, rich soil—a 6-in. layer of rotted manure, or manure and peatmoss to keep their roots cool—and an open, sunny place with good air circulation. For winter protection, hill soil up around them, and cover with spruce branches, straw, or any light covering which will protect them from winter sun.

When should ROSES be pruned back in the summer? How much pruning should they receive?   As soon as the rush of summer bloom is over. Prune back polyanthas to where individual rose stems leave main stem; hybrid teas more severely. A mulch of peatmoss in midsummer encourages fall bloom. As soon as first fall buds form, feed a balanced fertilizer. Climbing roses and hybrid perpetuals bloom on 2-year-old wood. Leave all vigorous canes of last season's growth. Cut out at the ground all wood older than this.

Our lot is entirely without shade. What TREES are the fastest growing and make good shade?   Siberian and Chinese Elm will grow rapidly and provide shade. *Acer dasycarpum* (Soft Maple) is also a fast grower and a more permanent tree.

OREGON

How can I grow CAMELLIAS?   See Tender Shrubs—Section II.

When should DAFFODIL bulbs be planted in Portland? Throughout the fall months; the earlier the better.

Should DAFFODILS be lifted annually and the soil fertilized before planting?   Lift only when bulbs become overcrowded and flowers begin to deteriorate—usually after being in the ground for 3 or 4 years. The bulbs are rich feeders and should be fertilized annually.

Will you give a good list of hardy EVERGREENS for 20° below zero; and the soil they require?   Blue Spruce, Norway Spruce, Douglasfirs, Concolor Firs, Scotch Pine, Ponderosa Pine, Austrian Pine, Mugho Pine, Juniper, both upright and spreading, any of the American Arborvitae, Alaska Cypress, California Nutmeg. Deciduous: *Betula nana* (Birch), Western Larch. They will grow in any good garden soil.

Will you name some FLOWERS that will bloom from spring to fall?   *Early:* narcissus, tulips, primulas, mertensia, *Anemone pulsatilla,* lily-of-the-valley. *Midseason:* aquilegia, *Aster subcoeruleus,* dicentra, anchusa, *Delphinium chinense, Campanula glo-*

merata, C. carpatica, digitalis, geum, hemerocallis, *Sidalcea rosea, Lilium candidum* (Madonna), *L. regale* (Regal), *L. tigrinum, L. umbellatum,* Iceland Poppy, peonies. *Late:* aconitum, *Anemone japonica, Clematis davidiana, Plumbago larpentiae,* gentians, early chrysanthemums.

What annual HERBS are grown in Oregon? What perennial herbs?   Annuals: Summer Savory, Sweet Marjoram, dill, chervil, Pot Marigold, coriander, Sweet Basil. Perennials: chives, tarragon, Sweet Woodruff, Common Balm, Curly Mint, Sweet Cicely, Wild Marjoram, rosemary, Winter Savory, Garden Thyme.

Do perennial HERBS require winter protection?   In colder sections some of them do. (See Herbs.)

Was presented with a double red HIBISCUS plant sent from southern California. Local nurseryman advises it is hardy in this climate. On his advice planted on west side of house to protect from east winds. Looks sick. What do you advise?   Herbaceous perennial species of hibiscus and the hardy shrub species (such as Rose-of-Sharon) will grow outside in the Northwest, but not tropical shrub species. We cannot tell from your description which kind yours is.

What is the best variety of Easter LILY to raise on Pacific coast, and how can I propagate and care for bulbs so they will flower at Eastertime? How are bulbs cared for after flowering?   Formosum (tall) and giganteum (low-growing) have long been favorites but are not now obtainable; growers are using an excellent one known as Croft variety. Start bulbs early in November; place single bulbs in 5-in. pots which have been provided with good drainage; use friable clay soil to which has been added a little old sifted manure; place an inch of soil in bottom; set bulbs and cover with soil; as foliage develops, add additional soil. Give a temperature of 65° to 75° F. and provide full light. Do not permit bulbs to dry out, but water sparingly. Grow only one stem. Spray with water or a weak nicotine solution for green fly. After blooming, plant bulbs outside; they usually require 2 years to recover from having been forced.

Where, and how, shall I plant LILIES-OF-THE-VALLEY for good blooms? My plants thrive but have no blooms.   On north side where they get plenty of light and filtered sunshine part of the day. Lily-of-the-valley, once established, becomes quite rampant. Plants must be confined by enclosing bed with cedar boards or in some similar way, otherwise they will not bloom freely.

They like a rich, woodsy soil containing a little well-rotted manure.

Will MAGNOLIAS live in northern Oregon?   Deciduous magnolia can be grown. Some evergreen varieties succeed in milder parts, but are not recommended for colder areas.

Shall I plant NANDINA and Mexican orange in sun or shade? One nurseryman says in sun and another says in shade. I am perplexed.   Full sun in Pacific Northwest. Neither plant is given a high rating for hardiness, so both should be placed in a protected situation.

How shall I care for OLEANDER that is 6 years old, buds each year but never blooms? Is it too cold here? Have it outdoors all the year around.   If plant does not suffer definite injury from frost, it is not too cold. Lack of sufficient light may cause lack of bloom. Prune previous year's shoots well back in spring.

Shall I plant PERNETTYA in sun or shade?   In the Pacific Northwest the plants do much better when planted in full sun.

How can I make PERNETTYA have more berries?   Three or more plants must be grown together; plants should be pruned annually, removing some of the old wood. Sometimes root pruning is necessary to prevent them from spreading and making too much sucker growth at the expense of fruiting.

When should ROSES be planted?   Plant in fall or spring (former preferably) in holes sufficiently wide and deep to accommodate roots without crowding. Set budded plants with bud about 2 ins. below surface of soil. Prune roots at time of planting. Shorten canes of fall-planted bushes; prune in spring. Prune spring-planted ones at time of planting. If soil is dry, water well. Surface dress with fertilizer after plants have become established.

Should ROSE bushes be planted in full sun, or where they have some shade?   A situation fully exposed to sun is best.

What makes SAGINA-MOSS (Lazyman's-lawn) turn brown in spots?   Air pockets which form under the "moss." Remove brown part and substitute a healthy piece of moss, first placing a little fresh soil and fertilizer in the hole. Sagina must be kept well pressed to the ground to avoid brown spots.

Will you suggest a few SHRUBS that will grow well at the coast in the briny atmosphere?   *Hypericum moserianum,* hydrangea, kerria, azalea, rhododendron, cydonia, deutzia, weigela, symphoricarpus, *Ilex aquifolium, Jasminum nudiflorum,* kalmia, *Viburnum tinus.*

Can you suggest locations for planting of SHRUBS—deutzia, Cydonia japonica, and pomegranate? In your state, growing conditions are so good that most shrubs are easy. Deutzias like well-drained soil with generous supply of humus; sun or part shade. *Cydonia japonica* (Japanese Quince) does well in any good soil in full sun. *Punica granatum* (pomegranate) needs deep, heavy soil, sun, and elbow room. Fertilize, if necessary, when planting by incorporating rotted dairy manure in soil below roots.

How shall I treat my VIOLETS to make them bloom? They do best in good loamy soil containing a little old manure and leafmold. To encourage plenty of blooms, runners must be removed. After plants of good size have flowered they should be lifted, divided, and replanted.

TENNESSEE

Will the pink AMARYLLIS grow outdoors in the climate of southern Tennessee? There are many so-called bulbous plants which belong to the amaryllis family. Those which are so frequently grown in pots are not reliable outdoor subjects. The best for your purpose is the one called "hardy amaryllis," frequently listed as *Amaryllis halli* but correctly known as *Lycoris squamigera*. The bulbs increase year after year in the open ground.

When should BOXWOOD be pruned in Tennessee? It is not customary to prune established boxwoods. Sometimes the smaller ones will send out precocious shoots which are cut off to retain the symmetry of the bush. Where pruning is necessary, this should be done during the growing season. Fall or winter pruning increases the danger of winter killing.

In Chattanooga BUDDLEIAS hold their green leaves all year. As they bloom on 1-year wood, where should they be cut back, to make the most flowers and the largest? The old, heavy canes should be cut back *to the ground*, in late fall or early winter. The strong younger shoots will bear larger blooms. If the entire plant is left undisturbed, you will have more blooms, but smaller ones.

If CANTERBURYBELL seeds are planted in a seedbed the latter part of winter, will they bloom that same summer? The canterburybell is a biennial plant and is best sown in late summer. Young plants may be transferred to the beds in early fall and given a light covering of leaves. These will bloom the following year. Seeds planted in late winter may be transplanted the following spring or fall for bloom the second year.

Will CAPEJASMINE stand the winters of this section (Johnson City, Tennessee? The capejasmine is a true gardenia, and so far there is no variety which is reliably hardy. It will stand 20° to 24° F. without damage. It blooms only on old wood, and if this is frozen back there will be no blooms the next year, even though the roots remain alive and the plant continues to send out new growth. In your section it would be far better to grow gardenias as tub plants: outdoors in spring, summer, and fall, and indoors during the cold winter months.

If DAHLIAS are left in ground over winter, will the new shoots bloom and do as well as if the bulbs had been taken up? Dahlias may be given extra covering and left in the open ground in your section. The clumps should be taken up in spring, however, divided, and replanted; such divisions will bloom just as well as those taken up and stored. The only danger is an occasional extremely severe winter during which they might be frozen.

What winter protection should be given ROSE trees planted in the upper South, where temperature goes to zero? Only the grafted head of a tree rose is likely to be damaged by zero weather. Dig the soil away from one side of the root, bend the plant down until the head touches the soil, and cover this head with mixed soil and leaves, pinning the mound down with a burlap sack. In spring this covering is taken off, the head pruned, and the soil packed around the roots to hold the tree upright again.

TEXAS

Will Japanese ANEMONE grow here? What location is best? Kind of soil? A partially shaded situation, sheltered from strong, drying winds, is best. They require a rich, moist soil, and a generous supply of water during dry periods.

Do I leave ANEMONE bulbs in the ground after they bloom? Are they supposed to come up year after year? It is better to lift the bulbs and store them in peatmoss or in dry sand until inspection shows that they are beginning to push for another season of growth.

Will you please give me some practical suggestions as to means of winter storage of tender tubers and BULBS, when basement or root-cellar facilities are not available? Tender bulbs can be lifted when the foliage turns brown or is frosted, and stored in containers of peat, sand, and bagasse, or rice hulls. The containers should be placed in a cool, shaded place. If they can be put in cold storage at about 50° F., they will keep very well.

How should I plant my CAMELLIAS? See Tender Shrubs.

When is the proper time to graft CITRUS fruit trees on trifoliate? When the bark will "slip" or separate easily from the wood. Ordinarily after a good rain during May, June, or July.

Do you think COLUMBINE and bleedingheart can be grown in central Texas? With good care columbine will succeed; and bleedingheart also if the soil is slightly acid and a sheltered position is given.

Will you give care for DAHLIAS? Is late planting best for here? Set out tubers about 10 days before average date of latest spring frost. This will vary for different sections of the state, but March should be right for the warmer sections, April planting for sections farther North. Set roots about 5 ins. deep in beds enriched with compost; tie plants to a stout stake as they grow; feed every 3 or 4 weeks with a balanced fertilizer. Dahlias must have plenty of water if you wish to cut an abundance of fine blooms.

Is it O.K. to leave DAHLIA bulbs in the ground until ready to plant in the spring, or should they be taken up in fall after stalks die? Both systems work. If you have been successful in leaving them in the ground, well and good. But if too many clumps have been disappearing, lift and carefully store in peat, sand, or similar material in a cool, shady place.

Can SHASTADAISIES be dug up in spring to permit the soil's being turned over and sweetened? They can be lifted, divided, and reset in spring, but autumn is much to be preferred, so the plants will have many well-established roots before warm weather.

Will DOGWOOD grow in this section? Yes, with proper preparation. A neutral or slightly acid soil, a high amount of organic matter, and good drainage are essential. Water freely in periods of drought and wrap the trunks with burlap for the first season or two.

When is the best time to set out DOGWOOD? During early winter, when they are without leaves. Dig as much of the roots as you can, protect from sun and wind, and set at the same level as they formerly grew. Wrap the trunks with cloth as a protection against sunscald and the entry of borers.

Will you list some of the best annual and perennial FLOWERS for this section of the Gulf Coast?   Annuals, for winter: alyssum, blanket flower, California Poppy, calliopsis, carnation, delphinium, larkspur, lupine, Moroccan toadflax, pansy, petunia, phlox, poppy, statice, sweetpea. Annuals, for summer: cosmos, flossflower, marigold, morningglory, nasturtium, portulaca, verbena, zinnia. Perennials: hemerocallis, Louisiana iris, Blue Sage, Stokes' Aster, violet, canna, chrysanthemum, four-o'clock, morea, shastadaisy, Transvaal Daisy, Golden Glow.

Are there any new or unusual FLOWERS easily grown in the extreme South? (Gulf coastal area.)   Practically all of the new annuals may be grown in the Gulf coastal area if fitted into the season that suits their needs. Hardy annuals during the autumn and winter; heat lovers, like marigolds, cosmos, and zinnias, during the hot, humid summers.

What is the best time to plant FLOWERS this far South?   Hardy annuals: alyssum, calendula, calliopsis, carnation, pansy, petunia, statice, sweetpea in the fall in warmer sections. Tender annuals for the summer: cosmos, flossflower, torenia, portulaca, nasturtium, and zinnia after danger of frost has passed. Perennials should be divided in the winter or when through blooming rather than in the spring.

What is the correct time to plant seeds of annual FLOWERS in Austin? To set out perennials?   For the cool-weather group —such as calendula, snapdragon, and pansy—October through December. For the heat-tolerant group—such as marigold and zinnia—March to April. Perennials should be divided in winter, December through February, or immediately after blooming.

Should LEAVES be left on the flower beds in our climate?   Yes, but do not let them pack down heavily over crowns of plants. New leaves should be added as the mulch decomposes.

What are the best FRUITS for this climate?   Oranges, grapefruit, peaches, pears, plums, bramble fruits, and figs.

What is a sure-fire remedy or preventive of borers in FRUIT TREES? (In the Southwest.)   It is generally agreed that there is no preventive. A remedy can be effected by using paradychlorbenzene. Your county agent, seedsman, or nurseryman can give the details of the treatment.

How can I grow GARDENIAS in Dallas?   A slightly acid soil, rich in organic matter; a mulch of oak leaves; and facilities for watering during dry times are essential. An occasional watering with a solution of copperas will supply iron, and periodic spraying with an oil emulsion will control whitefly and sooty mold.

What is the best location for GLADIOLI? Part shade or all sun? When is best time to plant for this part of the country? Gladioli are sun-demanding; corms should always be set in full sun. The planting time should be gauged by the time of tne latest killing frost for your section. Then plant about 2 or 3 weeks *ahead* of this date. Late February and early March for southern sections; 2 or 3 weeks later farther north in the state.

Is there a practical way to get rid of "Nut" or Coco GRASS? It is very difficult to eradicate once it gets beyond the hand-picking stage. Trials have shown that it is severely discouraged by growing a heavy cover of cowpeas on the plot for one or more summers. As soon as possible in early summer sow cowpeas thickly, fertilize well, and allow them to become thickly matted to shade the soil. The vines should be plowed or dug into the soil in October.

How can I kill Bermuda GRASS in beds where yard has been filled in? Digging the roots by hand is the only practical way to eradicate Bermuda Grass. Naturally this is a tiresome job; it must be repeated several times.

When is the time to plant California Privet HEDGE in central Texas? December to February. Cut the plants back heavily at planting time; set at the same level that the plants grew; water well at once.

What HERBS would you suggest for Gulf coast country, for growing on a commercial scale? Sage (*Salvia officinalis*) promises to be the best prospect for commercial production, following trials at experiment stations in this section.

When should HIBISCUS be moved? December to February. If plant is frosted in early winter, cut it back severely, and move it to the selected site.

What variety of HOLLY that will bear berries can best be grown here? What soil and treatment are required? The Chinese Holly (*Ilex cornuta*), the Dahoon Holly (*Ilex cassine*), American Holly, (*Ilex opaca*), varieties of all of which species succeed in this locality.

My HYDRANGEAS do not grow and bloom as they should. What kind of soil and fertilizer are best for them in southeast Texas? I used well-rotted leaves and barnyard fertilizer. Are they too rich for them? Your soil sounds all right, provided it is not strongly alkaline. Sulphur and alum will acidify soil; rotting leaves will help. Be sure not to prune after the wood is mature, as flower buds would be removed. Pinch or prune no later than July.

How can I make HYDRANGEAS, planted outdoors in Texas, bloom?   A soil not too alkaline, an abundance of organic matter, and water are essential. Severe competition from tree roots, winter killing, or late pruning can cause failure to bloom. The flower buds are formed before the plants go dormant in the fall.

How can I protect Dutch IRIS from cold?   When low temperatures are forecast, cover plants with excelsior, leaves, or some other mulch until the danger from that particular cold snap has passed. Generally the plants should be uncovered after 2 or 3 days. Newspapers or a single thickness of cloth is of no value.

Why do tall-bearded IRISES refuse to bloom along the Gulf coast?   Our light, sandy soils and lack of a real and prolonged dormant season combine to rule out this popular perennial for the Gulf coast. In some sections 1 or 2 varieties seem to be pretty much at home, but not like the semi-tropical perennials that really succeed here.

My yellow JASMINE is a beautiful shrub, three years old, and has had only 1 small bloom on it. Can you tell me why?   Jasmine requires plenty of sunshine. Possibly too much shade is the cause of your trouble.

Are LILACS and rhododendrons suitable for moist coastal areas?   These temperate shrubs are sure to be disappointing to you here. They must have a complete dormant period (induced by long, unbroken cold) and a heavy, rich soil. Better stick to the beautiful semi-tropical flowering shrubs that succeed in your section.

What LILIES will do well in semi-alkaline soil?   Easter Lilies, Madonna Lilies, (*L. candidum*), *L. chalcedonicum*, *L. croceum*, *L. martagon*, *L. testaceum* and other European types should all succeed if your soil is not too basic (alkaline). Of course the incorporating of acid organic materials will help in the culture of all of these and other lilylike plants.

Please advise if LYCORIS is adapted to this climate. What will make it bloom?   *Lycoris squamigera* should flower in the northern section of Texas if the bulbs are properly fed and watered and do not suffer too much root competition. *Lycoris radiata* will probably succeed in the southern sections under conditions of good culture and freedom from too many roots.

Rice hulls make very light soil, but are they too rich for PANSIES? If so, what besides sand should be used? Mixed with sandy soil, rice hulls make a good compost for pansies.

How many species of PASSION-FLOWER are there? Will any of these grow in Texas? A nineteenth-century botanist listed 184 species, and many more have been discovered since then. The fruits and flowers are of many kinds; some few of the fruits are edible, most are not. *Passiflora caerulea* and *P. manicata* should do well in gardens in southern Texas.

What is the best understock for PEACHES in the South, where root rot is prevalent in sections with high alkaline soil? Tennessee wild peaches are the most widely used understocks in all parts of Texas, but are not resistant to root rot.

Will PEONIES do well in central Texas in a black, waxy soil? If so, what varieties do best? No, peonies will not succeed in this climate. (See question on Peonies in South Carolina.)

What is the best time to divide and reset PERENNIALS in Austin? Autumn or winter; or immediately after flowering. In this way the roots will be widespread and well established before spring growth commences.

What is the best time for planting PERENNIALS? Fall. Practically all herbaceous perennials can be lifted in late fall, or very early winter, and reset.

Should RANUNCULUS bulbs remain in ground year after year? It is better to lift them each year after the foliage has died down and store in dry place.

Will you list some good ROCK GARDEN plants for use in this section? Probably the best groups are the true cacti and semitropical succulents that succeed out of doors in the South. The usual alpine rock garden plants used in the North will be a disappointment to you in Texas.

What ROSES are best for Southern gardens? The teas do fairly well if they have good care. Some old-fashioned roses, like Louis Philippe, Mme. Lombard, Minnie Francis, Duchesse de Brabant, and Safrano will thrive long years after many choice cutting roses have succumbed to this climate. Several Texas nurseries are specializing in these varieties for Southern gardens.

What makes ROSES die so quickly here? Black spot, dieback, crown gall, an excessively alkaline soil, lack of a distinct rest period—all contribute toward a short life for modern cutting roses.

Could I grow ROSES in a dry clay soil?   To do so successfully it will be necessary to improve the soil by the addition of compost, rotted leaves, sand, and other materials. An abundance of water is essential, and frequent feeding, during growing weather, with a balanced commercial fertilizer.

Will you tell me the proper time to set out new ROSE-BUSHES in southern Texas?   Early planting is strongly recommended for the South, December to February being best by all odds.

Is fall or spring best time to plant ROSES in west Texas? Fall planting is better by far. If the plants are set in December to February, roots can become established before top growth starts in the spring.

What is the cause of ROSES in Galveston, planted in either fall or spring, growing and blooming all summer, apparently strong and healthy, then suddenly dying in the fall? The trouble starts with black patches on the stems, while 25 per cent of bushes are not affected.   Patches on the canes are caused by the so-called dieback disease, for which no dependable control is known. Prune away diseased parts and mop the cuts with Bordeaux or sulphur paste. Black spots followed by yellow areas on the leaves are manifestation of black spot, which see.

Will you please give some information as to the enemies of ROSES in South and Southwest? Also what kinds are hardy for this section?   The greatest trouble is black spot, a fungous disease that can be controlled by the frequent use of Bordeaux spray or by dusting after every rain with 300-mesh sulphur. In the deep South so-called dieback is a serious trouble for which no dependable control is yet known. Old-fashioned varieties in the tea group are most dependable.

What SHRUBS shall I plant in southwestern Texas, where there is a dry climate, wind, and alkaline soil?   It is best to use natives, and some of the best of these are *Leucophyllum frutescens; Tecoma stans; Diospyros texana; Rhus virens* and other species of sumacs; several species of *acacia; Chilopsis linearis; Sophora secundiflora;* several species of salvia; *Clematis drummondi;* several species of *juniperus;* several species of yucca and agave.

May I have a list of flowering trees or SHRUBS for Houston? Trees: live oak, ash, hackberry, magnolia, mimosa, huisache, and junipers. Shrubs: crapemyrtle, pittosporum, photinia, privet, oleander, jasmine, forsythia, spirea, weigela, pyracantha, camellia, azalea, and gardenia.

What are some of the best SHRUBS for foundation plantings?
Azalea, camellia, podocarpus, euonymus, cotoneaster, pyracantha,
Japanese Box, Japanese Holly, jasmine, abelia, feijoa, and hi-
biscus.

**Why did ZEBRA-PLANT that came up from an old plant not
have the same white margin on the leaves that the old plant had?**
Many variegated plants will not come true from cuttings, particularly when sprouts come from the base of the plant as it
grows; try several highly variegated tip cuttings, discarding any
that "sport back."

UTAH

Are AZALEAS difficult to raise in the garden? If the soil
is slightly acid, moisture plentiful, and the location not too exposed to sun or high winds, the culture of hardy varieties is not
difficult.

**Can I have a list of ROCK GARDEN PLANTS hardy in
Utah?** The following should be hardy in Utah, at altitudes
below 6,000 ft.: any of the sedums, pinks (*dianthus*), dwarf
phlox (*P. subulata*), bellflower (*Campanula carpatica*), basket-
of-gold (alyssum), saponaria, globeflowers (trollius), coralbells
(heuchera), and violas. The last 3 should have part shade.

**Is there any fairly good climbing ROSE that will go through
the winter without covering in a climate where temperature occasionally goes from 10° to 15° F.?** Try Paul's Scarlet
Climber; south or east exposure is preferable. The new patented
Horvath setigera hybrid roses are very hardy. The following are
climbers: Federation, Hercules, and Thor.

**Have you a list of flowering SHRUBS and TREES that would
grow in an altitude of 6,000 ft. to make an attractive outdoor
living room?** Try French hybrid lilacs; they should do well
at this altitude. Recommended varieties are: Congo, Edith
Cavell, Leon Gambetta, Miss Ellen Willmott, Mme. Francisque,
Morel, Paul Thirion, Captaine Ballet, Marechal Foch, Mme. An-
toine Buchner, and President Fallieres. Other good shrubs would
be mockorange (Virginalis or Norma); Highbush Cranberry;
Wayfaring-tree. Small trees: Colorado Pink Locust; Hawthorn;
or Hopa Flowering Crab.

WASHINGTON

**When and in what kind of soil and location should ALSTRO-
MERIA be planted?** Plant tubers 5 to 6 in. deep in September

or early October in a rich, well-drained soil, and in full sun or partial shade; place the little eyes up and the tubers down.

Do ALSTROMERIAS require winter protection in the Pacific Northwest? Alstromerias make growth during the winter, and if the weather is cold should be mulched so that frosts do not freeze them down to the tubers, which are tender and will perish if once frozen.

What time should one take up DAHLIA bulbs? Lift as soon as early frosts have cut down the tops, usually in late October or early November.

Is there any secret to growing Cutleaf Weeping BIRCH trees? Every season I notice a few die off here in Yakima. It's heart-breaking to grow one for 6 or 7 years and then see it wither and die. The tree calls for no special culture. It likes a sandy loam soil. Being a shallow rooter, it must have plenty of moisture, particularly during dry periods. Leaf diseases and a birch borer are among its enemies. The borer is known to be somewhat prevalent in your section and may be responsible for the death of the trees.

When is the proper time to plant FRUIT trees in the Seattle, Washington, area? December is the ideal time. Planting, however, may be carried on through January and February.

How do I trim BOYSENBERRY, LOGANBERRY, and GRAPES in Seattle? Grapes—in February, cut back previous year's growth to 2 or 3 eyes. Remove weak canes. Loganberry and boysenberry—cut back all old wood to the ground as early as possible after fruit has been picked. This gives new shoots, which produce the next crop, a better chance to develop. Thin these, leaving only the strong ones, and nip off ends or tips.

What is the best lawn GRASS that needs no cutting? All lawn grasses require cutting if lawn is to look well and do well; some call for less cutting than others. White Dutch Clover seldom grows more than 2 or 3 ins. high; Chewing's Fescue is a low-grower; Annual Blue Grass stays within 2 ins. but is short-lived. Sagina-moss—"Lazyman's lawn" is sometimes used for lawns but must be rolled 2 or 3 times to prevent patches of it from turning brown.

What is LAZYMAN'S lawn, Moss-grass or Pearlwort? This is *Sagina subulata*, a creeping perennial, evergreen, hardy, bearing little white flowers, and in habits of growth similar to moss; but it is *not* a moss. It is used as a ground cover, also for planting between steppingstones, and sometimes for making lawns. It's much inclined to get humpy and must be kept flat by rolling or tamping. If this is neglected, the humps turn brown. Grass makes a much superior lawn and requires but little more care.

Are MONTBRETIAS hardy in Pacific Northwest? I lost mine last winter—the first time in 20 years. Montbretias are not always hardy, although in the milder parts of Washington they go through the average winter outside without being harmed. To be on the safe side, either mulch, or lift and store them in frost-free quarters for the winter.

What are some NUT trees that will grow in Spokane? The Black walnut and hardy filbert. Others, such as butternut and English Walnut, have been planted but do not long survive.

Would a RHODODENDRON be hardy in eastern Washington? Many fine rhododendrons may be grown in eastern Washington, provided they are given an acid soil, good drainage, some shade, and protection from cold winds. The soil in this area is alkaline and must be replaced with one that is on the acid side and which is kept so by an occasional application of aluminum sulfate or sulphur. Select only varieties of known hardiness.

What are a dozen or more good ROSES for a beginner in Washington? Bush roses—red: Crimson Glory, Etoile de Hollande, Christopher Stone. Pink: Madame Butterfly, Editor McFarlana, Comtesse Vandal. Yellow: McGredy's Yellow, Joanna Hill, Soeur Therese. White: McGredy's Ivory, Frau Karl Druschki. Blends: Mrs. Sam McGredy, Saturnia, Madame Henri Guillot, President Hoover. Climbing—Ruth Alexander, Elegance, Mme. Gregoire Staechelin.

In the Pacific Northwest can ROSES be transplanted any time during the winter? Yes, but November and December are the preferred months.

Will a TAMARIX hedge grow well in a rainy climate? Yes. It grows very rapidly in the Pacific Northwest. It should be pruned annually.

What are some SHRUBS that will do well on a dry, hot hillside exposed to the south? Tolerance of widely varying conditions makes the following shrubs grow almost anywhere in the Temperate Zone: *Berberis thunbergi* and *B. mentorensis; Cotoneaster acutifolia, C. divaricata,* and *C. salicifolia; Amorpha fruticosa,* and *A. canescens; Holodiscus dumosus; Mahonia repens; Caragana arborescens,* and *C. aurantiaca; Colutea arborescens;*

Hypericum prolificum; Ceanothus fendleri; Lonicera; *Pontentilla fruticosa; Prunus besseyi* and *P. Tomentosa;* rhus; *Rosa spinosissima,* and *R. woodsi; Shepherdia argentea; Symphoricarpos orbiculatus; Philadelphus microphyllus; Jamesia americana; Prunus tenella.*

Will you suggest SHRUBS that will do well in moist shade? *Mahonia aquifolium* and *M. repens; Euonymus radicans;* cornus; hydrangea; *Rhodotypos scandens;* Ribes; *Rubus deliciosus; Symphoricarpos albus,* and *S. orbiculatus; Viburnum lentago, V. carlesi,* and *V. burkwoodi; Arctostaphylos uva-ursi; Physocarpus opulifolius; Ptelea trifoliata; Lonicera involucrata; Genista tinctoria;* amelanchier; *Cotoneaster divaricata, C. horizontalis, C. acutifolia,* and *C. francheti.*

WISCONSIN

How and when should AZALEAMUMS be given winter protection in Kenosha County, Wisconsin? Apply a light covering of dry leaves, and top with evergreen branches, when soil is slightly frozen.

Are any varieties of AZALEAS or rhododendrons hardy as far North as Wisconsin? About the only plant in this group which is available in commerce and is hardy in the area mentioned is *Azalea mollis,* the Chinese Azalea. Some of the natives, like *A. viscosa,* which can be had from collectors, are winter hardy but don't like the hot summers of the Midwest.

Will BENT GRASS thrive in north central Wisconsin? Yes, provided you are willing to fuss with it. But for the home gardener, the less touchy, hardier grasses, such as blue grass, are far more satisfactory.

Is the Blue BEECH hardy in this Midwest climate? Yes. *Carpinus caroliniana* (Blue Beech or Hornbeam) is native from Minnesota to Florida, and is fully hardy if planted in rich, moist soil.

In this climate what is the best time to plant seeds of CANTERBURYBELLS? Plant in late May, to allow a full season's growth before the plants go through the winter. Carry over in the cold frame. Canterburybells all belong to the species *Campanula medium,* and all varieties are equally hardy, but none is easy to grow.

Can I grow the large-flowered CHRYSANTHEMUMS in the garden? These chrysanthemums are neither hardy nor early enough for Wisconsin. Consult your nearest Park Department concerning varieties for your section.

What is the proper method of planting and caring for DAPHNE cneorum in southeastern Wisconsin? *Daphne cneorum* likes a situation open to the sun, but sheltered from winter winds. An opening in a planting of evergreens which faces south is ideal. Plant slightly deeper than the plant stood in the nursery, and fill up to ground level with a mixture of half sand and half leafmold. A *p*H reaction of between 5.9 and 6.8 is satisfactory. Use balled and burlaped stock, and plant in spring.

What, if any, are the names of hardy APRICOTS for this section in Wisconsin? The only reliably hardy apricots for your region are the Manchurian sorts, and the hybrids of these developed by Prof. Hansen and the Manitoba Experiment Station. Some of these are Scout, Manchu, Mandarin, Golden Glow, Orange Sansin, Ninguta, and the straight Manchurian species. Don't expect too much in flavor from these; in some the flavor is quite strong and harsh, while in others it is green and sour. They are better canned and as sauce than when eaten raw.

What new FRUITS (cherries, plums, pears, grapes) are hardy in Wisconsin? All sour cherries are reasonably hardy, but where high winds prevail, better stick to the sand-cherry and plum hybrids which, while not so high in quality, do make good jams and pies. Of the true plums, a whole new series from the University of Minnesota look promising. Superior, Redcoat, Ember, and Pipestone are all good. Add some of the Hansen hybrids, Kaga and Sapa, for variety. The Beta Grape (a Concord-wild-grape hybrid) is reliably hardy but should be used only if Concord does not do well near you. Parker, Patten, and Bantam are three good new pears that can take it. Check with local nurserymen to see if older, tested sorts are hardy in your neighborhood, since most of those mentioned above are recommended largely because they will not winter kill, not for highest quality.

Is there a PEACH that will stand our winters? Yes, and no. The new peach, Hardee, has gone through some tough weather but has not yet been subjected to the lowest experienced in the Milwaukee area. It might be the answer. Stronger in flavor than peaches, but fully winter hardy, the new Manchurian apricots, such as Manchurian and Mandarin, are somewhat peachlike in quality.

What dwarf FRUIT trees will grow well in southeastern Wisconsin? Whatever standard varieties are hardy in your area. Dwarfness does not affect hardiness. Pears and apples, the two species most commonly dwarfed by grafting, should be 100 per cent hardy. However, don't overlook the possibility of growing full-sized varieties as semi-dwarfs, keeping them cut down to shrub forms. This is often more satisfactory for regions where apples do not do too well. Most apples in England are grown in bush form, by the way.

Can white, or green, GRAPES be raised in central Wisconsin?   The new Minnesota 66 is a green grape that has gone through 40° below zero. Worth trying, but not too sure, are the old green Niagara, the new yellowish Seneca, and the new early green Ontario.

Can you tell me what GRAPES and NUTS I can grow? The only grape that produces fair fruit and will survive your severe winter is the Concord-wild-grape hybrid, Beta. You are about on the northern limit of black walnut, hickory, and butternut.

Will the shrub LANTANA thrive in Wisconsin climate? What is meant by the shrub lantana is probably *Viburnum lantana,* the Wayfaringtree, which is hardy at Lake Geneva and possibly north of that point; *Viburnum carlesi* is about the same for hardiness, and is far superior in bloom and fragrance. *V. lantana* makes a splendid dense hedge.

Are PANSIES hardy in Wisconsin?   Not in the sense that they can be left outdoors without protection and survive. In Wisconsin, they can be started in cold frames, wintered with the glass on, and set out in spring.

When and how should PANSIES be started from seed? Pansy seed does not germinate satisfactorily at temperatures above 65° F. This means late seeding (about August 20) in your area. Plant in a cold frame in well-drained soil, not too heavy, and not too rich in nitrogen. Potash (which promotes tougher growth) helps the plants to winter over. Wait until snow flies and cover lightly with pine or spruce boughs, or with marsh hay, and apply the sash to the frames. Remove glass about April 1, and set plants in permanent position about May 1.

I have my ROSE bushes hilled up about 8 ins. Where and when should the tops be cut off?   Might as well wait until spring. The tops will have to be cut back to live wood anyway, and 1 cut is easier to make than 2. Also, the tops help catch and hold snow—the natural cover for roses.

Should a climbing ROSE be taken down from its trellis each year and covered with leaves over winter?   In Wisconsin, climbing roses should be laid down (a trellis hinged at the bottom so it can be dropped over without removing the canes is best) and covered. But do not cover with leaves; damp soil is much better. It keeps the canes moist and does not allow wind to blow off the covering.

Will you name the 12 best all-around varieties of hybrid tea ROSES for this territory? As with horses, so no 2 people can agree on "best bets" in roses. The reliable rose specialists and large American seed houses usually offer collections which are made up of roses satisfactory over a wide range of territory, beautiful in flower, and reasonable in price. You can do far worse than to trust to their expert judgment in this matter of variety.

What kinds of SHRUBS with red berries are hardy for northern Wisconsin? *Berberis thunbergi,* Crataegus (various); *Euonymus europaeus; Lonicera tatarica* (Bush Honeysuckle); *Malus hopa* (Hopa Crab); *Prunus tomentosa; Rosa palustris; Sambucus microbotrys* (Bunchberry Elder), *Symphoricarpus orbiculatus.*

What PERENNIALS should I plant for continuous bloom in Wisconsin for spring and summer? Achillea Perry's White, *A. filipendula;* aconitum; delphinium; aquilegia; *Artemisia lactiflora.* Asters: Mt. Everest, Harrington's Pink, Beechwood Challenger, Climax; *Dicentra spectabilis; Centaurea macrocephala;* chrysanthemum, earliest varieties; iris; dictamnus; peony; erigeron; hemerocallis; linum; lupine; *Papaver orientale* and *P. nudicaule;* Physostegia Vivid; *Phlox subulata, P. divaricata,* and *P. decussata; Trollius europaeus;* thalictrum.

When is TREE planting most successful, spring or fall? Unless one has the gift of long-range forecasting, this cannot be answered categorically. For most trees, the best time to plant is as soon as possible, since waiting merely means delay in getting the tree established. But certainly fall planting (any time after the leaves fall) is much to be preferred to the usual practice of waiting until trees are in leaf in May before setting out. Exceptions are the thin-barked trees like sycamore and birches, and those with fleshy roots like magnolias, which do best when planted as early as practicable in spring.

Can you suggest some reliable SHRUBS (flowering) for Wisconsin? Amelanchier; *Berberis thunbergi,* and *B. mentorensis; Buddleia alternifolia;* desmodium; *Euonymus europaeus; Exochorda racemosa; Hypericum prolificum,* syringa (lilac), various; Lonicera; *Physocarpus opulifolius; Prunus tomentosa* and *P. cis-*

tena; Rubus deliciosus, sambucus; spirea; viburnum; and species of brier roses.

WYOMING

Should I mulch my BLEEDINGHEART or in any way give it extra protection this winter?   A mound of leafmold or peatmoss over its crown would be helpful, but not absolutely necessary.

Will you be sure to tell us some good PERENNIALS to grow in the different climates of the state of Wyoming?   Variation in climate seems less a difficulty in Wyoming than quality and condition of soil. The following grow successfully where some protection from wind is possible: alyssum; *Centaurea macrocephala; Saponaria ocymoides; Pyrethrum hybridum;* peony; iris; oenothera; nepeta; lupine; linum; hemerocallis; *Heliopsis pitcheriana;* gypsophila; euphorbia; *Phlox subulata* and *P. decussata;* chrysanthemum; delphinium; Michaelmasdaisy; hollyhock; *Clematis integrifolia* and *C. recta;* anchusa.

What climbing ROSES would you recommend for Wyoming? Paul's Scarlet Climber, Silver Moon, Alida Lovett, Dr. W. Van Fleet, American Pillar.

What hybrid perpetual ROSES do well in Wyoming?   Hybrid perpetuals in regions of high altitude and short summer are of less value than in other regions. They incline strongly to mildew. Paul Neyron, Soleil d'Or, Mrs. John Laing, Frau Karl Druschki, are among the best. Floribunda roses do excellently in Wyoming and require little or no winter care.

Are there hybrid tea ROSES that will stand Wyoming winters? Select those not too double, and colors that do not fade in altitude sunshine. A few such are Edith Nellie Perkins, Etoile de Hollande, Joanna Hill, Editor McFarland, Caledonia, the McGredy introductions (any or all), Poinsettia, Mrs. E. P. Thom, Condesa de Sastago, Dame Edith Helen, and E. G. Hill.

SECTION X

Landscaping and Miscellaneous

INTRODUCTION

BY DONALD WYMAN

FEW OWNERS of small places can have all the landscaping done at one time. Usually it is extended over several years, a tree or two being added one season; a group of shrubs the next; a perennial border later; and so on.

But if a well-conceived plan—no matter how rough a one—is made in advance, many mistakes are avoided, and the result finally attained is lasting and more pleasing. This will save much time and money later on. Trees and shrubs are permanent fixtures, and should be given their place in the landscape plan only after careful thought and study.

Usefulness and beauty should be considered in that order. Think for a moment of the new house on a bare lot, with no planting whatsoever. Of course it looks bare, if not actually ugly. Trees, shrubs, and flowers, placed in the right situations, will make the house blend into the land, and at the same time fulfill many other desirable purposes. The trees will give shade in the summer and, if properly placed, help keep the building cool. Evergreens will help in the screening of objectionable views and aid in keeping the building warmer in the winter by shielding it from high winds.

Shrubs can be used for beauty and also for the necessary function of screening and hedgemaking, protecting the property from unwanted trespassers. Vines can be added for softening the harsh lines of buildings and to help beautify hard wall surfaces. Annuals, perennials, and bulbs can be planted for beauty and usefulness as well.

The reasons for placing trees, shrubs, and flower borders in definite areas, and in definite relation to each other, should be thought out *in advance of planting*. It is expensive and very time-consuming to "try" a tree for a year or two in a certain situation and then, later on, move it to another. If a specimen tree is wanted, and the Siberian Elm is selected, it is most disheartening to have this tree split from top to bottom by heavy winds or by snow and ice after it has been thriving for a number of years. It would have been far better to take more time at the beginning, when the plan for the landscaping was being made, to select a sturdy tree rather than a fast-growing but weak-wooded one.

The ideal around-the-house planting provides overhead shade and "ties the house to the ground" without obscuring walls or obstructing windows.

The selection of the right kind of plant material for the right place does take time, but pays in the end. In making the plan, the trees should be located first, then the evergreens, then the flower borders, shrubs, and vines—in about that order. A typical plan of this sort is shown on page 1289. In order to make such a plan intelligently, the gardener must have some knowledge of the different groups of plants, how they can be used, and the types of material available in each. In the following pages these groups are discussed.

Trees

Trees should be considered first because they are the largest and usually the most costly items on the home grounds, and because they require the most time to grow to the desired size. It may take years for a tree to become sufficiently large to give the effect we expect from it. First and foremost, the tree gives shade,

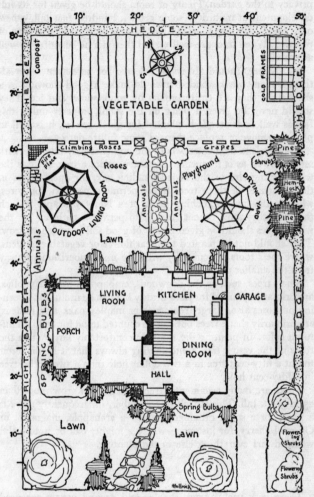

Typical landscape planting plan for a small place, showing the general layout of the entire plot. Detail plans for the different areas can be worked out later.

either to the house or to the terrace in the garden. It can be planted to obscure some objectionable view, or to aid in giving privacy to the garden. Plenty of room should be given for its full development at maturity (some grow a hundred feet tall, others only twenty-five feet)—a fact not always realized at the time of planting. When trees are well placed they can be beautiful as well as useful.

Sturdy trees should always be selected for permanence, for although many weak-wooded trees do make a good showing in a short time, they are easily broken by wind, snow, and ice. They should never be given a place on the small property unless this fact is well understood. If planted for quick results, it is well to plan to remove or replace them at some future date.

If a tree is to be located where the branches may interfere with service wires, as is frequently necessary, select a tree, such as the wide-arching elm or the wide-spreading oak, for open spaces in the branching of these trees freely permit a pathway for wires, whereas the close-branching habit of a Norway Maple is such that branches must be cut from it to permit a pathway for the wires. Trees should be given plenty of good soil in which to grow. They should not be planted too near flower or vegetable gardens, where their roots undoubtedly will take much nourishment away from the smaller plants.

Small trees, such as the dogwoods, crabapples, and magnolias, are primarily planted for their beauty but can be useful for screening purposes also. Large trees, such as maples, oaks, and lindens, are primarily shade trees but can be counted upon for brilliant autumn color. In planting dig the hole comfortably larger than the roots of the young tree, remembering always that it is far better to put a fifty-cent tree in a two-dollar hole than a two-dollar tree in a fifty-cent hole.

There are many ornamental trees that seldom grow more than 25 to 30 ft. tall. This is well to remember, for frequently there is a place for a small ornamental tree—a crabapple, magnolia, or Oriental cherry, for instance—where a mighty oak or stately elm would dwarf everything else in the planting.

Evergreens

These very useful trees, shrubs, and ground covers are used because of their winter appearance, keeping some of Nature's green foliage color the year 'round. Because of their dense habit of growth, they are especially valued as screening and windbreak plants, and the smaller ones as foundation plants next to the house. They require little attention when soil and climate are to

their liking, and are available in a wide assortment of sizes and
varieties.

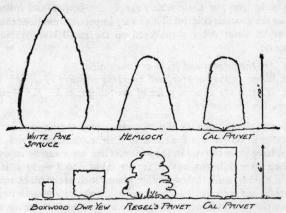

BOXWOOD   DWF. YEW   REGEL'S PRIVET   CAL. PRIVET

*In selecting shrubs and evergreens, for hedges especially, it is
important to consider habit of growth and ultimate height.*

Some of the evergreens—hemlocks, pines, and spruces—are
big trees. Many others are small trees, bushes, or even low,
creeping ground covers. As a group they are more difficult to grow
than deciduous plants, so they should be selected with care. Before purchasing an evergreen one should ascertain the soil and
climatic requirements of the particular kind desired. In the hot,
dry, windswept areas of the Midwest only a very few evergreens
survive. They need much more moisture in the summer than
conditions prevalent in those areas permit.

In the eastern part of the country there is a wide selection from
which to choose. Not only many species and varieties of the
narrow-leaved, cone-bearing evergreens do well, but also the many
bright-flowering, shrubby rhododendrons and evergreen azaleas.
These are truly worth while even though they need especially
prepared acid soil in which to grow. It should be remembered
that some are decidedly hardier than others, and in areas where
high winter winds and very low temperatures prevail only the
most rugged types should be selected, for many of the more tender
types may be injured by adverse weather conditions and show it
by the browning of their foliage. High and dry winds in early
spring are especially hard on all evergreens.   .

Shrubs

Shrubs ranging in height from 1 to 20 ft. make up the bulk

of the permanent planting after the trees and the evergreens have been properly placed. They are the plants that do the real bordering or hedging, or those which supply the flowers and fruits to make the grounds colorful. Three very important questions should be asked about every shrub used on the small home grounds, namely:

1. *Are the flowers and fruits ornamental?*
2. *When do they appear, and how long are they effective?*
3. *What is the autumn color of the foliage; and is the plant of interest in the winter?*

Some plants, such as the viburnums and the dogwoods, are colorful in flower and fruit and in their autumn hues, and may even have some interest in the winter. Their color can be enjoyed, during three different seasons, for a total of 6 to 8 weeks at least. On the other hand, there are other plants, such as the lilacs, mock-oranges, and weigelas, which are colorful only for a 2-week period when they are in flower, and have no interesting fruits or autumn color. When only a small amount of space is available, it is of the utmost importance to select shrubs which are colorful for several seasons, and so are of interest for a much longer time. Hence it pays well to find out the seasons of interest for the different shrubs, and to select the ones that have interest for several periods each year.

The ultimate size of the shrubs is very important; the taller ones should be used for backgrounds and screening purposes, while the smaller ones can be used as specimens in the foreground. Locating single-specimen plants is very difficult, even for the trained landscape architect. The most common mistake is to plant a specimen in the dead center of some lawn area. Usually this is absolutely wrong, for open lawn areas lend beauty and increase the apparent size of any property. So it is desirable to place specimens off center or at the side of lawn areas, leaving as long and clear a sweep of unobstructed lawn as possible.

Dense-growing shrubs, such as the barberries, privets, most of the shrub roses, yews, etc., are used as hedges. In fact, almost any shrub can be clipped enough to make it usable as a hedge plant, but the denser-growing types prove best and easiest to trim. Since there are more than one hundred kinds of plants that make good hedges, it is advisable to define clearly at first the exact reasons why a hedge is needed, then to select the plant material that most closely fills the bill. In this way you will be assured of a serviceable hedge, while at the same time you can select some material out of the ordinary which will lend considerable interest to the general appearance of the place. In placing a hedge, never put it on the exact center of a property line, for some future disgruntled neighbor would have the full right to dig up the half on his property. Prune hedges so that they are wider at the bottom than at the top, thus insuring sturdy branches from the ground up.

Vines

Vines are used either for beauty or for screening purposes, or both. They can be divided into two large groups, those that climb by clinging to a wall or support by means of small rootlike holdfasts (as the English Ivy), and those that climb by twining, like the bittersweets and honeysuckles. Never plant a clinging vine on a wooden house, for it will have to be removed every time the house is painted (and usually cannot be replaced), and the small holdfasts will injure the wood, aiding in its decay. Such vines are for stone and brick walls and tree trunks.

Twining vines can be used on wooden houses provided they have a trellis of some sort, or merely a single wire on which to twine. These supports may be made removable, at least at the top, so that the vine can be taken down and put up again at will, without seriously injuring the vine itself. The supports should be held 4 to 6 ins. away from the wooden boards. Or vines such as bittersweet, honeysuckle, and the Fiveleaf Akebia can be trained to twine around rainspouts. An established vigorous twiner will grow 2 stories high in 2 or 3 years, so that if twining on a rainspout it would not be a serious handicap to cut the vine to the ground when painting and repairs are necessary. Wisteria is frequently used, but often it proves too vigorous for the small home.

Clematis vines, like the Sweetautumn Clematis and the Jackman Clematis, and grapes, really belong to the twining group, for they climb by means of tendrils or modified tendrils. Some of the large-flowered clematis are difficult to grow, requiring just the right kind of limestone soil. Many annual vines, too, are available, some of which make a remarkable growth in one season. For a permanent screen, however, the perennial vines are best; but for flowers, it is difficult to surpass some of the annuals.

Basic Principles

In this, the last, but by no means the least important, section of this book, information has been included concerning the basic principles of landscaping for the small home and about special types of gardens.

Needless to say, these particular topics cannot be fully covered in question-and-answer form; but the number of questions received indicates a very widespread interest in them. Readers who seek further information are urged to procure, or to obtain from libraries, the books referred to in the following pages.

A careful study of the illustrations herewith will give the beginner definite suggestions as to how to attain pleasing results with his plantings and to solve some of the simpler problems of construction in laying out his place.

LANDSCAPE DESIGN AND PLANTING

DESIGN

Why should home grounds be "designed"?   To get the most efficient use out of them. Hit-or-miss planting never results in full or efficient use of the land, and it is pictorially ineffective.

What relationship has planting design to garden design? Garden design has to be carried out largely in terms of planting. This is to say that any plant used should be chosen because it has a definite place *in the design,* rather than merely because we like its flowers or foliage.

Which is the more important, the artistic or the practical, in designing a small property?   Neither; one supplements the other. Any garden, no matter how artistic its design may be, will be ineffective unless the layout is practical. If practical matters only are considered, however, the garden is unlikely to be an artistic success.

Is it necessary to make a plan of a garden?   For any but the very simplest of gardens a plan will be found to be a great help in carrying out your intentions. Only by planning ahead of time can you be sure that desirable color combinations will actually be achieved. Changes and rearrangements are more easily made on paper than in the garden itself. A plan is also most useful in estimating quantities; if the planting is not to be done all at once, it is essential.

Why should a garden be "balanced"?   Balance, whether symmetrical or irregular, gives a garden picture a feeling of stability and restfulness. A garden that lacks it will be less pleasing, although it may not be immediately apparent what the trouble is, particularly in a naturalistic composition.

What is the "garden axis" we read about? Why is it important? A garden axis is the center line of the composition. It is the basic line on which a design is built. Without it balance and symmetry, which give the garden a pleasing, restful appearance, are hard to develop.

What is a "terminal feature"?   This is a feature placed at the end of an axis in an oblong composition. It terminates the axis and turns one's attention back to the detail within the garden. A garden house, seat, pool, wall fountain, or group planting make suitable terminal features.

A tall, closely woven fence, secured by stout posts, makes a suitable screen where there is not room for a shrub border between garden and street or road.

What is meant by the term "focal point"?   A focal point is a point of highest interest in the development of the design, such as a pool, garden house, or a group of particularly striking plants. It serves as a center around which the design is built up.

In a square garden, where should the focal point be?   In the center, usually. In a square design the important lines lead to or from the center.

What is a vista?   A vista is a narrow view framed between masses of foliage. It tends to concentrate the observer's attention, rather than allowing it to spread over a wide panorama.

Must a flower garden be level?   A geometrical garden need not be level, but the slope should be away from the principal point from which the garden is seen, rather than from side to side. A naturalistic garden should have, if possible, a natural grade, irregular rather than level or smoothly sloping.

How do you decide on the size of a garden?   How large a garden can you take care of? Don't lay out more plantations than you can properly care for. A garden should be in scale with its surroundings, not too big for the house; nor so small as to seem insignificant. If the size of the property is limited, it is well to have the garden occupy the whole space instead of leaving a fringe of unusable space around it.

What is the rule for good proportion in the size of a garden? There is no hard-and-fast rule. Oblong areas are most effective when they are about one and a half times as long as they are wide; but the method of treating them and the surrounding foliage masses affect this considerably. Generally an oblong is better than a square; and an oval (on account of perspective) more effective than a circle.

How can you accent a planting? Is it necessary?   Plantings made up of all one kind of plant, or of a few similar varieties, are likely to be monotonous and uninteresting. By using an occasional plant of a different sort an accent is created that makes the planting more interesting. For example, a pointed evergreen in a group of flowering shrubs.

FORMAL AND INFORMAL GARDENS

What is the difference between a formal and a naturalistic garden?   Formal design uses straight lines and circular curves or arcs. Informal design uses long, free-flowing curves. Formality emphasizes *lines;* informality emphasizes *space.*

What is required in a formal garden?   A formal garden is essentially a composition in geometric lines—squares, oblongs, circles, or parts thereof. It need not be large, elaborate, or filled with architectural embellishment. Most gardens, on account of space limitations, are basically formal.

Which is the better suited to a small place, a formal or an informal garden?   Topography controls the type of design. On flat ground in proximity to buildings the rectangular (formal) type of design is easier to adapt. On rough land greater informality is desirable, particularly on slopes and in wooded areas.

PLANNING

What are the steps necessary to develop a small property?
Rough grading; staking out walks, drives, and garden area; plan
for drainage, if necessary; installation of utilities (water, gas,
sewage, etc.); preparation of planting areas; finish grading (topsoil); planting trees, shrubs, and perennials; making the lawn.

**Is there anything that can be done in advance of building on a
lot that would improve the land or save time later on? The lot is
100 × 100 ft., with trees, bushes, weeds, etc.** Clear out undesirable wild growths and trees where they are too thick. Avoid
destroying attractive native shrub masses in locations near the
property lines where they may be valuable as part of future shrub
borders. Plow and harrow the land. Get rid of roots and stones
and plant a cover crop, such as winter rye, until you are ready
to use the land.

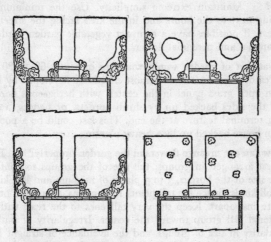

*Mistakes to avoid in planting. (Top) Leave lawn
areas open, free from beds or borders in center of
grass plots. (Below) Shrubs planted in polka-dot
pattern, and better arrangement of massing them in
borders.*

**We have a new home to garden completely, and very little
money to put into it. What do you advise concerning first plantings in our garden, to take away the bare, new look?** Shade
trees come first. Then important screen and background plant-

ings of shrubs, flowering trees, and evergreens. These are the framework of the landscape picture. Add details later.

I have just built a new home, with a large front yard, in a country town. What would be best to set out or plant?   Shade trees are important. Plant a few in such a way that they will throw their shade where it is most needed, and where they will compose best with the mass of the house. Shrub borders along the side property lines will help frame the picture. Avoid too much planting against the house, also isolated flower beds.

How would you go about designing a town-house garden area about 18 × 25 ft.? It is shady half the day.   In such a garden you will have to depend largely upon the pattern of the design and upon architectural accessories. The planting should be mostly specimen evergreens, vines, and spring bulbs. For the summer, a few annuals, either in pots or beds, will give color.

Can you suggest economical landscaping for a small temporary home?   Maintain extreme simplicity. Use the minimum of planting next to the house and in the area facing the street. In the rear, if possible, have a compact vegetable garden bordered with annual and perennial flowers.

What sort of garden would you plan in a plot 60 × 30 ft.?   An area of this sort is usually most effectively developed by having an open grass panel in the center, with herbaceous borders along the sides backed up by shrub borders, or hedges, and a strong terminal feature at the end. This last could be a pool or garden house backed up by a heavy planting.

How can one arrange flowers in the garden properly?   They are best arranged in groups; the size of the groups to conform to the size of the border, 3 to 5 plants of medium and low kinds, 3 of tall kinds. Space the tall plants 18 to 24 ins. apart, and others 9 to 12 ins. apart. Keep the very tall ones to the rear, with an occasional tall group toward the center. Irregularity of outline, irregularity in size of groups, and the avoidance of straight lines are among some of the things to be observed in arranging plants in a border.

What is the best way to arrange plants in a flower bed or border?   Plants in a flower border should be arranged according to height. Keep the low ones near the front edge and the tallest ones at the back. Occasionally, for accent, a tall plant can be brought farther forward than it normally would be. Of course in beds with a path on *both* sides of it, the tall plants would be placed in the center.

In arranging the mixed flower border, tall-growing sub-jects (such as delphiniums, hollyhocks, and digitalis) are kept to the rear.

How wide should a flower border be? To provide succession of bloom throughout the season a border 10 to 14 ft. wide is none too much. Narrower borders can be treated effectively for seasonal bloom, but there will be times when few if any flowers will be present. A width of 4 ft. is about the least that can be effectively planted.

How should I plan a perennial flower garden? Consult one or two good books that carry plans of such gardens. Select one that can be fitted easily into your scheme, and of a size you can manage. Consult a table of perennials that gives height, season of bloom and color. Study the plan well the first year after planting. Then is the time to do the real planning. (See other questions.)

Will you give suggestions for a practical mixed perennial and annual flower border? Two plans can be followed when combining annuals with perennials. One is to leave spaces in the border where annuals can be sown or plants set out early. The other is to raise annual plants for filling in bare spots as they occur. The former plan requires less work. Annuals generally are used to pick up the blooming period, which begins in July. In May, sow seeds of *Phlox drummondi,* alyssum, cosmos (early), marigold, zinnia, directly in the border. Obtain plants, or sow seeds in April, of lobelia, nicotiana, petunia, *Salvia farinacea.* Verbenas should be sown early in March. Annuals should, where possible, be planted near those perennials which do not bloom in summer.

I should like a mixed bed of irises, phlox, and chrysanthemums. How can I have blooms spring, summer, and fall? Is this possible? If so, how big a bed? How many plants, and how far apart should they be to make an effective planting? The size of the bed must depend upon how much time you have to devote to it. Time and labor are involved in maintaining a perennial planting. It takes a lot of each. (See questions about size.) Using irises, phlox, and chrysanthemums, so place them in the bed that at their particular season there is a good distribution of bloom. Don't use too much iris, or too large groups. Distribute in the same way a few varieties of the novae-angliae and novibelgi hardy asters for September bloom. Tie all these together with such perennials as *Achillea ptarmica,* anthemis, aquilegia, *Campanula persicifolia,* coreopsis, dictamnus, gypsophila. Plant in groups of 3, placing plants 15 ins. apart. Toward the edge use *Anemone japonica* varieties, dwarf asters (hardy), *Campanula carpatica, Dianthus deltoides* and *D. latifolius,* and geums. Plant in groups of 3, 6 to 12 ins. apart. For early spring, use tulips and narcissi interplanted in groups throughout the planting. Along the edge, plant arabis, aubrieta, *Alyssum saxatile* and *A. saxatile citrinum, Phlox subulata* varieties, and pansies. (See Chrysanthemums for other suggestions.)

Which perennial flowers are most satisfactory for a small garden? Any whose habit of growth and size of flower are not out of scale for a small area. A list of such are *Alyssum argenteum; Arabis albida;* aquilegia, various; dianthus, various; *Aster subcoeruleus* (Himalayan Daisy); bleedingheart; *Campanula carpatica* and *C. persicifolia;* lily-of-the-valley; *Delphinium chinense,* dwarf; candytuft; forget-me-not; chrysanthemum, dwarf; *Geum borisi;* Gypsophila Rosy Veil; heuchera, various; Hemerocallis Goldena; *Lychnis floscuculi; Nepeta mussini; Plumbago larpentae;* primula, various; pyrethrum; *Lilium tenuifolium, L. concolor,* and *L. flavum;* Iceland Poppy; peonies—*P. tenuifolia* and *P. latifolia,* Nellie, and Marie Jacquin; *Phlox divaricata* and *P. decussata* Jules Sandeau; *Veronica incana* and *V. amethystina.*

How can I plan for a continuous succession of bloom from early spring until late fall? First by having a wide planting space, at least 10 or 12 ft. in width, and by so planning that you have a few plants for each season in each part of the border.

Is it all right to plant roses and flowers together? Hybrid tea roses do not do well with other plants, but the floribundas, polyanthas, and hybrid perpetuals can be so used.

Backed by peonies and climbing roses, we have a rectangular bed 15 × 18 ft. What do you advise for a front planting? Interplant Regal Lily and *L. speciosum* among peonies. Enrich soil, plant solid with phlox, such as Africa, B. Compte, Count Zeppelin, Jules Sandeau, Mrs. Jenkins, Salmon Beauty. Edge with cushion chrysanthemums. For early color you could interplant between the phlox with small groups of cottage tulips and an edging of pansies.

BACKGROUNDS

Should a small garden be enclosed?   Yes. Any garden picture is more effective if the flowers can be seen against a background of shrubs, hedge, wall, or fence. Furthermore, views out of a garden tend to distract attention from the garden itself.

The charm of the half-hidden: an enclosing wall leads the imagination to beauty beyond.

Should flower borders and beds have a background?   Isolated flower beds with no background are rarely effective. Borders in front of shrubs, hedges, or walls make better places for color compositions.

What makes the best background hedge for a flower garden? Evergreens are probably better than deciduous shrubs because they do not grow so fast or provide such serious root competition. They are also effective in winter. Arborvitae, cedar, hemlocks, or Japanese Yew are suitable. (See also Hedges—Section II.)

I should like to plant a hedge for a background around my garden and have flowers in front. Would the hedge roots interfere with the flowers?   Yes, unless the flowers were planted at least 3 or 4 ft. away from the hedge. To prevent root interference, dig a trench about 3 ft. down, between the hedge and the flower border, and put in a thin wall of concrete to discourage the hedge roots from occupying the border.

I have a square area, about 40 ft. on a side, that I can enclose with a hedge and shrubbery, and which I would like to use for a flower garden. What arrangement of beds would you suggest? In such a definitely circumscribed area a geometrical pattern is almost mandatory. But it can be either a pattern of beds, planted with low bedding plants, or an open-center pattern where taller flowers and some shrubs are used in wide borders around the sides.

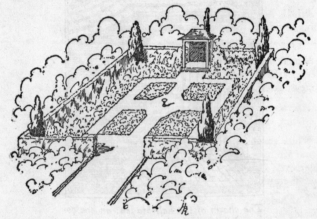

Typical enclosed formal garden of symmetrical design.

FLOWER BEDS

Our flower beds are best viewed from our porch. We use the porch more in July and August. What flowers should be used to give lots of color in these months?   Among the perennials: phlox, hollyhock, gaillardia, daylily, coreopsis, heliopsis, rudbeckia, penstemon, stokesia, and plantainlily are all good. Satisfactory annuals are zinnia, marigold, cosmos, salvia, ageratum, calliopsis, calendula, celosia, and cornflower.

What are "bedding" plants; and how are they used?   Bedding plants are low, compact annuals set out each year to form a definite pattern. They are most effective when used in a garden that is viewed from above.

Which type of plant makes the best edging for a flower bed? Low, compact evergreens, such as boxwood or Dwarf Teucrium give the most finished effect. Low, compact perennials, such as dwarf asters, armeria, and heuchera, give a softer effect. Perennials that can be sheared after flowering, such as candytuft and dianthus, can be used.

TO ATTRACT BIRDS

Which flowers attract birds? Birds are attracted by the seed of the plants and then only seed-eating birds. Sunflowers, *Eryngium amethystinum,* rudbeckia, coreopsis, poke, lily-of-the-valley, wild and species roses, partridge-berry, wild strawberry, wintergreen.

Which flowers can I plant that are most attractive to hummingbirds? Aquilegia, delphinium, monarda, phlox, penstemon, physostegia, tritoma.

Which vines attract birds? Vines that produce seeds or berries: bearberry, bittersweet, cranberry, dewberry, the grapes, the honeysuckles, Virginia creeper, morningglories.

Which evergreens attract birds? Redcedar, fir, hemlock, the pines, Canadian Yew, the junipers, arborvitae.

Which shrubs encourage birds? Most of the berried shrubs. Some are bayberry, benzoin, blackalder, blackberry, chokeberry, elderberry, hawthorn, holly, mulberry, shadbush, snowberry, the viburnums.

Which deciduous tree shall I plant to attract birds? Alders, White Ash, linden, beech, the birches, box elder, elm, hackberry, the oaks, hornbeam, larch, Black Locust, the maples, Mountain-ash, wild cherry.

BORDERS

Will you list a few low plants for edging or the front of a border of perennials? Aethionema (Persian Stonecress); *Ajuga genevensis* (Geneva Bugle); *Alyssum citrinum; Arabis alpina* fl. pl. (Double Rockcress); *Artemisia abrotanum* (Southernwood); dianthus in variety; *Globularia trichosantha* (globedaisy); heuchera in variety; *Jasione perennis* (Shepherd's Scabiosa); *Nepeta mussini; Phlox divaricata* (Canada Blue Phlox); *Polemonium reptans* (Greek Valerian); *Scutellaria baicalensis* (Azure Skullcap); *Silene schafta* (Autumn Catchfly); *Armeria maritima* (thrift); *Stokesia laevis* (Stokes Aster); *Veronica incana* (Woolly Speedwell); viola in variety.

Please give explicit plans for an effective border, mostly of perennials. I have a border on either side of a concrete walk in my back yard, 72 ft. long and 4 ft. wide. I should like to follow a well-planned design that would look well and furnish cutting flowers. How close together can plants in a border be placed? Plan and design your border, including such reliable cut-flower selections as peonies, irises, delphiniums, Regal and Madonna Lilies, together with hardy chrysanthemums for fall cutting. Toward the front of the border you should include such reliable bulbs as tulips, Dutch irises, and narcissi. All of the things mentioned are almost necessary to any good perennial border, but there are many other excellent perennials listed in flower catalogues from which to choose. For constant cutting it will be necessary for you to add some of your favorite annuals each year. The best rule for determining the distance between plants is to visualize them at their blooming season and give them sufficient space so that they will not be crowded by their neighbors. (See also Planning, this section.)

What are good companion plants for tall-bearded irises in a narrow border along driveway? Lupine, pink, veronica, doronicum, *Phlox suffruticosa*, geum, and delphinium.

FOR COLOR

Should a garden have a "color scheme"? If so, how do you make one? Restricted color schemes for small gardens have been overdone. Color harmony is important, and plants should be so placed that interesting color combinations result and violent clashes do not occur. Sometimes it is wise to rule out certain "difficult" colors, such as red and purple.

How important is good foliage in a color scheme? Are the flowers only to be considered? Good foliage should be considered because it creates a background for the flowers. Use strong-foliaged plants near or among weak-foliaged ones, or those whose foliage disappears. Often the foliage itself (which may be gray-green, yellow-green, or bluish-green) plays an important part in the color scheme.

How can I plan lovely color combinations in my garden? Effective color combinations in the garden must be thoughtfully worked out on paper beforehand. Make lists of plants according to color, and also time of bloom. Then with a large-scale plan of the garden and a set of colored crayons indicate their proposed position on paper before you start to plant.

Can you suggest some other BLUE FLOWERS besides larkspur and cornflowers? Ageratum, lobelia, browallia, torenia, Swanriver-daisy (brachycome), linaria, nigella, morningglory, scabiosa, *Aconitum fischeri,* forget-me-nots, aquilegia, aster, campanula, catananche, delphinium, clematis, echinops, mistflower, polemonium, *Salvia farinacea,* anchusa, cynoglossum, pulmonaria, ajuga. Bulbs: scilla, grapehyacinth, chionodoxa, hyacinth.

I plan to have a garden of primarily bright RED PLANTS. Can you name some? Zinnia, marigold, poppy, mallow, salvia, geranium, celosia, cardinalflower, nicotiana, hollyhock, penstemon, peony, beebalm, geum, Gaillardia Ruby, dahlia, rose, nasturtium, Heuchera Queen of Hearts, semperflorens begonia. Bulbs: tulip, tigridia, nerine.

Can you suggest some RED FLOWERS for a circular bed around my flagpole? I have planned to use dwarf blue ageratum with white sweet alyssum, but can find no bright red flower with dwarf and free-flowering habits. Try dwarf scarlet sage (salvia), dwarf red zinnia, cockscomb (celosia), red geranium, or verbena.

I have heard that gardens planted with only WHITE FLOWERS are effective. Are they? All-white gardens are often effective if one has room for background material such as evergreens and shrubs. They give a feeling of spaciousness and quiet. However, an all-white garden is likely to become tiresome unless one has space enough for other types of gardens and for borders of colorful plants.

What plants would you suggest for an all-white garden? Phlox, arabis, asters, chrysanthemum, larkspur, babysbreath, iberis, peony, platycodon, scabiosa, stokesia, yucca, veronica, alyssum, saponaria, petunia, poppy, nicotiana, sweetpea, morningglory, moonflower, arctotis. Bulbs: snowdrop, crocus, hyacinth, tulip, narcissus.

Will you suggest some bright YELLOW FLOWERS for the garden? Potentilla, thalictrum, oenothera, daylily, sunflower, zinnia, marigold, snapdragon, doronicum, chrysanthemum, dahlias, California Poppy, coreopsis, baptisia, *Alyssum saxatile,* anthemis, gaillardia, cosmos, celosia, calendula, nasturtium. Bulbs: crocus, daffodil, tulip, sternbergia.

FLOWERS FOR CUTTING

What are some desirable perennials for cut flowers, blooming in May and June, besides iris, etc.? *Doronicum caucasicum, Dicentra eximia, Dianthus plumarius* and varieties, *Delphinium belladonna, Alyssum saxatile citrinum, Saponaria ocymoides* *splendens, Pulmonaria saccharata, Phlox suffruticosa* and varieties, *Phlox divaricata,* Geum Fire Opal, *Anchusa myostidiflora.*

Can you tell me how to have cut flowers as early as possible, and for as long a time as possible?   Tall-bearded iris, Siberian iris, coreopsis, Delphinium Belladonna, *Eupatorium coelestinum,* gaillardia, geum, gypsophila, helenium, penstemon, physostegia, aster, chrysanthemum; spring bulbs.

Which flowers are best suited for show and cutting purposes? Tritoma, antirrhinum, aster, campanula, gaillardia, coreopsis, *Anemone japonica,* artemisia, chrysanthemum, and doronicum. Roses, delphinium, daffodil, tulip, peony, gladiolus, iris.

Which garden flowers are best for cutting, and last longest after being cut?   Aster, tritoma, chrysanthemum, helianthus, scabiosa, zinnia, aquilegia, *Stokesia lilacina, Verbena bonariensis,* celosia, and marigold.

Anticipating an August wedding, which white or pastel-colored flowers can we plant with which to decorate the church? White Shastadaisy, delphinium, chrysanthemum, phlox, aster, stock, scabiosa, gladiolus, and gypsophila.

FOR EDGING

What is a desirable perennial edging between lawn and border?   Dwarf Teucrium (*T. chamaedrys*), *Iberis sempervirens* Little Gem, *Dianthus caesius.*

I have a formal garden with 100 tulips and phlox at end. Which flowers are best to plant for edging and gradual build-up in size to height of phlox?   *Doronicum caucasicum, Phlox arendsi, Phlox divaricata, Dianthus plumarius, Anchusa myosotidiflora, Ajuga genevensis, Alyssum saxatile compactum, Anemone hupehensis, Anemone magellanica, Veronica spicata, Veronica incana,* dwarf asters, dwarf chrysanthemums.

Can you suggest some low edging plants with white flowers (not sweet alyssum) to plant where tulips have finished blooming?   Dwarf petunia; annual phlox; dwarf verbena.

I want to lay out a colonial garden using beds in some design. What shall I edge the beds with?   Dwarf box edging is typical. Dwarf teucrium and dwarf English Ivy can be substituted.

PLANNING FOUNDATION PLANTINGS
(See also Foundation Material—Section II.)

What kind of shrubbery would you plant in front of a new house with a 30-ft. frontage?   Use tall, upright-growing plants at the corners and low-growing, rounded masses between. Avoid too much planting. If the house foundation is low enough, leave some spaces bare to give the house the effect of standing solidly on the ground. Either deciduous or evergreen material is suitable.

A symmetrical balanced entrance planting.

We have large trees (oak, Gray Birch, maple, and ironwood). What should be planted near the house? The yard slopes toward the south and the house is new, so we are starting from scratch. Let the trees constitute the principal landscape feature. Use a minimum of planting near the house—vines on the foundation, a few shade-loving shrubs at the corners or either side of the entrance.

What is best for planting around a small house on a small acreage? Everyone has evergreens. Can't we have simplicity and still be different? Shrubs and vines are just as beautiful as evergreens and deserve wider use. The smaller the house the simpler the planting ought to be.

What is the best method of foundation planting for an "unbalanced" house—one with the door not in the center? An unbalanced composition for a foundation planting can be made extremely attractive. The fact that the door is not in the center will make it even more interesting. Naturally the doorway should be the point of interest, and your maximum height should begin on either side, tapering irregularly to the corners of the house where a specimen shrub or evergreen may go a little higher in order to break the sharp lines of the house corner. These corner accents should not be so tall as the main planting on either side of the doorway.

I want to plant flowers along the base of our house. Will you suggest what kind of flowers to plant?   Unless the house is an architectural jewel which should not be hidden, shrubs or vines, or both, as a background, with flowers planted in front of them, give a better effect than flowers which, alone, are apt to look too small and inadequate near a house foundation. Flowers to plant in front of shrubs by house: tulip, narcissus, crocus, *Scilla sibirica,* followed by dictamnus, polyantha roses, and *Phlox decussata.* Or use long drifts of one variety of annual, limited to one or two colors, such as Petunias Elks Pride and Snowdrift, or Heavenly Blue or Rosy Gem; or for a gay effect a good mixture of marigolds.

CAPE COD

How shall I landscape the front of our Cape Cod house? It was built about 1810 and during the 6½ years we have owned it every minute has been spent in restoring the old pine paneling within doors and developing the flower and vegetable gardens outside. There is the main house with front door in the center, an ell, and a long shed-garage combination. What treatment all along the front would you suggest?   Planting for a Cape Cod house should be very simple. A suitable planting is shown in the accompanying sketch. Shade trees are important and should be carefully placed. A small dooryard enclosed by a low picket fence often adds to the charm if the house sets far enough back from the highway to permit its being used.

The Cape Cod type of home calls for a low foundation planting, in keeping with its architectural lines.

We have a small home, Cape Cod. Which shrubs can be planted that would not be too expensive or difficult to grow? Among the "sure-fire" shrubs are *Amorpha nana;* berberis, various (barberry); *Caragana aurantiaca; Cotoneaster horizontalis; Deutzia gracilis; Euonymus alatus; Genista tinctoria;* broom; *Hypericum patulum* and *H. frondosum* (St. Johnswort); Philadelphus Mt. Blanc and P. Norma; wild roses; lilac; spirea.

COLONIAL

What can be done with a narrow front lawn between an old-fashioned house with a high porch and the street—which is lined with large, old maples?   Grass will probably not be very successful in such a place. Use *Vinca minor* or *Pachysandra terminalis* in place of it, and hide the porch foundation with a planting of laurel (*Kalmia latifolia*), rhododendron, or other shade-loving shrubs. Such a planting will require heavy applications of acid, humus-making fertilizer and frequent watering.

ENGLISH

Could you tell me what kind of foundation planting I could use for an English-type home?   The English style, being informal, calls for informal planting. Avoid symmetrically balanced groups of planting, or too much planting. Accent the doorways, the corners, and leave the rest open. Vines are important to soften brickwork or stone.

FARMHOUSES

Do you suggest landscaping a plot around a farmhouse?   A farm home needs planting, but it does not need the intensive landscape development that characterizes the average suburban home. Use a few well-placed clumps of hardy shrubs and small-flowering trees.

What native material can be collected in Maine that would be suitable for landscape use around a farmhouse?   Hemlock, witchhazel, winterberry, birch, Sugar Maples, Red Maples, pines, larch, arborvitae, Virginia Rose, blueberries, and many other shrubs. Take a walk through the woods there and see for yourself.

FRENCH

What sort of foundation planting is appropriate to an informal French house?   An informal house should have informal planting. Avoid rigid balance, and hold the planting down to the minimum. Use a few choice things rather than many ordinary

plants. Clumps of broad-leaved evergreens are particularly effective.

*The small
French - type
home calls for
simplicity in de-
sign of the
grounds and
planting.*

RUSTIC

We have a cabin among trees and woodland. We would like to
make the immediate grounds of the cottage look much nicer than
they now are. How could we go about it?   Underplant the
area with various kinds of native ferns and woodland wildflowers.

FOR HEDGES

See Section II.

HILLSIDE PLANTING

How could a rather steep hillside, partly wooded, be planted
to make it more attractive?   Such a wooded hillside could be
underplanted with native shrubs, evergreens, ferns, and woodland
wildflowers. An interesting system of trails leading through the
area would add to its interest.

SCREENS

How can I disguise my chicken house and yard so that they
will not injure the appearance of my property?   If the wire
of the chicken run is strong enough, you might plant a vine such
as honeysuckle on it. The house itself can be made less conspicuous by planting a group of pines and spruces around it. Or
the whole thing can be hidden behind a dense hedge.

Would a mixture of plants with various colored leaves or blossoms be satisfactory in an informal screening for enclosing a
yard?   Usually a suitable boundary screen consists of one
variety of shrub. Too varied a planting competes with the interest inside the garden instead of merely framing it. Variety in leaf,
flower, and fruit may be inside the boundary screen or in foundation plantings of buildings.

What type of shrubs make good informal screening for enclosing yard? Choice is determined by size of area to be enclosed and height of objects to be "screened out." Persian Lilac is excellent for areas of a quarter acre and larger. Smaller gardens may use *Rosa hugonis, Rosa rubrifolia,* Truehedge Columnberry, or privet, untrimmed.

SHRUBS

Should shrubs and small trees be used in a flower garden? Yes, an occasional compact-growing tree or shrub in the garden relieves the monotony of perennial and annual planting.

We plan to landscape a 3-acre tract. Will you name flowering shrubs that give a succession of bloom throughout the year? For spring: azalea, forsythia, lonicera, *Viburnum carlesi.* For summer: philadelphus, spirea, enkianthus, lilac, rhododendron. Later in season: *Hydrangea macrophylla* and buddleia. For autumn color: *Euonymus alatus, Cornus nuttalli,* Amur River Privet, *Stephanandra incisa,* and Smooth Sumac.

Can you suggest hardy shrubbery for a small country home? Standard varieties of deciduous shrubs, such as spirea, lilac, deutzia, philadelphus, and weigela, can always be relied upon to thrive with the minimum amount of care. Interest can be added to the planting by using some of the rarer varieties, such as Philadelphus virginalis, hybrid lilacs, and a few of the small-flowering trees, such as Flowering Crab, dogwood, and redbud.

FOR SHADE

See also Shady Environment—Section II.

There is no sun in my garden from September until May. What is the best way to treat a garden of this kind? Since the floral display in this garden will be effective only from late spring to early fall, make sure the garden background is interesting enough to make the garden attractive during the rest of the year. Use evergreen, berry-bearing shrubs and ones that have good, full color. Then for flowers select only those plants that bloom during the time when sunlight is available.

Will you suggest plants for a garden in an all-shade yard? Aconitum, ajuga, aquilegia, campanula, cimicifuga, dicentra, digitalis, ferns, funkia, hemerocallis, hesperis, lily-of-the-valley, thalictrum, tradescantia, trillium, valeriana, and viola are the principal shade-loving kinds of garden flowers. There are many varieties of most.

Which flowers are best for part shade?   Perennials for part shade: *Achillea filipendulina,* aconite, cimicifuga, digitalis, *Anemone japonica, Lobelia cardinalis,* mertensia, funkia, helleborus, daylily, trollius, primrose.

Which perennial flowers, tall, medium, low, may I use in a garden shaded by oak trees? What soil improvements should be made to overcome acidity from oaks?   Most perennial plants are not particular as to the acidity or alkalinity of soil. If there is overacidity from the leaves of your oak tree this may be corrected by an annual sprinkling of ground limestone worked shallowly into the topsoil. Your location should be ideal without treatment for all of your native wildflowers. The low-growing group would include cypripediums, woods ferns, etc. (See Woodland Wildflowers.) For taller plants you have a wide choice from such things as holly, mountain laurel, azalea, blueberries, and rhododendron. The combination of these should be an attractive planting.

Please name a few plants that will grow in dense shade, around base of large tree. Must I put them in pots on account of roots of tree?   Few plants will subsist on what's left in the soil after the roots of a large tree have filled the surface and used all available food. Try digging out pockets, filling them with good loam, and planting one of the following: *Viola canadensis, Mahonia repens, Vinca minor,* Kenilworth Ivy, pachysandra. Potted plants would be of only temporary value.

Which flower is the best to plant under a big maple tree where there are lots of roots and practically no sun? Altitude is 6,600 ft.   Norway Maple (*Acer platanoides*) foliage is so dense that few plants can survive both shade and the fight for root space and food. Deep watering of all maples encourages the development of deeper rooting, thus freeing the surface from this strangling network. Ground covers that accept the challenge of most maples are *Vinca minor, Mahonia repens,* pachysandra, *Sedum stoloniferum.*

Which plants would grow well along a shady wall?   *Euonymus radicans vegetus,* aquilegia, ladyslipper, hepatica, *Epimedium niveum, Plumbago larpentae,* dicentra, digitalis, sanguinaria, ferns, mertensia, anemone, primula, pulmonaria, aconitum, dodecatheon, thalictrum, *Anchusa myosotidiflora.* Trees which provide shade for plants in nature also supply abundant humus in the soil by their decayed leaves. Shade plants in the garden appreciate humus too.

SLOPES AND BANKS

See also Section II.

Will you suggest some shrubs or trees for the sloping terrace in front of my house? Roses such as Max Graf and *Rosa wichuraiana, Jasminum nudiflorum,* lonicera, bearberry, or dwarf, spreading evergreens.

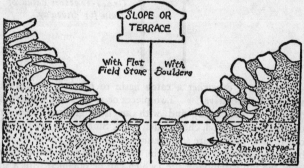

Method of placing stones to hold a slope or a terrace, without a wall.

How should a sloping area (15 × 3 ft.) along a driveway be planted? Fence or wall would be unsuitable. The location is sunny. Such a place is best treated by planting the slope with some easy-to-take-care-of, low, trailing shrub or perennial. *Phlox subulata alba, Teucrium chamaedrys, Juniperus chinensis sargenti,* or *Euonymus fortunei vegetus* would be suitable.

SURFACE DRAINAGE

What is a dry well, and what is it used for? A dry well is a pit dug 5 or 6 ft. deep, filled with stones and gravel. A pipe or sewer leading either from the house or from a poorly drained area leads into this, and provides drainage for difficult situations.

What can be done to prevent rain water from draining off the highway onto a sloping property, causing erosion? A low bank along the highway should be constructed, and at the lowest point in the gutter so created a catch basin can be installed to gather the water and lead it, through a pipe, to a place where it will do no harm. Such a catch basin can be simply 2 18-in. sewer tiles, one on top of the other, with a grating fitted into the top and a 4-in. side outlet about 1 ft. below the top. If there is a great deal of water, it may have to be a brick, concrete, or stone basin.

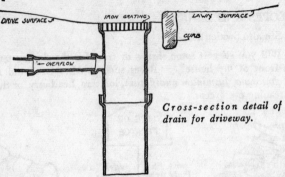

Cross-section detail of drain for driveway.

How can I construct a catch basin to take off surplus rain water from the drive?   Two pieces of 18-in. sewer tile, set one on top of the other, and with an iron grating fitted into the top, make a good, cheap catch basin. Smaller tile are too difficult to clean; larger are seldom needed. If the amount of water to be taken care of is large, a 4-in. or 6-in. tile pipe can be taken from the top catch-basin tile (which can be obtained with a side outlet) and carried some distance away to a low point where the water will do no harm, or to the storm sewer.

TREES

Should trees be removed from gardens?   Not necessarily. If the trees are fine old specimens, they should be left, and the garden designed around them using plants that will withstand shade; otherwise they should be taken out. Often trees form an important part of the garden's design.

Can you suggest desirable evergreens and deciduous trees for use in landscaping a suburban home?   See Section II.

GARDEN FEATURES AND ACCESSORIES

ARBORS

I want to buy an arbor for my garden on which to train roses. What type is best?   White-painted wooden arbors are inexpensive and look well. Get one that is sturdy and well designed. Rustic arbors, made from cedar or redwood, are also suitable.

BIRD BATHS

What type of bird bath is good for the small garden?   Any well-made concrete, marble, clay, wood, or stone bird baths that are available, as long as they are well designed and unobtrusive. Select a design which fits your garden plan. Homemade cement-and-field-stone bird baths are not usually desirable. For a small garden a height of 2½ ft. is about right. If the bath is detached from the pedestal, it will facilitate cleaning.

Are the bird baths which are set on the ground without a pedestal practical? Yes, they are very effective if well designed. Handmade ceramic or metal basins are interesting, or a hollowed stone may be used. They are usually placed in a sheltered spot surrounded by ivy or other ground cover, evergreens, or shrubs. It must be remembered, however, that this type bird bath can be used only where no cats are around to harm the birds when they use it.

How often should you clean bird baths? As often as they look dirty or stained, which is usually 2 or 3 times a week at least in warm weather. It will help to have a special scrubbing brush for the bird bath for removing scum around the edges.

What can be used to remove algae from a bird bath? Usually water or soapy water and a scrubbing brush are all that is necessary. Borax may be added, or a bleaching disinfectant. These, however, must be well rinsed off before filling the bath with water for the birds.

CURBINGS

Would you recommend brick or stone edging for a driveway or path? For a driveway, brick edging is somewhat too fragile unless the bricks are set in a heavy foundation of concrete. Then they are likely to be ugly. Granite paving blocks (Belgian blocks) are better because they are heavy enough to stay put without cement. For pathways, brick is ideal. Small rounded stones are useless for either purpose.

What sort of edging should I use for a brick walk? There are 3 standard sorts of edging: sawtooth, rowlock, and stretcher. For garden paths where there are no grass edges, sawtooth looks well, and it uses less brick than does rowlock. Against a lawn or grass edge rowlock is better because the mower can be run up on it and there is less hand clipping. Stretcher edging uses the least brick of all, but, since the bricks do not go down into the ground any farther than the bricks of the walk itself, it provides less stability for the walk.

What can I use to edge a driveway that will look well, but also make a strong, permanent edge? Granite paving blocks are ideal for this. They are so heavy they will stay in place without concrete to hold them. Do not let them stick up above the lawn area. Set them on end, with the short dimension parallel to the line of the driveway.

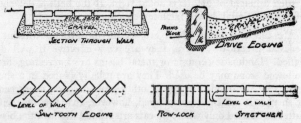

Types of edging for walks and drives.

Should flower beds be edged with stones, brick, or plants? Stone edgings are a nuisance, since the grass around them has to be hand clipped. Brick edgings have the same fault but in connection with gravel paths give a prim, quaint effect. In most cases edgings of flowering plants are more suitable.

DOORWAYS

The doorway of my house is a reproduction of an old colonial door, with leaded side lights and fanlight. How should I plant this so as to enhance rather than detract from its beauty? For an elaborate doorway, which is sufficiently interesting in itself, elaborate planting is unnecessary. Possibly the most effective thing would be to plant a big old lilac on either side of the door, train a light vine, possibly a large-flowered clematis, over the door itself, and leave it at that.

Suggestion for planting a colonial doorway.

Should planting either side of the front door always be alike on both sides? Certainly not. If the house is in an informal or picturesque architectural style, the planting should also be informal and picturesque. Use a tall, dark plant on one side, with a few smaller things around its base, and on the other side use something lighter, more graceful and spreading. Don't use too many kinds of plants and too many sorts of foliage.

A nicely balanced, but not symmetrical, front-door planting.

My colonial house seems to me to have a very plain doorway. How can I plant it to make it seem more important? Where the doorway is formal, but very plain, interest must be created through the planting. Use identical groups on either side, but select the various plants carefully for form texture and foliage color. Evergreens give great dignity and are less likely to get too large in a short time. Tall masses to accent the lines of the doorway, with more spreading plants around them, usually make the most effective arrangement.

DRIVEWAYS

What material do you recommend for the building of a driveway? Many materials make satisfactory driveways, but much depends on whether the drive is straight or curved, flat or sloping, in cold country or warm. A good, cheap driveway for a level drive in the New York area can be made of either cinders mixed with loam and sand or bank-run gravel. Either can be finished with grits or bluestone screenings. If there are curves or grades, crushed stone with a tar binder is practically mandatory.

How would you build a driveway on a steep slope to prevent washing? What material should be used? For a short driveway on a steep slope, granite paving blocks set in sand make an ideal material. They are rough enough to give good traction in icy weather, they need no maintenance, they are good-looking. For a long driveway, they may be too uneven for comfortable riding, and concrete, heavily scored to provide traction, may be better. But it is a hard, uncompromising-looking material.

I am building a driveway for my home. What sort of parking space for visiting cars do you recommend, and where should it be located?   Parking space for at least one guest car should be provided right at the front door or the path leading to it, so arranged that the use of the driveway by other cars is not prevented. (See next question.) Parking for a larger number of cars should be located at a distance from the front entrance of the house. It should be constructed of the same material as the driveway.

When guests come to the house and leave their cars before the front door, it is impossible for anyone else to use the driveway from the garage to the street. How can I avoid this situation?   Construct a pass court in front of the door wide enough so that a car can stand at the door and another pass it on the outside. The court should be about 30 ft. long and 16 ft. wide. Any interesting shape can be given it to make it a pleasing part of the landscape picture.

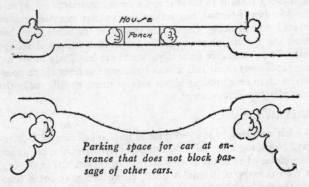

Parking space for car at entrance that does not block passage of other cars.

What is the most practical shape for a turn court at the garage on a small property?   The so-called Y-turn takes up the least space and yet provides for easy turning, either for your own car coming out of the garage, or for other cars using the driveway. The radius of the curves in the accompanying sketch should be 15 ft. to 20 ft., and it is important that the space into which the cars back be at least 14 ft. wide.

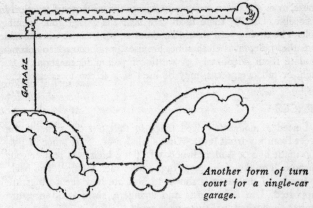

Another form of turn court for a single-car garage.

How large should a turn-around in front of the house be? The largest cars require a turning space about 60 ft. in diameter for making a complete turn without backing. An area of bluestone or gravel that large is often out of proportion to the house. It can be broken up with a grass island (but this should not have anything else planted in it). To make arrival at the house door easy, it is wise to distort the shape of the turn-around somewhat, making it more of an apple shape instead of a true circle.

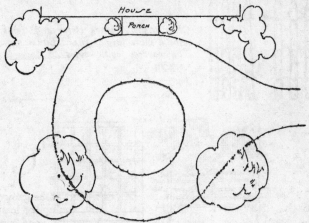

Turn-around for car.

DRYING YARD

How can one go about making a drying yard on the home grounds? Select a spot that will not be visible from the house, or one that can be separated from the garden and yet easily accessible. Usually there is an area near the garage that is suitable. The drying yard should be about 20 sq. ft. in size if one has a clothes pole, or, if clotheslines are used, large enough to accommodate them adequately. A wattle or paling fence about 6 ft. high, or tall evergreens, may be used as a screen to enclose the area.

FENCES

I need a moderate-priced fence to shut out the view of the street from my front lawn. What shall I use?   A fence of palings made of 1 × 4 in. redwood, 5 ft. 6 ins. high, will answer your purpose. The sketch on page 1324 shows such a fence. The back, or inside, of the fence is shown to indicate how the palings are supported. Use stout posts and stringers, since wind pressure against such a fence may be very great.

Where can I get a design for a picket fence?   The accompanying sketch shows a typical picket fence such as used to be seen often on village streets. Many modern picket fences are less substantially built, and hence tend to look flimsy. The effectiveness of such a fence depends largely on delicacy of detail, but it must also be, and look, strong.

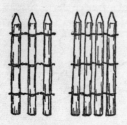

Rustic picket fence (left) and trellis for a more formal effect. Either may be covered with vines to form a screen.

Is a wattle fence appropriate for the home garden?   A woven wattle fence made of saplings or thin split logs is expensive, and because of this is not recommended for the small garden unless there is an objectionable view to be blocked or sturdy protection from animals to be provided. Wattle fences are excellent for such purposes as enclosing a drying yard, screening a highway, or to give privacy in a courtyard, small flower or herb garden.

What sort of fence is best for use along the highway in front of a farm where something elaborate would be out of place? A simple post-and-rail fence, such as the one in the accompanying sketch, has proved very satisfactory. It can be painted white, or, if made of dead chestnut, cypress, or redwood, left unpainted to weather. If it has to be made proof against small animals and chickens, wire can be attached to the inside.

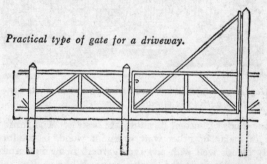

Practical type of gate for a driveway.

Shall I use perennials or annuals (a) for trellis fence; and (b) for chimney? How fast growing? (a) Ipomoea "Heavenly Blue"—annual, fast-growing; *Lathyrus latifolius*—perennial, fast-growing; *Clematis montana rubens*—perennial, strong grower. (b) *Euonymus fortunei vegetus*—perennial, fast-growing; *Ampelopsis lowi*—perennial, slow-growing; *Hedera helix "baltica"*—slow-growing, for north or northwest side only.

FOUNTAINS

Do you recommend putting a fountain into a small home garden? Elaborate fountains throwing large streams of water are rather expensive to maintain and too impressive for a small garden. A small fountain which drips water slowly over a shallow basin or a wall fountain that runs a tiny stream into a bowl are pleasing and in scale.

FURNITURE

Is it better to paint wooden garden furniture white or green? White is good for colonial or white frame homes. Almost any shade of green paint is likely to look artificial and out of place

with the green of the garden. Clear varnish, or a soft brownish
stain which brings out the grain of the wood may be used.

Is garden furniture recommended for the small garden?
Yes. It must be of good design, however, and suit the type of the
house. It should be comfortable, light weight (or heavy enough
to be placed permanently), resistant to weather, and preferably
of a color which will become part of the garden scene.

*'Garden seats should be placed where they will invite use—
not stuck out in the middle of a lawn.*

What kinds of garden furniture are best? The rustic type,
made of cedar or other water-resistant wood, if comfortable,
usually blends well with any type garden. Being inconspicuous,
it does not dominate the garden scene. White-painted wooden
furniture is desirable in some gardens, especially if the house is
also white. Metal furniture is comfortable, and good for outdoor
living rooms or terraces. Stone benches and tables are suitable
for the large garden. Cane or woven chairs may be used if not
subjected to bad weather. Canvas chairs are comfortable and
easy to move about, but also must be protected from rain.

GARDEN HOUSES

**What kind of garden house is most suitable for the small
garden?** A very simple house which fits the architecture
of the house and the landscape plan of the garden. The English
style, with a sloping tiled or thatched roof, is fitting for an
English-type garden. Rustic styles are good in a natural setting,
out of sight of the main house. Avoid fantastic or baroque styles.

GAME AREAS

How can I lay out a badminton court? Allow about 30 by
60 ft. of lawn space for a badminton court. (See also Lawns.)

**I want to make part of my garden into an area for a bowling
green and for horseshoe pitching. How much room is necessary?**

For a bowling green you should have a smooth grass area about 128 ft. sq. A gutter of sand 1½ ft. wide and about 6 ins. deep should surround this strip. For horseshoes, you will need an area 10 × 50 ft. The sand pit at either end should be 6 ft. sq., with a stout wooden or iron stake in the center.

How much room does a croquet lawn require? About 30 × 60 ft. A level, well-mowed area is essential for this game. (See Lawns.)

What games or equipment would be suitable for a children's game area? A wading pool, sandbox or sand pit, swings, see-saw, sliding board, ball court.

My children want a tennis court. What is the most practical type; and how should it be constructed? Clay courts are most satisfactory. See that the drainage of the area is good. Lay down tile lines across the area if necessary. Put in 6 ins. of good clay, tamped and rolled smooth. Let the whole court slope about 6 ins. from one end to the other, or 3 ins. from each end to a low point at the net line. Surface with an inch or less of fine sifted clay with a little sand mixed in.

What area is needed for a tennis court? The playing space of a double court is 38 × 78 ft., but at least 66 × 138 ft. is needed to give room at sides and ends for free play.

I would like to build a little shelter near our playground area for storing equipment and for spectators. Have you any suggestion? A simple 3-sided building of white clapboards, or of rustic logs or siding with an open front, might be constructed at the end of the area. The floor can be of stone or concrete. Closets could be built along one wall for storing tennis rackets, croquet mallets, etc. Allow one closet for sweaters, shoes, and other equipment. Comfortable lounging chairs should be at hand for spectators.

GATES

What kind of garden gate do you recommend? Wrought iron or wood (either rustic or painted). A paling gate would look well with a fence of the same material.

What kind of gate is best to use with a clipped privet hedge? A well-designed gate of stained, weathered, or painted wood, or wrought iron.

Do you recommend wire gates for gardens? Wire gates are not usually so decorative as wooden or iron gates. They are suitable for vegetable areas or dog runs.

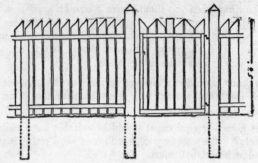

Gate for a picket fence.

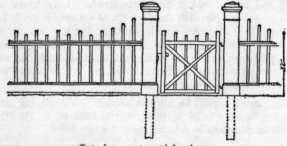

Gate for an open picket fence.

To be correct, must the planting either side of a garden gate or entrance be the same?   A symmetrically balanced arrangement is the usual thing, but it is often less interesting than an unsymmetrical treatment such as the one in the accompanying

Example of a balanced (but not symmetrical) gateway planting.

sketch. Here 3 elements—the vine on the wall, the urn filled with flowers, and the low, rounded shrub—have been balanced by the tall, dark evergreen on the other side. Such a treatment is easier to arrange when the position of the entrance, or conditions of shade, etc., make a symmetrical arrangement difficult. It is more lively and striking.

LAWNS

Should a garden have a lawn space in the middle?   Not all gardens should be so designed, but there are many advantages to this type of layout. A grass panel serves as a foreground to the floral displays in the beds and as a space for chairs and tables. Such a garden is easier to maintain than one made up of many small beds.

Where the house is below the street level, water may be drained away by sloping grade down from both house and street to form slight depression at a low point.

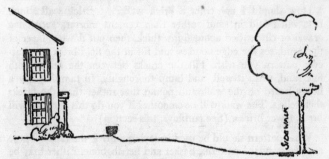

Grading: a flat terrace with a step, and curved slope to sidewalk is more attractive than a uniform grade from door to street.

How would you grade a front lawn where the house is small and is several feet below the highway level?   A gradual slope from the house up to the street is usually more pleasing than abrupt terraces. To prevent water draining toward the house, however, the grade should be carried down from the house slightly, to a low point from which the water can drain off to the sides before the slope up to the street begins. (See Lawns.)

PATHS

What materials are suitable for making paths? For an average flower garden, grass paths are usually best, for they present a green foreground for the garden picture. They need no maintenance other than what the lawn receives. Gravel or bluestone paths in the flower garden are likely to be a nuisance to take care of. Where a path must be dry, or at least passable in all sorts of weather, brick and flagstone are serviceable. Often it is possible to make a grass path more practical by laying a line of stepping-stones down its middle, or along either edge.

Should a path be laid out in a straight line or with a curve? Generally speaking, a path should be as direct as possible, because the purpose of it is to provide a passage between two points. However, a natural-looking path should follow the contour of the garden, curving around trees or shrubs that are in a direct line. Sharp curves are to be avoided, and all unnecessary turns. When a curve is to be made, it should have a long, gentle sweep. For very small paths, a straight line, with no curves at all, is advisable.

BRICK AND STONE

How should I construct a brick walk? Brick walks look best when laid in sand rather than cement mortar. Provide a gravel or cinder bed about 6 ins. thick, then put down a layer of fine sand, set the edge courses, and fill in the field brick in whatever pattern you wish. Fill the cracks between the bricks with fine sand, wash it well, and tamp thoroughly. In tamping, lay a heavy board on the walk and pound that rather than the bricks themselves. The walk will be smoother if you do this and you will break fewer bricks. (See curbings, this section)

What pattern should be used in laying a brick walk? There are two standard patterns, basket and herringbone. Either may be varied somewhat according to taste. The basket pattern is more economical, since there is no cutting of brick. The accompanying sketch shows basket pattern with a rowlock edge and herringbone with a sawtooth edge. In laying out the walk, set only one edge course first. Lay out a section of the field to see how the pattern is working out, then set the other edge. Do not decide on a predetermined width for the walk and then try to fit the pattern into it.

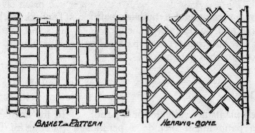

BASKET-PATTERN   HERRING-BONE

Two "patterns" for laying bricks for a walk.

FLAGSTONE

The front of my garage is about 50 ft. from street, joined to house; driveway level on one side; 4-ft. slope on other; no walk to house as yet. Would you suggest shrubs, rock garden, stone wall with flagstone walk, or low flowers?   A stone wall with flagstone walk to the front door would make the most dignified treatment. The front yard is usually no place for a rock garden or flowers of any sort.

GRAVEL

I have been thinking of putting in a gravel path. Is it commonly used in the garden?   Gravel paths are often used. They are inclined to look a bit formal and cold, however, and they are not so comfortable to walk upon as grass or tanbark.

STEPPINGSTONES

What sort of stones are suitable for a path of steppingstones? Water-washed flat stones with rounded edges are the most effective. If these are unobtainable, other flat stones or random slates or flagstones can be used, which are thick enough to bear the weight of traffic.

Is it possible to encourage the growth of moss? I want to put some between steppingstones.   Moss can be started only by transplanting sods of it from some place where it naturally grows. Find a variety that is growing under similar conditions of sun or shade. Probably you will get better results by using plants of *Arenaria verna caespitosa,* which can be purchased.

Will you suggest some plants for placing between steppingstones?   Various thymes, sedums, *Veronica repens, Mazus reptans, Potentilla tridentata, Achillea tomentosa, Tunica saxifraga.*

TANBARK

Do you recommend a tanbark path?   Tanbark paths are expensive and do not adapt themselves to the small garden so well as several other types of path. They are suitable for woodland, rose, or rock gardens.

PATIOS

Which plants are suitable for a patio?   In the northeast or north a patio might include a permanent planting of broad-leaved evergreens, an espaliered fruit tree (if there is a sunny wall), and a wisteria vine. Potted foliage plants (monstera, *Nephthytis afzelli,* dracaena, dieffenbachia, etc.) and potted geraniums, fuchsias, lantanas, begonias, and caladiums; crown-of-thorns and other succulents (such as crassulas) could be set out in warm weather. Patios in warm climates have a wider choice of plants, including such shrubs as oleanders, camellias, and gardenias; also bougainvillea and passiflora vines and other semi-tropical plant material.

I would like to have a patio garden. Would this be suitable with a colonial house?   Patio gardens are usually made within a courtyard or similar enclosure. They are of Spanish origin and suited to this type of dwelling. However, if you have or can arrange a suitable protected terrace or courtyard adjacent to your colonial house, you might use flat stones or flagging to pave the area, put potted plants in white containers instead of Spanish pottery ones and, by using colonial ornaments and furniture, arrange a fitting outdoor living room which would serve the same purpose as a patio.

PERGOLAS

What is a pergola?   A pergola is a passageway covered by an arbor which supports grapevines or large flowering vines. The structure is usually somewhat elaborate, with decorative columns and crosspieces. It is of Latin origin and is suitable to only a limited number of American gardens.

Is a pergola recommended for the small garden?   A pergola can be useful in the small garden for supporting a grapevine over a path and provide a practical as well as ornamental accessory. It is sometimes effective to put a pergola over the path to the garage, thus softening the harsh effect of the building and providing a place for vines. Whenever it is used, the pergola should provide a passageway from one place to another.

POOLS

How should a small pool be constructed? The accompanying sketch shows a simple concrete pool and the necessary plumbing connections. For the successful growing of aquatics the deep part of the pool should be 1½ ft., and if it is to be used at all by birds, some part of it should be shallow enough for them. They do not like water more than 2 ins. deep.

How shall I go about building a small pool? Excavate the ground about 6 ins. deeper on bottom and wider at the sides than you wish the pool to be. Insert drainage if pool is to be large enough to require it (see accompanying sketch); if it is very small, this will not be necessary. Fill hole with gravel layer, tamp down firm, or line with chicken wire. Pour cement, 1 part cement to 3 parts mixed sand and gravel. Add water enough so that mixture will spread evenly. Layer should be about 4 or 5 ins. thick. Next day finish with a coat of cement mortar, 1 part cement to 2 parts sand, applied with a trowel.

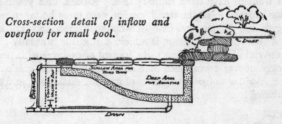

Cross-section detail of inflow and overflow for small pool.

How thick should the concrete walls of a garden pool be? The thickness of the walls of a pool depends on its size. A large pool naturally has to have thicker walls. For the average small pool (6 ft. or so in diameter) walls 6 ins. thick are sufficient. Some reinforcement in the form of wire or steel rods should be used.

How soon after finishing the construction of a small pool can plants be put in? Leave the pool filled with water for about 2 weeks, flushing occasionally, before planting or putting in fish.

I want to paint my pool blue. What kind of paint shall I use? There is a special paint available from seed or department stores for just this purpose.

I want to get some complete information on the construction of a small pool. Can you suggest some publication? The

Portland Cement Association, 347 Madison Ave., New York City, puts out a very helpful bulletin on this subject. You may obtain it from your local cement dealer.

What shape should a small pool be? It depends on your location and general garden design. If your garden is informal, an informally shaped pool would be best. This should be basically circular or "egg-shaped" with gently curving, irregular contours. By using the garden hose to lay out the shape of the pool, good curves may be attained. Avoid sharp curves and too many irregularities. Simplicity is the keynote.

I want to build a small informal pool. About what size should I make it? A good-looking small pool might be about 25 sq. ft. in size.

I want to build a small formal pool with a fountain and statue at the back. What shape would be best for the pool? A round or oblong formal pool is always good. If your garden is very formal, you could have a rectangular pool.

STATUARY

I want to have some statuary in my garden. Can you suggest some types? In the small garden, care must be taken not to overdo use of statuary. One well-designed piece, not too large, used as a center of interest, is sufficient. A statue is usually placed at the end of a vista or in a niche formed of evergreens. It needs a background of green plant material to fit it into the garden picture. Avoid use of pottery figures of gnomes, ducks, etc., and other novelties.

A simple treatment of steps in a steep bank—English Ivy for year-round greenery.

STEPS

Of what shall I build my garden steps? Steps of stone with brick or flagstone treads harmonize well in many gardens. All-brick steps often look too harsh and formal. Field stone is all right if you can find enough flat ones. Concrete is much too unyielding.

Grass steps held in place by steel bands imbedded in the turf are beautiful but hard to make and to maintain. For very informal situations, sod, gravel, or tanbark steps held up by field-stone or log risers are most effective. Sometimes the steps themselves are made of squared sections of cypress or Black Locust logs.

SUNDIALS

Do you recommend using a sundial in the garden?   A sundial is very effective in the right setting as the center of interest in a rose garden, or formal garden. It must, of course, be placed where the sun will hit it all day. The base can be planted with vines or low-blooming flowers. A sundial is usually placed at the axis where four paths meet, though a sunny position in a border or bed past which a path runs, is also good. Or it may occupy the center of a section of lawn.

TERRACES

How should I construct a flag terrace, and the steps down from it to the lawn?   The flagstone, 2 ins. or so thick, can be laid on a bed of cinders or gravel covered with a thin layer of fine sand. No mortar is needed if the flags are heavy enough to stay in place. Slate cannot be used so easily. Brick can be substituted for flag. Steps should have treads with at least 1 in. overhang, and there should be a solid concrete foundation under them. Ramps, parapets, or wing walls should be substantial and have copings with the same overhang as the step treads. Steps and walls should be laid in cement mortar.

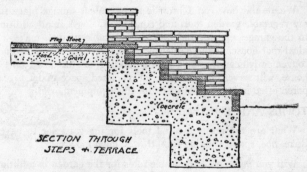

Cross-section detail for concrete and brick steps.

Which flowers will grow on a very windy terrace?   Dwarf phlox, astilbe, dianthus, *Eupatorum coelestinum, Gypsophila repens,* hemerocallis, iberis, lavandula, *Anchusa myosotidiflora.*

Will you suggest a plant giving a long period of bloom for the narrow border around my flagged lounging terrace?   Lantana. Purchase young blossoming plants from a florist or seed store and plant 18 ins. apart. They will grow into sturdy shrubs by mid-summer; not winter hardy. Try an edging of lobelia on the inside.

TOOL HOUSE

I want to fix up some space in my garage as a tool house and potting shed. How can I arrange this?   Build a long bench, at convenient height for standing, to be used for potting plants, mixing sprays, etc. Under this have drawers or shelves for pots, labels, and baskets, and bins for fertilizers and mulching materials. Over the bench, racks may be built for holding vases, and strips of wood nailed close to the wall will be convenient holders for small tools such as trowels, dibbers, and hand cultivators. A space against one wall should be left for the wheelbarrow and lawn mower. Wooden racks for rakes, hoes, and other long-handled tools (which are hung handle down) can be made by nailing a strip of wood on the wall, about 6 ft. above the floor. Pairs of tenpenny nails protruding from this hold the tools. Or an overhead hanging shelf may be notched on both sides to accommodate tool handles. Heads of tools are placed above the shelf. The garden hose needs a special rack where it will not be damaged by sharp tools. A stout 2-ft. bracket jutting out from the wall will be convenient for this purpose.

Where and how can I provide a convenient storage place for my vegetable garden tools and equipment?   A small addition to the garage, opening out into the vegetable garden, makes an ideal tool house. If the garden is fairly large and the garage not conveniently near, a small separate building, disguised as a garden house, will serve. On a sloping lot, enclosed space under a rear porch often makes a good place for this equipment.

TOOLS AND EQUIPMENT

What are the most essential tools for the gardener to have? Rake, hoe, spade, spading fork, trowel, lawn mower.

Will you name other desirable tools for the garden in addition to the main essentials?   Shovel, onion hoe, hedge shears, grass shears, pruning shears, wheelbarrow, hose, hand cultivator, scuffle hoe, pruning saw, sharp knife, sickle, dibber, lawn roller, lawn sprinklers, cultivator and wheel hoe, manure fork, watering can, lawn weeder, lawn edger, bamboo or steel grass rake.

What is an onion hoe? An onion hoe has a very shallow blade which cultivates only the upper surface of the soil without cutting into the soil or "hacking." It is convenient for cultivating close to plant rows.

What is a scuffle or Dutch hoe? A scuffle or Dutch hoe has a flat, sharp cutting blade which cultivates the upper part of the soil. It is efficient for making a dust mulch and for weeding.

What is a dibber? A dibber is a small rounded piece of wood about 6 ins. in length and 1 to 2 ins. in diameter shaped to a rounded point, used for making holes in which to set plants or bulbs. Sometimes dibbers are made of metal or have the point cased in brass. They may be bought, but they are easily made at home from broken tool handles. The dibber should not have a sharp point. This causes a small air space in the bottom of the plant hole.

I want to buy a complete set of garden tools. Do you have any suggestions? Never buy cheap tools; it doesn't pay. Buy good-quality tools from a reliable company. Avoid "novelties." Standard-type tools, suited to your needs, will usually give better results.

Should tools be cleaned after using? Yes, decidedly. Wipe them off thoroughly, with a piece of burlap or an old rag each time after using. Rub occasionally with a cloth dipped in oil.

I want to store my tools through the winter. What shall I clean them with first? Clean off all dirt and spots with an oily cloth.

What accessories or equipment is necessary for gardening? A line and reel, stakes, measuring rod (8 to 10 ft.), labels, basket, sprayers, dusters, tying material (twine and patent twisters), flowerpots, plant bands, bulb pans, seed sowers, flats, plant supports.

I have heard of "plant bands" but do not know what they are. Can you describe them? Plant bands are used, in place of flowerpots, for potting young plants and seedlings. They are made of very thin wood, and are square, thus taking up less room than ordinary flowerpots and making them easy to fit into a flat for carrying. They will collapse when empty, so are easily stored. More important, they are deep enough to allow ample room for root development and are easily removed so that a large ball of earth may be left on the plant when transplanting.

LABELS

What kind of labels do you suggest for seedling flats? Plain wooden labels, available in your local dime or seed store. Dip a corner of a clean rag in white paint and rub over the label. Then, while it is still wet, letter with an ordinary lead pencil.

What type label is best for greenhouse plants? Small border-type labels that fit down into the soil of the pot; or pointed wooden labels, in several lengths, like those recommended for flats.

What kind of label is best for the perennial border? Although border labels, similar to rock-garden labels, are sometimes recommended, they are inclined to heave during winter. Best results are usually obtained with wired labels fastened to garden stakes. These should be weatherproof and copper-wired.

What type labels would you suggest for a rock garden? Four- or 5-in. weatherproof markers that are plunged into the soil and provide an oblong space for writing. One type has a blank space for marking which slides into a glassine pane; another need only be marked with a pencil on the outside and will remain legible.

I want to buy some labels for my rose garden. What kind would be best? Most permanent are of metal with the lettering pressed in. These are wired to the plant. If these are not available, get waterproof wired wooden ones, mark in waterproof ink, and wire to the plant.

TOPIARY WORK

What is topiary work? Pruning of hedges, shrubs, or trees in specific shapes, as of animals, houses, balls, spools, figures, or geometric forms. Used only in formal gardens and primarily associated with medieval landscape design. Practiced today more in Europe than in America. Boxwood and yew, and less frequently, privet, are employed for this purpose.

VIEWS

I have read that a garden should not "compete with a view." Why? How is it prevented? The intimate detail of a garden suffers by comparison with a wide view into the surrounding landscape. It is usually wiser to surround the garden with an enclosure to shut off outside views, but if these are worth-while, provision should be made to take advantage of them from some point outside the garden.

My house is surrounded by trees, but there is a fine view now

obscured by foliage. What should I do? Do not hesitate to cut out trees to form a vista so that the view can be seen from some vantage point in the house or on the terrace. Often this can be achieved by removing lower branches rather than whole trees.

WALLS

Would a field-stone wall be satisfactory for fencing off a small garden? In some localities it would be appropriate. A field-stone wall is suited to a country property rather than a city or suburban plot.

How should I construct a retaining wall, to be built of field stones? Since it may be called upon to withstand considerable pressure, a dry wall must have an adequate foundation, and the stones must be firmly bedded. The accompanying sketch shows that the foundation is as wide or wider than the wall and goes down below frost level. The face of the wall slopes back slightly, and all the stones are set with the long dimension horizontal. Use squarish rather than rounded stones, and use as large ones as you can get. Avoid "chinking" with small stones.

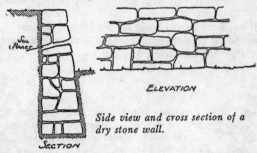

ELEVATION

Side view and cross section of a dry stone wall.

SECTION

How do you make soil pockets in a dry wall? As the wall is being laid up, leave gaps all the way through it, about 4 ins. in diameter. Be sure these openings slope downward toward the back of the wall to keep soil and plants from being washed out. See that the soil is continuous from the face of the wall to the soil back of the wall to permit moisture to penetrate to it constantly. Fill the holes thus made with rich soil. Be sure the stones above them make solid bridges over the holes.

WEATHER VANES

Should weather vanes be used on small properties? The use of weather vanes has been overdone in some sections. They are best used in the country, on barns, tool sheds, or other outbuildings. For a small place, get a simple style, not too large, to be used on the garage or garden house.

SPECIAL TYPES OF GARDENS

HERB GARDENS

WHAT TO GROW

Which herbs are annuals and which perennials? I am confused which ones to expect to come up a second year. The annual herbs most widely used are anise, dill, summer savory, fennel, coriander, and borage. The perennial herbs include horse-radish, lemon balm, winter savory, pot marjoram, sage, horehound, mint, tarragon, and beebalm. Parsley and caraway are, technically, biennials, but are grown as annuals. All of these grow in full sun and like a well-drained garden soil. Sow annuals as early in spring as weather permits, either in rows or broadcast.

Which herbs are the best to plant—annuals or perennials? This depends entirely upon your needs and garden facilities. A reasonably good selection of herbs includes both annuals and perennials.

Will you list 6 annual herbs for the kitchen garden? Basil, borage, chervil, parsley (really biennial but treated as an annual), Summer Savory, and Sweet Marjoram.

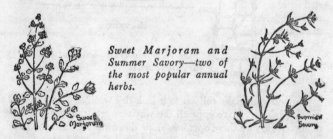

Sweet Marjoram and Summer Savory—two of the most popular annual herbs.

Which 6 perennial herbs do you suggest for the kitchen herb garden? Chives, horse-radish, mint, sage, tarragon, and thyme.

Which herbs do you suggest for a fragrant herb garden? Bergamot, lavender, lemonverbena, rosemary, scented geraniums, southernwood, sweet wormwood, lovage, valerian, lemon balm, sweetcicely, thyme, and costmary.

How should I start a small herb garden of a half-dozen

varieties of herbs?   Plant informally in little groups, taller plants more or less in back.

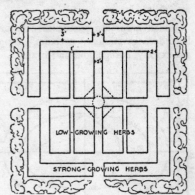

Design for a small formal herb garden.

What herbs may be grown successfully at home, and preserved for winter use?   Try the mints (if there is a moist spot in the garden, and care is taken to prevent the plants from overrunning their space); also sage, thyme, parsley, caraway, dill, and anise.

What are the best combinations of herbs for tea (as a beverage)?   For flavoring tea, try mints or lemonverbena. In combination, one authority suggests equal parts of elder flowers and peppermint; another, peppermint and lemonverbena. Sage and chamomile, each used alone, make tasty beverages. Never use a metal container.

Can you give some information on herbs—some to eat and some to smell?   Good herbs for flavoring: basil (sweet) for salads, soups, and tomato sauces; chives for salads and pot cheese; dill for pickles; fennel to eat like celery, or cooked; sweet marjoram, seasoning for stuffings, etc.; mints for teas and sauces; rosemary for seasoning roasts and chicken; sage for dressing; savory (summer) for flavoring vegetables, particularly string beans; thyme, seasoning for foods and salads; tarragon, to flavor vinegar, and in salads. Herbs for scent: beebalm, lavender, lemonverbena, mints, and scented geraniums.

Which herbs grow successfully in the house?   Basil, dittany of Crete, lemonverbena, parsley, rosemary, sweet marjoram, tarragon, and perhaps peppermint, if the room is cool and has plenty of light.

Which herbs do you suggest for an herbaceous border? Some of them grow too tall and scraggly.   Lavender, calendula, marjoram, rosemary, rue, sage, thyme, hyssop, and the gray artemisias.

Which herbs are particularly attractive to bees?   Thyme, lavender, germander, beebalm, lovage, hyssop, lemon balm, sweetcicely, borage, and marjoram.

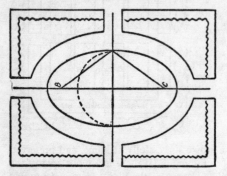

Method of laying out ellipses for a small herb garden. String is secured to stakes at B and C.

Can you name some herbs suitable for low hedges?   Hyssop, lavender, santolina, germander, southernwood, and rue. In fairly mild climates—rosemary.

Can you suggest herbs for a usable kitchen garden for the novice? Where can I get information as to their culture, preservation, and use?   The following are particularly good for a beginner's garden: sage, tarragon, parsley, chives, shallots, basil, dill, rosemary, some of the thymes, and sweet marjoram. For further information write The Herb Society of America, 300 Massachusetts Ave., Boston, Massachusetts.

Two of the most useful culinary herbs—Parsley and Chives — often grown in the vegetable plot.

Which geraniums are particularly suited for planting (in summer) in an herb garden?   These geraniums are botanically *Pelargonium.* The lemon-scented, peppermint-scented, apple-scented, and rose-scented are all good. (See Fragrant Gardens.)

Do any herbs endure shade? Many medicinal herbs grow well in shade, among them bloodroot, digitalis, ginseng, goldenseal, selfheal, and snakeroot.

Which herbs will tolerate part shade? Balm, bergamot, chervil, sweet fennel, tarragon, sweet woodruff, mints, angelica, sweetcicely, parsley, comfrey, and costmary.

Can you give me information on herbs suitable for an herb rock garden? The garden should be well drained and sunny; the soil on the lean side rather than overrich. Almost any of the lower-growing herbs can be used effectively, with a few taller ones for accents.

Of the varieties of herbs formerly imported, which ones can be grown in northern and central New York? Some of them are coriander, anise, fennel, dill, cumin, and sage.

What is ironweed? Several different plants have been shown me, but I want to be sure, as I wish to use it in an old-time medical recipe. The ironweed of eastern United States is *Vernonia noveboracensis*. It usually grows in moist places, is 3 to 6 ft. high, and has open-branched cymes with many purple flowers. A full description is given in Gray's *Manual of Botany*.

SOIL

What general type of soil is preferred by herbs? Ordinary well-drained garden soil, lean rather than rich, and not too acid, suits the majority. Mints prefer a fairly rich, moist soil.

Do herbs like sandy soils? With the possible exception of mints, which require considerable moisture, the great majority of herbs do very well in sandy soil if some humus is added and moisture is supplied in very dry weather.

I understand that most herbs need dry soil conditions. Can you suggest some for a moist, but not waterlogged, place? Angelica, bergamot, sweetcicely, sweetflag, yellow-stripe sweetflag, lovage, mints, parsley, English pennyroyal, snakeroot, valerian, and violets.

PLANTING

What is the best exposure for an herb garden? A southeast exposure is ideal, but any location that gets full sunshine during the growing season will do. The soil and cultural practices, which include winter protection, are equally important.

Must herbs be grown in an herb garden? No. They will thrive anywhere where soil and exposure are right: in the vegetable garden, by the kitchen door, in a dry wall (certain kinds), and good-looking ones in the flower border.

A decorative herb garden at the kitchen door.

CULTURE

What are the general cultural requirements for herbs?   A rather poor, well-drained sweet soil, warmth, sunlight, and a free circulation of air. Space the plants adequately, according to kind. Keep weeds down and surface soil tilled. This is a generalization; a number of herbs require distinctly different conditions.

What is the most practical arrangement of annual and perennial herbs—to interplant them, or to keep them separate? Plant the perennial kinds together and the annual kinds together. The area devoted to annuals can then readily be prepared afresh each spring and the perennial area is disturbed only every few years, when replanting becomes necessary.

Is it necessary to make more than one sowing of the various annual herbs each season?   Yes, if it is desired to pick them fresh throughout the summer. About 3 sowings of most are desirable, the last made in late June or early July.

Is watering important in the herb garden?   A few herbs (as mints) need generous supplies of moisture, but the majority develop their fragrances and flavors best when they are subjected to rather dry conditions; therefore, apply water with discrimination. Newly transplanted herbs and young plants need more attention in this respect than established plantings.

Should herbs be fertilized during the summer? The majority of true herbs require no fertilization. Feeding induces rank growth but does not favor the production of the essential oils which give to them their flavor and fragrance.

Can any non-hardy herbs be over-wintered successfully in a cold frame? Thyme, lavender, sage, and other "hardy" herbs which are often susceptible to winter killing can be kept over winter in a cold frame. Really tender subjects, like rosemary, pineapple sage, scented geraniums, and lemonverbena, must be kept in a temperature safely above freezing.

HARVESTING, CURING, AND STORING

Should herbs be washed before drying, and what is the appropriate time needed for this? What is a safe insecticide to use on these plants? Washing is not needed unless foliage is mud spattered. Time needed for drying varies according to kind and environment. A rotenone or pyrethrum insecticide is recommended.

How shall I cure herbs properly so as to retain their flavor? Dry as quickly as possible in a warm, airy, well-ventilated place, *without exposure to sun.*

How does one cure herb leaves for drying? Pick them just before the plants begin to flower, any time in the day after the dew has disappeared. Tie in bundles, each of a dozen stems or so. Hang in an airy, warm, but not sunny place. When they are completely dry and crisp, strip off leaves and put in tight jars. The leaves may also be stripped fresh, right after cutting, and placed in shallow screen-bottomed trays until dry.

When should herb seeds be harvested? When they have matured, and before they fall naturally from the plants.

How should herb seeds be dried? Collect the heads or seed pods and spread them in a tray made of screening, or in a thin layer on a cloth in a warm, well-ventilated room. Turn them frequently. At the end of a week or so they will be dry enough for threshing.

What is the best method of storing dried herbs? In airtight containers.

How can seeds in quantity, such as caraway, be best separated from stems and chaff? Remove as much of the stems as possible. Rub the heads or pods between the palms of the hands. If possible, do this outdoors where a breeze will help carry away the chaff. A kitchen strainer or screen is useful in the final cleaning.

GENERAL

What are "simples"?   Herbs that possess, or are supposed to possess, medicinal virtues.

What is the "Doctrine of Signatures"?   An ancient belief that plants, by the shape or form of their parts, indicated to man their medicinal uses. The spotted leaves of the lungwort showed that this plant was a cure for diseases of the lungs; the "seal" on the roots of Solomonseal promised the virtue of sealing or closing broken bones and wounds; and so on.

Can you recommend a good book on herbs and herb culture? *Herbs, How to Grow Them,* by Helen N. Webster; *Herbs, Their Culture and Uses,* by R. E. Clarkson; *Gardening with Herbs for Flavor and Fragrance,* by H. M. Fox; and *Old Time Herbs for Northern Gardens,* by M. W. Kamm, are all excellent.

Am interested in medicinal herbs. Are there any books on same?   *Try Growing Herbs,* by Helen M. Whitman, published by The Tool Shed Press, Bedford, New York; and *Medicinal Plants,* by Crooks and Sievers, published by the United States Department of Agriculture.

COMMERCIAL GROWING

Where can I obtain information on commercial herb growing? The following bulletins give information on this subject: *Circular 157,* New York State Agricultural Experiment Station, Geneva, New York; *Circular 83,* Vermont State College of Agriculture, Rutland, Vermont; *Circular 104,* Michigan State College of Agriculture, East Lansing, Michigan; *Bulletin 461,* Indiana College of Agriculture, Purdue, Indiana; *Circular 149,* Connecticut Agricultural Experiment Station, New Haven, Connecticut; and *Extension Circular 64,* Minnesota Agricultural College, University Farm, Minnesota. Also *Miscellaneous Publication 77, Circular 581,* and *Farmers' Bulletins Nos. 1184* and *1555,* all obtainable from Office of Publications, United States Department of Agriculture, Washington, D.C.

HERB WHEELS

I would like to put plants around the spokes of an old wagon wheel that I have. How would you suggest doing this?   A wagon wheel or oxcart wheel can be made the central feature of a small, formal herb garden. Select a level, sunny spot in the garden with enriched, well-prepared soil. Place the hub down into the ground and put a few plants of each variety in between the spokes. A narrow path edged with thyme can surround the wheel. Low-growing, compact plants are better for a wheel-planting than tall, straggly ones.

What culinary herbs would be best in a "wheel garden"? Thyme, chives, sage, parsley, mint, lemon balm, French tarragon, winter savory, sweet basil, sweet marjoram, chervil. Or the wheel can be planted exclusively with low-growing varieties of thyme.

Would you suggest some fragrant herbs that would look well planted in an oxcart wheel? Lemonverbena, mint, southernwood, rosemary, Rose Geranium, santolina, sweetcicely. (See Herbs.)

I want to plant some small, bright-blooming flowers in a wagon wheel. What would you suggest? Dwarf marigolds, zinnias, linaria, alyssum, lobelia, portulaca, ageratum, dwarf anchusas.

SPECIFIC HERBS

ANGELICA

How do you grow angelica and what is it used for? Sow in fall as soon as seed is ripe, thin out seedlings, and transplant following spring. Soil should be moist and fairly rich. Light shade is beneficial. The seeds are slow to germinate. The plant is biennial under some conditions, so it is better to sow a few seeds each year to maintain a supply. The stems and leafstalks are used for salads and candied to decorate confections; the seeds for flavoring and for oil.

ANISE

Can you give some information on growing anise? It is an annual, so it must be sown each year. The seeds should be fresh because old seed will not germinate. Sow when the soil has warmed a little (about beginning of May) in rows where the plants are to stand (anise does not transplant readily). Prepare the soil deeply and make it very fine. Sow in rows 15 ins. apart and thin the plants out to 9 ins. apart in the rows. Water in very dry weather.

BALM

Is balm difficult to grow? Is it a useful herb? Lemon balm or sweet balm (*Mellisa officinalis*) is a hardy perennial of easy culture. It can be grown from seeds sown in prepared soil in July or August; the seedlings are transplanted, when large enough, to their flowering quarters. Balm can also be propagated by division in spring. Any ordinary garden soil is satisfactory. The leaves of balm are used for seasoning, particularly liqueurs. They are also used for salads and for potpourris.

BASIL

Can you give me information on growing basil? When should I sow the seeds?   Seeds are sown outdoors after settled warm weather has arrived; or they are started indoors in April and the seedlings transplanted outdoors later. Allow 12 ins. apart between plants. Basil yields abundantly. When cut, it repeatedly sends out new growths. Plants can be lifted in the fall and potted for winter use if desired.

Sweet Basil

BORAGE

Is borage annual or perennial? Can it be grown from seed? An annual, easily grown from seed in any good garden soil. Sow in spring when all danger of frost is past. The seedlings can be transplanted if care is exercised, but the plants are better if grown undisturbed. About 15 ins. should be allowed between plants.

CARAWAY

How is caraway grown?   From seeds sown outdoors in late May in rows 2 ft. apart. The plants are thinned to about 9 ins. apart. The first year low-growing plants are formed; the second year seeds are produced; then the plants die. Seed is most abundantly produced if the soil is not too rich. Do not water much, as this tends to keep the stems soft and causes the blossoms to fall before setting seed. Dry, sunny weather favors this crop.

CHERVIL

How is chervil grown? From seeds sown in spring where the plants are to grow. Thin plants to stand 9 ins. apart. Light shade is beneficial. Chervil is an annual.

CHIVES

Can chives be grown from seeds or must I buy plants? They can be grown from seeds sown outdoors early in spring. Thin the little plants out to about ½ in. apart. They are hardy perennials, multiply rapidly, and need little attention. Divide every second year. They like a moderately moist soil.

CLARY

Clary dies out with me. Is it difficult to grow? Clary is a biennial and dies after flowering. Sow seeds in early spring; thin out to 6 ins. apart; as the plants develop pull out every other one. Those removed can be dried for use. The plants bloom and set seeds the second year. A rich soil is advantageous.

CORIANDER

Is it easy to grow coriander seed? Yes. Sow (thinly) in spring in well-drained, average soil and in sunny position. Thin out to stand 9 or 10 ins. apart. Plants and fresh seeds are unpleasantly scented, but ripe seeds become very fragrant as they dry.

COSTMARY

How is costmary grown? Propagate it from seeds or by root division. Plant in full sun or very light shade. Space plants about 3 ft. apart. Lift and replant every third year. A freely drained soil is needed.

Dill

DILL

How do you grow dill? Dill is a fast-growing annual that matures in about 70 days. Sow in early spring in well-prepared soil, in rows 2 ft. apart, where the plants are to stand. The plants grow about 3 ft. tall and make a good-sized bush. Thin out the seedlings to 3 or 4 ins. apart at first; later give a final thinning so that they stand a foot apart.

DITTANY OF CRETE

What is dittany of Crete and how is it grown in the herb garden? It is *Origanum dictamnus*. Increase it by seeds or cuttings. It is not hardy where winters are cold and must be wintered indoors in pots. A sandy soil, perfect drainage, and full sun are cultural desiderata.

FENNEL

Have you data on perennial fennel that grows 10 ft. tall? The common fennel (*Foeniculum vulgare*) has escaped to the wild down South and grows 8 ft. in height. In colder climates, fennel is less tall, rarely reaching 4 ft.

How is Florence fennel grown? As an annual. Seeds are sown in spring where the plants are to mature. The seedlings are thinned out to 6 ins. apart. The plants mature in about 60 days.

GINGER

Can ginger root be grown in New York State? Common ginger (*Zingiber officinale*) is a tropical plant adapted for culture only in warm climates. The wildginger (*Asarum canadense*) is a native of our own rich woodlands. It responds to cultivation if given a rich, rather moist soil.

DIGITALIS

Is the foxglove (digitalis) a perennial? No, a biennial, although occasionally a plant will persist for 3 years. Sow seeds each June. They like a well-drained soil that is deep and fairly moist.

Can digitalis (foxglove) be grown in partial shade? Yes, if you are growing it for its decorative effect; but when raised commercially for drug purposes it must be grown in full sun, as the valuable alkaloid does not develop satisfactorily in shade-grown plants.

HORSE-RADISH

See Section V.

HYSSOP

What are the cultural requirements of hyssop? Give this perennial full sun or light shade, and a warm, freely drained well-limed soil. Allow about a foot between plants. Trim plants back after flowering. Easily propagated by seeds, cuttings, or root division.

LAVENDER

What is the care and use of lavender?   Grows well in any well-drained soil, not too acid, in a dry, sunny place. Protect in winter with evergreen boughs; but, even with protection, plants 3 years old or more have a way of dying back in winter. Cut dead branches back in spring after new growth near base is fairly strong. It is best propagated from cuttings of the season's growth taken in the late fall or early spring. The plants are grown for ornament and fragrance. The flowers are used in perfumes, aromatic vinegar, sachets, and are tied into bundles for use in linen closets, etc.

How can I make lavender plants bloom?   They give much more prolific bloom, with better fragrance, if grown in a light, well-drained soil high in lime content. Rich or heavy soils encourage foliage growth rather than bloom.

When should lavender flowers be harvested?   Just as soon as they are fully open.

Can sweet lavender grow and live over winter as far North as Boston?   *Lavandula officinalis* should, if given good winter protection.

Do you have to protect thyme and lavender in winter, and how?   The true lavender, *Lavandula officinalis,* is hardier than others of its kind. However, it prefers a sheltered spot. Both lavender and thyme die during the winter because of excessive moisture rather than of cold. Salt hay or evergreen boughs are good mulches. It is safer, if there is any question about the drainage, to winter both of these plants, in the North, in a cold frame.

How can I start lavender from seed?   Seeds are rather slow to germinate, and the tiny plants grow slowly. Start seeds indoors in early spring, and set out the new plants after all danger of frost is past. Do not allow them to bloom the first year. Protect through first winter by placing them in a cold frame, if possible. A well-drained soil is essential to success.

Can I propagate lavender from cuttings?   Take 2-in. shoots off the main stems and branches in late fall or early spring, each with a "heel" (or portion of older wood) attached to its base. Cut the heel clean. Remove lower leaves for about 1 in. from base. Insert in well-packed sand in a cool greenhouse, and keep the sand moist. Slight bottom heat will help rooting. While roots are not more than ½ in. long, put up in small pots in a mixture of ½ sand, ½ soil. Keep in cool greenhouse for winter if fall-made cuttings, or in a cold frame if spring made.

LEMONVERBENA

How is lemonverbena grown?   Lemonverbena is a tender shrub which, in cold climates, must be taken in for the winter. Cut plants back in fall; water just enough to keep them from drying out. In February bring into the light, in a cool temperature. Repot and set out again in the garden when danger of frost is past.

When should cuttings of lemonverbena be made?   In fall, when the plants are trimmed back before being brought inside; or in spring, when new growth is made. Give same treatment as advised for cuttings of lavender.

LOVAGE

Is lovage suitable for a tiny herb garden?   Hardly. It is a perennial 6 or 7 ft. tall, and plants need to be spaced about a yard apart.

What soil and culture for the herb lovage that has flavor of celery?   Propagate by seeds sown in early fall, or by root division in spring. Provide a rich, moist soil in full sun or light shade.

MARJORAM

Can you winter over in the house a plant of marjoram dug up from the herb garden?   If you refer to sweet marjoram, this is the only way to keep it for another year. It is a tender perennial, sensitive to frost. Pot the plant in September, before there is any danger of frost, and let it get accustomed to its new quarters before bringing it indoors. Cuttings can be rooted in September, keeping the young plants indoors also. Pot marjoram is a hardy perennial.

In what soil and situation, and how far apart, should sweet marjoram plants be set?   Give light, well-drained, non-acid soil; full sun; space 9 or 10 ins. apart. This is a tender perennial that may be grown as an annual. Sow seed in spring. It is slow to germinate.

Are there any hardy perennial kinds of marjoram?   Yes. Pot marjoram, showy marjoram, and wild marjoram. Of these, pot marjoram is the best known for culinary purposes.

MINT

Would like a list of all mints that can be grown, and is there

a sale for them and where? The mints are very numerous. Write The Herb Society of America, 300 Massachusetts Ave., Boston, Massachusetts, with regard to these and to their marketability.

What is the culture of peppermint? How is oil extracted from it? Grows best in deep, rich, humusy soil which is open and well drained. The runners are planted in spring, 2 to 3 ft. apart, in shallow trenches. Keep well cultivated and free from weeds. When in full bloom the plants are cut and cured like hay. The oil is extracted by distillation with steam. For information concerning commercial cultivation ask the Department of Agriculture, Washington, D.C.

Why can't I start a successful mint patch? Mints are usually easy and very weedy. They like rich, humusy soil and plenty of moisture. Cultivate and weed them well. They should grow.

POTMARIGOLD

What is potmarigold? What is it used for? Is it hard to grow? *Calendula officinalis*—one of our most useful decorative annuals. As an herb, the flower heads are used for seasoning and coloring butter. It thrives best in cool weather. Sow outdoors in spring, or indoors in March for spring planting. Transplant 12 ins. apart. Sow again about July 1 for fall crop. The plants from this sowing will grow on into late fall and will survive light frosts.

Rosemary

ROSEMARY

What is the best way to grow rosemary? Rosemary is a tender shrub, not hardy in the North; but it may be plunged outdoors in a sunny, sheltered spot during the summer, and carried over winter in a cool, light room. Pot in well-drained soil to which a sprinkling of lime has been added. Propagate by cuttings.

What is the best protection for rosemary in this location? (Illinois.) It is a tender shrub and must be brought in for the winter in cold climates. If there is not space for so large a plant, make a few cuttings, which will root readily in moist sand and be ready to set out in the spring.

RUE

Is rue hardy in Northern gardens? Could you give its culture? Rue is hardy to Long Island, N. Y. It will not winter over outdoors in very severe climates, so it is much safer to keep it indoors during winter. It is easily grown from seeds sown early in spring in rows 18 ins. apart. Thin seedlings to 8 ins. apart, and again remove every other one. Keep the soil well cultivated. The leaves can be used whenever they are large enough. Any ordinary garden soil is satisfactory.

SAGE

Which variety of sage is used for culinary use?   *Salvia officinalis.*

I have been unsuccessful in growing sage. What are its needs? Sage enjoys best a sweet, well-drained, light sandy soil. Sow seeds in very early spring, or in August; or set out good-sized plants in early spring. Sage is not difficult. Give very little water; cultivate during the early part of the season. In spring give a light dressing of bone meal. Easily propagated by means of cuttings.

What are the methods of cultivating sage?   See preceding question. Transplant to permanent position when seedlings are 3 to 4 ins. high. Plant in rows 2 ft. apart with 12 ins. between the plants in the row. Cut back established plants in spring to let new growth develop. Do not overwater.

Can sage planted from seed be used and dried first year it is planted?   Yes. Don't strip the whole plant bare, however. Take only the largest leaves, or a branch here and there.

When is the best time to "pick" sage; and what is the best method of curing it?   Harvest in late summer. Cut shoots before they bloom, tie into bundles, and hang up; or strip leaves and place loosely in shallow trays in a warm, airy place, not exposed to sun.

How does one gather sage?   Shoots may be cut twice or three times during summer and early fall.

SAVORY

What kind of soil and culture does savory need?   There are 2 kinds of savory: summer savory (annual) and winter savory (perennial). Both grow best in a rather poor but well-limed soil, in an exposed sunny site. The annual kind is considered better than the perennial. The seeds are very small and are best sown indoors in pots and barely covered. Watering is done by immersing the pot in water, as the seeds wash out easily. Seedlings are set out when all danger of frost is over. Set seedlings in rows, 8 ins. between plants, 15 ins. between rows. The perennial sort can be handled in the same way.

SWEETCICELY

What are the garden requirements for growing sweetcicely? Sow seed in early fall, in well-drained average soil, and in light shade. When plants are mature they should stand 18 to 20 ins. apart. It is a hardy perennial and may be increased by root division.

SWEETFLAG

I want to grow sweetflag in my herb garden. Does it need full sun? Full sun is not necessary, but it must have moist soil. It is really a waterside plant. Propagate by division of rhizomes.

SWEET WOODRUFF

What conditions in the garden does sweet woodruff need? An open, rather moist soil, where drainage is good, and shade or partial shade. A fine perennial ground-cover plant in the right location.

TARRAGON

What soil for tarragon? Shade or sun? Almost any well-drained garden soil. Sun preferred, but will endure light shade.

Will you give me all information possible to grow tarragon? When to plant? Tarragon, a hardy perennial, needs a well-drained soil, moderately rich, with considerable lime. It does best in a lightly shaded location. This plant, since it seeds but little, is propagated by stem or root cuttings, or by division. Stem cuttings are taken any time during the summer, rooted in sand, and planted out. Root cuttings or divisions can be set out in early spring, 12 ins. apart. Do not use chemical fertilizer to force growth, as the quality of the leaves is affected by a too-rich diet.

THYME

I would like to grow thyme for seasoning. Will it stand our severe winters? (Western New York.) There are many varieties of the common thyme that may be used in the herb garden. The greatest menace to thymes during the winter is not so much cold as wetness. Wet crowns, caused by snow, will winter kill. One of the means of preventing this is to grow on rather poor soil, containing gravel or screened cinders. Do not feed in summer to force growth, and do not cut tops after September 1. A cold frame is an excellent place to keep thyme over the winter, where it will be dry. Otherwise, covering the plants with boxes to keep the snow off will help materially. Be certain their position is well drained to begin with. Seeds and plants are available from most houses listing herbs.

How can I grow common thyme? What soil? Shade? Sun? (Massachusetts.)   It is best grown on a light, well-drained soil. If the soil is inclined to heaviness, work in screened cinders or gravel. Seeds can be sown in early spring outdoors, or earlier in pots indoors. Transplant seedlings 6 ins. apart. When growth is advanced, do not water much; omit fertilizer, as this tends to force soft growth that will winter kill. Do not cut foliage after September 1, as this depletes vitality. Winter protection is given by covering with light evergreen boughs, or by using brushwood with a light covering of marsh or salt hay. Lift and divide every 2 or 3 years. Grow in full sun.

Will you name several creeping thymes for planting in steps and paths?   Mother-of-thyme (*Thymus serpyllum* and its variety *lanuginosus*); Caraway Thyme (*T. herba-barona*); British Thyme (*T. britannicus*).

WATERCRESS

How could I grow watercress for table use in my home garden that has no water?   Watercress is a plant of running water, growing in the edge of clear, fresh streams. It may be grown, after a fashion, in a moist spot in the garden, and the plants will last for a time in such a location if it is shady, but they will not live through the winter unless covered with water. They become true perennials only when grown in running water. As an alternative, you can grow the garden cress, or peppergrass. This is an annual, and furnishes salad in 3 to 4 weeks. Sow seed thickly in shallow drills 12 ins. apart. Make 2 sowings, 2 weeks apart in spring, and 2 sowings in August.

POTPOURRIS

Would you please tell me where I may obtain information for formulas for making rose jars, potpourris, and sachets?   A good book containing complete information on this subject is

Magic Gardens, by Rosetta E. Clarkson, published by the Macmillan Company.

What leaves and petals can be used for making potpourri?
Any leaves or petals that have a pleasing fragrance may be used. Some of the best are rose, lavender, lemonverbena, jasmine, marigold, stock, mignonette, heliotrope, violet, geranium, rosemary, lemon balm, mint, southernwood, santolina, pink, wallflower, thyme.

I want to make a potpourri of rose petals from my garden. How can I do this? Pick the rose petals (red holds its color best) when the flowers are in full bud but not completely blown. Spread them carefully on sheets of paper or strips of cheesecloth in a dry, airy room, away from the sun. Turn daily. Let them dry completely. This will take from a few days to a week. To each quart of petals add 1 oz. of orrisroot. Spices such as cloves, cinnamon, coriander, and mace may be added, if desired, ½ teaspoon of each. Keep in an airtight earthen jar.

What is "wet potpourri" and how is it made? Potpourri made by the wet method contains rose petals and the petals of any other fragrant flowers that are available. These are spread on cloths or papers to dry out partially. They are then packed in an earthenware jar with layers of table salt or coarse salt between. Add a layer of petals, then a sprinkling of salt, until the jar is filled. One oz. of orrisroot or violet powder is added, and, if desired, some cloves, allspice, and cinnamon. Put a weight on the petals and let them stand in the jar, covered, for several weeks before mixing. In addition to rose petals, lavender, lemonverbena leaves, and geranium leaves are the most commonly used ingredients.

What is a "fixative," and for what is it used in potpourris?
A fixative is used to retain the natural scent of leaves or petals and aids in preserving them. Orrisroot, violet powder, ambergris, and gum storax are common fixatives.

In making a sweet jar of flower petals, what can be used to keep the natural color of such flowers as delphinium, pansy, aconitum, and other colorful blooms? If the flowers are carefully dried, out of direct sunlight, they partially retain their color naturally. Orrisroot also seems to have a color-fixing effect.

ROCK GARDENS
PLANNING

To build, or not to build, a rock garden is the question with us. Answerman, what counsel? Can you fit this kind of garden properly into your home landscape without the effect being unnatural? Is there a bank or slope that could be utilized in making the garden? Have you access to natural rock material that could be used? If the area is all level, is there a section where low, natural rock outcrops could be simulated? The extent of the garden will be determined by the time, labor, and money that can be spent on it. A rock garden is costly to build and costly to maintain. These are the facts that need to be considered in deciding to build—or not to build.

Outcropping ledges of rock make an ideal setting for a rock garden. Where such a site is not available, every effort should be made to simulate the same effect.

Will I have as much in a rock garden as in other kinds of gardens? The floral display will be concentrated between early spring and mid-June. From then on your enjoyment will come mostly from pleasing mats and mounds and spreading foliage effects; these are decidedly worth-while.

Can I have flowers in a rock garden all summer long? Yes, by introducing a variety of small annuals and summer- and autumn-flowering bulbs. The use of these may relieve monotony; but it may easily be overdone and spoil the illusion of a mountain garden, which has but one main, brilliant burst of blossom, in the spring.

How can I best fit a rock garden into my place? Use, if you have it, a somewhat steep slope, not overhung by foliage. A natural ledge of porous rock, of acceptable, weathered appearance, and provided with deep fissures, is ideal. Where such a ledge lies buried, it pays to expose and use it.

What exposure is best for a rock garden? For easy-to-grow, sun-loving plants, such as many sedums, pinks and rockcresses, any exposure but a north one. For gardens containing also more finicky, choicer plants, if along a building or a fence, an east exposure; otherwise, an open slope facing east or northeast. As between south and north slopes, choose the latter.

Is there a rock-garden organization? Yes, the American Rock Garden Society, 57 Sanford Ave., Plainfield, New Jersey.

SOIL AND FERTILIZER

Should the rock-garden soil mixture be acid or alkaline? Some rock plants insist upon acid, some on alkaline soil. But most will do with an approximately neutral soil; it is, therefore, best to provide this kind of mixture throughout, and then to acidify or alkalize special areas for particular plants.

Do all rock-garden plants need a specially prepared soil? No. Many robust, easy-to-grow plants, such as most sedums, pinks, and rockcresses, will thrive in soil that would suit other garden plants. But in sharply drained places even these will be helped by an admixture of some peatmoss, to help retain moisture in summer.

What is a good average rock-garden mixture? Approximately 1 part each of good garden loam, fine leafmold, peatmoss, sand, and fine gravel (preferably ⅛-in. screen). The mixture should be gritty. It should let surface water penetrate promptly, but should be retentive enough to hold a reasonable supply of moisture.

What depth of prepared soil is desirable in a rock garden? About 1 ft. For gardens made above the surrounding grade, there should be, underneath, another foot of a coarse mixture of rubble and retentive ingredients, such as peatmoss or sphagnum moss, to act as a sponge.

In a rock garden is it necessary to provide the great depth of drainage that I read about in books? For gardens laid above the grade—no. In sunken gardens or in low-lying parts, unfailing provision must be made to prevent stagnant moisture below. In our dry summer climate we must think of drainage in reverse as well—of retaining some moisture below, which later will find its way back to the surface.

I have a rock garden at the side of my house and would like to rearrange it. Can you make any suggestions concerning soil preparation and enrichment? It should be deeply dug, and a liberal amount of peatmoss added. Also incorporate cinders, leafmold, a little bone meal, and a little tankage.

What is the best fertilizer to use for rock-garden plants, and when should I put it on? The majority of rock-garden plants should not be heavily fed; rich feeding causes soft growth which invites disease and leaves the plants subject to winter killing. Mix in fine bone meal and leafmold with the soil when preparing it, and in early spring dress established plantings with a top-dressing containing bone meal mixed with soil and leafmold.

CONSTRUCTION

What type of rock is best for rock gardens?   Any porous, weathered rock that will look natural in place. It is all the better if it is deep fissured. Use only one kind of rock throughout the garden.

What about tufa rock?   No rock is more acceptable to a wide diversity of plants than a soft, porous grade of tufa. But because of its glaring, bony color in sunny places it is not an attractive-looking material. In shade, and moisture, it quickly accumulates mosses and then becomes very beautiful.

Are large rocks desirable, or will small ones do as well? Construction should simulate Nature. She works with massive rocks. Therefore, in gardens large or small use rocks as large as you can handle; or match smaller ones together in such manner that they will create an effect of large masses.

Can you give me a few pointers on the placing of rocks? Embed the rockwork deeply enough to create an effect of natural outcroppings. Leave no lower edges exposed to betray superficial placing. Have the several rock masses extend in parallel directions, and carry out this principle even with the lesser rocks. Match joints and stratifications carefully. Try to get the rhythm of natural ledges and outcroppings.

How shall I build a rockery in a corner of my level lawn? In the foreground of corner shrubbery create the effect of a smoothish, shelved outcropping with several broad, low shelves. Push this arrangement back far enough for the shrubs to mask the sheer drop behind.

How should I arrange a rock garden and pool in the center of a small lawn without natural elevation of rock?   Create the effect of one large, flattish, or somewhat humped rock, broken, so as to provide two or more broad crevices for planting. Locate the pool, somewhat off-center, immediately against this rock effect.

Have you any suggestions for a little rock garden, of slight elevation, with shrubbery as a background?   Place or simulate the effect of one large, flattish outcropping, with fissures or wide joints for planting. Place the pool immediately against this rock mass. Your idea of a background of shrubs is excellent.

PLANTING

When is the best time to plant rock gardens?   If pot-grown plants are available and you can arrange to water and shade them carefully, planting may be done almost any time from spring to early autumn. Spring is a proper season everywhere. In moderately cold climates (as in lower New York State), September and October are also good months.

What rock-garden plants should one set out in early spring? (New Mexico.)   Any of the sedums, pinks (dianthus), dwarf phlox, primroses, painted daisies, bellflowers, and saponarias as well as most any other rock plants.

I am planting a rock garden. What distance between the plants will be necessary?   Much will depend upon the kind of plants you are using. If they are spreading kinds, such as cerastium, phlox, helianthemum, sedums, thyme, and dianthus, set the plants about 12 ins. apart. Plants that spread more slowly, such as primulas, sempervivums, saxifragas, candytufts, arenarias, aubrietas, douglasia, anemones, pulsatillas, and the dwarf achilleas, plant 6 to 8 ins. apart.

How deep should rock plants be set in the ground?   Most form a spreading top that either roots as it spreads or grows directly from a central root system. The crown of the plant must not be covered. Dig a hole with a trowel; gather the loose tops in the hand; hold the plant at the side of the hole, the crown resting on the surface, the roots extending into the hole while held in position; firm the soil around the roots. When the hole is filled, the crown should be resting on the surface. A good watering will then help establish it.

The soil on the slopes in my rock garden keeps washing out, especially after planting. How can I prevent this?   If a considerable stretch is exposed, set in a few good-sized rocks at irregular intervals and tilt them so that their upper surfaces slope downward into the hill. Into the surface 2 ins. incorporate screened cinders mixed with peat or leafmold. Set the plants in groups 9 to 12 ins. apart (depending on their size) and cover the spaces between the groups with peat or leafmold until the plants effect a covering.

CULTURE

What are the main items of upkeep in a rock garden? Weeding; thinning; repressing too-rampant growths; removal of old flower stalks; occasional division of robust plants; watering;

winter covering. For the choicer, high-mountain plants, maintain a gravel mulch about their base and top-dress with compost on steep slopes each spring.

When is the best time to trim and thin plants that begin to overrun a rockery?   Cut back the running kinds any time during their growing period.

Will you please discuss spring work in the rock garden? Remove winter covering when all danger of frost is over. If there is danger of cold winds and some plants have started to grow, uncover gradually. Firm back into the soil any plants that have been loosened. Replant as may be necessary. Top-dress with a mixture of 3 parts good soil, 1 part old, rotted manure, leafmold, or peatmoss, and 1 part coarse sand or screened cinders, with a 6-in. potful of fine bone meal added to each wheelbarrowload. When top-dressing, work this down around the crowns of the plants and over the roots of spreading kinds by hand. If a dry spell occurs in spring, give a good watering.

WATERING

How should the rock garden be watered and how often? With a fine sprinkler, so as to avoid washing the soil off the roots. Frequency of watering depends upon type of soil, amount of slope, kind of plants, and whether they are established or are newly planted, amount of shade, exposure, and of course weather. If dry spells occur in spring and early autumn, watering should be done in a very thorough fashion; toward late summer, unless a very prolonged dry spell occurs, watering should be confined to such plants as primulas, globeflowers, and other moisture-lovers. Ripening and hardening of most rock plants are necessary if they are to winter over properly.

WINTER PROTECTION

What is the best winter cover? When applied and when removed?   A single thickness of hemlock boughs is excellent. It is more quickly applied and removed than salt hay. Apply after the surface has frozen solid. It is needed, not as a protection against frost, but against thawing of the soil. Remove when danger of very hard frost seems past. Just when is always something of a gamble.

Is salt hay a good winter cover?   Yes, but it is not quickly removable in the spring. Use it lightly, lest you invite mice and kindred vermin.

WHAT TO GROW

Will you please name a dozen foolproof rock-garden plants, stating flower color and season? *Alyssum saxatile citrinum* (lemon-yellow; May), *Arabis albida* (double-flowered, white; April to May), *Arabis procurrens* (white, April to May), *Campanula carpatica* (blue; July), *Ceratostigma plumbaginoides* (blue; September to October), *Dianthus plumarius* (white and varicolored; June), *Phlox subulata* varieties (white, rose, dark rose, pink; May), *Sedum sieboldi* (rose; September to October), *Sedum album* (white; June), *Sedum ellacombianum* (yellow; July), *Thymus serpyllum coccineum* (deep rose; July), and *T. s. album* (white; June to July).

Can you give a list of some of the best rock plants for spring flowers? *Alyssum saxatile, Anemone pulsatilla, Arabis albida* (double-flowered), *Aubrieta deltoides, Corydalis halleri, Crocus* species, *Epimedium niveum, Scilla sibirica* and *S. bifolia*, and *Tulipa kaufmanniana.*

What are the best plants for a rockery for early spring and midsummer bloom? For early spring: *Tulipa kaufmanniana, Crocus* species, snowdrops, *Scilla sibirica*, and grapehyacinths. Non-bulbous plants: *Arabis albida, Aubrieta deltoides, Viola odorata*, primulas, *Anemone pulsatilla, Armeria caespitosa, Alyssum saxatile* and *A. saxatile luteum*, drabas, epimediums, *Erysimum rupestre*, and *Phlox subulata.* For midsummer bloom: *Dianthus plumarius, Campanula carpatica, Antirrhinum asarina, Bellium bellidioides, Campanula cochlearifolia, Carlina acaulis, Globularia cordifolia, Lotus corniculatus, Dianthus knappi, Linum alpinum, Linaria alpina, Nierembergia caerulea*, penstemons, *Rosa rouletti, Santolina viridis, Silene schafta*, and *Ceratostigma plumbaginoides.*

Will you list a few of the best rock plants to flower from about May 15 to early June? *Dianthus neglectus, D. plumarius, D. strictus, D. arenaria, Cymbalaria pallida, Dodecatheon* species, *Gentiana acaulis, Saxifraga* (encrusted species), and *Veronica teucrium rupestris.*

Can you name 12 good perennials suitable for rock gardens, which bloom at different periods? *Phlox subulata* and varieties (April to May), *Aubrieta deltoides* (May), *Alyssum saxatile* and its variety *luteum* (May), *Primula polyanthus* (May), *Dianthus plumaris* (June), *Campanula carpatica* (June), *Lotus corniculatus* (July), *Veronica spicata alba* (June to July), *Thymus serpyllum* and its varieties (July), *Calluna vulgaris* (August to September), *Ceratostigma plumbaginoides* (September to October).

Will you list late-flowering rock plants? *Ceratostigma plumbaginoides, Allium pulchellum, A. flavum, Antirrhinum asarina, Calluna vulgaris* and its varieties, *Chrysogonum virginianum*, colchicums, autumn crocuses, *Silene schafta, Saxifraga cortusaefolia*, and *Sedum sieboldi.*

What are the fastest-growing plants and vines for a rock garden? *Cerastium tomentosum, Ajuga reptans, Thymus serpyllum* and its varieties, *Lamium maculatum, L. m. album, Phlox subulata* and its varieties, *Arabis albida*, sedums, *Saponaria ocymoides, Lotus corniculatus, Campanula carpatica*, and *Asperula odorata.*

Should I try to furnish my new rock garden quickly with fast-growing plants, or do it gradually, with smaller plants? By all means the latter. Most people come to regret their first impatience, and wind up by rooting out the rampant growers, and replacing them with choicer, small plants; they are so much more delightful.

Which flowers are best to plant in a small rock garden? Such things as the drabas, *Aubrieta deltoides, Gypsophila repens, Myosotis alpestris, Nierembergia rivularis, N. caerulea, Primula vulgaris, Armeria caespitosa, Veronica teucrium rupestris, Androsace sarmentosa, A. villosa*, and *Rosa rouletti.* Avoid the use of coarse creeping plants; they will overrun the garden.

Can you suggest some plants for a very steep rock garden? *Thymus serpyllum* and its varieties, *Cerastium tomentosum, Sedum spurium, S. hybridum, Phlox subulata*, sempervivums, *Lotus corniculatus, Ceratostigma plumbaginoides, Antirrhinum asarina, Muehlenbeckia axillaris*, and *Campanula carpatica.*

Which perennial plants can I use for a very exposed location in a rock garden? *Arabis albida, Anemone pulsatilla, Phlox subulata* varieties, *Veronica teucrium rupestris, Cerastium tomentosum, Dianthus deltoides, D. plumarius, Lamium maculatum, Aquilegia canadensis, A. vulgaris, Campanula carpatica*, and *Dicentra eximia.*

Can you suggest a few small, decorative plants to fill small crevices in rocks and tiny pockets? My garden is in full sun. *Draba aizodes, Globularia repens (G. nana), Sedum dasyphllum, Sedum acre minus, Sedum anglicum minus*, and sempervivums (the tiny kinds).

Which are some good plants for shady corners in my rock garden, for spring flower? *Anemone nemorosa* (several kinds), *Brunnera macrophylla, Chrysogonum virginianum, Epimedium niveum, Iris cristata, Phlox divaricata laphami, Phlox stolonifera, Pulmonaria saccharata,* and *Saxifraga umbrosa.*

Which perennials, not over 10 ins. in height, bloom between June 15 and September 15, and are suitable for a rock garden in shade? *Chrysogonum virginianum, Corydalis lutea, Mitchella repens, Myosotis scorpioides, Sedum ternatum, S. Nevi, Allium Moly, Saxifraga cortusaefolia, Arenaria montana, Gentiana asclepiadea, Cymbalaria muralis, Scilla sinensis,* and *Dicentra formosa alba.*

Which are some small summer-blooming plants for the shady rock garden? *Chrysogonum virginianum, Cotula squalida, Mitchella repens, Sedum ternatum,* and *S. Nevi.*

Which are the most hardy rock-garden plants that will grow in semi-shade? *Primula polyanthus, P. veris, P. vulgaris,* epimediums, aubretias, aquilegias, *Iris verna, Phlox divaricata laphami, Chrysogonum virginianum, Viola odorata, V. priceana, Vinca minor, Lysimachia nummularia, Sedum ternatum, Ceratostigma plumbaginoides, Asperula odorata,* trilliums, erythroniums, and dodecatheons.

Will you name rock plants that will grow and bloom in the shade of a large oak tree? *Phlox divaricata laphami, Dicentra eximia, Chrysogonum virginianum, Asperula odorata,* erythroniums, trilliums, *Gaultheria procumbens, Mitchella repens, Iris verna, Vinca minor, Lysimachia nummularia,* and *Primula veris.*

Can you name several plants which will grow between rocks of a patio in very sandy soil; preferably fast growers? *Arenaria verna caespitosa, Thymus serpyllum* and its varieties, *Sedum acre, Dianthus deltoides, Muehlenbeckia axillaris, Mazus reptans,* and *Ajuga reptans.* Keep the soil reasonably moist.

Which rock plants require acid soil? Rhododendrons, azaleas, Mountain Laurel, pieris, shinleaf, partridge-berry, *Cypripedium acaule,* erythroniums, galax, and shortia.

Will you name a dozen or so of the choicest and most unusual plants that I may hope to grow in my rock garden? *Androsace lanuginosa, Androsace sarmentosa, Armeria caespitosa, Campanula cochlearifolia alba, Dianthus callizonus, D. neglectus, Saxifraga burseriana, S. irvingii,* and encrusted saxifragas.

Will all kinds of rock-garden plants grow successfully in a garden without rocks? Yes, although many of them look better against or between rocks.

ALPINES

What is the best site for alpines? A gentle slope facing northeast or northwest.

What soil is best for alpines? One that is not too rich. A neutral, porous soil, well drained, and with grit and cinders to lighten it, will be satisfactory for most alpine plants.

Need I know a lot about alpines to have a good rock garden? No. You may use, more or less exclusively, plants from high, intermediate, or low altitudes. A good rock garden need not be filled with "highbrow" plants. It should afford a happy glimpse of Nature's play with rocks and plants—be it in a mountain scree or on a roadside ledge.

Would you advise me, a beginner, to try an alpine garden? No. Most of the best rock gardens one sees are not alpine gardens, but bits of small-scale, intimate mountain or hillside scenery, with occasional patches of true alpine flora.

Why are alpine plants so difficult to grow? Because the conditions prevailing in lowland rock gardens are so utterly different from those at or above timber line: the heavy winter pack of snow, the short summer, pure, crisp air, and chilly baths of mountain mist. One must learn gradually to devise acceptable equivalents or approximations to these conditions.

Can you name a few alpine plants not too difficult for an amateur to grow? The following high-mountain plants (not all strictly alpines) are suggested: *Armeria caespitosa, Androsace lanuginosa, A. sarmentosa, Campanula cochlearifolia, Dianthus alpinus, D. callizonus, Douglasia vitaliana, Gentiana acaulis,* and saxifragas (encrusted and kabschia kinds).

What are the best alpine campanulas for the rock garden? Campanulas *allioni, alpina, cochlearifolia, elatines, fragilis, lasiocarpa, portenschlagiana, poscharskyana, pulla, raineri,* and *tommasiniana.*

What winter care should be given alpines? Cover lightly with evergreen boughs or salt hay after the ground is frozen—usually in December.

BULBS FOR ROCK GARDEN

How should chionodoxa (glory-of-the-snow) be used in the

rock garden? Scatter the bulbs in groups of 2 dozen or more in various places among low ground covers. They may also be used effectively beneath shrubs that may form a background to the garden.

Will you give a list of crocuses suitable for the rock garden? Spring-flowering: crocuses *aureus, biflorus, chrysanthus* and its varieties, *imperati, susianus, tomasinianus.* For autumn: *cancellatus albus, longiflorus, pulchellus, speciosus* and its varieties, *zonatus.*

Can you suggest some good narcissi for the rock garden? The best kinds are the small ones, such as *Narcissus minimus, cyclamineus, triandrus, t. albus* (angel's tears), *concolor, bulbocodium* (hoop-petticoat daffodil), and *B. citrinus.* The sweet jonquils and campernelles can also be used, such as *Narcissus jonquilla, j. flore-pleno,* and *odorus.*

Can you tell me kinds of tulips to plant in a rock garden and what conditions they need? The best are the species tulips, also called "botanical" tulips. These need well-drained soil and sunshine. Plant them about 6 or 7 ins. deep The following are among the best: *kaufmanniana, acuminata, clusiana* (Lady Tulip), *dasystemon, greigi, praecox, praestans, fosteriana* varieties, *sylvestris,* and *turkestanica.*

Which spring-flowering bulbs are suitable for the rock garden? Squills, glory-of-the-snow, snowdrops, spring-snowflakes, crocuses, grapehyacinths, miniature daffodils, and dogtooth violets, fritillaries, calochortuses, brodiaeas, and *Iris reticulata.*

Which bulbs are suitable for a rock garden at the side and front of the house? *Crocus* species (for fall and spring), *Galanthus nivalis* (snowdrops), *Leucojum vernum* (snowflake), *Chionodoxa luciliae* (glory-of-the-snow), muscari (grapehyacinths), scillas (squills), narcissi species, colchicums, Tulips *kaufmanniana,* and *dasystemon.*

When are small spring-flowering bulbs planted in the rock garden? In August plant snowdrops, winter-aconites, autumn-flowering crocuses, and colchicums. Plant the small daffodils and crocuses in September and others, mentioned in previous replies, in October.

I wish to plant a number of small bulbs in my rock garden. Should I dig up the other plants before planting the bulbs? How deep must I plant the bulbs? Unless the soil needs improving it is not necessary to remove the plants. Use a bulb trowel (a tool with a narrow concave blade), push it into the soil through the mat of plants, pull the handle toward you, and then push the bulb into the soil and smooth the plants back again. Plant these small bulbs in groups and closely together. The depth at which they are set should be, roughly, 3 times the depth of the bulb.

EVERGREENS

Can you tell me some evergreens for a rock garden which will withstand severe winter exposure?   *Taxus cuspidata, Juniperus communis, J. horizontalis, J. sabina tamariscifolia, Pinus mughus, Pieris floribunda,* and *Ilex glabra.*

Which are some small evergreens that may be used effectively in a rock garden?   *Juniperus procumbens nana* (for a low, flat spread), *Juniperus squamata prostrata* (to drape over a rock), *Juniperus horizontalis* "Bar Harbor"; the dwarfest and most compact of Japanese Yews and of hemlocks.

What soil does Daphne cneorum require?   This is a much-debated question. Its success seems to depend mostly upon climate. It does better in the cold parts of New England (with a winter covering, than in warmer climates. Plant in a well-drained soil, away from the fiercest sun.

SHRUBS

Will you suggest some shrubs to use in a rock garden near the front of my house?   Rhododendrons and azaleas are suitable. Mountain Laurel, *Daphne mezereum,* and *D. genkwa* would also look well against a taller evergreen background.

Will you name a few small shrubs that may look well in a small rock garden?   *Spiraea decumbens, S. bullata, Cotoneaster microphylla, Berberis verruculosa, Ilex crenata helleri.* In part shade and an acid, humusy soil, *Rhododendron obtusum* and its varieties, and *R. racemosum* should be satisfactory

Which shrubby plants would make a good background for our rock garden along the side of the garage?   In east to northeast exposures: rhododendrons, azaleas, laurel, pieris, Japanese holly, and *Mahonia aquifolium.* In sunnier exposures: *Berberis koreana, B. vernae, Symphoricarpos chenaulti,* and perhaps an upright yew.

I have a natural spot for a rock garden about 25 ft. long by 5 ft. wide, on a slope exposed to north and west winds. Are there any shrubs sufficiently hardy to winter in such a location? *Rhododendron mucronulatum, Daphne mezereum, Enkianthus campanulatus, Forsythia ovata,* and *Cercis chinensis* should do well.

SPECIFIC ROCK GARDEN PLANTS

What is the proper treatment of ALYSSUM SAXATILE which has grown "leggy"?   It is best to raise new plants from seed. This plant does not usually last much longer than 3 years. It is inclined to rot away during winter. If it survives, wait until new shoots appear near the base of the plant, then cut the leggy, long ones away.

Does AUBRIETA remain in bloom for a long period?   No. Its blooming season is short. However, it flowers in very early spring and is worthy of a place in the garden.

Are the plants called CINQUEFOILS suitable for the rock garden? Can you suggest a few?   Many cinquefoils (potentilla) are excellent, others are worthless weeds. *Potentilla nepalensis, tridentata,* and *verna* are worth trying. Give them full sun and well-drained, gritty soil.

How best to grow pinks in the rock garden?   Dianthuses do best in a well-drained, sunny position. Do not make the soil very rich and do not overwater them. They are good on gentle slopes, planted so that they can spread over the top of a rock, or in flat, well-drained pockets. Start with young, pot-grown plants if possible, and plant them out at about 9 ins. apart. Some kinds die after a time, so it is best to keep raising a few fresh plants each year.

What kinds of DIANTHUS do you suggest for a rock garden? *Dianthus deltoides* (Maiden-pink), *plumarius* (Grass-pink), *gratianopolitanus* (Cheddar-pink), and *neglectus* (Glacier-pink).

What can I do to make GENTIANA ANDREWSI grow? It appreciates a moist, semi-shaded situation, preferably on the edge of a pond, and a deep, humusy soil. Top-dress in spring with peatmoss mixed with a little cow manure.

Which IRISES are suitable for the rock garden?   Irises *reticulata, gracilipes, arenaria, pumila* (in many varieties), *dichotoma, minuta, cristata, cristata alba, lacustris, tectorum,* and its variety *album.*

What care should be given LEONTOPODIUMS that were raised from seeds?   The edelweiss likes a well-drained, limy soil, full sun in spring, semi-shade in summer, and light protection in winter. Either evergreen boughs or salt hay should be used, as leaves pack too hard and keep the plant waterlogged, which may result in rotting. From seed they should bloom well the second year. Carry the plants over in a cold frame, in pots, the first year.

Will you name a few PENSTEMONS that would grow in my rock garden? Are they difficult to grow?   *Penstemons glaber, heterophyllus, rupicola* and *unilateralis*. These are not difficult. They require gritty soil and do not like a position that becomes sodden in winter. They are not long-lived plants and in order to maintain them it is necessary to raise a few each year.

What soil is suitable for PHLOX subulata?   Any light, well-drained garden soil.

Where does Phlox subulata grow wild?   In the Eastern, Western, and Southern parts of the United States, on dry banks and in fields.

Do most of the Western species of phlox require scree conditions in the Eastern states?   Yes, they seem to do better under either scree or moraine conditions in the East.

What are some good kinds of phlox for a rock garden, not tall ones?   Some of the most suitable besides the various varieties of *Phlox subulata* are *Phlox amoena, divaricata* (and its variety *laphami*), *douglasi,* and *stolonifera.*

What conditions do PRIMULAS need in the rock garden? A rich, moist soil and a shady or semi-shady situation. Some, like *Primula pulverulenta,* grow best in almost boggy conditions along the sides of streams. Practically all need plenty of moisture. If very moist conditions cannot be given, grow them in shade.

Will you suggest some primulas for the rock garden?   Primulas: *polyantha, veris* (the cowslip), *farinosa, bulleyana, rosea, denticulata, frondosa,* and *japonica.*

What is the best place in the rock garden for SAXIFRAGAS? What kind of soil?   A partially shady situation facing east or west. Soil should be gritty, open, and well drained. Mix garden soil, leafmold, and stone chips, or screened cinders, in about equal proportion, and have a foot depth of this in which to plant. Limestone chips are beneficial for the encrusted saxifragas.

Which saxifragas are not too difficult to grow?   Saxifragas: *aizoon, apiculata, cochlearis, decipiens* (a mossy type, requiring partial shade), *hosti, macnabiana, and moschata.*

How many species and varieties of rock-garden SEDUMS are there?   Approximately 200. Perhaps not more than 50 distinct and useful kinds are available in nurseries.

Which are the best sedums? Sedums: *album, anglicum, brevifolium, caeruleum* (annual), *dasyphyllum, ewersi, kamtschaticum, lydium, middendorffianum, nevi, oreganum, populifolium, pilosum, reflexum, rupestre, sempervivoides, sexangulare, sieboldi, ternatum, stoloniferum, hybridum,* and the self-sowing biennial *nuttallianum.*

Can I get information regarding the culture of sedums? Most are easily propagated from cuttings taken in the fall or spring. They root best in sand, either in flats or in cold frames. When well rooted, transfer them into small pots or put them directly into their permanent places in the garden. The location should ordinarily be sunny, the soil sandy and well drained. Western-American sedums prefer a semi-shaded position.

Are the SUNROSES (helianthemums) hardy? Do they require much care? They are not very hardy; they thrive fairly well in the vicinity of New York but farther North they are doubtful subjects. They need no more care than ordinary rock-garden plants. Give them a well-drained soil in a sunny location. Protect them in winter with salt hay or evergreen boughs, and cut them back to within a few inches of their crowns in spring, to encourage fresh growth.

Do helianthemums survive the winter without protection? That all depends upon the winter, and upon where they are growing. In a sheltered spot they would probably come through. In an exposed position, cover them with evergreen boughs. They are not overhardy in lower New York State.

MORAINE GARDEN

Can you explain what a moraine garden is? How is it made? A moraine is constructed for the purpose of growing certain alpine plants from high altitudes. The garden contains little or no soil, the growing medium being mostly stone chips and shale. The important factor is water. The most complete moraines have cool water circulating below the growing medium so that the roots of the plants are in a cool, moist medium much as are alpines in their native haunts. A moraine can be built in a watertight basin 2 ft. deep and of any length and breadth. A foot-thick layer of stones is laid in the bottom. The remaining space is filled with a mixture of 5 parts crushed stone ($\frac{1}{2}$ in.), 1 part sand, and 1 part leafmold. Water is supplied during the growing season through a pipe at the upper end and the surplus is drawn off by one at the other end 12 ins. below the surface. Sub-irrigation is sometimes dispensed with and the garden is then known as a "scree."

Will you give me a list of plants suitable for a moraine garden?
Aethionema, androsace, *Arenaria montana, Dianthus sylvestris,*
Campanula speciosa, Silene acaulis, and saxifragas (the encrusted
kinds).

PATHS

**What are the most suitable kinds of paths for the rock garden
and how are they constructed?**   See Paths, this section.

PAVEMENT PLANTING

How are plants grown between the flags in a pavement?
For the plants to succeed, the flags should be laid on sand over-
lying several inches of soil. Watering during hot, dry weather is
very helpful.

How are plants arranged in a pavement planting?   Do not
overdo the planting or it will look untidy. Use for the most part
flat types of plants, with an occasional taller plant to relieve the
monotony.

How are plants planted between flagstones?   Planting is
first done as the flags are laid. When the spot for a plant is
selected, the plant is set so that when the surface is leveled for
the next flagstone, the top of the plant is resting at the correct
level. The stone may have to be chipped to avoid crushing the
plant.

Which plants are suitable for planting in a flagged walk?
Those that will withstand much walking are: *Festuca ovina
glauca, Arenaria verna caespitosa,* and *Tunica saxifraga.* Others
to use are *Thymus serpyllum* varieties, *Mentha requieni* (both
fragrant), *Alyssum montanum, Erinus alpinus,* and *Veronica
repens.*

POOLS

How do you construct a small pool for the rock garden?   See
Pool Construction, this section.

**I have a hillside rock garden with an uneven 6-ft.-diameter
pool. Will you give me advice as to plants for inside the pool
and for outside to hold up the dirt which seems to wash away
with each rain?**   Plant *Nymphoides peltatum* inside the pool.
Caltha palustris (marshmarigold) along the edge, also *Primula
rosea, Trollius europaeus,* and 2 or 3 *Lobelia cardinalis.* In between plant solid with *Myosotis scorpioides,* which will hold the
soil.

A pool for water lilies in a formal garden.

STEPS—PLANTING

I have some rough flagstone steps and wish to set some plants in them. How should I arrange them? What kind should I use? The width of the steps will have to be considered in the arrangement. The primary purpose of steps is to link certain areas. Plants, if used, are for decoration. Don't overplant and avoid regularity. Low plants should be used mostly with an occasional bushy one interspersed. The sides can be more thickly planted than the centers. (For kinds, see Pavement Plantings.)

WALL GARDENS

What exposure for a wall garden? Eastern, except for shade-loving plants such as ramondia, haberlea, *Saxifraga sarmentosa*, English Ivies, and certain ferns. For these a northern exposure.

What is the best type of rock for a wall garden? For an informal effect, any natural, porous rock with a good facing surface; squarish pieces, such as one might use for an ordinary dry wall, are best. A good wall garden can be made of bricks.

How does one make a wall garden? Much like a dry retaining wall, but the joints are packed with prepared soil and the stones are tilted backward to keep the soil from washing out and to direct the rain water toward the plant roots. To prevent squashing of roots, chink the horizontal joints with small pieces of stone. Place plants in position as the laying up proceeds, and firm the soil well at the back of the wall.

What special upkeep does a wall garden need? Upkeep is reduced by using suitably compact, small, rock-hugging plants. Remove all old flower stalks. Pull out weeds and excess seedlings. Prune and thin so as to maintain a balanced distribution of planting effect. On top of the wall, provide a watering trench or trough, and use it freely to prevent drying out in summer.

Wide terrace with planted dry wall.

How are plants planted in a wall? In a wall garden, building and planting are done at the same time. If the plants are located at the joints, the soil is packed in, the plant set, a little extra soil added, and then the stones are placed. Chips placed between the stones near the plants prevent them from sinking and squeezing the plants. If planting has to be done after building, the job is more difficult. The roots must somehow be spread out in a narrow space, and the soil rammed in with a piece of stick. Don't plant fast-growing plants near slow-growing ones or the latter will be smothered.

In planting a wall care must be taken to spot the plants with a natural-looking irregularity that avoids any studied pattern or design.

What summer upkeep is necessary for a rock wall? Keep plants well watered and weeded. Spray if necessary.

Can you tell me what spring care should be given a rockery

made in an old stone wall? Trim dead pieces off plants; fill washed-out cracks with new soil. Push heaved-out plants into soil or take them out altogether and replant.

What winter cover for a wall garden? Stick a row of pine boughs into the ground thickly enough to provide shade from the brightest sun of winter. Or place a row of two-by-fours, slanting against the wall, and over them stretch a burlap cover. The pine boughs will be better looking.

What winter care is necessary for a rock wall? Cover with evergreen boughs when the ground is frozen. Take off during early April.

Which plants are particularly suitable for use in a rock wall? All the sempervivums, Sedums: *hybridum, coccineum, nevi,* and *sieboldi, Nepeta hederacea,* Campanulas *carpatica: cochlearifolia,* and *rotundifolia, Silene caroliniana,* Linarias: *pallida* and *aequitriloba, Phlox stolonifera, Achillea ageratifolia,* and *Mazus reptans.*

WATER GARDENS
(*See also Pool Construction*)

PLANTING

What background materials should I use for my small informal pool? Small evergreens, yew, arborvitae, cedar, hemlock, azalea, laurel, rhododendron, leucothoe, euonymus, cotoneaster, daphne.

Can you tell me some flowering shrubs I can put around my pool? Viburnum, forsythia, abelia, mockorange, lilac, deutzia, kolkwitzia, spirea, azalea, rhododendron, laurel, lonicera. Shrub roses would also be a good choice here.

I want a formal-looking clipped hedge around the sides of my formal pool, which is at the rear of my garden. What would you suggest? Yew, hemlock, barberry, box (for sheltered positions), privet.

Can I have a successful fish pond in a plot about 9 × 15 ft.? How could anything so small be landscaped? Why not pave the area with flagstones, leaving wide cracks between stones? These could be planted with rock plants. The pool would be the central feature.

Have you any planting suggestions for rim of a pool? Astilbe, cardinalflower, Japanese iris, loosestrife, marshmarigold, rosemallow, Siberian iris.

Which flowering plants can be grown in a pool other than waterlilies? Floatingheart (*Nymphoides peltatum*); true forget-me-not; waterhyacinth (*Eichornia*); waterpoppy (*Hydrocleis*); water-snowflake (*Nymphoides indicum*). The last 3 are not winter hardy.

What can be used to break the monotonous flatness of a lily pool? Tall-growing water plants, such as American and Hindu Lotus; calla;* cattails (if pool is large); flowering rush; yellow and blue flags; taro;* water plantain.

With what flowers shall I border informal pool 6 × 10 ft.? *Spiraea venusta* and *S. filipendula, Iris ochroleuca, Trollius ledebouri, Lythrum salicaria,* hemerocallis, *Liatris pycnostachya, Myosotis palustris semperflorens.*

SPECIFIC WATER PLANTS

HINDU LOTUS

Which is the best way to keep sacred lotus through winter? If growing in a pond that is drained during the winter, cover the roots with a sufficient depth of leaves to prevent the frost penetrating to the tubers. When this plant is grown in water 2 or 3 ft. deep, usually no winter protection is necessary.

WATERHYACINTH

How can I grow waterhyacinth? Float in 6 ins. water above a box or tub containing 6 ins. or more of soil. Keep from drifting by confining within an anchored wooden hoop. Bring plants indoors before frost.

How do you winter waterhyacinths that have been in an outside pool? Bring them indoors before the leaves are injured by cold. Float them in a container of water which has 3 or 4 ins. of soil in the bottom. Keep in a sunny window in a temperature of 55° to 60° F.

WATERLILIES

What is proper soil for waterlilies? Heavy loam, composted for a year before use with cow manure in the proportion of 2 to 1. If this is out of the question, use rich soil from vegetable garden.

What shall I use to make waterlilies bloom better? Possibly your plants are starved. Divide and replant in the soil recom-

*Not winter hardy.

mended above, adding a 5-in. potful of bone meal to each bushel of soil.

How can I make waterlilies blossom in a small artificial pond? See answer to preceding question. Perhaps, however, the failure of your plants is due to insufficient sunshine. Waterlilies need full sun all day for best results.

How large should containers be for waterlilies? Depends on the variety. Small-growing kinds can be grown in boxes 15 × 15 × 10 ins., while the tropical varieties can be grown to advantage in sizes up to 4 × 4 × 1 ft.

In a small concrete pool is it better to cover the bottom with soil or use separate boxes for waterlilies? The lilies are better off if the bottom is covered with soil, but it is easier to avoid muddying the water in the pool if the soil is confined in wooden boxes or similar containers.

How deep should the water be over waterlilies? Six ins. to 3 ft. Preferably 1 ft. for tropical varieties, 1 to 2 ft. for hardy varieties, provided this is enough to prevent roots from freezing in winter.

What is the most practical way of caring for a waterlily pool in the winter? If the pool is small enough to be bridged by boards, do so and then cover with a sufficient thickness of straw or leaves to prevent the water from freezing. If the pool is drained and the lilies are growing in tubs, move the tubs together and cover around and over them with leaves held in place with wire netting or something similar.

Supposing the mud is not sufficiently deep to support the growth of waterlilies? Plant the lilies in rich soil in a shallow wicker or chip basket, or fruit crate with openings sufficiently wide to allow roots to emerge, then gently slide the planted container into the pond.

How often should waterlilies be divided? Whenever the container becomes so crowded that growth is poor—usually after 3 or 4 years.

Would colored pond lilies grow where wild white ones grow in a lake with muddy bottom? Yes.

Which waterlily can be grown in a pool fed from an underground stream? Water is cold the year around and is in dense shade. Waterlilies will not grow in such a location.

How can I plant HARDY WATERLILIES in a natural pond? If the pond has a rich mud bottom, merely tie a heavy sod or half brick to the tuber or rhizome and drop it in the pond where water is between 1 and 3 ft. deep.

When is the best time to plant hardy waterlilies?   When ice has left the pond in the spring, but they may be planted successfully up until mid-June.

Should hardy waterlilies be left outside in the pool through the winter? (New York.)   Yes, if they are growing in water so deep that there is no danger of the roots freezing—18 ins. should be enough in your locality.

How early can TROPICAL WATERLILIES be set out? (New York.)   Not until all danger of frost is past and the water has become warm—about the second week in June in the vicinity of New York.

How are tropical waterlilies planted?   Pot-grown plants are commonly used. A hole is scooped in the soil of the container deep enough to receive the ball of earth about the roots, then the roots are covered with soil, taking care not to bury the crown of the plant.

Can tropical waterlilies be kept through the winter as other bulbs are?   It is difficult to carry over tropical waterlilies unless one has a sunny greenhouse. When it is possible to find small tubers around the crown of the old plant, these may be gathered in the fall, stored in sand, protected from mice, and started in an aquarium in a sunny window in April.

Can I carry my Dauben Nymphaea over the winter?   Lilies of this type produce young plantlets on the leafstalks. If a greenhouse or sunny window is available, the plantlets can be gathered in the fall, planted in a watertight vessel about 12 ins. in diameter, filled to within 3 ins. of its rim with soil, the remainder of the container being filled with water.

Can tropical waterlilies be carried over the winter in this climate? (New York.)   Not out of doors. See answer to 2 preceding questions. Usually it is better to obtain new plants from dealers each spring.

During the past 2 summers some sort of leaf miner has eaten the leaves (making marks like Chinese ideographs) of my waterlilies. Consequently the leaves soon die. What are they and how may I get rid of them without injuring the fish in the pond?   The larvae of a midge—*Chirononus modestus.* Waterlily foliage is sensitive to insecticidal sprays, so it is best, whenever possible, to use mechanical means to get rid of pests; therefore pick off infested leaves as fast as they appear, and destroy by burning, which will ultimately eliminate the miner.

WILDFLOWER GARDENS

SOIL

What soil and fertilizer should be used for wildflower planting?
Generally speaking, the soil should approximate that in which the
plants grow naturally. Woodland plants thrive in rich leafmold.
Many prefer slightly acid soil. No artificial fertilizer should be
used; well-rotted compost is next best to natural leafmold.

What fertilizers are recommended for woodland wildflowers?
None. Leafmold is enough.

Should the soil around wildflowers be cultivated? The
weeds should be kept out, but the soil does not need cultivating.

PLANNING

What is the best location for a wildflower garden? This
depends on the type of flowers to be grown. Some wildflowers
grow naturally in woodlands, and others in a sunny meadow.
Try to make the condition in your garden most like the one
which the particular plants came from.

**Should a wildflower garden be attempted in an ordinary back-
yard garden? If so, what type?** No, not in general. However,
an informal sort of garden may be made, using the more common
types of either woodland flowers or meadow flowers.

**What plants go well with mertensia, bloodroot, and Dutch-
man's-breeches to fill in when their foliage dies down in late
spring?** Use Christmasfern or Evergreen Woodfern with mertensia and bloodroot; use spleenworts and grapeferns among the
Dutchman's-breeches. These ferns do not have crowding habits
and are almost evergreen. Their colors are good with the flowers
mentioned.

**Which wildflowers and trees can be established in dry, sandy,
stony soil?** Trees for dry, stony soil in your location are the
Redcedar (*Juniperus virginiana*) and the locust (*Robina pseudo-
acacia*). Many shrubs will grow, such as bayberry, barberry, scrub
oak, raspberries and blackberries, sumacs, blueberries. The black-
haw may assume the stature of a tree. Flowers include many of
the flowers of the open field—daisies, asters, blackeyedsusans,
everlasting.

PROPAGATION

Is it best to grow wildflowers from seed, or to buy the plants?
Choice plants may be started from seed. Plants of most varieties
may be purchased.

Which wild native plants may be started from seed and how is this done?   Practically all of the field flowers, such as asters, milkweeds, goldenrods. Also columbine, pale corydalis, climbing fumitory (vine), celandine poppy, bloodroot, Early Saxifrage, bishop's cap, foamflower, and painted cup. With more patience, try arbutus and Fringed Gentian. The seeds are best started in flats in a protected cold frame. Sow in early winter or spring, using a light, sandy, leafmoldy soil mixture.

What is a good all-around soil mixture in which to sow wild-flower seeds?   One half ordinary garden soil, ¼ leafmold, and ¼ coarse fresh-water sand, thoroughly mixed and worked through a ⅛-in. mesh sifter to remove all stones and lumps.

How long can wildflower seeds be kept before planting them?   Much depends on what kind they are. Some, such as trillium, bloodroot, and others that are produced in a more or less pulpy berry or pod, should be sown immediately before they dry at all; many other harder and thinner kinds can be kept for 5 or 6 months. A good general rule is to sow as soon as the seed is ripe, regardless of the time of the year.

Which kinds of wildflower seeds can be sown in a cold frame late in the fall?   Practically all of the perennial kinds, especially those which flower in midsummer or later. Keep the sash on the frame to protect from winter rains, and shade with slats or cheesecloth to prevent undue heating before spring.

I want to have thousands of beautiful kinds of wildflowers all over my meadow. Can't I get them by strewing handfuls of seed in all directions—a "wildflower mixture," you know, like I see advertised in the catalogues?   Sorry—but you can't. Only the toughest and commonest, such as daisies and goldenrod, will catch hold and grow, so all you'll really have in a couple of years will be a bumper crop of weeds. Rather raise the kinds you want from seed sown in a place where they won't be overrun, and set the plants out in the meadow when they're big enough to hold their own.

What wildflowers self-sow so quickly as to become pests if planted in the garden?   Goldenrod, cattails, wild carrot, jewelweed, ironweed, blackeyedsusan, sunflower, asters, golden ragwort, mullein, daisy, and many others.

COLLECTING

How can wildflowers be identified?   By a study of botany or by reference to a reliable illustrated book on the wildflowers growing in your locality.

Which wildflowers cannot be collected from the wild without breaking the conservation laws? Nearly every state has its own list of native plants under conservation, so a complete list of all protected species is impossible. Some of the more important kinds are trilliums, trailing arbutus, Mountain Laurel, all native orchids, anemone, lilies, dodecatheon, Fringed Gentian, cardinalflower, Birdsfoot Violet, bluebells, wild pink.

Where can wildflowers be obtained? There are special dealers in wildflowers throughout the country who carry all types of these plants.

How do you start a wildflower preserve? Start a wildflower preserve by acquiring a spot that already has enough trees and flowers and beauty to suggest preserving. Gradually bring in groups of plants which you wish to include and see that they are planted in situations such as they seek in nature. This involves a good working knowledge of the soil and other conditions which the plants prefer and matching these conditions in the places you plant them.

May a flower preserve be joined with an arboretum? It should be a splendid addition to an arboretum.

BOG

What conditions are necessary for a bog garden? Is it different from water gardening? Generally a swampy piece of ground, not under water, but where at all times there is plenty of moisture and usually too soft to walk upon. In water gardens the plants are immersed or floating. In bog gardens, the plants grow free above the soil.

Which plants grow in wet marshland? Swamp milkweed, marshmarigold, Joepyeweed, yellowflag, blueflag, cardinalflower, loosestrife, forget-me-not, sedges, marshmallow, water plantain, Yellow- and White-fringed Orchises, and many more.

Are tall-growing wildflowers, such as hibiscus, cardinalflower, and lobelia, suitable for the wild garden? Yes. They are best grown in the bog garden or in a moist border.

Which wildflowers are suitable for planting near a naturalistic pool in sun and shade? *Iris pseudacorus, Iris prismatica, Aruncus sylvestris, Vernonia noveboracensis, Anemone canadensis, Asclepias incarnata, Calla palustris, Caltha palustris, Chelone glabra, Gentiana andrewsi, Hypoxis hirsuta, Lilium superbum, Parnassia caroliniana.*

Which wildflowers do you suggest for the edge of a slow-

moving, shaded stream? Cardinalflower, boneset, turtlehead, Great Lobelia, Fringed and Bottle Gentians, forget-me-not, monkeyflower, mertensia, blueflag (iris), marshmarigold, American globeflower. A little distance from the stream, but where they profit by some of the moisture, you can grow Yellow lady-slipper, trilliums, Yellow Adders-tongue, Fringed Polygala, Solomonseal, false Solomonseal, foamflower, Jack-in-the-pulpit, White Violet, windflower (anemonella).

MEADOW

Can you give me some pointers on planning and setting out a meadow wild garden? The meadow where wildflowers are to be grown should be open, sunny, and preferably fenced with either a rustic fence or rock wall. The soil for common meadow flowers should be dry, porous, and preferably a little sandy. Most meadow flowers are easily grown from seed and then transplanted. Weeds should be kept away from the plants so that they are not choked out. Room should be allowed for them to reseed themselves and form natural-looking patches.

What are the general cultural requirements for growing meadow wildflowers in the garden? The conditions should be as much like those of a meadow as possible: full sun, plenty of room for the plants, and undisturbed conditions. The soil should be porous and loamy except for moist meadow plants.

What sun-loving wildflowers are suitable for rural garden planting to give color and succession of bloom? *Phlox amoena,* April to May; *Iris cristata,* May; *Corydalis glauca,* May to June; *Epilobium angustifolium,* June to July; *Gillenia trifoliata,* June to August; *Campanula rotundifolia,* June to October; *Cassia marilandica,* July to August; *Asclepias tuberosa,* July to August; *Aster linariifolius,* September; *Aster ericoides,* September to October.

Which wild plants will grow well in a sunny meadow? Daisies, blackeyedsusans, the goldenrods, butterflyweed, phlox, Joepyeweed, hawkweed (devil's-paint-brush), yarrow, thistles, ironweed, lupine, Pearly and Sweet Everlastings, American Artichoke, tansy, chicory; New England, Smooth, and New York Asters, trumpet creeper and Bush Honeysuckle, Queen Anne's lace, wild sweetpea.

WOODLAND

How can a woodland wild garden be planned and arranged? A woodland garden made for wild plants should simulate natural wild conditions. There should be shade and semi-shade formed by such trees as grow in the woods. The soil for wood plants should be rich and leafmoldy and slightly damp. The plants are best placed in natural-looking clumps around the base of the trees. A few rocks may be used as focal points, and plants placed around them.

How does one go about starting a wildflower garden beginning with a piece of wild woodland in Vermont? It's just a small patch about ¼ acre. How do you get cardinalflowers started to grow in such a garden? Start your wild garden by gradually replacing and replanting under and around trees, along paths, etc. You will have greatest success with the plants that grow naturally in Vermont woods. Cardinalflower (*Lobelia cardinalis*) likes the stream sides, will grow in partial shade almost in the water, although it sometimes thrives when transplanted to garden soil with less moisture.

Will bloodroot, trillium, and columbine grow under pine trees? If not, what will grow there? The plants mentioned grow well under oak trees. They will grow under pine trees if the shade is not too great and the soil is loamy. Why not try partridge-berry for ground cover, also the club mosses? Plant Christmasfern and Shieldfern. Pipsissewa and shinleaf (*Pyrola elliptica*) will be dainty but difficult additions, as well as wintergreen (*Gaultheria procumbens*) and bunchberry (*Cornus canadensis*).

What are the best methods of growing wild plants under shady conditions? Try to create the conditions in which the plants grow naturally. The amount of shade, moisture, and kind of soil are all important. If under oak trees, you may plant most of the early spring flowers, such as bloodroots, Dutchman's-breeches, partridge-berry, hepatica, bishop's cap, violets, shinleaf, woodbetony, and many ferns and club mosses, such as Shieldfern, polypody, Christmasfern, spleenworts. The club mosses include ground cedar, runningpine, and staghorn. The last, however, are very difficult to transplant.

What are the general cultural requirements for wildflowers? Such as grow in the woods? A leafmoldy soil, semi-shade, and undisturbed conditions.

What mulching materials are suitable for woodland wild plants? Fallen leaves and evergreen boughs.

Do woodland wildflowers require a mulch? A mulch of leaves is helpful.

When woodland wildflowers have been transplanted from their

natural habitat, should they be protected over winter?   Yes, especially the first year to prevent heaving.

Do woodland wildflowers require any special care in planting? They need the same careful planting as all flowers. Put them in well-dug soil with enough room for the roots and do not crowd them. Tamp the soil firmly around them.

My property is a Gray Birch grove. Which wildflowers can I plant in among the birches?   Under your Gray Birches you may grow speedwell (*Veronica officinalis*), violets, wild strawberries, Pearly Everlasting, pipsissewa, shinleaf, *Phlox divaricata*, Rue and Wood Anemones, mertensia. Ferns: Christmasfern, spleenwort, and polypody; the lycopodiums (club mosses.)

Can you suggest a group of native American wildflowers for planting in a wooded lot on home grounds?   *Aralia nudicaule, Aralia racemosa*, trilliums, *Dicentra eximia, Gillenia trifoliata, Shortia galacifolia, Tiarella cordifolia, Actaea alba* and *A. rubra*.

Which wildflowers will grow in a beech grove?   Springbeauty (claytonia), wild columbine, harebells, hepatica, violets, mertensia, *Phlox divaricata, Trillium grandiflorum,* Jack-in-thepulpit, Red Baneberry, the anemones, Yellow Ladyslipper (if moist), Solomonseal, false Solomonseal, bloodroot. Ferns: Walking and the woods ferns.

Which wildflowers will grow in a woodland where there are hemlocks and oaks?   A few are Pink Ladyslipper, Painted Trillium, Wood Lily (*L. philadelphicum*), arbutus, bellwort, *Iris verna*, wintergreen, Purple-fringed Orchis, Wood Anemone, partridge-berry, Wood Aster. Shrubs: rhododendron, wild azalea (Pinkster bloom), and laurel.

SPECIFIC WILDFLOWERS
ANEMONES

I have tried several times to transplant Rue Anemones (Anemonella thalictroides) from the woods, without success. What could be wrong?   They should be dug with a large ball of soil right after flowering, before the leaves die down. Take enough of the soil in which they are found to establish them in their new location. Plant in light shade. They require light, moist soil and are indifferent to acidity. The Wood Anemone (*A. quinquefolia*) requires moderate acidity.

What are the soil conditions required by the Wood Anemone (A. quinquefolia)?   Moist, open woodland. Likes the borders of streams. Must have moderately acid soil. Dig with a large ball of soil just after flowering.

ARBUTUS

What is the correct name for trailing arbutus or mayflower?
Epigaea repens.

How can I grow trailing arbutus? Best to get pot-grown
plants from a nursery, since they more easily adapt themselves
to changed soil conditions. Where arbutus grows in abundance
in nature there is usually a sandy base to the soil, often ancient
sandy river beds, or along the shore as on Long Island or the
pine barrens of New Jersey. Soil should be light, strongly acid,
and rich in organic matter, with good drainage.

BLUETS

**I should like to have a large patch of bluets (or quakerlady or
innocence, as they are called). How can this be done?** They
are best in a rather moist, acid soil, in full sun. If you get them
from the wild, put them in a place as much like the one they
were in as possible. They should reseed themselves and form a
patch.

**What kinds of bluets are there besides the common quaker-
lady?** Only one, if you are thinking of kinds that are worth
planting. This one is the Creeping Bluet (*Houstonia serpyllifolia*), from the southern Appalachians. It is a mat-forming,
rather short-lived perennial that flowers profusely for about 3
weeks in May. It will usually self-sow freely.

BLOODROOT

How is bloodroot transplanted? Take care to get the whole
root. Set it carefully in a well-dug soil in light shade, in August.
Indifferent to soil acidity.

*Dogtooth Violet (left) and
Bloodroot, two of our most
charming native spring
flowers.*

How may one germinate bloodroot seed?   Collect the seed capsules just before they burst open. When seeds have ripened, they may be planted immediately in a prepared spot in the garden where they are to stay.

BUTTERFLYWEED

Is butterflyweed difficult to transplant from the field to the garden?   *Asclepias tuberosa* is, as its scientific name implies, tuberous-rooted. In moving a mature specimen, a very large, thick ball of earth must be dug with it in order not to break the tubers. It can be transplanted in fall. Is one of the last things to appear above ground in spring.

Can I grow butterflyweed from seed?   Yes. Sow in fall or spring—preferably the latter. Transplant seedlings to place where they are to grow when about 6 ins. tall, being careful not to break the very long taproots. Give full sun and well-drained soil.

CARDINALFLOWER (LOBELIA CARDINALIS)

Is cardinalflower suitable for wild plantings?   Yes, if you have a moist, partly shaded situation. It is ideal for the edge of a stream or naturalistic pool.

How can cardinalflower be propagated?   By late-fall or early-spring sowing of fresh seed; by dividing large plants; and by pinning down a strong stalk on wet sand in August and half covering it with more sand until young plants start where the leaves join the main stem.

COLUMBINE

I have heard that wild columbine (Aquilegia canadensis) grows much taller and fuller in good garden soil than in the wild. Is this true?   Yes, but the improvement is limited to the stems and foliage; the flowers remain the same size. The result is a plant devoid of most of the grace and charm which make it so attractive in the wild. We recommend retaining its natural characteristics by giving it a rather poor, dryish soil.

What causes wild columbine to rot off at the crown when other things flourish around it?   Columbine is used to thin, poor, neutral soil. Perhaps your soil is too moist, or the roots may be burned by too much fertilizer. Or it may have been attacked by columbine borer.

CREEPING JENNY (LYSIMACHIA NUMMULARIA)

Where can I plant creeping Jenny?   In a low, damp, pasture-like location in the sun.

DUTCHMAN'S-BREECHES

What is the Latin name for Dutchman's-breeches? In what climate do they thrive? *Dicentra cucullaria.* The plant grows in thin woods and on rocky slopes, from New England south to North Carolina and west to South Dakota and Missouri. Prefers neutral soil.

FERNS

Which wild ferns can I plant in my woodland wildflower garden? Those which grow in your locality in wooded sections. Give them conditions as nearly as possible like those in which you find them. Among the best possibilities are Evergreen Woodfern, Christmasfern or Swordfern, Sensitivefern, Ostrichfern, Interruptedfern, Royalfern. (The last 3 need very moist situations.

Why can't I grow Walkingfern successfully in my rocky woodland? I give it just the kind of place it likes, but the leaves turn yellowish and just barely stay alive. Sounds as if the soil is acid, as is likely to be the case in a region where the rock ledges and outcrops are granite. Walkingfern appears to be a lime-lover, so we suggest having your soil tested for acidity.

In what section of the United States does the Climbingfern, Lygodium palmatum, grow as native? The Climbingfern, *Lygodium palmatum,* strangely enough is a native of fields in which shrubs are abundant, often in old river beds. It is found sporadically along the East coast and abundantly in the pine barrens of New Jersey.

GENTIANS

Is there any way to start or plant blue gentians? Fringed Gentians need a very moist situation in sun. Turn the soil, sow absolutely fresh seed on the surface in autumn, press it in, and cover with tow cloth to prevent washing. Remove tow cloth in spring as soon as frost is out of ground. Or, if you prefer, buy pot-grown seedlings.

Is Bottle Gentian a biennial? And is it hard to grow? Bottle or Closed Gentian (*Gentiana andrewsi*) is definitely a hardy perennial. It is easy to grow in rather heavy, dampish soil that is kept cool in summer by the shade of other plants.

HEPATICAS

What sort of soil is preferred by hepaticas? Can they be placed in a wildflower garden? There are 2 native hepaticas: *H.*

acutiloba, with pointed 3-lobed leaves, and *H. americana*, with rounded 3-lobed leaves. Common near Atlantic seaboard. Either can be planted in the home garden in shaded locations, near rocks, if soil is suitable. A neutral soil is preferred, though the last-named is considered more tolerant of acid.

IRIS

Which wild irises can be used in the garden?   *Iris cristata*, which needs a protected, moist situation and is indifferent to soil acidity. *I. verna*, wooded hills, very acid soil. *I. versicolor*, marshes, wet meadows, thickets; needs some sun. *I. prismatica*, marshes, swamps; full sun.

JACK-IN-THE-PULPIT

Can Jack-in-the-pulpits be grown in the wild garden?   Yes. Give them a deeply prepared soil. If they are transplanted from the woods, take care to get all of the roots and tubers.

LYCOPODIUMS (CLUB MOSSES)

When is the best time to transplant such things as princess-pine?   Transplant runningpine and other lycopodiums early in the spring before new growth starts. All club mosses are difficult to establish if conditions are not very close to their native habitats. May be moved any time if the place is damp enough.

MARSHMARIGOLD

Is it difficult to transplant marshmarigolds?   No, very easy. Dig or pull the plants gently from their position in marsh or stream. Do not let roots dry out. Replant promptly in similar situation in edge of stream or naturalistic pool.

How can I propagate marshmarigolds?   The simplest way is to divide the clumps in spring, right after flowering. Merely wash the mud away from around the roots so you can see what you're doing, and separate the numerous small crowns (with their roots and leaves) with your fingers. Replant at once in bog garden or in edge of slow-moving stream or near outlet of naturalistic pool.

MERTENSIA

Is mertensia easy to grow in the garden?   Yes. Though *Mertensia virginica* is found in very moist situations—chiefly along the edges of slow-moving streams—it is adaptable to partly shaded positions in the average garden.

How can I keep rabbits from eating up my mertensia plants?

The only way we know of is to get rid of the rabbits, by fair means or foul. Mertensia seems to be a special favorite of theirs in some localities.

ORCHIDS

How can I get wild orchids without breaking the conservation laws?   Purchase them from a wildflower specialist.

How many native American cypripediums (ladyslippers) are there? Which of these are suitable for use in the garden? There are about 10 native cypripediums, of which the following are the best for naturalistic gardening (none are suitable for gardens in the ordinary sense—they need special soil and care): *Cypripedium acaule* (pink); *C. montanum* (white); *C. parviflorum* (yellow); *C. pubescens* (yellow); *C. reginae,* white and rose; *C. candidum* (white.)

Can ladyslippers be transplanted to a semi-wild garden successfully? When should transplanting be done?   Yellow ladyslippers, both *Cypripedium parviflorum* and the larger *C. pubescens* and the Showy Ladyslipper, *C. reginae,* are transplanted with less risk than most other types. Best done in late summer or fall, but may be accomplished in spring if a firm root-ball is taken to prevent injury or disturbance to the roots.

Which of our native cypripediums are perennial? How deep should roots be set?   All are perennial. Roots should be set so that the growing bud, formed in fall, is just under the surface. Use rich woods soil, the surface kept from drying out with a thin layer of oak leaves. Whenever you transplant these cypripediums, take as much as possible of the soil in which they have been growing.

Can you tell me what to do with a moccasin plant after it is through blooming?   If by moccasin plant you mean our native Pink Ladyslipper, *Cypripedium acaule,* and if it is planted in a suitable place, you need do nothing after it blooms. An oak-leaf mulch in fall is desirable.

Does Showy Ladyslipper (Cypripedium reginae) require a neutral soil? (Minnesota.)   It generally is found in the wild where the soil is boggy and acid but is said to tolerate neutral soil.

ORCHIS

Where will I find the Showy Orchis?   The Showy Orchis (*Orchis spectabilis*) and the Pink Ladyslipper (*Cypripedium acaule*) inhabit rich, moist woods from Maine to Georgia, especially oak woods and hemlock groves. The Showy Orchis, however, is said to be tolerant of nearly neutral soil if rich enough.

Where will the Purple-fringed Orchis grow?   In woods, swamps, and meadows, or locations in the garden which simulate such conditions.

Where can I plant the White-fringed Orchis in my wild garden?   If you have a bog garden, plant it there. Native to swamps and bogs.

Can I grow the Yellow-fringed Orchis in my garden?   Perhaps, if you have a strongly acid, continuously moist wild garden.

PARTRIDGE-BERRY

Can partridge-berry be grown in the wild garden?   Yes, especially if it is damp. It requires an acid, rich woods soil.

PHLOX DIVARICATA

How can I get Phlox divaricata and what are its uses?   It can be purchased from many nurseries, especially those which deal in wild plants. Its uses are innumerable. Plant in open shade of deciduous trees. It blends well with mertensia, trilliums, and other plants of the open woodland. Self-sows.

PITCHERPLANT

Can pitcherplant (Sarracenia purpurea) be grown in the wild garden?   Yes. This is a good bog-garden subject.

SHOOTINGSTAR

Is shootingstar a good wild-garden subject?   Yes. *Dodecatheon meadia* is a showy wildflower suitable for woodland planting in slightly acid or neutral soil.

SPRINGBEAUTY (CLAYTONIA)

What are the cultural requirements of springbeauty (Claytonia)?   Damp, leafmoldy soil and full shade in summer.

TRILLIUM

Which trilliums are best for the wild garden?   *Trillium grandiflorum* (Large-Flowering White Trillium); *T. nivale* (small white, earliest); *T. luteum* (yellow); *T. stylosum* (rose); *T. californicum* (sessile type in white or red).

Can trilliums be purchased?   Yes, specialists in wild plants and some other nurseries list them.

How can trilliums best be propagated from seed?   The best way to propagate trilliums is by division of old, large clumps. Absolutely fresh seed, sown before it has a chance to dry, may germinate the following spring, but growth is very slow and all conditions have to be just right.

VIOLETS

Are violets dug up from the woods suitable for planting in the wild garden? Yes. They are easily transplanted.

What sort of conditions does Birdsfoot Violet need? Give a dryish, well-drained, sandy, very acid soil in full sun.

WINTERGREENS

Will you please name and describe some native wintergreens? Spotted Wintergreen (*Chimaphila maculata*) with white-veined lanceolate evergreen leaves; showy white flowers. Pipsissewa (*Chimaphila umbellata*), rather like the above but with wedge-shaped unmarked evergreen leaves and smaller flowers, sometimes blush pink. Shinleaf (*Pyrola elliptica*), oval basal leaves, persistent but not evergreen; white flowers on 5- to 10-in. stalks, in racemes. Round-leaved American Wintergreen (*Pyrola americana*), leaves basal, rounded; showy blush-white flowers on tall stalks. Creeping Wintergreen (*Gaultheria procumbens*), evergreen, blunt, aromatic leaves; creeping subterranean stems; blush flowers in leaf axils; edible red berries; 2 to 6 ins. tall. Flowering Wintergreen or Fringed Polygala (*P. paucifolia*), evergreen leaves; rose-purple, fringed flowers, or, sometimes, white; low-growing, and spreading.

How is pipsissewa (Chimaphila umbellata) propagated? By cuttings of new growth taken the first half of July and rooted in sand in a seed flat.

GARDENS OF OTHER TYPES

CHILDREN'S GARDEN

How much space would you suggest giving a child in which to make his own garden? This depends on the size of the child and on how much space is available. A little tot should have a tiny space—4 or 5 ft. square. The area may be increased as he grows older.

What would be a good location to give a child for a garden? A spot that has full sun all day, where the ground is in good condition and easily workable. Children are easily discouraged if their garden does not produce, so do not select any unfit "left-over" area.

Which plants would be suitable for a child to grow in his own garden?   Bright, easily grown annuals, which can be raised from seed: zinnias, marigolds, alyssum, scabiosa, and portulaca. These will give him an opportunity to learn how seeds are planted and what the plants look like as they come up. A few easy perennials might be given him to plant too. If a fence encloses his garden, morningglories can be used to cover it.

Will you list some easy vegetables that a child might grow from seed?   Carrots, beets, leaf lettuce, beans, radishes, and New Zealand spinach.

I am very much interested in planning a garden that will interest my children. Just what arrangement would you suggest? I have in mind something to go along with their own yard and playhouse.   Any garden for children should be scaled down to their size. They like intricate patterns and odd plants. Paths should be narrow, and all plants relatively small. Choose varieties that will stand the maximum amount of abuse. Leave plenty of play space.

CITY GARDENS

Will you give some hints on making a city garden?   The keynote of the city garden is simplicity. Remember that you cannot grow all the flowering plants that thrive in the country. If you have shade, plant interesting shrubs that will tolerate shady conditions, and some ground covers, such as pachysandra and ivy. Get a few pieces of suitable furniture and arrange them attractively. Pots of bright flowers, or window boxes, may be set about in sunny places. Vines are good for most city gardens, as they afford protection as well as greenery. (See also City Environment, Section II.)

ENGLISH GARDEN

How does one begin to plan an English country garden? Is there any set plan or style to follow?   This subject is too large to cover in a few words. Better consult such books as *Gardens for Small Country Houses,* by Gertrude Jekyll and Lawrence Weaver; *English Flower Garden,* by W. Robinson.

FRAGRANT GARDENS

I would like some fragrant annuals in my garden. What do you suggest?   Nicotiana, nasturtium, sweet alyssum, petunia, marigold, stock, heliotrope (tender shrub), mignonette, sweetpea.

Will you name some bulbs for a fragrant garden?   *Crocus versicolor* and *C. biflorus; Scilla italica* and *S. campanulata; Fritillaria imperialis;* hyacinths; narcissi (jonquils and hybrids; poetaz; poeticus; tazetta); tulips: Ambrosia, Arethusa, Dido, De Wet, Leda, Early Yellow Rose; lily-of-the-valley; scented irises (rhizomes, not bulbs); Liliums: *auratum, candidum, longiflorum, regale, speciosum;* tuberose.

What are some fragrant hardy flowers?   *Dianthus caesius* and varieties; *Dianthus caryophyllus* and varieties; scented bearded iris; lily-of-the-valley; *Viola odorata* and varieties; *Lavandula officinalis;* hemerocallis; buddleia; primula; clematis; sweetwilliam; monarda; phlox; peony; roses; Arabis Snowcap; salvia.

Which herbs shall I plant in a fragrant garden?   See Herbs.

Which flowers shall I plant for night fragrance?   Nicotiana; moonvine; petunia; *Pelargonium triste;* nightblooming waterlilies.

Will you tell me which geraniums to buy for fragrance? *Pelargonium tomentosum* (mint); *P. graveolens* (rose); *P. limoneum* (lemon); *P. odoratissimum* (nutmeg.)

What will give fragrance in the late garden?   Chrysanthemums, clematis, wallflowers.

Which shrubs shall I plant for fragrance?   Pink (winterbloom) and Swamp Azalea; *Jasminum nudiflorum* and *J. primulinum;* benzoin; magnolia; Flowering Almond; lilac; honeysuckle; daphne; *Forsythia ovata;* mockorange; strawberry-shrub; English Hawthorn; wisteria; witchhazel. Tender: lemonverbena; rosemary; heliotrope.

A "knot" design herb garden. The herbs used are: 1. Thyme or Roman Wormwood; 2. Sweet Violet or Santolina viridis; 3. Lavender cotton or dwarf Lavender; 4. Germander or Rosemary.

KNOT GARDENS

What is a knot garden?   A garden of low-growing plants or hedges planted in a formal, intricate design. Common to medieval landscape design, when colored sand was often used to form the paths or sections which outlined the beds. Now used in parks, herb gardens, and formal gardens.

What plant materials can be used for a knot garden?   Boxwood, artemisia, santolina, iresine; low-bedding flowers; herbs.

OUTDOOR LIVING ROOM

What is an "outdoor living room"?   An area with comfortable tables and chairs set aside for lounging and loafing. It should be secluded, at least partially walled in by evergreens, shrubs, or other plant material. It is desirable to have the outdoor living room away from the house, but easily accessible. The ideal "room" gives a view of the garden through an arch in the hedge or by leaving one side unscreened. It is often placed in the shade of a large tree. Some people like to include equipment for barbecues and picnics in this area.

Invitation to leisure: at least one corner of the garden, no matter how small, should be arranged for outdoor living.

We are planning a simple rose garden in an outdoor living room surrounded by poplar trees. Will you help us with the layout?   The typical rose garden is formal in design. Square or circular areas divided into small beds by narrow paths, and provided with a central feature such as a sundial, make an effective arrangement. (See also Roses and previous question.)

ROOF GARDENS

What soil mixture should be used to fill the boxes on a roof garden?   A good, friable loam is ideal. Avoid heavy clay or very sandy soil.

What kind of fertilizer should I use for the plants on my roof garden?   Liquid manure, or a complete commercial fertilizer.

Should one use a mulch on the soil in roof-garden boxes? Yes; a mulch will help prevent sudden drying out of the soil from wind and sun on the roof. Peatmoss, rotted manure, or leafmold could be used.

Can one grow vegetables successfully on a roof?   Yes, with full sun and good soil, a few can be grown. In boxes about 8 ins. deep grow lettuce, parsley, radishes, bush beans, endive, onions (from sets), New Zealand spinach, Swiss chard. Try stump-rooted carrots and beets. Tomatoes planted in deeper boxes, staked and sheltered so that they will not blow over, will probably thrive.

I would like to grow some herbs on my roof garden. Do you think they would be successful?   Yes, they probably would. Herbs are a good choice for the shallow boxes usually used on a roof. Try thyme, chives, parsley, mint, sage, and basil. (See Herbs for soil and culture.)

Will you give a list of annual flowers for growing on a roof? Marigolds, zinnias, ageratum, petunias, calendulas, alyssum, lobelia, portulaca, celosia, iberis, forget-me-nots, salvia, coreopsis, aster, scabiosa.

I am planning to make the boxes for plants on my roof garden. Can you give me some suggestions?   Your boxes should be made deep enough to hold 8 to 12 ins. of soil. They can be as wide as you like. Use cypress wood that will withstand water. Provide drainage holes in the bottom of each box so that the soil will not become sour. The inside of the boxes can be painted with asphaltum to protect the wood, and the outside with several coats of durable outdoor paint.

I want to grow some vines on my roof. How could I effectively support them?   Make an arbor over part of the roof. This would not only be a good support for your vines, but would also supply shade and some shelter on the terrace. Otherwise, use a trellis against the side of the building, or put vine supports along the side of the building on which to tie the vines.

What kind of furniture can I use for my roof garden?   Any comfortable, well-designed furniture that will withstand the weather. Avoid types that must be taken in each time it rains. Metal chairs and tables are good, if kept well painted, or stout wooden ones. If you care to be different, make your own furniture out of boxes and barrels, and paint with bright colors.

I want to make a roof garden that is good-looking but will not be expensive. Will you make some suggestions?   Edge the railing or wall with window boxes painted dark green or any color which fits your scheme. Grow such plants as petunias, ageratum, geraniums, alyssum, marigolds, and calendulas. Some potted plants can be arranged about the roof. If you can get some large boxes or barrels, try a few shrubs, such as privet or forsythia, or trees, such as cedars or yews, for a background. Train vines against the wall or building. Ivy, honeysuckle, or morningglories would do well. Comfortable chairs and tables will be needed.

What can be done on a flat roof, approximately 10 × 10 ft., on the west side of an apartment? Can dirt be put on the roof to sufficient depth to raise anything successfully?   Six to 8 ins. of soil will successfully grow many flowers or even a few vegetables. Check with engineer before putting this considerable weight on roof. Otherwise confine efforts to a few soil-filled boxes.

I have some large roof-garden boxes. How can I tell if the soil is sour? How can I fertilize the earth before we plant?   If in doubt, have a soil test made. For most plants add lime every 2 years. Bone meal and dried cow manure are excellent fertilizers; or use any complete commercial fertilizer. Do not mix lime and fertilizer at one time. Add lime in fall or very early spring, and fertilizer at planting time.

SUNKEN GARDENS

I have a natural spot for making a sunken garden. How can I plan this?   The sunken garden is viewed from above and the basic layout is very important because of this. An informal or untidy effect would spoil it. A formal garden, with a path running through the center, and a center of interest at the end, would probably work out well. If your garden is well drained, you might plan a formal rose garden; or an herb garden with thyme-planted steps and borders of fragrant plants around the four sides of the area in front of the walls. Leave the center in turf.

There is an old foundation on our property, where a house burned down. Would this make a good place for a sunken garden?   Yes, it should be excellent. You may have to provide drainage, if water collects in the foundation. Build steps down into the garden of the same kind of stones as the foundation. Perennials of doubtful hardiness and shrubs, which need much protection from cold winds, can be incorporated in your planting plan.

WINDOW BOX GARDENS

What special problems are involved in window-box gardening?
First provide appropriate boxes with holes in bottom for drainage.
Put in 2 or 3 ins. of cinders or broken brick, and fill with rich,
porous soil. Plant with appropriate material in spring. Regular
attention to watering is of prime importance. Fertilize as often
as necessary.

Can you give some pointers on making window boxes?
Make box to fit window space, but if the length is in excess of 3
ft. make in two sections. For good results the box should be not
less than 8 ins. deep and 10 ins. wide. Use cypress or white pine
at least 1 in. thick. Bore ½-in holes, 6 ins. apart, in bottom for
drainage.

What is the best soil for window boxes?   One that is rich,
with plenty of humus to retain moisture. Use 2 parts loam, 1 part
rotted manure or leafmold, with a 5-in. pot of bone meal mixed
with each bushel.

Are wooden window boxes better than those made of concrete?
They are inexpensive and less weighty to handle if they have
to be moved occasionally. On the other hand, they are less permanent.

Are the metal "self-watering" boxes satisfactory?   Yes; but
don't place too much reliance on the "self-watering" feature.

**Can an old hot-water tank (cylindrical) be used as a porch
box?**   Yes. Have a tinsmith cut out a strip equal to ⅓ to ½
of the circumference for the entire length. Punch holes in the opposite side to drain off surplus water.

**Is there any flowering plant suitable for window boxes which
will hold up all summer and be colorful?**   Lantana. Get
potted plants in May; usually then in flower, they will bloom
until frost. They stand heat, drought, and city conditions, but are
at their best when well watered and pruned occasionally to restrain lanky growth. Stand partial shade, but prefer full sun.
Balcony petunias are also good.

Which flowers grow in window boxes?   Among the most
satisfactory are begonias, geraniums, fuchsias, ageratum, petunias,
dwarf marigolds, torenias, pansies, sweet alyssum, morningglory,
vinca, sedum, balsam, portulaca, and lobelia.

Is there a blooming plant that will grow in window boxes under awning? (West Virginia.)   None that you can be sure of.

Try *Begonia semperflorens* varieties, petunias, and *Lobelia erinus* varieties.

What would you suggest for flowers (not tuberous begonias) for window boxes that are very shaded? Would like plenty of color. You will probably have difficulty with any flowering plant if the shade is heavy and continuous. Fuchsias, *Begonia semperflorens*, torenias, and lobelias will stand as much shade as any.

What shall I plant in a window box, outdoors, on north side? (Washington.) Flowering plants: begonias, fuchsias, lobelias, torenias. Foliage plants: aucuba, boxwood, Japanese Holly, Dwarf Yew, arborvitae, privet, English Ivy, vinca, Kenilworth Ivy.

What could we plant in outdoor front-stoop window boxes which will survive New York City winter climate, such as evergreen, yew, dwarf pine, etc.? Among the most satisfactory plants are small yew, arborvitae, Japanese Holly, privet, and English Ivy. All suffer, however, when the soil is frozen solid. Make sure soil is well soaked in fall. *Sedum acre* and *S. spectabile* will survive year in, year out.

What can be put in a window box (southern exposure) during the winter months? (Virginia.) Small evergreens, boxwood, arborvitae, junipers, spruces, with English Ivy and trailing myrtle to droop over edge. This material cannot be expected to thrive permanently, however, because of poor environment.

Is it necessary to put ivy and myrtle grown in window boxes into the ground for the winter? If the soil about their roots freezes solid, they cannot take up water to replace that lost by leaves, and the plants die. Place boxes on ground, pack manure or straw well about them, and cover with burlap or light layer of straw.

How early can pansies be planted in outdoor window boxes? (North Carolina.) Pansies are much hardier than most people realize. The established plants can be put in the outdoor window box as soon as the severe portion of winter is passed. Plants grown indoors should be hardened off by gradually exposing them to cooler temperatures before setting them in the outdoor boxes. March 15, or even earlier, in your locality, might be about right.

MISCELLANEOUS

CACTI FOR OUTDOORS

What are the hardiest kinds of cacti? *Opuntia compressa* (*vulgaris*), *O. fragilis, Echinocereus viridiflorus,* and *Pediocactus simpsoni.*

Are there any varieties of cactus, other than opuntia, that can be left outside all winter in south Jersey? You might try *Echinocereus viridiflorus* and *Pediocactus simpsoni.*

Will cactus from the Arizona desert thrive in Oklahoma? Those native from north of Phoenix will possibly grow if given a thoroughly well-drained and sheltered position.

Can spineless cacti of the type that Luther Burbank developed be grown in a climate which is hot and dry in the summer and cold and wet in the winter? No. The spineless opuntias do not thrive where wet winters are experienced.

What are names of some cacti that will live out of doors in south central North Carolina? *Opuntia compressa* (*vulgaris*), *O. fragilis, O. rhodantha,* (*O. xanthostemma*), *O. polyacantha, O. imbricata, O. basilaris, O. ursina, Echinocereus viridiflorus, E. reichenbachi, E. baileyi,* and *Pediocactus simpsoni.*

GOURDS

WHAT TO GROW

Will you tell me which gourds to grow for curing—gourds to be used for winter decoration? White pear, bicolor pear, goose egg, ringed pear, spoon, miniatures, ladle, warty hardhead, snake, lagenaria in variety.

Which kinds of gourds are suitable for bird houses? The ordinary dipper gourds as well as others of the lagenaria genus.

How can I produce dipper-type gourds? Have heard it is necessary to tape the neck of the gourd. Dipper gourds are known to seedsmen under that name and culture is the same as for other gourds. Shaping of necks is not ordinarily necessary for dipper gourds, but if you want to modify their shape this could be done.

CULTURE

Is there any fertilizer that will cause gourd plants to grow more rapidly? The same provisions that are made for cucumbers and melons will work well with gourds. Use a 5–10–5 fertilizer or a combination of manure and a smaller amount of fertilizer, or stable manure and superphosphate. Stable manure alone is also satisfactory.

How do you raise gourds?   Gourds are not particularly difficult to grow. They can be allowed to run on the ground but are better planted along a wire fence or provided with a trellis. General requirements are about the same as for cucumbers and melons—a moderately rich, well-fertilized soil with reasonable moisture supply. They thrive under a wide range of conditions, and most varieties of small gourds will mature in the Northern part of the country. Seed is sowed about 1 in. deep and plants are thinned to 2 or 3 ft. apart, according to varieties. Dusting may be necessary to control the striped cucumber beetle. In Northern climates plants may be started under glass as are cucumbers and muskmelons. Shallow cultivation should be practiced to control weeds.

What is the earliest date gourds can be planted?   Gourds are planted at about the same time as cucumbers, 2 or 3 weeks after average date of last killing frost in the spring or at about the time tomatoes are set out. Gourds will not stand frost.

How do you start gourds from seed?   Ornamental gourds are usually raised in pots from seed sown in April or May and transplanted out in June. Seed may also be sown outdoors when danger of frost is past.

Is there any pamphlet or booklet issued on the raising and use of ornamental gourds?   The following will be found helpful: "Useful and Ornamental Gourds," *Farmers' Bulletin 1849,* United States Department of Agriculture, Washington, D.C. "Gourds," by Hudson and Sando, *Bulletin 356,* University of Minnesota, St. Paul, Minnesota. *The Garden of Gourds,* by L. H. Bailey, The Macmillan Company, 60 Fifth Ave., New York.

How can one take care of gourds after they are picked so that they will not decay?   Gourds should be thoroughly matured on the vines before they are picked. They will not stand freezing if they are still succulent. If by necessity they are taken at the immature state, they should be handled with the utmost care and allowed to dry and cure indoors, but mold is likely to attack them. Some recommend washing gourds, but wiping with a soft cloth is probably better. Disinfectant solutions may be of some service, but not too much. To keep gourds in their natural state, waxing is one of the best methods, using ordinary floor wax and polishing lightly. Some use shellac, but this changes the color and appearance. Some also like to decorate and paint them in simple or fanciful fashion. Stems should be left on the gourds, removing them from vines by cutting. Maturity may be judged by feeling them, but it is not wise to test with the fingernail. They should be dry and the stem should be withered.

What is a good spray to combat the stem borer of gourds? It is best to grow the gourds on ground where curcubits have not been grown the previous year or where their refuse remains. Early summer squash may be used as a trap crop. When the borer is already at work in the vines, surgery is resorted to, cutting lengthwise of the vine with a thin knife to destroy the larvae, then the cut portion is covered with earth and little harm is done to the plant. Rotenone spray or dust applied 3 or 4 times may be effective in destroying the borers just after they are hatched.

Is there a gourd society in this country? Yes. The Gourd Society of America, Inc., Horticultural Hall, Boston, Massachusetts.

WEEDS

GENERAL

Can you keep weeds down; and how? By constantly attacking them while they are yet young, and above all by preventing them from seeding. On cultivated ground, use the cultivator and hoe, plus hand weeding; on lawns, hand weeding and good culture to encourage desirable grasses; on drives and paths, weed killers.

I have 6 acres, not worked for about 20 years, full of weeds. What is the best way to get rid of them? Is it best to plow in fall or spring? Maintain a bare fallow through one season. Plow in spring and harrow or plow shallowly at frequent intervals throughout summer, so the surface is never permitted to show any signs of green growth.

We intend fencing our lot (natural pickets) in spring. Adjoining are open fields. How can I keep down weeds at base of fence on the outside? If you are not planting too close to inside of fence, use regular weed killer, or a special weed-killing torch, made for the purpose. Otherwise, try spraying with ammonium sulfamate.

Would it be advisable to burn all dried-up flowers and weeds in our flower garden in early spring? (Due to illness, garden was

not tended in fall.) Under the circumstances the burning treatment would be satisfactory. The seeds produced by the weeds are already dispersed, however, so burning will not materially reduce the season's weed crop.

Is there any method other than burning trash or dry brush on a seedbed, to kill weed seeds? Burning is not very satisfactory, for weed seeds will stand considerable heat. A good method is to keep the bed moist to encourage germination and then to hoe 2 or 3 times (allowing 10 days between each hoeing) to destroy seedlings. Sterilization with chloropicrin (which see) is also effective, but special equipment is needed.

How can I get rid of weeds before and during growth of parsley, besides weeding when small? Hand weeding in the rows and frequent hoeing between the rows are the best methods for annual weeds. If the ground is infested with perennial weeds, these should be dug out to the last root before the parsley is sown.

In August I put turf-builder around a privet hedge. Six weeks later a broadleaf weed came in thick around hedges. Could it be the turf-builder? Turf-builder is a proprietary plant food that certainly does not contain weed seeds. It probably stimulated the growth of weeds present in the soil, thus proving its efficiency as a fertilizer.

Is there anything that will kill weeds, yet not destroy flowers or vegetables? While certain selective sprays have limited uses in the control of weeds in grainfields and in lawns, no substance has been (or probably ever will be) found to meet the requirements you state. This is because many weeds are closely related botanically to favorite flowers and vegetables.

What can be done to keep a cinder drive free from weeds? Procure a commercial weed killer from a dealer in horticultural supplies, and use according to directions. Crankcase drainings, diluted with kerosene so that they can be sprayed over the drive, are alternatives.

What is the name of a compound to put in paths between flower beds to eliminate weeds? Any good commercial weed killer will do this. Be careful not to let any of it get onto the flower beds, lawns, or other places where you desire vegetation to grow.

What is best to use in killing weeds in a brick drain? Providing the drain does not carry water into a pond or stream used by fish or animals, any commercial weed killer should prove effective.

How can I tell different kinds of weeds and grasses?   *Weeds* by Walter Conrad Muenscher (Macmillan, 1942) and *Just Weeds*, by Edwin Rollin Spencer (Scribner's, 1940) are two excellent books on this subject.

SPECIFIC WEEDS

Am planting a garden over an old asparagus bed and have tried many ways to kill the asparagus, even to digging up the crowns, but the stuff persists. How may I rid myself of this nuisance?   Keep digging. Every time an asparagus stem appears dig out the root from which it arises.

How can one get rid of bindweed on lawn without killing roses, trees, and shrubs by using poison?   You probably cannot. You might, however, try spraying it with the new poison-ivy eliminator, ammonium sulfamate. Alternative: dig out every scrap of bindweed root.

How can I exterminate an extremely hardy vine resembling a morningglory, having white flowers and seemingly endless roots?   Doubtless a bindweed, a pernicious weed with fleshy roots which descend several feet, every fragment of which will grow. Where it exists, either don't plant anything and constantly hoe, so that no leaves can build up a food store in the roots, or plant only low-growing crops which can be hoed frequently so that no vines can get started.

How can I get rid of Bermuda Grass?   Where ground freezes, plow or fork shallowly in fall so roots are exposed to air through winter. Farther South rely upon forking out and frequent cultivation; or smother with crop of fall-sown rye, followed by crop of cowpeas or velvet beans.

What can I do for Bermuda Grass in flower borders? (Tennessee.)   In your section, Bermuda Grass doubtless is a troublesome weed, but it is used to make lawns in the South. In the borders it must be kept down by frequent hoeing.

How can I clear land of blackberry vines?   Spray vines twice during season, when foliage is present, with ammonium sulfamate; strength, 1 lb. to 5 gals. of water. The solution reaches the roots through the vines and kills them.

Can you name a formula to kill buckthorn or plantain? At what time of year should it be used?   Dig out by hand or mow down and burn before seeding stage is reached.

We have some patches of Canada Thistle in our garden. Is digging them up the best remedy?   Yes, if the work is well done. Any pieces of root left in the soil will grow, however, and digging should be followed by repeated hoeings.

Narrowleaf Plantain, a deep-rooted pest in lawns; watch for and dig up seedling plants. (Right) The Broadleaved Plantain.

What is the best way to clean cattails and rushes from lake edge?   The only practicable method is to dig them out completely. If surface of lake could be lowered for a considerable period, they may die out from lack of moisture.

What method of controlling chickweed do you recommend to the home gardener?   In flower and vegetable garden, surface cultivation; remove *at once* every plant, with its spreading root system, as it appears, *and destroy*. In lawns, fertilize to encourage growth of grasses. Use lime if soil is at all too acid. Another method is to dust lightly with sulfate of ammonia on a dewy morning, and water well the same evening. More than one application may be necessary.

Chickweed: one of the worst pests in gardens. Remove plants—getting all the roots—in early spring, and burn.

In absence of sulfate of ammonia, what would be a good substitute for control of chickweed?   Hand weeding; frequent surface cultivation. For lawns, spray a solution of 1 lb. of iron sulfate to 1½ gals. of water over each 100 sq. ft. Temporary discoloration of the grass results from this treatment. Do not use on Creeping Bent lawns.

What is the best method of fighting crab grass? Pull every seedling as soon as big enough to recognize, thus preventing seeding (crab grass is an annual). Fertilize lawn generously to stimulate desired grasses. (See also Lawns.)

Crab grass: bane of the lawn maker. For control see Lawns (page 596).

How can creeping Jenny be eradicated? Creeping Jenny is a name applied to a golden-flowered lysimachia as well as to the white-flowered wild morningglory. The former is controlled by hand forking and frequent surface cultivation. (For control of wild morningglory, see other answers.)

How can I fight the curse of a neighbor's dandelion seed blowing into my yard? Three procedures are possible: eliminate dandelions on neighbor's property; dig out young dandelions as fast as they appear in your yard; learn to tolerate dandelions.

Dandelion: to control, cut tap root well below ground with an asparagus knife (see page 668) and prevent stray plants from seeding.

What is the best method for controlling dandelions? Digging them out. Alternate methods are: cut the plants off well below surface and drip a few drops of sulphuric acid onto the cut root; spray with an iron sulfate solution (1 lb. to 1½ gals. water) every 10 days.

How can one effectively destroy dock weeds? Specimens of small size can be pulled out when soil is very wet. With larger plants, cut tops off an inch below ground surface, pierce root with a skewer, and pour a few drops of sulphuric acid (or a large teacupful of salt) on cut surface.

What can be done to get rid of "dodder," also called lovevine, goldthread, strangleweed, Desire's-hair, and hellbind? Dodder is a parasitic annual. Cut down and burn all infected plants before the dodder has a chance to seed.

Will you suggest a remedy for much-branched, green, leafy weed with tiny daisy flowers each having 5 white petals? I think it is called galinsoga.   This is an introduction from tropical America. It is very sensitive to frost, but is an annual and so over-winters as seed. Hand pulling large plants *before seeds form* and cultivation to kill young ones are most practical remedies.

Is it possible to remove Johnsongrass or quackgrass from a vegetable garden so that it will not be back the next season? These are 2 distinct species. Both may be eliminated by forking out as much as possible by hand, taking pains to get every root, and then by repeatedly cultivating the surface throughout summer. Johnsongrass is particularly resistant, and vigorous methods must be used.

Lambsquarters is common in my garden. How do you keep it down?   This weed usually favors rich soils. It is controlled by cultivating and is easily hand pulled. When the plants are young, lambsquarters makes excellent greens.

We have a shrub called Mexican bamboo which is becoming a nuisance. How can it be eradicated?   This is *Polygonum cuspidatum*. If you want other plants to grow in same place, dig it out as thoroughly as possible, then cut every shoot off that appears when not more than an inch high. Otherwise use commercial weed killers.

I have a weed which grows very tall and multiplies rapidly, roots are red and run under the ground and sprout. What is the proper name and how can I kill it?   Probably *Polygonum cuspidatum*. Only relief other than poisoning ground with weed killer is to dig out all roots (which go very deep) and keep surface hoed afterward to kill any sprouts that appear.

What will kill moonvine or wild morningglory?   Dig out as much as possible, then keep the ground surface cultivated at frequent intervals so that no new shoot ever attains a height of more than 2 ins. before being cut off.

How can a fairly large patch of nettle in a field be eliminated? By repeatedly mowing so that the plants are never permitted to get more than a few inches high. Also, by spraying the plants when young with a commercial weed killer.

Nutgrass is a troublesome weed in my garden. Can you suggest a means of eliminating it?   This is not really a grass but a sedge which is partial to wet places. Drainage, followed by a year's clean cultivation, is the only real remedy.

What can be done to destroy petunia seedlings? I would like

to plant something else in the former petunia bed, but the petunias come up by the hundreds each year. Hand weeding and scuffle hoeing after the seedlings are up are the only practicable means. The hoeing will not only destroy the petunias but will also encourage the growth of whatever else you may plant in the bed.

Can you suggest any means of getting rid of plantain (both narrow- and broad-leaved) in quantity? Digging, even with a special tool, is slow and laborious. Plantains on lawns can be killed by using a pinch of salt in the center of each plant on a hot day. Two or 3 drops of sulphuric acid will also serve. There are compounds sold that will kill broad-leaved weeds in lawns when dusted on. (See Lawns.)

How can I get rid of poisonivy without spending a fortune? Syringe or spray the plants while green with fuel oil or crankcase oil thinned down with kerosene.

How can I eliminate poisonivy? By the use, according to the maker's directions, of the new Du Pont spray, ammonium sulfamate. By digging out the roots.

How may I get rid of poisonivy growing in a bed of lily-of-the-valley? Get someone immune to poisonivy to carefully dig up the bed. Transplant lily-of-the-valley to another location for 2 or 3 years. Meantime eliminate any ivy that appears on old site.

What is the poison-oak plant and how can it be destroyed? Poisonoak (*Toxicodendron quercifolium*) is similar to poisonivy (*T. radicans*), but has more oaklike leaves. Spray with ammonium sulfamate according to maker's directions.

Every summer my garden is invaded by purslane. What can I do? This is an annual that develops rapidly in warm weather and rich soil. Attack vigorously with hoe and cultivator while weeds are yet tiny. If plants get large, rake them up and burn or compost, otherwise they will root and grow again.

Which is the most effective way of ridding ground of quackgrass? It grows in soil around shrubbery and cannot be exposed to anything that would harm these plants. In the spring work the whole area over with a spading fork and carefully remove all underground stems of the grass. Follow this throughout the summer by forking out every piece of the grass that appears before the leaves are an inch high.

How can I eradicate redroot (pigweed)? Practice clean cultivation. Mow plants down before they reach the seeding stage.

How do you get rid of sandburs?   Practice clean cultivation. The plant is an annual and cannot reproduce if all plants are hoed or pulled out before they seed.

How can I destroy sheepssorrel and at the same time use the ground for vegetables and flowers?   Sheepssorrel is a sure sign of poor, infertile, and, usually, acid soil. Apply fertilizer generously and test for lime needs. Nitrogenous fertilizers are especially helpful.

How can I eradicate sumac?   The most satisfactory remedy is to grub out the roots.

Is there any method of destroying sumac other than digging it out?   Recommended method is to spread from 1 to 2 oz. of dry sodium chlorate around the base of each plant in November.

I have an old trumpetvine root in the ground and want to plant a fruit tree instead. How can I kill the heavy root so it won't take the strength from the fruit tree?   The only satisfactory procedure is to dig out the trumpetvine root and turn over and fertilize the soil before planting the fruit tree.

How can I get rid of white clover in my garden?   White clover in lawns may be discouraged by maintaining the soil on the acid side. Liming encourages its growth. If troublesome in flower and vegetable garden, hoeing and hand weeding are recommended.

What is best method of getting rid of white snakeroot? Grub out the roots.

How is the best way to get rid of wild carrot?   The plant is biennial and does not reproduce itself if it is cut down before it reaches the seeding stage.

Wild garlic is becoming troublesome. How shall I eliminate it?   A most pernicious weed, once established. If area is not too large, hand digging, followed by destruction of every bulb, is best. Cultivate surface frequently. Spray with fuel oil before flowering for 3 successive years.

How can wild grapevines and poisonivy be killed out? These seem to cover every rock and bit of space on our farm. Goldenrod and milkweed mingle with these weeds.   Du Pont's new spray, ammonium sulfamate, will control poisonivy and probably wild grapes as well. Otherwise the grapes must be dug out.

Can wild morningglory be exterminated around the trunk of

fruit trees without killing or damaging the trees?   Maintain a circle of bare ground around the tree and keep this clean of all growth by scuffle hoeing every few days throughout 2 successive growing seasons. As an alternative, cover infested area with heavy roofing paper for 2 seasons.

Poison Ivy (left); (right) Virginia-creeper, often mistaken for it.

How can I eradicate a weed called wild sweet potato which has white flowers similar to morningglory? Roots are too long to pull up or dig out.   Dig out as many roots as possible, then religiously cut off with a hoe every shoot that appears as soon as it is an inch or so above ground.

How can I get rid of wiregrass?   This name is applied to several distinct species of grasses, and also to a kind of rush. Several of these indicate soils low in fertility. Some are annuals, some perennials. Frequent cultivation and prevention of seeding are recommended treatments.

ODDS & ENDS

Will you explain the meanings of floriculture and horticulture? Horticulture covers the cultivation of all plants that may be grown in a garden. Floriculture is that branch of horticulture that deals with the growing of flowers—often used to denote the commercial culture of flowers outside and under glass.

What is meant by "deciduous" trees and shrubs?   Those which shed their foliage in the autumn. Some, which retain their dry leaves, all or partly, through the winter, like beech and some oaks, are commonly included in "deciduous" trees.

Is it possible that a chain or a peg fastened to a tree at a certain distance from the ground will ever be further from the

ground, no matter how old the tree?   No, there will be no elevation of anything driven into a tree at a given point.

How much sunshine and air circulation do most blooming plants need?   Some flowering plants are happiest in all the sunshine possible. Others appreciate shade during the hottest part of the day, and some are tolerant of a good deal of shade. All appreciate good air circulation but dislike drafts.

Will you tell me how to change the color of flowers? For instance, what would the procedure be if I wanted to raise a blue marigold?   Colors in flowers result from inheritance. You cannot get a blue marigold. In some instances (hydrangea) chemicals like aluminum added to the soil change the color from pink to blue.

Can I pollinate cotton flowers with pollen from tulip or poplar trees?   Yes, if pollen is available at the time cotton is in bloom. But if done in expectation of a "blessed event" you will certainly be disappointed, because there is no close family relationship between these plants.

What is the usual procedure in the treatment of seed by X ray for the origination of new varieties?   Both time of exposure and intensity of the rays seem to affect the results. Sometimes dormant seeds are irradiated and sometimes young flowers. Write to Research Laboratory, General Electric Co., Schenectady, New York.

Will you state what effect, if any, the moon has on planting gardens?   The moon has no effect on planting gardens.

What is the truth about planting in the signs of the zodiac? There is no scientific basis for these superstitions.

ADDRESSES OF AGRICULTURAL EXPERIMENT
STATIONS IN THE UNITED STATES

The name of city or town where station is located is given in *italics*. Example: address letter to Maryland State Experiment Station, *College Park*, Maryland.

Alabama: *Auburn*
Alaska: *College*
Arizona: *Tucson*
Arkansas: *Fayetteville*
California: *Berkeley*
Colorado: *Fort Collins*
Connecticut: *New Haven*
Connecticut: *Storrs*
Delaware: *Newark*
Florida: *Gainesville*
Georgia: *Coastal Plain Station, Tifton*
Hawaii: *Honolulu*
Idaho: *Moscow*
Illinois: *Urbana*
Indiana: *Lafayette*
Iowa: *Ames*
Kansas: *Manhattan*
Kentucky: *Lexington*
Louisiana: *Baton Rouge*
Maine: *Orono*
Maryland: *College Park*
Massachusetts: *Amherst*
Michigan: *East Lansing*
Minnesota: *St. Paul*
Mississippi: *State College*
Missouri: *College Station, Columbia*
Missouri: *Fruit Station, Mountain Grove*
Missouri: *Poultry Station, Mountain Grove*
Montana: *Bozeman*
Nebraska: *Lincoln*
Nevada: *Reno*

New Hampshire: *Durham*
New Jersey: *New Brunswick*
New Mexico: *State College*
New York: *State Station, Geneva*
New York: *Cornell Station, Ithaca*
North Carolina: *Raleigh*
North Dakota: *Fargo*
Ohio: *Wooster*
Oklahoma: *Stillwater*
Oregon: *Corvallis*
Pennsylvania: *State College*
Puerto Rico: *Federal Station, Mayaguez*
Puerto Rico: *Insular Station, Rio Piedras*
Rhode Island: *Kingston*
South Carolina: *Clemson*
South Dakota: *Brookings*
Tennessee: *Knoxville*
Texas: *College Station*
Utah: *Logan*
Vermont: *Burlington*
Virginia: *College Station, Blacksbury*
Virginia: *Truck Station, Norfolk*
Washington: *College Station, Pullman*
Washington: *Western Station, Puyallup*
West Virginia: *Morgantown*
Wisconsin: *Madison*
Wyoming: *Laramie*

BOOKS AND BULLETINS
FOR FURTHER INFORMATION

For the convenience of readers who would like to obtain more detailed information on special phases of gardening, we present the following list of books and bulletins, compiled by Miss Elizabeth C. Hall, librarian of the New York Botanical Garden:

ANNUALS

HOTTES, A. C. The Book of Annuals. *De La Mare.*
JENKINS, DOROTHY. Annual Flowers. *Barrows.*
FOLEY, DANIEL J. Annuals for Your Garden. *Macmillan.*

BIRDS

McKENNY, MARGARET. Birds in the Garden and How to Attract Them. *Reynal and Hitchcock.*
McATEE, W. L. Wildfowl Food Plants. *Collegiate Press* (Ames, Iowa).
POUGH, RICHARD H. Audubon Bird Guide. *Doubleday & Co.*

BOTANY

ROBBINS, W. J., and RICKETT, H. W. Botany. *Van Nostrand.*
PLATT, RUTHERFORD. This Green World. *Dodd, Mead.*
SALISBURY, E. J. The Living Garden. *Macmillan.*
ZIMMER, G. F. Popular Dictionary of Botanical Names and Terms. *Dutton.*

BULBS

WILDER, LOUISE BEEBE. Adventures with Hardy Bulbs. *Macmillan.*
WESTON, T. A. All About Flowering Bulbs. *De La Mare.*
WOOD, ALLEN H. Bulbs for Your Garden. *Garden City Pub. Co.*
WISTER, JOHN C. Bulbs for American Gardens. *Stratford.*

CACTI AND SUCCULENTS

HASELTON, SCOTT E. Cacti for the Amateur. *Abbey Garden Press.*
BROWN, J. R. Succulents for the Amateur. *Abbey Garden Press.*
ALEXANDER, E. J. Succulent Plants of New and Old World Deserts. *New York Botanical Garden.*
BORG, JOHN. Cacti. *Macmillan.*

CHRYSANTHEMUMS

CUMMING, ALEX. Hardy Chrysanthemums. *The American Garden Guild.*
LAURIE, ALEX. Chrysanthemums under Glass and Outdoors. *De La Mare.*
SCOTT, DR. ERNEST L. & ALEITA. Chrysanthemums for Pleasure. *Scott.*

COLD FRAMES AND HOTBEDS

SEATON, H. L. and others. Hotbeds and Cold Frames. *Mich. Agric. Ext. Bul. 20* (East Lansing, Mich.).

POST, KENNETH. Structures for Starting and Growing Ornamental Plants. *Cornell Agric. Ext. Bul. 468* (Ithaca, N. Y.).

NISSLEY, C. H. Starting Early Vegetable and Flowering Plants Under Glass. *Orange Judd.*

DAFFODILS

BOWLES, E. A. Handbook of Narcissus. *Hopkinson* (London).

ROYAL HORTICULTURAL SOCIETY. *Classified List of Daffodil Names* (London).

DAFFODIL YEAR BOOK. (*Joint issue of the Royal Horticultural Society and the American Horticultural Society*) (Washington, D.C.).

DAHLIAS

RILEY, MORGAN T. Dahlias. *Orange Judd.*

ROBERTS, J. LOUIS. Modern Dahlias. *Doubleday, Doran.*

ROCKWELL, F. F. Dahlias. *Macmillan.*

DECIDUOUS TREES

PIRONE, P. P. Maintenance of Shade and Ornamental Trees. *Oxford.*

FENSKA, RICHARD R. Tree Expert's Manual. *Dodd, Mead.*

HOTTES, A. C. Book of Trees. *De La Mare.*

COFFIN, MARIAN C. Trees and Shrubs for Landscaping Effects. *Scribner.*

DELPHINIUMS

BAILEY, L. H. Garden of Larkspurs. *Macmillan.*

LEONIAN, LEON H. How to Grow Delphiniums. *Doubleday, Doran.*

PHILLIPS, GEORGE A. Delphiniums, Their History and Cultivation. *Macmillan.*

EVERGREENS

BAILEY, L. H. Cultivated Conifers in North America. *Macmillan.*

KUMLIEN, L. L. Hill's Book of Evergreens. *D. Hill Nursery Co.* (Dundee, Ill.).

ROCKWELL, F. F. Evergreens for the Small Place. *Macmillan.*

FRUITS

KAINS, M. G. Grow Your Own Fruit. *Greenberg.*

AUCHTER, E. C., and KNAPP, H. B. Orchard and Small Fruit Culture. *Wiley.*

HEDRICK, U. P. Fruits for the Home Garden. *Oxford.*

GARDEN CLUB PROGRAMS

HUTTENLOCHER, FAE. The Garden Club Handbook. *Better Homes and Gardens.*

GRAYSON, ESTHER C., ed. Handbook For Flower Shows. *National Council of State Garden Clubs.*

GENERAL PLANT CULTURE

BAILEY, L. H. The Standard Cyclopedia of Horticulture. 3 vols. *Macmillan.*

FREE, MONTAGUE. Gardening; a Complete Guide to Garden Making. *Harcourt, Brace.*

MANNING, LAURENCE. The How and Why of Better Gardening. *Von Nostrand.*

TAYLOR, NORMAN, ed. The Practical Encyclopedia of Gardening. *Garden City Pub. Co.*

SEYMOUR, E. L. D., ed. The New Garden Encyclopedia of Gardening. *Wise.*

WISTER, JOHN C., ed. Woman's Home Companion Garden Book. *Doubleday.*

WOODRUFF, FLEETA BROWNELL. Better Homes & Gardens Garden Book. *Meredith Pub. Co.*

GLADIOLUS

ROCKWELL, F. F. Gladiolus. *Macmillan.*

GREENHOUSES

CHABOT, ERNEST. Greenhouse Gardening for Everyone. *Barrows.*

LAURIE, ALEX, and POESCH, G. H. Commercial Flower Forcing. *Blakiston.*

TAYLOR, K. S., and GREGG, E. W. Winter Flowers in the Sun-heated Pit. *Scribner.*

BAHR, FRITZ. Commercial Floriculture. *De La Mare.*

HERBS

WEBSTER, HELEN N. Herbs. *Hale.*

CLARKSON, ROSETTA E. Herbs, Their Culture and Uses. *Macmillan.*

FOX, HELEN M. Gardening with Herbs for Flavor and Fragrance. *Macmillan.*

————. Gardening for Good Eating. *Macmillan.*

HOUSE PLANTS

FREE, MONTAGUE. All About House Plants. *Doubleday.*

ROCKWELL, F. F., and GRAYSON, ESTHER. Gardening Indoors. *Macmillan.*

POST, KENNETH. Plants and Flowers in the Home. *Orange Judd.*

WILSON, HELEN VAN PELT, and JENKINS, DOROTHY. Enjoy Your House Plants. *Barrows.*

IRISES

MITCHELL, SYDNEY B., Iris for Every Garden. *Barrows.*

WISTER, JOHN C. The Iris. *Orange Judd.*

ROCKWELL, F. F. Irises. *Macmillan.*

AMERICAN IRIS SOCIETY. *Alphabetical Iris Check List.*

LANDSCAPING AND DESIGN

CAUTLEY, MARJORIE S. Garden Design. *Dodd, Mead.*

ROBINSON, F. B. Planting Design. *The American Garden Guild.*

GOLDSMITH, MARGARET O. Designs for Outdoor Living. *Stewart.*

ORTLOFF, H. S., and RAYMORE, H. B. Garden Planning and Building. *The American Garden Guild.*

LAWNS

SPRAGUE, H. B. Better Lawns for Homes and Parks. *The American Garden Guild.*

PARKER, CHARLES W. The Lawn. *Hale.*

LILIES

deGRAFF, JAN. The New Book of Lilies. *Barrows.*

MACNEIL, ALAN & ESTHER. Garden Lilies. *Oxford.*

SLATE, G. L. Lilies for American Gardens. *Scribner.*

PEONIES

BOYD, JAMES, ed. Peonies, the Manual of the American Peony Society. *Mt. Pleasant Press* (Harrisburg, Pa.)

ROCKWELL, F. F. Peonies. *Macmillan.*

HARDING, ALICE H. Peonies in the Little Garden. *Little, Brown.*

PERENNIALS

HOTTES, A. C. The Book of Perennials. *De La Mare.*

SEDGWICK, M. C., and CAMERON, ROBERT. The Garden Month by Month. *Garden City Pub. Co.*

ORTLOFF, H. S. Perennial Gardens. *Macmillan.*

PESTS

WESTCOTT, CYNTHIA. The Plant Doctor. *Lippincott.*

———. Gardener's Bug Book. *Doubleday.*

———. Plant Disease Handbook. *Van Nostrand.*

FELT, E. P., and RANKIN, W. H. Insects and Diseases of Ornamental Trees and Shrubs. *Macmillan.*

HEALD, F. D. Manual of Plant Diseases. *McGraw-Hill.*

PLANT BREEDING

HAYES, H. K., and IMMER, F. R. Methods of Plant Breeding. *McGraw-Hill.*

BAILEY, L. H. Plant Breeding. *Macmillan.*

LAWRENCE, W. J. C. Practical Plant Breeding. *Allen* (London).

CRANE, M. B., and LAWRENCE, W. J. C. The Genetics of Garden Plants. *Macmillan.*

POOLS AND ACCESSORIES (Construction)

RAMSEY, L. W., and LAWRENCE, C. H. Garden Pools, Large and Small. *Macmillan.*

LONGYEAR, WILLIAM. How to Make Garden Pools. *Doubleday, Doran.*

PROPAGATION

ADRIANCE, G. W., and BRISON, F. R. Propagation of Horticultural Plants. *McGraw-Hill.*

FAIRBURN, DR. DAVID G. Plant Propagation for the Garden. *Doubleday.*

KAINS, M. G., and McQUESTEN, L. M. Propagation of Plants. *Orange Judd.*

HOTTES, A. C. Plant Propagation. *De La Mare.*

ROCK GARDENS

SYMONS-JEUNE, B. H. B. Natural Rock Gardening. *Scribner.*

WILDER, LOUISE BEEBE. Pleasures and Problems of a Rock Garden. *Garden City Pub. Co.*

BISSLAND, J. H. The Rock Garden. *Hale.*

ROOF AND CITY GARDENS

McKENNY, MARGARET, and SEYMOUR, E. L. D. Your City Garden. *Appleton-Century.*

GOMEZ, NATALIE. Your Garden in the City. *Oxford.*

ROSES

ALLEN, DR. RAY C. Roses for Every Garden. *Macfarland.*

AMERICAN ROSE SOCIETY. What Every Rose Grower Should Know. *Amer. Rose Society.*

NICOLAS, J. H. Rose Manual. *Doubleday, Doran.*

McFARLAND, J. H. Modern Roses II. *Macmillan.*

SHRUBS

VAN MELLE, P. J. Shrubs and Trees for the Small Place. *Scribner.*

VAN DERSAL, WILLIAM. Ornamental American Shrubs. *Oxford.*

HOTTES, A. C. Book of Shrubs. *De La Mare.*

SOILLESS GARDENING

LAURIE, ALEX. Soilless Culture Simplified. *The American Garden Guild.*

SOILS AND FERTILIZERS

LYON, T. L., and BUCKMAN, H. O. The Nature and Properties of Soils. *Macmillan.*

MILLAR, C. E., and TURK, L. M. Fundamentals of Soil Science. *Wiley.*

TULIPS

HALL, A. D. Book of the Tulip. *Stokes.*

———. The Genus Tulipa. *Royal Horticultural Society* (London).

VEGETABLES

COULTER, FRANCIS C. A Manual of Home Vegetable Gardening. *Blue Ribbon Books.*

NISSLEY, CHARLES H. Pocket Book of Vegetable Gardening. *Pocket Books.*

VINES

HOTTES, A. C. A Little Book of Climbing Plants. *De La Mare.*

BEAN, W. J. Wall Shrubs and Hardy Climbers. *Macmillan.*

JENKINS, DOROTHY H. Vines for Every Garden. *Doubleday, Doran.*

WATER GARDENS

PERRY, FRANCES. Water Gardening. *Scribner.*

NIKLITSCHEK, ALEXANDER. Water Lilies and Water Plants. *Scribner.*

SAWYER, ROBERT V., and PERKINS, E. H. Water Gardens and Goldfish. *De La Mare.*

WEEDS

MUENSCHER, W. C. Weeds. *Macmillan.*

GEORGIA, A. E. A Manual of Weeds. *Macmillan.*

SPENCER, E. R. Just Weeds. *Scribner.*

SEED WORLD. Weeds and Weed Seeds. *Seed World* (Chicago).

WILDFLOWERS

AIKEN, G. D. Pioneering with Wild Flowers. *Daye.*

BIRDSEYE, CLARENCE & ELEANOR. Growing Woodland Plants. *Oxford.*

McKENNY, MARGARET. The Wild Garden. *Doubleday, Doran.*

ROBERTS, E. A., and REHMANN, ELSA. American Plants for American Gardens. *Macmillan.*

WHERRY, EDGAR T., Ph.D. Wildflower Guide. *Doubleday.*

FLOWER, FRUIT, AND TREE SOCIETIES OF THE UNITED STATES AND CANADA

(*with Secretaries*)

AFRICAN-VIOLET SOCIETY OF AMERICA, Neil C. Miller, Layton's Lake, Penns Grove, N.J.

AMERICAN AMARYLLIS SOCIETY (branch of AMERICAN PLANT LIFE SOCIETY).

AMERICAN BEGONIA SOCIETY, Mrs. A. N. Hartwell, 1719 Alamitos Ave., Monrovia, Cal.

AMERICAN CAMELLIA SOCIETY, Sam P. Harn, Box 2398, University Station, Gainesville, Fla.

AMERICAN CARNATION SOCIETY, Leland T. Kintzele, P.O. Box 1138, Denver 1, Col.

AMERICAN DAHLIA SOCIETY, Andrew J. Mulcahy, 20 Marshal Ave., Floral Park, N.Y.

AMERICAN DELPHINIUM SOCIETY, Carl Grant Wilson, 22150 Euclid Ave., Cleveland 17, Ohio.

AMERICAN FERN SOCIETY, Miss Edith Scamman, Gray Herbarium, Harvard University, Cambridge, Mass.

AMERICAN FORESTRY ASSOCIATION, S. L. Frost, 919 17th St. N.W., Washington 6, D.C.

AMERICAN FUCHSIA SOCIETY, Mrs. Ellen L. O'Brien, California Academy of Sciences, Golden Gate Park, San Francisco 18, Cal.

AMERICAN HIBISCUS SOCIETY, J. K. Brower, P.O. Box 51, Palm Beach, Fla.

AMERICAN HORTICULTURAL COUNCIL, J. Franklin Styer, Concordville, Pa.

AMERICAN HORTICULTURAL SOCIETY, Dr. W. Andrew Archer, 821 Washington Loan & Trust Bldg., Washington, D.C.

AMERICAN IRIS SOCIETY, Geddes Douglas, Franklin Road, Brentwood, Tenn.

AMERICAN NATURE ASSOCIATION, James A. O'Hearn, 1214 16th St. N.W., Washington 6, D.C.

AMERICAN ORCHID SOCIETY, Gordon W. Dillon, Botanical Museum, Harvard University, Cambridge 38, Mass.

AMERICAN ORIENTAL POPPY SOCIETY (no record since 1948).

AMERICAN PELARGONIUM SOCIETY (no record since 1948).

AMERICAN PENTSTEMON SOCIETY, Mrs. Edward M. Babb, 213 Lambert St., Portland, R. 5, Maine.

AMERICAN PEONY SOCIETY, George W. Peyton, Box 1, Rapidan, Va.

AMERICAN PLANT LIFE SOCIETY, E. Frederick Smith, P.O. Box 2398, Stanford University, Cal.

AMERICAN POMOLOGICAL SOCIETY, W. D. Armstrong, Princeton, Ky.

AMERICAN POPPY SOCIETY (no record since 1948).

AMERICAN PRIMROSE SOCIETY, Mrs. Earl A. Marshall, 1172 S.E. 55 Ave., Portland 15, Ore.

AMERICAN RHODODENDRON SOCIETY, Mrs. Ruth M. Hansen, 3514 N. Russet St., Portland, Ore.

AMERICAN ROCK GARDEN SOCIETY, Mrs. Dorothy Ebel Hansell, 19 Pittsford Way, Summit, N.J.

AMERICAN ROSE SOCIETY, R. C. Allen, 1316 Derry St., Harrisburg, Pa.

AMERICAN SOCIETY FOR HORTICULTURAL SCIENCE, Dr. Freeman S. Howlett, Ohio Agricultural Experiment Station, Wooster, Ohio.

AMERICAN SOYBEAN ASSOCIATION, George M. Strayer, Hudson, Iowa.

AMERICAN SWEET PEA SOCIETY (no record since 1948).

AMERICAN ZINNIA SOCIETY, C. L. Derr, 1940 Queens Road, Pasadena, Cal.

BROMELIAD SOCIETY, Victoria Padilla, 647 S. Saltar Ave., Los Angeles 40, Cal.

BULB SOCIETY, no sec'y, but office at: 2446 Huntington Drive, San Marino, Cal.

CACTUS AND SUCCULENT SOCIETY OF AMERICA, Miss Mary Glade, 7600 Verdugo Crestline Drive, Tujunga, Cal.

CAMELLIA SOCIETY OF AMERICA (American Camellia Society).

CHRYSANTHEMUM SOCIETY OF AMERICA, James Mikkelsen, P.O. Box 1536, West End Station, Ashtabula, Ohio.

CYMBIDIUM SOCIETY, Edwin L. Reed, 2026 Marengo Ave., S. Pasadena, Cal.

EPIPHYLLUM SOCIETY OF AMERICA, Mrs. Martha Maxwell, 500 Grove Place, Glendale 6, Cal.

GOURD SOCIETY OF AMERICA, Mrs. Dora Walker, Horticultural Hall, 300 Massachusetts Ave., Boston 15, Mass.

HEMEROCALLIS SOCIETY, George E. Lenington, Box 39, Kansas City, Mo.

HERB SOCIETY OF AMERICA, Mrs. Frances R. Williams, 234 Highland Ave., Winchester, Mass.

HOLLY SOCIETY OF AMERICA, Harry W. Dengler, Extension Service, College Park, Md.

NATIONAL CHRYSANTHEMUM SOCIETY, Carl Toepler, 86 Van Buren Ave., Teaneck, N.J.

NATIONAL GLADIOLUS SOCIETY, Mrs. Helen E. Bolton, 6728 2nd St. N.W., Washington, D.C.

NATIONAL PECAN ASSOCIATION (no record since 1948).

NATIONAL SHADE TREE CONFERENCE, L. C. Chadwick, Dept. of Horticulture, Ohio State University, Columbus, Ohio.

NATIONAL SNAPDRAGON SOCIETY, Helen Windmiller, 2997 S. Hight St., Columbus, Ohio.

NATIONAL TULIP SOCIETY, Felix R. Tyroler, 37 West 43 Street, New York 18, N.Y.

NEW ENGLAND GLADIOLUS SOCIETY (national in scope), Miss Marian P. Ayer, 12 Newbury Park, Needham, Mass.

NORTH AMERICAN LILY SOCIETY, Dr. Forrest Kendall, Douglaston, N.Y.

NORTHERN NUT GROWERS ASSOCIATION, J. C. McDaniel, State Capitol, Nashville 3, Tenn.

WILD FLOWER PRESERVATION SOCIETY, Edna L. Stone, 3740 Oliver St. N.W., Washington 15, D.C.

CANADA LILY SOCIETY, Arthur Peiffer, 520 Duke St., Preston, Ont., Canada.

CANADIAN ALPINE ASSOCIATION (no record since 1948).

CANADIAN FORESTRY ASSOCIATION, Norton J. Anderson, 679 Belmont St., Montreal 3, Que., Canada.

CANADIAN GLADIOLUS SOCIETY, Mrs. J. A. Carleton, 166 Willow Road, Guelph, Ont., Canada.

CANADIAN HORTICULTURAL COUNCIL, L. F. Burrows, 262 Wellington St., Ottawa, Canada.

CANADIAN IRIS SOCIETY, L. Laking, Royal Botanical Gardens, Hamilton, Ont., Canada.

ROSE SOCIETY OF ONTARIO, John H. Berry, 108 Southvale Drive, Leaside, Toronto 17, Ont., Canada.

Index

Index

Abelia, 304, 306
Abies concolor, 347
Abutilon, 901
  greenhouse, 154
  propagation, 901
Acacia, 380
  greenhouse, 154
Acanthopanax, 306
Accent in landscaping, 1296
Accessories, garden, 1314-36
Achimenes, 249
Acidanthera, 249
Acidification of soils, 34-36
Acidity
  preferences of common plants, 33-
  34
  vegetable garden, 639-40
Acid
  leafmold, 37
  levulinic, 87
  soils, 9, 34-35; fertilizer for, 36
Aconite (Aconitum), 226
  regional, Colorado, 1215
  troubles, 1047-48
African Daisy, 176, 180
African Lily, 249
African-Violet, 902-7
  culture, 902-4
  fertilizer for, 902
  origin, 906-7
  propagation by cuttings, 905-6; by
  division, 905
  temperature for, 902
  troubles, 904-5, 1048-49; lice,
  1049; mealy bug, 904, 1048;
  mildew, 904; red spider, 905
  varieties, 906
  watering, 902-3
Agapanthus, 249
  indoors, 978
Ageratum
  annual, 176
  hardy, 223
  troubles: root aphids, 1048; white
  fly, 1048
Aglaonema simplex, 930
Agrico fertilizer, 81
Agricultural drain tile, 30; lime,
  38-39
Ailanthus, 270-71
Air circulation for blooming plants,
  1406
Akebia, 400
Alabama, regional problems, 1190-
  94

annuals for, 1190
perennials for, 1190
individual plants:
  apple, 1191; azaleamum, 1191;
  azaleas, 1191; bulbs, 1191; camellia, 1191; crapemyrtle, 1191-
  92; daylilies, 1192; fruit trees,
  1192; fuchsia, 1192; gladiolus,
  1192; grass, Bermuda, 1192;
  grass, nut, 1192; herbs, 1192;
  iris, 1193; nandina, 1193; orange,
  1193; pansies, 1193; peony,
  1193; rhododendron, 1193; rock-
  garden plants, 1194; roses, 1194;
  tulips, 1194
Albizzia julibrissin rosea, 325
Alcohol for mealy bugs, 1048
Alfalfa, 7, 60, 63
Alkaline soil, 9
  improving, 37-38
Alleghenyvine, 398
Allium, 240, 721
Allspice tree, greenhouse, 154-55
Almond, 863
  flowering, 306
  regional, California, 1204
Alpines, 1362
  for beginner, 1362
  difficult, 1362
  not difficult, 1362
  site for, 1362
  soil for, 1362
  winter protection for, 1362
Alstroemeria, 249
  Alstroemeria aurantiaca, 249
  regional, Washington, 1279-80
Aluminum, 4
  sulfate, 9
Alyssum
  annual, 176, 1365
  hardy, 215
  Alyssum saxatile, 1365
  indoors, 926
  troubles, 1049
Amarcrinum
  troubles, 1049
Amaryllis (hippeastrum), 250
  Amaryllis belladonna, 250
  Amaryllis formosissima, 258
  Amaryllis halli, 246
  fertilizer for, 979
  greenhouse, 155
  hardy, 246
  indoors, 978-81
  planting, 978
  regional; Florida, 1216; Georgia,

1419

troubles, 1151
varieties, 695
Cedar
Cedar-of-Lebanon, 346
Japanese Temple, 346
Red (*see* Juniper), 349–50
regional, California, 1206
troubles, 1061; apple rust, on apple, 792, 1175; cedar, 1061; crabapple, 1068; hawthorn, 1089; red spider, 1061; rust, 1036, 1061
Celeriac, 699
Celery, 695–99
blanching of, 698
blight, 698, 1151
culture, 695–98
storage of, 698–99
storage outdoors, 663
troubles, 1151; seed treatment, 1151; slugs, 1151; tarnished plant bug, 1151
varieties, 699
Centaurea, 179
regional, North Florida, 1221
Centipede, 1009
Grass, 1219, 1241
Cercis, 294
Cereus, night-blooming, 967–68
Chaenomeles, 327–28
Chaenomeles japonica alpina, 327
Chaenomeles lagenaria, 327
Chamaecyparis obtusa nana, 347
Charcoal, 74
Chastetree, 310–11
Chayote, 699–700
Chemical
fertilizer, 76
gardening, 89
indoors, 89
Chemistry of compost heap, 69
Cherry, 794–97
cross-pollination, 795
culture, 794–96
fertilizer for, 794
flowering, 284
planting, 794
pruning, 794–95
regional: Illinois, 1228; Kansas, 1237; Missouri, 1251; Minnesota, 1246
soil for, 794
sour, 766
sweet, 766
troubles, 796–97, 1177–78; aphids, 1177–78; birds, 797; circulio, 797–98; leaf spot, 1178; rot, 1178; slugs, 1038; spraying, 1177–78; worms, 1178
varieties, 766
Chervil, 1345
Chestnut, 863–64
Chinese, blight-resistant, 863
soil for, 863

Chicken manure, 53
Chickweed, 1400
Chicory, 700–1
culture, 700
cutting of, 701
forcing of, 700
Child's garden, 1387–88
location, 1387
planning, 1388
plants for, 1388
space, 1387
vegetables for, 1388
Chimaphila, 1387
Chimney, perennials and annuals for, 1321
Chinch bug, 1009–10
creosote for, 1010
in grain, 1010
Chinese Cabbage, 701
storage of, 701
Chinese Elm, 273–74
for hedge, 390
Chinese-evergreen, 930
Chinese Jujube or Date, 857–58
Chineselantern
troubles, 1061
Chinese-sacred-lily, 989
Chionanthus, 288
Chionodoxa, 242
for rock garden, 1362–63
Chives, 701–2, 1345
cookery of, 702
culture, 701–2
indoors, 900
Chlorine, 46
Chlorophyll, 4
Chlorophytum variegatum, 937
Chloropicrin, 1010
for fungi, 1010; insects, 1010; nematodes, 1010; soil sterilization, 1039–40; weeds, 1010
Christmas Begonia, 909
Christmas Cactus, 968–70
Christmasrose, 219–20
Christmas tree, 347–48; regional, Missouri, 1252
Chrysanthemum, 456–69
culture of, 460
fertilizer, 457
greenhouse, 158
indoors, 940
Introduction, 456
planting, 458
problems, 463
propagation of, 465
regional: Arizona, 1195; California, 1206; Illinois, 1228; Iowa, 1234–35; Louisiana, 1240; Michigan, 1242; Mississippi, 1249; Missouri, 1252; Wisconsin, 1282–83
soil preparation, 457

transplanting, 458
troubles, 467, 1061–65; aphids, 467, 1063–64; caterpillars, 1064; crown gall, 1065; crown rot, 1063; cucumber beetle, 1064; diabrotica beetle, 1064; dodder, 1063; gall midge, 1065; grasshoppers, 1064; leaf nematodes, 467, 1062; leaf spot, 467; Mexican bean beetle, 1064; mildew, 467, 1062–63; septoria leaf spot, 1063; stalk borer, 1065; termites, 1065; verticillium wilt, 1061–62
varieties, 467
winter care of, 459

Cineraria, 913–14
greenhouse, 159
propagation from seed, 913–14

Cinnamomum camphora, 930
Cinquefoil, 1365
Cissus, 961–2
Cissus antarctica, 962
Cissus rhombifolia, 961
Citrus fruits, 949–50
indoors, 949–50
varieties for, 950
regional: California, 1207–8; Florida, 1217; Texas, 1273
troubles, 1065; aphids, 1065; mealy bug, 1065; nematode-resistant, 1032; scale, 1065; white fly, 1065

City
annuals for, 100–1
bulbs for, 101
environment, 100–3
environmental problems, 103
evergreens for, 101
ferns in house in, 955
flowering trees for, 102
gardens, 1388
designing, 1298
making, 1388
ground covers for, 101–2
house plants in, 894–95
lawn for, 102, 569–70
perennials for, 101
plant material for, 100–3
rock garden for, 102
roses for, 102
shrubs for, 102
trees for, 102–3
vines for, 103

Cladrastis lutea, 296
Clary, 1345
Clay, 1
blue, 14
gray, 14
pipe, 15
red, 15
rocky, 15
white, 15
yellow. 15

Clay soil, 10, 13, 36
coal ashes on, 13
fertilizer for, 14
improvement of, 13–14
plants for, 16

Claytonia, 1386
Cleft grafting, 139, 780
Clematis, 402–4
culture, 402–3
propagation, 404
pruning, 403–4
regional, Michigan, 1245
species and varieties, 402
troubles, 1066–67; blister beetles, 1066; stem rot, 1066

Climbers (*see* Vines), 394–406
regional, Arizona, 1195
Central Florida, 1218

Climbingfern, 1383
Climbing roses, 449–50
pruning, 437
regional: Illinois, 1231; Minnesota, 1249; Wyoming, 1286
varieties, 450
winter protection of, 433

Clivia, 254
indoors, 984

Clover, 7, 60
Crimson, 60, 63
Red, 60
Sweet, 60
White, 560–61
as weed, 1404

Club mosses, 1384
Clubs, hydroponic, 89
Coal ashes, 31–32
on clay soil, 13
on vegetable garden, 639

Cobaea scandens, 397
Coco Grass, 1275
Codiaeum, 931
Codling moth
on apple, 791, 1173–74; pear, 804; quince, 1186
biological control, 1006
spray for, 1171

Cod-liver oil, 88
Coffee grounds, 74
Coke ashes, 32
Colchicine, 87
Colchicum, 242
Cold frames, 140–43
care of plants in, 141–43
construction of, 140
fertilizer for, 143
forcing in, 142
starting plants in, 141
vegetables in, 671
winter protection for, 143

Coleus
indoors, 931
troubles, 1066

1424

Collard troubles, 1151–52
Colocasia, 254
Color
combinations in garden, 1304
foliage for, 1304
planning for, 1304–5
Colorado, regional problems, 1215–16
annuals and perennials for, 1215–16
individual plants:
boysenberry, 1215; ground cover, 1215; monkshood, 1215; pansy, 1216; roses, 1216; sweetpea, 1216
soil, 1194–95
Columbine, 220–21
regional: Central Florida, 1218; Texas, 1273
troubles, 1067; borer, 1067; crown rot, 1067; leaf miner, 1067; red spider, 1067
wild, 1382
Commercial fertilizers, 7, 81
"complete," 79, 80
in vegetable garden, 639
Complete commercial fertilizers, 79, 80
Compost, 63
formula, 6
for lawns, 590–91
heap, 64
chemistry of, 69
diseases and pests in 68, 1010
leaf, 66
mushroom, 67
special problems, 67
Contact insecticides, 1000, 1010–11
Convallaria, 242–43
Cooperia, regional: Mississippi, 1249
Copper, 46
Copper oxide, for seed treatment, 1037
Coralbell
mealy bug on, 1027
Coriander, 1345
Corktree, 274
Corms, hardy, 236–48
propagation of, 128–29
Corn, sweet, 702–5
culture, 702–3
troubles, 1152–53; bacterial wilt, 1153; borer, 704, 1152–53; chinch bugs, 1010; crows, 704; ear worm, 704, 1152; Japanese beetle, 1023, 1153; seed treatment, 1037; smut, 704, 1153; squirrels, 1153; wire worms, 1047
varieties, 704–5
when to pick, 662

Cornelian Cherry, 313
Cornflower, 179
Cornus (see also Dogwood), 286–88, 312–13
Corrosive sublimate
for dahlias, 1070
Cosmos, 179–80
troubles, 1068; Japanese-beetle resistant, 1023
Costmary, 1345
Cotinus, 295
Cotoneaster, 311
regional, California, 1208
Cottonseed meal, 4, 71
Cover Crops
for fruit orchard, 771–72
lawns, 587–88
vegetable garden, 641–42
Cow manure, 55
Cowpeas, 6, 60
Crabapple, 285; troubles, 1068–69; rust, 1068; aphids, 1068–69; cankerworm, 1069; woolly aphids, 1068–69
Varieties, 285
Bechtel, 285
Carmine, 285
Dolgo, 285
flowering, 285
Sargent, 285
Toringo, 285
Crab Grass, 596–98, 1401
in lawn, 596–98
Crab meal, 74
Cranberry, 853–54
culture, 853
as fertilizer, 74
propagation, 853
pruning, 854
soil for, 853
Cranberrybush, dwarf, 332
Crapemyrtle, 311–12
indoors, 950
regional, Alabama, 1191; Illinois, 1228; Louisiana, 1240; Ohio, 1265
troubles, 1068
Crassula, 973
Crawfish, 1011
Creeping Fig, 960
Creeping Jenny, 1382
as weed, 1401
Crimson Clover, 60, 63
Crinum, varieties, 254
indoors, 984
Crocosmia, 258
Crocus, 243
regional, Michigan, 1242–43
for rock garden, 1363
troubles, 1069
Croquet Lawn, 1323

Crotalaria, 60
Croton, 931
Crown Imperial, 244
Crown-of-thorns, 973
Crown rot, 1011
    of aconite, 1048; campanula,
    1059–60; carrot, 1151; colum-
    bine, 1067; delphinium, 1073;
    iris, 1096; larkspur, 1098–99;
    lupine, 1104; penstemon, 1111;
    sedum, 1130; stocks, 1132
Crucifers, troubles, 691
Cryolite, 1012
    for blister beetle, 1007, 1012; cu-
    cumber beetle, 1012; flea beetle,
    1016–17; Mexican bean beetle,
    1012; vegetables, 1042
Cryptanthus, indoors, 931
Cryptomeria, 346
    dormant spraying, 1014
Cube, 1011
Cucumber, 705–8
    crossing of cucumber and musk-
    mellons, 706
    culture, 705–6
    fertilizer for, 706
    picking of, 706
    training of, 706
    transplanting of, 706
    troubles, 707, 1154–55; anthrac-
    nose, 707; bacterial wilt, 707;
    beetles, 707, 718, 742, 1154;
    leaf spot, 707; lice, 1154–55;
    mosaic, 1155; scab, 707; seed
    treatment, 1037–38; squash bug,
    1154; white fly, 1155
    varieties, 707
Cucumber Tree, 291
Cultivation
    of plants, 119
    roses, 423
    soil, 28–29
    vegetables, 655–57
Cultivators, garden, 29
    for vegetables, 656
Culture
    annuals, 166–68
    bulbs, hardy, 238–39
    bulbs, tender, 248
    chrysanthemums, 460
    dahlias, 525
    delphiniums, 472
    evergreens, 337–42
    gladiolus, 537
    gourds, 1395–97
    gravel, 88
    greenhouse, 149–54
    herbs, 1340–1
    irises, 479
    lilies, 490
    narcissi, 507
    peonies, 497
    perennials, 209–10
    roses, 421

sand, 88
shrubs, deciduous, 262–63
    ericaceous, 367–68
soilless, 88
trees, deciduous, 262–63
tulips, 515
vegetables, 673–758
water, 88
Cup-and-saucer vine, 398
Cuprocide
    for seed treatment, 1037
Curbings, 1315–16
    ground covers for, 107
Currant, 761, 854–57
    culture, 854
    fertilizer for, 854
    planting, 854
    propagation from cuttings, 856
    pruning, 855
    regional: Minnesota, 1246
    soil for, 854
    troubles, 856–57, 1178–79;
    aphids, 856, 1178; blister rust,
    white-pine, 857, 1178; currant
    worm, 856; fruit fly, 1179; leaf
    spot, 857
    varieties, 766, 856
Cutting and exhibition
    flowers for, 1305–6
    roses for, 425
Cuttings, 129–33
    half-ripe wood, 129
    hardwood, 129
    leaf, 133–34
    propagation by, 129–33
    propagation of perennials by, 213–
    14
        roses by, 444
        trees and shrubs by, 270
    root, 133–34
    root stimulants for, 131–32
    rooted, care of, 132
    rooting medium for, 131
    softwood, 129
Cutworm, 1011–12
Cyanogas
    for ants, 1002; mealy bugs, 1026;
    woodchucks, 1047
Cycas revoluta, 937
Cyclamen, 940–43
    propagation, 942
        from seed, 942
    repotting, 942
    troubles, 942, 1069–70
    bacterial soft rot, 1069; mite,
    942, 1069–70
Cydonia, 327–28
Cymbalaria muralia, 962
Cyperus alternifolius, 938
    propagation, 938
Cypress, 347
    Dwarf Hinoki, 347
    Monterey for hedge, 390
    regional, California, 1208

Hoe, Dutch, 1333
  onion, 1333
  scuffle, 656, 1333
Holly (*see* Ilex), 362–65; American, 362–65; Chinese, 264; English, 362–65
  culture, 362–65
  indoors, 932
  propagation, 364–65
  pruning, 364
  regional: California, 1210; Indiana, 1233; Iowa, 1235; Michigan, 1244; Texas, 1275
  sex of trees, 363–64
Hollyfern, 957
Hollyhock, 225
  troubles: Japanese beetle, 1021; red spider, 1091; rust, 1090–91
Home vegetable garden, 602–758
Honey locust, 275
Honeysuckle, 315, 405–6; Bush, 315; Amur, 315; Blueleaf, 315; Fragrant, 315; Morrow, 315; Tatarian, 315
  troubles, 1091
Hormones, 87
Hornbeam, 275
Horseshoe-pitching area, 1322–33
Horsechestnut, 275–76
Horse manure, 58
Horse-radish, 710
Horticulture, meaning of, 1405
Hosta troubles, 1091
Hose, "porous," 669
Hotbeds, 143–45; heating, 144–45; making, 143; ventilating, 145; watering, 145; winter protection, 145
Hotkaps, 655, 670
  use of, for muskmelon, 716
House plants, 869–992
  annuals and biennials as, 925–26
  autumn care, 885
  bulbs, 975–92
  cacti, and succulents, 965–75
  drainage, 880
  easy to grow, 895
  environment, 887–88
  exposure, 885–87
  feeding, 880–81
  ferns, 954–58
  flowering, 901–25
  foliage, 928–38
  gift, 938–47
  humidity, 871, 895
  Introduction, 869–78
  lifting in autumn, 877
  potting, 879–80
  potting soil, 875–76
  propagation from slips, 892–93
  pruning and training, 873

  repotting, 874–75, 879–80
  rest period, 878
  sanitation, 890–92
  in shade, 886
  shrubs, 947–54
  soil for, 878–79
  summer care, 884–85
    quarters, 876–77
  syringing, 890
  temperature, 870–71, 883–84
  troubles, 888–90, 1091–94; aphids, 889, 1092; insect control, 1093; lice, 1092; maggots, 1092; mealy bugs, 889, 1091; mildew, 1094; mosquitoes, 1094; nematodes, 1094; red spider, 889–90, 1093; scale, 890, 1092; white fly, 890, 1092; worms, 1093
  ventilation, 873, 884
  vines, 958–64
  watering, 872–3, 881–2
  for winter bloom, 894
Houstonia serpyllifolia, 1381
Hoya carnosa, 964
Humidity greenhouse, 150
  house plants, 871, 895
Humus, 1, 47–48
  for lawns, 588–90
  in soil, function of, 47
Hyacinth, 245
  indoors, 988
  regional: Nebraska, 1256; Texas, 1275–76
Hybrid perpetual roses, 451
  sweetbriar, 455
  tea, 452–53
Hybridizing perennials, 214
  roses, 447
Hydrangea, 315–20; Bigleaf, 315; Climbing, 315, 406; French, 316–18; *Hydrangea macrophylla rosea*, 315; *Hydrangea petiolaris*, 315; Oakleaf, 315–17, Panicle, 315; Pegee, 316–17
  changing color of, 318–19
  culture, 315–16
  greenhouse, 160
  indoors, 943–44
  troubles, 1094; leaf spot, 1094; mildew, 1094
  varieties, 315
Hydrated lime, 38–39
Hydrogen, 4
Hydroponic clubs, 89
Hydrosme, 256
  Hydrosme rivieri, indoors, 988
Hymenocallis, indoors, 989
Hyssop, 1346–47
Iberis sempervirens, 217
Idaho, regional problems, 1226–27
  individual plants:
    daisies, 1226
    hedges, 1226

Landscaping, 1287–1336; accent in, 1296; backgrounds in, 1301–2; balance in, 1295; banks, 1313; evergreens in, 1290–91; focal point in, 1295; garden axis in, 1295; garden pools in, 1329–30; proportion in, 1296; shrubs in, 1291–93; slopes, 1313; temporary home, 1298; terminal feature in, 1295; trees in, 1288–90; vines in, 1293–94; vista in, 1295; with shrubs, 1311

Lantana
indoors, 953
regional, Wisconsin, 1284
Weeping, indoors, 953

Lapeirousia, 258

Larch, 276

Larkspur, 180
troubles, 1098–99

Larvacide, 85, 1010
for fungi, 1010; insects, 1010; nematodes, 1010; soil sterilization, 1039–40; weeds, 1010

Lath house, regional, California, 1204

Lathyrus latifolius, 227

Laurel for hedge, 391

Laurus, 380

Lavender, 1347–48; care, 1347; harvesting, 1347; propagation from cuttings, 1347–48; from seeds, 1347; regional, Missouri, 1253; winter protection, 1347

Lawns
basic requirements, 543–54
Bent, 570–77
from stolons, 574–75
calendar of operations, 552
care of new, 549, 579–81
city, 102, 569–70
composts for, 590–91
cover crops for, 587–88
diseases, 551, 593–94
drainage, 557
edging, 586–87
grading, 547, 552–54
grass seed mixtures, 548, 558–60
humus and peatmoss for, 588–90
for landscape effects, 1325–26
liming, 592–93
maintenance of established, 581–84
manures for, 591–92
moss, 577–78
mowers, 584–85
mowing, 550, 584
peatmoss for, 588–90
pests, 595–96
play areas, 567–68
preparation
of soil for, 546–47
for sowing, 555–56
quantity of seed needed, 563
regional: Alabama, 1192; Califor-

nia, 1200–1; Florida, 1219; Georgia, 1223–24; Iowa, 1235; Kansas, 1238; Louisiana, 1241; Mississippi, 1250; New Mexico, 1258–59; North and South Carolina, 1261; North and South Dakota, 1263; Oklahoma, 1266; Texas, 1275; Washington, 1280; Wisconsin, 1282
rehabilitation of old, 578–79
rolling, 587
seeding and sodding, 548
service areas, 568
shaded areas, 566–67
sodding, 565–66
soil for Bent, 570
sowing, 562
sowing slopes and terraces, 563
troubles, 593–96; 1099; brown patch, 576; chinch bugs, 576, 1099; damping off, 576; dogs, 1099; fungous diseases, 1017–20; Japanese beetle, 577, 1021; May beetle grubs, 576; moles, 1099; pythium, 576; sod webworm, 577; sunscald, 576
types of turf, 544
watering, 550, 585–86
weed control, 550, 596–600
weeds and pests, 575–77

Layering
kinds of, 134–35
propagation by, 134–36
roses, 446

Lead arsenate, 1024–25
for Asiatic beetle, 1004; bag-worms, 1005; caterpillars, 1111; earthworms, 1015; fall canker-worm, 1016; grub-proofing, 1024–25; Japanese beetle, 1022; leaf miners, 1050; slugs, 1038; ter-mites, 1045; white grubs, 1046

Leaf composts, 66

Leaf cuttings, 133–34

Leaf miners
of arborvitae, 1050; birch, 1055; boxwood, 1056; columbine, 1067; delphinium, 1076

Leafmold, 37, 47, 71
acid, 37
oak, 37

Leaf spots, 996

Leather dust, 75

Leaves, 66
structure of, 92

Leeks, 712

Legumes, 62
inoculant powders for, 63

Lemon, indoors, 949
regional, California, 1207

Lemon oil, 1025

Lemon-scented geranium, 922, 1389

Nevada regional problems, 1257–58
  individual plants:
    azalea, 1257–58
    fruit trees, 1258
    roses, 1258
New Mexico regional problems, 1258–60
  individual plants and problems:
    dahlias, 1258
    fruits, bush, 1258
    fruits, tree, 1258
    garden, irrigated for flowers, 1260
    grass, 1258
    lawn, 1258–59
    roses, 1259–60
    soil, 1194–95
    strawberries, 1260
New Zealand spinach, 740
Nicotine dust, 1031
  for slugs, 1038
Nicotine sulfate, 1031
  for aphids, 1002; cyclamen mite, 1029; lace bugs, 1024; leaf miners, 1050; spittle bugs, 1041; thrips, 1085
Nitrate of soda, 4, 77
  applied to vegetable garden, 634
Nitrogen, 4–5, 44–45
  deficiency, 44
  for vegetable garden, 633
Norfolk-Island-Pine, 933
  regional, California, 1211
North and South Carolina, regional problems, 1260–63
  individual plants:
    camellia, 1260–61
    evergreens, 1261
    gardenia, 1260–61
    grass, 1261
    nandina, 1261
    pansy, 1262
    peony, 1252
    perennials, 1262
    roses, 1262
    shrubs, 1263
    sweetpea, 1263
    trees, 1263
North and South Dakota, regional problems, 1263–64
  individual plants:
    daffodils, 1263
    Grass, Kentucky Blue, 1263
    Lily, Regal, 1263–64
    nut trees, 1264
    peony, 1264
    perennials, 1264
    roses, 1264
    tulip, 1264
Nutgrass, 1275, 1402
Nutmeg Geranium, 1389
Nut trees, 861–68
  culture, 861–62

  grafting, 862
  regional: Illinois, 1232; Iowa, 1235; Michigan, 1244; North and South Dakota, 1264; Washington, 1281; Wisconsin, 1284
  soil for, 861
  what to grow, 862
Nutrient solutions, 89–90, 169
Nutrients, plant, 44
  soil and plant, 3
Nutrition elements of plant, 44
Nyssa sylvatica, 282
Oak, 280–81; Black, 280; Pin, 280–81; Red, 280–81; Scarlet, 280; White, 280–81
  flowers under, 114
  leafmold, 37
  regional, California, 1211
  troubles, 1109; borers, 1109; scale, 1109
Oats, 6, 60
Ohio, regional problems, 1264–65
  individual plants:
    apples, 1264
    gerberas, 1265
    herbs, 1265
    perennials, 1265
    roses, 1265
    shrubs, 1265
    strawberry, 1265
Oil, 1014, 1033
  emulsion, 1014, 1033
  miscible, 1014, 1033
  sprays, 1033
  white, 1014
Oklahama, regional problems, 1266–68
  individual plants:
    berries, 1266
    daphne, 1266
    delphinium, 1266
    flowers for honey, 1266
    flowers for shade, 1266
    fruits, small, 1266
    fruit trees, 1266
    gladiolus, 1266
    Grass, Bermuda, 1266
    ground cover, 1266–67
    lawn, 1266
    peony, 1267
    perennials, 1267
    roses, 1267
    trees, 1268
Okra, 718–19
Oleander
  indoors, 953–54
  outdoors, 384
  regional: California, 1211; Florida, 1220; Oregon, 1270
  troubles, 1109
Onions, 719–22
  culture, 719–20
  flowering, 240

indoors, 945–47
propagation from cuttings, 946–47
regional, Arkansas, 1196
troubles, 1117
Poisonivy, 1403
Poison-oak, 1403
Pole beans, 678–82
Polianthes, 257
Polianthes tuberosa, 257
Pollination fruit, orchard, 775–77
Polyantha roses, 454
Polygala
Fringed, 1387
Polygala paucifolia, 1387
Polygonum cuspidatum, 1402
Pomegranate, indoors, 935
outdoors, 385
propagation, 935
regional, California, 1211
Pomo green, 1043
for Japanese beetle, 1022
Pools
construction of, 1329
flower border for, 1372
hedge around formal, 1371
informal, 1330
in landscaping, 1329–30
lilies for, 1372–74
painting, 1329
tall plants for lily, 1372
for rock garden, 1368
walls of pools, 1329
Poplar, 281–82
flowers under Lombardy, 115
troubles, 1117
Poppy
annual, 185
hardy, 230–32
Oriental, 230–32
perennial, 230–32
regional, Arkansas, 1196; Georgia, 1224
Shirley, 185
Portulaca, 185
Potash, 44, 46
muriate of, 78
for vegetable garden, 633
Potassium, 3, 4, 5
chloride, 6
deficiency, 46
Potato, 728–34
beetle, 734
certified seed, 729
"culls," 734
culture, 732
digging, 734
fertilizers for, 730
mulching, 732
planting of, 731
problems, 733–35
seed, 729–30
soil for, 729

preparation of for planting, 729–30
spraying, 735
storage of, 734
Sweet, 743–45
troubles, 734–35, 1158–61; black heart, 1160–61; blight, 1158; blister beetle, 1159–60; flea beetle, 734, 1017; leaf hopper, 1160; potato bug, 734, 1159; scab, 735, 1159; seed treatment, 1159; spraying, 735; virus diseases, 1160; wireworms, 1047
varieties, 735–36
Pothos, 936, 963
Potmarigold, 1349
Potpourris, 1352–53; fixative, 1353; making, 1353; of rose petals, 1353; wet, 1353
Potting
house plants, 879–80
greenhouse plants, 152
soil, 875–76
Prairie Rose (*Rosa setigera*), 455
Praying Mantis, 1033–34
Primrose, 232, 924–25
Chinese, propagation of, 924–25; Evening, nematode-resistant, 1032; Fairy, 924; Giant-fringed, 924
greenhouse, 161–62
indoors, 924–25
rock-garden, 1366
varieties: *Primula grandiflora fimbriata,* 924; *Primula malacoides,* 924–25; *Primula obconica,* 924–25; *Primula sinensis,* 924–25
Principles of fertilization, 79
Privet, 326; Amur River, 326; California, 392; Ibolium, 392; Regal, 326; Waxleaf, 392
for hedge, 391–93
planting, 391
propagation, 393
regional, Minnesota, 1247
troubles, 1117
Propagation, general, 94, 128–40
by budding, 138, 779–81; cuttings, 129–33; division, 214; grafting, 136–40, 779–81; layering, 134–36; runners, 136; seeds, 128, 168–75; stolons, 136; suckers, 136
abutilon, 901
African-violet, 905–6
annuals, 168–75
by cuttings, 175
indoors, 168–73
outdoors, 173–75
from seed, 168–75
Aralia sieboldi, from seed, 928
asparagus "ferns" from seed, 929
azaleas, 373, 939
begonia, 910–12
blackberry, 838

Black Walnut, from seed, 867
bloodroot, from seed, 1382
blueberry, 849
bougainvillea by cuttings, 893
boxwood, 360–61
bulbs, 128–29
butterflyweed, from seed, 1382
cactus, 968
camellia, 382–83
cardinalflower, from seed, 1382
clematis, 404
corms, 128–29
cranberry, 853
currant, from cuttings, 856
cyclamen, from seed, 942
dahlia, 530
daphne, 361–62
delphinium, 474
dieffenbachia, 932
ferns, 958
figs, by layering, 858
foliage plants, from seed, 928
fruit, 779–81
　budding, 779–81
　grafting, 779–81
geraniums, by cuttings, 920–21
gladiolus, 540
gloxinia, 987
gourds, 1396
grape, by cuttings, 830–31
holly, 364–65
house plants: by division, 892;
　from seeds, 892; slips, 892–93
iris, 483
ivy, indoors, 960
Jerusalem-cherry, from seed, 945
lavender, by cuttings, 1347–48;
　from seed, 1347
lemonverbena, by cuttings, 1348
Leopard-plant, 932
lilac, 324–25
lilies, 492
marica, 923
narcissus, 509
oleander, 384
pandanus, 934
passion-flower, 962
peach, 799, 801
peony, 501
perennials, 212–14
persimmon, from seed, 861
"pick-a-back" plant, 893
poinsettia, by cuttings, 946–47
pomegranate, 935
Primrose, Chinese, 925
pyracantha, 367
raspberry, 844
rhododendron, 379
rhubarb, 738
roses, 443–46
rubber plant, 936
　from slips, 893
sansevieria, 937
shrubs, deciduous, 304
strawberry, 814
trees and shrubs, deciduous, 270

trees, evergreen, 344–45
tubers, 129
tulip, 519
wildflowers, from seed, 1375–76
Proportion in landscaping, 1296
Pruning
　apple, 784–86
　blackberry, 838
　boysenberry, 840
　cherry, 794–95
　clematis, 403–4
　to control plant troubles, 123–24
　cranberry, 854
　currant, 855
　daphne, 361
　dewberry, 842
　espalier fruit trees, 807
　fig, 858
　filbert, 864
　fruit, orchard, 772–73
　general, 122–24
　gooseberry, 856
　grapes, 825–30
　holly, 364
　house plants, 873
　lilac, 322–24
　peach, 800
　pear, 803–4
　plants, 98–99
　plum, 805
　quince, 861
　raspberry, 842
　roses, 434
　　climbing, 437
　　floribunda and hugonis, 440
　　hybrid perpetual, 440
　　hybrid tea, 441
　　old-fashioned, 442
　　polyantha, 442
　　rambler, 439
　　shrub, 442
　　tree, 443
　shrubs, deciduous, 302–3
　tomatoes, 750
　trees, 122–24
　　evergreen, 342–43
　tools, 124
Prunus (*see* Plum); *Prunus pis-*
　sardi, 294; *Prunus triloba*, 306
Pseudotsuga taxifolia, 347
Pteris fern, 957–58
Pteris struthiopteris, 958
Pumpkin, 736–37
　culture, 736
　troubles, 1161; cucumber beetle,
　1161; seed treatment, 1037; vine
　borer, 1161
　varieties, 737
Purslane, 1403
Puschkinia, 247
Pyracantha, 366–67; *Pyracantha*
　coccinea, 366; *Pyracantha coccinea*
　lalandi, 366
　culture, 366

regional, California, 1212
troubles, 1118
Pyrethrum, 232
for: aphids, 1034; blister beetle, 1007; crambid moth, 1030; Mexican bean beetle, 1034; other insects, 1034
Pyrola, 1387; *Pyrola americana,* 1387; *Pyrola elliptica,* 1387
Quack grass, 1402–3
Quakerlady, 1381
Quercus phellos, regional, Florida, 1221
Quicklime, 39
Quince, 861
Baltzi, 327; Columbia, 327; Corallina, 327; Double Scarlet, 327; Macrocarpa, 327; *Rubra grandiflora,* 327
flowering, 327–28
grafting, 861
pruning, 861
soil for, 861
troubles, 1186–87
varieties, 766
Rabbit manure, 4, 59
Rabbitfootfern, 957
Rabbits, 1034–36
Radish, 737
troubles, 1161
varieties, 737
Rainlilies, regional, Mississippi, 1249
Rambler rose, 454
pruning, 439
varieties, 454
Ranunculus, 257
greenhouse, 162
indoors, 991
regional, Texas, 1277
Raspberry, 842–46
black, 766
purple-cane, 766
red, 766
mulch for, 844
planting, 842
propagation, 844
pruning, 842
regional, Idaho, 1226; Iowa, 1236; Minnesota, 1248
support for, 843
transplanting, 842
troubles, 844–45, 1187–88; cane borer, 1188; crown gall, 1187; diseases, 1187; fruit worm, 1188; insects, 1187–88; Japanese beetles, 1188
winter protection, 843
varieties, 845–46
Rats, 1027
Raw bone flour, 70
Raw ground limestone, 39
Red clay, 15

Red clover, 60
Red copper oxide, for seed treatment, 1037
Red spider, 1028–29
Red squill, 1027
Redbud, regional, Georgia, 1222
Redcedar, 349–50
Redroot, 1403
Redwood burl, 936
Refuse, burning, 28
Regal Lilies, 489–90
Regional garden problems, 1190–1286
Repotting
geraniums, 917
house plants, 874–75, 879–80
in greenhouse, 152
plants, 152
Retinospora, dormant spray for, 1014
Rhododendron, 376–80
culture, 377
fertilizer for, 378
planting, 377
propagation, 379
regional: Alabama, 1193; Illinois, 1230; Michigan, 1245; Missouri, 1253; Texas, 1276; Washington, 1281
for shaded foundation material, 106
soil for, 377–78
soil preparation for, 377
troubles, 380, 1118; aphids, 1118; armillaria root rot, 1003; black vine weevil, 1118; borers, 1118; lace bugs, 1118; sooty mold, 1118
what to grow, 376
winter protection, 378–79
Rhubarb, 738–39
cutting, 738
forcing, 739
propagation of, 738
troubles, 1161; crown rot, 1161; curculios, 1161; Japanese beetle, 1023
varieties, 739
Robinia, 328
Rock garden, 1353–71
bulbs for, 1362–64
small, 1363–64
chionodoxa, 1362–63
for city garden, 102
construction of, 1356
crocuses, 1363
culture, 1357–58
drainage, 1355
evergreens, 1364
exposure, 1354
flowers, 1354
in landscape plan, 1354
iris, 1365

1451

Frost Maps

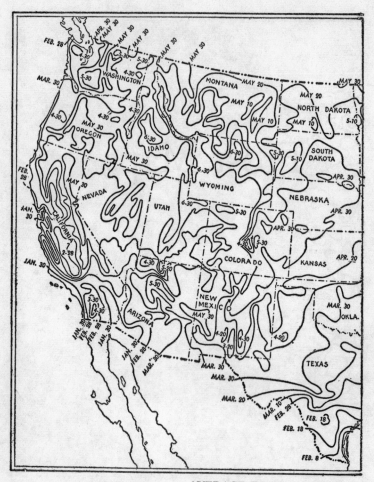

AVERAGE DATE OF LAST

"Tender" vegetables and flowers—those likely to be injured or killed by a light frost—should not be planted out until after danger of a late frost is past. *Seeds* of tender subjects (such as beans or corn) may be planted a few days earlier, as it will take them a week or ten days to germinate.

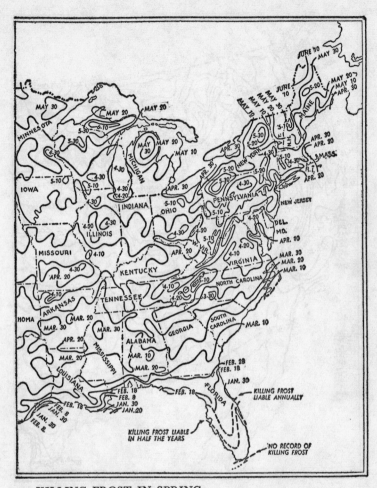

KILLING FROST IN SPRING

Local conditions—such as elevation above sea level, exposure to or protection from prevailing winds, and proximity to large bodies of water—may advance or delay the dates indicated on maps by a few days to a week or more. (Figures on the map—such as 4-20, 5-10—indicate dates, April 20, May 10, etc.)

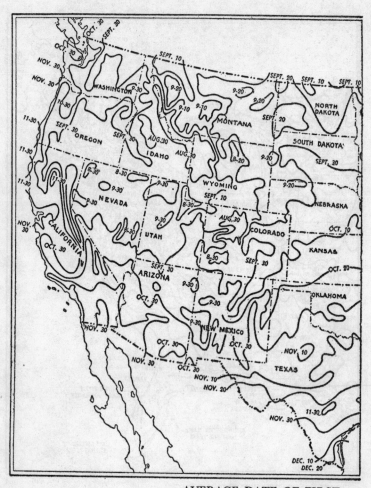

AVERAGE DATE OF FIRST

Hardy shrubs, roses, perennials, bulbs, and many fruits are usually planted in autumn about the time of, or just after, the first killing or "hard" frosts have checked growth. Many of these can be planted up until the time the ground begins to freeze, but in most instances earlier planting is advisable.

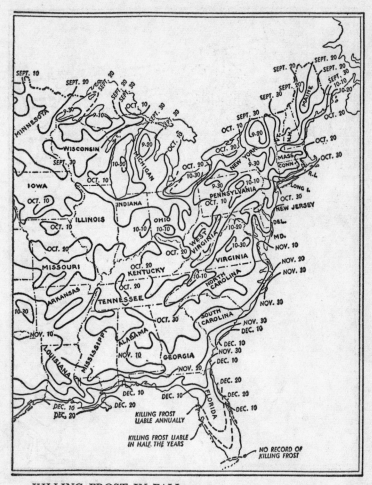

KILLING FROST IN FALL

If there is a period of a few weeks between planting and the time the ground begins to freeze, the newly set out plants or bulbs have an opportunity to make some root growth, and thus become established in their new positions. As in the case of spring frosts, local conditions will advance or delay the average dates (indicated on map) by a considerable period.